**Kodansha's Dictionary of
Basic Japanese Idioms**

Kodansha's Dictionary of
Basic Japanese Idioms

Jeff Garrison
Kayoko Kimiya
George Wallace
Masahiko Goshi

KODANSHA INTERNATIONAL
Tokyo • New York • London

SYMBOLS USED IN THIS BOOK

  related information about the entry under discussion or about a word or phrase appearing in a sample sentence.

  a cross-reference to a synonym, antonym, or other related word or phrase in this dictionary.

Also variant reading or script for the idiom under discussion.

Based on four titles in Kodansha International's Power Japanese series: *"Body" Language* by Jeff Garrison (1990), *Communicating with Ki: The "Spirit" in Japanese Idioms* by Jeff Garrison and Kayoko Kimiya (1994), *Kanji Idioms* by George Wallace and Kayoko Kimiya (1995), and *Animal Idioms* by Jeff Garrison and Masahiko Goshi (1996).

Distributed in the United States by Kodansha America, Inc., 575 Lexington Avenue, New York N.Y. 10022, and in the United Kingdom and continental Europe by Kodansha Europe Ltd., 95 Aldwych, London WC2B 4JF. Published by Kodansha International Ltd., 17-14 Otowa 1-chome, Bunkyo-ku, Tokyo 112-8652, and Kodansha America, Inc.

Copyright © 2002 by Kodansha International Ltd.
All rights reserved. Printed in Japan.
ISBN 4-7700-2797-4
First edition, 2002
02 03 04 05 06 07 08 09 10 9 8 7 6 5 4 3 2 1

CONTENTS

Preface 6

DICTIONARY 9

Index 643

PREFACE

Kodansha's Dictionary of Basic Japanese Idioms is based on four previously published books in Kodansha International's Power Japanese series: *"Body" Language* by Jeff Garrison (1990), *Communicating with Ki: The "Spirit" in Japanese Idioms* by Jeff Garrison and Kayoko Kimiya (1994), *Kanji Idioms* by George Wallace and Kayoko Kimiya (1995), and *Animal Idioms* by Jeff Garrison and Masahiko Goshi (1996). The content of these books has been rearranged into alphabetical order by Japanese entry word, minor changes have been made in the text, more extensive cross-references have been added, and an index has been appended. It is hoped that the resultant book will make the study of Japanese idioms much more convenient.

Students who are approaching idioms for the first time may want to know exactly what an idiom is. The third edition of the *American Heritage Dictionary* defines the word as "a speech form or an expression of a given language that is peculiar to itself grammatically or cannot be understood from the individual meanings of its elements, as in *keep tabs on*." This simply means that students of the English language may know the individual meanings of *keep*, *tab*, and *on*, but still not understand what the phrase *keep tabs on* means.

The same applies to the Japanese language. For example, students may know the individual words in the phrase 肩を持つ *kata o motsu* (*kata* = shoulder, *o* = particle indicating a direct object, *motsu* = hold), but still not understand what the phrase as a whole means ("to side with or support someone"). To learn the meaning, there is no choice but to look the phrase up in a dictionary and commit it to memory. If idioms like this cropped up only occasionally in writing or conversation, they would not represent a problem worth fretting about, but the fact is that idioms are just as widely used in Japanese as they are in English. This is because they are often the most concise, efficient, and pointed way of expressing what one wants to say.

Thus students must first learn idioms in order to understand everyday conversation and written material. This can be called a passive use of idioms—to understand them us they are presented by an outside source, so that you can at least grasp the intent of what is being conveyed.

The second reason students must study idioms is proactive, since it is only through idioms that students can hope to express their thoughts effectively and avoid awkward paraphrasing. Better to learn them than to be continually stopped in the midst of a paraphrase by your Japanese conversant with a sudden "Oh, you mean *kata o motsu,*" or whatever, providing exactly the right phrase for what you wanted to say.

There are many other reasons why idioms must, or should, be learned, not the least of which is the fact that idioms often serve as pivotal points for jokes. For instance, you could play on the Biblical admonition that "you should not cast pearls before swine" 豚に真珠 *buta ni shinjū*, meaning, of course, that you shouldn't give something important to a person who cannot understand its value. If a certain Tanaka-san is just that obtuse person, you could say, "Don't cast pearls before Tanaka-san" 田中さんに真珠 *Tanaka-san ni shinjū*. Or let us say that in your place of work there is a British person who is known for his crafty political maneuvering. Let us further say that a Japanese, making use of a common expression, refers to him as an "wily old raccoon" 古狸 *furu-danuki*. You could play on this idiom and respond by saying that "the only thing worse than a wily old raccoon is a wily old Brit" 古狸より古イギリス人が恐ろしい *furu-danuki yori furu-Igirisu-jin ga osoroshii*.

The idioms appearing in this book are basically of two types: idiomatic words and phrases (such as those cited above) and expressions composed of four Chinese characters (commonly called 四字熟語 *yoji-jukugo* "four-character compounds"). These compounds are generally not thought of as idioms but either simply as compound nouns or as adages and proverbs.

Among the compound nouns might be counted 年功序列 *nenkō-joretsu* ("seniority") and 意識不明 *ishiki-fumei* ("unconscious"), which, though they are fairly straightforward, need some interpretation to be understood and therefore can be considered within the idiom bailiwick. The adage or proverb type definitely need explanation to be understood. Examples are 呉越同舟 *goetsu-dōshu* ("the Go and the Etsu in the same boat") and 十人十色 *jūnin-tōiro* ("ten people, ten colors"). This type can be considered idiomatic in the sense that their exact meaning is not clear from the surface meaning of the individual words.

In conclusion, it might be noted that a good number of the idioms involve the character 気 *ki*. These words and phrases are extremely important in expressing moods and feelings, and without at least minimal knowledge of them it is nearly impossible to carry on a normal conversation. Starting with 元気 *genki* (original *ki*), as in お元気ですか *Ogenki desu ka* "How are you?" and going on to heavy, light, long, short, warped, and crazed *ki*, and ending perhaps with そういう気がしました *sō iu ki ga shimashita* "That's the way I felt about it," innumerable ways are provided for expressing feelings and thoughts.

All in all, idioms are not only useful—in fact, indispensable—to speaking and understanding Japanese, but they can also be a great deal of fun to learn, to explore, and, yes, to play with.

Editorial Department,
Kodansha International

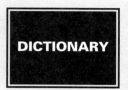

abi-kyōkan 阿鼻叫喚 "screaming in hell"
pandemonium, like a scene out of hell

戦闘の後の町は、まさに阿鼻叫喚の巷だった。
Sentō no ato no machi wa, masa ni abi-kyōkan no chimata datta.
After the battle the town looked like a scene from hell.

爆発事故で、工場は阿鼻叫喚の場となった。
Bakuhatsu-jiko de, kōjō wa abi-kyōkan no ba to natta.
After being hit by that explosion, the factory looked like something out of Dante's *Inferno*.

☙ Originally 阿鼻 and 叫喚 are the names of two of the eight burning hells of Buddhism. In Sanskrit the two hells are called Avici and Raurava.

abu 虻 horsefly

Anyone who has been bitten by one knows a little of what horses and cattle must go through and at least one reason they have long tails. The females of this species are bloodsuckers. They'll take a piece out of your hide if you give 'em a chance.

Abu are counted *ippiki* 一匹.

Abuhachi torazu 虻蜂取らず "catch neither the horsefly nor the bee"
try to do two things and fail at both; fall between two stools

そんなに欲張っても虻蜂取らずになったら元も子もないよ。
Sonna ni yokubatte mo abuhachi torazu ni nattara moto mo ko mo nai yo.
Let your greed get the better of you and you'll end up falling flat on your face.

彼はいろいろな事業に手を出しすぎて、結局虻蜂取らずとなった。
Kare wa iroiro na jigyō ni te o dashisugite, kekkyoku abuhachi torazu to natta.

He overextended by branching out into all kinds of businesses and went bust.

🐝 There are several variations of this expression: *abu mo hachi mo torazu* 虻も蜂も取らず, *abu mo torazu hachi mo torazu* 虻も取らず蜂も取らず, and *abu mo torazu hachi ni sasareru* 虻も取らず蜂に刺される. The first two are reconfigurations of the idiom as it appears in the entry; the third translates literally as "not only fail to catch the horsefly, but get stung by a bee (in the process)." A similar expression is *nito o ou mono wa itto o (mo) ezu* 二兎を追う者は一兎を（も）得ず, precisely the same as (and perhaps derived from) the English "If you run after two hares, you will catch neither." It is effectively the opposite of *isseki-nicho* 一石二鳥, or "(killing) two birds with one stone."

☞ *isseki-nichō* 一石二鳥

ago あご jaw(s), chin

It means the lower jaw, both upper and lower jaws, or the chin. When you hear *ago ga yowai* at ringside, you know that some boxer has a "weak" or "glass" jaw. Contrarily, about a guy who can really take a punch, you say *ago ga tsuyoi*.

Figurative meanings of *ago* include excessive talking or jawing and, less commonly, food or chow. Idioms exemplifying these meanings are included in the following selection.

Ago de (hito o) tsukau **あごで（人を）使う** "Use someone with one's jaw."
boss someone around, be bossy

あの会社の社長は、あごで人を使うので嫌われている。
Ano kaisha no shachō wa, ago de hito o tsukau no de kirawarete iru.
A lot of people don't like the president of that company because he's such a slave driver.

彼は使用人をあごで使っていた。
Kare wa shiyō-nin o ago de tsukatte ita.
He was really cracking the whip.

This expression is presumably from the unpopular habit among some Japanese of ordering people around by motioning with their chin and a slight flick of the head.

Ago ga deru / ago o dasu **あごが出る／あごを出す** "one's jaw is sticking out"
be bushed, worn out, done in, dog tired, dragging ass

歩き過ぎて、あごが出た。
Arukisugi de, ago ga deta.
I'm beat (dead tired, burned out) from walking so far. / I'm all walked out.

こんな重労働が毎日続いたら、さすがの彼女もあごを出すだろう。
Konna jū-rōdō ga mainichi tsuzuitara, sasuga no kanojo mo ago o dasu darō.
If the workload keeps up like this much longer, even she's going to drop in her tracks.

☞ *ashi ga bō ni naru / ashi o bō ni suru* 足が棒になる／足を棒にする, *hirō-konpai* 疲労困憊; *genki* 元気

Ago ga ochiru **あごが落ちる** "one's jaw falls"
mouthwatering, delicious, succulent, yummy, fit for a king

この店のミートローフはあごが落ちるほどうまい。
Kono mise no mītorōfu wa ago ga ochiru hodo umai.

This place has got some meatloaf that'll get your juices flowing.

ああ、おいしい。あごが落ちそうなくらい。
Ā oishii. Ago ga ochisō na kurai.
Ummm, this is fit for a king.

Also ほっぺたが落ちる *hoppeta ga ochiru.*

aimai-moko 曖昧模糊 "vague and indistinct"
~とした, ~としている vague, hazy, patchy, wishy-washy

そんな曖昧模糊とした説明で納得できると思ってるのかね。
Sonna aimai-moko to shita setsumei de nattoku dekiru to omotte 'ru no ka ne.
Do you really think you can convince me with such a wishy-washy explanation?

あいつの話は何だか曖昧模糊としていて、訳が分からなかったよ。
Aitsu no hanashi wa nandaka aimai-moko to shite ite, wake ga wakaranakatta yo.
The guy just went on and on in such a vague and roundabout way that I had no idea what he was talking about.

僕にも確信があるわけじゃなくて、曖昧模糊とした印象に過ぎないんだけどね。
Boku ni mo kakushin ga aru wake ja nakute, aimai-moko to shita inshō ni suginai n' da kedo ne.
It is just a vague impression; it is not that I'm absolutely sure about it.

akusen-kutō 悪戦苦闘 "a difficult battle, a bitter struggle"

a long hard fight; 〜する to fight desperately (with one's back to the wall, against heavy odds)

悪戦苦闘の末、明け方になってやっとレポートを書き終わったよ。
Akusen-kutō no sue, akegata ni natte yatto repōto o kakiowatta yo.
After a long hard slog I finally managed to finish my report by dawn.

かれこれ半年も悪戦苦闘の毎日だったけど、来月からは少し楽になりそうなんだ。
Karekore hantoshi mo akusen-kutō no mainichi datta kedo, raigetsu kara wa sukoshi raku ni narisō nan da.
For the past six months it's been nose to the grindstone all the way, but from next month it looks like things'll get easier.

忙しい日にバイトの子に休まれちゃって、朝から悪戦苦闘だよ。
Isogashii hi ni baito no ko ni yasumarechatte, asa kara akusen-kutō da yo.
We've been rushed off our feet all morning, thanks to that part-timer taking the day off just when we needed her most.

※ バイト (*baito*) is the shortened form of アルバイト (*arubaito*), meaning part-time job. It is a loanword coming from the German word for work (Arbeit).

anchū-mosaku 暗中模索 "searching in the dark"

〜する to grope blindly in the dark, to be (all) at sea, to be at a (total) loss

どこから始めたらいいのか、まだ暗中模索だよ。
Doko kara hajimetara ii no ka, mada anchū-mosaku da yo.
I'm still totally in the dark as to where to begin.

大変なのは分かるが、いつまでも暗中模索の状態が続いてるのはちょっと困るな。
Taihen na no wa wakaru ga, itsu made mo anchū-mosaku no jōtai ga tsuzuite 'ru no wa chotto komaru na.
I realize things are difficult, but your continued cluelessness is not making our life any easier.

暗中模索しているうちに、ふっと良い考えがひらめいたんだ。
Anchū-mosaku shite iru uchi ni, futto yoi kangae ga hirameita n' da.
There I was, wondering what on earth I should do when suddenly I had a great idea.

aoiki-toiki 青息吐息 "blue breath, exhaling breath (i.e., a sigh)"

be in great distress, have a hard time of it

元金どころか利子を払うだけで青息吐息の毎日なんだ。
Gankin dokoro ka rishi o harau dake de aoiki-toiki no mainichi nan da.
Pay back the initial loan? You've got to be kidding! I'm busting a gut just trying to meet the interest payments.

早く人員を補充してくれなきゃ。こっちはもう青息吐息だよ。
Hayaku jin'in o hojū shite kurenakya, kotchi wa mō aoiki-toiki da yo.
They're gonna have to give us some extra staff soon; we're only just managing to keep our heads above water.

ari 蟻 ant

Ants appear often in folk tales, owing to their social behavior and other fanciful similarities to humankind. Any unusal activity by ants is also thought to presage events. For example, when ants are observed fighting, it is believed to warn of impending rain.

Ants are counted *ippiki* 一匹, or *ichiwa* 一羽, and the latter is not used exclusively of the winged varieties.

Ari-jigoku 蟻地獄 "a doodlebug"
quicksand, a trap

借金の蟻地獄にはまった彼はとうとう会社の金に手を出した。
Shakkin no ari-jigoku ni hamatta kare wa tōtō kaisha no kane ni te o dashita.
Having fallen deeply in debt, he ended up dipping into corporate funds.

彼は新興宗教にうっかり引っかかり、蟻地獄に落ちる思いであった。
Kare wa shinkō-shūkyō ni ukkari hikkakari, ari-jigoku ni ochiru omoi de atta.
After falling in with some new religion, he began to feel trapped.

蟻地獄のような売春組織にひっかかった彼女はその後行方がわからなくなった。
Ari-jikoku no yō na baishun-soshiki ni hikkakatta kanojo wa sono ato yukue ga wakaranaku natta.
She was never heard from again once she had been sucked into the quicksand of organized prostitution.

🐜 The doodlebug is the larva of the ant lion. This energy-efficient creature lies in ambush at the bottom of a conical sand trap for ants that slide down that slippery slope into its arthropodan mandibles. Despite parallels with Kobo Abe's *Woman in the Dunes,* there is no evidence that the female of the species is particularly rapacious. As for the idiom, it derives from the trap its namesake constructs, and is used of a condition into which one has fallen and from which escape is all but impossible. Perhaps taking a hint from entomology, enterprising city planners in Japan have devised an ingenious concrete contraption (much to the delight of harried mothers) that resembles the doodlebug's lair, only much bigger. Placed strategically in city parks, these *ari-jigoku* effectively restrict a child's wanderings, freeing the mother for a few moments of peace and prattle.

Ari no haideru suki mo nai **蟻の這いでる隙もない** "without space for so much as an ant to crawl out"
completely surrounded, sealed off, cordoned off

強盗が立てこもった民家の周りには蟻の這いでる隙もないほどの警官が包囲した。
Gōtō ga tatekomotta minka no mawari ni wa ari no haideru suki mo nai hodo no keikan ga hōi shita.

The house where the robber was holed up was sealed off watertight by the police. / Nobody could possibly get through the police cordon around the house where the robber was hiding out.

国連の平和維持部隊は包囲され蟻の這いでる隙もなかった。
Kokuren no heiwa-iji-butai wa hōi sare ari no haideru suki mo nakatta.
United Nations peacekeepers were completely sealed off from the outside.

❧ Used most commonly of, or by, law enforcement or the military.

Ari no ikketsu **蟻の一穴** "an ant hole"
a tiny mistake can lead to disaster

蟻の一穴とならないよう、もう一度チェックしよう。
Ari no ikketsu to naranai yō, mō ichido chekku shiyō.
I'm going to look this over again to make sure there's nothing in here that could be my undoing.

作業員の不注意が蟻の一穴となり、その現場は一瞬にしてがれきの山となった。

Sagyō-in no fu-chūi ga ari no ikketsu to nari, sono genba wa isshun ni shite gareki no yama to natta.
A simple slipup by one of the workers turned the construction site into a mountain of rubble in an instant.

✣ From an ancient parable about a 10,000-foot dike that collapsed due to a single tunnel dug by an ant, this idiom is often used as an admonition against oversight or omission.

ashi 足 leg, foot

People, dogs, insects, tables and chairs all have them. Squid have them, too. *Ashi* can be used to mean either the whole leg or just the foot. Another meaning is mode of transportation, or more colloquially, one's wheels. So *ashi ga nai* doesn't mean that the speaker has met with some terrible accident, it just means that his car is in the shop or he has no way of getting around. *Ashi* can also mean money or "bread" when preceded by *o*, presumably because of the way it just seems to run away from you. Finally, for all you scatologists out there, the third or middle leg is the same in Japanese, *sanbon-me no ashi*.

↬ *hitoashi-chigai* ひと足違い, *ni-no-ashi o fumu* 二の足を踏む

Ageashi o toru **あげ足を取る** "grab someone's leg when it's in the air"
pick at, trip someone up

彼女は、人のあげ足を取っては喜んでいる。
Kanojo wa, hito no ageashi o totte wa yorokonde iru.
She gets a kick out of finding fault with what people say.

人のあげ足ばかり取るのは、良いことではない。
Hito no ageashi bakari toru no wa, yoi koto de wa nai.
It's not right to just trip people up all the time.

Ashi ga bō ni naru / ashi o bō ni suru 足が棒になる／足を棒にする "one's legs become sticks"

be so tired that one's legs feel like rubber bands

足が棒になるまで歩き回った。
Ashi ga bō ni naru made arukimawatta.
I walked my legs off.

足を棒にして安いアパートを探し回った。
Ashi o bō ni shite yasui apāto o sagashi mawatta.
I walked around looking for a cheap apartment until I was practically dead on my feet (thought I would drop).

☞ *ago ga deru / ago o dasu* 顎が出る／顎を出す, *hirō-konpai* 疲労困憊

Ashi ga chi ni tsukanai 足が地に着かない "one's feet aren't touching the ground"

---

(1) be extremely excited (2) be unrealistic, not have one's feet on the ground, impractical, have one's head up in the clouds

(1) 3ヵ月先の旅行のことばかり考えて、足が地に着かない。
Sankagetsu-saki no ryokō no koto bakari kangaete, ashi ga chi ni tsukanai.
I feel as if I'm walking on air, the way I'm always thinking about the trip we're going on three months from now.

(2) 彼は夢ばかり追っていて足が地に着いていない。
Kare wa yume bakari otte ite ashi ga chi ni tsuite inai.
He's always up in the clouds somewhere, chasing a pipe dream.

Also 地に足が着いていない *chi ni ashi ga tsuite inai.*

Ashi ga deru 足が出る "one's feet are sticking out"
run over the budget, be in the red

新年会で足が出た。
Shinnen-kai de ashi ga deta.
The New Year's party ran over the budget (ended up in the red).

節約したつもりだったが、今回の旅行も結局足が出てしまった。
Setsuyaku shita tsumori datta ga, konkai no ryokō mo kekkyoku ashi ga dete shimatta.
I tried to keep expenses down on the recent trip but ended up in the hole anyway.

Ashi ga hayai 足が早い "have fast feet"

(1) be a fast runner (2) (of food) spoil quickly

(1) 彼は足が早い。
Kare wa ashi ga hayai.
He's fast on his feet. / He can really fly.

(2) 生ものは足が早いので、特に梅雨どきには注意して下さい。
Namamono wa ashi ga hayai no de, toku ni tsuyu-doki ni wa chūi shite kudasai.
Fresh foods go bad quickly, so be very careful during the rainy season.

Ashi o arau 足を洗う "wash one's feet"
wash one's hands of, be through with

Now here is one that's interesting because it is similar in concept—washing something dirty off—but different in the part of the body chosen to express the decision to turn over a new leaf.

やくざの世界から足を洗うことにした。
Yakuza no sekai kara ashi o arau koto ni shita.
I made up my mind to go straight. / I decided to wash my hands of the mob.

そろそろ独身生活から足を洗おうと思っている。
Sorosoro dokushin-seikatsu kara ashi o araō to omotte iru.
I think I've had just about enough of being footloose and fancy-free.

☞ *te o kiru* 手を切る

Ashi o hakobu 足を運ぶ "carry one's feet"
go, come, visit

こんな田舎までわざわざ足を運んでくれて、ありがとうございます。
Konna inaka made wazawaza ashi o hakonde kurete, arigatō gozaimasu.
Thank you for coming all the way out here to the countryside to see us.

彼は情報を集めに、毎日証券会社へ足を運んだ。
Kare wa jōhō o atsume ni, mainichi shōken-gaisha e ashi o hakonda
He went to his broker's every day to keep up on the latest developments.

Don't be tempted to use this next one like the literal English equivalent. It doesn't have anything to do with teasing anyone, but it is easy to understand why it means to hold someone back.

Ashi o hipparu 足を引っ張る "pull someone's leg"
interfere, get in someone's way, hold someone back, cramp someone's style, skewer, hobble
---

同じ職場の人間の足を引っ張るようなことはしたくない。
Onaji shokuba no ningen no ashi o hipparu yō na koto wa shitaku nai.
I don't want to stand in the way of any of my co-workers.

今回の選挙では、野党は自分で自分の足を引っ張った面もある。
Konkai no senkyo de wa, yatō wa jibun de jibun no ashi o hippatta men mo aru.
To some extent, the opposition was its own worst enemy in the recent elections.

Ashi o mukeru **足を向ける** "point one's feet toward"

(1) go toward, head for (2) [in the phrase 足を向けては眠れない *ashi o mukete wa nemurenai*] never do anything to hurt someone

(1) 東北地方に足を向けて旅立った。
Tōhoku-chihō ni ashi o mukete tabidatta.
We set out on a trip (headed out) for the Tōhoku area.

(2) あの方に足を向けては眠れない。
Ano kata ni ashi o mukete wa nemurenai.
I could never do anything to hurt him (after all he's done for me).

Ashi o ubau **足を奪う** "steal one's feet or legs"
strand someone, take away someone's wheels

その電車の脱線事故は、6000人の足を奪った。
Sono densha no dassen-jiko wa, rokusen-nin no ashi o ubatta.
The train derailment left 6,000 people stranded.

大雪で、大勢の通勤客の足が奪われた。
Ōyuki de, ōzei no tsūkin-kyaku no ashi ga ubawareta.
Many commuters were left without transportation by the snowstorm.

atama 頭 **head**

What better place to start than at the top, which in Japanese is *atama kara,* or, literally, "from the head"? In addition to its obvious reference to a division of the body, *atama* shares many other meanings with its English equivalent, including mind, intelligence, and top or beginning. An example of which is *atama o hitsuyō to shinai shigoto,* meaning "a job that it doesn't take any smarts or brains to do."

Some idioms, such as *atama no teppen kara ashi no tsumasaki made* (from the top of one's head to the tip of one's toes), are the same both literally and figuratively in English. You can even count cattle, horses, and other large mammals like whales as you would in English, but the pronunciation of the character for *atama* changes to *tō,* so five head of horses is *go-tō no uma.*

Atama dekkachi　頭でっかち　"big (large) headed"

---

(1) (of the size of a person's head) big-headed, have a big head (2) (of an institution) top-heavy, too many chiefs and not enough Indians (3) (of a person or way of thinking) academic, intellectual, pointy-headed

(1) あいつは頭でっかちだな。
Aitsu wa atama dekkachi da na.
Look at the size of that guy's head, would you.

(2) あそこは天下りの役員ばかりで、頭でっかちな会社だ。
Asoko wa amakudari no yakuin bakari de, atama dekkachi na kaisha da.
That company is top-heavy, with former government officials filling the management ranks.

(3) 頭でっかちな意見は説得力に欠ける。
Atama dekkachi na iken wa settoku-ryoku ni kakeru.
Pointy-headed (ivory-tower) opinions are unconvincing.

あいつは頭でっかちだ。
Aitsu wa atama dekkachi da.
He's such a conehead.

Atama ga agaranai 頭が上がらない "can't lift up one's head"
can't stand up to someone, be no match for someone

あいつは女房に頭が上がらないらしい。
Aitsu wa nyōbō ni atama ga agaranai rashii.
Word is that he's no match for his wife (is henpecked). / I hear his wife wears the pants in the family.

どうして彼は社長に頭が上がらないのだろう。
Dō shite kare wa shachō ni atama ga agaranai no darō.
Why do you suppose he can't stand up to the boss?

Atama ga furui 頭が古い "one's head is old"
be behind the times, be of the old school

お父さんは頭が古いよ。
Otōsan wa atama ga furui yo.
Oh, Dad, you're so out of it. / You're such an old fogy, Dad.

私の頭が古いのか、同棲する人たちの考えは理解できない。
Watashi no atama ga furui no ka, dōsei suru hitotachi no kangae wa rikai dekinai.
Maybe I'm just old-fashioned, but I can't understand people who live together without being married (who shack up).

☞ *atama ga katai* 頭が固い

Atama ga ii 頭がいい "one's head is good"
be smart, sharp, bright, quick

鈴木さんは頭がいいですね。
Suzuki-san wa atama ga ii desu ne.
Suzuki's a pretty sharp (bright) guy. / Suzuki has got a good head on his shoulders.

彼女は頭のいい人が好きです。
Kanojo wa atama no ii hito ga suki desu.
She goes for smart (intelligent) guys.

☞ *atama ga kireru* 頭が切れる, *atama no deki ga chigau* 頭の出来が違う, *atama no kaiten ga hayai* 頭の回転が早い; *atama ga nibui* 頭が鈍い, *atama ga warui* 頭が悪い, *chi no meguri ga warui* 血の巡りが悪い

Atama ga ippai **頭がいっぱい** "one's head is full"
be preoccupied, obsessed with something

彼は来週提出する論文の事で頭がいっぱいだ。
Kare wa raishū teishutsu suru ronbun no koto de atama ga ippai da.
All he can think about is the report he has to turn in next week. / He's got a lot on his mind, what with the report he's got to turn in next week.

彼は今娘の結婚のことで頭がいっぱいです。
Kare wa ima musume no kekkon no koto de atama ga ippai desu.
He's got this thing (a bee in his bonnet) now about getting his daughter married off.

Atama ga itai **頭が痛い** "one's head hurts"

---

(1) have a headache, one's head hurts (2) worry over something

(1) 二日酔いで頭が痛い。
Futsuka-yoi de atama ga itai.
I've got a headache from being hung over.

(2) ローンの事を考えると頭が痛い。
Rōn no koto o kangaeru to atama ga itai.
Just thinking about that loan makes me sick.

どうして頭の痛い問題ばかり起きるのだろうか。
Dō shite atama no itai mondai bakari okiru no darō ka.

Why is it that every problem has got to be such a hassle? / Why does everything have to be such a pain in the neck?

Atama ga katai 頭が固い "have a hard head"
be stubborn, pigheaded, unreceptive to change

彼は頭が固い。
Kare wa atama ga katai.
He is hardheaded.

年をとると頭が固くなるものだね。
Toshi o toru to atama ga kataku naru mono da ne.
I guess the older you get the more set in your ways you become.

☞ *atama ga furui* 頭が古い; *atama ga yawarakai* 頭が柔らかい

Atama ga kireru 頭が切れる "one's head cuts"
be a quick thinker, quick on one's feet

あの弁護士は本当に頭が切れる。
Ano bengo-shi wa hontō ni atama ga kireru.
That lawyer is really sharp. / That lawyer is really on the ball.

☞ *atama ga ii* 頭がいい, *atama no deki ga chigau* 頭の出来が違う, *atama no kaiten ga hayai* 頭の回転が早い; *atama ga nibui* 頭が鈍い, *atama ga warui* 頭が悪い, *chi no meguri ga warui* 血の巡りが悪い

Atama ga nibui 頭が鈍い "one's head is dull"
be dull-witted, slow-witted

こんなに説明してもわからないとは、彼はちょっと頭が鈍いのかな。

Konna ni setsumei shite mo wakaranai to wa, kare wa chotto atama ga nibui no ka na.
He must be a little slow (thick) if he still doesn't understand after all the explaining I've done.

☞ *atama ga warui* 頭が悪い, *chi no meguri ga warui* 血の巡りが悪い; *atama ga ii* 頭がいい, *atama ga kireru* 頭が切れる, *atama no deki ga chigau* 頭の出来が違う, *atama no kaiten ga hayai* 頭の回転が早い

Atama ga sagaru **頭が下がる** "one's head lowers"
admire, take one's hat off to someone.

佐々木さんの勤勉さには頭が下がる。
Sasaki-san no kinben-sa ni wa atama ga sagaru.
You've really got to hand it (take your hat off) to Sasaki for how hard he works.

盲導犬の忠実さに頭の下がる思いがした。
Mōdōken no chūjitsu-sa ni atama no sagaru omoi ga shita.
I was really impressed by how loyal Seeing Eye dogs are.

Atama ga warui **頭が悪い** "one's head is bad"
be dim-witted, slow, soft in the head, not playing with a full deck

---

あいつは本当に頭が悪い。
Aitsu wa hontō ni atama ga warui.
That guy's so stupid! / God, he's dumb! / What a lame-brain (knucklehead)!

このコンピュータのソフトは頭が悪い。
Kono konpyūta no sofuto wa atama ga warui.
This computer software is the pits (not up to snuff).

頭の悪いやりかたをして失敗した。

Atama no warui yarikata o shite shippai shita.
I blew it because of the stupid way I tried to do things.

☞ *atama ga nibui* 頭が鈍い, *chi no meguri ga warui* 血の巡りが悪い; *atama ga ii* 頭がいい, *atama ga kireru* 頭が切れる, *atama no deki ga chigau* 頭の出来が違う, *atama no kaiten ga hayai* 頭の回転が早い

Atama ga yawarakai 頭が柔らかい "one's head is soft"
be flexible, receptive to new things

あの先生は年の割りに頭が柔らかい。
Ano sensei wa toshi no wari ni atama ga yawarakai.
That teacher is pretty open-minded for someone her age.

頭が柔らかいから子供は物覚えが早い。
Atama ga yawarakai kara kodomo wa mono-oboe ga hayai.
Kids pick up things so quickly because they are still impressionable.

☞ *atama ga katai* 頭が固い

Atama kara 頭から "from the head"

(1) from the start (2) out of hand, right off

(1) もう一度頭から歌いましょう。
Mō ichido atama kara utaimashō.
All right, let's sing it again from the top.

(2) 政府の正当性を頭から否定するむきもある。
Seifu no seitō-sei o atama kara hitei suru muki mo aru.
There are some who dispute the very notion that the government is legitimate at all.

Atama ni kuru 頭に来る "come to one's head"

(1) get mad, get angry, pop one's cork (2) flip one's lid, flip out, freak out

(1) 頭に来た、もう我慢できない！
Atama ni kita, mō gaman dekinai!
Boy, does that burn me up! I'm not taking it any more!

彼の横柄な態度は、全く頭に来る。
Kare no ōhei na taido wa, mattaku atama ni kuru.
His arrogance really gets me! / He acts so big, it really pisses me off.

(2) あんなかっこうをして、彼女は頭に来たんじゃないか。
Anna kakkō shite, kanojo wa atama ni kitan ja nai ka.
She must have gone off her rocker (lost her marbles), the way she's dressed.

Atama no deki ga chigau 頭の出来が違う "one's head is made differently"
be (a lot) smarter than someone else

東大出は頭の出来が違うね。
Tōdai-de wa atama no deki ga chigau ne.
University of Tokyo grads do seem to have more on the ball.

君と僕では頭の出来が違うよ。
Kimi to boku de wa atama no deki ga chigau yo.
You and I are in different leagues, friend.

↬ *atama ga ii* 頭がいい, *atama ga kireru* 頭が切れる, *atama no kaiten ga hayai* 頭の回転が早い; *atama ga nibui* 頭が鈍い, *atama ga warui* 頭が悪い, *chi no meguri ga warui* 血の巡りが悪い

Atama no kaiten ga hayai　頭の回転が早い　"one's head turns over fast"
smart, quick-witted, quick on the uptake

彼女は頭の回転が早い。
Kanojo wa atama no kaiten ga hayai.
She's as smart as a whip. / She has a mind like a steel trap.

☞ *atama ga ii* 頭がいい, *atama ga kireru* 頭が切れる, *atama no deki ga chigau* 頭の出来が違う; *atama ga nibui* 頭が鈍い, *atama ga warui* 頭が悪い, *chi no meguri ga warui* 血の巡りが悪い

Atama no kuroi nezumi　頭の黒い鼠　"a black-headed rat"
a snitcher, a thief in the family (who steals from the family)

買い物から帰ってきたら引き出しの中の5千円札が無くなっていたので、これは頭の黒い鼠の仕業とピンときた。
Kaimono kara kaette kitara hikidashi no naka no gosen-en satsu ga nakunatte ita no de, kore wa atama no kuroi nezumi no shiwaza to pinto kita.
When I came home from shopping and discovered five thousand yen missing from the drawer, I knew it was the work of someone in the family.

まさかわが家に頭の黒い鼠がいるとは思わなかった。
Masaka wagaya ni atama no kuroi nezumi ga iru to wa omowanakatta.
I never imagined we'd have a little snitcher in the family.

❀ Used all but exclusively of a person, often a child, either a family member or roommate, who pilfers from those living under the same roof. From the facts that rats prosper in and around human habitations, that things disappear when they forage successfully, and that, when something in the home is discovered missing and a rat is unlikely to have an interest in that object, comes this idiom's attribution of blame to someone in the household. The fact that Japanese have black hair provides the final element of the idiom, which is often used jocularly. Can be used in other group situations like co-workers in an office, when one discovers someone has been into the candy on one's desk.

☞ *nezumi* 鼠

Atama o hiyasu **頭を冷やす** "cool one's head"
cool down, cool off, relax, take it easy, calm down, settle down

---

散歩でもして頭をひやしてこよう。
Sanpo de mo shite atama o hiyashite koyō.
I think I'll take a walk and try to cool down.

頭を冷やして出直してこい。
Atama o hiyashite denaoshite koi.
Come back and give it another try when you've mellowed out a little.

Atama o kakaeru **頭を抱える** "hold one's head in one's hands"
be at a loss for an answer, don't know what to do

むずかしい問題に皆は頭を抱えた。
Muzukashii mondai ni mina wa atama o kakaeta.
Everyone was at their wit's end trying to solve the problem. / The problem had everyone stumped (wringing their hands).

盗難事件続発に校長は頭を抱え込んだ。
Tōnan jiken zokuhatsu ni kōchō wa atama o kakaekonda.
The principal was tearing her hair out trying to figure out what to do about all the thefts that had been taking place.

Atama o sageru **頭を下げる** "lower one's head"

(1) bow to (in greeting) (2) give in to, bow to

(1) 彼は深々と頭を下げて挨拶した。
Kare wa fukabuka to atama o sagete aisatsu shita.
He greeted us with a deep bow.

(2) あんな奴に頭を下げて取り引きを頼む気はないね。
Anna yatsu ni atama o sagete torihiki o tanomu ki wa nai ne.
I've got no intention of kowtowing to a guy like that just to get him to do business with us. / There's no way I'm going to go to that guy on my hands and knees and beg him to cut a deal with us.

Atama o tsukau **頭を使う** "use one's head"
use one's head (noodle)

ちょっと頭を使えば金もうけの道はいくらでもある。
Chotto atama o tsukaeba kane-mōke no michi wa ikura de mo aru.
There are all kinds of ways to make money if you just use your head (the old bean) a little.

頭は生きている間に使わなくっちゃ。
Atama wa ikite iru aida ni tsukawanakutcha.
I figure that as long as you are alive and kicking you should use your head for something besides a hatrack.

ateuma 当て馬 "an applied horse"

a plant, decoy; (of a political candidate sent out to test the waters or divide the opposition) a stalking horse, a spoiler

当て馬を使って相手の出方を見てみよう。
Ateuma o tsukatte aite no dekata o mite miyō.
Let's see if we can draw them out by sending in a decoy.

あの人は単に当て馬候補にされただけさ。
Ano hito wa tan ni ateuma kōho ni sareta dake sa.
That candidate's just a stalking horse.

✌ Metaphoric use derives from the original meaning of a stallion used to discover or encourage the readiness of a mare to mate.

awabi あわび（鮑） abalone

This increasingly less common shellfish lends its moniker to the lexicon of love from the observation that although it is a true univalve, it appears to be a bivalve missing one of its two shells and is, hence, in search of its other (better?) half. It is otherwise lexically undistinguished.

Awabi are counted *ichimai* 一枚.

Awabi no kataomoi 鮑の片思い "an abalone's one-sided love"
unrequited love, one-sided love, carrying a torch for someone

---

おまえはいつも鮑の片思いだなあ。どうしてもてないんだろう。
Omae wa itsumo awabi no kataomoi da nā. Dōshite motenai n' darō.
You're always in love with some chick that doesn't even know you're alive. Wonder why you can't find yourself a woman.

Awabi is often deleted from the expression altogether.

佳子さんの片思い、もう3年にもなるんだって。
Yoshiko-san no kataomoi, mō sannen ni mo naru n' datte.
They say Yoshiko's been carrying the torch for three long years.

☞ *sōshi-sōai* 相思相愛

baimei-kōi 売名行為 "name-selling activity"

self-advertisement; a publicity stunt; publicity seeking

彼女は「女優の売名行為だ」という陰口にも負けず、ボランティア活動を続けている。
Kanojo wa "Joyū no baimei-kōi da" to iu kageguchi ni mo makezu, borantia-katsudō o tsuzukete iru.
The actress didn't let snide remarks about it all being a publicity stunt prevent her from continuing her volunteer work.

誠意があるか単なる売名行為かは、見る目のある人にはすぐわかってしまうさ。
Seii ga aru ka tannaru baimei-kōi ka wa, miru me no aru hito ni wa sugu wakatte shimau sa.
Anyone with half an eye can tell in an instant whether something is meant sincerely or is only done for publicity.

baji-tōfū 馬耳東風 "the east wind (blowing in) a horse's ear"

have no effect, (like) water off a duck's back; go in one ear and out the other

The east wind 東風 here refers to the warm wind heralding the arrival of spring, usually called *harukaze* 春風. The origin of this four-character compound dates from a poem written in the Tang dynasty in ancient China by the poet Rihaku 李白. Here is a free and easy translation of his poem: "After suffering the hardships of the long cold winter, people rejoice at the arrival of the warm winds of spring, but our joy is not shared by the horses of the field." Maybe the horses knew something Rihaku didn't: spring may mean warm winds and pretty flowers for poets, but it also means backbreaking work for farmers and their work animals.

俺は全身全霊をこめて話をした積もりだけど、あいつには馬耳東風だった。

Ore wa zenshin-zenrei o komete hanashi o shita tsumori da kedo, aitsu ni wa baji-tōfū datta.

I put body and soul into telling him all about it, but it seemed to go in one ear and out the other.

聞いていないのか、聞いていても馬耳東風なのか、分からないんだ。

Kiite inai no ka, kiite ite mo baji-tōfū na no ka, wakaranai n' da.

I don't know whether he simply didn't hear or whether he heard and just couldn't care less.

仕事に熱中している彼女に縁談の話をしても今は馬耳東風だな。

Shigoto ni netchū shite iru kanojo ni endan no hanashi o shite mo ima wa baji-tōfū da na.

She's so wrapped up in her work right now that if you try to talk to her about marriage, it just goes in one ear and out the other.

TVゲームに夢中になっている人間に何を言っても馬耳東風だ。

Terebi gēmu ni muchū ni natte iru ningen ni nani o itte mo baji-tōfū da.

You might as well go talk to the wall as to someone engrossed in playing Nintendo.

❧ In Japanese there are several idioms expressing the idea of giving something of value to someone who does not appreciate its worth. One of these 馬の耳に念仏 (*Uma no mimi ni nenbutsu*, "A Buddhist prayer in a horse's ear") is similar to 馬耳東風 (both having the characters for "horse's ear" in common), so care should be taken not to confuse the two expressions. Two further idioms with a similar meaning are 猫に小判 (*Neko ni koban*, "Giving gold coins to a cat") and 豚に真珠 (*Buta ni shinju*, "Casting pearls before swine"). The difference between 馬耳東風 and 馬の耳に念仏 on the one hand and 猫に小判 and 豚に真珠 on the other is that the former can only be used when something intangible is concerned, e.g., advice. The latter can be used for both tangible and intangible things.

☞ *buta ni shinju* 豚に真珠, *neko ni koban* 猫に小判, *uma no mimi ni nenbutsu* 馬の耳に念仏

bakyaku o arawasu 馬脚を露す "expose the horse's legs"

give oneself away, show one's true colors, reveal one's true character, betray oneself, reveal one's cloven foot (hoof)

あいつ善人ぶっているがいつか馬脚を露すぞ。
Aitsu zennin butte iru ga itsuka bakyaku o arawasu zo.
He's faking being a nice guy. Give him some time and he'll give himself away.

彼はとうとう馬脚を露し、麻薬密売に手を染め始めた。
Kare wa tōtō bakyaku o arawashi, mayaku-mitsubai ni te o somehajimeta.
Eventually he showed his true colors by beginning to sell drugs.

🐎 From the stage, *bakyaku*—literally "horse's legs"—meant the person dressed in a horse suit playing the role of the legs. For it to become apparent through some mishap or otherwise that the horse was really played by actors was to "expose the horse's legs," and later, by extension, to inadvertently reveal something one had attempted to conceal.

bankoku-kyōtsū 万国共通 "ten thousand countries in common"

universal, the same everywhere

笑顔は万国共通の挨拶ですね。
Egao wa bankoku-kyōtsū no aisatsu desu ne.
A smile is a universal greeting the world over.

地球の環境問題は、万国共通の課題だろう。
Chikyū no kankyō-mondai wa, bankoku-kyōtsū no kadai darō.
The earth's environmental problems are of concern to all people everywhere.

bari-zōgon 罵詈雑言 "abusive language, rude words"

abusive language, cursing and swearing, insults; 〜を浴びせる (*abiseru*) to shower someone with abuse; to call someone names (every name in the book)

酒の席とはいえ、罵詈雑言を浴びせられて、黙っているわけにはいかなかったんだ。
Sake no seki to wa ie, bari-zōgon o abiserarete, damatte iru wake ni wa ikanakatta n' da.
Even considering that everyone had had a few drinks, I just couldn't sit there after being showered with abuse like that.

日本語より英語のほうが罵詈雑言の種類は多いような気がするけど、どう。
Nihongo yori eigo no hō ga bari-zōgon no shurui wa ōi yō na ki ga suru kedo, dō.
I've got a sneaky feeling there are more ways of insulting someone in English than in Japanese. What do you think?

社長は総会屋たちの浴びせかける罵詈雑言にじっと耐えていた。
Shachō wa sōkaiya-tachi no abisekakeru bari-zōgon ni jitto taete ita.
The president sat there stoically while the hoodlums at the shareholders' meeting rained down invective on him.

↷ *biji-reiku* 美辞麗句

bashauma 馬車馬 "a carriage horse"

a workhorse, a hard worker

彼は死ぬまで馬車馬のように働き続けた。
Kare wa shinu made bashauma no yō ni hatarakitsuzuketa.

He worked like a dog until his dying day.

彼、馬車馬のように働いてるけど、一体いつ寝てるんだ？
Kare, bashauma no yō ni hataraite 'ru kedo, ittai itsu nete 'ru n' da?
Wonder when a guy who works like a horse (slaves away) like he does ever gets any sleep?

🐎 From the way a carriage horse wearing blinders goes about its job singlemindedly. The idiom commonly appears followed by *no yō ni hataraku*.

biji-reiku 美辞麗句 "beautiful language, charming phrases"

pretty words, flowery language, highfalutin phrases, purple prose

内容のお粗末さを美辞麗句でごまかそうとしているのが見え見えさ。
Naiyō no osomatsusa o biji-reiku de gomakasō to shite iru no ga miemie sa.
It's as clear as day that they're trying to cover up for the lack of content by using flowery language.

美辞麗句を連ねてあるが、要するに断りの返事だよ。
Biji-reiku o tsuranete aru ga, yōsuru ni kotowari no henji da yo.
They've strung together lots of highfalutin phrases, but what they're basically saying is the answer's no.

☞ *gaikō-jirei* 外交辞令, *tamamushi-iro* 玉虫色; *bari-zōgon* 罵詈雑言

bōin-bōshoku 暴飲暴食 "violent drinking, violent eating"

make a pig of oneself, overeat and overdrink, stuff oneself stupid with food and drink

暴飲暴食はやめなさい。「腹も身の内」だよ。
Bōin-bōshoku wa yamenasai. "Hara mo mi no uchi" da yo.
Stop making such a pig of yourself. Remember, you are what you eat.

🖎 腹も身の内 (*hara mo mi no uchi*) is a Japanese saying with no direct equivalent in English. Paraphrased it means "Your stomach is part of your body too, you know, so you'd better take care of it."

お前みたいに毎日暴飲暴食を続けてると、いまに胃をこわすよ。
Omae mitai ni mainichi bōin-bōshoku o tsuzukete 'ru to, ima ni i o kowasu yo.
If you go on stuffing yourself full of food and drink, you'll ruin your stomach.

bōjaku-bujin 傍若無人 "as if there were no one around" (*in old Japanese* 若 *means "as if"*)

arrogance, audacity, insolence, defiance, recklessness

彼の傍若無人な自己主張には、腹が立つより先に呆れてしまう。
Kare no bōjaku-bujin na jiko-shuchō ni wa, hara ga tatsu yori saki ni akirete shimau.
I'm not so much angry at his outrageous selfishness as simply amazed.

あんな傍若無人のふるまいが通るのも、社長の娘と結婚してるからだ。
Anna bōjaku-bujin no furumai ga tōru no mo, shachō no musume to kekkon shite 'ru kara da.
The reason he can get away with such outrageous behavior is that he's married to the boss's daughter.

buta ぶた (豚) pig, swine

The three hundred or so varieties of swine known to Japan are reviled as filthy, ugly beasts, a reputation these descendants of wild boars have been encumbered with, perhaps due to the conditions of their domesticity, i.e., living in sties. Although cops don't get called *buta* by protestors, jails do earn the unofficial appellation *butabako*, or pig box, presumably for the unsanitary conditions encountered inside. The pig's oink is *būbū* ブーブー (the same as a fart), and it is counted *ippiki* 一匹 or *ittō* 一頭.

Buta 豚 "pig"

1. (someone ugly) a pig, two-bagger; (dirty or slovenly) a pig, slob, scuzzball; (someone who is fat or overeats) a pig, a chow hound; (someone stupid) a dumbell, fool, dimwit, knucklehead, airhead

   この豚！
   Kono buta !
   You swine (pig, fat ass, dimwit)!

   あの豚野郎、今度会ったらただじゃおかねえ。
   Ano buta yarō, kondo attara tada ja okanē.
   That mother! He's gonna get what's coming to him next time.

🕯 Used to revile someone, it is often followed by *yarō* 野郎, when describing a man, or *onnamata* 女又, when referring to a woman who is an object of scorn.

2. (of such things as a bad hand in cards or a losing lottery ticket) a loser; nothing; come up short

   またブタだ！
   Mata buta da!
   Not another shitty hand!

   この間宝くじ2万円も買ったのに全部ブタだったよ。
   Kono aida takarakuji niman-en mo katta no ni zenbu buta datta yo.

I shelled out 20,000 yen for lottery tickets a while ago, and damned if every last one of them wasn't a loser.

Buta mo odaterya ki ni noboru **豚もおだてりゃ木に登る** "Even a pig will climb a tree if you flatter it."
flattery will get you a long way

「えー、あの人がその借金の面倒みるって本当に約束したの。」
"Ē, ano hito ga sono shakkin no mendō miru tte hontō ni yakusoku shita no."
"No way! He really promised he'd loan you the money?"

「豚もおだてりゃ木に登るっていうだろう。」
"Buta mo odaterya ki ni noboru tte iu darō."
"Like they say, a little flattery goes a long way."

豚もおだてりゃ木に登るっていうけど、どうやってあの女優に出演を承諾させたの？
Buta mo odaterya ki ni noboru tte iu kedo, dō yatte ano joyū ni shutsuen o shōdaku saseta no?
I know a little flattery will go a long way, but just how did you talk that actress into agreeing to appear in the production?

Buta ni shinju **豚に真珠** "pearls to pigs"
casting pearls before swine; a waste

そんな高級なピアノ買ったって、豚に真珠だよ。
Sonna kōkyū na piano katta tte, buta ni shinju da yo.
Buying an expensive piano like that for him is like casting pearls before swine.

こんな年寄りがワープロ持っても、豚に真珠ですよ。
Konna toshiyori ga wāpuro motte mo, buta ni shinju desu yo.
What a waste it is for an old guy like me to have a word processor.

✌ A linguistic import, this comes from the New Testament. Although there is no consensus, some feel this expression is used exclusively about material objects rather than abstractions.

☞ *baji-tōfū* 馬耳東風, *neko ni koban* 猫に小判, *uma no mimi ni nenbutsu* 馬の耳に念仏

Butabako 豚箱 "pig box"
a jail, the clink, the cooler, the slammer

俺、若い頃極道して豚箱入れられたことあるんだ。
Ore, wakai koro gokudō shite butabako irerareta koto aru n' da.
I went astray when I was young and ended up doing time.

お前そんなことしてると豚箱にぶち込まれるぞ。
Omae sonna koto shite 'ru to butabako ni buchikomareru zo.
Keep it up and you'll be cooling your heels in jail.

✂ From the filthy crowded conditions associated with such places.

Butagoya 豚小屋 "pigpen"
(a small filthy house, apartment, or room) a pigpen, pigsty

なんだこの部屋はまるで豚小屋だなあ、すこしは掃除しろよ。
Nan da kono heya wa maru de butagoya da nā, sukoshi wa sōji shiro yo.
God, what a pigsty! Ever thought about cleaning it up a little?

こんな豚小屋から早く引っ越したいよ。
Konna butagoya kara hayaku hikkoshitai yo.
I can't wait to move out of this dump.

byōki 病気 "sick *ki*"

1. condition; disease, sickness, illness

父が心臓の病気で先日入院しましてね。
Chichi ga shinzō no byōki de senjitsu nyūin shimashite ne.
Yeah, Dad went into the hospital the other day for a heart condition. / My father was hospitalized the other day with heart disease.

彼の病気はかなり重いようで、心配なんですが。
Kare no byōki wa kanari omoi yō de, shinpai nan desu ga.
He appears to be quite seriously ill, and it has me worried (we're worried).

病気が直ったらまた一緒に山へ行こうよ。
Byōki ga naottara mata issho ni yama e ikō yo.
Let's go hiking again once you get better (recover, get over your illness).

毎日そんなに飲んでるとしまいには病気になるよ。
Mainichi sonna ni nonde 'ru to shimai ni wa byōki ni naru yo.
Keep drinking like that and you'll end up sick.

この病気にかかったら、とにかく安静にしていることですね。
Kono byōki ni kakattara, tonikaku ansei ni shite iru koto desu ne.
Rest is the most important thing when you come down with this sickness.

病気の人は悲観的になりがちだから、気をつけてあげなくちゃ。
Byōki no hito wa hikan-teki ni narigachi da kara, ki o tsukete agenakucha.
Sick people can quickly become pessimistic, so you've got to keep an eye on them.

病気の時はお互い様なんだから、遠慮しないで。
Byōki no toki wa otagaisama nan da kara, enryo shinai de.
Everybody gets sick sometime, so don't hesitate to ask for something if you need it.

変な病気うつされたんじゃないでしょうね。
Hen na byōki utsusareta n' ja nai deshō ne.
You didn't, like, catch something [from him/her], did you? [While *hen na byōki* may mean "a strange or unusual disease," it is also common slang for venereal disease, as is *myō na byōki*.]

悪い病気でなければいいんですが。
Warui byōki de nakereba ii n' desu ga.
I hope it's not the big C. [*Warui byōki* is often a euphemism for "cancer."]

あいつほとんどビョーキだぜ。
Aitsu hotondo byōki da ze.
Dude's sick [in the head] (waaay out there), man. [*Byōki* written in katakana, this trendy usage has yet to stand the test of time.]

🎖 An illness is commonly described as being either *karui* 軽い (slight, not serious; literally "light") or *omoi* 重い (serious; literally "heavy"). *Byōki ni naru* is used about any disease, illness or sickness, while use of *byōki ni kakaru* is reserved for contagious diseases.

☞ *karada o kowasu* 体を壊す

2. (of a bad habit or shortcoming) one's old tricks

あいつ例の病気がぶり返したんじゃないか。
Aitsu rei no byōki ga burikaeshita n' ja nai ka.
I see he's up to his old tricks again.

また悪い病気が始まったら、臭い飯を食うことになるぞ。
Mata warui byōki ga hajimattara, kusai meshi o kuu koto ni naru zo.
Start up again and you'll end up behind bars.

chi 血 blood

The blood that courses through our bodies carries more than the nutrients necessary to sustain life. It is thought, poetically at least, to be an important determinant in the formation of our very nature. Idioms with *chi* are often used in describing certain strong emotions and degrees of intelligence. To be related is to "share the same blood." Beyond the realm of idioms, mates are chosen or rejected on the basis of blood type, and Japanese never seem to tire of asking one's blood type and then proceeding to explain every observed personality trait by whether one is type A, B, or O. About the only thing that even comes close to this national fascination with blood is the Western notion of zodiac signs, which, by the way, are themselves nearly as common a topic of light conversation in Japan as in the West.

Chi ga sawagu 血が騒ぐ "one's blood clamors"
get excited, (all) worked up, hopped up, hot and bothered, be hot to trot

---

祭りの太鼓の音を聞いただけで血が騒いだ。
Matsuri no taiko no oto o kiita dake de chi ga sawaida.
The juices started flowing at the mere sound of the festival drums.

毎年、フットボールのシーズンになると血が騒ぐのです。
Mainen, futtobōru no shīzun ni naru to chi ga sawagu no desu.
He starts racing his motor every year when football season rolls around.

Chi no meguri ga warui 血の巡りが悪い "have bad circulation"
be slow on the uptake, be dense

あの人は血の巡りが悪いらしくて、つまり、ちょっと鈍いのですよ。
Ano hito wa chi no meguri ga warui rashikute, tsumari, chotto nibui no desu yo.
That guy is just a little thick, I'm afraid. / That guy's so slow— there must be something wrong upstairs.

☞ *atama ga nibui* 頭が鈍い, *atama ga warui* 頭が悪い; *atama ga ii* 頭がいい, *atama ga kireru* 頭が切れる, *atama no deki ga chigau* 頭の出来が違う, *atama no kaiten ga hayai* 頭の回転が早い

Chi o miru 血を見る "see blood"
lead to bloodshed, come to bloodshed

いい加減にしないと血を見るぞ。
Ii kagen ni shinai to chi o miru zo.
You're cruisin' for a bruisin', buddy. / Keep it up if you want your ass kicked.

血を見たくなければ、俺の言う通りにしろ。
Chi o mitaku nakereba, ore no iu tōri ni shiro.
Do what I say and nobody will get hurt.

最初は小さな争いだったが、とうとう血を見ることになった。
Saisho wa chiisa na arasoi datta ga, tōtō chi o miru koto ni natta.
It started out as just a little tiff, but it wasn't long before people started getting hurt.

Chi o wakeru 血を分ける "share blood"
be related by blood, be blood relations

あの二人は血を分けた兄弟だ。
Ano futari wa chi o waketa kyōdai da.
They're real brothers.

私に血を分けた兄がいるとは、知らなかった。
Watashi ni chi o waketa ani ga iru to wa, shiranakatta.
I never knew I had an older brother.

Also 血を引く *chi o hiku,* 血がつながっている *chi ga tsunagatte iru.*

chidori ちどり（千鳥） plover

The name *chidori* literally means "a thousand birds," and is thought to have come from the fact that the wee riparians are usually seen in large flocks. Twelve of the world's sixty or so species of plovers can be found in Japan's marshlands and along its shores. Unlike its three-toed namesakes, which are known to be vigorous walkers, the five-toed variety, often sighted primarily during hours of darkness in towns and cities across the nation, seems to have an inordinate amount of difficulty ambulating, particularly in a straight line. Plovers, considered winter birds in Japan, are counted *ichiwa* 一羽.

Chidoriashi 千鳥足 "plover legs"
wobbly (rubbery) legs

> 飲み過ぎたその客は千鳥足で店を出て行った。
> *Nomisugita sono kyaku wa chidoriashi de mise o dete itta.*
> The tipsy patron staggered out of the joint on rubbery legs.

> 千鳥足だったから家に着くのにいつもの倍かかったよ。
> *Chidoriashi datta kara ie ni tsuku no ni itsumo no bai kakatta yo.*
> With my legs feeling like rubber bands, it took me twice as long as usual to get home.

❧ Used primarily of the way a drunk walks, from the manner in which the plover crosses its legs one over the other as it darts about in search of a meal. Research has shown that the plover's unique walk is, in fact, a ploy which allows it to catch unsuspecting prey.

chikuba no tomo 竹馬の友 "stilt friends"
a childhood friend, a friend from childhood

> 竹馬の友は何年会ってなくても不思議と話がはずむ。
> *Chikuba no tomo wa nannen atte 'nakute mo fushigi to hanashi ga hazumu.*
> It's really weird how you can get together with a childhood friend after years and still find plenty to talk about.

❧ The word for stilts originally meant a branch of bamboo, with the attached leaves bringing up the rear, ridden around like a horse by children. Later it was used to describe the tall poles (made of bamboo in Japan) with places to put your feet that provide children with a new perspective on life as well as yet another opportunity to injure themselves. As an independent word, 竹馬 is read *takeuma*.

chō 蝶 butterfly

A symbol of beauty, there are over 250 known varieties of this diurnal four-winged insect in Japan. Unlike their poor sisters, the moths, butterflies rest with their wings folded vertically and show no monomaniacal or suicidal tendencies when exposed to light. Also called *chōchō* or *chōcho* 蝶蝶, their flight is expressed onomatopoeically in Japanese as *hirahira to tobu* ヒラヒラと飛ぶ, or fluttering. They are counted in various ways: *ichiwa* 一羽, *ippiki* 一匹, or *ittō* 一頭, the last usually reserved for counting large mammals.

Chō yo hana yo 蝶よ花よ "O butterfly, O flower"
shower affection on one's darling daughter (son), bring up one's daughter (son) like a princess (prince)

蝶よ花よと育てられた彼女はわがままばかり言っている。
Chō yo hana yo to sodaterareta kanojo wa wagamama bakari itte iru.
Pampered all her life, she's always got to have her own way.

長い間子宝に恵まれなかったその夫婦は一粒種の娘を蝶よ花よと育てた。
Nagai aida kodakara ni megumarenakatta sono fūfu wa hitotsubudane no musume o chō yo hana yo to sodateta.
Childless for many years, the doting couple brought up their darling daughter like a princess.

🐍 Similar to *neko kawaigari* 猫かわいがり, in the sense of showering affection on someone, *chō yo hana yo* differs in that it is used specifically about bringing up one's own child, almost always a daughter. Accordingly, it appears almost exclusively with the verb *sodatsu* 育つ.

chōda no retsu 長蛇の列 "a long snake line"

a long line, a queue

そのラーメン屋の前は昼どきになると長蛇の列ができる。
Sono rāmen-ya no mae wa hirudoki ni naru to chōda no retsu ga dekiru.
There's always a long line of people in front of that ramen shop when lunchtime rolls around.

祭日のディズニーランドはどこのアトラクションも長蛇の列だ。
Saijitsu no Dizunīrando wa doko no atorakushon mo chōda no retsu da.
There's a long line snaking around in front of every attraction at Disneyland on holidays.

🐍 From the resemblance of a line of people to the body of a snake.

chototsu-mōshin 猪突猛進 "the boar's wild rush"

reckless, foolhardy, madcap; straight ahead (and damn the torpedos)

猪突猛進の彼にこの仕事を任せない方がいい。
Chototsu-mōshin no kare ni kono shigoto o makasenai hō ga ii.
He's so foolhardy that we'd better not put him in charge of this project.

彼女の性格は一言で言うと猪突猛進型です。
Kanojo no seikaku wa hitokoto de iu to chototsu-mōshin-gata desu.
You could characterize her personality in a word, "reckless."

✌ From the way a wild boar runs straight ahead full-blast, looking neither right nor left, and its inability to change directions quickly. Not the kind of thing you'd want to have somebody say about you.

chūto-hanpa 中途半端 "halfway and incomplete"

half-finished, half-done, halfhearted, incomplete, half-baked

あいつは口だけは達者だけど、やることは中途半端なんだ。
Aitsu wa kuchi dake wa tassha da kedo, yaru koto wa chūto-hanpa nan da.
He talks up a storm, but he botches up everything he does.

いつまでも中途半端な態度だと、彼女に振られちゃうよ。
Itsu made mo chūto-hanpa na taido da to, kanojo ni furarechau yo.
If you don't start treating her a bit more seriously, she'll leave you, you know.

こんな中途半端なやり方じゃ、効果が上がらないのは目に見えてるよ。
Konna chūto-hanpa na yarikata ja, kōka ga agaranai no wa me ni miete 'ru yo.
It should be obvious to anybody that this half-baked way of doing things is not going to produce results.

「中途半端は何もしないのと同じ」と上司に怒鳴られた。
"Chūto-hanpa wa nani mo shinai to onaji" to jōshi ni donarareta.
The boss bawled me out, saying, "Doing half a job is the same as doing nothing at all."

↪ *mushikui* 虫食い, *shirikire-tonbo* 尻切れとんぼ

chūya-kenkō 昼夜兼行 "going both day and night"

(work) day and night, flat out, around the clock

締切が迫って来たので、昼夜兼行で原稿を書いています。
Shimekiri ga sematte kita no de, chūya-kenkō de genkō o kaite imasu.
With the deadline for my book approaching, I'm writing day and night.

このままじゃ納期に間に合わないぞ、今日から工場は昼夜兼行だ。
Kono mama ja nōki ni ma ni awanai zo, kyō kara kōjō wa chūya-kenkō da.
At this rate we'll never make the delivery on time, so starting today the factory's going on a 24-hour shift.

☞ *fumin-fukyū* 不眠不休

daikon-yakusha 大根役者 "a radish actor"

a ham actor, a lousy (poor) actor

若い頃「大根役者」と言われたのに奮起して、押しも押されもしない名優になった。
Wakai koro "daikon-yakusha" to iwareta no ni funki shite, oshi mo osare mo shinai meiyū ni natta.
Called "a ham actor" while young, he was inspired to become one of the best actors around.

いくら顔が良くても、あんな大根役者じゃどうしようもないよ。
Ikura kao ga yokute mo, anna daikon-yakusha ja dō shiyō mo nai yo.
I don't care how handsome he is; the guy's still hopeless as an actor.

daitan-futeki 大胆不敵 "bold and daring"

audacious, daredevil, undaunted, intrepid, brave, as bold as brass, fearless; to not know the meaning of fear

その武将は大胆不敵な人物だった。

Sono bushō wa daitan-futeki na jinbutsu datta.
The general was incredibly courageous and brave.

泥棒は大胆不敵にも正面玄関から出入りしたらしい。
Dorobō wa daitan-futeki ni mo shōmen-genkan kara deiri shita rashii.
The burglar was as bold as brass, apparently entering and exiting by the front door.

dani だに (壁蝨) **tick**

This eight-legged parasite is related to spiders but liked a lot less, wherever it is found. Urban infestations of the hearty bloodsuckers have caused apartment dwellers headaches—and a lot of itching and scratching—in recent years. Ticks are counted *ippiki* 一匹.

Dani だに "tick"
a hood, gangster, punk; a good-for-nothing, parasite, scumbag

---

あいつはこの町のだにだから、早くいなくなればいいんだ。
Aitsu wa kono machi no dani da kara, hayaku inaku nareba ii n' da.
He's like a plague on the town. The sooner he's outa here the better.

あんなだにのような奴、ろくな死に方しないよ。
Anna dani no yō na yatsu, roku na shinikata shinai yo.
A punk like that's gonna end up face down in some alley.

🐛 By extension from the fact that ticks are parasites sucking the lifeblood of others, this expression is usually used of those involved in underworld activities or the likes.

danson-johi 男尊女卑 "men respected, women despised"

the custom of treating women as inferior to men; male chauvinism

表向きは男女平等なんて言ってても、大企業ほど本音は男尊女卑なんだから。
Omotemuki wa danjo-byōdō nante itte 'te mo, dai-kigyō hodo honne wa danson-johi nan da kara.
Although in public they like to talk about sexual equality, in truth big corporations are deeply chauvinistic.

今時そんな男尊女卑の考え方をしてたら、結婚してくれる女性なんかいないよ。
Imadoki sonna danson-johi no kangaekata o shite 'tara, kekkon shite kureru josei nanka inai yo.
With a chauvinistic attitude like yours, you'll never find a woman to marry you in this day and age.

dasoku 蛇足 "snake's feet"

unnecessary, extraneous; tits on a boar

そんな話は蛇足だ。
Sonna hanashi wa dasoku da.
That's completely unnecessary.

彼女がその講演で最後に話したことは蛇足だった。
Kanojo ga sono kōen de saigo ni hanashita koto wa dasoku datta.
What she said at the very end of the lecture amounted more and less to flogging a dead horse.

蛇足ですが、私は昆虫採集が趣味です。
Dasoku desu ga, watashi wa konchū-saishū ga shumi desu.
Needless to say, collecting insects is my hobby.

このレポートは蛇足の部分が多すぎる。
Kono repōto wa dasoku no bubun ga ōsugiru.
There's too much padding in this paper. / This report has got a lot of fluff in it.

🐍 Can be used both of objects and of behavior. From an ancient Chinese tale of some friends who bet a round of drinks on who among them could paint a snake the fastest. One of the men was much quicker at the task than his friends and decided in his leisure to add legs to his creation. Upon seeing this, another painter asked how he could put legs on a reptile that originally had none, and he relieved the man of his prize before he could quaff his victory libation.

dobunezumi どぶ鼠 "a sewer rat"

a rat, a scoundrel

あの老舗が潰れたのはどぶ鼠のせいだ。
Ano shinise ga tsubureta no wa dobunezumi no sei da.
That long-established business went under thanks to the skulduggery of one of its employees.

このどぶ鼠が、ちょっと目を離すとろくなことしない。
Kono dobunezumi ga, chotto me o hanasu to roku na koto shinai.
You're always up to something the minute I take my eyes off you.

🐍 Actually a brown, or Norway rat, this rodent is known for carrying the plague. Idiomatic usage is limited to an employee who embezzles from his employer or otherwise bites the hand that feeds him.

dojō どじょう (泥鰌) loach

Unfamiliar to most Westerners, these small freshwater fish, variously said to be related to minnows or carps, are common in streams, marshes, and rice paddies throughout Japan. They are eaten in a variety of ways, including as a tabletop casserole dish called *yanagawa* 柳川, in which the little critters are boiled alive with eggs. Their futile attempts to escape the increasing heat drives them headlong into a pattern radiating away from the center of the pot, creating a delightful artistic, if not culinary, motif for the enjoyment of cold-blooded diners. Many Tokyo restaurants specializing in loach dishes advertise their menu by corrupting the four-phonetic character name *dojō* どじょう as *dozeu* どぜう. By deleting a phonetic character they avoid a word composed of four letters, the Japanese word for four, *shi,* being homonymous with that for death. Anything in fours is considered inauspicious.

Dojō hige **どじょうひげ** "a loach mustache"
a thin (sparse) mustache

あのどじょうひげのお爺さん知ってる？
Ano dojō hige no ojiisan shitte 'ru?
You know that old guy with the skinny little mustache?

考え事をするときどじょうひげを引っ張るのが父の癖だった。
Kangaegoto o suru toki dojō hige o hipparu no ga chichi no kuse datta.
My dad always used to tug at his thin mustache when he was thinking about something.

🐟 From the resemblance of such a mustache to the ten barbels growing around the mouth of a loach.

Yanagi no shita ni itsumo dojō wa inai **柳の下にいつもどじょうはいない** "There is not always a loach under the willow."
there is a limit to luck (from the tale of a man who once caught a loach under a certain willow tree but was never able to repeat the feat)

去年のダービーでは大穴を当てたが、柳の下にいつもどじょうはいないということか。
Kyonen no dābī de wa ōana o ateta ga, yanagi no shita ni itsumo dojō wa inai to iu koto ka.
Last year I made a killing on a sleeper in the derby, but no such luck this year.

前の試験はたまたまヤマが当たっただけでしょう。柳の下にどじょうは二匹いないよ。
Mae no shiken wa tamatama yama ga atatta dake deshō. Yanagi no shita ni dojō wa nihiki inai yo.
I just lucked out on the last test. No way it'll ever happen again.

dokuritsu-doppo 独立独歩 "standing by oneself, walking by oneself"

independence, self-reliance, standing on one's own two feet

子供たちには、まず独立独歩の精神を身につけさせたいと思っているんです。
Kodomo-tachi ni wa, mazu dokuritsu-doppo no seishin o mi ni tsuke-sasetai to omotte iru n' desu.
Above all I want to instill in my children a spirit of independence.

独立独歩の道を歩むべく、このたび脱サラする決心をいたしました。
Dokuritsu-doppo no michi o ayumu beku, kono tabi datsusara suru kesshin o itashimashita.
I have decided to quit the company because I feel I must branch out and stand on my own two feet.

dokushin-kizoku 独身貴族 "single aristocrats"

single people who can live very comfortably as they have no spouse to support (or live with their parents); footloose and fancy-free single people

独身貴族の生活が楽しめるのも今のうちだよ。せいぜい遊んでおきなさい。
Dokushin-kizoku no seikatsu ga tanoshimeru no mo ima no uchi da yo. Seizei asonde okinasai.
Now's the time to enjoy your bachelor status, so get out there and have some fun (sow some wild oats) while you can!

家の息子は、独身貴族っていうんでしょうかねえ、優雅で気ままな暮らしをしてますよ。
Uchi no musuko wa, dokushin-kizoku tte iu n' deshō ka nē, yūga de kimama na kurashi o shite 'masu yo.
I suppose that's what they call being young, free, and single. Our son's certainly enjoying the nice things of life, doing exactly as he pleases.

礼子さんの今度のマンションすごいわよ。やっぱり独身貴族は違うわね。
Reiko-san no kondo no manshon sugoi wa yo. Yappari dokushin-kizoku wa chigau wa ne.
Reiko's new apartment is really something. Things are certainly different when you're single and have money to spare.

ebi えび（海老） shrimp / prawn / lobster

Among these auspicious crustaceans, lobsters are often served on commemorative occasions in Japan when normal shrimp or prawns won't do, though there is basically no linguistic distinction among the three. Why they are thought to be auspicious is unclear, though one theory points to the bent shape of their back, suggesting old age and longevity. Shrimp are counted *ichio* 一尾, *ippiki* 一匹, and *ippon* 一本.

Ebi de tai o tsuru　海老で鯛を釣る　"catch a sea bream with a shrimp"

do things the easy way; get a lot of bang for your buck, maximize returns and minimize effort, profit handsomely from a small investment, make a killing; throw a sprat to catch a mackerel

---

「バラの花束なんか持ってどうしたんだい。」
"Bara no hanataba nanka motte dō shita n' dai."
"What're you up to, carrying a bouquet of roses and all?"

「今日は、念願の彼女と初デートなんだ。よくいうだろう『海老で鯛を釣れ』って。」
"Kyō wa, nengan no kanojo to hatsu dēto nan da. Yoku iu darō 'ebi de tai o tsure' tte."
"Today's my first time out with that chick I've had my eye on, and I'm just trying to make the most of it."

大した努力もしないで、海老で鯛を釣ろうとしてもだめだな。
Taishita doryoku mo shinai de, ebi de tai o tsurō to shite mo dame da na.
Trying to make a killing without making much of an effort just isn't going to work.

🦐 Possibly from the plentifulness of shrimp and their diminutive size compared to sea bream. Used of attempts to spend little time, money, or effort to attain one's grandiose goals. Often shortened to *ebi (de) tai* 海老（で）鯛.

eiko-seisui　栄枯盛衰　"flourish and wither, prosper and perish"

the rise and fall of human affairs; the ups and downs of life; the many vicissitudes of life

栄枯盛衰は世の習いと思ってあきらめるほかないぞ。
Eiko-seisui wa yo no narai to omotte akirameru hoka nai zo.
Son, you have to take the fortunes and misfortunes of life as the way of the world and learn to live with them.

「平家物語」は平家の栄枯盛衰を描いている。
"Heike monogatari" wa Heike no eiko-seisui o egaite iru.
The *Heike Monogatari* is a story depicting the rise and fall of the Heike clan.

fugen-jikkō 不言実行 "silent action"

action speaks louder than words; 〜の人 a quiet man of action

私は古い人間かもしれないが、不言実行が好きだ。
Watashi wa furui ningen ka mo shirenai ga, fugen-jikkō ga suki da.
I may be old-fashioned, but I like getting things done without a lot of fuss.

不言実行は、ともすれば不言不実行になってしまうおそれがあるよ。
Fugen-jikkō wa, tomosureba fugen-fujikkō ni natte shimau osore ga aru yo.
If you are not careful, getting things done without a lot of fuss can end up meaning getting nothing done at all.

☙ Japanese who are articulate and good at expressing their ideas are not always popular. Getting on with things without talking about them (不言実行) is seen as a virtue. Many people have commented on how the Japanese prefer intuitive ways of communicating over verbal ones. There is "the art of the belly" (腹芸 *haragei*; the intuitive way of guessing what the other means), and "the transferal of one's true intent from one heart to another" (以心伝心 *ishin-denshin*). This is not altogether a wholly Japanese phenomenon; after all, we do say in English "Actions speak louder than words," and a fair number of Hollywood's biggest male stars are more famous for their action-packed performances than their mastery of the English language. The saying "Silence is golden" exists in both languages (the Japanese being 沈黙は金, *chinmoku wa kin*).

fugu-taiten 不倶戴天 "cannot bear (carry) the same sky"

irreconcilable (foes)

あいつは俺のいわば不倶戴天の敵なんだ。
Aitsu wa ore no iwaba fugu-taiten no teki nan da.
That guy's what you might call a mortal enemy.

青山さんと赤坂さんは、昔から不倶戴天の間柄だ。
Aoyama-san to Akasaka-san wa, mukashi kara fugu-taiten no aidagara da.
Aoyama and Akasaka have been at each other's throats for as long as I can remember.

fuhen-futō 不偏不党 "without bias and free from party affiliation"

impartial, neutral, non-partisan, fair, unbiased, independent

公務員は政治的には不偏不党が建前だ。
Kōmu-in wa seiji-teki ni wa fuhen-futō ga tatemae da.
Civil servants are supposed to be free of political bias.

長田教授は学閥に属さないで不偏不党の、いわば一匹狼だ。
Nagata-kyōju wa gakubatsu ni zokusanai de fuhen-futō no, iwaba ippiki-ōkami da.
Professor Nagata is what you might call a lone wolf, not aligning himself with any academic clique.

fūkō-meibi 風光明媚 "The scenery is clear and beautiful."

beautiful scenery, picturesque

こんな風光明媚なところで、老後をすごしたいものだね。
Konna fūkō-meibi na tokoro de, rōgo o sugoshitai mono da ne.
I would love to spend my retirement in a place as picturesque as this.

昔は風光明媚だったこの海岸も、すっかり観光化して汚れてしまったよ。
Mukashi wa fūkō-meibi datta kono kaigan mo, sukkari kankō-ka shite yogorete shimatta yo.
In the old days this beach used to be so beautiful, but now it's been totally spoilt by tourism.

fukurō ふくろう（梟） owl

This usually nocturnal carnivore is common in the forests of Japan but appears to have never inspired the notions of wisdom or omniscience that are commonly attributed to its Western counterparts. Its only characteristic worthy of lingiustic note in Japanese appears to be its activity at night, a trait it shares with owls everywhere. The protrusions on its head, by the way, are tufts of feathers, not ears, though they are sometimes called that.

The owl's cry is variously *hōhō* ホウホウ or *gorosukehohho* ゴロスケホッホ. They are counted *ippiki* 一匹 or *ichiwa* 一羽.

Fukurō ふくろう（梟） "owl"
a night owl, a person who stays up late, a night person

そんなふくろうみたいな生活してると体こわすよ。
Sonna fukurō mitai na seikatsu shite 'ru to karada kowasu yo.
You'll ruin your health living like a night owl like that.

彼女がふくろうのような仕事をしているのは、誰にも言わないが大きな夢があるらしい。
Kanojo ga fukurō no yō na shigoto o shite iru no wa, dare ni mo iwanai ga ōki na yume ga aru rashii.
She doesn't let on to anybody, but the reason she's working till all hours of the night is that she's pursuing a dream of hers.

✤ From the owl's nocturnal habits.

fukuro no (naka no) nezumi 袋の（中の）ねずみ
"a rat in a sack"

(of a person) someone trapped (like a rat); (of a situation) the jig is up

君は袋のねずみだ、人質を解放して、投降しなさい。
Kimi wa fukuro no nezumi da, hitojichi o kaihō shite, tōkō shinasai.
You're trapped. Release your hostages and give yourself up.

あいつはもう袋のねずみ同然だ、どこへも逃げられない。
Aitsu wa mō fukuro no nezumi dōzen da, doko e mo nigerarenai.
The guy's up shit creek without a paddle. There's no place for him to go.

袋のねずみにされた容疑者は投降した。
Fukuro no nezumi ni sareta yōgi-sha wa tōkō shita.
Surrounded, the suspect gave himself up to the police

✤ From the plight of a rat that has been chased into a sack and has no way to escape.

☞ *kyūso neko o kamu* 窮鼠猫を噛む

fumin-fukyū 不眠不休 "without sleep, without rest"

(to work hard) with no sleep or rest, day and night, twenty-four hours a day, non-stop, round-the-clock

不眠不休の勤務が続いて、過労死がひと事とは思えなくなった。
Fumin-fukyū no kinmu ga tsuzuite, karō-shi ga hitogoto to wa omoenaku natta.
Since I've been working flat out for quite a while, it's beginning to dawn on me that dying from overwork isn't just something that happens only to other people.

救援隊の不眠不休の活動のおかげで、多くの生存者が救出された。
Kyūen-tai no fumin-fukyū no katsudō no okage de, ōku no seizon-sha ga kyūshutsu sareta.
Many survivors were rescued thanks to the round-the-clock efforts of the emergency services.

医師は不眠不休で、患者の容態を見守った。
Ishi wa fumin-fukyū de, kanja no yōtai o mimamotta.
The doctor maintained a round-the-clock vigil, closely monitoring the patient's condition.

furudanuki 古狸 "an old raccoon dog"

a sly old fox, a wily (crafty) old dog

あの古狸また新入社員をいびってるらしいぞ。
Ano furudanuki mata shinnyū-shain o ibitte'ru rashii zo.
That wily old dog is at it again, giving the new employees a hard time.

あの人は古狸だからうかつなこと言うな。
Ano hito wa furudanuki da kara ukatsu na koto iu na.

Watch what you say around him, he's a sly old fox.

✌ Used exclusively of older men.

☞ *furugitsune* 古狐 (of older women), *tanuki* 狸

furugitsune 古狐 "an old fox"

a sly old bitch, a wily old bat, a cunning old battle-ax, a grimalkin

あの古狐め、いつか思い知らせてやる。
Ano furugitsune-me, itsuka omoishirasete yaru.
I'll show the old witch some day.

古狐と呼ばれていた彼女もいまではその面影もなくひっそりと暮らしている。
Furugitsune to yobarete ita kanojo mo ima de wa sono omokage mo naku hissori to kurashite iru.
Everybody used to call her a wily old bat, but you sure couldn't tell from how quietly she's living now.

✌ Used almost exclusively of women.

☞ *furudanuki* 古狸 (of men), *kitusne* 狐, *megitsune* 牝狐

fushō-fuzui 夫唱婦随 "the husband speaks, the wife obeys"

a loving couple (where the wife is happy to play second fiddle to her husband)

いまどき夫唱婦随が理想だなんて言ってるから、結婚相手が見つからないんじゃないの。
Imadoki fushō-fuzui ga risō da nante itte 'ru kara, kekkon-aite ga mitsukaranai n' ja nai no.
It's precisely because you say you're looking for a woman to be at your beck and call that you can't find anyone to marry you!

このごろでは夫唱婦随ならぬ婦唱夫随の家庭も多いんじゃないでしょうか。
Konogoro de wa fushō-fuzui naranu fushō-fuzui no katei mo ōi n' ja nai deshō ka.
These days there seem to be a good many families in which the wife not only washes her husband's pants but wears them, too.

fuyō-fukyū 不要不急 "unnecessary and not urgent"

not pressing, not vital

回線が混雑していますので、不要不急の電話は避けて下さい。
Kaisen ga konzatsu shite imasu no de, fuyō-fukyū no denwa wa sakete kudasai.
The phone lines are very busy so please don't make a call unless it is really urgent.

午後から大雪になる見込みですから、不要不急の用事の場合は出かけないほうがいいでしょう。
Gogo kara ōyuki ni naru mikomi desu kara, fuyō-fukyū no yōji no bāi wa dekakenai hō ga ii deshō.
The outlook is for heavy snow from the afternoon, so unless you have urgent business, you'd be better off staying in.

gaden-insui 我田引水 "(to) my ricefield (I) draw water"

self-seeking, promoting one's own interests, turning every argument in one's own favor, every miller draws water to his own mill

あいつと話してるといつも我田引水で腹が立つよ。
Aitsu to hanashite 'ru to itsumo gaden-insui de hara ga tatsu yo.
Talking with him drives me up the wall; he's only concerned with looking after his own interests.

まったく我田引水もいいところだ。
Mattaku gaden-insui mo ii tokoro da.
I've had more than enough of his enlightened self-interest.

いつも自分に都合のいいようにしかとらないんだな。我田引水もいい加減にしろよ。
Itsumo jibun ni tsugō no ii yō ni shika toranai n' da na. Gaden-insui mo ii kagen ni shiro yo.
You only see things in the best possible light for yourself. Stop being so self-centered.

☞ *jiga-jisan* 自画自賛, *shiri-shiyoku* 私利私欲

gaijū-naigō 外柔内剛 "soft on the outside, hard on the inside"

gentle on the outside, tough on the inside; gentle in appearance, but sturdy in spirit (often used to describe people who are hard on themselves but easy on others)

おとなしそうに見えるのに、頑固なんだよね。典型的な外柔内剛だよ。

Otonashisō ni mieru no ni, ganko nan da yo ne. Tenkei-teki na gaijū-naigō da yo.
> She looks like the quiet type, but she's stubborn as hell. She's one of those people who has an easygoing manner but is actually as tough as nails.

先生は外柔内剛で、人には優しいが自分には厳しい。
Sensei wa gaijū-naigō de, hito ni wa yasashii ga jibun ni wa kibishii.
> Our teacher's kind to others, but he really comes down hard on himself.

✧ The opposite to this four-character compound is 内柔外剛 *naijū-gaigō*, which is only different from the above entry in that the first and third characters have changed places.

gaikō-jirei 外交辞令 "diplomatic language"

just being polite (diplomatic)

そんな外交辞令をまともにうける奴があるか。
Sonna gaikō-jirei o matomo ni ukeru yatsu ga aru ka.
> Anyone with half a brain could see he was just being diplomatic (polite).

単なる外交辞令のつもりだったのに、先方は脈があると思ったらしいんです。
Tannaru gaikō-jirei no tsumori datta no ni, senpō wa myaku ga aru to omotta rashii n' desu.
> It was only meant as a polite formality, but it seems the other guy took it as meaning he has a chance.

☞ *biji-reiku* 美辞麗句, *tamamushi-iro* 玉虫色

gaikō-shuwan 外交手腕 "diplomatic talent (skill)"

diplomacy

彼は若いけど見事に外交手腕を発揮して、条約をまとめ上げた。
Kare wa wakai kedo migoto ni gaikō-shuwan o hakki shite, jōyaku o matomeageta.
Though still young, he showed great diplomacy in concluding (drawing up) the treaty.

彼の外交手腕には、まったく舌を巻いたよ。
Kare no gaikō-shuwan ni wa, mattaku shita o maita yo.
I have to take my hat off to his tact and diplomacy.

gakureki-shakai 学歴社会 "school-record society"

a society which places great importance on scholastic credentials and educational background (i.e., which school you went to)

学歴社会の弊害が言われて久しいが、一向に改善されていない。
Gakureki-shakai no heigai ga iwarete hisashii ga, ikkō ni kaizen sarete inai.
It's long been said that our society's obsession with academic credentials is harmful, but nothing's ever been done to improve the situation.

息子は学歴社会に反発して、大学へは進学しないと言い出した。
Musuko wa gakureki-shakai ni hanpatsu shite, daigaku e wa shingaku shinai to iidashita.
Reacting against the Japanese obsession with scholastic background, our son says he's not going to university.

gamaguchi がま口 "a toad's mouth"

1. (coin) purse

今どき、がま口なんていう人はあまりいないよ。

Imadoki, gamaguchi nante iu hito wa amari inai yo.
Nobody calls a coin purse a *gamaguchi* anymore.

2. (literally) a big mouth

あの漫画の主人公の特徴はがま口のような口です。
Ano manga no shujinkō no tokuchō wa gamaguchi no yō na kuchi desu.
The hero of that cartoon's got a giant mouth.

gan がん (雁) wild goose

These majestic, gregarious water birds come to Japan in the late fall to stay until early spring, when they once again return north. Often living in noisy flocks and known for their vigilance, geese can be found resting on sandbars in rivers or on islands to gain a measure of protection from their natural enemies, which include man. Given how long they have been hunted here, one cannot but wonder why they continue to return. The head of the traditional Japanese tobacco pipe, or *kiseru* きせる, and other kinds of pipes are called *gankubi* 雁首, or goosenecks, from their resemblance to the bird's head and neck when not outstretched in flight. A similar observation has led to a peculiar type of American trailer hitch, which mounts in the bed of a truck instead of on the rear bumper, being called a "gooseneck."

Geese are known for their distinctive honk, which is *gangan* ガンガン. They are counted *ichiwa* 一羽 or *ippiki* 一匹.

Gankubi soroeru 雁首そろえる "line up goosenecks"
line up, form up

何だ、兄弟三人雁首そろえて、小遣いでもねだりに来たのか。
Nan da, kyōdai sannin gankubi soroete, kozukai de mo nedari ni kita no ka.
What's this? The three of you all lined up, thinking you're gonna get

your old dad to cough up some money?

今部長が四人雁首そろえて社長室に入って行ったけど何かあったのかなあ？
Ima buchō ga yonin gankubi soroete shachō-shitsu ni haitte itta kedo nani ka atta no ka nā?
I wonder what's up. All four department heads just marched into the president's office.

🦢 Possibly from the unique diagonal or "V" flying formations of these migratory birds in which they line up their outstretched necks with near perfection. A slang expression for head or neck, *gankubi* now appears almost exclusively in *gankubi o soroeru,* an often derogatory and sometimes jocular expression used of a limited number of people (as few as two qualify) lining up for some specific purpose.

gashin-shōtan 臥薪嘗胆 "lying on firewood, licking liver"

sustained determination and perseverance; struggling against difficulties for the sake of vengeance; going through thick and thin (fire and water) to avenge oneself against one's enemies

In ancient China the Go and the Etsu were at war. After fifteen years of conflict, Kōsen, the Etsu king, led his troops to victory over the Go, whose leader Kōryo was slain in battle. Kōryo's son, Fusa, was determined to avenge his father. Every night he slept on a pile of firewood, to inflame his desire for revenge. It obviously did the trick as within three years he won the Battle of Kaikei, where he defeated the Etsu king Kōsen. Kōsen pleaded for mercy and was allowed to return home after a period of imprisonment. His shame at having surrendered to his fallen foe's son weighed heavily upon him and he resolved to restore his pride the only way he knew how—by beating Fusa in battle. To give himself courage to carry out this endeavor, he covered the floor of his bedroom with the livers of wild animals (in Japanese the character for liver also means courage). He licked up all the liver to give him courage, and thus fortified, set out with his faithful retainer Hanrei to wreak terrible revenge upon Fusa. It took them twenty-two years, but eventually they did it.

> 前回の選挙では落選したが、3年間の臥薪嘗胆の末に当選することができた。
> *Zenkai no senkyo de wa rakusen shita ga, sannen-kan no gashin-shōtan no sue ni tōsen suru koto ga dekita.*
> I was a loser in the last election, but I managed to get elected this time after three years of keeping my nose to the grindstone.

> 臥薪嘗胆の浪人生活の末、志望校に合格した。
> *Gashin-shōtan no rōnin seikatsu no sue, shibō-kō ni gōkaku shita.*
> Taking a year out to resit my entrance exams was tough, but it paid off in the end when I got accepted by the university I wanted to go to.

浪人 (*rōnin*): In feudal Japan a samurai without a lord and master was called a 浪人 ("a wave-person," being someone condemned to wander about by himself, belonging to no group, a virtual outcast from society). Nowadays this term is used to describe students who are unsuccessful in entering university at the first attempt. Those rōnin who fail their exams two (or three) years running are called 二浪 (*nirō*) or 三浪 (*sanrō*).

gejigeji げじげじ (蚰蜒)　house centipede

Just why this and other caterpillar-like critters are so despicable is unclear. One suggestion is that they have fifteen pairs of legs, not the fifty it would take to make them full-fledged centipedes. They are counted *ippiki* 一匹.

Gejigeji **げじげじ（蚰蜒）** "house centipede"
a creep, jerk, rat, skunk, bastard

あのげじげじやろうめ。
Ano gejigeji yarō me!
That creepy son of a bitch!

僕は小さい頃げじげじと呼ばれていた。
Boku wa chiisai koro gejigeji to yobarete ita.
They used to call me "creep" when I was little.

🌿 Of a strongly disliked person. Used most commonly by children.

↝ *kemushi* 毛虫

Gejigeji-mayuge **げじげじ眉毛** "millipede eyebrows"
bushy (thick and shaggy) eyebrows

あのげじげじ眉毛のお爺さん相当な資産家らしいよ。
Ano gejigeji-mayuge no ojiisan sōtō na shisan-ka rashii yo.
That old guy with the bushy eyebrows is supposed to be filthy rich.

細川さんとこの男の人達はお爺さんから孫までみんなげじげじ眉毛だね。
Hosokawa-san toko no otoko no hitotachi wa ojiisan kara mago made minna gejigeji-mayuge da ne.
All the men in the Hosokawa clan, from grandfather to grandson, have thick, shaggy eyebrows.

🌿 From the resemblance of such eyebrows to caterpillars. Can be pejorative. Seldom used of women.

genki 元気 "original *ki*"

energy, vitality; (good) health

シロが最近元気がないので心配だ。
Shiro ga saikin genki ga nai no de shinpai da.
I've been a little worried the way Shiro [a dog] has been moping around lately.

なんとなく元気が出ないよ。
Nan to naku genki ga denai yo.
I just don't seem to have any energy.

子供たちは元気いっぱい踊った。
Kodomo-tachi wa genki ippai odotta.
The children danced energetically.

そんな顔しないで、もっと元気を出して。
Sonna kao shinai de, motto genki o dashite.
Don't look so glum. Cheer up!

山田さんを元気づけるためにみんなで飲みに行こう。
Yamada-san o genki-zukeru tame ni minna de nomi ni ikō.
Let's all go out for a drink to cheer Yamada up.

今日は、悟ずいぶん元気がいいなあ。
Kyō wa, Satoru zuibun genki ga ii nā.
Hey Satoru, you're sure bright-eyed and bushy-tailed (full of vim and vigor) today.

これ飲んでごらんよ、元気がつくから。
Kore nonde goran yo, genki ga tsuku kara.
Take this. It'll make you feel better.

さ、みんな、外へ出て元気よく遊ぼう。
Sa, minna, soto e dete genki yoku asobō.
All right, everybody, it's time to go out and play. [A teacher to his or her pupils.]

お元気でお過ごしのご様子、お喜び申し上げます。
Ogenki de osugoshi no goyōsu, oyorokobi mōshi agemasu.
I'm happy to hear you are well. [In a somewhat formal letter.]

☞ *genki (na)* 元気(な)

genki (na) 元気(な) "original *ki*"

active, cheerful, energetic, lively

皆様お元気ですか。
Mina-sama ogenki desu ka. [in a letter]
How is everyone?

いつも元気なぼうやねえ。
Itsumo genki na bōya nē.
You're a cheerful little fella, aren't you.

じゃ、みなさん、名前を呼ばれたら元気にお返事しましょうね。
Ja, mina-san, namae o yobaretara genki ni ohenji shimashō ne.
OK, everybody, when I call your name, I want you to answer in a loud voice.

☞ *genki* 元気

~gimi 〜気味 [following a noun] "a taste of *ki*"

a dash, a hint of, a little, somewhat; a touch; a tendency to be ~ , on the ~ side

今日は風邪気味なのでお先に失礼します。
Kyō wa kaze-gimi na no de osaki ni shitsurei shimasu.
I feel like I'm coming down with a cold, so I think I'll call it a day.

最近太り気味で服がきつくなってきた。

Saikin futori-gimi de fuku ga kitsuku natte kita.
My clothes are too tight now 'cause I've put on a little weight lately.

息子はこのごろ怠け気味で、成績が下がってきちゃったのよ。
Musuko wa kono goro namake-gimi de, seiseki ga sagatte kichatta no yo.
My son's gotten rather lazy recently, and his grades are beginning to show it.

おばあちゃんがちょっとボケ気味で心配してるんです。
Obāchan ga chotto boke-gimi de shinpai shite 'ru n' desu.
We're concerned that Grandma might be getting a little senile.

☞ *kimi* 気味, *kokimi-yoi* 小気味よい

gishin-anki 疑心暗鬼 "a suspicious mind (produces) dark demons"

a feeling of suspicion (a doubt) gnaws at one, suspicions eat away at one, paranoid

イアゴーの告げ口が、オセロの胸に疑心暗鬼を生じさせた。
Iagō no tsugeguchi ga, Osero no mune ni gishin-anki o shōjisaseta.
Iago's talebearing awakened in Othello's heart a terrible suspicion.

親友が僕の悪口を陰で言いふらしていると聞いて、疑心暗鬼に陥ったよ。
Shin'yū ga boku no warukuchi o kage de iifurashite iru to kiite, gishin-anki ni ochiitta yo.
When I heard that a good friend was bad-mouthing me behind my back, I felt that I could no longer trust anyone.

連絡が遅いから、何かあったんじゃないかと、疑心暗鬼になっていたんだ。
Renraku ga osoi kara, nani ka atta n' ja nai ka to, gishin-anki ni natte ita n' da.
As time ticked on and still no word came, I began to think something awful must have happened.

goetsu-dōshū 呉越同舟 "the Go and the Etsu in the same boat"

bitter enemies (placed by fate) in the same boat, adversity makes strange bedfellows, to be united by ties of common interest

元の与党と野党第1党が、呉越同舟の連立内閣を組んだ。
Moto no yotō to yatō daiittō ga, goetsu-dōshū no renritsu-naikaku o kunda.
The cabinet was formed by a coalition of convenience between the former ruling party and their ex-arch rivals, who used to be the main opposition party.

あの二人が一緒にゴルフに行ったとは、呉越同舟だね。
Ano futari ga issho ni gorufu ni itta to wa, goetsu-dōshū da ne.
Those two hate each other's guts, so it's odd they should go off and play golf together.

❧ The Go and the Etsu were two rival states in ancient China which were always at war with each other. (See note at *gashin-shōtan*.)

gokuraku-ōjō 極楽往生 "rebirth in paradise"

an extremely pleasant death, a painless death, to leave (this world) and be reborn in paradise, to die peacefully (in one's bed), to pass away in peace

極楽往生を願っていたおじいさんは、苦しまずに亡くなった。
Gokuraku-ōjō o negatte ita ojīsan wa, kurushimazu ni nakunatta.
Grandpa had always hoped for a peaceful death and that's what he got, slipping away quietly and painlessly.

❧ Originally used to mean being reborn in Buddhist heaven after leaving this world. Now used to mean simply to die a peaceful death. In addition, someone who is a carefree, happy-go-lucky type is mockingly called *goku-raku-tonbo* 極楽とんぼ (a paradise dragonfly).

gongo-dōdan 言語道断 "words cannot express" (originally "the ultimate truth of Buddha's teaching cannot be expressed by (mere) words," but now used pejoratively)

unspeakable, unutterable, unmentionable, outrageous, unpardonable, inexcusable, preposterous, absurd, abominable, shocking, scandalous, beyond description

こんな初歩的なミスだらけのレポートを出すなんて、言語道断だね。
Konna shoho-teki na misu darake no repōto o dasu nante, gongo-dōdan da ne.
It is inexcusable to hand in a report so full of rudimentary mistakes as this.

「金さえ払えば文句なかろう」だと？言語道断な言い種だ。
"Kane sae haraeba monku nakarō" da to? Gongo-dōdan na iigusa da.
What do you mean "I'm paying, so what do you have to complain about?"
What a despicable thing to say!

gori ごり（鮴） goby

These small freshwater, spiny-finned fishes are known to school and swim upstream dozens of kilometers to visit relatives during the summer holidays. Apparently it's the only time of year they can get away from work around the estuaries, where they usually attach themselves to rocks by way of a unique ventral suction disk formed by their pelvic fins, which are joined together.

Gobi are counted *ichibe* 一尾 or *ippiki* 一匹.

Gorioshi ごり押し "goby push"
ram (push) through; steamroll, bulldoze

そういうごり押しをするからおまえはみんなから嫌われるんだ。
Sō iu gorioshi o suru kara omae wa minna kara kirawareru n' da.
That's why nobody wants to have anything to do with you, 'cause you're always ramming stuff down their throats.

あの代議士ごり押しして急行を自分の駅に臨時停車させて問題になった。
Ano daigi-shi gorioshi shite kyūkō o jibun no eki ni rinji-teisha sasete mondai ni natta.
He's the representative that caused all the fuss when he forced an express train to make an unscheduled stop at his station.

それはごり押しですよ。あの成績では、息子さんを入学させるわけにはいきません。
Sore wa gorioshi desu yo. Ano seiseki de wa, musuko-san o nyūgaku saseru wake ni wa ikimasen.
You are asking far too much. There is no way your son can be accepted at the school with those grades.

※ From the tremendous efforts expended by these tiny fish to swim long distances upstream to spawn.

gori-muchū 五里霧中 "five *ri* in the fog"

in a fog, all at sea, bewildered, at a total loss (what to do); to not have the foggiest idea what to do, to not have a clue

初めてフランスへ行った時は、全然言葉が分からなくて、五里霧中でしたよ。
Hajimete Furansu e itta toki wa, zenzen kotoba ga wakaranakute, gori-muchū deshita yo.

The first time I went to France, I couldn't understand a word of what was being said. I was totally at sea.

畑違いの企画を任されて、いまだに五里霧中の状態なんです。
Hatake-chigai no kikaku o makasarete, imada ni gori-muchū no jōtai nan desu.
They've put me in charge of a project that's outside my field. I still haven't got a clue what I should be doing.

❦ A *ri* is a unit of distance (approximately equivalent to two and a half miles) that was used in ancient China and Japan. This four-character compound is said to derive from the trick once practised by a Chinese mystic of conjuring up a thick fog to engulf his enemies and make them lose their sense of direction. Care should be taken when writing this expression as people sometimes confuse the third character with the character for dream (夢), whose *on*-reading is also *mu*. Perhaps this is because in Japanese the compound 夢中 (*muchū*) is commonly used in the phrase 夢中になる, which means to become engrossed/absorbed in (something).

gyokuseki-konkō 玉石混淆 "jewels and stones mixed together"

a mixture of the good and the bad

新入社員も、以前は粒が揃っていたけど、このごろじゃ玉石混淆だよ。
Shinnyū-shain mo, izen wa tsubu ga sorotte ita kedo, kono goro ja gyokuseki-konkō da yo.
We always used to get a well-balanced crop of new recruits in the old days, but of late it's been a mixed bag.

どんな有名作家の作品でも、やはりある程度は玉石混淆になりますね。
Donna yūmei-sakka no sakuhin de mo, yahari aru teido wa gyokuseki-konkō ni narimasu ne.

It doesn't matter how famous the writer is, there will always be some second-rate work mixed in with the masterpieces.

❧ This expression can also be written as 玉石混交.

gyūho (ushi no ayumi) 牛歩（牛の歩み）"a cow's gait"

a very slow walk; last-ditch stalling (slowdown) tactics [in parliament]

野党はその法案に反対の立場から、投票に牛歩戦術で対抗した。
Yatō wa sono hōan ni hantai no tachiba kara, tōhyō ni gyūho-senjutsu de taikō shita.
The opposition party resorted to plodding up to cast its ballots when the bill it opposed came to (up for) a vote.

美術館の行列は牛の歩みだった。
Bijutsu-kan no gyōretsu wa ushi no ayumi datta.
The line at the art museum was moving at a snail's pace.

❧ This expression is most commonly used to describe one of the more senseless if amusing tactics employed by an outnumbered opposition party in the lower house of Japan's Diet. Facing certain defeat, members of the minority party line up to cast their ballots against a bill and proceed to plod toward the ballot box in the chamber by walking more slowly than the beasts of burden from which the expression takes its inspiration. Hours can pass, seasons come and go, and mountains tumble into the sea before the foregone conclusion, defeat, is official. It's a great argument for live coverage of the Diet, and gives new meaning to voting with your feet.

gyūjiru 牛耳る "grasp a cow's ear"

control, dominate, hold sway over; take charge of, lead, run (the show), shepherd, steer

現在、日本の政界を牛耳る人物がいない。
Genzai, Nihon no seikai o gyūjiru jinbutsu ga inai.
No single person rides herd over the Japanese political world right now.

一部の人間に牛耳られたあの会社には将来は望めないだろう。
Ichibu no ningen ni gyūjirareta ano kaisha ni wa shōrai wa nozomenai darō.
Controlled by a small group of people, a company like that doesn't have much of a future.

🐄 Shortened and made into a verb from the expression *gyūji o toru* 牛耳を執る, literally "grasp a cow's ear," this is exactly what the fabled feudal rulers of ancient China are said to have done at a meeting where they swore allegiance to one another at the behest of the leading member of the alliance, who then cut off the ear of a sacrificial cow, divided it up among those in attendance, and each of them sucked blood from their share of the dismembered ear. Sort of a different twist to a blood oath, less painful for all except the cow.

ha 歯 tooth, teeth

As a part of the mouth and therefore associated with speech, *ha* figures in many expressions concerning how things are said, whether deviously or straightforwardly. The most graphic of the idioms, though, is one that likens an empty space to a mouth missing some teeth, perhaps from the fact that an unfilled theater seat or vacant house is dark like the gap left by a missing tooth.

Ha ga nuketa yō 歯が抜けたよう "like missing teeth"
sparse

客席は、歯が抜けたように空席ができていた。
Kyakuseki wa, ha ga nuketa yō ni kūseki ga dekite ita.
There were empty seats all around the hall. / The audience was conspicuous by its absence.

街に移り住む人が増えて、その村では歯が抜けたように家々がなくなっていった。
Machi ni utsurisumu hito ga fuete, sono mura de wa ha ga nuketa yō ni ie-ie ga nakunatte itta.
With so many people moving into town, the village seems like a graveyard.

Ha ga tatanai 歯が立たない "one's teeth don't stand up"
be too difficult for one, one is no match for something or someone

あの男には全く歯が立たない。
Ano otoko ni wa mattaku ha ga tatanai.
I'm no match for him. / He's way out of my league. / I can't hold a candle to him

こんなに難しい問題は、私にはとても歯が立たない。
Konna ni muzukashii mondai wa, watashi ni wa totemo ha ga tatanai.
A problem like this is way over my head.

Ha ga uku (yō na) 歯が浮く（ような） "one's teeth are floating"

(1) (about a grating sound) set one's teeth on edge (2) (about someone's behavior, especially flattery) nauseating, disgusting; make one want to gag

(1) 私は黒板を爪でひっかいた時の、あの歯の浮くような音が大嫌いだ。

Watashi wa kokuban o tsume de hikkaita toki no, ano ha no uku yō na oto ga daikirai da.
Oh, the sound of someone scratching their fingernails on a blackboard really drives me up the wall (sets my teeth on edge).

(2) 歯の浮くようなお世辞はよしてください。
Ha no uku yō na oseji wa yoshite kudasai.
Don't you think you're laying (spreading) it on a little thick there? How about knocking it off. / I've just about had enough of your damn brown-nosing.

結婚式とはいえ、あれだけ歯の浮くようなスピーチもめずらしい。
Kekkon-shiki to wa ie, are dake ha no uku yō na supīchi mo mezurashii.
Even for a speech at a wedding, it's unusual to lay it on so thick.

Ha ni kinu o kisenu 歯に衣を着せぬ "don't wear any clothes on one's teeth"
be frank, outspoken, forthright; speak one's mind

その評論家は歯に衣を着せぬことで有名だ。
Sono hyōron-ka wa ha ni kinu o kisenu koto de yūmei da.
That critic is famous for the way she gets right to the point (says exactly what she thinks).

彼は歯に衣を着せずにものを言う男だ。
Kare wa ha ni kinu o kisezu ni mono o iu otoko da.
He gets right to the point. / He doesn't beat around the bush (mince his words). / He speaks his mind.

☞ *biji-reiku* 美辞麗句, *gaikō-jirei* 外交辞令

Hagire ga ii / hagire ga warui　**歯切れがいい／歯切れが悪い**
  "feel good (bad) when you bite down on something"
[positive] clear, articulate, terse, to the point; [negative] sloppy, evasive

その話になると、彼女は急に歯切れが悪くなった。
Sono hanashi ni naru to, kanojo wa kyū ni hagire ga waruku natta.
She suddenly started beating around the bush when the subject came up.

委員長の歯切れのいい答弁は評判がよかった。
Iin-chō no hagire no ii tōben wa hyōban ga yokatta.
The chairperson's crisp reply was favorably received.

hachi 蜂 bee

Bees don't figure in stories that Japanese moms tell their preteen daughters in order to prepare them for life, if they tell them anything. The principal aspects of apian behavior that warrant lexical attention appear to be industriousness, activity, and the ability to inflict pain, though the word for beehive, *hachi no su* 蜂の巣, can be used metaphorically to describe the riddling of something, such as a body with bullet holes lying on the mean streets of Tokyo. The bee lends its name to a tiny bird as well, the *hachidori* 蜂鳥, or "bee bird," which is better known in the West as a hummingbird. The sound bees make when flying is *bunbun* ブンブン or *būn* ブーン. They are counted *ippiki* 一匹.

↝ *hatarakibachi* 働き蜂, *nakitsura ni hachi* 泣き面に蜂

Hachi no su o tsutsuita yō　**蜂の巣をつついたよう**　"like having poked a beehive"
be thrown into utter confusion, be a madhouse; commotion

証券業界はそのニュースに蜂の巣をつついたような騒ぎだった。
Shōken-gyōkai wa sono nyūsu ni hachi no su o tsutsuita yō na sawagi datta.
The securities industry was thrown into utter confusion at the news. / All hell broke loose in the securities industry when the news was released.

ポケベルの新製品の注文が殺到し、営業部は蜂の巣をつついたようだった。
Pokeberu no shin-seihin no chūmon ga sattō shi, eigyō-bu wa hachi no su o tsutsuita yō datta.
The sales department turned into a madhouse (There was pandemonium in the sales department) when orders for our new pagers started pouring in.

🐝 This is a false friend, for while it may sound like the English idiom "stir up a hornet's nest," there is no sense of creating trouble or arousing anger in the Japanese. Rather, the idiom evokes a sense of the excitement and confusion of jillions of tiny flapping wings when a hive, belonging to a bunch of bees who were minding their own business, has been disturbed.

hada 肌 skin

Hada derives its figurative meaning of "firsthand experience" from the fact that as a layer of cells covering the body it houses the tactile organs of sense, the nerve endings. It also has the meaning "temperament," so if your skin feels good about someone it's an indication that you can get along with that person.

An example of *kanji* giving way to *katakana*, *sukinshippu* is a late eighties coinage taken from the English words "skin" and "friendship," and indicates the bond created by physical or personal contact between humans, as between parent and child.

↪ *hito-hada nugu* 人肌脱ぐ

Hada de kanjiru 肌で感じる "feel something with one's skin" experience firsthand
---

雪国の冬の厳しさを肌で感じることができた。
Yukiguni no fuyu no kibishisa o hada de kanjiru koto ga dekita.
I saw firsthand just how hard winter can be in the snow country.

人々がどんなに民主主義を願っているか、肌で感じた。
Hitobito ga donna ni minshu-shugi o negatte iru ka, hada de kanjita.
I saw for myself just how strongly people long for democracy.

Hada ga au 肌が合う "skin gets along with someone else's"
get along [usually in a negative sentence]

外国人とはどうも肌が合わない。
Gaikoku-jin to wa dō mo hada ga awanai.
I just don't seem to hit it off with foreigners.

彼女とは肌が合わない。
Kanojo to wa hada ga awanai.
I don't get along with her. / She rubs me the wrong way.

☞ *ki ga au* 気が合う, *uma ga au* 馬が合う

Hada ni au 肌に合う "suit one's skin"
suit, be well suited for, be right for one

このスキンクリームは私の肌に合わない。
Kono sukinkurīmu wa watashi no hada ni awanai.
This skin cream isn't right for my skin. / This isn't the right skin cream for me.

今の仕事は僕の肌に合っている。
Ima no shigoto wa boku no hada ni atte iru.
The job I have now suits me just fine. / I'm perfectly happy with my job.

Hada o yurusu **肌を許す** "allow someone to have one's skin"

give in to a man's demands for sex, give oneself to a man, sleep with a man

彼女はボーイフレンドに肌を許した。
Kanojo wa bōifurendo ni hada o yurushita.
She went all the way (went to bed) with her boyfriend.

☞ *mi o makaseru* 身を任せる

hakike 吐き気 "vomiting *ki*"

nausea, feeling sick to one's stomach

薬の副作用からか、ひどい吐き気におそわれた。
Kusuri no fuku-sayō kara ka, hidoi hakike ni osowareta.
I don't know if it was the medicine I took or what, but I started feeling sick to my stomach.

乗り物酔いで吐き気がする。
Norimono-yoi de hakike ga suru.
I feel carsick.

食べ物を見ただけで吐き気を催すんです。
Tabemono o mita dake de hakike o moyōsu n' desu.
Just the sight of food turns my stomach.

これでも音楽かよ。吐き気がするぜ。
Kore de mo ongaku ka yo. Hakike ga suru ze.
You call this music? Makes me wanna barf.

昨日見たホラー映画は吐き気を催すような場面の連続で、途中でやめたよ。

Kinō mita horā-eiga wa hakike o moyōsu yō na bamen no renzoku de, tochū de yameta yo.

There were so many gory scenes in the horror flick I went to yesterday that I left halfway through.

☞ *kibun ga warui* 気分が悪い, *kimochi ga warui* 気持ちが悪い

hakuri-tabai 薄利多売 "(to make) a thin (small) profit and sell a lot"

narrow margin and high turnover

当店では薄利多売をモットーに、少しでも良い品をお求めやすいお値段で、ご提供いたしております。

Tōten de wa hakuri-tabai o mottō ni, sukoshi de mo yoi shina o omotomeyasui onedan de, goteikyō itashite orimasu.

The motto at our shop is a narrow margin with high turnover; we endeavor to supply good products at reasonable prices.

薄利多売の代表は、何と言ってもディスカウントストアなどの量販店でしょうね。

Hakuri-tabai no daihyō wa, nanto itte mo disukaunto-sutoa nado no ryōhanten deshō ne.

No matter how you look at it, the most representative example of narrow-margin high-turnover selling is the large-volume discount store.

hana 鼻 nose

We've all heard of horses or candidates for political office and other dubious characters winning something by a nose. Well, you can say the same thing in Japanese, at least about the ponies. *Hana no sa de katsu*—"win by a nose"—will do the trick. Aside from that part of the face that Japanese lay a finger on in reference to themselves, when we think they should be pointing to their chest, *hana* refers also to the sense of smell, as in the first of the idioms below.

Hana de warau 鼻で笑う "laugh with one's nose"
snort derisively, mock

あの男はまだ子供さ、と彼は鼻で笑った。
Ano otoko wa mada kodomo sa, to kare wa hana de waratta.
"That guy never grew up," he sniffed.

彼女は僕たちの計画を鼻で笑った。
Kanojo wa boku-tachi no keikaku o hana de waratta.
She dismissed our plan with a snort.

Hana ga kiku 鼻が利く "one's nose works"

---

(1) have a good sense of smell (2) have a nose for

(1) 僕は鼻が利くので、遠くでタバコを吸っていても臭いでわかる。
Boku wa hana ga kiku no de, tōku de tabako o sutte ite mo nioi de wakaru.
I've got a good nose, so I can tell when someone's smoking even if they're quite far away.

(2) あいつは本当にもうけ話には鼻が利く男だ。
Aitsu wa hontō ni mōke-banashi ni wa hana ga kiku otoko da.
The guy can really sniff out a deal. / He's got a nose for making money.

Hana ni kakeru 鼻にかける "hang something on one's nose"
be proud of, boast about, go on and on about

彼は名門の出だということを鼻にかけていた。
Kare wa meimon no de da to iu koto o hana ni kakete ita.

He was bragging about graduating from a famous college.

彼女は、息子を有名な幼稚園に通わせていることを鼻にかけていた。
Kanojo wa, musuko o yūmei na yōchi-en ni kayowasete iru koto o hana ni kakete ita.
She prided herself on sending her son to some famous kindergarten.

↪ *hana o takaku suru* 鼻を高くする

Hana ni tsuku 鼻に付く "hit one's nose"
be up to here with something, be sick (and tired) of something, have had about all of something that one can stand

---

彼女には彼のいばった態度が鼻についた。
Kanojo ni wa kare no ibatta taido ga hana ni tsuita.
She was pretty fed up with his hoity-toity attitude.

あのレストランは味は良いのだが、ボーイ達の気取った態度がどうも鼻につく。
Ano resutoran wa aji wa yoi no da ga, bōi-tachi no kidotta taido ga dō mo hana ni tsuku.
The food at the restaurant is OK, but I haven't got much use for the waiters' pretentious attitude.

↪ *ki ni iranai* 気に入らない (see under *ki ni iru* 気に入る), *ki ni kuwanai* 気に食わない

Hana no shita ga nagai 鼻の下が長い "The space below one's nose is long."
be soft on women, like the ladies, be a lady-killer, have a roving eye

---

「叔父さんは鼻の下が長い」と叔母さんが怒ってましたよ。
"Oji-san wa hana no shita ga nagai" to oba-san ga okotte mashita yo.

My aunt is really pissed about the way my uncle is always sniffing around the girls.

隣の酒屋のおやじは若い女の子が来ると、鼻の下を長くして喜ぶ。
Tonari no saka-ya no oyaji wa wakai onna no ko ga kuru to, hana no shita o nagaku shite yorokobu.
The guy who runs the liquor store next door gets that twinkle in his eye every time a young gal comes in the door.

Hana o takaku suru 鼻を高くする "put one's nose up"
be proud as a peacock

高校野球で優勝したので、校長はすっかり鼻を高くした。
Kōkō-yakyū de yūshō shita no de, kōchō wa sukkari hana o takaku shita.
The principal is so proud that the team won the high-school baseball tournament you'd think he was going to pop all the buttons on his shirt.

売り上げが1位となり、支店長は鼻を高くしている。
Uriage ga ichi-i to nari, shiten-chō wa hana o takaku shite iru.
The manager is all puffed up since his branch came out number one in sales.

Also 鼻が高い *hana ga takai.*
↬ *hana ni kakeru* 鼻にかける

Hanappashi(ra) ga tsuyoi 鼻っ柱が強い "The pillar of one's nose is strong."
stand one's ground, be defiant, ornery, feisty

彼は彼女の鼻っ柱の強いところが気に入っていた。
Kare wa kanojo no hanappashira no tsuyoi tokoro ga ki ni itte ita.
He liked the way she wouldn't take any guff (shit) off anyone.

彼女は鼻っぱしが強いけど、意外にやさしいところもある。

Kanojo wa hanappashi ga tsuyoi kedo, igai ni yasashii tokoro mo aru.
She's a feisty gal, but she can be surprisingly sweet, too.

Also 鼻っ張りが強い *hanappari ga tsuyoi.*
☞ *ki ga tsuyoi* 気が強い; *ki ga yowai* 気が弱い

hanshin-fuzui 半身不随 "half one's body does not obey"

partial paralysis, paralyzed on one side (of one's body)

お隣りのおじいちゃんは、去年の冬脳梗塞で倒れて以来、半身不随で寝たきりです。
Otonari no ojī-chan wa, kyonen no fuyu nō-kōsoku de taorete irai, hanshin-fuzui de neta kiri desu.
The old guy living next door has been bedridden with partial paralysis since he had a stroke last winter.

わが国の経済は、いまや半身不随の病人に例えられるほど、行き詰まっている。
Wagakuni no keizai wa, imaya hanshin-fuzui no byōnin ni tatoerareru hodo, ikizumatte iru.
Our nation's economy can be compared to a partially paralyzed patient: we're stuck and we can't move.

hanshin-hangi 半信半疑 "half believing, half doubting"

incredulous, doubtful, dubious, somewhat suspicious

自分の目が信じられず、半信半疑で銀行へ行ったが、本当に当たりくじだった。

Jibun no me ga shinjirarezu, hanshin-hangi de ginkō e itta ga, hontō ni atari-kuji datta.

I couldn't believe my eyes and went to the bank thinking it couldn't be true, but I had really won the lottery.

すっかりあきらめていたので、合格の知らせが着いてもまだ半信半疑だった。

Sukkari akiramete ita no de, gōkaku no shirase ga tsuite mo mada hanshin-hangi datta.

I had given up all hope, so when news of my exam success reached me, I couldn't believe it was true.

happō-bijin 八方美人 "an eight-directions beauty"

somebody who tries to please everyone (be everybody's friend)

彼女は八方美人だからね、誰にどう言えばいいかよく心得てるよ。
Kanojo wa happō-bijin da kara ne, dare ni dō ieba ii ka yoku kokoroete 'ru yo.
She tries to keep on everyone's good side, and is perfectly aware of what to say and when.

あの八方美人め！ みんなにいい顔しやがって。
Ano happō-bijin-me! Minna ni ii kao shiyagatte.
That flunkey really pisses me off! There's no end to his apple polishing.

政府の福祉政策は八方美人的で、結局誰も満足していない。
Seifu no fukushi-seisaku wa happō-bijin-teki de, kekkyoku dare mo manzoku shite inai.
The government's welfare policy tries to be all things to all people, so it ends up satisfying no one.

hara 腹 **stomach, belly**

English speakers make up their mind, native speakers of Japanese make up their bellies. So when Japanese intend to do something adventurous, something calling for a great deal of resolve—such as leaving the family business to their daughter to manage—they might say something like *Keiei o musume ni makaseru hara da,* or "I intend to leave the running of the company to my daughter." Another colorful expression with *hara, Kochira no hara wa itamanai,* might best be translated as "It's no skin off my nose" or "It's not costing me a thing." Neither *onaka,* a polite synonym for *hara,* or *i,* a more anatomical term, figure in very many idioms.

☞ *(hara no) mushi ga osamaru* 腹の虫が治まる (see under *mushi* 虫), *jibara o kiru* 自腹を切る

Hara (ga) heru 腹（が）へる "one's stomach decreases"
get hungry, be hungry

ああ、腹へった。何か食べるものある？
Ā, hara hetta. Nani ka taberu mono aru?
I'm starving. Is there anything to eat around here?

腹がへっては戦が出来ぬ。
Hara ga hette wa ikusa ga dekinu.
An army marches on its stomach.

Also おなかがへる *onaka ga heru.*

Hara ga deru 腹が出る "one's stomach sticks out"
have a little potbelly, have a spare tire

運動もしないで飲んでばかりいると腹が出るよ。
Undō mo shinai de nonde bakari iru to hara ga deru yo.
If you keep drinking like that and don't get any exercise, you're going to end up with a spare tire (a beer belly).

年のせいか、最近腹が出てきた。
Toshi no sei ka, saikin hara ga dete kita.
I must be getting old. I'm starting to get a potbelly.

Hara ga kuroi / haraguroi　腹が黒い／腹黒い　"have a black stomach"
be evil, be blackhearted, be scheming

あの男は親切そうに見えるが、実は腹が黒い。
Ano otoko wa shinsetsu-sō ni mieru ga, jitsu wa hara ga kuroi.
That guy looks like he's nice, but he's really a bastard (scumbag).

年寄りをだますような腹黒いまねはするな。
Toshiyori o damasu yō na haraguroi mane wa suru na.
Don't be a louse, cheating old people like that.

☞ *seiren-keppaku* 清廉潔白

Hara ga tatsu / hara o tateru　腹が立つ／腹を立てる　"one's stomach stands"
get angry, get bent out of shape, get hot under the collar

今度ばかりは腹が立った。
Kondo bakari wa hara ga tatta.
I'm really mad (pissed) this time. / I've really got my Irish (my back) up this time.

そんなささいなことで腹をたてるのはよしなさい。
Sonna sasai na koto de hara o tateru no wa yoshinasai.

Don't get so riled (worked) up over something so stupid.

☞ *ki ga tatsu* 気が立つ

Hara o kimeru / hara ga kimaru 腹を決める／腹が決まる "decide one's stomach"
make up one's mind, decide, resolve

大学に行くか就職するか、そろそろ腹を決めなければならない。
Daigaku ni iku ka shūshoku suru ka, sorosoro hara o kimenakereba naranai.
I've got to make up my mind pretty soon whether to go to college or to get a job.

よし、これで腹が決まった。どんなことがあってもこの計画は実現させるぞ。
Yoshi, kore de hara ga kimatta. Donna koto ga atte mo kono keikaku wa jitsugen saseru zo.
That does it. My mind is made up. I'm going through with the project now, no matter what.

☞ *ichinen-hokki* 一念発起

Hara o watte hanasu 腹を割って話す "cut one's stomach and talk"
have a heart-to-heart talk

今夜は腹を割って話そう。
Kon'ya wa hara o watte hanasō.
Let's talk things out tonight.

腹を割って話してみて本当によかった。
Hara o watte hanashite mite hontō ni yokatta.
I sure did the right thing by having a heart-to-heart with him about it.

haran-banjō 波瀾万丈 "Small waves and big waves rise 10,000 feet."

eventful, stormy, full of ups and downs, checkered

波瀾万丈の人生でしたが、何も後悔はしていません。
Haran-banjō no jinsei deshita ga, nani mo kōkai wa shite imasen.
I've led a checkered life, but I regret nothing.

祖父の一生はまさに波瀾万丈で、僕に文才があれば、小説に書きたいくらいだ。
Sofu no isshō wa masa ni haran-banjō de, boku ni bunsai ga areba, shōsetsu ni kakitai kurai da.
Granddad's life was full of incident, and if I had any talent as a writer, I'd write a novel about it.

hatarakibachi 働き蜂 "worker bee"

someone who works like a dog, a workhorse, a hard worker, a workaholic, a grind

働き蜂と呼ばれる日本人も少しずつ労働時間短縮を目指し始めている。
Hatarakibachi to yobareru Nihon-jin mo sukoshi zutsu rōdō-jikan tanshuku o mezashihajimete iru.
Even the hard-working Japanese are gradually beginning to cut back on the number of hours they work.

連休が終わると家族サービスで疲れきった「働き蜂」たちがオフィスに戻ってきた。
Renkyū ga owaru to kazoku-sābisu de tsukarekitta "hatarakibachi"-tachi ga ofisu ni modotte kita.
The nation's workhorses returned to harness today completely exhausted from a long weekend of quality time with their families.

🐾 It's difficult to think of an example for this expression which isn't about the Japanese. The nuance of being a grind is strong, though there is also a sense of industriousness and, perhaps, a slight tinge of resignation as one takes one's place in the traces.

hato はと (鳩) **pigeon or dove**

This municipal scourge is as prevalent in Japanese cities as anywhere else, especially around train stations, under overpasses, and in parks. The far more beautiful wild dove is, unfortunately, far less common. Still, it symbolizes peace and prosperity in Japan as elsewhere. And yes, those peace-loving folks who are always willing to try to see the other guy's side of things are doves in Japanese, too. And as with their natural enemies the hawks, *-ha* ～ 派 is attached to describe them as a faction.

The coo of doves and pigeons is *poppo* ポッポ. In baby talk, both pigeons and their coo are *poppo*. They are counted *ichiwa* 一羽.

☞ *kyūshu* 鳩首

Hato ga mamedeppō o kutta yō na **鳩が豆鉄砲を食ったような**
  "like a pigeon that has just been hit by a pea shooter"
astounded, astonished, blown away, floored

なんだそんな鳩が豆鉄砲を食ったような顔して。
Nan da sonna hato ga mamedeppō o kutta yō na kao shite.
What are you looking so flabbergasted about?

死んだはずの夫が帰ってきたので、妻は鳩が豆鉄砲を食ったような顔で言葉も出ず立ち尽くした。
Shinda hazu no otto ga kaette kita no de, tsuma wa hato ga mamedeppō o kutta yō na kao de kotoba mo dezu tachitsukushita.

Dumbfounded, she just stood there open-mouthed when her supposedly dead husband suddenly turned up.

🕊 Of the wide-eyed expression imagined to resemble that of a pigeon that has just been hit by a beanshooter. Not used about dangerous or life-threatening situations.

↬ *me o maruku suru* 目を丸くする

hebi 蛇 snake, serpent

Less in the grass than the paddies, snakes nevertheless fare little better in Japanese than in English, their lowly position inspiring the linguistic muse to a few waggish observations about their not needing feet, or humans inviting trouble by rustling around in the bushes where snakes repose. In need of some serious PR work in Japan, snakes are commonly held to be mysterious, fearsome, loathsome, and creepy. Snakes were formerly thought to enjoy eternal life because of their ability to molt.

Snakes are fairly common in Japan but seldom poisonous. Only the *mamushi*, a kind of pit viper, is widely distributed and feared (for good reason). One snake, the boa, or *uwabami* 蟒蛇, has lent its moniker to a person who drinks a lot, perhaps from a folk tale in which an eight-headed, eight-tailed snake is conquered and a beautiful maiden rescued by a prince who gets the beast drunk by bringing eight casks from which it quaffs its fill. One less common proverb not included as an entry, *ja no michi wa hebi* 蛇の道は蛇, literally, "a snake (knows) the path of snakes," is similar to the English "Set a thief to catch a thief" or, more commonly among children, "It takes one to know one."

When written as the sixth sign of the Chinese and Japanese zodiac calendar, the character 巳 is employed. Snakes are counted *ippiki* 一匹 or, less commonly, *ichio* 一尾.

☞ *chōda no retsu* 長蛇の列, *dasoku* 蛇足, *ryūtōdabi* 竜頭蛇尾, *yabuhebi* やぶ蛇

Hebi ni niramareta (mikomareta) kaeru **蛇ににらまれた（見込まれた）蛙** "a frog being watched by a snake" cannot move or get away

be frozen in fear, transfixed (paralyzed) with fear; (like) a deer caught in the headlights

浮気の現場を妻におさえられて彼はまるで蛇ににらまれた蛙だった。
Uwaki no genba o tsuma ni osaerarete kare wa maru de hebi ni niramareta kaeru datta.
He was frozen with fear when his wife caught him in bed with another woman.

蛇に見込まれた蛙のように彼女はその男の言うなりだった。
Hebi ni mikomareta kaeru no yō ni kanojo wa sono otoko no iu nari datta.
Like a deer caught in a car's oncoming headlights, she found herself at his beck and call.

✺ Graphic metaphorical expression illustrating the paralysis induced by fear when prey are confronted by a natural enemy.

Hebi no namagoroshi **蛇の生殺し** "half-killing a snake"

1. (literally) leave something half-dead (on its last legs)

その部隊は村民全員を蛇の生殺し状態にして、村を去った。
Sono butai wa sonmin zen'in o hebi no namagoroshi jōtai ni shite, mura o satta.
The unit left the villagers to die after beating them to within an inch of their life.

マスコミがこぞって犯人扱いにしたので、まるで蛇の生殺し状態となったそのタレントはとうとう自殺に追い込まれた。
Masukomi ga kozotte hannin-atsukai ni shita no de, maru de hebi no namagoroshi jōtai to natta sono tarento wa tōtō jisatsu ni oikomareta.
Branded as a criminal by the press and left twisting in the wind, the celebrity was driven to commit suicide.

🐍 From the notion of beating a snake half dead (within an inch of its life) and then leaving it to die; the kind of thing young boys seem compelled to do.

2. leave something half-done (-finished), do something half-assed

あの人の仕事はいつでも蛇の生殺しだね。
Ano hito no shigoto wa itsu de mo hebi no namagoroshi da ne.
Every job he does is either half-finished or half-baked.

うちのような零細企業がこの不景気に銀行の融資を打ち切られたら蛇の生殺しだ。
Uchi no yō na reisai-kigyō ga kono fu-keiki ni ginkō no yūshi o uchikiraretara hebi no namagoroshi da.
Small businesses like ours will be left high and dry if banks cut us off in the middle of an economic downturn like this.

↬ *chūto-hanpa* 中途半端

heiki (na) 平気(な) "undisturbed *ki*"

1. don't care, be indifferent, insensitive; [*heiki de ~ o suru*] make no bones about doing, be unconcerned; nonchalance, calmness, unperturbedness

ゆうべのことなどなかったかのように平気な顔をしている。
Yūbe no koto nado nakatta ka no yō ni heiki na kao o shite iru.
She's acting as if nothing happened at all last night.

人気のない暗い道だって平気で歩けるわよ。
Hitoke no nai kurai michi datte heiki de arukeru wa yo.
I don't think anything of walking down dark, deserted streets.

何度注意しても平気な顔してまた遅れてくるんだよ。
Nando chūi shite mo heiki na kao shite mata okurete kuru n' da yo.
You can chew him out all you want; he still turns up late with a couldn't-care-less look on his face.

レバーは平気だけどモツはだめなんだ。
Rebā wa heiki da kedo motsu wa dame nan da.
Liver doesn't bother me (I don't mind liver), but the guts, now, they're a different story.

「禁煙」の張り紙の前で平気でタバコを吸っている。
"Kin'en" no harigami no mae de heiki de tabako o sutte iru.
Guy's puffing away right in front of the "no smoking" sign like it wasn't even there!

2. without effect, without feeling a thing

僕は水割り2杯までなら平気だけど。
Boku wa mizuwari nihai made nara heiki da kedo.
I can handle a couple whisky-and-waters without any problem, but more than that and . . .

このビルは関東大震災並みの地震が起こっても平気なんだってさ。
Kono biru wa Kantō-daishinsai nami no jishin ga okotte mo heiki nan datte sa.
They say this building can take an earthquake as strong as the Great Kanto Earthquake, no sweat.

慣れると平気になってしまうらしいね。
Nareru to heiki ni natte shimau rashii ne.
You'll get over it once you get used to it. / Once you get used to it, apparently it's no big deal.

あんなもの見た後で平気でいられるわけないだろう。

Anna mono mita ato de heiki de irareru wake nai darō.
After seeing something like that, you can hardly expect me to act the same as always.

☞ *heiki no heiza* 平気の平左

heiki no heiza 平気の平左

cool as a cucumber, unflappable

大丈夫だよ、僕は何を言われても平気の平左だから。
Daijōbu da yo, boku wa nani o iwarete mo heiki no heiza da kara.
Don't worry about me, I'm Mr. Cool. I don't give a hoot what people say.

☞ *heiki (na)* 平気(な), *ki ni shinai* 気にしない (see under *ki ni suru* 気にする)

heso へそ navel, belly button

For all practical purposes, *heso* just means somebody's belly button. But a stretch of the imagination allows Japanese to use *heso* in reference to things that resemble belly buttons in one way or another—pooched out or sunken—like the little dimple in a bean-paste bun. This is not, however, a particularly common usage. One interesting combination that is frequently heard is *hesomagari,* or a "bent navel," that is, a screwball, a crank, or someone who otherwise deliberately deviates from the norm.

Heso ga cha o wakasu へそが茶を沸かす "one's navel boils tea"
be a big laugh, be a million laughs

あいつが今では中学校の先生だとは、へそが茶を沸かす。

Aitsu ga ima de wa chūgakkō no sensei da to wa, heso ga cha o wakasu.
Imagine him a junior high school teacher—that's priceless (a riot).

あの汚職議員のキャッチフレーズが「クリーン…」とは、へそが茶を沸かす。
Ano oshoku-giin no kyatchi-furēzu ga "kurīn . . ." to wa, heso ga cha o wakasu.
That sleazy politician's "clean so-and-so" slogan has got to be the joke of the century.

Heso o mageru へそを曲げる "bend one's navel"
get cross, be in a bad mood, get pushed out of shape

みんなに子供扱いされて、彼女はへそを曲げてしまった。
Minna ni kodomo-atsukai sarete, kanojo wa heso o magete shimatta.
She was all out of sorts because everyone was treating her like a child.

彼は気に入らないことがあるとすぐへそを曲げる。
Kare wa ki ni iranai koto ga aru to sugu heso o mageru.
He gets bent out of shape every time something doesn't go his way.

---

higai-mōsō 被害妄想 "injury delusions"
a persecution complex, paranoia

会社が彼を首にしようとして電話を盗聴してるなんて、完全な被害妄想だよ。
Kaisha ga kare o kubi ni shiyō to shite denwa o tōchō shite 'ru nante, kanzen na higai-mōsō da yo.
He's completely paranoid, convinced the company's bugged his phone and is out to sack him.

あの人の場合、被害妄想と誇大妄想が一緒になっていて、自分

は素晴らしく能力があるのに、回りの人たちに妬まれて邪魔
されていると思ってるんだ。

*Ano hito no bāi, higai-mōsō to kodai-mōsō ga issho ni natte ite, jibun wa
subarashiku nōryoku ga aru no ni, mawari no hitotachi ni netamarete
jama sarete iru to omotte 'ru n' da.*

That guy not only has a persecution complex but delusions of grandeur,
too. He's convinced he's brilliantly talented but is being held back by
people around him who are jealous of his abilities.

hihi ひひ (狒狒) baboon

Since they are not native to Japan, it comes as no surprise that baboons figure in no parables or proverbs. That they are considered the closest thing in the wild kingdom to lecherous middle-aged or elderly men is due, some suggest, to their resemblance to bearded old geezers. Baboons are counted *ittō* 一頭.

Hihi ひひ "baboon"
a dirty old man, an old lech

このひひおやじ何を考えているんだ？
Kono hihi-oyaji nani o kangaete iru n' da?
You dirty old man, what've you got in mind now?

あのひひ爺酔ったふりして私のおっぱい触りまくったのよ。
Ano hihi-jijī yotta furi shite watashi no oppai sawarimakutta no yo.
That old lech acted like he was drunk so he could feel me up.

❦ Commonly followed by *jijī* 爺 or *oyaji* おやじ.

↬ *hana no shita ga nagai* 鼻の下が長い

hiji ひじ elbow

What you see is what you get, only one expression with *hiji,* namely *hijideppō* ("elbow-gun"). *Hiji,* aside from a few rare cases, just doesn't mean anything else. An elbow is an elbow—except on a chair, when it becomes an arm. An armchair is a *hiji-kake isu,* or literally, "chair with elbow rest."

You'll run into the behavioral counterpart of the first meaning of *hijideppō* on the crowded morning rush-hour trains in Japan. If you're really unlucky, you may get firsthand experience of the second.

Hijideppō o kurawasu (kuu) **ひじ鉄砲を食らわす（食う）** "give someone an elbow-gun to eat"

---

(1) jab someone with one's elbow (2) rebuff someone

(1) 彼女は、思いきり痴漢にひじ鉄砲を食らわした。
Kanojo wa, omoikiri chikan ni hijideppō o kurawashita.
She really let some pervert have it with her elbow.

(2) 彼は、彼女にひじ鉄砲を食わされて、しょんぼりしていた。
Kare wa, kanojo ni hijideppō o kuwasarete, shonbori shite ita.
He was moping around because she gave him the cold shoulder.

面接に行った会社からひじ鉄砲を食ってしまった。
Mensetsu ni itta kaisha kara hijideppō o kutte shimatta.
The company I tried to interview with wouldn't even give me the time of day.

hinkō-hōsei 品行方正 "exemplary behavior"

exemplary behavior, good (irreproachable) conduct, high morals, upstanding (moral) character

あまりに品行方正なので、とんでもない裏があるんじゃないか
とかえって疑ってしまうよ。

Amari ni hinkō-hōsei na no de, tondemonai ura ga aru n' ja nai ka to kaette utagatte shimau yo.

He is a man of such upstanding morals, you actually end up suspecting he must have some awful skeletons in the cupboard (closet).

彼は品行方正で、女にも金にも悪い噂など聞いたことがない。

Kare wa hinkō-hōsei de, onna ni mo kane ni mo warui uwasa nado kiita koto ga nai.

He is a man of unimpeachable morals. I have never heard the slightest rumor of dalliances or financial irregularities.

hirō-konpai 疲労困憊 "tiredness and exhaustion"

〜する to be totally exhausted, knackered, done in, beat, worn out, dog-tired

麻雀で疲労困憊だなんて、誰も同情しないよ。

Mājan de hirō-konpai da nante, dare mo dōjō shinai yo.

Exhausted from playing mahjong? You're not going to get much sympathy for that.

徹夜が二日も続いたから、みんな疲労困憊している様子だ。

Tetsuya ga futsuka mo tsuzuita kara, minna hirō-konpai shite iru yōsu da.

We've been up for the last two nights without a wink of sleep, and everybody's dog-tired.

今思えば当時は連日の残業で、心身ともに疲労困憊していたん
だなあ。

Ima omoeba tōji wa renjitsu no zangyō de, shinshin tomo ni hirō-konpai shite ita n' da nā.

Now that I think about it, what with overtime every night, we were just downright exhausted, both mentally and physically.

⇨ *ago ga deru / ago o dasu* あごが出る／あごを出す, *ashi ga bō ni naru / ashi o bō ni suru* 足が棒になる／足を棒にする; *genki* 元気

hitai 額 forehead

Foreheads can take a real beating in Japan. The greater the presence, the lower down you've got to go and the longer you've got to stay there. None but the very devout or contrite really slap their foreheads on the floor in a deep bow from the sitting position, but there is an expression that brings such a scene to mind, *hitai o kosuritsukeru yō ni fukaku atama o sageru,* or bow so deeply that one almost scrapes one's forehead. Fact of the matter is, if you're into the Zen thing you'll find yourself scraping the *tatami* with your forehead during the morning rituals a whole lot more than you might think necessary.

Hitai o atsumeru **額を集める** "collect foreheads"
discuss, put your heads together, compare notes, huddle

役員全員が額を集めて話合った。
Yakuin zen'in ga hitai o atsumete hanashiatta.
The directors all had a little powwow.

家事の分担について、家族が額を集めて相談した。
Kaji no buntan ni tsuite, kazoku ga hitai o atsumete sōdan shita.
The whole family got together to work out who was going to do what around the house.

Neko no hitai **猫の額** "cat's forehead"
(of a plot of land) tiny, minuscule

私の家には猫の額ほどの小さな庭が付いています。
Watashi no ie ni wa neko no hitai hodo no chiisa na niwa ga tsuite imasu.
My house has got a yard that's about the size of a postage stamp.

hito-hada nugu 一肌脱ぐ "take off a layer of skin"

help, give (lend) a helping hand, give one's right arm for someone

彼は彼女のために一肌脱ぐことにした。
Kare wa kanojo no tame ni hito-hada nugu koto ni shita.
He decided to do what he could for her. / He made up his mind to go the extra mile for her.

彼は、その友人のためなら、一肌でも二肌でも脱ぐつもりだった。
Kare wa, sono yūjin no tame nara, hito-hada de mo futa-hada de mo nugu tsumori datta.
He was ready to give his friend the shirt off his back.

hitoashi-chigai 一足違い "one step different"

just barely

一足違いでしたね。彼はたった今会社を出たところです。
Hitoashi-chigai deshita ne. Kare wa tatta-ima kaisha o deta tokoro desu.
You're a second too late. He just stepped out of the office.

一足違いで、彼女とすれ違いになってしまった。
Hitoashi-chigai de, kanojo to surechigai ni natte shimatta.
I just missed her by a hair.

hitoke 人気 "people's *ki*"

a sign that someone is around; [~ *ga nai*] unpopulated, empty, not a sign of anyone

屋台を出すなら、もっと人気がある所にすればいいのに。
Yatai o dasu nara, motto hitoke no aru tokoro ni sureba ii no ni.
If you're going to set up a stall to sell food, wouldn't it be better to do it in a place where there are more people around?

旅館の裏手は人気もなく、広間の宴会の音も聞こえなかった。
Ryokan no urate wa hitoke mo naku, hiroma no enkai no oto mo kikoe-nakatta.
There wasn't anybody around in the rear of the inn, and you couldn't even hear the party being held in the banquet room.

この公園は夜になると人気がなくなるから、女の人は一人で歩かない方がいいのよ。
Kono kōen wa yoru ni naru to hitoke ga nakunaru kara, onna no hito wa hitori de arukanai hō ga ii no yo.
There aren't many people in the park after dark, so it's probably not a good idea for a woman to go there alone.

✌ Almost always appears in the negative. See note at *ninki* for tips on when the characters are read as *hitoke* or *ninki*.

hitsuji ひつじ (羊) sheep

This docile animal comes off about the same in Japan as its cousins elsewhere, figuring in few idioms that would make it proud and several that draw upon its perceived docility or stupidity. The word *hitsuji* is said to have been formed from the *hi* for *hige* 髭, or beard, the *tsu* つ for the possessive particle *no*, and the *ji* じ for cow. A sheep, in other words, is a cow with a beard.

The sheep's bleat is *mēmē* メーメー. They are counted as *ippiki* 一匹 or *ittō* 一頭. When the sheep is the eighth of the twelve signs in the Chinese zodiac, it is written 未.

Hitsuji no yō (na/ni) 羊のよう（な／に） "like a sheep"
docile(ly), mousy (mousily), sheepish(ly), timorous(ly), very quiet(ly)

普段は羊のようにおとなしい彼が怒鳴ったんだからよっぽどひどいこと言われたに違いないよ。
Fudan wa hitsuji no yō ni otonashii kare ga donatta n' da kara yoppodo hidoi koto iwareta ni chigai nai yo.
For a sheepish (rabbity) guy like him to up and shout like that, somebody must have said something pretty bad to him.

羊のような人ほど一度怒りだすと手が付けられないことが多いね。
Hitsuji no yō na hito hodo ichido okoridasu to te ga tsukerarenai koto ga ōi ne.
When someone who's usually a pussycat (milquetoast) explodes in anger, you've just got to keep your distance.

🐑 From the fact that sheep seldom rise up in rebellion against shepherds.

Hitsujigumo 羊雲 "a sheep cloud"
a fluffy (fleecy) cloud, a (altocumulus) floccus

今日は絵に描いたような大きな羊雲が空に浮かんでいました。
Kyō wa e ni kaita yō na ōki na hitsujigumo ga sora ni ukande imashita.
The sky was full of big, picture-perfect fleecy clouds today.

さとし君の描く雲はいつも羊雲だね。
Satoshi-kun no kaku kumo wa itsumo hitsujigumo da ne.
All the clouds you draw are big fluffy ones, Satoshi.

↪ *iwashigumo* 鰯雲

hiza ひざ knee

Meanings of *hiza* include both that part of the leg that kids skin all the time as well as the same part of their pants that, if not already worn through, then almost always seems to stick painfully to the wound. *Hiza* also means one's lap.

You know how when you suddenly understand something, you slap your thigh? Well, the Japanese slap their knee, *hiza o utsu*. Maybe there really *is* something to what they say about Japanese having short legs.

Hiza o majieru **ひざを交える** "mix knees"
get together informally

首相は、野党の党首とひざを交えて話し合った。
Shushō wa, yatō no tōshu to hiza o majiete hanashiatta.
The prime minister had an informal chat (friendly talk) with the leaders of the opposition parties.

ひざを交えて話し合えば、彼もわかってくれるかもしれない。
Hiza o majiete hanashiaeba, kare mo wakatte kureru ka mo shirenai.
If you have a little heart-to-heart with him, he'll probably understand.

Hiza o tsukiawaseru **ひざを突き合わせる** "shove one's knees against someone else's"

---

(1) sit right across from (2) have a friendly chat with, have a tête-à-tête

(1) あの人と3時間もひざを突き合わせていたら、肩がこっちゃったよ。
Ano hito to san-jikan mo hiza o tsukiawasete itara, kata ga kotchatta yo.
Three hours of being holed up with him really did me in. / Boy, have I got a stiff neck after three hours of sitting shoulder to shoulder (cheek by jowl) with him.

駅周辺の再開発について、商店主たちはひざを突き合わせて話し合った。
Eki-shūhen no sai-kaihatsu ni tsuite, shōtenshu-tachi wa hiza o tsuki-awasete hanashiatta.
The shop owners all got together to discuss redevelopment plans for the area around the station.

(2) 仲間とひざを突き合わせて、将来の計画を話し合った。
Nakama to hiza o tsukiawasete, shōrai no keikaku o hanashiatta.
He and his friends sat around and talked over their plans for the future.

hone 骨 bone

In addition to meaning the bones that support the body of animals, birds, and fish, *hone* also can mean the framework or ribs in a fan, umbrella, *shōji,* or other man-made object. It can also refer to a person who is the heart or backbone of an organization, an essential element or aspect of something, or the quality of perserverance or spunk and hard work.

One of my favorite expressions with *hone* is *honeorizon*—literally, "breaking bones and losing." An English approximation might be something like "busting your ass for nothing."

Hone ga oreru / hone o oru 骨が折れる／骨を折る "one's bones break"
be a lot of work, not be easy, be difficult; take pains, try (push) hard, bust ass

---

この計画を彼に承諾させるのは、骨が折れるだろう。
Kono keikaku o kare ni shōdaku saseru no wa, hone ga oreru darō.
It's going to be an uphill battle trying to get him to go along with this plan.

田中さんに骨を折ってもらったおかげで、今日の会は大成功でした。
Tanaka-san ni hone o otte moratta okage de, kyō no kai wa daiseikō deshita.
We owe the success of today's meeting to all the efforts Mr. Tanaka has made on our behalf.

Hone o uzumeru 骨を埋める "bury one's bones"
(stay somewhere) forever, the rest of one's life

僕は、今度の会社に骨を埋める覚悟でがんばるよ。
Boku wa, kondo no kaisha ni hone o uzumeru kakugo de ganbaru yo.
I've made up my mind to work hard and stick it out at my new job.

3年間のボランティアとして来たが、今ではこの国に骨を埋めるつもりだ。
San-nenkan no borantia toshite kita ga, ima de wa kono kuni ni hone o uzumeru tsumori da.
I came to this country as a volunteer on a three-year stint but now I intend to be buried here.

Hone(mi) o oshimazu (oshimanai) 骨（身）を惜しまず（惜しまない） "don't regret one's bones"
spare no pains, give something one's all, hold back nothing

彼は骨身を惜しまず働いて、今の地位を築いた。
Kare wa honemi o oshimazu hataraite, ima no chii o kizuita.
He rose to his present position by dedicating himself entirely to the job.

骨を惜しんでいるようでは、いい職人になれないよ。
Hone o oshinde iru yō de wa, ii shokunin ni narenai yo.
You'll never make much of a craftsman if you don't put everything you've got into your work.

Honemi o kezuru 骨身を削る "scrape off one's bone marrow"

toil, slave, bust ass; suffer greatly

商家に嫁いだ祖母は、骨身を削って働いた。
Shōka ni totsuida sobo wa, honemi o kezutte hataraita.
My grandmother married into a family of merchants and worked her fingers to the bone.

あの頃は骨身を削るような生活をしていた。
Ano koro wa honemi o kezuru yō na seikatsu o shite ita.
Times were tough back then. / I used to work like a slave in those days.

honki 本気 "real *ki*"

earnestness, seriousness, sincerity; no fooling, for real

みんなは信じていないが、彼は本気なんですよ。
Minna wa shinjite inai ga, kare wa honki nan desu yo.
No one believes him, but he's not playing around (he's serious).

私は正気じゃないかも知れないが、本気だ。
Watashi wa shōki ja nai kamo shirenai ga, honki da.
I may not be sane (in my right mind), but I am serious.

会社をやめて田舎へ帰るって聞いたんだが、本気なのか？
Kaisha o yamete inaka e kaeru tte kiita n' da ga, honki na no ka?
I heard you were quitting work and going back to your hometown. Are you serious?

君が本気なら私もできるだけのお手伝いはしよう。
Kimi ga honki nara watashi mo dekiru dake no otetsudai wa shiyō.
If you mean what you say, I'll do what I can to help.

honki de ~ o suru 本気で〜をする "to do ~ with real *ki*"

be serious about something, get behind something

本気で販売戦略を展開すれば絶対売れるはずだ。
Honki de hanbai-senryaku o tenkai sureba zettai ureru hazu da.
If we throw ourselves into the sales strategy, I know the product will move.

政府は本気で流通の規制緩和を進める構えだ。
Seifu wa honki de ryūtsū no kisei-kanwa o susumeru kamae da.
The government appears to be serious about relaxing distribution regulations.

本気でやりさえすれば1日でできる仕事だ。
Honki de yari sae sureba ichinichi de dekiru shigoto da.
Get serious about it, and you can polish the job off in a day.

僕は君のことを本気で心配しているんだよ。
Boku wa kimi no koto o honki de shinpai shite iru n' da yo.
In all seriousness (No kidding), I'm worried about you.

☞ *ki o ireru* 気を入れる, *mi o ireru* 身を入れる

honki ni naru 本気になる "to become real *ki*"

get serious, get down to business, get down to it

本気になればもっと成績が上がるのは確かなんだけどねえ。
Honki ni nareba motto seiseki ga agaru no wa tashika nan da kedo nē.
I know she could get better grades if she just buckled down (got serious).

迷いに迷ったが、やっと本気になった。
Mayoi ni mayotta ga, yatto honki ni natta.
I might have fooled around for a long time, but I now I'm ready to get down to business.

もっと本気になって聞いて下さい。
Motto honki ni natte kiite kudasai.
Listen to what I'm saying, would you.

うちのやつが本気になって怒り出すと怖いぞ。
Uchi no yatsu ga honki ni natte okoridasu to kowai zo.
It's scary as hell when the old lady really gets pissed off (flies into a rage, flies off the handle).

honki ni suru 本気にする "to make into real *ki*"

take someone seriously, take someone at his word

本気にするかどうかは君次第だが、僕は嘘はついていない。
Honki ni suru ka dō ka wa kimi shidai da ga, boku wa uso wa tsuite inai.
It's up to you whether you take me at my word, but I'm not just talking through my hat.

子供達ははじめは父の言うことを本気にしなかった。
Kodomo-tachi wa hajime wa chichi no iu koto o honki ni shinakatta.
The kids didn't believe their father at first.

そういう冗談をいちいち本気にしていたら身が持たないぞ。
Sō iu jōdan o ichi-ichi honki ni shite itara mi ga motanai zo.
If you take every little joke seriously, you'll screw yourself up.

honmatsu-tentō 本末転倒 "the beginning and the end reversed"

getting one's priorities all wrong (mixed up); putting the cart before the horse

教師が学生から注意されるなんて、本末転倒じゃないか。情けない。

Kyōshi ga gakusei kara chūi sareru nante, honmatsu-tentō ja nai ka. Nasake-nai.

When the students start correcting their teachers, you know something is drastically wrong. A pretty sad situation if you ask me.

節税のために借金するなんて本末転倒だと思うけどなあ。

Setsuzei no tame ni shakkin suru nante honmatsu-tentō da to omou kedo nā.

Taking out a loan just to reduce your taxes makes me think you've got your priorities all wrong.

hotaru 蛍 firefly

Nature's original "thousand points of light," the two dozen or so species of fireflies found in Japan, especially the luminous ones, have long been thought to embody the souls of the dead. Just how this quaint folk belief squares with decadent romanticists of yesteryear who used the firefly as a metaphor for passionate love remains unclear, for there is no indication that these Heian aristocrats were necrophiles.

One thing that is clear is that most Japanese associate the firefly with the nation's version of "Auld Lang Syne," *Hotaru no Hikari*「蛍の光」. Unfortunately, fireflies are seldom around to be enjoyed in today's urban environment unless you shell out a few bucks to buy a handful at your local friendly department store—which is exactly what some parents are forced to do when summer vacation rolls around and the kids are given their summer homework. The collecting of such insects remains the number one assignment in many grammar schools.

Hotaru-zoku 蛍族 "firefly clan"

someone, usually a husband, who has to go out on the veranda to smoke (because of growing concern over the effects of secondary smoke on others, especially children); a glowworm

この団地も夜になると蛍族があちらこちらに見られる。
Kono danchi mo yoru ni naru to hotaru-zoku ga achira kochira ni mirareru.
The glowworms are out in force around this apartment complex once night falls.

蛍族にとって冬は厳しい。
Hotaru-zoku ni totte fuyu wa kibishii.
Winter's tough on people who have to go out of the house to smoke.

🕯 From the lambent glow of lighted cigarettes in the darkness. A poetic expression in deference to those driven from their homes by spouses and children more interested in longevity than they are.

hyappatsu-hyakuchū 百発百中 "one hundred shots, one hundred in the center"

hitting the bull's-eye every time, hitting the mark ten times out of ten, always (bang) on target, 100 percent accurate

この局の天気予報はこのところ百発百中だから、今日は傘を持って行った方がいいよ。
Kono kyoku no tenki-yohō wa kono tokoro hyappatsu-hyakuchū da kara, kyō wa kasa o motte itta hō ga ii yo.
This channel's weather forecasts have been 100 percent accurate recently, so you'd better take an umbrella with you today.

長島さんの動物的なカンは、百発百中とは行かないまでも、かなりよく当たるらしい。

Nagashima-san no dōbutsu-teki na kan wa, hyappatsu-hyakuchū to wa ikanai made mo, kanari yoku ataru rashii.

Mr. Nagashima's animal instinct is not quite infallible, but he gets things right pretty often.

百発百中は難しいけど、十のうち八つくらいは予想が当たる。

Hyappatsu-hyakuchū wa muzukashii kedo, jū no uchi yattsu kurai wa yosō ga ataru.

Getting ten out of ten is not easy, but I can usually get about eight out of ten right.

i no naka no kawazu 井の中の蛙 "a frog in a well"

a babe in the woods, a naive person

井の中の蛙になるのを恐れて彼女は独立を決心した。

I no naka no kawazu ni naru no o osorete kanojo wa dokuritsu o kesshin shita.

Afraid that she would end up not knowing anything about the ways of the world, she resolved to set out on her own.

たかが地区大会に優勝したぐらいで有頂天になっては井の中の蛙じゃないか。

Takaga chiku-taikai ni yūshō shita gurai de uchōten ni natte wa i no naka no kawazu ja nai ka.

Don't you think getting all worked up over something like winning at the regional level is a bit parochial?

֍ Shortened from the now less common proverb, *I no naka no kawazu taikai o shirazu* 井の中の蛙大海を知らず, or "The frog in the well knows nothing of the great ocean."

ichibu-shijū 一部始終 "the whole thing from beginning to end (from start to finish)"

the full particulars, all the details, the whole story (from beginning to end), the complete rundown from A to Z, all the ins and outs

犯行の一部始終が、防犯ビデオに録画されていた。
Hankō no ichibu-shijū ga, bōhan-bideo ni rokuga sarete ita.
The security cameras recorded the whole scene on video, from beginning to end.

少年は犯行の一部始終を見ていた。
Shōnen wa hankō no ichibu-shijū o mite ita.
The boy watched as the crime in its entirety unfolded before his very eyes.

一部始終が分かって、やっと納得したよ。
Ichibu-shijū ga wakatte, yatto nattoku shita yo.
Now that I know the whole story, I'm perfectly happy with the situation.

ichigo-ichie 一期一会 "in one lifetime, one meeting"

a once-in-a-lifetime meeting

この歳になると、どの出会いも一期一会と思って大切にしていますよ。
Kono toshi ni naru to, dono deai mo ichigo-ichie to omotte taisetsu ni shite imasu yo.
When you get to be my age, every time you meet someone you think of it as a unique opportunity and make the most of it.

一期一会と思えば、人と言い争う気持ちもなくなりますね。
Ichigo-ichie to omoeba, hito to iiarasou kimochi mo nakunarimasu ne.
When you think of each and every moment as precious, you don't feel like getting involved in arguments with people.

❧ Originally part of the teaching of the tea ceremony: every occasion of extending hospitality to another person is a particular opportunity never to recur in one's lifetime, so one should try to make the occasion perfect.

ichijitsu-senshū 一日千秋 "one day (is like) a thousand autumns"

to look forward to something eagerly; 〜の思い to wait impatiently for something (and while you wait, time seems to tick by so slowly that one day seems to last forever)

一日千秋の思いで、この日を待っていました。
Ichijitsu-senshū no omoi de, kono hi o matte imashita.
I feel as though I have been waiting for this day forever.

結果が発表されるまでの1週間は、一日千秋の思いだったよ。
Kekka ga happyō sareru made no isshūkan wa, ichijitsu-senshū no omoi datta yo.
The week I spent waiting for my results to come out was one of the longest of my life.

ichimō-dajin 一網打尽 "with one (throw of the) net, catch the lot"

a wholesale arrest; 〜にする to catch, to arrest the whole gang in one go (in one big raid, in one big roundup, in one fell swoop)

これで麻薬密売組織は一網打尽だ。
Kore de mayaku-mitsubai-soshiki wa ichimō-dajin da.
With this raid we'll catch the whole drug smuggling ring in one fell swoop.

暴走族を一網打尽にするため、特別班が出動した。

Bōsō-zoku o ichimō-dajin ni suru tame, tokubetsu-han ga shutsudō shita.
Special police units were mobilized in the raid to round up the motor-bike gangs.

集団スリは、刑事たちに一網打尽にされた。
Shūdan-suri wa, keiji-tachi ni ichimō-dajin ni sareta.
The team of pickpockets was rounded up as the detectives closed in.

ichimoku-ryōzen 一目瞭然 "clear at a glance"

clearly, obviously, as clear as day(light), evidently, plain to see, obvious, you could tell right away that . . .

ここが長い間空き家だったのは一目瞭然だな。
Koko ga nagai aida akiya datta no wa ichimoku-ryōzen da na.
It's plain to see that this house has been empty for a long time.

彼がもう相当飲んでるのは一目瞭然よ。
Kare ga mō sōtō nonde 'ru no wa ichimoku-ryōzen yo.
You don't have to be Sherlock Holmes to see he's had a few drinks already.

何が起こったかは一目瞭然だった。
Nani ga okotta ka wa ichimoku-ryōzen datta.
It was patently obvious what had happened.

こんな一目瞭然の間違いを見逃すなんて、たるんでるんじゃないか。
Konna ichimoku-ryōzen no machigai o minogasu nante, tarunde 'ru n' ja nai ka.
To miss such a glaring mistake really beggars belief. Get a grip, man!

☞ *me ni miete* 目に見えて

ichinen-hokki 一念発起 "arouse the single mind"

〜する to make up one's mind (to do something)

リストラで会社に居づらくなったよ、一念発起して脱サラするかな。
Risutora de kaisha ni izuraku natta yo, ichinen-hokki shite datsusara suru ka na.
What with the restructuring, life at the office isn't getting any easier. Maybe I'll just take the plunge and strike out on my own.

❦ 脱サラ (*datsusara*) is a compound of 脱 (escaping) and サラ, a shortened form of サラリーマン (company employee). Together they refer to the ever-increasing phenomenon of disgruntled white-collar workers who quit their companies and the rat race (usually to do something slightly "alternative," such as open a bar, become a musician, or free-lance).

これからしばらくはマイホームの買い時だと聞いて一念発起したらしく急に貯金を始めた。
Kore kara shibaraku wa maihōmu no kaidoki da to kiite ichinen-hokki shita rashiku kyū ni chokin o hajimeta.
He heard that now's a good time to buy, so apparently he immediately started saving up for his own home.

❦ Owning one's own home is the dream of many Japanese, especially those living in or around Tokyo and Osaka, where land prices are still so astronomical that a detached house on a tiny plot of land is about as affordable as a mansion in Manhattan or a palatial penthouse in Paris.

☞ *hara o kimeru* 腹を決める

ichiren-takushō 一蓮托生 "on the same lotus leaf, trust one's life (with the others')"

being born on the same lotus leaf in Buddhist heaven; casting one's lot with another; being in the same boat; thrown together by a quirk of fate; facing the same fate

俺たちは一蓮托生だ。自分だけ逃げようったって、そうは行かないぞ。
Ore-tachi wa ichiren-takushō da. Jibun dake nigeyō 'tta tte, sō wa ikanai zo.
We're in this together. If you're thinking of making a run for it by yourself, buddy, just think again.

密告するのは勝手だけど、あんたも一蓮托生で刑務所行きだぜ。
Mikkoku suru no wa katte da kedo, anta mo ichiren-takushō de keimusho-yuki da ze.
Go on then, squeal on me. See what good it does you. We're in this together, and we'll both end up going to jail.

与党と野党は、結局一蓮托生だったわけだ。
Yotō to yatō wa, kekkyoku ichiren-takushō datta wake da.
So, it turns out the ruling and opposition parties were working in cahoots.

✢ Originally this expression came from Buddhism and referred to the belief that people who loved each other in this world would be joyfully reunited in paradise, spending eternity together on a lotus leaf. Now the expression has come to take on a radically different meaning and is used in situations when people are thrown together and find themselves in dire straits.

iiki いい気 "good *ki*"

(be on) an ego trip, self-satisfaction, cockiness, conceit, vanity; (~ になる; ~ *ni naru*) let something go to one's head, think one is hot stuff (shit)

いい気になってると今にしっぺ返しされますよ。
Iiki ni natte 'ru to ima ni shippegaeshi saremasu yo.
Let your head get too big and they'll turn the tables on you real quick.

親の気も知らないでまったくいい気なものだ。
Oya no ki mo shiranai de mattaku iiki na mono da.
You're so self-centered. Couldn't care less about your parents' feelings.

おとなしくしてりゃいい気になりやがって。
Otonashiku shite 'rya iiki ni nariyagatte.
Big man! Think your shit doesn't stink, huh. / What are you gloating about, asshole? (more literally, "If I keep quiet, you start acting big.")

☙ *Iiki* is found almost exclusively in the two expressions appearing above: *iiki ni naru* and *iiki na mono*. Bear in mind that although the former is critical of a person's high estimation of himself, the latter, although critical, is less so and of a different character—being complacent or happy-go-lucky, especially when consideration of others is thought necessary, which is to say, almost all of the time in Japan. A synonym for *iiki ni naru* is *tengu ni naru* 天狗になる (literally, "become a flying goblin," from the long-nosed mythical monster's reputation for arrogance). One for *iiki na mono* is *nonki* 呑気. The latter is included in this book.

iki-shōchin 意気消沈 "spirits sinking"

with a heavy heart, with a sinking heart; 〜する to be depressed (dejected, discouraged, downhearted), to be down in the dumps, to have the mopes (the blues), to feel like you have had all the wind knocked out of you

滑り止めの大学に落ちてから、すっかり意気消沈してしまってるんだよ。
Suberidome no daigaku ni ochite kara, sukkari iki-shōchin shite shimatte 'ru n' da yo.

Not getting into that university really bummed me out; it was my fail-safe choice.

😼 滑り止めの大学 (*suberidome no daigaku*): In Japan students usually apply to about half a dozen different universities. The university they most want to enter is referred to as their 第1志望校 (*daiichi shibō-kō*, their first-choice); their second-choice is 第2志望校 (*daini shibō-kō*), their third 第3志望校 (*daisan shibō-kō*), ad infinitum. Just in case they fail the entrance exams to all their principal choices, most high school students sit the exam for a less academically challenging university. In colloquial Japanese 滑る (*suberu*; to slip, slide) is a euphemism for failing an exam. When you fail your first-to-nth-choices, your *suberidome* is the university where you put a stop to your "slide."

そんなに意気消沈することないよ。君のせいじゃないんだから。
Sonna ni iki-shōchin suru koto nai yo. Kimi no sei ja nai n' da kara.
Don't let it get you down. After all, it wasn't your fault.

☞ *ki ga shizumu* 気が沈む; *iki-yōyō* 意気揚々

iki-tōgō 意気投合 "spirits joining (spirits fusing)"

mutual understanding, affinity, sympathy; 〜する to be like-minded, to find a kindred spirit, to get on like a house on fire, to be on the same wavelength, to speak the same language, to hit it off with someone, to see eye to eye with someone

寿司屋のカウンターで隣合った人と意気投合しちゃってね。
Sushiya no kauntā de tonariatta hito to iki-tōgō shichatte ne.
I really hit it off with this guy who was sitting next to me at the sushi bar.

鈴木さんとはすっかり意気投合して、家族ぐるみのつき合いをしていますよ。
Suzuki-san to wa sukkari iki-tōgō shite, kazoku-gurumi no tsukiai o shite imasu yo.

Ol' Suzuki and me, we're great buddies, always inviting each other's family around.

iki-yōyō 意気揚々 "spirits soaring"

triumphant(ly), exultant(ly), elated(ly), in triumph, in high spirits; 〜と、〜とする to be in good cheer, to be in a buoyant mood, to be over the moon, to be cock-a-hoop, to be as pleased as Punch

大口の契約がとれたって、意気揚々と報告して来たよ。
Ōguchi no keiyaku ga toreta tte, iki-yōyō to hōkoku shite kita yo.
He's just told me about that big new contract he pulled. He was practically walking on air.

合格発表を見に行った娘が、意気揚々としてもどって来た。
Gōkaku-happyō o mi ni itta musume ga, iki-yōyō to shite modotte kita.
My daughter went to check out her exam results and came back on cloud nine.

※ A synonymous expression is 意気軒昂 (*iki-kenkō*).

社長は「この製品は絶対売れる」と意気軒昂だ。
Shachō wa "Kono seihin wa zettai ureru" to iki-kenkō da.
The boss is all fired up about the product, saying it is sure to sell.

∞ *iki-shōchin* 意気消沈

ikka-danran 一家団欒 "one family all together"

the whole family happily united, a happy home, a happy family

子供たちが大きくなって、昔のような一家団欒の時間が少なくなったよ。

Kodomo-tachi ga ōkiku natte, mukashi no yō na ikka-danran no jikan ga sukunaku natta yo.

Since the kids have grown up, we don't seem to spend as much time together as we used to.

一家団欒といっても、家じゃみんながテレビの方を見ていてあまり話はしないんだ。

Ikka-danran to itte mo, uchi ja minna ga terebi no hō o mite ite amari hanashi wa shinai n' da.

I wouldn't say we're one big happy family. There's not much talking, what with everybody staring at the TV.

ikkaku-senkin 一攫千金 "(with) one grab (get) a thousand (pieces of) gold"

making a fortune at a stroke, a bonanza; to get rich quick, to strike oil; to strike it rich, to hit the jackpot, to make a killing

一攫千金を夢見て、馬券を買うときはいつも大穴を狙ってる。

Ikkaku-senkin o yumemite, baken o kau toki wa itsumo ōana o neratte 'ru.

He's always putting his money on the horses, going for the big win that'll make him an overnight millionaire.

一攫千金を狙うことばかり考えないで、地道に働きなさい。

Ikkaku-senkin o nerau koto bakari kangaenai de, jimichi ni hatarakinasai.

Instead of dreaming up ways of getting rich quick, why don't you try doing some honest work for a change?

毎年ジャンボ宝くじを買ってるけど、まだ一攫千金の夢は夢のままだよ。

Maitoshi janbo-takarakuji o katte 'ru kedo, mada ikkaku-senkin no yume wa yume no mama da yo.

Every year I buy tickets for the grand slam lottery, but my dreams of hitting the jackpot have yet to come true.

バブルの崩壊以後、一攫千金の儲け話はなくなった。
Baburu no hōkai igo, ikkaku-senkin no mōkebanashi wa nakunatta.
Since the bubble economy burst, you don't hear so much talk of people getting rich overnight.

※ The correct way to write this expression is 一攫千金 but it can also be written 一獲千金. In either case the pronunciation is the same. A synonymous expression is 濡れ手で粟 (*nurete de awa*), which literally translated means "(to grasp) millet grain with wet hands."

ikken-rakuchaku 一件落着 "one matter settled and done"

the matter has been settled; it's all done and dusted

何カ月にも渡った捜査が実って、事件は一件落着した。
Nankagetsu ni mo watatta sōsa ga minotte, jiken wa ikken-rakuchaku shita.
After an investigation that lasted many months, the case was successfully concluded.

これでやっと一件落着したと思ったのに、また横槍が入ったんだって？
Kore de yatto ikken-rakuchaku shita to omotta no ni, mata yokoyari ga haitta n' datte?
Just when I thought it was all over, now you tell me someone else is meddling in the matter?

※ There is a long-running Japanese TV drama called *Tōyama no Kin-san* (遠山の金さん), which is set in feudal times. At the end of every episode the hero, Kin-san (a young judge), always brings the villains to book uttering his weekly punchline of *ikken-rakuchaku* ("That sews up another case for this week, boys.")

ikki 一気 "one *ki*"

all at once, at a stretch, in one shot, without stopping

途中で休むとペースが崩れるから、一気にやってしまおう。
Tochū de yasumu to pēsu ga kuzureru kara, ikki ni yatte shimaō.
We're gonna lose momentum if we take a break, so let's just forge ahead and finish it up.

おなかが減っていたので弁当を一気に食べたら、どんな味か分からなかった。
Onaka ga hette ita no de bentō o ikki ni tabetara, donna aji ka wakaranakatta.
I was so famished I wolfed (scarfed) down my lunch without even tasting it.

一気、一気、一気。
Ikki! Ikki! Ikki!
Chugalug, chugalug!

In a full sentence, *ikki* appears exclusively with the particle *ni* as *ikki ni*.

☞ *ikki-nomi* 一気飲み

ikki-ichiyū 一喜一憂 "one joy, one sadness"

〜する to alternate between hope and despair; to be up in the clouds one minute, down in the dumps the next; to be on an emotional rollercoaster; to swing from joy to sorrow

その程度のことで、一喜一憂するんじゃない。
Sono teido no koto de, ikki-ichiyū suru n' ja nai.
Don't get worked up over a little thing like that.

試合は接戦で、点が入る度にそれぞれのチームの応援団が一喜一憂している。
Shiai wa sessen de, ten ga hairu tabi ni sorezore no chīmu no ōendan ga ikki-ichiyū shite iru.
It was a close game and each time somebody scored, the cheerleaders went into ecstasies of pleasure or pain.

たいして貯金があるわけじゃないのに、利率が変わるたびに一喜一憂してしまうんです。
Taishite chokin ga aru wake ja nai no ni, riritsu ga kawaru tabi ni ikki-ichiyū shite shimau n' desu.
I haven't got much in the way of savings but even so, every change in the interest rates has me either jumping for joy or ready to jump off a cliff.

ikki-nomi 一気飲み "a one-*ki* drink"

chugalug, guzzle

毎年4月には若い人の一気飲みによる急性アルコール中毒が多い。
Mainen shigatsu ni wa wakai hito no ikki-nomi ni yoru kyūsei-arukōru-chūdoku ga ōi.
Every April lots of young people get acute alcohol poisoning from chugalugging.

🍶 The Japanese college student's favorite pastime, drinking, takes on heroic proportions as *ikki-nomi* during the early days of a new "academic" (I use the word loosely) year, when clubs, circles, and classes get together for parties, or *konpa*, at which the major activity, in addition to scouting out the new guys and gals, is consuming massive quantities of beer, often amid shouts of *ikki, ikki, ikki!* from other students still on their feet.

ikkyo-ichidō 一挙一動 "one gesture and one move"

every move one makes

彼女の一挙一動は絵になってるじゃないか。
Kanojo no ikkyo-ichidō wa e ni natte 'ru ja nai ka.
She looks the part no matter what she does.

有名な人になると、一挙一動に注目されて不自由でしょうね。
Yūmei na hito ni naru to, ikkyo-ichidō ni chūmoku sarete fujiyū deshō ne.
Once you become famous, every little move you make is under the spotlight; it must be a strain.

一挙一動まで監視されてるみたいで嫌だよ。
Ikkyo-ichidō made kanshi sarete 'ru mitai de iya da yo.
It's horrible. I feel like I'm being watched whatever I do.

iku-dōon 異口同音 "(from) different mouths (come) the same sound"

〜に with one voice, by common consent, unanimously, as one, all of one accord

葬儀の参列者は、異口同音に彼の人柄のよさを口にした。
Sōgi no sanretsu-sha wa, iku-dōon ni kare no hitogara no yosa o kuchi ni shita.
All the mourners at the funeral were unanimous in their praise of his good character.

「ビートルズのようなすぐれたバンドは、もう二度と現れないだろう」と音楽ファンは異口同音に言う。
"Bītoruzu no yō na sugureta bando wa, mō nido to arawarenai darō" to ongaku-fan wa iku-dōon ni iu.

All music buffs are agreed: there will never be another band quite like the Beatles.

同僚は異口同音に今辞表を出したら損だと忠告してくれた。
Dōryō wa iku-dōon ni ima jihyō o dashitara son da to chūkoku shite kureta.
All my colleagues without exception advised me against handing in my resignation now.

✤ Care should be taken when writing this four-letter compound. Japanese schoolchildren often mistakenly write it as 異句同音. Other expressions meaning "unanimously" include 口を揃えて (*kuchi o soroete*) and 口々に (*kuchiguchi ni*). When various people use exactly the same words, you can use either 異口同音 or 口を揃えて, but not 口々に, as this is used when people say similar things (but each person uses a slightly different expression).

imi-shinchō 意味深長 "meaning, deep and long"

very meaningful, of profound significance, fraught (pregnant) with meaning, speaking volumes

彼がさっき言ったことは、意味深長だよ。
Kare ga sakki itta koto wa, imi-shinchō da yo.
What he just said is of great significance. / What he said a moment ago really ought to be listened to.

ずいぶんと意味深長な発言だったね。
Zuibun to imi-shinchō na hatsugen datta ne.
That was a very profound comment, wasn't it? / You really hit the nail on the head with what you said back then, didn't you?

彼は意味深長な笑いを浮かべて彼女の話を聞いていた。
Kare wa imi-shinchō na warai o ukabete kanojo no hanashi o kiite ita.
He listened to what she was saying with a smile on his lips that spoke volumes (with a meaningful smile on his lips).

✣ In colloquial Japanese it is very common to abbreviate this four-character compound and simply say (or write) イミシン (*imishin*).

> 彼の発言、ずいぶんイミシンじゃないか。
> *Kare no hatsugen, zuibun imishin ja nai ka.*
> I'd say there was something behind what he said, wouldn't you?

> イミシンな返事だったなあ。なんかワケアリだぜ。
> *Imishin na henji datta nā. Nanka wakeari da ze.*
> There was more to that answer than met the eye. He must be up to something.

ingin-burei 慇懃無礼 "politely insolent"

feigned politeness, being overpolite, being ever so polite

> あの人の慇懃無礼な言い方が、嫌で嫌で仕方がないんだ。
> *Ano hito no ingin-burei na iikata ga, iya de iya de shikata ga nai n' da.*
> I really can't stand his way of talking. He's so fawningly polite it makes me sick.

> 前もって連絡しなかったこちらも悪かったけれど、先方の断り方は実に慇懃無礼だった。
> *Mae-motte renraku shinakatta kochira mo warukatta keredo, senpō no kotowarikata wa jitsu ni ingin-burei datta.*
> I was at fault for not making contact beforehand, but the way they turned me away was absolutely the worst kind of insincere politeness.

inki (na) 陰気(な) "shadowy *ki*"

1. (of a person's attitude, countenance or mood) blue, gloomy, long-faced, melancholy; (of a person's temperament or personality) brooding, lugubrious, morose, saturnine, sulky, sullen, taciturn

中村さんはいい人なのに第一印象が陰気だからずいぶん損をしている。
Nakamura-san wa ii hito na no ni daiichi-inshō ga inki da kara zuibun son o shite iru.
Nakamura's a nice guy, but on first impression he seems so sullen that people don't really appreciate him.

そんな陰気な顔しないで、笑って、笑って。
Sonna inki na kao shinai de, waratte, waratte.
Wipe that hangdog look off your face and try a smile.

☞ *yōki (na)* 陽気(な)

2. (of a place or its atmosphere) dark, depressing, dreary, gloomy

深刻な問題を取り上げているのに、決して陰気な作品ではない。
Shinkoku na mondai o toriagete iru no ni, kesshite inki na sakuhin de wa nai.
For all the seriousness of its subject matter, this work isn't a bit gloomy.

この家は日当たりが悪くて少し陰気だね。
Kono ie wa hiatari ga warukute sukoshi inki da ne.
This house doesn't get much sun. It's a little too dreary for me.

inoshishi いのしし(猪) wild boar

Hunted since ancient times in Japan, this stout omnivore is known for the havoc it wreaks on crops as well as its mad rushes and observed inability to change direction quickly. The compound *inoshishi-musha* 猪武者 was formerly used to describe a reckless samurai and through the years has been applied to anyone who rushes headlong into things without considering the consequences.

The meat, variously called *yamakujira* ("mountain whale"—from earlier days when consumption of wild meat was taboo but whale meat accepted) and *botan* ("peony"), is rarely seen in Japan today and is therefore prized.

Wild boars are counted *ittō* 一頭 or *ippiki* 一匹. Written 亥, the boar is twelfth among the twelve signs of the Chinese zodiac.

Chototsu-mōshin 猪突猛進 "the boar's wild rush"
reckless, foolhardy, madcap; straight ahead (and damn the torpedos)

猪突猛進の彼にこの仕事を任せない方がいい。
Chototsu-mōshin no kare ni kono shigoto o makasenai hō ga ii.
He's so foolhardy that we'd better not put him in charge of this project.

彼女の性格は一言で言うと猪突猛進型です。
Kanojo no seikaku wa hitokoto de iu to chototsu-mōshin-gata desu.
You could characterize her personality in a word, "reckless."

猪 From the way a wild boar runs straight ahead full-blast, looking neither right nor left, and its inability to change directions quickly. Not the kind of thing you'd want to have somebody say about you.

inu 犬 dog

Dogs have been hanging around long enough to warrant mention in the *Kojiki,* Japan's oldest extant historical work. And although they figure in numerous expressions, the images elicited are generally the result of the dog's inferior qualities.

An interesting insight into how man's best friend was thought of in earlier days can be gained from a look at the word for a useless or shameless samurai, *inuzamurai* 犬侍, or a "dog samurai." The word possibly derives from the fact that dogs, unlike domesticated animals such as cows or horses, are relatively unproductive and, according to one source, display a particularly beastly lack of decorum by copulating in public.

In addition to the more common *koinu* 小犬, puppies are also called *inukoro* 犬ころ. They are counted *ippiki* 一匹 or *ittō* 一頭.

Written 戌, the dog is eleventh among the twelve signs of the Chinese zodiac.

☞ *kaiinu ni te o kamareru* 飼い犬に手を噛まれる, *ken'en (inu to saru) no naka* 犬猿（犬と猿）の仲, *makeinu* 負け犬, *makeinu no tōboe* 負け犬の遠吠え

Inu 犬 "dog"

a (police) spy, mole, plant, an informant, a shamus; ass-licker, a brown-noser, cat's paw, flunky, lackey, sycophant, stooge, stool pigeon, toady, yes-man; a slave (to the passions)

おまえ一生政府の犬でいるつもりか。
Omae isshō seifu no inu de iru tsumori ka.
Are you gonna spend your whole life informing for the government?

あいつは社長の犬だから、気をつけて話せよ。
Aitsu wa shachō no inu da kara, ki o tsukete hanase yo.
Watch out when you talk to that guy. He's the boss's lackey.

おまえいつからあんな奴の犬に成り下がったんだ。
Omae itsu kara anna yatsu no inu ni narisagatta n' da.
Since when have you fallen so low that you're ratting on your friends for him?

あいつはどうも犬のような気がする。
Aitsu wa dōmo inu no yō na ki ga suru.
I get the feeling the guy's a plant.

おまえが（警察の）犬だということがばれたらコンクリート詰めだぞ。
Omae ga (keisatsu no) inu da to iu koto ga baretara konkurīto-zume da zo.
You'll end up dressed in concrete if word ever gets out that you're working for the pigs.

🐾 Often written in katakana, this use of *inu* is possibly from the dog's quality of compliance to its owner's wishes.

Inu ga nishi mukya o wa higashi **犬が西向きゃ尾は東** "A dog's tail points east when the dog points west."

obviously; needless to say; plain at the nose on your face

犬が西向きゃ尾は東、卒業なんか無理だよ。学校に行ってないんだから。
Inu ga nishi mukya o wa higashi, sotsugyō nanka muri da yo. Gakkō ni itte 'nai n' da kara.
It's no surprise that you're not going to graduate. You never go to class.

彼女は「犬が西向きゃ尾は東」式のことしか会議で発言しない。
Kanajo wa "Inu ga nishi mukya o wa higashi" shiki no koto shika kaigi de hatsugen shinai.
The only remarks she made at the meeting were of the most obvious sort, like the sun rises in the east.

そういうの、犬が西向きゃ尾は東っていうんだよ。
Sō iu no, inu ga nishi mukya o wa higashi tte iu n' da yo.
Does a bear shit in the woods?

🐾 As can be seen in the last example, like similar English retorts, this expression is also used in response to a comment the speaker feels is patently true or false. Unlike its English equivalents, this and similar Japanese expressions are seldom used as rhetorical responses to a question by another person.

Inu mo arukeba bō ni ataru **犬も歩けば棒に当たる** "If a dog walks around enough, it is likely to get hit with a stick."

---

1. (of bad fortune) trouble lurks, be out of luck

「犬も歩けば棒に当たる」で散歩してたら頭に鳥の糞が落ちてきた。

"Inu mo arukeba bō ni ataru" de sanpo shite 'tara atama ni tori no fun ga ochite kita.

Some bird shit on my head when I went out for a walk. Guess it just wasn't my day.

昨日の夜はまさに「犬も歩けば棒に当たる」で、渋谷で得体の知れない奴らに金をせびられた。
Kinō no yoru wa masa ni "Inu mo arukeba bō ni ataru" de, Shibuya de etai no shirenai yatsura ni kane o sebirareta.

You really just never know what's gonna happen. There I was out walking around Shibuya, minding my own business last night, when a bunch of guys I didn't know from Adam came up and started hassling me for money.

2. (of good fortune) every dog has his day, be in luck, be one's lucky day

昨日は犬も歩けば棒に当たるで、パチンコで結構稼いだよ。
Kinō wa inu mo arukeba bō ni ataru de, pachinko de kekkō kaseida yo.
I made out like a bandit yesterday playing pachinko. Hey, it's like they say, every dog has his day.

犬も歩けば棒に当たるだよ、いいバイトが見つかった。
Inu mo arukeba bō ni ataru da yo, ii baito ga mitsukatta.
I lucked into this great part-time job.

🐕 Dogs and their human friends are likely to meet with something unexpected if they are active in anyway at all. It is obviously safer for one and all to stay home in bed. Of the definitions above, the second and more recent meaning derives from a mistaken use of the phrase, and now appears to be more common than the original.

Inu mo kuwanai **犬も食わない** "Even a dog will turn up its nose." avoid something like the plague; won't touch something with a ten-foot pole

夫婦喧嘩は犬も食わない。
Fūfu-genka wa inu mo kuwanai.
No one in his right mind wants to get mixed up in someone else's marital spat.

そんなくだらない話犬も食わないよ。
Sonna kudaranai hanashi inu mo kuwanai yo.
I can't imagine anyone showing any interest in something that stupid.

🐾 Derives from the observation that dogs are notoriously omnivorous, and if a dog won't touch something, it has to be pretty bad. It appears only in the negative, and predominately in reference to domestic quarrels.

Inu-chikushō **犬畜生** "a dog from hell"
a beast, a cur

あいつは犬畜生にも劣る。
Aitsu wa inu-chikushō ni mo otoru.
He's lower than pond scum.

犬畜生だってそんなことはしないよ。
Inu-chikushō datte sonna koto wa shinai yo.
Even a lowly cur wouldn't do something like that.

🐾 Obviously derogatory, the word can be used in response to a person's speech or behavior.

Inuji ni **犬死に** "a dog's death"
die a dog's death, die in vain

彼は結局犬死にした。
Kare wa kekkyoku inuji ni shita.
He died like a dog in the end.

彼は過労死したにもかかわらず、賠償金はわずかで、会社のために犬死にしたことになった。
Kare wa karō-shi shita ni mo kakawarazu, baishō-kin wa wazuka de, kaisha no tame ni inuji ni shita koto ni natta.
Despite the fact that overwork killed him, the company paid such a piddling sum in damages that his death was truly in vain.

✌ Although appearing most commonly in verb form, *inuji ni suru,* it can also be used to express futility or effort that goes unrewarded. In such cases, it is followed by *dōzen* 同然, as in the following example:

それじゃあ、犬死に同然だ。
Sore jā, inuji ni dōzen da.
That amounts to throwing away your life for nothing.

Inukaki 犬かき "dog scratching"
dog-paddle

俺犬かきしかできないんだ。
Ore inukaki shika dekinai n' da.
The only thing I can do is dog-paddle.

競泳パンツで犬かきしてたのを友人たちに見られて稔は二度と海水浴に行くことはなかった。
Kyōei-pantsu de inukaki shite 'ta no o yūjin-tachi ni mirarete Minoru wa nido to kaisui-yoku ni iku koto wa nakatta.
Minoru never went to the beach again after his friends caught him dog-paddling in a pair of really cool Speedos.

✌ Also, but less commonly, *inu-oyogi* 犬泳ぎ.

ippan-kōkai 一般公開 "general opening"

open to the public; on general release

あの寺の宝物は普段は一般公開されていないから、今がチャンスだよ。

Ano tera no hōmotsu wa fudan wa ippan-kōkai sarete inai kara, ima ga chansu da yo.

That temple's sacred treasures aren't usually open to the public, so now's your chance to see them.

僕は、一般公開の前のプレヴューで見たんだけど、評判通りいい映画だったね。

Boku wa, ippan-kōkai no mae no purevū de mita n' da kedo, hyōban-dōri ii eiga datta ne.

I saw the film at a preview before it went on general release. It was as good as it's cracked up to be.

ippatsu-shōbu 一発勝負 "One shot decides who wins."

go for broke; all or nothing

最後のレースでは、一発勝負で大穴をねらった。
Saigo no rēsu de wa, ippatsu-shōbu de ōana o neratta.
In the last race I went all out for the big win.

これ以上交渉を続けても拉致があかないよ。そろそろ一発勝負に出た方がいい。

Kore ijō kōshō o tsuzukete mo rachi ga akanai yo. Sorosoro ippatsu-shōbu ni deta hō ga ii.

There's no point continuing any further with the negotiations—we're getting nowhere. We'd better go for broke.

ippiki ōkami 一匹狼 "a single wolf"

a lone wolf, loner, maverick

彼は出版業界の一匹狼で通っている。
Kare wa shuppan-gyōkai no ippiki ōkami de tōtte iru.
He's known in the publishing industry as a maverick.

一匹狼だったその男の居所を知る者はいない。
Ippiki ōkami datta sono otoko no idokoro o shiru mono wa inai.
Nobody knows the whereabouts of that loner.

ippo-temae 一歩手前 "one step before"

one step short of, on the verge of, (barely) inches away from

彼女とは婚約する一歩手前まで行ってたんだが、些細なことから喧嘩別れしてそのままになってしまったんだ。
Kanojo to wa kon'yaku suru ippo-temae made itte 'ta n' da ga, sasai na koto kara kenka-wakare shite sono mama ni natte shimatta n' da.
We were on the verge of getting engaged when we had a row over something petty and split up, and that's the way things have stayed.

受話器を置いてハッと気がついたら、もう火事の一歩手前でした。それ以来、天ぷらを揚げてるときは電話に出ないことにしてるんです。
Juwa-ki o oite hatto ki ga tsuitara, mō kaji no ippo-temae deshita. Sore irai, tenpura o agete 'ru toki wa denwa ni denai koto ni shite 'ru n' desu.
Just as I hung up, I was surprised to find that I almost had a fire on my hands. Since then, I've made it a practice never to answer the phone while deep-frying tempura.

iroke 色気 "colored *ki*"

1. sex appeal

この女優さんはもう50を過ぎているのにまだまだ色気があるね。

Kono joyū-san wa mō gojū o sugite iru no ni mada mada iroke ga aru ne.
This actress may never see fifty again, but she's still a turn-on.

彼女は色気たっぷりの仕草で歩く。
Kanojo wa iroke tappuri no shigusa de aruku.
She's got one sexy walk. / She's got all these sexy (foxy) little moves when she walks.

この俳優はこぼれるような色気で中年女性を魅了している。
Kono haiyū wa koboreru yō na iroke de chūnen-josei o miryō shite iru.
This actor's oozing with so much sex appeal that he sweeps middle-aged women off their feet.

❦ While the original meaning of *iroke* appears to have been the sexual quality of a woman that arouses a man's interest, the definition has now been expanded to include the same sort of quality in a man by which he arouses interest in a woman. And though lexical legitimacy has yet to be bestowed upon gay use of the term, such use is common. Gender aside, it is plain and simple sex appeal.

2. [in the phrase *iroke nuki*] women

今日は色気抜きの会だから飲むだけが楽しみだ。
Kyō wa iroke-nuki no kai da kara nomu dake ga tanoshimi da.
No gals at the party today, so the only fun thing to do is drink.

たまには色気抜きの飲み会もいいものだ。
Tama ni wa iroke-nuki no nomikai mo ii mono da.
A stag party's all right too sometimes.

❦ Derivative from the first sense, the term as seen in the above expressions originally referred to the absence of women who, by profession, entertained men in drinking establishments—geisha or hostesses traditionally, so-called "companions" today. Later usage expanded to include female office workers who were—and, in less enlightened companies, still are—expected to wait on their male co-workers and bosses at office parties and the like. From the perspective of such hidebound males, a get-together with no female employees in attendance is still referred to as *iroke nuki no kai.* Contemporary sensitivities require that students of the language be aware that many now feel that this phrase is a form of sexual discrimination.

☞ *onnakke* 女気

3. desire (for), interest (in)

> この合併の話には先方も色気を示している。
> *Kono gappei no hanashi ni wa senpō mo iroke o shimeshite iru.*
> The other party is also showing interest in the merger, too.

> 上田選手もうちへの移籍に色気があるようだ。
> *Ueda-senshu mo uchi e no iseki ni iroke ga aru yō da.*
> Ueda seems to want to be traded to our team.

☞ *ki ga aru* 気がある

iroke yori kuike 色気より食い気 "eating over colored *ki*"

be more interested in food than sex, like food better than sex

> 彼は色気より食い気だから、当分恋人は無理だね。
> *Kare wa iroke yori kuike da kara, tōbun koibito wa muri da ne.*
> He's more interested in feeding his face than women, so it'll be a while before he finds himself a girl.

> うちの娘は色気より食い気で、友だちとの会話もどこのケーキ屋さんがおいしいかとかそんなことばかりだ。
> *Uchi no musume wa iroke yori kuike de, tomodachi to no kaiwa mo doko no kēkiya-san ga oishii ka to ka sonna koto bakari da.*
> My daughter's more interested in eating than she is in boys. All she and her friends ever talk about is stuff like where you can get good pastries.

🌿 When used about men, *iroke yori kuike* indicates the subject is more interested in eating—and by extension a woman who can cook—than he is in how good-looking a woman is. But when a woman is the subject, the expression can be interpreted two ways: either she is less interested in *attracting* men than she is in eating, or she is less interested in *attractive* men than eating. *Iroke yori kuike* is similar—by a slight stretch of the imagination—to *hana yori dango* 花より団子 ("dumplings before flowers," or less literally, substance over appearance), but the latter is somewhat broader in scope, used to describe a general preference for things of substantive importance rather than beauty or appearance.

iroke-zuku 色気づく "colored *ki* adheres"

become interested in (awaken to) sex, start to notice boys (girls); become sexually attractive

一郎の奴、いつまでも子供だと思ってたが、そろそろ色気づいてきたかな。
Ichirō no yatsu, itsu made mo kodomo da to omotte 'ta ga, sorosoro iroke-zuite kita na.
I was beginning to think the sap would never rise in old Ichirō (good ol' Ichirō), but it looks like he's finally starting to get that gleam in his eye.

隣の娘はいつの間にか色気づいてきたなぁ。
Tonari no musume wa itsu-no-ma ni ka iroke-zuite kita nā.
The girl next door is really starting to fill out. / The girl next door has started taking an interest in boys all of a sudden.

Although yet to attain lexical respectability in the sense of a person, usually an adolescent woman, becoming sexually attractive, this meaning of *iroke-zuku* is common in speech. The translation in the immediately preceding example would be the meaning as understood by most native speakers of the language.

ishiki-fumei 意識不明 "consciousness unclear"

unconscious, senseless

倒れてしばらくは意識不明で、このまま駄目になるんじゃないかと思われたそうだ。
Taorete shibaraku wa ishiki-fumei de, kono mama dame ni naru n' ja nai ka to omowareta sō da.
I was unconscious for some time after I collapsed, and apparently they thought that might be the end of me.

事故に会った人は3人で、そのうち1人は意識不明の重体です。
Jiko ni atta hito wa sannin de, sono uchi hitori wa ishiki-fumei no jūtai desu.
Of the three people involved in the accident, one of them is unconscious and in serious condition.

ishin-denshin 以心伝心 "from one heart to another"

immediate communication from one mind to another, telepathy, telepathic communication between people, tacit understanding, intuitively shared thoughts or feelings, to be able to read each other's mind

これ以上言わせるなよ、以心伝心だろう。
Kore ijō iwaseru na yo, ishin-denshin darō.
Don't make me spell it out. You must know what I'm getting at, surely.

父の気持ちは以心伝心でよく分かった。
Chichi no kimochi wa ishin-denshin de yoku wakatta.
Dad didn't have to say a word. I knew exactly what he was thinking.

俺とあいつは以心伝心の間柄なんだ。
Ore to aitsu wa ishin-denshin no aidagara nan da.

He and I know each other so well that we can tell what the other's thinking.

☞ *isshin-dōtai* 一心同体

isse-ichidai 一世一代 "one generation, one lifetime"

once in a lifetime

今回の独立開業は、僕にとっては一世一代の大ばくちなんですよ。
Konkai no dokuritsu-kaigyō wa, boku ni totte wa isse-ichidai no ōbakuchi nan desu yo.
I'm taking the chance of my life starting up this new business on my own.

一世一代の決断をして、衆議院選挙に出ることにしました。
Isse-ichidai no ketsudan o shite, shūgi-in senkyo ni deru koto ni shimashita.
Taking what might be the most important decision of my life, I've decided to run as a candidate in the parliamentary elections (for the House of Representatives).

isseki-nichō 一石二鳥 "one stone, two birds"

to kill two birds with one stone

そうしてもらえると、一石二鳥でこちらも助かりますよ。
Sō shite moraeru to, isseki-nichō de kochira mo tasukarimasu yo.
If you would do that, we could kill two birds with one stone, which would be a big help to me.

一石二鳥どころか、一石三鳥をねらった欲張りな案なんです。
Isseki-nichō dokoro ka, isseki-sanchō o neratta yokubari na an nan desu.
Isn't this idea great? We're aiming not to kill two birds with the one stone, but three!

※ A synonymous expression to this is 一挙両得 (*ikkyo-ryōtoku*). Of the two expressions, 一石二鳥 is by far the more commonly used.

↪ *abuhachi torazu* 虻蜂取らず

isshin-dōtai 一心同体 "one heart, the same body"

of one heart and mind, as one mind and body

「夫婦は一心同体」というのは幻想じゃないでしょうか。
"Fūfu wa isshin-dōtai" to iu no wa gensō ja nai deshō ka.
When they say man and wife are of one heart and mind, isn't that just a fantasy (illusion)?

おまえと俺とは一心同体なんだから、何でも打ち明けてくれよ。
Omae to ore to wa isshin-dōtai nan da kara, nan de mo uchiakete kure yo.
We're one and the same, you and me. You can tell me anything.

↪ *ishin-denshin* 以心伝心

isshin-ittai 一進一退 "one forward, one back"

ebb and flow, back and forth, dingdong, seesaw; two steps forward, two steps back

父の病状は一進一退で、楽観は出来ないそうだ。
Chichi no byōjō wa isshin-ittai de, rakkan wa dekinai sō da.
Some days Dad's condition gets better, some days worse. There isn't a lot of room for optimism, I'm told.

政府間交渉は一進一退を繰り返している。
Seifu-kan kōshō wa isshin-ittai o kurikaeshite iru.

The governments' negotiations are an endless repetition of two steps forward, two steps back.

isshō-kenmei 一生懸命 "one lifetime laying down one's life"

with all one's might, (try) as hard as one can, with all one's heart and soul, putting all one's energy into

もっと一生懸命やりなさい。
Motto isshō-kenmei yarinasai.
Come on! You can do better than that!

どんなに一生懸命に勉強しても、おれはどうせ頭が悪いんだからだめなんだよ。
Donna ni isshō-kenmei ni benkyō shite mo, ore wa dōse atama ga warui n' da kara dame nan da yo.
No matter how hard I study, I'm never going to make it 'cause I just don't have the brains.

❦ Originally written 一所懸命 with the character for "place." This dates from the time in feudal Japan when a samurai would lay down his life to defend his territory.

☞ *muga-muchū* 無我夢中

isshoku-sokuhatsu 一触即発 "one touch, immediate explosion"

a touch-and-go situation, a potentially explosive situation, a volatile situation, sitting on a powder keg

政府軍とゲリラの間の緊張が高まり、一触即発の状態にある。

Seifu-gun to gerira no aida no kinchō ga takamari, isshoku-sokuhatsu no jōtai ni aru.

The tension between the government troops and the guerilla forces has reached such a pitch that the situation could blow up at any moment.

隣のご夫婦は普段から喧嘩が絶えず、一触即発の関係だ。
Tonari no gofūfu wa fudan kara kenka ga taezu, isshoku-sokuhatsu no kankei da.

The couple next door do nothing but quarrel, the least thing setting them off.

大物政治家の突然の逮捕で、永田町は一触即発の緊張感に包まれた。
Ōmono seiji-ka no totsuzen no taiho de, Nagatachō wa isshoku-sokuhatsu no kinchō-kan ni tsutsumareta.

With the sudden arrest of a high-ranking politician, the whole government was thrown into an volatile state of high tension.

※ 永田町 (Nagatachō) is the area in central Tokyo where the Diet and the Prime Minister's residence are located. Just as in England we often say Whitehall when we mean the British government (likewise Americans often say Capitol Hill), in Japan they often use Nagatachō to refer to the Diet and/or the government.

itachi いたち (鼬) weasel

Not exactly man's best friend in Japan, the weasel comes off little better in Japanese than in English. Like the fox, it is believed to be the harbinger of bad luck when encountered and was formerly thought to breathe fire. As can be inferred from the examples below, it is believed to be mischievous and cunning. Weasels are counted *ippiki* 一匹.

Itachi-gokko **いたちごっこ** "play weasel"
the cat and mouse game; (go) round and round

東京の路上駐車の問題は、警察とドライバーのいたちごっこに
終わっている。
*Tōkyō no rojō-chūsha no mondai wa, keisatsu to doraibā no itachi-gokko
ni owatte iru.*
There's no end in sight to the endless game of cat and mouse played out
on the streets of Tokyo between police and drivers who park illegally.

ハッカーとの長年のいたちごっこを終結に向かわせる研究にメ
ーカーは注目している。
*Hakkā to no naganen no itachi-gokko o shūketsu ni mukawaseru kenkyū
ni mēkā wa chūmoku shite iru.*
Manufacturers are pinning their hopes on research that promises to bring
an end to years of going round and round with hackers.

🥀 Derived from a very primitive form of one-upsmanship, idiomatic usage
of *itachi-gokko* has its origins in a game by the same name played by children in the late Edo period (1600–1868) in which two children face each other
and repeat the phrase *itachi-gokko, nezumi-gokko* (play weasel, play rat)
while pinching the back of the other's extended hands and placing their own
on top to have it pinched in return until the stack rises out of reach, or until
they lose interest or can no longer bear the pain (which usually comes first).
The game possibly developed from the observation of the struggle for survival
between the weasel and its prey the rat. The term *-gokko* is a suffix meaning play or game, as in *oisha-san-gokko* お医者さんごっこ, or play doctor.

Itachi no saigoppe いたちの最後っぺ "a weasel's last fart"
a parting shot, a last gasp retort; a last ditch effort

いたちの最後っぺよろしく、彼は会社の秘密を暴露して、辞め
て行った。
*Itachi no saigoppe yoroshiku, kare wa kaisha no himitsu o bakuro shite,
yamete itta.*
His parting shot upon quitting was to expose corporate secrets.

泥棒は、いたちの最後っぺよろしく、盗んだ金の一部をバラま

いて捜査員の追尾を振り切ろうとした。
Dorobō wa, itachi no saigoppe yoroshiku, nusunda kane no ichibu o baramaite sōsa-in no tsuibi o furikirō to shita.
The thief scattered some of the money he had stolen in a last ditch effort to throw the police off his trail.

※ From the weasel's documented ability to emit a foul odor from its anal glands when all other means of escape have failed. The expression is frequently used with *yoroshiku,* which means "just like."

☞ *makeinu no tōboe* 負け犬の遠吠え

itchō-isseki 一朝一夕 "one morning, one evening"

in a day, overnight, in a short time, in the twinkling of an eye

人は一朝一夕に変わるものじゃないから、長い目で見てやろう。
Hito wa itchō-isseki ni kawaru mono ja nai kara, nagai me de mite yarō.
People don't change overnight. We've gotta be patient on this one.

そういう問題は、一朝一夕には解決しないよ。
Sō iu mondai wa, itchō-isseki ni wa kaiketsu shinai yo.
This isn't the sort of problem that can be solved overnight, you know.

※ This expression is always followed by a negative clause. Thus you cannot say 一朝一夕に〜する. The correct usage is 一朝一夕には〜しない／出来ない.

itchō-ittan 一長一短 "one long, one short"

having both merits and demerits, both good points and bad points, both pros and cons

応募者は結構集まったが、どの人も一長一短だね。

Ōbo-sha wa kekkō atsumatta ga, dono hito mo itchō-ittan da ne.
We've had quite a lot of applicants, but they are all much of a muchness.

どちらの案にも一長一短があって、決めかねているんだよ。
Dochira no an ni mo itchō-ittan ga atte, kimekanete iru n' da yo.
Both proposals have their good and bad points, which makes choosing between them difficult (so I can't make up my mind).

※ This expression is used when comparing two or more items, all of which have their good points and their bad points. You cannot use it when simply talking about one thing. Thus you can't say あの人には一長一短がある to mean "He has good points and bad points." However, it's okay to say あの人を採用した場合には一長一短がある, because in this situation you are comparing two alternatives—whether to hire him or not—and talking about the pros and cons of each.

ittō-ryōdan 一刀両断 "cut in half (in two) with one sword"

〜する to take a drastic step or measure, to solve a problem once and for all, to cut the Gordian knot, to deal with a matter decisively, to strike at the heart of the matter

「責任は相手にある」と一刀両断のもとに言い放った。
"Sekinin wa aite ni aru" to ittō-ryōdan no moto ni iihanatta.
He took the situation by the scruff of its neck and laid the blame clearly at the other guy's feet.

我々の販売促進策は、まだ生温いと社長に一刀両断された。
Wareware no hanbai-sokushin-saku wa, mada namanurui to shachō ni ittō-ryōdan sareta.
The boss really laid it on the line (put the knife in) when he told us our ideas for increasing sales were half-baked.

iwashi いわし（鰯） sardine

Appreciation for this lowly regarded but always numerous plebe of the oceans is growing as other more highly prized delectables vanish from the plundered seas. Sardines, fresh or preserved in salt, have been eaten as common fare by Japanese for centuries and figure in several idioms expressive of numerousness or the color gray. A dull sword was known as an *iwashi*, perhaps because of its namesake's slender, silvery body (which isn't much good for cutting anything), and a rusted sword was called an *akaiwashi*, from the red hue the salted sardine takes on. The fact that *iwashi* expire almost immediately after being removed from water is part of their image in the Japanese mind (note that the right side of the character for *iwashi* means "weak").

Iwashigumo いわし雲 "sardine cloud"
a small, white, fleecy cloud; a cirrocumulus; a mackerel cloud; (of a sky in which such clouds appear) a mackerel sky

今日はいわし雲が出ていた。
Kyō wa iwashigumo ga dete ita.
There was a mackerel sky today.

真冬にいわし雲とは珍しいな。
Mafuyu ni iwashigumo to wa mezurashii na.
It's unusual for there to be these small, fleecy clouds in wintertime.

⚜ Colloquial word for such clouds. Closely tied to autumn, their mention brings to mind that season. There are apparently two theories of the word's origin, one based on the notion that such cloud formations resemble schooling sardines, the other that ancient fishermen believed that the appearance of such clouds signaled a large catch of sardines. The formations were also thought to portend heavy rain and winds, a meteorologically sound observation since these clouds, which form high in the troposphere, are often the high-level blowoff of deeper precipitating clouds farther upwind. They are, according to meteorologist R. A. Rangno, "the smoke from the fire."

☞ *hitsujigumo* 羊雲

iyake ga sasu 嫌気が差す " disagreeable *ki* gets in"

be disgusted with, be up to here with; have had enough of

堂々めぐりで結論が出ない会議には嫌気が差すもんね。
Dōdō-meguri de ketsuron ga denai kaigi ni wa iyake ga sasu mon ne.
Don't you get fed up with meetings where endless talk never leads to any conclusions?

❀ *dōdō-meguri*: literally, to go repeatedly around a Buddhist temple as a ritual; to repeat something *ad nauseam*.

安月給に嫌気が差して、会社をやめた。
Yasu-gekkyū ni iyake ga sashite, kaisha o yameta.
I got sick and tired of being paid next to nothing, so I quit my job.

☞ *ki ni iru* 気に入る

jakuniku-kyōshoku 弱肉強食 "The weak (are) meat (for) the strong (to) eat."

the law of the jungle, the survival of the fittest, only the strong survive, it's a dog-eat-dog world

野生動物は、弱肉強食の自然界で生きている。
Yasei-dōbutsu wa, jakuniku-kyōshoku no shizen-kai de ikite iru.

Wild animals inhabit a world where the only law is eat or be eaten. (Animals in the wild live according to the law of the jungle.)

きれいごとを言ったって、所詮世の中は弱肉強食なんだよ。
Kireigoto o itta tte, shosen yo no naka wa jakuniku-kyōshoku nan da yo.
For all your fine words, it is still a dog-eat-dog world.

৺ In Japanese schools, students are often tested on their knowledge of four-letter compounds. They are sometimes presented with compounds with two of their component characters missing, and have to fill in the blanks correctly. In the case of 弱肉強食 the first and third characters are usually left blank (i.e., □肉□食). In one apocryphal case a hungry fifteen-year-old was said to have written 焼肉定食 (*yakiniku-teishoku*, a popular and inexpensive lunch of Korean-style beef served with rice and miso soup). Obviously his concerns in life were more culinary than classical.

jibara o kiru 自腹を切る "cut one's own stomach"

foot the bill, pay for something when one doesn't really have to

得意先の接待に、彼は自腹を切った。
Tokuisaki no settai ni, kare wa jibara o kitta.
He dug deep to entertain some of his best clients.

そんな高いパソコンに自腹を切るとは、すごいね。
Sonna takai pasokon ni jibara o kiru to wa, sugoi ne.
So you paid for an expensive computer like that out of your own pocket. That's really something.

jibō-jiki 自暴自棄 "self-abuse, self-abandonment"

desperation, despair; 〜になる to abandon oneself to despair, to be in total despair

あいつ彼女にふられて以来、自暴自棄になってるみたいだぜ。
Aitsu kanojo ni furarete irai, jibō-jiki ni natte 'ru mitai da ze.
It seems he's been in total despair ever since he was given the elbow by his girlfriend.

その程度のことで、そんなに自暴自棄になる必要はないのに……。
Sono teido no koto de, sonna ni jibō-jiki ni naru hitsuyō wa nai no ni . . .
I don't know why you have to get all bent out of shape over some little thing like that.

🦊 The last two characters of this compound (自棄) can also be pronounced *yake* when written as a two-character compound (though nowadays most people write this simply as やけ, using hiragana). The meaning is the same as above, and it is commonly used in the expressions やけになる (*yake ni naru*, to feel desperate and lose control of oneself) and やけ酒を飲む (*yakezake o nomu*, to drown one's sorrows in drink or take to drink out of desperation).

jiga-jisan 自画自賛 "(one's) own drawing, (one's) own praise"

〜する to blow one's own trumpet, to sing one's own praises; to pat oneself on the back

この人の回想録は自画自賛の話ばかりで、おもしろくも何ともない。
Kono hito no kaisō-roku wa jiga-jisan no hanashi bakari de, omoshiroku mo nan to mo nai.
His memoirs are as dull as ditch water; all he does is paint a pretty picture of himself.

おばあちゃんは近ごろ俳句に凝っていて、一句出来る度に自画自賛してるよ。
Obāchan wa chikagoro haiku ni kotte ite, ikku dekiru tabi ni jiga-jisan shite 'ru yo.
Granny's become really keen on haiku recently. It's funny—every time she writes a new one, she pats herself on the back.

🐌 This expression derives from the practice of one's teacher writing a few words of praise in the corner of one's painting, and then adding his seal (of approval) to authenticate the comments as his own. Without this favorable comment from one's *sensei*, a picture has little value. To add the all-important critique oneself is not only highly disreputable but also self-serving and smug.

☞ *gaden-insui* 我田引水, *shiri-shiyoku* 私利私欲

jigō-jitoku 自業自得 "self-deed, self-gain (one's own deeds, one's own rewards)"

you reap what you sow; you made your bed, now you have to lie in it; you've got nobody to blame but yourself; you deserve what you get; it serves you right; you asked for it

こう言っちゃ何だが、あいつが破産したのは自業自得さ。
Kō itcha nan da ga, aitsu ga hasan shita no wa jigō-jitoku sa.
I suppose I shouldn't say this, but if he's gone bankrupt, he's only got himself to blame.

勉強せずにファミコンばかりしてたんだから、試験に落ちても自業自得だよ。
Benkyō sezu ni famikon bakari shite 'ta n' da kara, shiken ni ochite mo jigō-jitoku da yo.
Since you were playing computer games all the time instead of studying, it'll be your own fault if you fail the exams.

jiki-shōsō 時期尚早 "The timing is too early."

the time is not yet ripe for (doing something), to jump the gun, to be premature

今からそんな心配までするのは、時期尚早というものだよ。
Ima kara sonna shinpai made suru no wa, jiki-shōsō to iu mono da yo.
It's much too early to be getting all worried about that now.

時代を先取りした法律だったが、時期尚早だという声が多く、廃案になってしまった。
Jidai o sakidori shita hōritsu datta ga, jiki-shōsō da to iu koe ga ōku, haian ni natte shimatta.
The law was made with an eye to the future, but it was repealed when many voiced the opinion that it was ahead of its time.

jiko-manzoku 自己満足 "self-satisfaction"

complacent satisfaction with oneself or one's accomplishments, self-congratulation, smugness

おだてられて、自己満足してるだけだよ。
Odaterarete, jiko-manzoku shite 'ru dake da yo.
A little flattery, and look how proud he is of himself.

単なる自己満足に終わってしまっては、進歩がないな。
Tannaru jiko-manzoku ni owatte shimatte wa, shinpo ga nai na.
If it ends up as an exercise in self-satisfaction, nothing will be achieved at all.

jiko-tōsui 自己陶酔 "self-intoxication"

self-conceit, self-admiration, to think yourself the center of the universe, to be in love with yourself, to be narcissistic

自己陶酔してるんじゃないの。馬鹿みたい。
Jiko-tōsui shite 'ru n' ja nai no. Baka mitai.
I'd stop thinking I was God Almighty if I were you. Grow up!

あの時代は甘っちょろい自己陶酔にひたっている暇はなかった。
Ano jidai wa amatchoroi jiko-tōsui ni hitatte iru hima wa nakatta.
In that day and age there just wasn't time for us to get carried away with our own brilliance (with an inflated sense of our own worth).

jikyū-jisoku 自給自足 "self-providing, self-satisfying"

self-sufficiency, self-supporting, self-reliant; 〜する to be self-sufficient

自給自足の生活って、実際にはそりゃ大変らしいよ。
Jikyū-jisoku no seikatsu tte, jissai ni wa sorya taihen rashii yo.
Seems trying to live a life of self-sufficiency is really tough.

この国の農業は、まだ自給自足の段階に達していない。
Kono kuni no nōgyō wa, mada jikyū-jisoku no dankai ni tasshite inai.
This country's nowhere near being agriculturally self-sufficient.

いざという時に、自給自足でやっていける国がいくつあるだろうか。
Iza to iu toki ni, jikyū-jisoku de yatte ikeru kuni ga ikutsu aru darō ka.
If push came to shove, I wonder how many countries could really get by without outside help.

友だちに、会社を辞めて田舎に古い家買って、自給自足してる奴がいるよ。
Tomodachi ni, kaisha o yamete inaka ni furui ie katte, jikyū-jisoku shite 'ru yatsu ga iru yo.
I've got this friend who quit his job, bought an old house out in the country, and is now living off the land.

食料の自給自足体制が整っていないわが国では、食料安保が大きな問題だ。
Shokuryō no jikyū-jisoku taisei ga totonotte inai wagakuni de wa, shokuryō-anpo ga ōkina mondai da.
Since the country has no system of self-sufficiency to fall back on, we have to consider the need for a treaty guaranteeing sufficient food supplies.

✤ Agricultural self-sufficiency is a Japanese worry that Westerners often find difficult to understand. Many Japanese (especially those who lived through the Second World War when food was in short supply) still feel it is essential that Japan be able to produce enough food (in particular, rice) to feed itself, without relying upon imports. This perhaps accounts in part for the fact that they are prepared to buy home-grown rice rather than imported rice, even though it is more than twice the price.

jimon-jitō 自問自答 "ask oneself, answer oneself"

a soliloquy, a monologue, thinking aloud; 〜する to think aloud, to wonder to oneself, to ask oneself

どこで間違ったのかと自問自答してみたが、答えは出なかった。
Doko de machigatta no ka to jimon-jitō shite mita ga, kotae wa denakatta.
I wondered to myself where I might have gone wrong, but I just couldn't think of an answer.

これからどうしたらいいかと、彼は長い間自問自答して、結局は田舎に帰ることにした。
Kore kara dō shitara ii ka to, kare wa nagai aida jimon-jitō shite, kekkyoku wa inaka ni kaeru koto ni shita.
After long deliberation as to what he should do from now on, he finally decided to go back to his hometown.

jinkai-senjutsu 人海戦術 "a human-sea strategy"

adopt human wave tactics, send in a sea of bodies (to deal with a problem or a situation)

もう時間がない！原始的だが全員集めて人海戦術で行こう。
Mō jikan ga nai! Genshi-teki da ga zen'in atsumete jinkai-senjutsu de ikō.
We're running out of time. It's primitive, I know, but let's get everybody together and throw them into the fray.

この国は、人海戦術を駆使して、短期間のうちに経済発展を遂げた。
Kono kuni wa, jinkai-senjutsu o kushi shite, tan-jikan no uchi ni keizai-hatten o togeta.
This country mobilized its people and through sheer weight of numbers made incredible economic progress in a very short time.

jishin-manman 自信満々 "full of confidence"

brimming with confidence, supremely confident

試験の前は自信満々だったが、手も足も出なくて惨めだった。
Shiken no mae wa jishin-manman datta ga, te mo ashi mo denakute mijime datta.
Before the exam I was brimming with confidence, but I just wasn't up to it and failed miserably.

彼女、スタイルには自信満々で、いつも体にぴったりの服着てる。
Kanojo, sutairu ni wa jishin-manman de, itsumo karada ni pittari no fuku kite 'ru.
She's supremely confident of her good figure and always wears tight-fitting clothes.

jitchū-hakku 十中八九 "eight or nine out of ten"

ten to one; in nine cases out of ten; in all probability

十中八九間違いないと思いますが、もう一度確認の電話を入れてみます。
Jitchū-hakku machigai nai to omoimasu ga, mō ichido kakunin no denwa o irete mimasu.
There's next to no mistake about it, but I'll call once more just to be sure.

最終面接まで行ったんだったら、もう十中八九内定だよ。
Saishū-mensetsu made itta n' dattara, mō jitchū-hakku naitei da yo.
If they asked you to come in for the final interview, you've almost got the job sewn up, I'm sure.

🌱 The expression 九分九厘 (*kubu-kurin*) is virtually synonymous. Its degree of certainty is a bit higher (at 99 percent) than 十中八九 (80–90 percent), but in general the two expressions are used interchangeably, both meaning "almost definitely."

jiyū-jizai 自由自在 "free and at will"

freely, to one's heart's desire, with wonderful dexterity, fluency in (languages etc.), unrestricted, unrestrained

この報道カメラマンは、世界中を自由自在に飛び回って活躍している。
Kono hōdō-kameraman wa, sekai-jū o jiyū-jizai ni tobimawatte katsuyaku shite iru.
This photojournalist flies round the world wherever he pleases, shooting assignments.

子供たちは自由自在に壁を塗り始めた。
Kodomo-tachi wa jiyū-jizai ni kabe o nurihajimeta.

The children began painting the wall in any way that struck their fancy.

首謀者は、手下を自由自在に操って、次々と犯罪を犯していった。
Shubō-sha wa, teshita o jiyū-jizai ni ayatsutte, tsugitsugi to hanzai o okashite itta.
Manipulating his henchmen as freely as puppets on a string, the ringleader went on to commit one crime after another.

彼は自由自在にはさみを使って、あっと言う間に複雑な切り絵を完成させた。
Kare wa jiyū-jizai ni hasami o tsukatte, atto iu ma ni fukuzatsu na kirie o kansei saseta.
Using the scissors as if they were a part of his own hand, he completed a complex cutout in no time at all.

jōjō-shakuryō 情状酌量 "circumstances (taken into) consideration"

taking mitigating circumstances into consideration when dealing with an offender; clemency, leniency

これだけの事件を起こしたんだ。情状酌量の余地はないよ。
Kore dake no jiken o okoshita n' da. Jōjō-shakuryō no yochi wa nai yo.
There can be no room for clemency in a case such as this (as big as this).

弁護士は被告人の不幸な生い立ちを述べて、情状酌量を訴えた。
Bengo-shi wa hikoku-nin no fukō na oitachi o nobete, jōjō-shakuryō o uttaeta.
The lawyer spoke of the defendant's unhappy childhood, and pleaded for clemency.

今日で今週3回目の遅刻だぞ！　もう情状酌量の余地はないな。
Kyō de konshū sankai-me no chikoku da zo! Mō jōjō-shakuryō no yochi wa nai na.
Today is the third time you've been late this week! Don't expect to be let off lightly.

juken-jigoku 受験地獄 "examination hell"

the intense competition among Japanese students for acceptance at junior high schools, high schools, and universities

女房は、子供に受験地獄を経験させたくないからって、エスカレーター式の有名幼稚園に入れようとしてるんだ。
Nyōbō wa, kodomo ni juken-jigoku o keiken sasetaku nai kara tte, esukarētā-shiki no yūmei-yōchien ni ireyō to shite 'ru n' da.
My wife says she doesn't want to put our kids through the gruelling experience of preparing for secondary school and college exams, so she's trying to get them into a famous kindergarten where they can get a free pass into its affiliated schools.

大学受験が、受験地獄とか受験戦争とか呼ばれるようになったのは、いつごろからだろうか。
Daigaku-juken ga, juken-jigoku to ka juken-sensō to ka yobareru yō ni natta no wa, itsugoro kara darō ka.
I wonder when studying for university entrance exams came to be known as "exam hell" and "exam war."

jūnin-toiro 十人十色 "ten people, ten colors"

so many men, so many minds; one man's meat is another man's poison; it takes all kinds (to make a world)

みんなの意見は十人十色で、とてもまとまりそうにないよ。
Minna no iken wa jūnin-toiro de, totemo matomarisō ni nai yo.
With everyone being of a different mind, it's unlikely we'll be able to wrap this one up smoothly.

異性の好みは十人十色で、だから世の中うまくいくのかな。
Isei no konomi wa jūnin-toiro de, dakara yo no naka umaku iku no ka na.
About the opposite sex, there are as many different tastes as there are people; maybe that's what makes the world go round.

🐾 三人三様 (*sannin-san'yō*) or 三者三様 (*sansha-san'yō*)—literally, three people, three ways—are synonymous expressions, though the numbers involved are different.

junpū-manpan 順風満帆 "sails full of a favorable wind"

with the wind in one's sails, swimmingly, full steam ahead, (smooth sailing) with the wind at one's back

子役として人気が出て以来、順風満帆の女優人生を歩んできた。
Koyaku toshite ninki ga dete irai, junpū-manpan no joyū-jinsei o ayunde kita.
Since coming to popularity while still a child, she has sailed through life as a successful actress.

これまでは必ずしも順風満帆じゃなかったけど、やっと俺にも運が向いてきたらしい。
Kore made wa kanarazushimo junpū-manpan ja nakatta kedo, yatto ore ni mo un ga muite kita rashii.
Things haven't always gone smoothly up until now, but at last my luck seems to have taken a turn for the better.

junshin-muku 純真無垢 "pure and clean"

innocent, as pure as the driven snow

彼女の純真無垢な心に触れて、私のすさんでいた心も洗われたような気がする。
Kanojo no junshin-muku na kokoro ni furete, watashi no susande ita kokoro mo arawareta yō na ki ga suru.
Meeting somebody as pure and innocent as her makes me feel as though I've been made whole again.

彼は純真無垢で、思ったことを素直に言ってるだけなんだが、生意気だと誤解されていじめられているみたいだ。
Kare wa junshin-muku de, omotta koto o sunao ni itte 'ru dake nan da ga, namaiki da to gokai sarete ijimerarete iru mitai da.
He simply says what he thinks in all innocence, but they take it as impertinence and pick on him.

☞ *hara ga kuroi / haraguroi* 腹が黒い／腹黒い

jūō-mujin 縦横無尽 "the length and breadth, inexhaustible"

freely, in all directions, vigorously, tirelessly

ひび割れが、壁中に縦横無尽に走っている。
Hibiware ga, kabejū ni jūō-mujin ni hashitte iru.
The wall is just a maze of cracks from top to bottom.

この本の中で、著者はわが国の土地政策について縦横無尽に語っている。
Kono hon no naka de, chosha wa wagakuni no tochi-seisaku ni tsuite jūō-mujin ni katatte iru.
In this book the author expresses his far-reaching opinions about our national land policy.

今回のイベントでは、彼の縦横無尽な活躍ぶりが目立った。
Konkai no ibento de wa, kare no jūō-mujin na katsuyaku-buri ga medatta.
His tireless efforts on behalf of the event this time were quite remarkable.

ka 蚊 mosquito

With around a hundred species of this diminutive pest indigenous to Japan, it is not surprising to discover that it figures in a number of common idioms, none of which are particularly flattering. The mosquito is said to have metamorphosed from the dead body of an ogre, whose curse upon humanity the female of the family, with its elongated proboscis, is banefully adapted to carry out. It wasn't too long ago that Japanese spread their futons out under mosquito nets during the summer for protection from the pesky bloodsuckers. Idioms that incorporate the insect are generally of delicate or otherwise insubstantial things. The sound associated with the mosquito is *būn* ブーン. It is counted *ippiki* 一匹.

Ka ni sasareta hodo ni mo omowanu 蚊に刺されたほどにも思わぬ "consider something to be less than a mosquito bite"
(of a person) don't care a bit, could(n't) care less; (of an inconvenience) a fleabite

---

あいつ先生に怒られても、蚊に刺されたほどにも思ってないよ。
Aitsu sensei ni okorarete mo, ka ni sasareta hodo ni mo omotte 'nai yo.
He doesn't give a shit if the teacher gets mad at him. / It doesn't mean diddly squat to him if the teacher goes ballistic.

あの人は相当な資産家だから、今回の株下落も蚊に刺されたほどに思っていない様子だったよ。
Ano hito wa sōtō na shisan-ka da kara, konkai no kabu-geraku mo ka ni sasareta hodo ni omotte inai yōsu datta yo.
He's pretty well off so it doesn't look like the recent decline in the stock market is any big deal to him.

たいていの大企業にとって住民からの訴訟は蚊に刺されたほどに思わぬものだ。
Taitei no dai-kigyō ni totte jūmin kara no soshō wa ka ni sasareta hodo ni omowanu mono da.
A law suit by some citizen is about as troublesome to most big businesses as a fleabite.

🦋 The idiom is always negative, reflecting the view that there is no influence or change as a result of the action to which it refers.

↪ *kaeru no tsura ni shonben (shōben)* 蛙の面に小便

Ka no naku yō na koe　**蚊の鳴くような声**　"a cry like a mosquito's"
a faint (barely audible, thin) voice, a whisper

そんな蚊の鳴くような声では面接に落ちてしまうよ。
Sonna ka no naku yō na koe de wa mensetsu ni ochite shimau yo.
You'll never make it beyond the interview if you mumble like that.

彼は蚊の鳴くような声で先生の質問に答えた。
Kare wa ka no naku yō na koe de sensei no shitsumon ni kotaeta.
He answered the teacher's question in a barely audible voice.

🦋 From the all but inaudible sound made by the wings of the dipterous pest. Often used of a timid person or one who lacks self-confidence.

Ka no namida　蚊の涙　"a mosquito's tear"
(of an amount of money) very little, next to nothing

今年の昇給は蚊の涙だ。
Kotoshi no shōkyū wa ka no namida da.
The raise I got this year didn't amount to much. / I didn't get shit for a raise this year.

そんな蚊の涙ほどの報酬では、人は集まらない。
Sonna ka no namida hodo no hōshū de wa, hito wa atsumaranai.
You're not going to get many job applicants by offering a pittance like that.

↪ *suzume no namida* 雀の涙

Ka-tonbo　蚊トンボ　"a mosquito dragonfly"

a crane fly; a skinny person; a rail, a rattlebones, skinnybones; (of a tall person) a beanstalk, bean pole

鈴木さんは蚊トンボのような人。
Suzuki-san wa ka-tonbo no yō na hito.
Suzuki's a regular bean pole.

「どんなのがタイプ？」
"Donna no ga taipu?"
"What kinda guys do you like?"

「蚊トンボは嫌ね。」
"Ka-tonbo wa iya ne."
"No skinnybones for me."

❦ Of a tall, thin person, often used jocularly. While the long-legged crane fly resembles a large mosquito, it is not one. Nor does it bite. This idiom is included here for convenience only.

kachiki (na)　勝ち気（な）　"victorious *ki*"

feisty, competitive, hates to lose, strong-minded, strong-willed, tough

勝ち気な性分で、いつもトップを走っていないと気が済まない。
Kachiki na shōbun de, itsumo toppu o hashitte inai to ki ga sumanai.
She's so competitive that she's got to be right up there at the top or she's not satisfied.

子供の時から勝ち気で負けず嫌いだったしさ。
Kodomo no toki kara kachiki de makezu-girai datta shi sa.
She's been like that since she was a kid, just hated to lose.

❦ Of a person, usually a woman or child, who will do just about anything not to end up on the losing side in an argument. Regularly used disparagingly or with minimal, grudging approval of a woman who refuses to knuckle under to a man.

☞ *ki ga tsuyoi* 気が強い

kaeru or *kawazu* 蛙 frog

If you're French you can relax; no Japanese is going to call you a *kaeru* because of your nation's nuclear policies. They might call you something else, but at least it won't be "Frog." These most common of amphibians have yet to be driven into extinction in Japan, less, no doubt, because of environmental concern than long-standing governmental protection of rice farmers, rice paddies, and hence our vocal green buddies, who enjoy a worldwide reputation for forewarning of rain by croaking. It is from their croaking, which, by the onomatopoeic way, is *kerokero* ケロケロ or *kuwa'-kuwa'* クワックワッ, that Japanese children, especially those brought up in the country hearing the soothing evening serenade, often head for home on a warm summer evening after a day of play intoning their own homophonic play on words, *Kaeru ga naku kara kaero* 蛙がなくから帰ろ, literally, "The frogs are croaking so let's go home."

The *kerokero* voice of a frog is said to resemble the Japanese phrase *kaerō*, or "Let's go home." The infinitive of the verb "to return" or "to go home" *kaeru* is also a homophone for the word for frog. Some simple words and phrases of interest include *kaeruashi* 蛙足, literally "frogleg," and meaning the frog kick as employed in the breast stroke, which in turn, and perhaps not coincidentally, is called *kaeru-oyogi* 蛙足泳ぎ, or "frog swim." There is also *kaerutobi* 蛙跳び, or "leapfrog," though only in the sense of a game children play; and *kaeru-nyōbō* 蛙女房, a complicated play on words that originates from the fact that a frog's eyes are on the top of its head (目が上にある, *me ga ue ni aru*) and that a common word for wife in Japanese, *tsuma*

妻, can also be pronounced *me,* and if she is older, she is above, or *ue,* her husband; hence a *kaeru-nyōbō* is a woman who is older than her husband.

Frogs are counted *ippiki* 一匹.

☞ *gamaguchi* がま口, *i no naka no kawazu* 井の中の蛙, *otamajakushi* おたまじゃくし

Kaeru no ko wa kaeru 蛙の子は蛙 "The child of a frog is a frog."
---

1. like father, like son; like mother, like daughter; what is born of a cat will catch mice

> 蛙の子は蛙、手先が器用なのは親譲りだ。
> *Kaeru no ko wa kaeru, tesaki ga kiyō na no wa oyayuzuri da.*
> I get my manual dexterity from my parents. It's in the blood.

> やっぱり蛙の子は蛙だね、彼の息子も結局会社を辞めて家業を継いだよ。
> *Yappari kaeru no ko wa kaeru da ne, kare no musuko mo kekkyoku kaisha o yamete kagyō o tsuida yo.*
> His son's a chip off the old block, all right. In the end, he quit his job and followed in his father's footsteps, taking over the family business.

2. ordinary parents have ordinary children

> 俺の子供が東大なんて入れるものじゃないよ、蛙の子は蛙、変な夢を見たと思って諦めよう。
> *Ore no kodomo ga Tōdai nante haireru mono ja nai yo. Kaeru no ko wa kaeru, hen na yume o mita to omotte akirameyō.*
> I guess it was too much to expect that one of my kids could get into the University of Tokyo. Better just chalk it up to experience, I guess.

☞ *tobi ga taka o umu* 鳶が鷹を生む

Kaeru no tsura ni shonben (shōben) 蛙の面に小便 "piss on a frog's face"
(like) water off a duck's back, not faze someone

先生がもう卒業出来ないって言っても、あいつには蛙の面に小便だよ。
Sensei ga mō sotsugyō dekinai tte itte mo, aitsu ni wa kaeru no tsura ni shonben da yo.
It doesn't faze him if teachers tell him that he's not going to graduate; he could care less.

皆がいくらいじめてもまるで蛙の面に小便、あいつは鈍いのか強いのかわかんないね。
Mina ga ikura ijimete mo maru de kaeru no tsura ni shonben, aitsu wa nibui no ka tsuyoi no ka wakannai ne.
No matter how bad a time everybody gives him, it's like water off a duck's back. It's hard to tell if he's really tough or just a bit dim.

🕊 A graphic if disgusting idiom illustrating the futility of talking to a person who is either too brazen, dull-witted, or insensitive to listen. Less common is *kaeru no tsura ni mizu,* or "water on a frog's face."

↪ *ka ni sasareta hodo ni mo omowanu* 蚊に刺された程にも思わぬ, *nakitsura ni hachi* 泣き面に蜂

kai かい（貝） shellfish

Kai is the generic term for shellfish of all kinds, univalves and bivalves included. These aquatic animals have been part of the Japanese diet since the earliest times, with kitchen middens containing pottery shards and shell refuse from the Jomon period and beyond, providing researchers with a significant source of information about the lifestyles and diets of early inhabitants of the archipelago.

Kai no yō ni (kuchi o tsugumu) 貝のように（口をつぐむ）
"(close *one's* mouth) like a clam"

keep one's mouth shut, clam up, close up like a clam, button one's lip

彼は貝のようにその件については口をつぐむばかりだ。
Kare wa kai no yō ni sono ken ni tsuite wa kuchi o tsugumu bakari da.
He clammed up (was closemouthed) about the incident.

貝のように口を閉ざした男は、その罪を一身に背負って死んでいった。
Kai no yō ni kuchi o tozashita otoko wa, sono tsumi o isshin ni shotte shinde itta.
The man took full responsibility for the crime upon himself and went to the grave without ever breaking his silence.

※ From the bivalve's ability to shut down completely, and the difficulty one has in attempting to pry it open once it has closed.

kaiinu ni te o kamareru 飼い犬に手を噛まれる
"be bitten by one's pet dog"

be double-crossed (stabbed in the back) by someone trusted; warm a snake in one's bosom

山川の独立は社長にとってまさに飼い犬に手を噛まれた出来事だった。
Yamakawa no dokuritsu wa shachō ni totte masa ni kaiinu ni te o kamareta dekigoto datta.
Yamakawa going independent was seen as an act of betrayal by the boss.

マネージャーに金を横領されたタレントは飼い犬に手を噛まれたと有名になった。
Manējā ni kane o ōryō sareta tarento wa kaiinu ni te o kamareta to yūmei ni natta.

Some celebrity got a lot of press for being double-crossed by her manager, who was embezzling money from her.

🐝 Used when the one doing the betraying is a trusted subordinate or someone otherwise indebted to the person betrayed. Similar to the English expression "bite the hand that feeds one," but the Japanese version is always used from the point of view of the person having his or her hand bitten.

kami 髪 hair   *ke* 毛 hair

Both *kami* and *ke* mean hair, but it's usually the former you'll use when referring to human hair. *Ke* alone, although it does mean human hair, is most often used for fur. Sometimes they're even used together, as in *Kami no ke ga mijikai,* or "He has short hair."

There aren't many idioms with either *kami* or *ke.* Those included, however, are graphic, the first one depicting what in English would be a matter of the heart.

Ke no haeta yō na 毛の生えたような "like something with hair on it"
not much more than, little more than

マンションといってもアパートに毛の生えたようなものさ。
Manshon to itte mo apāto ni ke no haeta yō na mono sa.
They call it a condo, but it's really just a glorified apartment.

あの教授は学生に毛の生えた程度の知識しかない。
Ano kyōju wa gakusei ni ke no haeta teido no chishiki shika nai.
That prof doesn't know much more than a student. / That professor is little more than a glorified student.

Ushirogami o hikareru (omoi)　**後ろ髪を引かれる（思い）**　"feel like the hair on the back of one's head is being pulled"
reluctantly, with a heavy heart

彼は後ろ髪を引かれる思いで故郷を後にした。
Kare wa ushirogami o hikareru omoi de kokyō o ato ni shita.
He left his hometown with a heavy heart.

彼女は後ろ髪を引かれる思いで年老いた母のいる家を出た。
Kanojo wa ushirogami o hikareru omoi de toshioita haha no iru ie o deta.
It was hard for her to leave her old mother alone. / She almost couldn't find it in her heart to leave her aged mother alone at home.

kamo　かも（鴨）　wild duck

Of the approximately thirty or so species known to visit Japan, all but a few are migratory. The lucky ones winter in the nation's lakes and rivers before returning north in the spring; the unlucky ones end up in a variety of delectable dishes, including *kamonabe* 鴨鍋, or duck soup.

Ducks are considered to be easy marks in much the same way an English speaker would think of pigeons, presumably because they are good hunting.

Ducks are counted *ichiwa* 一羽.

Kamo (ii kamo)　**鴨（いい鴨）**　"a duck (good duck)"
a pigeon, sucker, dupe, patsy; an easy mark

おい見ろ、鴨が向こうから歩いてきたぞ。
Oi miro, kamo ga mukō kara aruite kita zo.
Check out that pigeon coming this way.

お前は人がいいから、キャッチセールスのたぐいのいい鴨なんだよ。

Omae wa hito ga ii kara, kyatchi-sērusu no tagui no ii kamo nan da yo.

You're too nice for your own good. Somebody like those guys selling stuff on street corners is gonna take you to the cleaners some day.

🖎 From the notion that ducks are slow to get airborn and thus easy marks for hunters.

Kamo ga negi o shotte kuru 鴨が葱を背負ってくる "a duck coming (to dinner) with a load of leeks on its back"

more than one can ask (hope) for, a dream come true; someone just asking for it

---

育児でヘトヘトになっているとき、たまたま親がおむつを持って来たんで、思わず「鴨か葱を背負って来た」と心の中で叫んだね。

Ikuji de hetoheto ni natte iru toki, tamatama oya ga omutsu o motte kita n' de omowazu "Kamo ga negi o shotte kita" to kokoro no naka de sakenda ne.

Just as I was about worn to a frazzle from looking after the baby, Mother came visiting with a bunch of diapers. I could hardly keep from crying out, "What a godsend!"

借金返済に困っているところに弟が宝くじに当たったと駆け込んできたんだから、まさに「鴨葱」だった。

Shakkin-hensai ni komatte iru tokoro ni otōto ga takarakuji ni atatta to kakekonde kita n' da kara, masa ni "kamo-negi" datta.

Just as I was wondering how to pay off this loan, my kid brother came prancing in, saying he won at the lottery. Well, what more could you ask for.

🖎 At the very minimum, two things are necessary to prepare *kamo nabe* 鴨鍋, or duck soup: a duck and some leeks. So it's just too good to be true when a duck comes waddling up with those very same leeks on his back, just when your gastric juices are starting to flow. This phrase is often given in abbreviated form: *kamo-negi*.

Kamo ni suru　鴨にする　"make a duck"
sucker someone, make a patsy out of someone

今度加納を麻雀に誘って鴨にしてやろう。
Kondo Kanō o mājan ni sasotte kamo ni shite yarō.
I'm gonna get Kano to play some mah-jongg with us next time and clean him out.

この前はポーカーでいい鴨にされたよ。
Kono mae wa pōkā de ii kamo ni sareta yo.
They saw me coming the other day when I played poker. / I got suckered (duped) into playing poker the other day.

Kamo no mizukaki　鴨の水掻き　"a duck's paddling"
unappreciated or unnoticed hard work; toil (done) in obscurity

自営業は気楽に見えるかも知れないがその実鴨の水掻きです。
Jieigyō wa kiraku ni mieru kamo shirenai ga sono jitsu kamo no mizukaki desu.
It may look like a carefree way to make a living, but there's a lot of unseen hard work that goes into being in business for yourself.

彼は会社でやり手に見られているが、実際は鴨の水掻きなんじゃないのかなあ。
Kare wa kaisha de yarite ni mirarete iru ga, jissai wa kamo no mizukaki nan ja nai no ka nā.
At the office he's got a reputation for being a fast worker, but I can't help thinking that behind the scenes he's got his nose to the grindstone.

🐾 From the observation that while ducks may look like they are tooling along effortlessly in the water, in fact they are paddling away like mad under the surface.

kan no mushi かんの虫 "the childhood sickness bug"

a source of peevishness

この薬は赤ちゃんのかんの虫によく効きます。
Kono kusuri wa aka-chan no kan no mushi ni yoku kikimasu.
This medicine does wonders for a baby that's always fretting.

この子はよく泣くけど、かんの虫でも悪いのだろうか？
Kono ko wa yoku naku kedo, kan no mushi de mo warui no darō ka?
Little thing's always crying. I wonder if maybe she's not just sensitive?

🐇 Actually a kind of childhood nervous disorder, when all else fails you can blame just about any problem an infant might have which leads to crying on a "bug," supposedly inside its tiny body. Hunger, pain, unpleasantness, unease, and diaper rash, all—well almost all—qualify.

☞ *mushi* 虫

kanjō-inyū 感情移入 "emotion moves in"

empathy

想像力の豊かな人は、感情移入が容易に出来る。
Sōzō-ryoku no yutaka na hito wa, kanjō-inyū ga yōi ni dekiru.
People with vivid imaginations find it easy to empathize with others.

相手に感情移入し過ぎては、冷静な判断ができなくなるよ。
Aite ni kanjō-inyū shisugite wa, reisei na handan ga dekinaku naru yo.
If you sympathize with people too much, you won't be able to make rational decisions.

kankodori 閑古鳥 cuckoo

This is the old word for a cuckoo, which is more commonly known today as a *kakkō* かっこう (郭公). Whatever it's called, and it is called pretty much the same thing worldwide because of its distinctive cry (*kakkōkakkō* カッコウカッコウ), this brazen migratory bird lays its eggs in the nests of other unsuspecting birds and then merrily goes about its business while its young are raised by surrogate—and unsuspecting—parents.

Kankodori ga naku 閑古鳥が鳴く "The cuckoo cries."
business is slow (bad), the place is empty

近ごろこの商店街でも閑古鳥が鳴いている。
Chikagoro kono shōten-gai de mo kankodori ga naite iru.
Even this shopping arcade (mall) has been dead (like a morgue) lately.

今年は冷夏でどこのプールでも閑古鳥が鳴いている。
Kotoshi wa reika de doko no pūru de mo kankodori ga naite iru.
It's been so cold this summer that swimming pools are empty everywhere.

バブル経済も破綻して夜の銀座では閑古鳥が鳴きだした。
Baburu keizai mo hatan shite yoru no Ginza de wa kankodori ga nakidashita.
Now that the economic bubble has burst, the streets of the Ginza are all but deserted at night.

🐦 Perhaps from an association with the lonesome cry of the cuckoo in quiet, remote areas. Referring to a lack of customers, visitors, or spectators, this idiom can be used about shops, bars, museums, even sporting events, practically anywhere money is made by selling services or products to customers.

kanzen-muketsu 完全無欠 "perfect, flawless"

absolute perfection, absolutely perfect, faultless, flawless

お前は完全無欠の女性を求めているから、結婚のチャンスがないんだよ。
Omae wa kanzen-muketsu no josei o motomete iru kara, kekkon no chansu ga nai n' da yo.
You don't have a hope in hell of getting married. You're too busy looking for the perfect woman.

今人気があるのは、昔のような完全無欠のヒーローより、むしろどこか抜けている人間的な人だ。
Ima ninki ga aru no wa, mukashi no yō na kanzen-muketsu no hīrō yori, mushiro doko ka nukete iru ningen-teki na hito da.
These days the big crowd-pullers are the slightly wacky kind of guys who are light-years away from the too-good-to-be-true superheroes of old.

※ You can only use this expression when referring to people. If you want to say a plan is perfect, for example, you have to use a different expression, such as 完璧 (*kanpeki*).

kao 顔 face

Though women still spend a great deal of time making it up, the younger generation of Japanese men also seem more inclined to spend time doing their faces. It hasn't quite reached the point where they go to the men's room after eating to "fix their face" or *kao o naosu,* but times are changing, and sales of men's cosmetics are skyrocketing.

The three basic meanings of *kao,* besides the part of the body to which it refers, are influence, a look or countenance, and the all-important social concept "face."

∽ *ōki na kao o suru* 大きな顔をする, *ukanai kao o suru* 浮かない顔をする

Kao ga hiroi **顔が広い** "one's face is broad"
have a wide circle of acquaintances

遠藤さんはとても顔が広い。
Endō-san wa totemo kao ga hiroi.
Mr. Endo really gets around. / That Endo sure knows a lot of people.

あなたは顔が広いそうですが、誰かよい人を紹介してもらえませんか。
Anata wa kao ga hiroi sō desu ga, dare ka yoi hito o shōkai shite moraemasen ka.
Since you seem to have so many contacts, how about introducing us to someone that you think would be good (for the job)?

🕯 Don't go running off and asking people to "lend you their face" without first making sure that they are either close friends or way, way down the social scale. It's not exactly a polite expression.

Kao ga kiku / kao o kikaseru **顔が利く／顔を利かせる** "one's face works (takes effect)"
have influence, be influential, have contacts

流通関係に顔が利く友人を紹介しましょう。
Ryūtsū-kankei ni kao ga kiku yūjin o shōkai shimashō.
I'll introduce you to a friend of mine who has some pull in distribution circles.

どこも予約でいっぱいだったが、斎藤さんが顔を利かせて新年会の会場をとってくれた。
Doko mo yoyaku de ippai datta ga, Saitō-san ga kao o kikasete shinnen-kai no kaijō o totte kureta.

Everyplace was booked up, but Saitō pulled some strings and found us a place to hold our New Year's party.

Kao ga tsubureru / kao o tsubusu 顔がつぶれる／顔をつぶす
"one's face is crushed"

lose face, have one's good name tarnished, get a black eye

紹介した人が会社で盗みを働き、私の顔はすっかりつぶれてしまった。
Shōkai shita hito ga kaisha de nusumi o hataraki, watashi no kao wa sukkari tsuburete shimatta.
My name was sure mud when they discovered that the guy I had introduced was stealing stuff from the office.

よくも俺の顔をつぶしてくれたな。
Yoku mo ore no kao o tsubushite kureta na.
You've really seen to it that I'll never be able to hold my head up around here again, haven't you. / You really screwed things up for me, didn't you, buddy? / Thanks a lot for the black eye.

Kao o dasu 顔を出す "stick out one's face"

---

(1) show up, go to, attend, put in an appearance (2) visit

(1) 先日、10年ぶりの同窓会に顔を出した。
Senjitsu, jūnen-buri no dōso-kai ni kao o dashita.
I went to my first class reunion in ten years the other day.

彼はパーティーに顔を出してすぐ帰った。
Kare wa pātī ni kao o dashite sugu kaetta.
He put in a brief appearance at the party and then left.

(2) 時々顔を出して下さいね。
Tokidoki kao o dashite kudasai ne.

Don't make yourself scarce. / Don't be a stranger. / Come around and see us once in a while.

Kao o kasu **顔を貸す** "lend one's face"
go (along) with someone at their request; go to someone

そこの喫茶店まで顔を貸してくれ。
Soko no kissaten made kao o kashite kure.
Come along to the coffee shop with me.

おい、ちょっと顔貸しな。
Oi, chotto kao kashi na.
Hey, come here a minute. / Yo, get over here.

Kao o tsunagu **顔をつなぐ** "connect one's face"
cultivate a (business) relationship.

彼らに顔をつないでおけば、後で役に立ちますよ。
Karera ni kao o tsunaide okeba, ato de yaku ni tachimasu yo.
If we keep in touch with them, it will be of some use to us later.

顔をつなぐために、そのパーティーに出席した。
Kao o tsunagu tame ni, sono pātī ni shusseki shita.
I went to the party just to be seen. / I attended the party to maintain some contacts I have.

karada 体 body   *mi* 身 body

Except for a few instances when *mi* appears in a particular idiom, *karada* is the word you want for the physical body. *Karada* may mean either the entire body, as in *Karada ga itai* (My body aches all over), or it can mean just the trunk. *Karada* can also refer to the body as an object of sex, and one such idiom is included below. Finally, *karada* can be used when speaking of one's health, as in *Karada no guai wa ikaga desu ka,* a handy phrase to remember when you want to inquire after the health of someone who has been feeling poorly.

The meanings of *mi* are more numerous than those of *karada*. In addition to the physical body, *mi* can be meat or flesh, whether human, animal, or fish. It can also mean one's person or self, as well as one's social standing or position. Lastly, *mi* is that part of the sword that slides into the scabbard, the blade.

⇨ *mi ni amaru* 身に余る, *mi ni naru* 身に成る, *mi ni oboe ga aru* 身に覚えがある, *mi ni shimiru* 身にしみる, *mi ni tsukeru* 身につける, *mi o hiku* 身を引く, *mi o ireru* 身を入れる, *mi o katameru* 身を固める, *mi o ko ni suru* 身を粉にする, *mi o makaseru* 身を任せる

Karada ga aku　体があく　"one's body opens"
be free.

日曜日なら体があくけれども。
Nichiyōbi nara karada ga aku keredomo.
Sunday would be fine with me. / I'll be free on Sunday.

12月は仕事に追われ、とても体のあく暇がなかった。
Jūni-gatsu wa shigoto ni oware, totemo karada no aku hima ga nakatta.
I was so busy with work in December that I didn't have any time to myself.

Karada o haru　体を張る　"stretch out one's body"
risk one's life, lay (put) one's life on the line, lay one's life down

---

彼らは体を張って伐採に反対した。
Karera wa karada o hatte bassai ni hantai shita.
They laid their lives on the line to stop the logging operation.

体を張ってでも君を守ってみせる。
Karada o hatte de mo kimi o mamotte miseru.
I'd risk my life for you. / I'd lay down my life for you.

Karada o kowasu **体を壊す** "destroy one's body"
become ill, ruin one's health, be down

彼女は体を壊すまで働き続けた。
Kanojo wa karada o kowasu made hatarakitsuzuketa.
She worked herself sick.

去年の夏、体を壊して2ヵ月ほど入院していました。
Kyonen no natsu, karada o kowashite ni-kagetsu hodo nyūin shite imashita.
I got sick and spent two months in the hospital last summer.

⇨ *byōki ni naru* 病気になる

karasu からす（烏） crow

This big, black, boisterous bird is an all too common sight and sound in the cities of Japan, where its cacophonous caw awakens entire neighborhoods, and its strong beak allows it to plunder the thin plastic garbage bags that line the streets every other weekday morning. Such characteristics have led this stout-billed bully—a "gregarious songbird" according to the dictionaries—to stand for a loud or coarse person, a loiterer, someone with disgusting table manners, or a scatterbrain. As if that were not bad enough, the crow's grating caw is generally held to presage bad news or the visitation of evil, and superstition once held that the future could be divined from its cry.

One word that has fallen into disuse but warrants mention here for its colorfulness is *karasugane* 烏金, or "crow money," a high-interest, one-day loan that must be repaid early the next day when the crows start cawing, which is to say at daybreak.

The crow's caw is *kākā* カーカー. They are counted *ichiwa* 一羽.

↪ *sanba-garasu* 三羽がらす, *ugō no shū* 烏合の衆

Karasu no ashiato 烏の足跡 "crow's footprints"
crow's-feet

あら、烏の足跡だわ。いやねぇ。
Ara, karasu no ashiato dawa. Iya nē.
My goodness! I've got crow's-feet around my eyes.

あの人烏の足跡があるからそんなに若くないよ。
Ano hito karasu no ashiato ga aru kara sonna ni wakaku nai yo.
He's got crow's-feet around his eyes, so he can't be all that young.

※ Exactly the same usage as in English. (And the same sinking feeling seems to accompany first notice of them, too.)

Karasu no gyōzui 烏の行水 "a crow's bath"
a hurried bath, a spit bath, a quick dip

時間がなかったので烏の行水になった。
Jikan ga nakatta no de karasu no gyōzui ni natta.
I was short on time so I just made do with a spit bath.

今風呂に入ったと思ったら、烏の行水だね。
Ima furo ni haitta to omottara, karasu no gyōzui da ne.
Boy, that was a quick bath. I could swear you just got in.

※ From the crow's hurried bathing habits.

karite kita neko 借りてきた猫 "a borrowed cat"

be a pussycat; (uncharacteristically) quiet or well mannered; be lamblike

花子は叔父さんの家に行くのが初めてだったので、借りてきた猫のようだった。
Hanako wa ojisan no ie ni iku no ga hajimete datta no de, karite kita neko no yō datta.
Hanako was uncharacteristically well behaved because it was the first time she visited her uncle.

毒舌の彼も奥さんの前では借りてきた猫だ。
Dokuzetsu no kare mo okusan no mae de wa karite kita neko da.
He's usually pretty poison-tongued, but he's a regular pussycat around his wife.

🐱 One of my personal all-time favorites. From the observation that a cat in unfamiliar surroundings, subdued and uncertain, appears well behaved. But put his rambunctious self on home turf and you've got a horse of a different color, so to speak. Often followed by *no yō* or *mitai.*

↩ *neko* 猫

kata 肩 shoulder

Aside from the bodily "shoulder," *kata* refers to that part of a shirt or jacket which goes by the same name in English, that section of the road where you pull off to change a flat or relieve yourself, and other shoulderlike protuberances such as the shoulder of a mountain.

Generally speaking, idioms with *kata* concern work or responsibility and the pressures resulting from them. There are several idioms, however, that express a person's attitude or bearing.

By the way, when a Japanese sports announcer says the right fielder has a strong shoulder, *kata ga tsuyoi,* he means, of course, that he has a strong arm.

Kata ga koru 肩が凝る "have frozen shoulders"

(1) have a stiff neck (2) feel ill at ease, get (be) uptight

(1) 肩が凝ったので、マッサージをしてもらった。
Kata ga kotta no de, massāji o shite moratta.
My neck was stiff so I got a massage.

(2) 社長がいると肩が凝る。
Shachō ga iru to kata ga koru.
I feel ill at ease whenever the boss is around.

肩の凝らない本を読みたいな。
Kata no koranai hon o yomitai na.
I'd like to do a little light reading.

Kata ni kakaru 肩にかかる "be on one's shoulders"
be one's responsibility

団長という責任が彼の肩にかかっていた。
Danchō to iu sekinin ga kare no kata ni kakatte ita.
The responsibilities of being group leader were squarely on his shoulders.

この国の将来は君たちの肩にかかっている。
Kono kuni no shōrai wa kimi-tachi no kata ni kakatte iru.
The future of the nation is in your hands.

Kata no chikara o nuku 肩の力を抜く "remove the strength from one's shoulders"
relax, shake it out

もっと肩の力を抜いて、気楽にやりなさい。
Motto kata no chikara o nuite, kiraku ni yarinasai.
Don't be so uptight. Take it easy and try it.

ふっと肩の力をぬいたら、いろいろなものが見えてきた。
Futto kata no chikara o nuitara, iroiro na mono ga miete kita.
As soon as I just relaxed a little, things began to fall into place.

Kata o ireru / kata-ire suru　**肩を入れる／肩入れする**　"put one's shoulder into something"
get behind something, be enthusiastic about something, support something, back something

---

彼の学校は、昔からバスケット部に特に肩を入れている。
Kare no gakkō wa, mukashi kara basuketto-bu ni toku ni kata o irete iru.
His school has always been especially supportive of the basketball team.

その組合は、ある政党に肩入れしている。
Sono kumiai wa, aru seitō ni kata-ire shite iru.
The union is putting its weight behind a certain political party.

Kata o motsu　**肩を持つ**　"hold someone's shoulder"
side (up) with someone, support someone

田中さんの肩を持つわけではないが、彼に対する批判は間違っている。
Tanaka-san no kata o motsu wake de wa nai ga, kare ni taisuru hihan wa machigatte iru.
I don't mean to take sides with Mr. Tanaka, but the criticisms of him are not justified.

あなたはどうして彼女の肩ばかり持つのですか。
Anata wa dō shite kanojo no kata bakari motsu no desu ka.
Why are you always on her side? / Why are you always going to bat for her?

Kata o naraberu　**肩を並べる**　"line up shoulders"

(1) shoulder to shoulder (2) be on a par with, be neck and neck with, measure up to

(1) 久しぶりに父と肩を並べて駅まで歩いた。
Hisashiburi ni chichi to kata o narabete eki made aruita.
For the first time in ages my father and I walked side by side to the train station.

(2) 彼と肩を並べる力士はいない。
Kare to kata o naraberu rikishi wa inai.
There is no other sumo wrestler that can even touch (come close to, hold a candle to) him. / He's head and shoulders above the rest of the wrestlers.

戦後、日本は経済大国として、先進国と肩を並べるようになった。
Sengo, Nihon wa keizai-taikoku toshite, senshin-koku to kata o naraberu yō ni natta.
Japan has grown to rival (joined the ranks of) the great economic powers of the world since the end of World War II.

Kata-tataki　**肩たたき**　"tapping someone on the shoulder"
early retirement

私も、そろそろ肩たたきを覚悟する年になった。
Watashi mo, sorosoro kata-tataki o kakugo suru toshi ni natta.
I've reached the age where I'm likely to be put out to pasture pretty soon.

Katagawari o suru　**肩代わりをする**　"switch shoulders"
take over (for someone)

君の借金は、私が肩代わりしましょう。

Kimi no shakkin wa, watashi ga katagawari shimashō.
I'll pay off your loan for you.

katagi 堅気 "firm *ki*"

(of a person) serious, straight; reliable; (of an occupation) real, regular, legitimate, legit

暴力団も昨今では堅気の世界のビジネスに参入してきた。
Bōryoku-dan mo sakkon de wa katagi no sekai no bijinesu ni sannyū shite kita.
Organized crime has recently begun to branch out into legitimate business undertakings.

早く堅気になって奥さんを安心させてあげなさい。
Hayaku katagi ni natte okusan o anshin sasete agenasai.
Why don't you hurry up and get a real job, man, so your wife can stop worrying.

暴力団員の更正の難しさを訴えても、堅気の人はほとんど関心を示さない。
Bōryokudan-in no kōsei no muzukashi-sa o uttaete mo, katagi no hito wa hotondo kanshin o shimesanai.
You can argue all you want about the difficulty of reforming gang members, but your average Joe Blow could hardly care less.

❦ In contrast to the traditional, socially unacceptable gangland livelihoods, which include gambling, prostitution, and bar ownership or employment, *katagi* refers to the occupations, lifestyles, or ways of living of those who walk the straight and narrow.

kawaige (ga) nai かわい気（が）ない "without cute (charming) *ki*"

without charm or cuteness; that's not very nice

顔は可愛いのに言うことは実にかわい気がないのさ。
Kao wa kawaii no ni iu koto wa jitsu ni kawaige ga nai no sa.
For such a good-looking chick there's sure nothing lovable about the way she talks.

素直に喜べばいいのに、かわい気のないやつだな。
Sunao ni yorokobeba ii no ni, kawaige no nai yatsu da na.
It'd sure be nice if you could just show some appreciation (show how much you like it), but, no, you've got to be a sourpuss.

🞰 *Kawaige (ga) nai* is used almost exclusively in the negative, describing a lack of charm that is unexpected or unseemly.

☞ *ki ga tsuyoi* 気が強い

kazamidori 風見鶏 "a bird that looks at the wind"

a weathercock, an opportunist, an unprincipled person who follows the majority

あいつは風見鶏だから同僚からは信頼されていない。
Aitsu wa kazamidori da kara dōryō kara wa shinrai sarete inai.
The guy's such an opportunist that none of his co-workers trust him.

昔風見鶏と言われた日本の首相がいたが、その後政治スキャンダルで辞任した。
Mukashi kazamidori to iwareta Nihon no shushō ga ita ga, sono go seiji sukyandaru de jinin shita.
A long time ago there used to be a Japanese prime minister that every-

body called the weathercock, but he resigned because of some political scandal.

🐇 This bird (*tori*) is really a chicken (*niwatori*). But the character can be pronounced *tori,* and is, in fact, so pronounced at meat markets all around the country. Ask for *toriniku*, or "bird meat," and you'll get chicken and not sparrow or pheasant. The weathervane usage is similar to the English and derives from the similarity of such a person to the erratic gyrations of the figurine atop buildings. Roosters make the sound *kokekokkō* コケコッコウ.

Ke no haeta yō na 毛の生えたような "like something with hair on it"

not much more than, little more than

マンションといってもアパートに毛の生えたようなものさ。
Manshon to itte mo apāto ni ke no haeta yō na mono sa.
They call it a condo, but it's really just a glorified apartment.

あの教授は学生に毛の生えた程度の知識しかない。
Ano kyōju wa gakusei ni ke no haeta teido no chishiki shika nai.
That prof doesn't know much more than a student. / That professor is little more than a glorified student.

kedakai 気高い "high *ki*"

aristocratic, blue-blooded, noble; exhalted, grand, imposing, regal

彼女の指には気高いグリーンのエメラルドが輝いていた。
Kanojo no yubi ni wa kedakai gurīn no emerarudo ga kagayaite ita.
A majestic green emerald sparkled from its perch on her finger.

皇族になられる前からも気高い雰囲気の方でした。
Kōzoku ni narareru mae kara mo kedakai fun'iki no kata deshita.
There was a noble air about her even before she became a member of the Imperial family.

kehai 気配 "sign of *ki*"

an indication, a sign

部屋は真っ暗だったが誰かいる気配がした。
Heya wa makkura datta ga dare ka iru kehai ga shita.
The room was pitch black, but I sensed (felt) that someone was there.

電気はついているのに家の中に人のいる気配が全くないね。
Denki wa tsuite iru no ni uchi no naka ni hito no iru kehai ga mattaku nai ne.
The lights are on, but there's no indication at all that anybody's home.

2階で何か動く気配がしなかったかい。
Nikai de nanika ugoku kehai ga shinakatta kai.
Did you hear something move upstairs?

🐇 Not to be confused with 気配り *kikubari*.

kemushi 毛虫 "hairy bug"

caterpillar

---

kemushi 毛虫 "hairy bug"
a creep, crud, jerk, rat, skunk, bastard

あのタレント、小さい頃はこの近所では毛虫と呼ばれてたんだよ。
Ano tarento, chiisai koro wa kono kinjo de wa kemushi to yobarete 'ta n' da yo.
That celebrity used to be known as a creep around this neighborhood when he was little.

昔はよくおとなしい子を「弱虫毛虫はさんで捨てろ！」と言ってからかったことがあるよ。
Mukashi wa yoku otonashii ko o "yowamushi kemushi hasande sutero!" to itte karakatta koto ga aru yo.
Way back when, I used to tease quieter kids, saying "Cry baby, cry baby, nobody likes a cry baby!"

※ Used by children pejoratively to describe a strongly disliked person.

↪ *gejigeji* げじげじ （蚰蜒）

ken-en (inu to saru) no naka 犬猿（犬と猿）の仲
"dog-and-monkey relationship"

be at each other's throats all the time, get along like cats and dogs; be bad blood between

伊藤さんと鈴木さんは犬猿の仲だ。
Itō-san to Suzuki-san wa ken-en no naka da.
There's bad blood between Ito and Suzuki.

環境保護団体と大企業は往々にして犬と猿である。
Kankyōhogo-dantai to dai-kigyō wa ōō ni shite inu to saru de aru.
Environmental groups and big business are always going round and round like cats and dogs.

※ The two variations of this idiom appear to enjoy similar frequency of use, though some sources claim the former may be slightly more common.

Idiomatic usage is thought to have originated from the Japanese fairy tale *Momotarō* 「桃太郎」 in which two retainers, a dog and a monkey, began to fight over the reward after the ogre had been banished to an outlying island.

ki 気 *ki*

The idioms and patterns given immediately below, and also in independent entries, feature *ki* in an integral—and relative—role in which its meaning changes depending on what comes before it (i.e., when *ki* follows one of three types of modifier: the sentence-ending form of a verb, the sentence-ending form of an "*i*" adjective, or the "*na*" form of a "*na*" adjective) and after it. The most common structures in which *ki* so appears include ~ *ki ga aru,* ~ *ki ga suru,* ~ *ki da,* and ~ *ki ni naru,* the swung dash " ~ " representing the modifier which determines the meaning of *ki* in the pattern. Broadly speaking, there are two types of pattern.

The first type of modifier ends in the so-called "dictionary" form of a verb expressing some form of action. *Ki* in this case takes on such meanings as plan, intention or inclination. When the degree of certainty is high in this usage, *ki* is interchangeable with *yotei* 予定 or *keikaku* 計画.

The second type ends either in the dictionary form of a verb expressing a condition (examples of this type of verb include *wakaru, dekiru,* and *iru*); or in the past, present continuous (~ *te iru*), past continuous (~ *te ita*) tenses of a verb, or in an adjective. In this case, ~ *yō na* is usually found attached to the preceding part. Here, *ki* has the sense of "feeling" and may be replaced by *kibun* 気分.

In both of the above types, *kimochi* 気持ち may be considered a synonym and, with the exception of the ~ *ki ga suru* pattern, so may *tsumori*.

~ *ki da* ～気だ "*ki* is"

1. be going to, be inclined to, intend to, plan to

   優勝できなかったら丸坊主になる気だ。
   Yūshō dekinakattara marubōzu ni naru ki da.
   I'm gonna shave my head if we don't win the championship.

   大学へ行く気なら学費ぐらいはなんとかしてやるから頑張れ。
   Daigaku e iku ki nara gakuhi gurai wa nan to ka shite yaru kara ganbare.
   If you're planning to go to college, I'll do what I can to come up with the money for your tuition. Go for it.

   あいつ本当にカンニングする気らしいぜ。
   Aitsu hontō ni kanningu suru ki rashii ze.
   He really intends to cheat. / He's really gonna cheat.

   今のところは参加する気でいますが、はっきりした返事はもうしばらくお待ち下さい。
   Ima no tokoro wa sanka suru ki de imasu ga, hakkiri shita henji wa mō shibaraku omachi kudasai.
   At the moment I'm inclined to take part, but please wait a little longer for my final decision.

☞ *~ ki ga aru* 〜気がある

2. feel like, think like

   たった半年暮らしただけでその国のことがすべて分かったような気でいる。
   Tatta hantoshi kurashita dake de sono kuni no koto ga subete wakatta yō na ki de iru.
   I only lived there for six months, but I feel as though I got to know the country inside out.

   オーディションに受かっただけなのに、もう大女優になった気らしい。
   Ōdishon ni ukatta dake na no ni, mō dai-joyū ni natta ki rashii.
   She acting like she's a big movie star even though all she did was pass the audition.

清水の舞台から飛び降りた気で転職しましたよ。
Kiyomizu no butai kara tobiorita ki de tenshoku shimashita yo.
It was a big step for me to change jobs. / I felt I was jumping off the deep end when I changed jobs.

大船に乗った気で、安心してお任せ下さい。
Ōbune ni notta ki de, anshin shite omakase kudasai.
Just relax, you're in safe hands. Leave everything to me.

🞳 *ōbune ni notta*: literally, "ride on a big ship," a set phrase often followed by *yō de*.

催眠術にかかっている間は犬になった気でいたのかい。
Saimin-jutsu ni kakatte iru aida wa inu ni natta ki de ita no kai.
What, did you feel like you'd turned into a dog when you were under hypnosis?

☞ ~ *ki ni natta* 〜気になった、~ *ki ni natte iru* 〜気になっている (see ~ *ki ni naru*)

ki de ki o yamu 気で気を病む "*ki* gets ill due to *ki*"

get all worked up about nothing, work oneself into a lather, worry oneself sick (unnecessarily)

彼女の場合は世間体を気にし過ぎて、「気で気を病む」の見本みたいなもんだ。
Kanojo no bāi wa seken-tei o ki ni shisugite, "ki de ki o yamu" no mihon mitai na mon da.
The way she's so uptight about appearances and all, she's your classic worrywart.

気で気を病むということもありますから、あまり思い詰めない方がいいですよ。

Ki de ki o yamu to iu koto mo arimasu kara, amari omoitsumenai hō ga ii desu yo.

You know what they say about worrying yourself sick about nothing. If I were you, I'd try not to take things to heart so much.

🖙 The sense of the idiom is that by taking something too much to heart, *ki ni shisugite* 気にしすぎて, one can become psychologically distressed.

☞ *yamai wa ki kara* 病は気から

ki ga arai 気が荒い "*ki* is rough"

temperamental, excitable, volcanic

ある程度気が荒い馬でないとよい競走馬にはならないそうだ。
Aru teido ki ga arai uma de nai to yoi kyōsō-ba ni wa naranai sō da.
They say an animal has got to be somewhat temperamental to make a good racehorse.

気が荒い人が多い職場なので、けんかが絶えない。
Ki ga arai hito ga ōi shokuba na no de, kenka ga taenai.
There're so many contentious people where I work that there's no end to the arguing.

☞ *ki ga yasashii* 気が優しい

(ni) ki ga aru 気がある "there is *ki*"

be interested in, take to, have a place in one's heart for, be keen on, take a fancy to

この話には十分気があるんだが、いろいろとこちらにも事情があってねえ。

Kono hanashi ni wa jūbun ki ga aru n' da ga, iroiro to kochira ni mo jijō ga atte nē.

We're interested enough in the project; it's just that you have to realize that there are other considerations involved for us here.

今度の縁談には十分気があるんだ。
Kondo no endan ni wa jūbun ki ga aru n' da.
She's very interested in the latest marriage proposal.

あいつはどうやら昭子さんに気があるらしいが、彼女の方は全然あいつに気のある素振りは見せない。
Aitsu wa dō yara Akiko-san ni ki ga aru rashii ga, kanojo no hō wa zenzen aitsu ni ki no aru soburi wa misenai.
It looks like he's got the hots for Akiko all right, but she's showing no signs that she even knows he's alive.

❅ While ~ *ni ki ga aru* means to be interested in something, as does the expression ~ *ni kyōmi ga aru*, unlike the latter it connotes a sometimes strong desire for the object of affection—usually someone or something of sexual or financial interest—rather than a passing or dispassionate interest. You would use the expression ~ *ni kyōmi ga aru* if you were interested in soccer, or following a particular athlete's career as a sports commentator, while you would use ~ *ni ki ga aru* about that same athlete if you were bent on luring him to play for your team or going out on a date with him. This idiom, by the way, should not be confused with ~ *ki ga aru* preceded by the dictionary form of a verb and exemplified under the *ki* entry. (See following entries.)

☞ *ki ga nai* 気がない

~ *ki ga aru*　〜気がある　"the *ki* to do ~ exists"

feel like, be interested in, be ready to, be up for, intend to, want to

結婚する気があるのかないのか、はっきりしてちょうだい。
Kekkon suru ki ga aru no ka nai no ka, hakkiri shite chōdai.
Come on, just make up your mind whether you want to get married or not.

就職する気があるんだったら、そろそろ活動しなくちゃだめだよ。
Shūshoku suru ki ga aru n' dattara, sorosoro katsudō shinakucha dame da yo.
If you're thinking about getting a job, you're going to have to get on the ball and start looking around pretty soon.

買う気があるなら値段の交渉してみたら？
Kau ki ga aru nara nedan no kōshō shite mitara?
If you're interested in buying, why don't you try to get them to come down on the price?

ダイエットする気はあるんだけど、ついつい甘い物に手が出ちゃうのよね。
Daietto suru ki wa aru n' da kedo, tsuitsui amai mono ni te ga dechau no yo ne.
I want to diet, but I just can't seem to stay away from (keep my hands off) the sweets.

※ Attached to the dictionary form of the verb, ~ *suru ki ga aru* expresses a present desire or intention to do something. The related expression ~ *ki ni naru* (〜気になる) suggests that a change from a previous state has resulted in the desire or intention to do something. ~ *Ki ga aru* is often replaced by ~ *ki da*. In the first three of the above four examples, ~ *suru ki ga aru* and ~ *ki da* are interchangeable; in the fourth they remain interchangeable but ~ *ki da* imparts a firmer sense of resolve to drop a few pounds. While ~ *ki ga aru* implies that there are several possible courses of action from which a particular one has been chosen, ~ *ki da* implies that either none exist or at least that they are not considered viable alternatives.

☞ ~ *ki ni naru* 〜気になる, ~ *ki da* 〜気だ

ki ga au 気が合う "*ki*'s match"

get along (well); be compatible, like-minded, on the same wave length; hit it off

あの人とは最初に紹介されたときから気が合う。
Ano hito to wa saisho ni shōkai sareta toki kara ki ga au.
He and I've hit it off ever since we were first introduced.

どうせ飲むなら、会社の上司とじゃなくて気の合う者同士で行きたいよ。
Dōse nomu nara, kaisha no jōshi to ja nakute ki no au mono dōshi de ikitai yo.
If I've got to go out drinking, I'd sure rather do it with people I get along with instead of my boss.

山田さんはいい人だとは思うんだけど、なぜか気が合わない。
Yamada-san wa ii hito da to wa omou n' da kedo, naze ka ki ga awanai.
I'm sure Yamada is a fine person, but the chemistry is just not right for us.

🎍 Expresses the sympathetic feelings between like-minded individuals rather than agreement among them on any particular matter.

↪ *hada ga au* 肌が合う, *uma ga au* 馬が合う

ki ga chigau 気が違う "*ki* is different"

go (be) crazy, nuts, out of one's mind; be off one's rocker

あの日以来気が違ったように勉強している。
Ano hi irai ki ga chigatta yō ni benkyō shite iru.
He's been studying like mad from that day on.

🎍 *Ki ga chigau* is used almost exclusively in its metaphoric sense in the phrase *ki ga chigatta yō ni* or as a rhetorical question in *ki de mo chigatta n' ja nai ka*. The standard expressions for "mentally ill" are *seishin ni ijō o kitasu* 精神に異常を来す or *seishin-byō ni naru* 精神病になる.

↝ *kichigai* 気違い

ki ga chiisai 気が小さい "*ki* is small"

feel inhibited; be chickenhearted, fainthearted, lily-livered, meek; be a chicken, a weenie

田中さんはふだんは気が小さいのに、飲むと人が変わってしまう。
Tanaka-san wa fudan wa ki ga chiisai no ni, nomu to hito ga kawatte shimau.
Tanaka's usually such a wimp, but when he gets a few drinks in him he becomes a different person.

そんなことでくよくよ悩むとは、君も意外と気が小さいんだな。
Sonna koto de kuyokuyo nayamu to wa, kimi mo igai to ki ga chiisai n' da na.
I never figured you for such a weenie that you'd fret over something like that.

↝ *ki ga yowai* 気が弱い, *nomi no shinzō* 蚤の心臓, *shinzō ga yowai* 心臓が弱い

ki ga chiru 気が散る "*ki* is scattered"

be (get) distracted, break one's concentration, lose it

気が散るから計算中は話しかけないでくださいね。
Ki ga chiru kara keisan-chū wa hanashikakenai de kudasai ne.

Don't talk to me when I'm trying to add stuff up 'cause I'll lose track of where I am (break my concentration).

気が散って勉強できないからもっとテレビの音小さくしてよ。
Ki ga chitte benkyō dekinai kara motto terebi no oto chiisaku shite yo.
I can't concentrate on studying (keep my mind on my studies) with the TV so loud. Turn it down, would you?

☞ This is what happens to you when your *ki* "gets taken" (*ki o torareru*).

~ *ki ga deru* 〜気が出る "the *ki* to do ~ comes out"

want to do, feel like doing

勉強する気が出るように、お父さんからも話してやって下さいな。
Benkyō suru ki ga deru yō ni, otōsan kara mo hanashite yatte kudasai na.
You have a talk with him too, Father, and see if you can't motivate (get) him to study.

彼も失業保険が切れそうになってやっと仕事を探す気が出てきたようだね。
Kare mo shitsugyō-hoken ga kiresō ni natte yatto shigoto o sagasu ki ga dete kita yō da ne.
What with his unemployment benefits coming to an end, it seems he's finally decided to look for a job.

☞ ~*ki ni naru* 〜気になる

ki ga fureru 気がふれる "*ki* is touched"

be touched, unbalanced, be out of one's mind

戦争中は気がふれるほど辛い経験をしました。

Sensō-chū wa ki ga fureru hodo tsurai keiken o shimashita.
During the war I experienced some things so terrible that I feared for my sanity.

そんなにいくつも難問をかかえて、気がふれない方が不思議だ。
Sonna ni ikutsu mo nanmon o kakaete, ki ga furenai hō ga fushigi da.
With all the problems you have, it's a wonder that you are able to maintain a balanced outlook.

✤ Literary.

☞ *ki ga chigau* 気が違う, *ki ga kuruu* 気が狂う, *ki ga hen ni naru* 気が変になる

ki ga fusagu　気がふさぐ　"*ki* closes up"

be blue, be in low spirits, be low, get depressed

この地方の冬は曇の日ばかりで実に気がふさぐね。
Kono chihō no fuyu wa kumori no hi bakari de jitsu ni ki ga fusagu ne.
The way it's overcast every day during the winter in this region can really get depressing.

わけもなく気がふさいで、何をするのも嫌なんです。
Wake mo naku ki ga fusaide, nani o suru no mo iya nan desu.
I'm just moping around all the time and can't get into doing anything at all.

✤ Commonly heard in conversation with *ki* omitted and no change in meaning. See the examples below.

最近ひどくふさいでるじゃないか、お前。
Saikin hidoku fusaide 'ru ja nai ka, omae.
You've really been bummed out lately, haven't ya? / You've sure been draggin' ass lately.

ふさいだ顔していったいどうしちゃったの。
Fusaida kao shite ittai dō shichatta no.
What's the long face all about? / How come you're so down in the mouth?

↪ *ki ga meiru* 気が滅入る, *ki o harasu* 気を晴らす

ki ga hairu 気が入る "*ki* comes in"

get into doing something, be enthusiastic about something, put one's mind to doing something

気が入ると実にいい絵を描く人だ。
Ki ga hairu to jitsu ni ii e o kaku hito da.
He can really paint when he puts his mind to it (gets into it).

ずいぶん気の入った仕事ぶりだ。
Zuibun ki no haitta shigoto buri da.
She's really into her work.

✦ Compared to *ki o ireru*, *ki ga hairu* implies that there is less effort or intentionality involved.

↪ *ki o ireru* 気を入れる

ki ga hareru 気が晴れる "*ki* clears up"

feel better, relieved, lighthearted, like a weight has been lifted from one's shoulders

このあいだからひっかかっていたことが解決して、やっと気が晴れた。
Kono aida kara hikkakatte ita koto ga kaiketsu shite, yatto ki ga hareta.

That stuff I'd had on my mind finally got worked out, so I feel like it's clear sailing from here on out.

亭主と喧嘩してむしゃくしゃしてたんだけど、パチンコしたら気が晴れちゃった。
Teishu to kenka shite mushakusha shite 'ta n' da kedo, pachinko shitara ki ga harechatta.
I got all worked up fighting with my old man, but felt a whole lot better after playing pachinko for a while.

※ Unlike *ki ga raku ni naru* 気が楽になる, which expresses only a freedom from concern or worry, and *ki ga karuku naru* 気が軽くなる, which signals the relief arising from completion of some duty (usually a job), *ki ga hareru* can also express a return to calm once anger has subsided.

↪ *ki ga shizumu* 気が沈む

ki ga haru 気が張る "*ki* is stretched out"

be anxious, strung-out, tense, under stress, uptight; [〜の〜] stressful, nerve-racking

今日見えるのは気難しい人ばかりだからほんとうに気が張るわ。
Kyō mieru no wa kimuzukashii hito bakari da kara hontō ni ki ga haru wa.
I'm uptight because I'm meeting a bunch of really difficult people today.
 / The people I'm supposed to see today are all difficult to please, so I'm kind of anxious about it.

気の張る集まりじゃありませんから、ぜひ一度どうぞ。
Ki no haru atsumari ja arimasen kara, zehi ichido dōzo.
You ought to try to make it to one of our little get-togethers. They're not pretentious at all.

今はまだ気が張っているから元気そうだが、一段落してからが心配だ。

Ima wa mada ki ga hatte iru kara genkisō da ga, ichi-danraku shite kara ga shinpai da.

She seems lively enough now while she's still keyed up, but I'm worried what'll happen when things settle down a bit.

☞ *ki ga yasumaru* 気が休まる, *ki ga yurumu* 気が緩む

ki ga hayai 気が早い "*ki* is fast"

be hasty, impatient; get ahead of oneself

まだ恋人もいないのにもう結婚式場を予約したなんて、ずいぶん気が早いね。

Mada koibito mo inai no ni mō kekkon-shikijō o yoyaku shita nante, zuibun ki ga hayai ne.

Don't you think you're jumping the gun a little, reserving a wedding chapel when you haven't even got a girlfriend?

気の早い吉田さんは、生まれたばかりの息子の大学進学の心配をしている。

Ki no hayai Yoshida-san wa, umareta bakari no musuko no daigaku-shingaku no shinpai o shite iru.

That Yoshida's so far ahead of himself that he's already worrying about his newborn son getting into college.

☞ *sekkachi (na)* せっかち(な)

ki ga hayaru 気がはやる "*ki* hurries"

be hasty, impatient, impetuous, rash

気がはやって新記録が出せなかった。
Ki ga hayatte shin-kiroku ga dasenakatta.

I tried too hard and was unable to set a new record.

落ち着いてよ。気がはやるとうまくいかないからさ。
Ochitsuite yo. Ki ga hayaru to umaku ikanai kara sa.
Take it easy! You'll screw everything up if you get impatient.

↪ *ki ga seku* 気が急く

ki ga hazumu 気が弾む "*ki* bounces"

become buoyant, get excited, be in high spirits

春のイタリア旅行のことを考えると気が弾むよ。
Haru no Itaria ryokō no koto o kangaeru to ki ga hazumu yo.
I get excited (hyped) just thinking about our trip to Italy in the spring.

気が弾んで、つい鼻歌が出ちゃった。
Ki ga hazunde, tsui hanauta ga dechatta.
I was so high that I found myself humming a little tune.

ki ga hen (na) 気が変（な） "strange *ki*"

bonkers, cracked, crazy, have a screw loose, have lost one's marbles, insane, mad, off one's rocker

あんた気が変なんじゃないの、そんな夢みたいなことばかり言って。
Anta ki ga hen nan ja nai no, sonna yume mitai na koto bakari itte.
Don't you think you're going off the deep end, always talking about your pie-in-the sky dreams?

このがらくたに100万円も払ったなんて、気が変なのか。

Kono garakuta ni hyakuman-en mo haratta nante, ki ga hen na no ka.
You paid a million yen for a piece of junk like this! Are you out of your mind?

🕉 Note that the meaning of this phrase is not synonymous with *hen na ki ga suru* 変な気がする (to feel funny about *something*) and *hen na ki ni naru* 変な気になる (to feel a sudden urge *toward the opposite sex* or to feel a unexpected temptation *to pilfer or steal*).

☞ *ki ga hen ni naru* 気が変になる

ki ga hen ni naru 気が変になる "*ki* becomes strange"

go crazy, nuts; flip out, lose it, lose one's marbles

忙しくて忙しくて、もう気が変になりそうだ。
Isogashikute isogashikute, mō ki ga hen ni narisō da.
I'm so busy I feel like I'm gonna go nuts.

どうして東京の人はこんな満員電車に毎日乗って気が変にならないんだろう。
Dōshite Tōkyō no hito wa konna man'in densha ni mainichi notte ki ga hen ni naranai n' darō.
I wonder how Tokyoites keep from flipping out riding these crowded trains every day.

🕉 As with *ki ga chigau*, used primarily in a metaphoric sense.

☞ *ki ga chigau* 気が違う, *ki ga hen (na)* 気が変(な), *ki ga kuruu* 気が狂う, *ki ga fureru* 気が触れる

ki ga heru 気が減る "*ki* diminishes"

be depressed, down, worn down

毎月のように預金金利が下がるので気が減るよ。
Maitsuki no yō ni yokin-kinri ga sagaru no de ki ga heru yo.
It's such a bummer to sit and watch interest rates on savings accounts head south almost every month.

この不景気で注文が少なくなって気が減る思いだ。
Kono fu-keiki de chūmon ga sukunaku natte ki ga heru omoi da.
It's depressing the way orders keep declining during the recession.

彼の節約ぶりには見ている方が気が減る。
Kare no setsuyaku-buri ni wa mite iru hō ga ki ga heru.
He's so frugal that it's almost pathetic.

※ Similar to *ki ga meiru* 気が滅入る, *gakkari suru* がっかりする and *genki ga naku naru* 元気がなくなる insofar as it expresses a sense of depression, the source of that depression is primarily material or financial loss or penury in the case of *ki ga heru*. There is, by the way, no *ki ga hette iru* (present progressive tense), as the idiom describes a condition rather than the process of falling into such a condition.

↔ *ki ga shizumu* 気が沈む, *ki ga meiru* 気が滅入る

ki ga hikeru 気が引ける "*ki* pulls in"

feel funny, diffident, timid, timorous, can't get into it

こんな恰好だから入るの気が引けるよ。
Konna kakkō da kara hairu no ki ga hikeru yo.
It just doesn't feel right going in dressed like this.

彼の誘いを断ってこのまま帰るのは少し気が引ける。
Kare no sasoi o kotowatte kono mama kaeru no wa sukoshi ki ga hikeru.
I can't very well simply leave after turning him down the way I did.

まわりの人がそうそうたるメンバーだったので、気が引けて何も発言できなかった。
Mawari no hito ga sōsō-taru menbā datta no de, ki ga hikete nani mo hatsugen dekinakatta.
With all the heavyweights there, I couldn't bring myself to speak up.

ki ga hikishimaru 気が引き締まる "*ki* tightens"

be determined (resolved) to do something

正装すると気が引き締まるものだね。
Seisō suru to ki ga hikishimaru mono da ne.
There's something about getting dressed up that makes you feel like a new person.

辞令をもらって、気が引き締まる思いがした。
Jirei o moratte, ki ga hikishimaru omoi ga shita.
I had pause to reflect on things when I received my official notice of appointment.

☞ *ki o hikishimeru* 気を引き締める

ki ga ii 気がいい "*ki* is good"

amiable, good-hearted, good-natured, have a good disposition, pleasant; laid-back

彼は気がいいからまわりの人にずいぶんと利用されている。
Kare wa ki ga ii kara mawari no hito ni zuibun to riyō-sarete iru.
He's such an easygoing guy (a big softie, a pussycat) that he's always letting people take advantage of him.

息子は気がよすぎて人に頼まれたことは断れないので、将来が心配だ。
Musuko wa ki ga yosugite hito ni tanomareta koto wa kotowarenai no de shōrai ga shinpai da.
I'm worried about my son's future because he's just too nice (softhearted) for his own good. He can't say no when someone asks him to do something.

タローは気のいい犬で、猫に餌を横取りされても怒らない。
Tarō wa ki no ii inu de, neko ni esa o yokodori sarete mo okoranai.
Taro's such a good-natured dog that he doesn't even get mad when some cat snatches his food away.

☞ *ki no ii hito* 気のいい人

ki ga karui 気が軽い "*ki* is light"

feel lighthearted, relieved, feel like a load has been lifted from one's shoulders

今月のノルマが達成できてしばらくは気が軽い。
Kongetsu no noruma ga tassei dekite shibaraku wa ki ga karui.
I'm gonna be walking on air now that I've made my quota for this month. / What a load off my mind it is to have met my quota this month.

とりあえず第二志望の学校に受かったので気が軽くなった。
Toriaezu daini-shibō no gakkō ni ukatta no de ki ga karuku natta.
Knowing that I've at least made it into my second-choice school is a big relief.

✣ *Ki ga karui* is used to describe a feeling of lightheartedness which is normally the result of some felicitous event or state of affairs in the past. Such being the case, it differs somewhat in usage from its most obvious antonym *ki ga omoi*, which looks forward—literally—to the ominous future for its referent. *Ki ga karuku naru* is also to be distinguished from its near synonym *ki ga hareru* in that the former describes a feeling of relief upon completion of some duty or distasteful task such as work or study, while the latter results more from a clearing of the air and return to normalcy after that anxious moment when you were sure the teacher spotted your crib sheet or after the prolonged gloom of a languid stock market has suddenly lifted.

☞ *ki ga omoi* 気が重い

ki ga katsu 気が勝つ "*ki* is victorious"

hard-nosed, opinionated, spirited, strong-minded, strong-willed, unyielding

気が勝った人で、ひとから注意されると猛烈に反発するんだよ。
Ki ga katta hito de, hito kara chūi sareru to mōretsu ni hanpatsu suru n' da yo.
A strong-willed woman, she'll jump on anybody who tries to give her advice.

姉貴は気が勝ってて絶対弱音は吐かないんだ。
Aneki wa ki ga katte 'te zettai yowane wa hakanai n' da.
My big sister's a real competitor. No way she'll ever give up. / My big sister is her own woman. You won't hear her moaning and groaning about anything.

✣ Used only in the ~ *katta* or ~ *katte iru* forms, often (though not always) disparagingly of a woman who "doesn't know her place," i.e., one who has her own opinions and is unwilling to go along with what a man tells her.

☞ *ki ga tsuyoi* 気が強い

ki ga kawaru 気が変わる "*ki* changes"

blow hot and cold, change one's mind, feel differently about, flip-flop, have a change of heart, think better of

なにしろしょっちゅう気が変わるんだから、こっちはたまったもんじゃないさ。
Nanishiro shotchū ki ga kawaru n' da kara, kotchi wa tamatta mon ja nai sa.
No way I'm gonna just let it slide the way he's always going and changing his mind every few minutes.

気が変わりやすい人だから、早くはんこをもらってしまったほうが勝ちだよ。
Ki ga kawariyasui hito da kara, hayaku hanko o moratte shimatta hō ga kachi da yo.
He's so fickle that you'd be better off getting him to sign on the dotted line as soon as you can.

出不精のお父さんの気が変わらないうちに家族旅行の計画を立てることにした。
Debushō no otōsan no ki ga kawaranai uchi ni kazoku-ryokō no keikaku o tateru koto ni shita.
My dad's not much for going out, so we started making plans for the family vacation before he had any second thoughts.

環境が変われば気も変わるだろう。
Kankyō ga kawareba ki mo kawaru darō.
When you're in different surroundings, you'll look at things differently.

☞ *uwakippoi* 浮気っぽい, *uwaki na* 浮気な (both mentioned, though not exemplified, under *uwaki* 浮気)

ki ga ki ja nai 気が気じゃない "*ki* is not *ki*"

be beside oneself with worry, be worried to death, not be oneself (because of worry)

買ったばかりの株が下がり始めて毎日気が気じゃない。
Katta bakari no kabu ga sagarihajimete mainichi ki ga ki ja nai.
What with that stock I just bought starting to drop, I'm worrying myself sick every day.

あと1分で新幹線が出るっていうのに姿が見えないんだもの、気が気じゃなかったわよ。
Ato ippun de shinkan-sen ga deru tte iu no ni sugata ga mienai n' da mono, ki ga ki ja nakatta wa yo.
I was pulling my hair out with you nowhere in sight and the bullet train leaving in one minute.

Also 気が気で(は)ない *ki ga ki de (wa) nai.*
↝ *sensen-kyōkyō* 戦々恐々

ki ga kiku 気が利く "*ki* works"

1. be considerate, tactful, thoughtful

彼は若いがなかなか気が利く。
Kare wa wakai ga nakanaka ki ga kiku.
He may be young, but he's really quite considerate. / He's got pretty good judgement for someone his age.

さすがに秘書の経験が長いだけあって気が利く方ですね。
Sasuga ni hisho no keiken ga nagai dake atte ki ga kiku kata desu ne.
It must be all that secretarial experience that has made her so thoughtful.

お茶も出してないのか。まったく気が利かないな。

Ocha mo dashite nai no ka. Mattaku ki ga kikanai na.
Hasn't even served the tea, huh? I don't know where her head is at (What can she be thinking?).

↔ *ki ga tsuku* 気がつく (#2), *ki ga mawaru* 気が回る, *ki o kikasu* 気を利かす

2. be bright, on the ball, quick, sharp, smart, witty

あんな気の利かない奴は見たことない。
Anna ki no kikanai yatsu wa mita koto nai.
I've never seen such a numbskull (dimwit, knucklehead, loser).

そういうのを気が利きすぎて間が抜けてるっていうんだ。
Sō iu no o ki ga kikisugite ma ga nukete 'ru tte iu n' da.
That's what you call being too smart for your own good. / That's a case of thinking you've got all the bases covered, only to find you've forgotten the obvious thing.

あんな場では気の利いた冗談の一つも言って上手に逃げろよ。
Anna ba de wa ki no kiita jōdan no hitotsu mo itte jōzu ni nigero yo.
When you get stuck in a situation like that, you've gotta lay something witty on 'em to get out of it. / When something like that happens, you've gotta do some fancy footwork to extricate yourself.

3. chic, cool, just right

この服のデザインはなかなか気が利いているね。
Kono fuku no dezain wa nakanaka ki ga kiite iru ne.
These threads are really a cool design.

彼の誕生日に何か気の利いた贈り物したいんだけど、何がいいかしら。
Kare no tanjō-bi ni nanika ki no kiita okurimono shitai n' da kedo, nani ga ii kashira.
I'd like to give him the perfect gift for his birthday. I wonder what'd be good.

🕸 When modifying a noun as in senses 2 and 3, the idiom appears almost exclusively as *ki no kiita*.

ki ga kuruu 気が狂う "*ki* is deranged"

go crazy, insane, mad, nuts; flip out, lose it, lose one's mind

今日は気の狂う暑さだね。
Kyō wa ki no kuruu atsusa da ne.
It's hot enough today to drive you up the wall.

その母親は気が狂うほど子供に会いたがっている。
Sono haha-oya wa ki ga kuruu hodo kodomo ni aitagatte iru.
She (that mother) wants desperately to see her child.

彼女はその知らせを聞いて気も狂わんばかりに泣き出した。
Kanojo wa sono shirase o kiite ki mo kuruwan bakari ni nakidashita.
She started bawling like crazy when she heard the news.

🕸 Somewhat more formal than *ki ga chigau*, *ki ga kuruu* can be used colloquially to mean "mentally ill," although its primary use is metaphoric.

↬ *ki ga chigau* 気が違う, *ki ga fureru* 気がふれる, and *ki ga hen ni naru* 気が変になる

ki ga magireru 気が紛れる "*ki* is diverted"

be diverted, forget (one's worries)

皆と一緒にいる時は気が紛れるが、一人になるととても淋しい。
Minna to issho ni iru toki wa ki ga magireru ga, hitori ni naru to totemo sabishii.

Being out with friends is a great distraction, but boy do I get lonely when I'm by myself.

滝本さんからの電話のおかげで気が紛れた。
Takimoto-san kara no denwa no okage de ki ga magireta.
Thanks to Takimoto's call, I forgot all my worries (for a while).

↬ *ki o magirawasu* 気を紛らわす

ki ga mawaru 気が回る "*ki* goes around"

be thoughtful, considerate; be full of (good) ideas

おじょうちゃんはまだ小さいのにずいぶん気が回るのね。
Ojōchan wa mada chiisai no ni zuibun ki ga mawaru no ne.
For such a little girl, you sure are thoughtful.

忙しかったからそこまで気が回らなかった。
Isogashikatta kara soko made ki ga mawaranakatta.
I was so busy I didn't even think of doing that.

そこまで気が回らないよ。
Soko made ki ga mawaranai yo.
Hey, I can't think of everything, you know.

※ Not to be confused with its cognate *ki o mawasu* 気を回す, which means to be suspicious and is used critically of others.

↬ *ki ga kiku* 気が利く (#1), *ki ga tsuku* 気がつく (#2)

ki ga meiru 気が滅入る "*ki* is downcast"

be depressed, bummed out, down; one's heart sinks

雨の日は気が滅入る。
Ame no hi wa ki ga meiru.
Rainy days get me down. / I get bummed out on rainy days.

これ以上気が滅入る話は聞きたくない。
Kore ijō ki ga meiru hanashi wa kikitaku nai.
Enough of all these depressing stories.

そんなこと言わないでよ。そうじゃなくても気が滅入ってるんだから。
Sonna koto iwanai de yo. Sō ja nakute mo ki ga meitte 'ru n' da kara.
Come on, don't give me that! I'm depressed enough as it is.

君の話を聞いているうちにだんだん気が滅入ってきたよ。
Kimi no hanashi o kiite iru uchi ni dandan ki ga meitte kita yo.
I'm getting bummed out just listening to you.

⇨ *ki ga heru* 気が減る, *ki ga omoi* 気が重い, *ki ga shizumu* 気が沈む; *ki o harasu* 気を晴らす

ki ga mijikai 気が短い "*ki* is short"

1. be hotheaded, hot-tempered, quick-tempered, short-tempered, touchy, volcanic; have a short fuse

家の親父は気が短くてすぐ怒鳴るから、話の切り出し方が難しい。
Uchi no oyaji wa ki ga mijikakute sugu donaru kara, hanashi no kiri-dashi-kata ga muzukashii.
The way my dad's always flying off the handle, it's not easy to bring up the subject.

結婚するまで夫があんなに気の短い人とは思わなかった。
Kekkon suru made otto ga anna ni ki no mijikai hito to wa omowanakatta.
I had no idea my husband had such a short fuse until after we were married.

2. antsy, hasty, impatient, rash, restless

気が短い人はエレベーターに乗るとすぐ「閉」のボタンを押す。
Ki ga mijikai hito wa erebētā ni noru to sugu "hei" no botan o osu.
Impatient people push the "close" button as soon as they get in an elevator.

そんな気の短いこと言わないで、もう少し時間をくれないか。
Sonna ki no mijikai koto iwanai de, mō sukoshi jikan o kurenai ka.
Think you could back off a bit and give me just a little more time?

☞ *ki ga hayai* 気が早い, *tanki (na)* 短気(な); *ki ga nagai* 気が長い, *kinaga (ni)* 気長(に)

ki ga momeru 気が揉める "*ki* gets crumpled"

be anxious (to find out about something), wring one's hands (over something)

結果がどうなったか気が揉めるんだが、こちらから聞くわけにもいかないしね。
Kekka ga dō natta ka ki ga momeru n' da ga, kochira kara kiku wake ni mo ikanai shi ne.
I'm anxious to find out how things turned out, but I can't very well ask, now can I?

昨日は例の件で気が揉めて、一日中何も手につかなかったよ。
Kinō wa rei no ken de ki ga momete, ichinichi-jū nani mo te ni tsukanakatta yo.

Yesterday I was so worried about you-know-what that I didn't get a thing done all day.

☞ *ki o momu* 気を揉む

ki ga muku　気が向く　"*ki* moves toward"

be (feel) inclined to do, be in the mood to do, feel like doing

気が向くと頑張るけど、長続きしないんだよねえ。
Ki ga muku to ganbaru kedo, nagatsuzuki shinai n' da yo nē.
He works hard when he has a mind to, but he never sticks to anything for long.

気が向いたときにいつでもいらしてください。
Ki ga muita toki ni itsu de mo irashite kudasai.
Come visit any time you take a notion to.

誘われていることはいるんだが、どうも気が向かないよ。
Sasowarete iru koto wa iru n' da ga, dōmo ki ga mukanai yo.
I've been invited all right, but I just can't get motivated to go.

足の向くまま気の向くままに世界中を旅してみたいものだ。
Ashi no muku mama ki no muku mama ni sekai-jū o tabi shite mitai mono da.
I'd love to be able to travel around the world wherever my fancy took me.

☞ *noriki ni naru* 乗り気になる, *kinori suru* 気乗りする (see under *ki ga noru* 気が乗る)

ki ga nagai　気が長い　"*ki* is long"

1. (of a person) patient, laid-back, have a long fuse

   彼は気が長いから何ヵ月でも待ってくれると思うよ。
   Kare wa ki ga nagai kara nankagetsu de mo matte kureru to omou yo.
   He's a patient guy. I imagine he'll wait months for you if he has to.

   大陸の国民は島国の国民より気が長いようだ。
   Tairiku no kokumin wa shimaguni no kokumin yori ki ga nagai yō da.
   People living on continents seem to have a lot more patience than islanders.

2. (of events and processes) a slow business, take a lot of patience

   百年前に造り始めたこの教会は完成までにもう百年かかるそうだが、気が長い話だね。
   Hyakunen-mae ni tsukurihajimeta kono kyōkai wa kansei made ni mō hyakunen kakaru sō da ga, ki ga nagai hanashi da ne.
   Imagine it taking another hundred years to finish this church that was started a hundred years ago! They're really in it for the long haul!

   そんなに気の長いこと言ってると彼女他の人と結婚しちゃうよ。
   Sonna ni ki no nagai koto itte 'ru to kanojo hoka no hito to kekkon shichau yo.
   She's gonna up and marry some other guy if you keep drawing things out.

☞ *kinaga (ni)* 気長(に); *ki ga mijikai* 気が短い

~ *ki ga nai* 〜気がない "the *ki* to do ~ doesn't exist"

not be ready to, be unready to, don't feel like, don't intend to

買う気がないのに冷やかしたのかい。
Kau ki ga nai no ni hiyakashita no kai.

What did you do, just go around window shopping and pestering the clerks even though you never intended to buy anything?

借りる気はなかったが、一応比較のためにアパートを見せてもらうことにした。
Kariru ki wa nakatta ga, ichiō hikaku no tame ni apāto o misete morau koto ni shita.
I had no intention of renting the apartment, but I had them show it to me anyway for the sake of comparison.

☞ *~ki ga aru* 〜気がある

ki ga nai 気がない "no *ki*"

feel blah, be lackadaisical, be listless; be uninterested (in), not be interested (in), have no taste for, not like

気がないのなら早くそう言ってあげた方が彼女のためだよ。
Ki ga nai no nara hayaku sō itte ageta hō ga kanojo no tame da yo.
If you don't feel anything for her, the sooner you tell her the better off she'll be.

もったいぶって気がない素振りなんかしてると彼に逃げられちゃうわよ。
Mottai-butte ki ga nai soburi nanka shite 'ru to kare ni nigerarechau wa yo.
If you keep playing it cool like you're not interested in him, he's going to find himself someone else.

※ *mottai-buru*: literally, "act no thing"; to put on airs (when there is no justification)

なんだか気のない返事だね。
Nan da ka ki no nai henji da ne.
That's a half-assed (lukewarm) answer if I've ever heard one.

✌ Not to be confused with ~ *ki ga nai*.

☞ *ki ga aru* 気がある

ki ga noru 気が乗る "*ki* mounts up"

get enthusiastic, get going, get into, get turned on (to), get all hopped up (about)

気が乗ると一晩中でもワープロに向かって仕事をする。
Ki ga noru to hitoban-jū de mo wāpuro ni mukatte shigoto o suru.
I'll pound away on the word processor all night long when I'm on a roll.

あいつ気が乗ったら平気で徹夜もするぜ。
Aitsu ki ga nottara heiki de tetsuya mo suru ze.
Hey, when he gets all pumped up about something, he'll stay up all night, no sweat.

今度の計画にはあまり気が乗らない。
Kondo no keikaku ni wa amari ki ga noranai.
I'm not too hot on (can't get too worked up about) the project.

社内旅行は申し込みはしたが何となく気が乗らない。
Shanai-ryokō wa mōshikomi wa shita ga nan to naku ki ga noranai.
I applied to go along on the company trip this time, but for some reason I just can't seem to get excited about it.

一応こちらの話は聞いてくれたんですが、あまり気が乗らない様子でした。
Ichiō kochira no hanashi wa kiite kureta n' desu ga, amari ki ga noranai yōsu deshita.
They listened to what I had to say, but they didn't show much interest.

✌ The idiom is most often encountered in the negative.

↪ *kinori (ga) suru* 気乗り(が)する, *noriki (na)* 乗り気(な), *ki ga muku* 気が向く; *kinori-usu (na)* 気乗り薄(な), *ki ga susumanai* 気が進まない

ki ga nukeru 気が抜ける "*ki* slips out"

1. be (feel) disappointed, let down, bummed out; lose heart

そんなこと言わないでよ。こっちまで気が抜けるじゃないか。
Sonna koto iwanai de yo. Kotchi made ki ga nukeru ja nai ka.
Cut it out. Whaddya want to do, bum me out too?

張り切っていたのに雨で試合が中止になって、気が抜けた。
Harikitte ita no ni ame de shiai ga chūshi ni natte, ki ga nuketa.
I was really up for the game, so it was a big letdown when it got rained out.

日本チームが代表になれなかったので、サッカーファンもすっかり気が抜けてしまった。
Nihon-chīmu ga daihyō ni narenakatta no de, sakkāfan mo sukkari ki ga nukete shimatta.
Japanese soccer fans were down in the dumps when the national team failed to make the cut.

経営者側からの回答は気が抜けるような内容だった。
Keieisha-gawa kara no kaitō wa ki ga nukeru yō na naiyō datta.
The response from management was a big disappointment (disappointing / disheartening).

2. go (be) flat, stale; lose (all the) fizz

気が抜けるとまずいから早く飲んでしまおう。
Ki ga nukeru to mazui kara hayaku nonde shimaō.
We'd better drink up 'cause it's no good once it goes flat.

気の抜けたビールも料理に使えるから捨てなくてもいいよ。
Ki no nuketa bīru mo ryōri ni tsukaeru kara sutenakute mo ii yo.

You can use stale beer to cook with so you don't have to throw it away.

気が抜けた風船みたいにしょんぼりしている。
Ki ga nuketa fūsen mitai ni shonbori shite iru.
He sure looks deflated (like somebody took the wind out of his sails). [From another meaning of *ki ga nukeru* not included here, "to be punctured or lose air."]

☞ *ki o nuku* 気を抜く, *ki o yurumeru* 気を緩める

ki ga ōi 気が多い "there is a lot of *ki*"

1. like to play the field, like the ladies (men), be flirtatious; be fickle

あいつ今3人の女性とつきあってるらしいよ。相変わらず気が多いな。
Aitsu ima sannin no josei to tsukiatte 'ru rashii yo. Aikawarazu ki ga ōi na.
That guy's in his usual fine form, going out with three chicks at the same time.

おとなしそうな顔して、あんな気の多い女とは知らなかった。俺、くやしいよ。
Otonashisō na kao shite, anna ki no ōi onna to wa shiranakatta. Ore, kuyashii yo.
She looked like such a quiet girl, how was I to know she'd be screwing around on me. Jeez, that pisses me off.

☞ *uwaki* 浮気, *uwakippoi* 浮気っぽい, *uwaki suru* 浮気する

2. want to do everything (a lot of things), capricious, have a lot of irons in the fire, [～多すぎて] spread oneself (a little) thin

娘が就職活動中なんだが、結構気が多くてなかなか決まらないんだ。
Musume ga shūshoku katsudō-chū nan da ga, kekkō ki ga ōkute nakanaka kimaranai n' da.

My daughter's looking for a job right now, but there are so many things she wants to do she just can't seem to make up her mind.

彼は気が多くていろんな趣味を持っている。
Kare wa ki ga ōkute ironna shumi o motte iru.
He's an inquisitive guy with a lot of hobbies.

☙ Similar to *utsurigi* (*na*) 移り気(な), but while *utsurigi* (*na*) indicates that the person is always flitting from one thing or person to another, *ki ga ōi* suggests that several interests (flames?) hold the person's attention at the same time.

ki ga okenai 気が置けない "unable to place *ki*"

feel at ease (with someone), easy to be around; (of a situation) informal, relaxed

気が置けない友人と飲むのが一番のストレス解消法だよ。
Ki ga okenai yūjin to nomu no ga ichiban no sutoresu kaishō-hō da yo.
Having a drink with a friend you can open up to is the best way I know to unwind.

こういう気の置けない会だと時間のたつのが早いね。
Kō iu ki no okenai kai da to jikan no tatsu no ga hayai ne.
Time really flies at get-togethers like this.

彼女は気の置けない人だからお友達も多いらしいわ。
Kanojo wa ki no okenai hito da kara otomodachi mo ōi rashii wa.
She's so easy to talk to that she's got lots of friends.

☙ A contemporary example of how language may change to take on an opposite meaning, usage of *ki no okenai hito* among young people seems to indicate a misconstruction of its meaning, possibly due to the *okenai* element, "unable to place," taken to imply that the person in question is unworthy of trust; that is, that one shouldn't *place* one's *ki* in him or her. Though it is still too early for this recent trend to enjoy lexicographic respectability, the trend bears watching. Students of the language should be aware that although both meanings are in use, only the original is widely accepted.

ki ga ōkiku naru 気が大きくなる "*ki* grows large"

be (feel) expansive, flushed, uninhibited; let it all hang out; don't sweat the small stuff (shit)

酔うと気が大きくなってできもしない事を約束する癖がある。
You to ki ga ōkiku natte deki mo shinai koto o yakusoku suru kuse ga aru.
Every time I tie one on I start feeling my oats and go around making all kinds of promises that I can't deliver on.

宝くじが当たったので気が大きくなってやたら買い物しまくったら足が出てしまった。
Takarakuji ga atatta no de ki ga ōkiku natte yatara kaimono shimakuttara ashi ga dete shimatta.
In a liberal mood after winning the lottery, I went on a shopping spree and blew all the money I'd won, and then some.

~ *ki ga okoru* 〜気が起こる "the *ki* to do ~ happens"

get in the mood to do, bring oneself to do

原稿を書く気が起こるまでしばらくテレビゲームでもやろうっと。
Genkō o kaku ki ga okoru made shibaraku terebigēmu de mo yarō tto.
Maybe I ought to play a video game for a while until I get in the mood to start working on the manuscript.

あまりのことに泣く気も起こらなかった。
Amari no koto ni naku ki mo okoranakatta.
Things were so terrible that I couldn't even cry.

コーチに馬鹿にされて猛烈に練習する気が起こった。
Kōchi ni baka ni sarete mōretsu ni renshū suru ki ga okotta.
I went all out in practice when the coach made fun of me.

☞ ~ *ki ni naru* 気になる

ki ga omoi 気が重い "***ki* is heavy**"

be (feel) blue, bummed out, down, low, heavyhearted

19日までにあと15も例文を作らなければならないので気が重い。
Jūku-nichi made ni ato jūgo mo reibun o tsukuranakereba naranai no de ki ga omoi.
It's depressing to think that I've got to come up with fifteen more example sentences by the nineteenth.

仕事とはいえ結果的にはあの人を裏切ることになると思うと気が重い。
Shigoto to wa ie kekka-teki ni wa ano hito o uragiru koto ni naru to omou to ki ga omoi.
I know it comes with the job, but it makes me feel bad to think that it amounts to stabbing him in the back.

✌ Used of the way one feels when facing a disagreeable situation or distasteful task rather than of an emotional state resulting from some unpleasant event, past or present. The latter meaning is more appropriately expressed with either *ki ga shizumu* 気が沈む or *ki ga meiru* 気が滅入る, both of which are included herein.

☞ *ki ga fusagu* 気がふさぐ, *ki ga shizumu* 気が沈む, *ki ga meiru* 気が滅入る; *ki ga karui* 気が軽い

ki ga raku (na) 気が楽（な） "easy *ki*"

(of a person) be relieved, feel lighthearted; (of a condition) easy, a snap, a piece of cake, no sweat; a relief

今度のプロジェクトほど気が楽な仕事は珍しい。
Kondo no purojekuto hodo ki ga raku na shigoto wa mezurashii.
Jobs as easy as this project are few and far between.

林さんならよく知っているから気が楽だよ。
Hayashi-san nara yoku shitte iru kara ki ga raku da yo.
If it's Ms. Hayashi, it won't be a big deal because I know her quite well.

☞ *ki ga raku ni naru* 気が楽になる, *ki o raku ni motsu* 気を楽に持つ, *ki o raku ni suru* 気を楽にする, *kiraku (na)* 気楽(な)

ki ga raku ni naru 気が楽になる "one's *ki* relaxes"

be a relief, be relieved, feel better, feel like a weight has been lifted from one's shoulders, feel lighthearted, feel relieved

本当のことを話せば気が楽になるよ。
Hontō no koto o hanaseba ki ga raku ni naru yo.
You'll feel a whole lot better if you just tell us what really happened. / It'll be a relief if you just tell the truth.

今年の確定申告も終わって、気が楽になったなあ。
Kotoshi no kakutei-shinkoku mo owatte, ki ga raku ni natta nā.
What a load off my mind it is to have finished filing this year's tax return and all.

気が楽になったら急にお腹がすいてきた。
Ki ga raku ni nattara kyū ni onaka ga suite kita.
With that off my mind, I got hungry all of a sudden.

☞ *ki o raku ni suru* 気を楽にする, *ki ga raku (na)* 気が楽(な), *kiraku (na)* 気楽(な), *nonki (na)* 呑気(な)

ki ga seku 気が急く "*ki* hurries"

be in a hurry, in a rush; champ at the bit

約束の時間を10分も過ぎているので、気が急く。
Yakusoku no jikan o juppun mo sugite iru no de, ki ga seku.
Ten minutes late already, I've gotta step on it.

気ばかり急いて一向にはかどらないよ、困ったもんだ。
Ki bakari seite ikkō ni hakadoranai yo, komatta mon da.
I'm running around like a chicken with its head cut off but not making a bit of headway.

☞ *ki ga hayaru* 気がはやる

~ *ki ga shinai* ~気がしない "the key not to do ~"

1. don't feel (like doing)

あれ以来、もう何もする気がしないのさ。
Are irai, mō nani mo suru ki ga shinai no sa.
Ever since, I just haven't felt like doing anything.

いくら勧められてもそんな物は買う気が全然しないよ。
Ikura susumerarete mo sonna mono wa kau ki ga zenzen shinai yo.
Doesn't matter how hard they try to persuade me, I'm not at all interested in buying anything like that.

やめた、やめた、食う気しない。
Yameta, yameta, kuu ki shinai.
Nope, I've changed my mind. I don't feel like eating anymore.

Beware—the antonym of ~ *ki ga shinai* is not ~ *ki ga suru*.

☞ ~ *ki ni naranai* 〜気にならない (examples under ~ *ki ni naru* 〜気になる)

2. don't feel, don't get the feeling, don't think

彼はほめているつもりだろうが、あれではほめられている気がしないさ。
Kare wa homete iru tsumori darō ga, are de wa homerarete iru ki ga shinai sa.
He may think it's a compliment, but it sure doesn't feel that way.

あんな少しじゃ飲んだ気がしねえ。もう1軒行こうぜ。
Anna sukoshi ja nonda ki ga shinē. Mō ikken ikō ze.
You call that drinkin'? I haven't even got a buzz, man. Whaddya say we hit another bar.

🐚 While *taberu ki ga shinai* 食べる気がしない means the same as *tabetaku nai* 食べたくない, namely that one does not want to eat, *tabeta ki ga shinai* 食べた気がしない means something akin to "that was so bad (such a small amount, etc.) that I don't feel that I've eaten at all."

☞ ~ *ki ga suru* 〜気がする, ~ *ki ni naru* 〜気になる

ki ga shirenai 気が知れない "can't understand someone's *ki*"

be beyond one, be unable to figure out

こんな悪趣味な服を着る人の気が知れないな。
Konna aku-shumi na fuku o kiru hito no ki ga shirenai na.
I just can't understand how someone could be such a fashion criminal.

あんないい娘をふるなんてあいつの気が知れない。
Anna ii ko o furu nante aitsu no ki ga shirenai.
I just can't figure that guy out, dumping a nice girl like her.

旦那にあんな好き勝手なことさせて、まったく彼女の気が知れないわ。
Danna ni anna suki-katte na koto sasete, mattaku kanojo no ki ga shirenai wa.
It's beyond me why she lets her husband do whatever he wants all the time.

✌ Found preceded by possessive ~ *no* 〜の.

ki ga shizumaru 気が静まる "*ki* quiets down"

calm down, regain one's composure, settle down

彼の気が静まるのを待ってもう一度話してみよう。
Kare no ki ga shizumaru no o matte mō ichido hanashite miyō.
I think I'll give him a chance to settle down before I talk to him again.

ようやく気が静まったらしい。
Yōyaku ki ga shizumatta rashii.
Looks like she's finally cooled off.

☞ *ki ga ochitsuku* 気が落ち着く, *ki o shizumeru* 気を静める; *ki ga tatsu* 気が立つ

ki ga shizumu 気が沈む "*ki* sinks"

become melancholy, become sad, be saddened, get depressed, down, bummed out

入院している姪のことを思うと気が沈む。
Nyūin shite iru mei no koto o omou to ki ga shizumu.
My heart sinks every time I think of my niece in the hospital.

天気が良くないせいか今朝から気が沈んで何もしたくない。
Tenki ga yoku nai sei ka kesa kara ki ga shizunde nani mo shitaku nai.
I don't know if it's the weather or what, but I've been blue since this morning and haven't felt like doing a thing.

⚜ Used of a feeling one gets when thinking of something unpleasant in the past or present, and to be distinguished from *ki ga omoi* (see note thereunder).

☞ *iki-shōchin* 意気消沈, *ki ga fusagu* 気がふさぐ, *ki ga omoi* 気が重い, *ki ga heru* 気が減る, *ki ga meiru* 気が滅入る; *ki ga hareru* 気が晴れる

ki ga soreru 気が逸れる "*ki* is distracted"

get distracted, stop paying attention

どんなにおもしろい講義でもやはりときどき気が逸れる。
Donna ni omoshiroi kōgi de mo yahari tokidoki ki ga soreru.
No matter how interesting a lecture is, your mind wanders now and then.

ふと気が逸れた瞬間に包丁で指を切ってしまった。
Futo ki ga soreta shunkan ni hōchō de yubi o kitte shimatta.
I cut my finger with the kitchen knife the second I stopped paying attention to what I was doing.

☞ *ki ga chiru* 気が散る, *ki o sorasu* 気を逸らす

ki ga sumu 気が済む "*ki* is finished"

be content, satisfied; have enough, have had one's fill

俺が悪かった。気が済むまで殴ってくれ。
Ore ga warukatta. Ki ga sumu made nagutte kure.
It's all my fault. Go ahead, pound on me to your heart's content.

あなたの気が済むようにしてちょうだい。
Anata no ki ga sumu yō ni shite chōdai.
Feel free to do what you want. / Suit yourself.

言いたいことは全部言って、やっと気が済んだ。
Iitai koto wa zenbu itte, yatto ki ga sunda.
I feel better now that I've finally had my say.

こんなことぐらいじゃまだ気が済まないぜ。
Konna koto gurai ja mada ki ga sumanai ze.
This is hardly enough to satisfy me. / I'm not finished with you yet, man.

☞ *(hara no) mushi ga osamaru* (腹の)虫が治まる (see under *mushi* 虫)

~ *ki ga suru* ～気がする "the *ki* to do ~ does"

believe, feel (like), get the notion (that), think

君となら うまくやっていけそうな気がするんだ。
Kimi to nara umaku yatte ikesō na ki ga suru n' da.
I get the feeling that you and I are going to do just fine together.

熱がありそうな気がする。学校は休もうかな。
Netsu ga arisō na ki ga suru. Gakkō wa yasumō ka na.
I feel kinda like I've got a fever. Maybe I ought to cut (skip) school today.

彼の言い分も分かる気がするが、やはり賛成できない。

Kare no iibun mo wakaru ki ga suru ga, yahari sansei dekinai.
I think I understand what he's saying, but I just can't go along with it.

たかが一泊旅行にこんな大きな荷物持って行くのはカッコ悪い気がする。
Takaga ippaku ryokō ni konna ōki na nimotsu motte iku no wa kakko warui ki ga suru.
I get the feeling (it strikes me) that taking a big suitcase like this on a little overnighter is gonna look pretty stupid.

ちょっと覗いてみたい気もするなあ。
Chotto nozoite mitai ki mo suru nā.
You know, I'd kinda like to take a peek.

この人から離れられなくなってしまうような気がした。
Kono hito kara hanarerarenaku natte shimau yō na ki ga shita.
I felt like I might not be able to go back to a life without him.

あの人にはどこかで会ったような気がするんだが、どこだったか思い出せない。
Ano hito ni wa doko ka de atta yō na ki ga suru n' da ga, doko datta ka omoidasenai.
I've got the feeling that I've met him somewhere before, but I can't remember where.

ちょっと路地を入っただけで戦前の東京に迷い込んだような気がした。
Chotto roji o haitta dake de senzen no Tōkyō ni mayoikonda yō na ki ga shita.
I felt like I had stepped back in time to prewar Tokyo almost as soon as I got on the back streets.

※ Less definite than ~ *to omou*, ~ *ki ga suru* is a somewhat evasive way of saying what you think. That is, it is an artful—some would say typically Japanese—way of avoiding responsibility for suggesting an idea or a strong commitment to one. Add *yō na*, as in *yō na ki ga suru*, and you're practically a seasoned politician who is just impossible to pin down. While *yō na* can be appended to any usage of *ki ga suru*, it is especially recommended when the word preceding the expression is any part of speech other than an adjectival verb (形容動詞) to make the expression more natural. This may arise from basing one's comments on something only dimly remembered. Finally, the negative of *ki ga suru*, *ki ga shinai* (which see) appears to be seldom used when the future is being spoken of.

ki ga susumanai 気が進まない "*ki* doesn't go forward"

be disinclined, unwilling, reluctant

悪い話じゃないと思うんだけど、今一つ気が進まないんだ。
Warui hanashi ja nai to omou n' da kedo, ima hitotsu ki ga susumanai n' da.
I don't think it's a particularly bad deal; it's just that I can't get real enthusiastic about it.

あまり気が進まないのなら無理にとは言わない。
Amari ki ga susumanai no nara muri ni to wa iwanai.
If you don't feel like doing it, I'm not going to force you. / If you can't get into doing it, I won't twist your arm.

⚜ While the positive form of this idiom can be found, it is all but exclusively seen in dictionaries and seldom, if ever, occurs in speech.

↪ *ki ga noranai* 気が乗らない (see under *ki ga noru* 気が乗る); *ki ga noru* 気が乗る, *noriki (na)* 乗り気(な)

ki ga tashika (na) 気が確か(な) "certain *ki*"

be all there, in one's right mind, sane, together; have both oars in the water

年はとっても気は確かだ。
Toshi wa totte mo ki wa tashika da.
I may be getting along in years, but I still know the score (what time it is).

あんな待遇のいい会社をやめるなんて、気が確かとはとても思えない。
Anna taigū no ii kaisha o yameru nante, ki ga tashika to wa totemo omoenai.
You ought to have your head examined, quitting a company that's as good to its employees as yours is.

彼女に誘われて断った？　気は確かかい？
Kanojo ni sasowarete kotowatta? Ki wa tashika kai?
What are you, one brick short of a load, turning her down when she asked you out?

また金利が下がるらしいが、日銀総裁は気が確かなのか。
Mata kinri ga sagaru rashii ga, Nichi-gin sōsai wa ki ga tashika na no ka.
With interest rates apparently headed down again, I've got to wonder if the governor of the Bank of Japan knows what he's doing.

✌ Appears regularly in rhetorical questions.

↬ *shōki* 正気, *ki o tashika ni motsu* 気を確かに持つ; *ki ga chigau* 気が違う, *ki ga hen (na)* 気が変(な)

ki ga tatsu 気が立つ "*ki* stands up"

be (get) agitated, aroused, flustered, hot, on edge, ruffled, wrought up

気が立つのはよく分かるが、もっと穏やかに話し合えないものかな。
Ki ga tatsu no wa yoku wakaru ga, motto odayaka ni hanashiaenai mono ka na.
I know it upsets you, but we ought to be able to talk this thing out more calmly.

こちらもつい気が立って失礼なことを言ってしまった。
Kochira mo tsui ki ga tatte shitsurei na koto o itte shimatta.
I got a little excited (on edge) myself and got out of line.

今は気が立っているから誰が何を言っても無理だと思うよ。
Ima wa ki ga tatte iru kara dare ga nani o itte mo muda da to omou yo.
He's so edgy (worked up) now that I don't think he gives a hoot what anyone says.

❦ Not to be confused with *hara ga tatsu* 腹が立つ, which always means to get angry, *ki ga tatsu* most commonly implies only agitation although it can be used synonymously with *hara ga tatsu*.

☞ *hara ga tatsu* 腹が立つ

ki ga togameru 気がとがめる "*ki* blames (itself)"

be conscience-stricken, repentant; blame oneself; feel a pang of conscience, guilty, sorry, remorseful; regret

あのときひどいこと言ってしまって、今でも気がとがめる。
Ano toki hidoi koto itte shimatte, ima de mo ki ga togameru.
Some of the terrible things I said then still bother me. / I still feel bad about some of the horrible things I said then.

気がとがめて彼の顔がまともに見られなかった。
Ki ga togamete kare no kao ga matomo ni mirarenakatta.
I felt so guilty I couldn't even look him square in the eye.

人を裏切ってちっとも気がとがめない奴の気が知れないなあ。
Hito o uragitte chittomo ki ga togamenai yatsu no ki ga shirenai nā.
I just can't understand how somebody could think nothing of double-crossing a friend like that.

自分が悪いことをしたとは思わないから、全然気がとがめない。

Jibun ga warui koto o shita to wa omowanai kara, zenzen ki ga togamenai.
I'm not a bit sorry, 'cause I don't feel I did anything wrong.

ki ga tōku naru 気が遠くなる "*ki* grows distant"

1. black (pass) out, faint, go out like a light, lose consciousness, slip into unconsciousness (darkness); feel faint, light-headed

君は血を見ると気が遠くなるから、医者にはなれないね。
Kimi wa chi o miru to ki ga tōku naru kara, isha ni wa narenai ne.
You might as well forget ever becoming a doctor, the way you pass out (get dizzy) every time you see blood.

満員電車に揺られてるうちに気が遠くなった。
Man'in densha ni yurarete 'ru uchi ni ki ga tōku natta.
The train was packed, and I started feeling woozy as it rocked back and forth.

↝ *ki o ushinau* 気を失う, *kizetsu suru* 気絶する

2. (of a person) be stupefied; (of something) humongous, dizzying, stupendous

息子が警察に逮捕されたと聞かされたときは、気が遠くなりそうだった。
Musuko ga keisatsu ni taiho sareta to kikasareta toki wa, ki ga tōku narisō datta.
I was stupefied (flabbergasted) when I was told that my son had been arrested by the police.

あの星の光は、気の遠くなるような長い時間かかって地球へ届いたんだよ。
Ano hoshi no hikari wa, ki no tōku naru yō na nagai jikan kakatte chikyū e todoita n' da yo.

The light from that star took so long to reach the Earth that it makes your head spin to think about it.

今週中にしなければならない仕事を考えると気が遠くなる。
Konshū-chū ni shinakereba naranai shigoto o kangaeru to ki ga tōku naru.
It blows my mind just to think of all the work I've got to get done this week. / I kinda go blank when I think of everything I've got to take care of this week.

株の損失は気が遠くなるような額だ。
Kabu no sonshitsu wa ki ga tōku naru yō na gaku da.
My stock losses are staggering (mind-boggling).

🕯 Although the expression literally means to faint or lose consciousness (*ki o ushinau* 気を失う), it is widely used in a metaphoric sense in conjunction with ~ *narisō da* or ~ *naru yō na* to express shock, amazement, or astonishment at some vast quantity.

ki ga tsuku 気がつく "*ki* gets attached"

1. be aware of, realize, pick up on, [eventually] come to one, dawn on one, think of

ふっと気がつくともう40なのよね。
Futto ki ga tsuku to mō yonjū na no yo ne.
I was forty almost before I knew it. / It's like all of a sudden I was forty, you know. / The big four-oh snuck right up on me.

あっちの席の人ずっとあなたのこと見てるわよ。気がついた？
Atchi no seki no hito zutto anata no koto mite 'ru wa yo. Ki ga tsuita?
The guy sitting over there has been eyeing you for quite a while. Did you notice?

気がついた時にやっとかないと忘れちゃうよ。
Ki ga tsuita toki ni yattokanai (= yatte okanai) to wasurechau yo.

If I don't do it when it comes (occurs) to me, I'll forget all about it.

もういい加減に気がついてもいいはずだけど。
Mō iikagen ni ki ga tsuite mo ii hazu da kedo.
Jeez, it's really about time she woke up and smelled the coffee (saw the light).

気がつかないふりをしてるに決まってるよ。
Ki ga tsukanai furi o shite 'ru ni kimatte 'ru yo.
I bet he's just pretending like he hasn't noticed.

さっきから手を振っているのにまだ気がついてくれないんだ。
Sakki kara te o futte iru no ni mada ki ga tsuite kurenai n' da.
I've been waving at her for a while now, but she still hasn't seen me.

これは気がつきませんで、失礼しました。
Kore wa ki ga tsukimasen de, shitsurei shimashita.
Sorry I didn't notice you were empty. (said, for example, while pouring someone's beer)

☞ *kuzuku* 気づく

2. attentive, considerate, thoughtful

まだお若いのによく気がつく娘さんですね。
Mada owakai no ni yoku ki ga tsuku musume-san desu ne.
My, what a thoughtful young lady she is!

細かいことには気のつかない子だけどばりばり仕事を片づけるんだ。
Komakai koto ni wa ki no tsukanai ko da kedo baribari shigoto o katazukeru n' da.
She's not very attentive to detail, but she does pump out the work.

☞ *ki ga kiku* 気が利く (#1), *ki ga mawaru* 気が回る

3. regain consciousness, come back to one's senses, come to, come around, wake up

もうすぐ麻酔がさめて気がつくはずだ。
Mō sugu masui ga samete ki ga tsuku hazu da.
He should be coming around soon, now that the anesthesia is wearing off.

気がついたら駅のベンチで寝ていた。
Ki ga tsuitara eki no benchi de nete ita.
When I came to, I was lying on a bench in the station.

↪ *ki o ushinau* 気を失う, *kizetsu suru* 気絶する

ki ga tsumaru 気が詰まる "*ki* gets clogged"

feel ill at ease, uncomfortable, uneasy

あんな堅苦しい気が詰まる会じゃ懇親会にはならないさ。
Anna katakurushii ki ga tsumaru kai ja konshin-kai ni wa naranai sa.
How can they possibly think a formal, stuffy party like that could ever be a "mixer?"

お作法の先生と一緒だもの、気が詰まって食事どころじゃなかったわ。
Osahō no sensei to issho da mono, ki ga tsumatte shokuji dokoro ja nakatta wa.
I was with an etiquette teacher, for heaven's sake! I was so self-conscious there was no way I could have actually eaten anything.

今日みたいに気の詰まるような思いをしたのは初めてだよ。
Kyō mitai ni ki no tsumaru yō na omoi o shita no wa hajimete da yo.
I've never felt as uncomfortable as I did today.

↪ *kizumari (na)* 気詰まり(な)

ki ga tsuyoi 気が強い "*ki* is strong"

determined, hardheaded, headstrong, iron-jawed, strong-willed, tenacious, feisty, game, gutsy, plucky, spunky, stubborn, tough, willful; have a mind of one's own, stand one's ground, put one's foot down

隣の奥さんは見るからに気が強そうな人だ。
Tonari no okusan wa miru kara ni ki ga tsuyosō na hito da.
You can tell that guy's wife next door is one tough cookie just from the look of her.

✌ *miru kara ni*: at a glance (it is plain to see); a set phrase.

彼女は仕事はできるが気が強過ぎて同僚としてはやりにくい。
Kanojo wa shigoto wa dekiru ga ki ga tsuyosugite dōryō toshite wa yarinikui.
She does her job, but she's just too ornery to work with.

✌ *Ki ga tsuyoi* describes a character trait, and while it can be either neutral or approbatory in the sense of "resolute," it is more often derogatory, especially when used about someone the speaker feels should be compliant—a woman or a subordinate in the workplace—and connotes contrariness or intractability. By comparison, *tsuyoki (na)* is neutral and describes an attitude or stance on a particular issue.

Also 気強い *kizuyoi* [preceeding a noun].
☞ *hanappashi(ra) ga tsuyoi* 鼻っ柱(ら)が強い, *kachiki (na)* 勝ち気(な), *ki o tsuyoku motsu* 気を強く持つ, *tsuyoki (na)* 強気(な); *ki ga yowai* 気が弱い, *nomi no shinzō* 蚤の心臓

ki ga wakai 気が若い "*ki* is young"

young at heart

おじいちゃんはいくつになっても気が若いね。
Ojīchan wa ikutsu ni natte mo ki ga wakai ne.
It doesn't matter how old you get, Grandpa, you'll always be young at heart.

気だけは若いが体力の方はもうだめだ。
Ki dake wa wakai ga tairyoku no hō wa mō dame da.
I feel young at heart, but the old body is going downhill fast. / The spirit is willing but the flesh is weak.

ki ga yasashii　気が優しい　"*ki* is gentle"

compassionate, gentle, kind, nice, sweet, warm

北嶋医院の看護婦さんはみんな美人で気が優しい。
Kitajima-iin no kangofu-san wa minna bijin de ki ga yasashii.
All the nurses at the Kitajima Clinic are good-looking, and nice too.

「気は優しくて力持ち」なんて桃太郎みたいな人だね。
"Ki wa yasashikute chikara-mochi" nante Momotarō mitai na hito da ne.
"Gentle-natured and strong," huh—sounds like [that legendary boy born from a peach] Momotaro or something.

気の優しい息子で、いつも私のことを心配してくれる。
Ki no yasashii musuko de, itsumo watashi no koto o shinpai shite kureru.
My son's so considerate, always thinking of me.

ki ga yasumaru　気が休まる　"*ki* rests"

recharge one's batteries, relax, rest, take a breather, unwind

康子さんといる時だけは気が休まる。

Yasuko-san to iru toki dake wa ki ga yasumaru.
The only time I can really unwind is when I'm with Yasuko.

毎日毎日仕事に追われて気の休まる暇もない。
Mainichi-mainichi shigoto ni owarete ki no yasumaru hima mo nai.
It's just work, work, work every day, with no time to even catch my breath.

騒々しくて全然気の休まらない喫茶店だったね。
Sōzōshikute zenzen ki no yasumaranai kissa-ten datta ne.
With all the racket going on, that coffee shop was certainly no place to relax.

☞ *kiyasume* 気休め, *ki o yasumeru* 気を休める; *ki ga haru* 気が張る

ki ga yowai 気が弱い "*ki* is weak"

be fainthearted, meek, timid, unassertive, weak-kneed, weak-willed; be a pussycat, a pushover

気が弱くて、「いや」と言えないでキャッチ・セールスにひっかかった。
Ki ga yowakute, "iya" to ienai de kyatchi-sērusu ni hikkakatta.
I'm such a weenie I can't even bring myself to say no to those high-pressure salesmen that buttonhole you on the street.

面接にやってきたのは40代後半の気の弱そうな男性だった。
Mensetsu ni yatte kita no wa yonjū-dai kōhan no ki no yowasō na dansei datta.
The guy who showed up for the interview was some wimpy-looking guy in his late forties.

Also 気弱い *kiyowai* [in front of a noun].
☞ *ki ga chiisai* 気が小さい, *koshi ga yowai* 腰が弱い, *yowaki (na)* 弱気な; *ki ga tsuyoi* 気が強い

ki ga yowaru 気が弱る "*ki* weakens"

lose one's zest for life, slow down, weaken

病気の時は誰だって気が弱るものですよ。
Byōki no toki wa dare datte ki ga yowaru mono desu yo.
I don't care who you are, getting sick is bound to take something out of you (take some of the fun out of life).

僕も最近歳のせいかずいぶんと気が弱ってきちゃってねえ。
Boku mo saikin toshi no sei ka zuibun to ki ga yowatte kichatte nē.
I don't know if it's age or what, but I don't look forward to getting up in the morning nearly as much as I used to.

ki ga yurumu 気が緩む "*ki* loosens"

drop one's guard, let one's guard down, let up, relax

ふっと気が緩む瞬間があるんだ。
Futto ki ga yurumu shunkan ga aru n' da.
There's always a moment when you lower your guard (without realizing it). / You can't stay on top of things every second.

酒で気が緩んで、本音が出てしまった。
Sake de ki ga yurunde, honne ga dete shimatta.
The drink loosened my tongue, and before I knew it I'd spoken my mind.

こんな初歩的なミスをするなんて、気が緩んでるぞ。
Konna shoho-teki na misu o suru nante ki ga yurunde 'ru zo.
Your mind's not on what you're doing, making a simple mistake like this.

☞ *ki ga haru* 気が張る

ki mo shiranai de 気も知らないで "without even knowing *ki*"

could(n't) care less about how someone feels

人の気も知らないで呑気なものだ。
Hito no ki mo shiranai de nonki na mono da.
You're one happy-go-lucky gal. Couldn't care less about my feelings, could you.

親の気も知らないで娘は二人とも好き勝手をしています。
Oya no ki mo shiranai de musume wa futari tomo suki-katte o shite imasu.
Neither of our daughters give so much as a thought to how we feel, they're both so self-centered.

隣の息子は親の気も知らないで高校をやめてしまった。
Tonari no musuko wa oya no ki mo shiranai de kōkō o yamete shimatta.
Our neighbor's son up and quit high school without a thought for his parents' feelings.

※ The *hito no ki* and *oya no ki* seen in the first two example sentences above, while literally meaning "a person's *ki*" and "a parent's *ki*" respectively refer in fact to that of the speaker, and in this way are similar to saying that someone could care less "about how other people feel," when a native speaker of English understands that it is the speaker's feelings that are being hurt.

ki mo sozoro 気もそぞろ "*ki* is restless"

can't keep one's mind on, have trouble concentrating on

彼女朝から気もそぞろで間違えてばかりいるよ。
Kanojo asa kara ki mo sozoro de machigaete bakari iru yo.
She's been distracted since morning and making a lot of mistakes.

今は気もそぞろだから何を言っても無駄だと思うな。
Ima wa ki mo sozoro da kara nani o itte mo muda da to omou na.
It won't do you any good to talk to her now; her mind's someplace else.

☞ *ki ga ki ja nai* 気が気じゃない

ki ni iru 気に入る "come into *one's ki*"

like, take a fancy to, take to

この条件なら先方も気に入るでしょう。
Kono jōken nara senpō mo ki ni iru deshō.
I'm sure these conditions will be to their liking as well.

気に入ってもらえてうれしいよ。
Ki ni itte moraete ureshii yo.
I'm sure glad you like it.

この子は気に入ったおもちゃを持たせておけば、何時間でもおとなしく遊んでくれるから助かります。
Kono ko wa ki ni itta omocha o motasete okeba, nanji-kan de mo otonashiku asonde kureru kara tasukarimasu.
It's great because if you give her a toy she likes she'll play with it quietly for hours.

父は気に入らない人とは話もしない。
Chichi wa ki ni iranai hito to wa hanashi mo shinai.
Dad won't even give the time of day to somebody he doesn't like.

☞ *oki ni mesu* お気に召す, *oki-ni-iri* お気に入り; *ki ni kuwanu* 気に食ぬ

ki ni kakaru 気にかかる "hang on *ki*"

be bothered by, concerned about; have something on one's mind, think about, worry (about)

内緒だけど夫より猫の健康の方が気にかかるのよ。
Naisho da kedo otto yori neko no kenkō no hō ga ki ni kakaru no yo.
Just between you and me, I worry more about my cat's health than my husband's.

試合の結果が気にかかって、早く会議が終わらないかとばかり思っていた。
Shiai no kekka ga ki ni kakatte, hayaku kaigi ga owaranai ka to bakari omotte ita.
The outcome of the game was on my mind so much that all I could think of was how soon the meeting would end.

※ Believe it or not, there is a subtle distinction to be made between this and *ki ni kakeru* (see below). *Ki ni kakeru* is usually used after the fact or source of immediate concern has passed to indicate that concern lingers, while *ki ni kakaru* is more immediate.

↬ *ki ni naru* 気になる, *ki ni kakeru* 気にかける, *kigakari* 気がかり, *kigakari (na)* 気がかり(な)

ki ni kakeru 気にかける "hang *something* on one's *ki*"

be concerned about, worry about

母は私のことを気にかけるあまり、毎日2回も電話をよこす。
Haha wa watashi no koto o ki ni kakeru amari, mainichi nikai mo denwa o yokosu.

My mother is so worried about me that she calls twice a day.

僕の健康を気にかけてくれるのはありがたいが、仕事のことには口を出さないでほしい。
Boku no kenkō o ki ni kakete kureru no wa arigatai ga, shigoto no koto ni wa kuchi o dasanai de hoshii.
It's nice that you worry so much about my health and all, but I'd really appreciate it if you'd not tell me how to do my job.

See note under *ki ni kakaru*.

↝ *ki ni suru* 気にする, *kigakari* 気がかり, *kigakari (na)* 気がかり(な)

ki ni kuwanai 気に食わない "not eaten by *ki*"

don't like, don't care (much) for, dislike, get on one's nerves, go against the grain, have no use for, make one sick, rub one the wrong way

俺はそもそもあいつの顔が気に食わねぇ。
Ore wa somosomo aitsu no kao ga ki ni kuwanē.
Can't stand the fucker's looks in the first place.

新入りのくせにでかい態度で気に食わない野郎だぜ。
Shin-iri no kuse ni dekai taido de ki ni kuwanai yarō da ze.
The new guy makes me sick the way he swaggers around like he owned the place.

🐰 Much rougher and more vulgar than *ki ni iranai*. There is no affirmative of the *ki ni kuwanai* form.

↝ *ki ni iranai* 気に入らない (see under *ki ni iru* 気に入る), *hana ni tsuku* 鼻につく

~ ki ni naru　～気になる　"become ki to do ~"

1. be (get) in the mood to do, feel like doing, want to do

あまり興味がない分野の本も書評でほめてあると読んでみる気になる。
Amari kyōmi ga nai bun'ya no hon mo shohyō de homete aru to yonde miru ki ni naru.
I feel like reading books even in fields I'm not particular interested in when they've gotten good reviews.

しばらくは未練もあったが、最近やっとあきらめる気になった。
Shibaraku wa miren mo atta ga, saikin yatto akirameru ki ni natta.
For a while there I just couldn't let go, but recently I've finally resigned myself to things.

人間、死ぬ気になれば何でも出来る。
Ningen, shinu ki ni nareba nan de mo dekiru.
Human beings can do anything if they go about it as if there was no tomorrow.

金山さんもやっと結婚する気になったらしいよ。
Kanayama-san mo yatto kekkon suru ki ni natta rashii yo.
It looks like Kanayama is finally warming up to the idea of getting married.

いくらおいしいって言われても、生玉子だけは食べる気にならないんだ。
Ikura oishii tte iwarete mo, nama-tamago dake wa taberu ki ni naranai n' da.
Raw eggs are the one thing I can't bring myself to eat, no matter how good people say they are.

両親から顔を見るたびにうるさく言われるが、見合いをする気にはなれない。
Ryōshin kara kao o miru tabi ni urusaku iwareru ga, miai o suru ki ni wa narenai.
My parents bug me about it every time I see them, but I'm not into (I can't see) doing the arranged marriage thing.

☞ *ki ga deru* 気が出る

✣ The dictionary form of the verb in the above examples is often replaced by ~ *shiyō to iu* 〜しようというbefore *ki ni naru* with no significant change in meaning. Examples of this structure follow.

父が手術を受けようという気になってくれて私たちも一安心だ。
Chichi ga shujutsu o ukeyō to iu ki ni natte kurete watashi-tachi mo hito-anshin da.
Now that Dad's ready to have the operation, it's a big relief for the whole family.

真面目に働こうという気になりさえすれば、仕事はすぐ見つかるよ。
Majime ni hatarakō to iu ki ni nari sae sureba, shigoto wa sugu mitsukaru yo.
All you've got to do is get serious about working and you'll find a job right away.

あの人を殺して自分も死のうという気になったこともあります。
Ano hito o koroshite jibun mo shinō to iu ki ni natta koto mo arimasu.
At one point I was all set to kill him and then die myself.

✣ There is an important distinction—implied if not explicit in the original Japanese—between ~ *ki ga aru* 〜気がある, which is simply descriptive of one's present state of mind, and ~ *ki ni naru* 〜気になる, which implies that ones present thoughts on the topic of discussion are different from before.

☞ *ki ga aru* 〜気がある, ~ *ki ga okoru* 〜気が起こる

2. feel like one has already done something when one hasn't

応募葉書を出しただけなのにもう抽選に当たった気になっている。
Ōbo-hagaki o dashita dake na no ni mō chūsen ni atatta ki ni natte iru.
I may have just mailed in the postcard, but I already feel like a winner.

旅行案内を読んで行った気になれるんだから、安上がりだね。
Ryokō annai o yonde itta ki ni nareru n' da kara, yasuagari da ne.

It's a cheap way to travel when you feel like you've already been there just from reading the travel brochure.

パン屋さんでちょうど焼たてのパンが買えると得したような気になるね。
Panya-san de chōdo yakitate no pan ga kaeru to toku-shita yō na ki ni naru ne.
You get the feeling that you've really lucked out when you go to a bakery and they've just put out the fresh stuff, don't you.

❧ Similar to ~ (*yō na*) *ki ga suru* 〜(ような)気がする, the expressions are interchangeable in the three examples above without altering the meaning. While ~ *ki ga suru* 〜気がする is a straightforward description of one's present state of mind, however, (*shita yō na*) *ki ni naru* 〜気になる suggests a *fanciful* change in one's attitude or feeling, or that one's present feelings on the topic of discussion are somehow different from before.

ki ni naru 気になる "become *ki*"

bother, be bothered by, be (have something) on one's mind, be disturbing, be (get) on one's nerves, wonder about, worry about, be worrying

きちょうめんな人だから壁の絵がちょっと曲がっても気になるらしい。
Kichōmen na hito da kara kabe no e ga chotto magatte mo ki ni naru rashii.
He's such a stickler for detail that if there's a picture on the wall that's even a little bit cockeyed, it bothers him.

隣の部屋の話し声が気になって勉強できない。
Tonari no heya no hanashigoe ga ki ni natte benkyō dekinai.
I can't study with all the jabbering going on next door.

気にしている素振りはみせないが、内心気になっているに違いない。

Ki ni shite iru soburi wa misenai ga, naishin ki ni natte iru ni chigainai.
He may act as if it's nothing, but down deep it's got to be getting to him.

今日の試合が気になってゆうべはよく眠れなかった。
Kyō no shiai ga ki ni natte yūbe wa yoku nemurenakatta.
I couldn't sleep last night thinking about the game today.

彼女の欠点も気にならないどころかえって可愛いぐらいだ。
Kanojo no ketten mo ki ni naranai dokoro ka kaette kawaii gurai da.
I not only don't mind her foibles, I actually think they're kind of cute.

彼女が別れ際に何を言おうとしたのか気になる。
Kanojo ga wakare-giwa ni nani o iō to shita no ka ki ni naru.
I can't help wondering what she was about to say just before we parted ways.

ボロ車なので都心で走ると他人の目が気になる。
Boro-guruma na no de toshin de hashiru to tanin no me ga ki ni naru.
My car's such a junker that I get self-conscious when I'm driving downtown.

まだ気になることが一つだけ残っている。
Mada ki ni naru koto ga hitotsu dake nokotte iru.
There's just one other thing that still bothers me.

美人の新入社員が気になって見積もり書の計算をまちがえた。
Bijin no shinnyū-shain ga ki ni natte mitsumori-sho no keisan o machigaeta.
I couldn't get my mind off the good-looking new woman in the office and ended up messing up the estimate I was working on.

宝くじの当選番号発表が気になって仕事が手につかない。
Takarakuji no tōsen-bangō happyō ga ki ni natte shigoto ga te ni tsukanai.
I can't get any work done, thinking about what number is going to win the lottery.

こうやって料理すればにんにくの臭いも気になりませんよ。
Kō yatte ryōri sureba ninniku no nioi mo ki ni narimasen yo.
If you cook it like this, the garlic odor won't bother you.

気になるお値段ですが、三枚組み特別価格は￥13、900でお買い得です。

Ki ni naru onedan desu ga, sanmai-gumi tokubetsu-kakaku wa ichiman-sanzen-kyūhyaku-en de okaidoku desu.

And now for what you have all been waiting for, our special, one-time-only price of ¥13,900 for a package of three.

☞ *ki ni suru* 気にする, *ki ni kakaru* 気にかかる

~ *ki ni saseru* ～気にさせる

make someone (want to) do something, convince someone to do something, bring someone around

「お子さんを勉強する気にさせるのはお母さんの役目ですよ」と言われた。
"Okosan o benkyō suru ki ni saseru no wa okāsan no yakume desu yo" to iwareta.
She told me, "It's a mother's job to make her children want to study."

弟を結婚する気にさせようと両親はいろんな手を使っている。
Otōto o kekkon suru ki ni saseyō to ryōshin wa ironna te o tsukatte iru.
My parents are pulling out all the stops to get my younger brother in the mood to marry.

ki ni sawaru 気に障(触)る "to touch *ki*"

annoy, bother, get to one, irritate

あいつの一言一言が気に障る。
Aitsu no hitokoto hitokoto ga ki ni sawaru.
Every little thing he says gets on my nerves.

いったい何が谷川さんの気に障ったんだろう。

Ittai nani ga Tanikawa-san no ki ni sawatta n' darō.
I wonder just what it was that rubbed Ms. Tanikawa the wrong way.

正直に言います。お気に障ったらお許し下さい。
Shōjiki ni iimasu. Oki ni sawattara oyurushi kudasai.
I'll be frank, and I hope you'll forgive me if what I say offends you.

↝ *ki o waruku suru* 気を悪くする

ki ni suru 気にする "make into *ki*"

be bothered by, care, have something on one's mind, let something get to one, mind, pay attention to, take something to heart

彼のこと気にしないで。
Kare no koto ki ni shinai de.
Forget him! / Don't let him bother you!

気にすんなよ。
Ki ni sun' na yo.
Don't sweat it, man! / Hang loose!

✌ *sun' na*: a contraction of *suru na*

あの人に言われたことなんて気にすることはないよ。
Ano hito ni iwareta koto nante ki ni suru koto wa nai yo.
Don't worry about what he says. / Don't let anything he says bother you.

体重を気にして、コーヒーはブラックで飲んでいる。
Taijū o ki ni shite, kōhī wa burakku de nonde iru.
I drink my coffee black because I'm watching my weight.

この間のことは気にしていませんから忘れてください。
Kono aida no koto wa ki ni shite imasen kara wasurete kudasai.
What happened the other day is water under the bridge as far as I'm concerned (I'm not going to make an issue of what happened the other day), so just forget it.

鹿は人間を気にする様子もなくゆっくり歩いていった。
Shika wa ningen o ki ni suru yōsu mo naku yukkuri aruite itta.
The deer was ambling along and didn't appear at all concerned about the people.

学生は授業が終わる時間を気にして時計ばかり見ている。
Gakusei wa jugyō ga owaru jikan o ki ni shite tokei bakari mite iru.
The students are doing nothing but looking at their watches, the main thing on their minds being when the class will end.

田中の奴、鈴木さんを気にしてカッコつけてるんだ。
Tanaka no yatsu, Suzuki-san o ki ni shite kakko tsukete 'ru n' da.
Tanaka's acting cool 'cause he's got the hots for Suzuki.

☞ *ki ni naru* 気になる, *ki ni tomeru* 気に止める

ki ni tomeru 気に止める "stop in *ki*"

be aware of, notice, occur to, pay attention to, bear in mind

最初は通りの暗さを気に止めていなかったが、だんだん不安になった。
Saisho wa tōri no kurasa o ki ni tomete inakatta ga, dandan fuan ni natta.
At first it didn't register just how dark the street was, but pretty soon I got nervous about it.

こうした問題をまったく気に止めていないようだ。
Kōshita mondai o mattaku ki ni tomete inai yō da.
None of these problems appears to affect him in the slightest.

❈ *kōshita*: = *kono yō na*

年寄りの言うことも少しは気に止めるものだ。
Toshiyori no iu koto mo sukoshi wa ki ni tomeru mono da.
You can't entirely ignore what old folks say.

これだけは気に止めて、くれぐれも無茶なことはするな。
Kore dake wa ki ni tomete, kuregure mo mucha na koto wa suru na.
There's one thing I want you to bear in mind: whatever you do, don't go overboard.

標識を気に止めないで走っていたら道に迷ってしまったよ。
Hyōshiki o ki ni tomenai de hashitte itara michi ni mayotte shimatta yo.
I was just going along on my merry way, not paying any attention to the road signs, and I ended up getting lost.

☞ *ki ni suru* 気にする

ki ni yamu 気に病む "to sicken *ki*"

worry (needlessly) about, fret over, stew

そんなこと気に病むなよ。
Sonna koto ki ni yamu na yo.
Don't let a silly thing like that bother you.

彼女は噂をよく気に病むたちなんだ。
Kanojo wa uwasa o yoku ki ni yamu tachi nan da.
She's the type that's always fretting about some rumor or other.

🌑 Similar to *ki ni suru*, but the person about whom it is used is much more deeply troubled, morbidly even, by the cause of concern.

☞ *ki ni suru* 気にする

ki no doku (na) 気の毒(な) "poison of *ki*"

pitiful, regrettable, sad, unfortunate

お気の毒でしたね。
Oki no doku deshita ne.
That's too bad. / I'm sorry to hear that. / I'm so sorry.

地震の被災者の方々は本当にお気の毒ですね。
Jishin no hisai-sha no katagata wa hontō ni oki no doku desu ne.
It's really terrible (a pity) about the earthquake victims.

あいつが首になったことなんか、気の毒でも何でもない。自業自得さ。
Aitsu ga kubi ni natta koto nanka, ki no doku de mo nan de mo nai. Jigō-jitoku sa.
I don't feel a bit sorry for him. It's his own fault he got the ax.

小山君には一人で責任を取らせてしまって気の毒なことをしたね。
Koyama-kun ni wa hitori de sekinin o torasete shimatte ki no doku na koto o shita ne.
It's regrettable that we had to let Koyama take all the blame for what happened.

山下さんは気の毒に8人の奥さんを次々に病気で亡くした。
Yamashita-san wa ki no doku ni hachinin no okusan o tsugitsugi ni byōki de nakushita.
Poor old Yamashita lost all eight of his wives to illness.

ki no ii hito 気のいい人 "a person with good *ki*"

an amiable person, a good person, a personable person, a person with a good disposition

厚さんのように気のいい人は珍しいですよ。
Atsushi-san no yō ni ki no ii hito wa mezurashii desu yo.
People as good-natured as Atsushi are rare.

彼は気のいい人で決して他人の言うことを悪くとらない。

Kare wa ki no ii hito de kesshite tanin no iu koto o waruku toranai.
He's such a prince that he'd never take anything the wrong way.

☞ *ki ga ii* 気がいい

ki no mochiyō 気の持ちよう "way of holding one's *ki*"

one's frame of mind, how one looks at it (things)

幸福か不幸かは最終的には本人の気の持ちようによるもんだ。
Kōfuku ka fukō ka wa saishū-teki ni wa honnin no ki no mochiyō ni yoru mon da.
Fortune or misfortune ultimately depend on how you look at things. / Whether a person is happy or not ultimately depends on how he views things.

気の持ちようひとつで人生180度変わるんですよ。
Ki no mochiyō hitotsu de jinsei hyakuhachijū-do kawaru n' desu yo.
A change in your frame of mind can completely turn your life around.

ki no sei 気のせい "because of *ki*"

it's all in one's head (imagination), must be imagining things, be a figment of one's imagination

電話鳴らなかった？ 気のせいかな。
Denwa naranakatta? Ki no sei ka na.
Did the phone ring, or am I just imagining things?

近ごろときどき胸のあたりが痛むので医者へ行ったら気のせいだと言われた。藪医者め！

Chikagoro tokidoki mune no atari ga itamu no de isha e ittara ki no sei da to iwareta. Yabu-isha me!

You know, I've been having these chest pains lately so I went to the doctor, and you know what that quack told me? "It's all in your head."

太った人が暑がりなのは気のせいではなく、科学的根拠がある。
Futotta hito ga atsugari na no wa ki no sei de wa naku, kagaku-teki konkyo ga aru.

There's more to fat people feeling hot all the time than their imaginations; there's a scientific reason for it.

気のせいか、この人には貴族の風格が漂っている。
Ki no sei ka, kono hito ni wa kizoku no fūkaku ga tadayotte iru.

I don't know if it's all in my head or what, but there's something aristocratic about that person.

ki no yamai 気の病 "illness of *ki*"

an illness brought on by emotional fatigue, a psychosomatic illness, neurosis

家族からも気の病だと言われて相手にしてもらえない。
Kazoku kara mo ki no yamai da to iwarete aite ni shite moraenai.
Even my family tells me that it's all in my head and won't take me seriously.

この患者さんは検査でも異常はないし、気の病の要素が強いから神経科受診を勧めた。
Kono kanja-san wa kensa de mo ijō wa nai shi, ki no yamai no yōso ga tsuyoi kara shinkei-ka jushin o susumeta.
Since nothing irregular showed up on the tests we ran on this patient and there is reason to believe his illness is largely psychosomatic, I recommended that he see someone in neurology.

↣ *ki de ki o yamu* 気で気を病む

ki o haku 気を吐く "spit *ki* out"

(of speech) talk up a storm; (of behavior) do a good job, outdo oneself, put on a good show, work out

中山さんは自信満々で盛んに気を吐いている。
Nakayama-san wa jishin-manman de sakan ni ki o haite iru.
Nakayama's brimming with confidence and going all out.

同窓会では旧友と大いに気を吐き合った。
Dōsō-kai de wa kyūyū to ōi ni ki o hakiatta.
I talked up a storm with an old friend at the reunion.

ki o harasu 気を晴らす "clear up *one's ki*"

divert oneself, do something to take one's mind off one's problems, [do something to] forget one's troubles

気を晴らすのに何かいい方法はないだろうか。
Ki o harasu no ni nanika ii hōhō wa nai darō ka.
You don't know a good way I can get my mind off my troubles, do you?

少し外へ出て気を晴らさないとこのままでは病気になってしまうよ。
Sukoshi soto e dete ki o harasanai to kono mama de wa byōki ni natte shimau yo.
If you don't get out to clear the air, you'll end up making yourself sick.

☞ *ki ga fusagaru* 気がふさがる, *ki ga meiru* 気が滅入る

ki o haritsumeru 気を張りつめる "to draw *ki* taut"

be on edge, on one's toes; be tense, under a strain, under a lot of pressure

受験生たちはみんな気を張りつめた表情で教室へ向かった。
Jukensei-tachi wa minna ki o haritsumeta hyōjō de kyōshitsu e mukatta.
All those taking the test headed for the classroom with tense looks on their faces.

朝から気を張りつめていて、すっかり肩がこっちゃったよ。
Asa kara ki o haritsumete ite, sukkari kata ga kotchatta yo.
I've been under such a strain since morning that now I've got a stiff neck.

❀ *Ki o haritsumeru* describes a more intense form of concentration or tension than *ki o haru*.

☞ *ki ga haru* 気が張る; *ki ga yasumaru* 気が休まる

ki o haru 気を張る "stretch *ki* out"

be ready (for anything), be on one's guard, be on the lookout for

そんなに気を張らなくても大丈夫だよ。
Sonna ni ki o haranakute mo daijōbu da yo.
You don't have to be so uptight.

試合中は気を張ってるから寒さなんか感じないのさ。
Shiai-chū wa ki o hatte 'ru kara samusa nanka kanjinai no sa.
I'm so focused during a game that a little cold doesn't even register.

☞ *ki ga haru* 気が張る, *ki o hikishimeru* 気を引き締める

ki o hikishimeru 気を引き締める "tighten *ki*"

get oneself worked up for, screw oneself up for (to do) something, steel oneself

気を引き締めるために当分酒を断とうと思う。
Ki o hikishimeru tame ni tōbun sake o tatō to omou.
I'm going to lay off the booze for a while and get my act together.

中日まで全勝の貴錦はいっそう気を引き締めていた。
Nakabi made zenshō no Takanishiki wa issō ki o hikishimete ita.
With a perfect win record going into the ninth day of the tournament, [the Sumo wrestler] Takanishiki was really psyched up.

チーム全員が気を引き締めて決勝戦に臨んでもらいたい。
Chīmu zen'in ga ki o hikishimete kesshō-sen ni nozonde moraitai.
I want everybody on the team to pull himself together and get focused on the championship.

油断大敵だ。気を引き締めてかかれ。
Yudan-taiteki da. Ki o hikishimete kakare.
Letting up now is the worst thing you can do. You've gotta want it. Now go out there and give 'em hell!

☞ *ki ga hikishimaru* 気が引き締まる

ki o hiku 気を引く "pull *ki*"

get someone to notice (pay attention to) one, sound (feel) someone out (about how he or she feels about oneself)

彼はしきりと私の気を引くような素振りを見せているのよ。
Kare wa shikiri to watashi no ki o hiku yō na soburi o misete iru no yo.
He's doing his best to attract my attention.

あの人の気を引こうといろいろ試してみたが、全く反応がない。
Ano hito no ki o hikō to shite iroiro tameshite mita ga, mattaku hannō ga nai.
I've tried everything I can think of to get him to notice me, but there's been absolutely no reaction.

🐧 Used of someone trying indirectly to gain the attention and affection of the opposite sex, it has nothing to do with whistling or waving arms.

ki o ireru 気を入れる "put *one's ki* into"

get into doing something, get enthusiastic about something

好きでもないことに気を入れるのは実に難しい。
Suki de mo nai koto ni ki o ireru no wa jitsu ni muzukashii.
It's really hard to get into doing something that you don't like.

もっと気を入れて勉強しないと、いつまでたっても試験には受からないよ。
Motto ki o irete benkyō shinai to, itsu made tatte mo shiken ni wa ukaranai yo.
If you don't buckle down and study, you're never going to pass the test.

🐧 Compared to *ki ga hairu*, *ki o ireru* implies that conscious effort is involved.

↪ *honki de ~ o suru* 本気で〜をする, *ki ga hairu* 気が入る, *koshi o ireru* 腰を入れる, *mi o ireru* 身を入れる

ki o kikasu 気を利かす "to work *ki*"

[try to] be thoughtful, considerate; use one's head

少し気を利かすことも覚えなくちゃ、秘書としては失格だね。
Sukoshi ki o kikasu koto mo oboenakucha, hisho toshite wa shikkaku da ne.
You've got to learn to be more thoughtful. As it is, you can't call yourself a secretary.

気を利かしたつもりが、余計なお節介になってしまった。
Ki o kikashita tsumori ga, yokei na osekkai ni natte shimatta.
Trying to be considerate (helpful) just ended up causing more problems.

気を利かして若い二人だけにしてあげた。
Ki o kikashite wakai futari dake ni shite ageta.
Realizing that I might be a third wheel, I left the two young folks to themselves.

🕸 Unlike *ki ga kiku*, which is most commonly used about others, *ki o kikasu* is used primarily of oneself, indicating a conscious act of will or intention, or when advising others to act a certain way.

Also 気を利かせる *ki o kikaseru*.
☞ *ki ga kiku* 気が利く

ki o kubaru　気を配る　"distribute *ki*"

pay attention to, take care (to), be careful (to), take pains (to)

もう少し身だしなみに気を配るようにしたらどうだい？
Mō sukoshi midashinami ni ki o kubaru yō ni shitara dō dai?
Don't you think you ought to pay a little more attention to your appearance?

平等になるように気を配ったが、それでも一部の人から苦情が出た。
Byōdō ni naru yō ni ki o kubatta ga, sore de mo ichibu no hito kara kujō ga deta.
I was careful to arrange things equitably, but there were still complaints from some people.

出発日によって航空運賃が違うから、スケジュールの調整には気を配るべきだ。
Shuppatsu-bi ni yotte kōkū-unchin ga chigau kara, sukejūru no chōsei ni wa ki o kubaru beki da.

You should take care when deciding your itinerary because airline ticket prices vary depending on the date of departure.

See note at *kizukau* 気遣う for explanation of differences among this entry, *kizukau*, and *ki o tsukau* 気を使う.

☞ *ki o tsukau* 気を使う, *kikubari* 気配り

ki o magirawasu 気を紛らわす "divert *ki*"

divert one's attention, find a diversion, get (take) one's mind off

僕たちが心配しなくても、彼には気を紛らわす方法はたくさんあるさ。
Boku-tachi ga shinpai shinakute mo, kare ni wa ki o magirawasu hōhō wa takusan aru sa.
There's nothing for us to worry about 'cause there are plenty of things he can do to take his mind off his problems.

昼間はパチンコしたり映画に行ったりして適当に気を紛らわしている。
Hiruma wa pachinko shitari eiga ni ittari shite tekitō ni ki o magirawashite iru.
I'm doing what I can to keep my mind off my problems by playing pinball and going to the movies during the day.

⚜ Not to be confused with the related expression *kimagure na* 気紛れ(な), which means "capricious," "fickle" or "whimsical," *ki o magirawasu* indicates intention to escape from an unpleasant emotional state, and in this respect also differs slightly from its cognate *ki ga magireru*, which, although used to describe the same phenomenon, does so by depicting the resulting relief as a natural course of events rather than one specifically sought after or willed.

Also 気を紛らわせる *ki o magirawaseru*.

↪ *ki ga magireru* 気が紛れる

ki o mawasu 気を回す "rotate *one's ki*"

be mistrustful, (overly) suspicious, suspecting, uptight; get the wrong idea, take something (someone) wrong

そこまで気を回す必要はない。
Soko made ki o mawasu hitsuyō wa nai.
I think you're reading too much into the situation.

君は気を回し過ぎるよ。
Kimi wa ki o mawashisugiru yo.
You try to read between the lines too much. / You think too much.

❦ Not to be confused with its cognate *ki ga mawaru* 気が回る, which means to be thoughtful or considerate. *Ki o mawasu* is used critically of one who is thought to be either too suspicious, always looking for an ulterior motive which doesn't exist, or worrying needlessly about insignificant things.

ki o momu 気を揉む "crumple *ki*"

be anxious; fret, fuss, stew, worry

君が気を揉むのも無理はないが、連絡があるまで待つよりしかたないだろう。
Kimi ga ki o momu no mo muri wa nai ga, renraku ga aru made matsu yori shikata nai darō.
It's understandable that you'd be sweating things out, but there's not much you can do except wait for them to contact you.

お父さんが気を揉んでもどうしようもないんだから、少し落ち着いたら。
Otōsan ga ki o monde mo dō shiyō mo nai n' da kara, sukoshi ochitsuitara.
It's not going to do you any good to get all worked up, Dad. Why don't you just try to relax?

まったくいくつになっても親に気を揉ませる娘だ。
Mattaku ikutsu ni natte mo oya ni ki o momaseru musume da.
When are you going to start acting your age so your parents don't have to worry about you all the time?

☞ *ki ga momeru* 気が揉める

ki o motaseru 気を持たせる "give someone *ki* to hold"

get someone's hopes up, raise someone's expectations

気を持たせられてさ、脈があると思ったのが甘かった。
Ki o motaserarete sa, myaku ga aru to omotta no ga amakatta.
The way she got my hopes up, I thought I had a chance. Guess it was wishful thinking.

🌿 *myaku ga aru*: literally, "have a pulse"; figuratively, have a future. When used of relations between the sexes, indicates a hope that one may gain the favor of another.

さんざん気を持たせておきながら土壇場で逃げてしまった。
Sanzan ki o motasete okinagara dotanba de nigete shimatta.
He led me on, then dumped me at the last minute.

ki o ~ motsu 気を〜持つ "hold *one's ki* (in some way)"

to assume a (certain) attitude

In general, the expressions mentioned below (see their separate entries) are used when advising someone or describing the attitude of a person who is preparing to deal with a difficult situation. An adverb, the *-ku* form of an *-i* adjective, or the *ni* form of a *na* adjective appears in the ellipsis. With the exception of *ki o shikkari motsu,* the idioms that follow are each related to another similar expression included in this book. The differences between them and *ki ga tashika (na), ki ga tsuyoi, ki ga nagai*, and *ki ga raku (na)* are as follows.

The distinction between *ki ga tsuyoi* and *ki o tsuyoku motsu* is representative of the others. While the former is used of those perceived to be more tenacious or stubborn than normal, and thus describes an uncommon personality trait, the latter is an admonition not to waver or weaken in the face of some disasterous or trying situation—not, in other words, to become fainthearted or *ki ga yowai*, the opposite of *ki ga tsuyoi*. A person who is described as *ki o tsuyoku motte iru,* therefore, is not necessarily particularly strong-willed. Similarly, *kiraku na* describes a laid-back personality and *ki o raku ni shite* a relatively relaxed situation while *ki o raku ni motte* encourages someone who has already tensed up not to do so, or at least to remain as unperturbed as possible.

---

ki o nagaku motsu 気を長く持つ "hold *ki* for a long time"
be patient, persevere, stick to something

外国との合弁事業の成功には気を長く持つことが必要です。
Gaikoku to no gōben-jigyō no seikō ni wa ki o nagaku motsu koto ga hitsuyō desu.
Making a go of an international joint venture requires patience (a long-term commitment).

焦って失敗するより、気を長く持ってよい結果を待ちましょう。
Asette shippai suru yori, ki o nagaku motte yoi kekka o machimashō.
Instead of getting impatient, why don't we hang on and see how it turns out.

↪ *ki ga nagai* 気が長い

ki o nomareru 気を呑まれる "have one's *ki* swallowed"

be overpowered; be set back on one's heels, be taken aback

会場の熱気にすっかり気を呑まれてしまった。
Kaijō no nekki ni sukkari ki o nomarete shimatta.
I was overcome by the excitement that swept the place.

最初から最後まで気を呑まれっぱなしだったよ。
Saisho kara saigo made ki o nomareppanashi datta yo.
I was simply overwhelmed from beginning to end.

ki o nuku 気を抜く "take *ki* out"

let up, relax, become (get) careless, goof off

気を抜くと、思わぬところで失敗するよ。
Ki o nuku to, omowanu tokoro de shippai suru yo.
Start daydreaming and you'll screw up when you least expect to.

リハーサルはうまくいったのでつい気を抜いたのがよくなかった。
Rihāsaru wa umaku itta no de tsui ki o nuita no ga yoku nakatta.
The rehearsal went so well that I sort of relaxed, and that was a mistake.

最後まで気を抜かないできちんとやりなさい。
Saigo made ki o nukanai de kichin to yarinasai.
No sloughing off. Don't let up till you've finished everything.

❧ Distinguished from its cognate *ki ga nukeru* insofar as it indicates intentionality or willfulness.

☞ *ki ga nukeru* 気が抜ける, *ki o yurumeru* 気を緩める; *ki o ireru* 気を入れる

ki o ochitsukeru 気を落ち着ける "calm *ki* down"

calm oneself down, regain one's composure, settle down

大失敗の後、気を落ち着ける間もなく次の仕事にかからねばならなかった。
Daishippai no ato, ki o ochitsukeru ma mo naku tsugi no shigoto ni kakaraneba naranakatta.
Right after this major screw-up I had to pull myself together and start right in on another job.

気を落ちつけて最初からもう一度話して下さい。
Ki o ochitsukete saisho kara mō ichido hanashite kudasai.
Now calm down and start again from the beginning.

Also 気を落ち着かせる *ki o ochitsukaseru.*
☞ *ki o shizumeru* 気を静める

ki o otosu 気を落とす "drop *ki*"

be (become) dejected, depressed, despondent, disheartened, downcast

よくあることだから、気を落とすことはないさ。
Yoku aru koto da kara, ki o otosu koto wa nai sa.
It could happen to anybody, don't let it get you down. / Happens all the time, man. Don't sweat it.

南田さんは3年もつきあっていた彼女にふられて気を落としている。
Minamida-san wa sannen mo tsukiatte ita kanojo ni furarete ki o otoshite iru.
Minamida's bummed out 'cause this gal he'd been going out with for three years dumped him.

気を落とさないで。またいいこともあるよ。
Ki o otosanaide. Mata ii koto mo aru yo.
Don't get so discouraged. Things will start looking up before long.

☞ *kiochi suru* 気落ちする

ki o raku ni motsu 気を楽に持つ "hold *ki* easily"

calm oneself, relax, take it easy

面接試験では気を楽に持って自分の言葉で話しなさい。
Mensetsu-shiken de wa ki o raku ni motte jibun no kotoba de hanashinasai.
When you go for the interview, just relax and speak as you normally do.

堅くならないで、どうぞ気を楽にお持ち下さい。
Kataku naranai de, dōzo ki o raku ni omochi kudasai.
Try not to tense up; just go ahead and relax.

☞ *ki ga raku (na)* 気が楽(な), ki o ~ motsu 気を〜持つ

ki o raku ni suru 気を楽にする "relax *one's ki*"

relax, make oneself at home

気を楽にするために何回か深呼吸してみた。
Ki o raku ni suru tame ni nankai ka shin-kokyū shite mita.
I took several deep breaths to try and relax.

そこへ横になって気を楽にしてください。
Soko e yoko ni natte ki o raku ni shite kudasai.
Lie down there and relax, please.

☞ *ki ga raku (na)* 気が楽(な), *ki ga raku ni naru* 気が楽になる, *ki o raku ni motsu* 気を楽に持つ, *kiraku (na)* 気楽な

ki o shikkari motsu 気をしっかり持つ "hold *ki* firmly"

be brave, be strong, brace up, buck up, hang tough

傷は浅いですよ。気をしっかり持ちなさい。
Kizu wa asai desu yo. Ki o shikkari mochinasai.
It's a shallow wound. Hang in there.

気をしっかり持って聞いて下さい。残念なお知らせです。
Ki o shikkari motte kiite kudasai. Zannen na oshirase desu.
You've got to be brave now. I've got some bad news.

⚜ Used to urge someone not to give in to pain, not to lose consciousness. No similar expression using *ki*.

☞ *ki o ~ motsu* 気を〜持つ

ki o shizumeru 気を静める "quiet *ki* down"

calm down, get a grip (on oneself), get hold of oneself, settle down

気を静めてよく聞いてほしいんだ。
Ki o shizumete yoku kiite hoshii n' da.
Simmer down now and listen.

まずはこれでも飲んで気を静めることだ。
Mazu wa kore de mo nonde ki o shizumeru koto da.
The first thing you've got to do is take (drink) this and try to calm yourself down.

↝ *ki ga shizumaru* 気が静まる, *ki o ochitsukeru* 気を落ち着ける

ki o sogu 気をそぐ "shave off *ki*"

dampen, dishearten, throw cold water on, throw a wet blanket on

せっかくやる気になってるのに気をそぐようなこと言うもんじゃないよ。
Sekkaku yaru ki ni natte 'ru no ni ki o sogu yō na koto iu mon ja nai yo.
Why are you trying to discourage him just when he's getting into it?

あの人の一言ですっかり気をそがれてしまった。
Ano hito no hitokoto de sukkari ki o sogarete shimatta.
One word from him was all it took to put a damper on my enthusiasm.

ki o sorasu 気を逸らす "divert *ki*"

1. let one's mind wander, lose concentration, stop paying attention, wool-gather

機械での作業中に気を逸らすのは事故につながる。
Kikai de no sagyō-chū ni ki o sorasu no wa jiko ni tsunagaru.
If you let yourself get distracted when you're operating machinery, it could lead to an accident.

気を逸らさないでちゃんと聞きなさい。
Ki o sorasanai de chanto kikinasai.
Quit fooling around and pay attention.

2. break someone's concentration, distract, divert someone's attention, get someone's attention

俺がサツの気を逸らすから、その間にお前は裏口へ回れ。
Ore ga satsu no ki o sorasu kara, sono aida ni omae wa uraguchi e maware.
While I'm distracting the cop, you go around to the back.

先生の気を宿題から逸らそうとして皆で次々に質問した。
Sensei no ki o shukudai kara sorasō to shite minna de tsugi-tsugi ni shitsumon shita.
Everyone was asking all kinds of questions, trying to make the teacher forget about the homework assignment.

☞ *ki ga soreru* 気が逸れる

ki o tashika ni motsu 気を確かに持つ "hold *ki* certainly"

brace up, hang on, hold on, ready oneself, summon one's courage

母さん、気を確かに持ってくれ。父さんの病気はもう手遅れだそうだ。
Kāsan, ki o tashika ni motte kure. Tōsan no byōki wa mō te-okure da sō da.
Brace yourself, Mom. They say there's nothing they can do now for Dad.

取り乱すんじゃない。気を確かに持つんだ。

Torimidasu n' ja nai. Ki o tashika ni motsu n' da.
Don't go to pieces on me now. Get hold of yourself.

☞ *ki ga tashika (na)* 気が確か(な), *ki o ~ motsu* 気を〜持つ, *shōki* 正気

ki o torareru 気を取られる "have one's *ki* taken"

one's mind is taken off something, get distracted

運転中に窓の外に気を取られると危険だよ。
Unten-chū ni mado no soto ni ki o torareru to kiken da yo.
Don't let yourself get distracted while you're driving. It's dangerous.

派手な喧嘩に気を取られているうちに財布をすられたらしいんです。
Hade na kenka ni ki o torarete iru uchi ni saifu o surareta rashii n' desu.
I guess I must have had my pocket picked while my attention was diverted by a loud argument.

前の席の美人に気を取られて、講義が耳に入らなかった。
Mae no seki no bijin ni ki o torarete, kōgi ga mimi ni hairanakatta.
I got distracted by this raving beauty sitting in front of me in class and didn't hear a thing the prof said.

🕸 For what it's worth, the result of having your *ki* "taken" (*ki o torareru*) is that your *ki* "disperses" (*ki ga chiru*).

☞ *ki ga chiru* 気が散る

ki o torinaosu 気を取り直す "grab hold of *ki* again"

buck up, collect oneself, collect one's thoughts, pull oneself together, regroup

今は先のことを心配するよりまず気を取り直すことだ。
Ima wa saki no koto o shinpai suru yori mazu ki o torinaosu koto da.
Right now it's more important for you to pull yourself together than worry about the future.

人生これからなんだから、気を取り直して頑張れよ。
Jinsei kore kara nan da kara, ki o torinaoshite ganbare yo.
Look, you've got your whole life ahead of you, so just pull yourself together and keep plugging away.

西村さんは少し気を取り直したらしく、笑顔も見せるようになった。
Nishimura-san wa sukoshi ki o torinaoshita rashiku, egao mo miseru yō ni natta.
Nishimura seems to have perked up a bit and has even started to smile.

ki o tsukau 気を使う "use *ki*"

1. (of people) look after, take (good) care of, take pains

添乗員というのは気を使うわりに感謝されない仕事だよ。
Tenjō-in to iu no wa ki o tsukau wari ni kansha sarenai shigoto da yo.
For all the pains they take, tour conductors don't get much respect. / Being a tour conductor is a thankless job that requires a lot of painstaking work.

どうぞもう気を使わないでください。
Dōzo mō ki o tsukawanai de kudasai.
Don't worry about me. / Don't mind me.

あまり気を使われるとかえって窮屈な思いをする。
Amari ki o tsukawareru to kaette kyūkutsu na omoi o suru.
It's actually an imposition when someone's always fussing over you.

へんに気を使わずに遠慮なく言ってもらった方がいい。
Hen ni ki o tsukawazu ni enryo naku itte moratta hō ga ii.
Why don't you tell me what you think without worrying how I'm going to feel about it (take it).

2. (of things or events) pay attention to, be uppermost in one's thoughts

どの都市も水源地の環境保全にはかなり気を使っている。
Dono toshi mo suigen-chi no kankyō-hozen ni wa kanari ki o tsukatte iru.
Urban areas all over are paying close attention to the protection of their watersheds.

営業でよく外を歩くので、靴には人一倍気を使う。
Eigyō de yoku soto o aruku no de, kutsu ni wa hito-ichibai ki o tsukau.
I'm pounding the pavement all the time on my sales route, so I pay a lot more attention to my shoes than most people do.

食事にも気を使い、自然食品を買うようにしている。
Shokuji ni mo ki o tsukai, shizen-shokuhin o kau yō ni shite iru.
I also watch what I eat and try to buy natural foods when I can.

アメリカ人が健康に気を使い出して20年もたっています。
Amerika-jin ga kenkō ni ki o tsukaidashite nijū-nen mo tatte imasu.
Twenty years have already passed since Americans first began to pay attention to their health.

細かいところにまで気を使ったデザインですよね。
Komakai tokoro ni made ki o tsukatta dezain desu yo ne.
They sure have paid close attention to detail in this design.

🐙 See the note at *kizukau* 気遣う for the differences among this entry, *kizukau*, and *ki o kubaru* 気を配る.

↪ *ki o kubaru* 気を配る, *kizukau* 気遣う, *kigane (o) suru* 気兼ね(を)する

ki o tsukeru 気をつける "put *ki* on"

be attentive (to), be careful, take note of, take care (of)

気をつけて。
Ki o tsukete.
Be careful. / Take care. / Have a good time. [A common expression when parting company.]

今回は見逃すが、この次からよく気をつけるようにしなさい。
Konkai wa minogasu ga, kono tsugi kara yoku ki o tsukeru yō ni shinasai.
I'm going to overlook (I'm not going to make an issue of) it this time, but you'd better be a little more careful from now on.

夜はまだ冷えますから、どうぞお体にはお気をつけて。
Yoru wa mada hiemasu kara, dōzo okarada ni wa oki o tsukete.
The nights still get chilly, so take good care of yourself. [A typical ending for a letter written in early spring.]

気をつけてよく見ると小さい虫がたくさん葉の裏にいた。
Ki o tsukete yoku miru to chiisai mushi ga takusan ha no ura ni ita.
If you look really carefully, you can see all kinds of tiny insects on the underside of the leaf.

これからの季節に気をつけたいのが食中毒だ。
Kore kara no kisetsu ni ki o tsuketai no ga shoku-chūdoku da.
One thing you want to watch out for this time of year is food poisoning.

痛い！　気をつけろよ。あぶないなあ。
Itai! Ki o tsukero yo. Abunai nā.
Ouch! Watch it, huh. You're going to hurt somebody.

🕸 By the way, The Japanese military equivalent of the English "Attention!" is *"Ki o tsuke!"*

☞ *ki o kubaru* 気を配る

ki o tsuyoku motsu 気を強く持つ "hold *ki* strongly"

keep the faith, be resolute, be steadfast, be strong, be unwavering

子供たちのためにもあなたが気を強く持って頑張って下さい。
Kodomo-tachi no tame ni mo anata ga ki o tsuyoku motte ganbatte kudasai.
For the children's sake too, you must be strong.

こんなことぐらいでへこたれないで、気を強く持とうよ。
Konna koto gurai de hekotarenai de, ki o tsuyoku motō yo.
Hey, don't let something like this get you down. Pull yourself together.

☞ *ki ga tsuyoi* 気が強い, *ki o ~ motsu* 気を〜持つ

ki o ushinau 気を失う "lose *ki*"

black out, faint, go out like a light, lose consciousness, pass out, slip into unconsciousness (darkness)

ボクシングではスパーリング中に打たれて気を失うことも珍しくない。
Bokushingu de wa supāringu-chū ni utarete ki o ushinau koto mo mezurashiku nai.
In boxing it's not all that uncommon to get knocked out when you're just sparring.

大統領は即死だったが夫人は気を失っただけで無事だった。
Daitōryō wa sokushi datta ga fujin wa ki o ushinatta dake de buji datta.
The president died instantly, but his wife just fainted and emerged unscathed.

✤ Entails a complete loss of consciousness, unlike *ki ga tōku naru* which usually means *feeling* faint.

↪ *ki ga tōku naru* 気が遠くなる (#1), *kizetsu suru* 気絶する; *ki ga tsuku* 気がつく (#3)

ki o waruku suru　気を悪くする　"make *ki* bad"

feel bad; have one's feelings hurt, take offense, be offended

あそこまで言えばいくら友だちでも気を悪くするさ。
Asoko made ieba ikura tomodachi de mo ki o waruku suru sa.
I don't care how good a friend he is, when you say something like that it's bound to hurt his feelings.

気を悪くしたみたいですぐ帰ってしまった。
Ki o waruku shita mitai de sugu kaette shimatta.
She must have been offended (gotten her nose out of joint), the way she up and left.

どうぞお気を悪くなさらないで下さい。
Dōzo oki o waruku nasaranai de kudasai.
Please don't take offense. / Don't take it the wrong way.

↪ *kibun ga warui* 気分が悪い, *ki ni sawaru* 気に障る; *ki o yoku suru* 気をよくする

ki o yasumeru　気を休める　"rest *ki*"

kick back, relax, rest

しばらく休暇でもとって気を休める必要があると医者に言われた。
Shibaraku kyūka de mo totte ki o yasumeru hitsuyō ga aru to isha ni iwareta.
The doctor told me that I ought to take some time off and get a little R&R.

一晩ゆっくり寝て気を休めなさい。話はそれからだ。
Hitoban yukkuri nete ki o yasumenasai. Hanashi wa sore kara da.
Relax and get a good night's sleep. We can talk after that.

🐝 As with other such idioms with either ~ *ga* or ~ *o*, the distinction between *ki ga yasumaru* and *ki o yasumeru* is one of intentionality. Neither should be confused with *ki ga raku ni naru* 気が楽になる or *ki o raku ni suru* 気を楽にする, which mean to "relax" as from a state of nervous agitation. The idioms in this entry are used of a condition of reduced mental activity or stress and the resulting relaxation and refer to a psychological state, although this state is often accompanied by physical inactivity.

☞ *ki ga yasumasu* 木が休まる, *kiyasume* 気休め

ki o yoku suru 気をよくする "make *ki* good"

be buoyed up, encouraged; be in a good mood; flatter oneself

何か気をよくすることがあったらしく朝から機嫌がいい。
Nanika ki o yoku suru koto ga atta rashiku asa kara kigen ga ii.
Something uplifting must have happened to her; she's been in a good mood since morning.

五回のホームランで気をよくしたタイガースは勢いに乗って楽勝した。
Gokai no hōmuran de ki o yoku shita Taigāsu wa ikioi ni notte rakushō shita.
A fifth-inning home run gave the Tigers a lift that carried them on to victory.

彼女と一回だけデートしたぐらいで気をよくするもんじゃないぞ。
Kanojo to ikkai dake dēto shita gurai de ki o yoku suru mon ja nai zo.
You went out with her, like, one time? So what!

思いがけずほめられてすっかり気をよくした。
Omoigakezu homerarete sukkari ki o yoku shita.
I was on cloud nine when she unexpectedly paid me a compliment.

新製品の大ヒットで、社長はかなり気をよくしている。
Shin-seihin no daihitto de, shachō wa kanari ki o yoku shite iru.
The boss is in seventh heaven since that new product's proved so popular.

↪ *kibun ga ii* 気分がいい; *ki o waruku suru* 気を悪くする

ki o yurumeru 気を緩める "loosen *one's ki*"

ease off, let up, relax

気を緩めるつもりはなかったが、どうも疲れが出たようだ。
Ki o yurumeru tsumori wa nakatta ga, dōmo tsukare ga deta yō da.
I never intended to let up, but I guess I must have just been tired or something. / I didn't mean to be careless, but, you know, I was tired and all.

気を緩めないで、もっと真面目にやれ。
Ki o yurumenai de, motto majime ni yare.
Quit goofing off! Pay attention to what you're doing.

🖎 Whereas *ki ga yasumaru* 気が休まる and its cognate *ki o yasumeru* 気を休める are used to describe an action thought to be required for good mental health and therefore carry positive connotations, *ki ga yurumu* and *ki o yurumeru* (together with their synonyms *ki ga nukeru* 気が抜ける and *ki o nuku* 気を抜く) are used of a relaxation incompatible with whatever activity is presently being undertaken and carry negative connotations. The activity may be driving, attending a meeting, or working, something which, in any case, requires one's full attention. As with other ~ *ga* and ~ *o* constructions, the latter indicates that the action is controllable by the agent, while the former indicates the opposite—namely that what happens is beyond control.

☞ *ki ga nukeru* 気が抜ける(#1), *ki o nuku* 気を抜く

ki o yurusu 気を許す "allow *ki*"

1. relax, drop one's guard, let one's guard down, let up

   男に気を許すなよ。
   Otoko ni ki o yurusu na yo.
   Don't let your guard down around men. / Keep those guys at arm's length.

   消防署の当直は夜中でも気を許すことは出来ない。
   Shōbō-sho no tōchoku wa yonaka de mo ki o yurusu koto wa dekinai.
   A fireman on duty can't relax even in the middle of the night.

   あの人との交渉では決して気を許してはならない。
   Ano hito to no kōshō de wa kesshite ki o yurushite wa naranai.
   You have to keep on your toes every minute when you're negotiating with her.

   犯人が気を許した瞬間、警官は彼を取り押さえた。
   Hannin ga ki o yurushita shunkan, keikan wa kare o toriosaeta.
   The police overpowered the criminal the second he relaxed his guard.

☞ *ki ga yurumu* 気が緩む, *ki o yurumeru* 気を緩める, *ki o nuku* 気を抜く

2. open up to someone, let someone into one's heart

   あんな奴に気を許したのが間違いだった。
   Anna yatsu ni ki o yurushita no ga machigai datta.
   I should have never let a guy like him into my life.

   俊雄さんには気を許して何でも話せる。
   Toshio-san ni wa ki o yurushite nan de mo hanaseru.
   I can open up to Toshio and tell him everything.

ki wa kokoro 気は心 "*ki* is heart"

it's the thought that counts, a token of one's appreciation (gratitude)

この程度のことしかできないが、まあ「気は心」と思ってくれ。
Kono teido no koto shika dekinai ga, mā "ki wa kokoro" to omotte kure.
I couldn't get you anything really nice, but I just wanted you to know that my heart's in the right place.

つまらないものですが、「気は心」で、どうぞお受け取りください。
Tsumaranai mono desu ga, "ki wa kokoro" de, dōzo ouketori kudasai.
[It's really nothing, but] I hope you'll accept this small token of my appreciation.

🐾 Used when giving a gift to convey the idea that while the gift or amount of money may be small, the thought behind it is sincere.

↪ *kimochi* 気持ち (#2)

kiai 気合い "matching *ki*s"

backbone, fight, heart, spirit

若の富士の顔は気合いが入っていた。
Wakanofuji no kao wa kiai ga haitte ita.
One look at (the sumo wrestler) Wakanofuji's face and you could tell that he was psyched up.

「気合いを入れろ」とコーチに発破をかけられた。
"Kiai o irero," to kōchi ni happa o kakerareta.
The coach fired me up (lit a fire under me) by yelling "Fight!"

気合いの足りない人間は若くてもダメだ。
Kiai no tarinai ningen wa wakakute mo dame da.

I don't care how young you are, you're no good to me without any get-up-and-go.

kibarashi 気晴(ら)し *"ki* clearing"

a change of pace, (for) a change, diversion, relaxation

家にばかり閉じこもっていないで、たまには気晴らしをしに出かけなさい。
Uchi ni bakari tojikomotte inai de, tama ni wa kibarashi o shi ni dekakenasai.
Don't just shut yourself up in the house all the time; get out and do something for a change.

気晴らしに駅前のパチンコ屋へちょっと行ってくるよ。
Kibarashi ni ekimae no pachinko-ya e chotto itte kuru yo.
I'm going to the pachinko parlor in front of the station for a while to relax (to calm my nerves, veg out).

☞ *ki o harasu* 気を晴らす

kibun 気分 *"ki* portion"

feeling(s), mood, the way one feels

気分はどう？
Kibun wa dō?
How do you feel? / How are you doing (feeling)?

要は気分の問題だ。
Yō wa kibun no mondai da.
Just depends how you look at it (feel about it).

好きでもない人から交際を申し込まれて複雑な気分だ。
Suki de mo nai hito kara kōsai o mōshikomarete fukuzatsu na kibun da.
I've got mixed feelings about being asked out by someone I'm not really interested in.

とても旅をしたい気分じゃないのよ、いまは。
Totemo tabi o shitai kibun ja nai no yo, ima wa.
Right now I'm in no mood to take a trip.

土曜の夜じゃね。どうしても勉強する気分にならないもんね。
Doyō no yoru ja ne. Dōshite mo benkyō suru kibun ni naranai mon ne.
Saturday night? Hey, man, no way I can get in the mood to crack the books.

みんな揃いも揃ってアンニュイな気分だった。
Minna soroi mo sorotte annyui na kibun datta.
A feeling (atmosphere) of ennui pervaded the place. / For one and all, the general feeling was one of tedium.

✌ *soroi mo sorotte*: one and all, every last one

寝る前にこれを飲めば、気分がさわやかになってよく眠れる。
Neru mae ni kore o nomeba, kibun ga sawayaka ni natte yoku nemureru.
If you take this before you go to bed, you'll feel a whole lot better and sleep soundly.

高揚した気分が少しは落ち着いてきた。
Kōyō shita kibun ga sukoshi wa ochitsuite kita.
I don't feel quite as worked up as I did before.

誰も作品をほめなかったので、彼は気分を害したらしい。
Dare mo sakuhin o homenakatta no de, kare wa kibun o gaishita rashii.
I guess his feelings got hurt when no one had anything good to say about his artwork.

タバコは健康に悪いが、気分転換には役立つ。
Tabako wa kenkō ni warui ga, kibun-tenkan ni wa yakudatsu.
Cigarettes may be bad for your health, but they're sure great for a change of pace.

kibun ga ii 気分がいい *"ki* is good"

1. feel great, feel well

    おじいちゃん、今朝は気分がいいですか?
    Ojīchan, kesa wa kibun ga ii desu ka?
    Are you feeling all right this morning, Grandpa?

    気分がよくなるまでここで安静にしていなさい。
    Kibun ga yoku naru made koko de ansei ni shite inasai.
    Stay here and rest until you start feeling better.

2. charming, delightful, pleasant

    素直に「はい」と言ってもらえると気分がいい。
    Sunao ni "Hai" to itte moraeru to kibun ga ii.
    It'd really be nice if she'd simply say, "Yes."

    空気はおいしいし、景色もいいし、ここは本当に気分のいい所だ。
    Kūki wa oishii shi, keshiki mo ii shi, koko wa hontō ni kibun no ii tokoro da.
    Fresh air, beautiful scenery—this is truly a delightful place.

☞ *ki o yoku suru* 気をよくする, *kimochi ga ii* 気持ちがいい; *kibun ga warui* 気分が悪い

kibun ga warui 気分が悪い *"ki* is bad"

1. feel ill, sick, sick to one's stomach; have an upset stomach

    気分が悪い人は手を挙げて申し出てください。
    Kibun ga warui hito wa te o agete mōshidete kudasai.
    If you're not feeling well, please let me know by raising your hand.

電車の中で気分が悪くなった。
Densha no naka de kibun ga waruku natta.
I started feeling sick on the train.

気分が悪くならないうちに乗り物酔いの薬を飲んでおこう。
Kibun ga waruku naranai uchi ni norimono-yoi no kusuri o nonde okō.
Think I'll take some motion sickness medicine before I start feeling sick.

2. sickening, unpleasant

気分の悪い虐殺場面だったよね。
Kibun no warui gyakusatsu-bamen datta yo ne.
That was one sickening massacre scene, wasn't it.

けんかして以来、あいつの声を聞くだけで気分が悪い。
Kenka shite irai, aitsu no koe o kiku dake de kibun ga warui.
Ever since I had that argument with him, it makes me sick just to hear his voice.

☞ *ki o waruku suru* 気を悪くする, *kimochi ga warui* 気持ちが悪い; *kibun ga ii* 気分がいい

kibun-ya 気分屋

a moody person, someone who blows hot and cold

彼みたいな気分屋は客商売には向かないだろう。
Kare mitai na kibun-ya wa kyaku-shōbai ni wa mukanai darō.
I doubt that a moody person like him is suited to dealing with customers.

kichigai 気違い "differing *ki*"

(of a person) a crackpot, loony, lunatic, madman, maniac, nut, psycho, screwball; (of a mental state) insanity, madness; (of a temporary condition) crazy, insane, nuts, off one's rocker, way out there

Kichigai and its derivatives (as well as, to a lesser extent, *ki ga kuruu*, *ki ga fureru*, *ki ga hen ni naru*, and *kyōki*) are now considered by many to be politically incorrect and highly discriminatory or offensive in almost any situation. Words and phrases that appear innocuous to the non-native can often be sources of ill will. Today both literal and figurative usage of these words is shunned by newspapers and broadcast media, though the latter (figurative meaning) remains common in colloquial speech. Even in figurative form, however, there is a wide range of acceptability according to the degree of metaphorical sense. *Eiga-kichigai* (a movie freak), for example, would likely have the widest range of acceptance and seem free of any negative implications, but even it would be found unacceptable by those who are particularly sensitive to this aspect of language. Thus the student is advised to proceed with utmost caution in this area, and beginning and intermediate students might do best to study the vocabulary here more for comprehension than actual use in speech. In particular, *kichigai* and its derivatives should be avoided when referring to someone with a mental disability, whether in a literal or figurative sense. The examples given in this book are of the type mostly likely to be encountered in conversation among people who possess no special awareness of this aspect of the language.

 私の息子は大学に入るために気違いのようになって（気違いみ
  たいに）勉強しています。
Watshi no musuko wa daigaku ni hairu tame ni kichigai no yō ni natte (kichigai mitai ni) benkyō shite imasu.
My son is studying like crazy in order to get into college.

☞ *ki ga kuruu* 気が狂う, *ki ga fureru* 気が触れる, *ki ga hen ni naru* 気が

変になる, *kichigai-jimiru* 気違いじみる, *kichigai-zata* 気違い沙汰, *kyōki* 狂気; *ki ga tashika* 気が確か, *shōki* 正気

~ *kichigai* 〜気違い "different-*ki*'ed"

(preceded by a noun) an addict, a buff, devotee, enthusiast, fan

若い頃は映画気違いと言われたが、今では有名な映画評論家だ。
Wakai koro wa eiga-kichigai to iwareta ga, ima de wa yūmei na eiga-hyōronka da.
They called him a movie freak when he was young, but look at him now—a famous film critic.

ギャンブル気違いの亭主を持って、彼女も苦労してるに違いないよ。
Gyanburu-kichigai no teishu o motte, kanojo mo kurō shite 'ru ni chigainai yo.
With that dyed-in-the-wool gambler husband she's strapped with, life can't be easy.

私は自他ともに認める猫気違いだ。
Watashi wa jita-tomo ni mitomeru neko-kichigai da.
Everyone knows what a nut I am about cats. / Everyone knows how cat-crazy I am.

☞ *kichigai* 気違い

kichigai-jimiru 気違いじみる "to be a little different-*ki*'ed"

(a little bit) crazy, cracked, nutty

そんな気違いじみたスケジュールで働いたら、からだこわします。
Sonna kichigai-jimita sukejūru de hataraitara, karada kowashimasu.
You're going to ruin your health if you work at an idiotic pace like this.

kichigai-zata 気違い沙汰 "crazy affair"

madness, lunacy

こんな時期に借金で新しく設備投資をするなんて気違い沙汰だ。
Konna jiki ni shakkin de atarashiku setsubi-tōshi o suru nante kichigai-zata da.
It's sheer madness to make capital outlays on borrowed money in this [economic] climate.

☞ *kichigai* 気違い

kidate 気立て "*ki* standing"

disposition, nature, temperament

気立てがいい娘さんで、近所でも評判がいいですよ。
Kidate ga ii musume-san de, kinjo de mo hyōban ga ii desu yo.
She's so sweet (good-natured) that everyone in the neighborhood likes her.

気立てがやさしい子で、迷い犬や捨て猫を見ると放っておけないらしい。
Kidate ga yasashii ko de, mayoi-inu ya sute-neko o miru to hōtte okenai rashii.
She's so kindhearted that she has to take care of every lost dog and stray cat she comes across.

✤ Generally used of a person's nature when it is thought to be good, *kidate* is never used in conjunction with negative words or phrases.

kido-airaku 喜怒哀楽 "joy, anger, sadness, and pleasure"

(the gamut of) human emotions

彼があんなに喜怒哀楽を見せるとは、意外だったなあ。
Kare ga anna ni kido-airaku o miseru to wa, igai datta nā.
It was a real surprise to see him show such emotion.

普段は一切喜怒哀楽を表情に出さない人なのにね。
Fudan wa issai kido-airaku o hyōjō ni dasanai hito na no ni ne.
Usually he never shows the slightest trace of emotion.

昔は、喜怒哀楽の情を露にするのは、はしたないと教えられたものだよ。
Mukashi wa, kido-airaku no jō o arawa ni suru no wa, hashitanai to oshierareta mono da yo.
In the old days we were always taught that showing your feelings (giving vent to your emotions) was just not done.

↫ *kimochi* 気持ち

kidoru 気取る "to take *ki*"

1. act big; be affected, conceited, fake, phony, pompous; put on airs

たまには気取って二人で高級レストランへ行くのも楽しいものだよ。
Tama ni wa kidotte futari de kōkyū resutoran e iku no mo tanoshii mono da yo.
It's fun sometimes to put on the dog and go out to an expensive restaurant.

何よ！ 気取って！
Nani yo! Kidotte!

You must really think you're something! / Who do you think you are?

🥬 Anyone who fits the above descriptions is a *kidori-ya* 気取り屋.

2. pass oneself off as, pretend to be, pose as

彼は改革派を気取りながらいち早く寝返った。
Kare wa kaikaku-ha o kidorinagara ichi-hayaku negaetta.
He made like he was a reformer and all, but he was the first to go over to the other side.

当時の私は物わかりの良い女を気取っていた。
Tōji no watashi wa monowakari no yoi onna o kidotte ita.
Back then I passed myself off as a worldly wise and sophisticated woman.

kigakari 気がかり "something hanging on one's *ki*"

a concern, headache, worry; something on one's mind

入院している母がたったひとつの気がかりです。
Nyūin shite iru haha ga tatta hitotsu no kigakari desu.
The only thing that bothers me is my mother in the hospital.

売り上げが伸び悩んでいるのが気がかりだ。
Uriage ga nobinayande iru no ga kigakari da.
I'm a little worried about the sluggish sales.

西田さんの気がかりはアメリカへ留学している娘らしい。
Nishida-san no kigakari wa Amerika e ryūgaku shite iru musume rashii.
Nishida's chief concern (big worry) is apparently the safety of his daughter who's studying in the United States.

☞ *ki ni kakaru* 気にかかる, *ki ni kakeru* 気にかける, *ki ni suru* 気にする, *kigakari* 気がかり

kigakari (na) 気がかり(な) "a *ki* hanging"

bothersome, troubling, worrisome

決して気がかりな相手ではなかった。
Kesshite kigakari na aite de wa nakatta.
As an opponent, he wasn't worth losing a night's sleep over.

今いちばん気がかりなことは夫の働き過ぎです。
Ima ichiban kigakari na koto wa otto no hatarakisugi desu.
What's bothering me most now is my husband working too hard for his own good.

☞ *ki ni kakaru* 気にかかる, *ki ni naru* 気になる, *ki ni suru* 気にする

kigamae 気構え "the build of *one's ki*"

anticipation, preparedness, readiness

彼の場合、普通の学生とは気構えが違う。
Kare no bāi, futsū no gakusei to wa kigamae ga chigau.
He's different from other students in the way he approaches things.

しっかりした目的意識と気構えがなければ、成功しないよ。
Shikkari shita mokuteki-ishiki to kigamae ga nakereba, seikō shinai yo.
You'll never make a go of it unless you've got a clear goal in mind and you're prepared to see things through.

お互いに一歩もゆずらない気構えだった。
Otagai ni ippo mo yuzuranai kigamae datta.
They both had their heels dug in and weren't about to budge an inch.

kigane 気兼ね "pile up *ki*"

uneasiness, discomfort (after taking into account how someone else feels and modifying one's behavior accordingly)

僕はなぜかあの人には気兼ねがあって、率直にものが言えないんだ。
Boku wa naze ka ano hito ni wa kigane ga atte, sotchoku ni mono ga ienai n' da.
There's something about that guy that keeps me from saying what I think when I'm around him.

どうぞ気兼ねなく分からないことは何でも聞いて下さい。
Dōzo kigane naku wakaranai koto wa nan de mo kiite kudasai.
Please feel free to ask about anything you don't understand.

↪ *kigane (o) suru* 気兼ね(を)する, *kizukai* 気遣い; *kiyasui* 気安い, *kigaru (na)* 気軽(な)

kigane (o) suru 気兼ね(を)する

feel (somehow) constrained, uneasy, uncomfortable

彼女はそんなに気兼ねする性質には見えないが、意外だね。
Kanojo wa sonna ni kigane suru tachi ni wa mienai ga, igai da ne.
She sure doesn't look the type to be ill at ease around people, but you never know, I guess.

周りの人に気兼ねをして、かわいそうなぐらい小さくなっている。
Mawari no hito ni kigane o shite, kawaisō na gurai chiisaku natte iru.
He's so intimidated by the people around him it's almost sad. / He's so self-conscious that it's almost pathetic.

↪ *kigane* 気兼ね, *ki o tsukau* 気を使う

kigaru (na) 気軽（な） "light *ki*"

be easygoing, laid-back; lighthearted

結婚とかなんとか難しいこと言わないで、気軽なつきあいをしようよ。
Kekkon to ka nan to ka muzukashii koto iwanai de, kigaru na tsukiai o shiyō yo.
Come on now, don't get all uptight about gettin' married and stuff. Let's just have a good time together.

遠慮なく気軽に遊びに来てくださいね。
Enryo naku kigaru ni asobi ni kite kudasai ne.
Don't hesitate to just drop by some time when you're in the mood.

栄養たっぷりでしかも気軽に作れるメニューをご紹介しましょう。
Eiyō tappuri de shikamo kigaru ni tsukureru menyū o goshōkai shimashō.
And now I'd like to introduce some dishes that are both nutritious and a snap to prepare.

↪ *kisaku (na)* 気さく(な)

※ An advertising industry favorite, *kigaru ni* is used—somewhat hopefully—to allay the fears of prospective customers who might be reluctant to enter a certain place of business, a mahjong parlor, for example (thinking it might be a hangout for punks and hustlers), or an expensive-looking restaurant (out of concern that they will be stuck with picking up a large tab), or even an optician's. I recently received junk mail from a optician inviting me to "drop by anytime" (*Okigaru ni o tachiyori kudasai*) to have my glasses cleaned or adjusted.

kigokoro 気心 "*ki* heart"

one's feelings, one's heart and mind, one's innermost thoughts

やっぱり学生時代のお友だちがいちばん気心が分かってるわ。
Yappari gakusei-jidai no otomodachi ga ichiban kigokoro ga wakatte 'ru wa.
I swear, there's no one who can really understand you like an old schoolmate.

気心の知れた友人とは、しばらく会ってなくてもすぐ話が弾むもんだね。
Kigokoro no shireta yūjin to wa, shibaraku atte 'nakute mo sugu hanashi ga hazumu mon da ne.
It's amazing how really good friends who haven't met for a while can find all kinds of things to talk about when they do get together.

中井さんっていつまでたっても気心の知れない人だなあ。
Nakai-san tte itsu made tatte mo kigokoro no shirenai hito da nā.
Nakai is someone you can just never seem to get close to (get to know).

※ Anyone about whom you would use *kigokoro no shireta* is, of course, a *ki no okenai hito* 気の置けない人. Er, that is unless we're talking about those teenagers busily redefining the term. They'll drive you up the wall. See the note at *ki ga okenai*.

kigurai 気位 "rank of *ki*"

pride, self-esteem, self-respect; arrogance, vanity; be stuck up, think one's shit doesn't stink

あいつエリートだという気位ばかりで、実力は全然ないさ。
Aitsu erīto da to iu kigurai bakari de, jitsuryoku wa zenzen nai sa.
He's as proud as can be about being a member of the "elite," but he is absolutely worthless on the job.

家柄を鼻にかけた気位の高い人で、私は好きになれない。
Iegara o hana ni kaketa kigurai no takai hito de, watashi wa suki ni narenai.
She's all wrapped up in how great her pedigree is and all. I haven't got any use for her, though.

kigurō 気苦労 "hard work for *ki*"

anxiety, care, mental anguish, pains, worry

出世コースに乗ったら乗ったで、人には言えない気苦労があるらしいよ。
Shusse-kōsu ni nottara notta de, hito ni wa ienai kigurō ga aru rashii yo.
Once you're on the fast track, you come under a lot of strain that you can never really explain to others.

結構気苦労の多い職場みたい。
Kekkō kigurō no ōi shokuba mitai.
It sounds like a workplace where you've got to worry a lot about interpersonal relations.

京子も家の中がいざこざ続きで、気苦労が絶えないんですって。
Kyōko mo ie no naka ga izakoza-tsuzuki de, kigurō ga taenai n' desu tte.
According to Kyoko, all the hassles at home are a constant source of concern (worry) for her.

おふくろと女房の間に挟まって気苦労してるぜ、まったく。
Ofukuro to nyōbō no aida ni hasamatte kigurō shite 'ru ze, mattaku.
Hey, man, let me tell you, being caught between my mother and my old lady is wearing me out (is no fun).

kihin 気品 *"ki* quality"

dignity, refinement

このホテルのロビーは格調が高く、調度品にも気品が漂っている。
Kono hoteru no robī wa kakuchō ga takaku, chōdo-hin ni mo kihin ga tadayotte iru.
The lobby of this hotel is a study in elegance, right down to the finely appointed furnishings.

気品のある顔立ちの老婦人が入って来た。
Kihin no aru kaodachi no rōfujin ga haitte kita.
An elderly matron (of dignified mien) entered.

新人作家だが、気品のある文章を書く。
Shinjin-sakka da ga, kihin no aru bunshō o kaku.
Though she's a new author, her writing is elegant.

豪華な中にも気品に満ちたウエディングドレスでございます。
Gōka na naka ni mo kihin ni michita uedingu-doresu de gozaimasu.
It is truely a magnificent and yet throughly refined wedding gown, ma'am.

kiji きじ（雉） pheasant

This resident game bird, though seldom seen, makes its home in the foothills and fields of Japan, appears in such well-known Japanese folk tales as *Momotaro* 桃太郎, and was designated the national bird in 1947 (a little-known bit of trivia that might win you a couple of beers at the local *izakaya*). The idioms included here indicate that the bird's intelligence is not the characteristic that propelled it to become a national symbol. The high-pitched cry of pheasants—well, the males anyway, the one that gets them in trouble during the hunting season—is *kenkēn* ケンケーン. They are counted *ichiwa* 一羽.

Kiji mo nakazuba utaremai 雉も鳴かずば打たれまい "even a pheasant will not be shot if it remains quiet"
stay quiet and stay out of trouble

> 「雉も鳴かずば打たれまい」ここはひとつじっと様子を見ていろ。
> *"Kiji mo nakazuba utaremai" koko wa hitotsu jitto yōsu o mite iro.*
> Let's just lay low for a while and see which way the wind blows.

> この件については他言無用に願いますよ。雉も鳴かずば打たれまいというでしょう。
> *Kono ken ni tsuite wa tagon-muyō ni negaimasu yo. Kiji mo nakazuba utaremai to iu deshō.*
> We'd best keep this to ourselves (under our hats). You know what they say about loose lips sinking ships.

✌ A graphic expression of inviting danger by drawing attention to oneself.

kiki-ippatsu 危機一髪 "danger (crisis), a hair's breadth (away)"

at the critical moment, in the nick of time, a close shave, a close call, by the skin of one's teeth, touch-and-go; to hang by a hair

> ホームから線路に落ちた酔っぱらいは、危機一髪のところで救出された。
> *Hōmu kara senro ni ochita yopparai wa, kiki-ippatsu no tokoro de kyūshutsu sareta.*
> The drunkard who toppled off the platform onto the tracks was saved just in the nick of time.

> 危機一髪だったよ。もう少しで浮気がばれるとこだった。
> *Kiki-ippatsu datta yo. Mō sukoshi de uwaki ga bareru toko datta.*

It was a close call, I can tell you. My wife was this far away from finding out about my affair.

あわや正面衝突かと思ったが、危機一髪で難を免れた。
Awaya shōmen-shōtotsu ka to omotta ga, kiki-ippatsu de nan o manukareta.
I was convinced I was gonna crash right into him but managed to swerve away at the last moment.

💥 This expression is written with the character for hair (髪), but sometimes you might come across it written as 危機一発. This was the punning title given to a 007 James Bond film, with 髪 being replaced by 発 (here meaning a shot from a gun). Due to the film's popularity many people now write the expression this way.

kikotsu 気骨 "a boned *ki*"

[～がある] (have) backbone, (have the strength of one's) convictions

上田君は今時の学生には珍しく気骨があるな。
Ueda-kun wa imadoki no gakusei ni wa mezurashiku kikotsu ga aru na.
Ueda's not like most students these days; he's actually got convictions.

なかなか気骨のある人物じゃないか。
Nakanaka kikotsu no aru jinbutsu ja nai ka.
He's got real backbone.

頑固なのも困るが、お前たちには気骨がなさ過ぎるぞ。
Ganko na no mo komaru ga, omae-tachi ni wa kikotsu ga nasasugiru zo.
I'm not saying you've got to be stubborn, but you guys are far too wishy-washy.

💥 By convention *kikotsu ga aru* is not used in reference to women. The idiom itself is not sexist; rather, usage reflects the fact that historically women have not been in positions requiring (encouraging?) them to express their views. The consensus of the authors is that when a woman sticks by her guns, however praiseworthy that effort may be, words like *kachiki* and *namaiki* (both of which are included in this book) would be used, suggesting that it is not her place to have an opinion, much less to defend it.

The characters 気骨 have a variant reading, *kibone*, with a different meaning, "anxiety" or "pains." This word is most commonly found in the phrase *kibone ga oreru* 気骨が折れる, which means to be emotionally exhausted or "worn to a frazzle." It is derived by adding *ki* to the expression *hone ga oreru* 骨が折れる, which literally means "break a bone."

中間管理職は想像していた以上に気骨が折れるよ。
Chūkan-kanrishoku wa sōzō shite ita ijō ni kibone ga oreru yo.
Being in middle management takes a lot more out of you than I ever thought it would.

↬ *kigurō* 気苦労, *kizukare* 気疲れ

kikubari 気配り "doling out *ki*"

attention, care, pains

道子さんのさりげない気配りが嬉しかったのよ。
Michiko-san no sarigenai kikubari ga ureshikatta no yo.
The way Michiko was so attentive without being obtrusive was really nice.

いくら若いからと言っても、もう少し気配りをするべきだ。
Ikura wakai kara to itte mo, mō sukoshi kikubari o suru beki da.
Sure he's young and all, but just the same he's got to pay more attention to how his actions affect other people.

気配りが足りなくて、不愉快な思いをさせてしまった。
Kikubari ga tarinakute, fu-yukai na omoi o sasete shimatta.

I'm afraid I was a little tactless and ended up offending him.

岡田さんはいつもまわりを大事にする典型的な気配りの人だ。
Okada-san wa itsumo mawari o daiji ni suru tenkei-teki na kikubari no hito da.
Mr. Okada is a typical caring person, always seeing to the needs of those around him.

細かい気配りが行き届いたすばらしいパーティーだったね。
Komakai kikubari ga yukitodoita subarashii pātī datta ne.
That was one great party, wasn't it. The preparations were so thoroughgoing.

🖐 Contrasted to *kizukai*, which describes the care for others that arises naturally from a gentle, caring person, *kikubari* describes more the artifice or technique necessary, particularly in Japanese society, to insure that human relations remain congenial and work gets done. So while *kizukai* is greatly appreciated, some degree of *kikubari* is expected, indeed demanded, from adults in Japan. It should not, by the way, be confused with 気配 *kehai*.

☞ *kizukai* 気遣い, *ki o kubaru* 気を配る, *ki o tsukau* 気を使う

kimae 気前 "front of *ki*"

generosity, largess, munificence

お前の親父は気前がいいなあ。うちのはケチでだめだ。
Omae no oyaji wa kimae ga ii nā. Uchi no wa kechi de dame da.
Your old man is really generous. Mine's so stingy.

大山さんっていつも気前よくおごってくれるから大好き。
Koyama-san tte itsumo kimae yoku ogotte kureru kara daisuki.
I really like Koyama, because he always picks up the tab when you go out with him.

✌ Always in conjunction with the adjective *ii* or adverb *yoku*.

kimagure 気まぐれ "a diversion of *ki*"

a whim, caprice

僕の気まぐれにつきあってくれてありがとう。
Boku no kimagure ni tsukiatte kurete arigatō.
Thanks for going along with me on the spur of the moment.

親父の気まぐれにふりまわされるのはもうご免だ。
Oyaji no kimagure ni furimawasareru no wa mō gomen da.
I'm sick and tired of my dad getting these burrs under his saddle all the time.

あの時のプロポーズは一時の気まぐれだったって言うの？
Ano toki no puropōzu wa ichiji no kimagure datta tte iu no?
So, are you telling me that you proposed to me on a whim, or what?

☞ *kimagure (na)* 気まぐれ(な)

kimagure (na) 気まぐれ（な） "*ki* diverted"

capricious, whimsical, spur-of-the-moment

彼女の気まぐれな行動には私たちも困っている。
Kanojo no kimagure na kōdō ni wa watashi-tachi mo komatte iru.
Her capricious behavior is giving us a lot of headaches too.

君も気まぐれな恋人を持って大変だな。
Kimi mo kimagure na koibito o motte taihen da na.
With that fickle girlfriend of yours, I can see life's not easy for you either.

☞ *kimagure* 気まぐれ

kimama (na) 気まま(な) "as *ki* likes"

willful, selfish; carefree

たまには気ままな一人旅がしてみたいなあ。
Tama ni wa kimama na hitori-tabi ga shite mitai nā.
Once in a while I'd like to just take off on a trip all by myself.

あんまり勝手気ままな人なので誰も相手にしないんだ。
Anmari katte kimama na hito na no de dare mo aite ni shinai n' da.
He's way too full of himself for anybody to take him seriously.

独身の頃は休日は気ままに過ごせたものだけど、今じゃそういうわけにもいかないね。
Dokushin no koro wa kyūjitsu wa kimama ni sugoseta mono da kedo, ima ja sō iu wake ni mo ikanai ne.
When I was single, I used to be able to do anything I felt like on my days off, but those days are gone now.

☞ *kigaru (na)* 気軽(な)

kimazui 気まずい "distastful *ki*"

awkward, ill at ease, sensitive, strained, tense, uncomfortable

例の件以来、彼と会ってもなんとなく気まずい。
Rei no ken irai, kare to atte mo nan to naku kimazui.
Ever since, there's been a certain awkwardness between us when we meet.

会議は気まずい雰囲気の中で始まった。
Kaigi wa kimazui fun'iki no naka de hajimatta.
The conference began in an atmosphere of unpleasantness (a constrained atmosphere).

kimi 気味 "a taste of *ki*"

a [usually bad, strange, or uncanny] feeling or sensation

いい気味だ。
Ii kimi da.
It serves him (you) right!

いくら作り物と分かっていてもやはり気味が悪い。
Ikura tsukurimono to wakatte ite mo yahari kimi ga warui.
Even though you know it's not real, it still gives you the creeps.

二十歳の男がそんなに品行方正だったらかえって気味が悪いよ。
Hatachi no otoko ga sonna ni hinkō-hōsei dattara kaette kimi ga warui yo.
On the contrary, for a twenty-year-old to be that well behaved is kind of weird. / There's something eerie about a twenty-year-old guy who's that polite.

なんだか薄気味悪い客だったねえ。
Nandaka usu-kimi-warui kyaku datta nē.
He was kind of a creepy customer (client), wasn't he?

あの家は殺人事件以来空き家で、誰も気味悪がって近づかない。
Ano ie wa satsujin-jiken irai akiya de, dare mo kimi-warugatte chikazukanai.
That house has been vacant ever since somebody got murdered there, and everybody's so spooked that no one will go near the place.

⚜ Although there are idioms in which the word appears to have a positive meaning—*ii kimi da*, or less commonly *kimi ga ii*—both express a feeling of satisfaction upon learning that someone disliked has suffered disappointment or failure and finally gotten what he or she deserves. In practice, *kimi* is found almost exclusively in negative expressions such as *kimi ga warui* and its variant *kimi no warui* or the derivative *kimi-warui.*

☞ *~gimi* 〜気味

kimo 肝 liver

One of the few internal organs that figures in a significant number of idioms, the liver, or *kimo* in Japanese, also carries both meanings of the English word "guts": the innards collectively and the qualities of strength, fortitude, and bravery. A word of caution, however, is in order. *Kimo* is not used to refer to that cut of meat that so many children have nightmares about. At a restaurant, a butcher shop, or even a *yakitori* shop the word is *rebā,* the *katakana* approximation of the English "liver."

Kimo ni meijiru 肝に銘じる "impress on one's liver"
take something to heart

> 資源には限りがあるということを、一人一人が肝に銘じるべきである。
> *Shigen ni wa kagiri ga aru to iu koto o, hitori-hitori ga kimo ni meijiru beki de aru.*
> We should all bear in mind that the earth's resources are limited.

> 二度と同じ過ちを犯さぬよう、肝に銘じておきなさい。
> *Nido to onaji ayamachi o okasanu yō, kimo ni meijite okinasai.*
> Take this lesson to heart so that you won't end up making the same mistake again.

Also 肝に銘ずる *kimo ni meizuru.*

🐍 There is an important distinction between the next two expressions, although the English may on occasion be similar. *Kimo o tsubusu* is used to express surprise; *kimo o hiyasu*, to express fear or danger.

Kimo o hiyasu 肝を冷やす "have a cold liver"
be scared (half) to death, terrified, scared stiff, scared spitless, nearly shit one's pants

---

高層ビルの最上階にいる時に地震が起きたので、本当に肝を冷やした。
Kōsō-biru no saijō-kai ni iru toki ni jishin ga okita no de, hontō ni kimo o hiyashita.
I was on the top floor of a skyscraper when the earthquake hit. It scared the wits out of me.

会社に金の使い込みがばれてしまったのかと、肝を冷やした。
Kaisha ni kane no tsukaikomi ga barete shimatta no ka to, kimo o hiyashita.
Let me tell you, I was scared shitless when I thought they'd discovered that I had been siphoning off the company's money.

Also 肝が冷える *kimo ga hieru.*
↪ *kimo o tsubusu* 肝を潰す, *koshi ga nukeru / koshi o nukasu* 腰が抜ける／腰を抜かす

Kimo o tsubusu 肝をつぶす "crush one's liver"
be frightened out of one's wits, be blown away

怪物のお面をつけて飛び出してきた子供に、肝をつぶした。
Kaibutsu no omen o tsukete tobidashite kita kodomo ni, kimo o tsubushita.
Some kid wearing a monster mask jumped out and scared the wits out of me.

目の前でオートバイ事故が起きた時は、肝をつぶすかと思った。
Me no mae de ōtobai-jiko ga okita toki wa, kimo o tsubusu ka to omotta.

It really floored me when that motorcycle accident happened right in front of my eyes.

Also 肝がつぶれる *kimo ga tsubureru.*
☞ *kimo o hiyasu* 肝を冷やす, *koshi ga nukeru / koshi o nukasu* 腰が抜ける／腰を抜かす

Kimo(ttama) ga chiisai 肝（っ玉）が小さい "have a small liver"
be yellow, yellow-bellied, chicken-livered, chickenhearted, lily-livered, fainthearted, weak-kneed

---

彼はボクサーのくせに、肝っ玉の小さいところがあった。
Kare wa bokusā no kuse ni, kimottama no chiisai tokoro ga atta.
For a boxer, there was something about the guy that made him seem like a candy ass.

あの子は肝が小さくて、大きな音がするだけでびくっとする。
Ano ko wa kimo ga chiisakute, ōki na oto ga suru dake de bikutto suru.
That kid's such a sissy (scaredy-cat) that he flinches every time there's even a loud noise.

kimochi 気持ち "*ki* holding"

1. feelings, the way one feels

まだ気持ちの整理がつかないんだろう。
Mada kimochi no seiri ga tsukanai n' darō.
I don't think she's sorted out her feelings about it yet. / I think she still has mixed feelings about it.

お気持ちはよく分かりますとも。
Okimochi wa yoku wakarimasu tomo.
I know exactly how you feel.

後は君の気持ち次第だよ。
Ato wa kimi no kimochi shidai da yo.
It's up to you from here on out.

あなたならこんな時どんな気持ちがする？
Anata nara konna toki donna kimochi ga suru?
How would you feel (What would you think) if you were in my place?

今はまだあの人を許す気持ちにはなれないわ。
Ima wa mada ano hito o yurusu kimochi ni wa narenai wa.
I still can't (I'm still not ready to) forgive him.

張りつめていた気持ちが彼の一言で一度に楽になりましたよ。
Haritsumete ita kimochi ga kare no hitokoto de ichido ni raku ni narimashita yo.
All the tension I had been feeling just melted away when he spoke to me.

からだの心配より「休んではいけない」という気持ちの方が強かった。
Karada no shinpai yori "Yasunde wa ikenai" to iu kimochi no hō ga tsuyokatta.
I was more concerned about missing work than I was about my health.

ああ、いい気持ちだった。やっぱり温泉はいいなあ。
Ā, ii kimochi datta. Yappari onsen wa ii nā.
Oh, man, that felt great! There's nothing like a hot spring.

☞ *kimochi (ga) ii* 気持ち(が)いい, *kimochi (ga) warui* 気持ち(が)悪い

2. a (small) token of one's appreciation

ささやかですが、私どもの気持ちでございます。
Sasayaka desu ga, watakushi-domo no kimochi de gozaimasu.
This is a mere token of our gratitude.

ほんの気持ばかりですが、どうぞお納めください。
Hon no kimochi bakari desu ga, dōzo oosame kudasai.
I hope you will accept this small gift as a token of my appreciation.

⇨ *ki wa kokoro* 気は心

3. a bit, hair, tad

裾を気持ち短くしてもらいたいんですが。
Suso o kimochi mijikaku shite moraitai n' desu ga.
I'd like to have the hem raised just a smidgen.

その絵、気持ち上にずらした方がいいんじゃないの。
Sono e, kimochi ue ni zurashita hō ga ii n' ja nai no.
Wouldn't that picture be better just a shade higher?

kimochi (ga) ii 気持ち（が）いい "the way *ki* is held is good"

feel good, feel great

1. (of a person's or animal's pleasant sensation) feel good

早起きすると気持ちがいいなあ。
Hayaoki suru to kimochi ga ii nā.
It feels so good to get up early.

タマのやつ気持ちよさそうに日溜まりに寝そべってるよ。
Tama no yatsu kimochi yosasō ni hidamari ni nesobette 'ru yo.
Tama [the cat] is napping happily in the sunlight.

2. (of a thing) pleasant, pleasing

気持ちのいい朝だなあ。
Kimochi no ii asa da nā.
What a wonderful morning! / A morning like this makes you happy to be alive.

さっぱりした気持ちのいい人ですよ。

Sappari shita kimochi no ii hito desu yo.
He's a very refreshing person to be around.

⇨ *kibun ga ii* 気分がいい; *kimochi (ga) warui* 気持ち(が)悪い

kimochi (ga) warui 気持ち(が)悪い "the way *ki* is held is bad"

1. (of a person's or animal's unpleasant sensation) feel bad

   気持ちが悪いんだったら、この薬をお飲みなさい。
   Kimochi ga warui n' dattara, kono kusuri o onominasai.
   Take this medicine if you don't feel well (if you're feeling under the weather).

   靴がビショビショで、気持ち悪いよ。
   Kutsu ga bishobisho de, kimochi warui yo.
   These shoes are soaking wet. They feel terrible.

   飲み過ぎて気持ち悪くなっても知らないぞ。
   Nomisugite kimochi waruku natte mo shiranai zo.
   Don't come crying to me if you drink too much and get sick.

2. (of a thing) disagreeable, disgusting, unpleasant

   彼女があんまり機嫌がいいと気持ちが悪いね。
   Kanojo ga anmari kigen ga ii to kimochi ga warui ne.
   It gives you the creeps when she gets in such a good mood.

   気持ちの悪い絵にしか見えないけど、これが傑作なの？
   Kimochi no warui e ni shika mienai kedo, kore ga kessaku na no?
   I don't see anything except a disgusting painting. How can this be a "masterpiece"?

☞ *kibun ga warui* 気分が悪い, *mune ga warui* 胸が悪い; *kimochi ga ii* 気持ちがいい

kimuzukashii 気難しい "difficult *ki*"

hard to get along with, cross-grained, difficult, fussy, touchy

家の父は気難しいから母はいつも腫れ物にさわるようにしてる。
Uchi no chichi wa kimuzukashii kara haha wa itsumo haremono ni sawaru yō ni shite 'ru.
My dad's such a grouch that Mom's got to tiptoe around him.

いつもニコニコしていらしてそんな気難しい方のようには見えないけどねえ。
Itsumo nikoniko shite irashite sonna kimuzukashii kata no yō ni wa mienai kedo nē.
He sure doesn't look like he's that hard to please, the way he always has a smile on his face.

kinaga (ni) 気長(に) "long *ki*"

patient(ly), long-suffering; persistent(ly), enduring(ly)

まだ若いんですから気長に見守ってあげましょうよ。
Mada wakai n' desu kara kinaga ni mimamotte agemashō yo.
He's still young, so let's give him a chance. / He's still young, so let's not jump to conclusions about him.

そんなに結果を急がないでもっと気長に考えなさい。
Sonna ni kekka o isoganai de motto kinaga ni kangaenasai.
Don't be in such a hurry to get results. Put a little more thought into it. / Keep your shirt on, and give it some more thought.

↪ *ki ga nagai* 気が長い, *ki o nagaku motsu* 気を長く持つ (see under *ki o ~ motsu* 気を〜持つ)

kingyo きんぎょ (金魚) goldfish

Perhaps as much a part of teaching human fry responsibility for the care of animals in Japan as in the West, goldfish are said to have been first introduced from China early in the fifteenth century and, typically, improved upon. Since their introduction they have become the most common freshwater fish to take up residence in Japanese homes and to sacrifice their lives in the interest of the larger and more demanding pets that inevitably follow in their tiny wakes (pun intended).

Sold at shrine festivals held throughout Japan during the summer, goldfish are netted by children with small paper nets from troughs at outdoor stalls after paying a small fee to the vendors, only then to be carried home, gasping for life in plastic baggies by proud anglers who have just unwittingly experienced an essential early childhood social indoctrination ritual: to fish in Japan is to stand shoulder to shoulder with dozens of others who have traveled far and paid a fee to those who stock moats, ponds, and rivers with hungry fish. Be that as it may, goldfish are so closely associated with summer that they have even been bestowed with the cultural seal of approval, classification as a "seasonal word" in *renga* and haiku connoting summer.

Kingyo no fun 金魚の糞 "goldfish crap"
a tagalong, shadow, hanger-on; someone you just can't seem to shake (off)

斉藤君の妹は金魚の糞のように、どこに行くにもお兄さんと一緒だ。

Saitō-kun no imōto wa kingyo no fun no yō ni, doko ni iku ni mo oniisan to issho da.
Saito's little sister is always tagging along after him everywhere he goes.

そのバンドのファン達は金魚の糞だ。一日中彼らの後を追いかけ廻した。
Sono bando no fan-tachi wa kingyo no fun da. Ichinichi-jū karera no ato o oikakemawashita.
A bunch of groupies followed the band around all day.

✄ This colorful metaphoric use will be readily identified (by anyone who has ever had goldfish) with the difficulty the fish have shaking off their own excrement. Also, but less commonly, *kingyo no unko* 金魚のうんこ.

kinken-seiji 金権政治 "power-of-money politics"
money politics; plutocracy

選挙の度に金権政治の打破が叫ばれるが、結局何も変わっちゃいない。
Senkyo no tabi ni kinken-seiji no daha ga sakebareru ga, kekkyoku nani mo kawatcha inai.
Every time there's an election there's lots of talk about doing away with money politics, but in the end nothing ever changes.

このところ投票率が下がり続けているのは、国民が金権政治に愛想をつかしたからだろう。
Kono tokoro tōhyō-ritsu ga sagaritsuzukete iru no wa, kokumin ga kinken-seiji ni aiso o tsukashita kara darō.
The reason why the voter turnout keeps going down, I suppose, is because the general public is fed up with money politics.

kinori (ga) suru 気乗り(が)する "get *ki* mounted"

an interest (in), an inclination (to do); a notion (to do)

あまり気乗りするアイデアじゃないが背に腹はかえられない。
Amari kinori suru aidea ja nai ga se ni hara wa kaerarenai.
It's not exactly one of my favorite ideas, but I suppose we'll just have to bite the bullet on this one.

🌿 *se ni hara wa kaerarenai*: literally, "can't change one's stomach into one's back"; to be unavoidable, no way out.

先生は熱心に進めてくれる会社だが、どうも気乗りがしない。
Sensei wa nesshin ni susumete kureru kaisha da ga, dōmo kinori ga shinai.
My teacher is really pushing (enthusiastically recommending) this company [as a place of work], but there's something about it that turns me off.

☞ *ki ga noru* 気が乗る, *noriki (na)* 乗り気(な), *ki ga muku* 気が向く; *kinori-usu (na)* 気乗り薄(な)

kinori-usu (na) 気乗り薄(な) "weak-mounted *ki*"

lukewarm, unenthusiastic, halfhearted

大暴落以来、一般投資家は優良株にも気乗り薄だ。
Dai-bōraku irai, ippan tōshi-ka wa yūryō-kabu ni mo kinori-usu da.
Ever since the market crashed, private investors have even been shying away from the blue chips.

気乗り薄な返事だったから、もう一度当たってみます。
Kinori-usu na henji datta kara, mō ichido atatte mimasu.
Their reply was pretty lukewarm, so I'll try them again.

🌿 Appears most commonly in the negative.

↝ *ki ga noru* 気が乗る, *noriki (na)* 乗り気(な), *ki ga muku* 気が向く

kiochi suru 気落ちする　"be dropped *ki*"

be discouraged, despondent; feel low; lose heart

北山君は今年も試験に受からなかったのですっかり気落ちしている。
Kitayama-kun wa kotoshi mo shiken ni ukaranakatta no de sukkari kiochi shite iru.
Kitayama's down in the dumps 'cause he failed the exam again this year.

気落ちした父を慰めようと、姉夫婦が子供を連れて遊びに来た。
Kiochi shita chichi o nagusameyō to, ane-fūfu ga kodomo o tsurete asobi ni kita.
My sister and her husband came over with their kids to cheer Dad up.

↝ *ki o otosu* 気を落とす

kioi 気負い　"taking on *ki*"

ardor, enthusiasm, fervor, intensity, zeal

彼には、うちの社は俺でもっているという気負いがある。
Kare ni wa, uchi no sha wa ore de motte iru to iu kioi ga aru.
He's worked himself up into thinking that the company couldn't get along without him.

昔の日記は若さ故の気負いがあふれていて、読むのが面はゆいのさ。
Mukashi no nikki wa wakasa yue no kioi ga afurete ite, yomu no ga omohayui no sa.

My old diaries are so full of the boundless enthusiasm of youth that it's kind of embarrassing to read them now.

気負いを捨てて肩の力を抜けば、楽になれるよ。
Kioi o sutete kata no chikara o nukeba, raku ni nareru yo.
Simmer down and relax, and things will smooth out a little.

☞ *kiou* 気負う

kiokure (ga) suru 気後れ(が)する "one's *ki* falls behind"

lose one's nerve, back down, back out, chicken out, cop out

あなたは気後れするようには見えないが、意外ですね。
Anata wa kiokure suru yō ni wa mienai ga, igai desu ne.
I sure never figured you for the type to get cold feet.

準備はしていたが、いざとなると気後れがして何も言えなかった。
Junbi wa shite ita ga, iza to naru to kiokure ga shite nani mo ienakatta.
I was all prepared, but I chickened out when the chips were down and couldn't get a word out.

あなたの方が正しいのだから、気後れしないで堂々としていなさい。
Anata no hō ga tadashii no da kara, kiokure shinai de dōdō to shite inasai.
You're the one who's right, so don't back down now. Give 'em hell.

kiou 気負う "to take on *ki*"

get into, get worked up, screw oneself up (to do something), work oneself up

気負うのもいいが、過ぎると傲慢になるおそれがあるよ。
Kiou no mo ii ga, sugiru to gōman ni naru osore ga aru yo.
There's nothing wrong with psyching yourself up, but go too far and you can end up trying to lord it over everybody.

俺が、俺が、と気負っていた昔が嘘のようだ。
Ore ga, ore ga, to kiotte ita mukashi ga uso no yō da.
Sometimes it doesn't seem possible the way I used to think I could do just about anything.

☞ *kioi* 気負い

kiraku (na) 気楽（な） "easy *ki*"

(of a person) carefree, easygoing, happy-go-lucky, laid-back; (of a condition) can handle it, comfortable, no complaints

お前も気楽な奴だな、まったく。
Omae mo kiraku na yatsu da na, mattaku.
You're one laid-back kind of guy, aren't you.

定年後は気楽な隠居生活で、子供たちから「サンデー毎日」と冷やかされている。
Teinen-go wa kiraku na inkyo-seikatsu de, kodomo-tachi kara "Sandē Mainichi" to hiyakasarete iru.
I've got to put up with the kids teasing me about living the life of Riley now that I'm comfortably retired.

※ *"Sandē Mainichi"*: a play on the name of a weekly magazine and the fact that, for the man in our sentence, virtually every day (*mainichi*) is Sunday.

そんなに堅いこと言わないで、もっと気楽にやりましょうよ。
Sonna ni katai koto iwanai de, motto kiraku ni yarimashō yo.
Quit being so difficult. Let's just take it easy, OK.

独り者は気楽でいいね。
Hitorimono wa kiraku de ii ne.
Must be great being footloose and fancy-free.

☞ *ki ga raku ni naru* 気が楽になる, *ki o raku ni motsu* 気を楽に持つ, *ki o raku ni suru* 気を楽にする, *ki ga raku (na)* 気が楽(な), *nonki (na)* 呑気(な); *kizumari (na)* 気づまり(な)

kiryoku 気力 "power of *ki*"

drive, energy, heart, inner strength, mettle, (emotional) staying power, vitality, willpower

このプロジェクトには、気力、体力、知力のすべてが要求されている。
Kono purojekuto ni wa, kiryoku, tairyoku, chiryoku no subete ga yōkyū sarete iru.
Energy, intelligence and stamina are all required for this project.

生き続けようという気力を失った。
Ikitsuzukeyō to iu kiryoku o ushinatta.
She lost the will to live.

彼の場合は気力だけで持ちこたえたようなものだ。
Kare no bāi wa kiryoku dake de mochikotaeta yō na mono da.
He hung on almost by sheer intestinal fortitude.

kisaku (na) 気さく(な) "free *ki*"

easy to get along with, laid-back, natural, relaxed, unaffected

有名人なのに偉ぶらない気さくな方ですね。
Yūmei-jin na no ni eraburanai kisaku na kata desu ne.

She's very unassuming and easygoing for a celebrity, isn't she.

彼とは気さくに話ができるから、飲みに行っても楽しい。
Kare to wa kisaku ni hanashi ga dekiru kara, nomi ni itte mo tanoshii.
It's fun to go out for a drink with him because he's so easy to talk to.

もっと気さくに誰とでも話せる性格になりたいよ。
Motto kisaku ni dare to de mo hanaseru seikaku ni naritai yo.
I wish I had the kind of personality that lets you talk openly to all kinds of people.

☞ *kigaru (na)* 気軽(な); *kimuzukashii* 気難しい

kishō-kachi 稀少価値 "rareness value"

scarcity value

今時あんな純情な人、稀少価値があるわね。
Imadoki anna junjō na hito, kishō-kachi ga aru wa ne.
In this day and age people as pure as that are worth their weight in gold.

そんなにきれいじゃないけど、稀少価値があるから高価なんだ。
Sonna ni kirei ja nai kedo, kishō-kachi ga aru kara kōka nan da.
It's not that beautiful to look at, but it is valuable because of its rarity.

🐇 This expression can also be written as 希少価値.

kishoku-manmen 喜色満面 "a joyful color fills (one's) face"

a face full of joy, beaming with joy, all smiles and joy, smiling from ear to ear, delight written all over one's face, a face lit up with joy, grinning like a Cheshire cat, as pleased as Punch

祐二はたくさんお年玉をもらって、喜色満面だった。
Yūji wa takusan otoshidama o moratte, kishoku-manmen datta.
With all the money he'd received from his relatives over the New Year, Yuji looked as pleased as Punch.

  お年玉 (*otoshidama*) is the traditional gift of money given by parents (and other adult relations) to their children at New Year.

父は露天風呂に入りながら喜色満面で熱燗を飲んでいる。
Chichi wa rotenburo ni hairinagara, kishoku-manmen de atsukan o nonde iru.
Dad's sitting out in the open-air bath drinking hot sake with a look of profound contentment on his face.

  露天風呂 (*rotenburo*) is an open-air bath at a hot spring, of which there are many all over Japan. It is sometimes jokingly said that a Japanese man is happiest when sipping hot sake (*atsukan*) in a hot *rotenburo* (at which point he is supposed to say 極楽、極楽 [*gokuraku, gokuraku*], which means "Ah, what paradise!").

連戦連勝で、監督は喜色満面だね。
Rensen-renshō de, kantoku wa kishoku-manmen da ne.
Our manager's all smiles because of our recent unbeaten streak.

kisō-tengai 奇想天外 "an unusual idea (falls down from) the sky"

fantastic, out of the ordinary

あんな奇想天外な作戦が、まさか成功するとは思わなかったよ。
Anna kisō-tengai na sakusen ga, masaka seikō suru to wa omowanakatta yo.
I would never have believed that such a weird strategy would work out so well.

ずいぶんと奇想天外なデザインだけど、買う人いるのかなあ。
Zuibun to kisō-tengai na dezain da kedo, kau hito iru no ka nā.
It's a pretty off-the-wall design, but are people gonna want to buy it?

kitsune きつね (狐) fox

The fox, like the badger, was formerly believed capable of assuming many shapes as well as causing other things to change appearance in order to startle, deceive, or beguile humans. One popular folk tale has the guileful fox inviting a man out for a walk on a country road, where it then proceeds to deceive him by showing him a leaf that it has transformed into a gold coin. English words evoking foxes, like the verbs "fox" or "outfox," conjure up similar devious characteristics.

In a tale which shows possible, if distant linguistic similarities to the English use of fox to describe a sexually attractive young woman, a fox takes the shape of a beautiful woman to marry a man. Positive linguistic parallels pretty much end there, for in Japan these wily creatures rarely come off well in idiomatic usage. *Megitsune,* written with the characters for woman 女 and fox 狐, for example, is closer to bitch or vixen in English than to fox. Still, the identification of these secretive carnivores with cunning and craftiness in both languages indicates an astounding commonality of experience and imagination.

Foxes were also believed capable of possessing human beings, a notion that no doubt led to expressions like *kitsune ni tsumamareru,* which is included here.

In an interesting aside, there is even a word in Japanese, written (infrequently) with the characters for fox and odor 狐臭, that means tragomaschalia—"B.O." for most of us—and a "disease" in Japan. Fortunately, there is no evidence that it is carried or spread by our foxy friends, though ancient Japanese appear to have noticed that foxes do have a distinct, strong odor.

The fox's bark in Japanese is *konkon* コンコン. It is counted *ippiki* 一匹 or *ittō* 一頭.

↪ *furugitsune* 古狐, *megitsune* 牝狐

Kitsune ni tsumamareru **狐につままれる** "be bewitched by a fox"
be baffled, befuddled, foxed, puzzled, mystified; be at a loss

---

1,000万円の賞金とは狐につままれたような話だ。
Issenman-en no shōkin to wa kitsune ni tsumamareta yō na hanashi da.
Winning a ten million yen prize is just too good to be true.

君のような美人が僕とつき合ってくれるなんて、なんだか狐につままれたような話だな。
Kimi no yō na bijin ga boku to tsukiatte kureru nante, nan da ka kitsune ni tsumamareta yō na hanashi da na.
It's really baffling why a beautiful girl like you would go out with me.

たった1時間道端に立っただけでこんな報酬になるなんてきっと狐につままれているにちがいない。
Tatta ichiji-kan michibata ni tatta dake de konna hōshu ni naru nante kitto kitsune ni tsumamarete iru ni chigai nai.
There's something funny going on here! I can't believe that I could earn this much money just standing by the road for an hour.

✥ From the belief that the fox can change its appearance to deceive humans comes this metaphoric use when something unbelievable occurs.

Kitsune no yomeiri **狐の嫁入り** "a fox becomes a bride"

---

1. a sudden shower when the sun is shining, a sun shower

なんだ？狐の嫁入りか？
Nan da? Kitsune no yomeiri ka?
What's this? A sun shower?

晴れているのに雨が……まるで狐の嫁入りだね。

Harete iru no ni ame ga . . . maru de kitsune no yomeiri da ne.
Raining even though the sun is out . . . just like a sun shower.

2. (from its resemblance to a procession of lanterns formerly carried at a wedding procession) a large number of will-o'-the-wisps or foxfires

子供の頃おばあちゃんから裏山で狐の嫁入りを見たと聞かされ怖かった。
Kodomo no koro obāchan kara urayama de kitsune no yomeiri o mita to kikasare kowakatta.
I remember being scared when I was little and my grandma told me about seeing will-o'-the-wisps deep in the mountains.

Kitsune soba (udon) きつねそば（うどん） "fox *soba (udon)*"
buckwheat (wheat) noodles in broth and topped with a piece of fried tofu

---

きつねそばひとつください。
Kitsune soba hitotsu kudasai.
I'll take the *kitsune* soba.

週に1回はきつねうどんを食べないと気がすまない。
Shū ni ikkai wa kitsune udon o tabenai to ki ga sumanai.
I don't feel right unless I eat *kitsune udon* at least once a week.

❦ No, Japanese don't eat fox. These noodles derive their name from the belief that foxes like fried tofu, a belief borne out by the fact that the stylized guardian foxes known as *inari* bracing the *torii* of Shinto shrines are often presented with fried tofu offerings.

Kitsune to tanuki no bakashiai 狐と狸の化かし合い "the fox and the badger trying to outsmart each other"
try to outfox (outsmart) each other

冷戦時代の米ソのスパイ活動は狐と狸の化かし合いであった。
Reisen-jidai no Bei-So no supai katsudō wa kitsune to tanuki no bakashiai de atta.
U.S. and Soviet spy operations during the Cold War were a constant game of one-upsmanship (cat and mouse).

そのライバル会社の商戦は、狐と狸の化かし合いで、もう何年も続いている。
Sono raibaru-gaisha no shōsen wa, kitsune to tanuki no bakashiai de, mō nannen mo tsuzuite iru.
Those two rival companies have been trying to outsmart each other for years.

🦊 Both the fox and badger were formerly thought to be masters of deception, a belief that found its way into the language in this idiom, which now enjoys wide use.

Kitsunebi 狐火 "a fox fire"
fox fire; will-o'-the-wisp, ignis fatuus, jack-o'-lantern

あの山はよく狐火が見えるらしい。
Ano yama wa yoku kitsunebi ga mieru rashii.
They say that you can see a lot of fox fires on that mountain.

子供たちはその山の狐火の話を聞いて怖くなった。
Kodomo-tachi wa sono yama no kitsunebi no hanashi o kiite kowaku natta.
The children got scared when they heard stories of the fox fires on the mountain.

🦊 From the old belief that foxes breathed fire. There are also folk tales of foxes carrying lanterns in their own version of a wedding procession. Also called *onibi* 鬼火, or ogre fire.

Kitsuneme 狐目 "fox's eyes"
thin, sharp eyes

この狐目の男に見覚えはありませんか？
Kono kitsuneme no otoko ni mioboe wa arimasen ka?
Do you remember ever seeing this man with thin eyes before?

眼鏡をかけてるから気がつかないけど、彼女どっちかというと狐目してるよね。
Megane o kakete 'ru kara ki ga tsukanai kedo, kanojo dotchi ka to iu to kitsuneme shite 'ru yo ne.
It's hard to tell when she's wearing glasses, but her eyes are kind of thin.

✄ Not, by Japanese standards of physical beauty, the kind of eyes you want to have.

kiyasui 気安い "*easy ki*"

relaxed, familiar, friendly

気安い友人が何人もいて、俺は本当に幸せ者だ。
Kiyasui yūjin ga nannin mo ite, ore wa hontō ni shiawasemono da.
I'm a lucky guy to have so many friends I feel comfortable around.

あの先生には気安く何でも話せるってみんな言ってるよ。
Ano sensei ni wa kiyasuku nan de mo hanaseru tte minna itte 'ru yo.
Everyone says that that professor is very approachable (easy to talk to).

困ったことができたらいつでも気安く相談に来たまえ。
Komatta koto ga dekitara itsu de mo kiyasuku sōdan ni kitamae.
Any time you have a problem, feel free to come and talk it over.

あんな気安い言い方をされると不愉快だ。
Anna kiyasui iikata o sareru to fu-yukai da.
It's not very pleasant to be spoken to so offhandedly.

気安くあだ名を呼ばないでくださいな。
Kiyasuku adana o yobanai de kudasai na.

Don't get so familiar that you're going around calling me by my nickname.

☞ *ki ga okenai* 気がおけない, *kigaru (na)* 気軽(な), *kiraku (na)* 気楽(な); *kigane (o) suru* 気兼ね(を)する

kiyasume 気休め "a *ki* rest"

[empty] comfort, consolation, encouragement, reassurance, solace

単なる気休めと分かってはいるが、何かしないではいられないんだ。
Tannaru kiyasume to wakatte wa iru ga, nanika shinai de wa irarenai n' da.
I know it's only for my own peace of mind, but I can't just stand by and do nothing.

そんな気休めはもう聞きあきたんだろう。
Sonna kiyasume wa mō kikiakita n' darō.
You've gotta be sick and tired of everybody patting you on the back, telling you things will be all right.

気休めばかり言わないで本当のことを教えて下さい。
Kiyasume bakari iwanai de hontō no koto o oshiete kudasai.
I want the truth, not a pat on the back. / Don't just tell me everything's going to be all right. Give it to me straight.

試験が始まるまでの間、気休めに単語カードをもう一度見直した。
Shiken ga hajimaru made no aida, kiyasume ni tango-kādo o mō ichido minaoshita.
I spent the time until the test began looking over my word cards one more time just to reassure myself.

海外旅行に出かける前に、気休めに英会話教室に通っている。
Kaigai ryokō ni dekakeru mae ni, kiyasume ni ei-kaiwa kyōshitsu ni kayotte iru.

She's going to an English conversation school before she goes abroad, just to ease her mind.

🦂 Say there's something that's got you wringing your hands, but you know there's nothing you can do that will really improve matters. You've just got to do *something*. Doing something will at least allow your *ki* to relax (*ki ga yasumaru*). That *something* is a *kiyasume*. When used in reference to a comment by another person, the expression is replete with negativity, expressing an awareness of how hollow the comment is.

↪ *ki ga yasumasu* 気が休まる, *ki o yasumeru* 気を休める

kiyō-binbō 器用貧乏 "dexterous and poor"

Jack of all trades and master of none, fixer-upper, handyman, talented amateur

彼は何でも一応要領よくこなすんだけど、しょせん器用貧乏なんだよね。

Kare wa nan de mo ichiō yōryō yoku konasu n' da kedo, shosen kiyō-binbō nan da yo ne.

He can take on anything and do a decent job, but when all is said and done he's nothing but a fixer-upper.

器用貧乏って言われたくないから、何か一つのことを徹底的にマスターしたいんだ。

Kiyō-binbō tte iwaretaku nai kara, nanika hitotsu no koto o tettei-teki ni masutā shitai n' da.

I don't want to be thought of as "a Jack of all trades but master of none," so I'm going to make myself into an expert at something.

kiyo-hōhen 毀誉褒貶 "praise and criticism"

mixed opinion, divergent views, one extreme or the other

この政治家は、見方によって毀誉褒貶いろいろだ。
Kono seiji-ka wa, mikata ni yotte kiyo-hōhen iroiro da.
Depending on your point of view, that politician's either a hero or a crook.

毀誉褒貶は世の習いと言うけれど、それにしてもこの人の評判は両極端だね。
Kiyo-hōhen wa yo no narai to iu keredo, sore ni shite mo kono hito no hyōban wa ryō-kyokutan da ne.
They say you can't please all the people all of the time, but even so, opinions on this guy run to extremes.

kizetsu suru 気絶する "cut off *ki*"

black out, faint, fall unconscious

幸い気絶しただけで怪我はなかったんです。
Saiwai kizetsu shita dake de kega wa nakatta n' desu.
Fortunately, I just fainted and wasn't injured at all.

金額を聞いて気絶しそうになったよ。
Kingaku o kiite kizetsu shisō ni natta yo.
I nearly passed out when I heard how much it was.

࿓ A noun form of *kizetsu* also exists but is virtually never encountered.

☞ *ki ga tōku naru* 気が遠くなる, *ki o ushinau* 気を失う

kizewashii 気ぜわしい "*ki* busy"

be harried, hounded, in a tizzy, in a dither; feel rushed; be restless

ぎりぎりまで寝てるから、朝はいつも気ぜわしいんだ。
Girigiri made nete 'ru kara, asa wa itsumo kizewashii n' da.
I like to sleep till the last minute, so I'm always running around like mad (a chicken with its head cut off) in the morning.

気ぜわしく机の上を片づけて、飛ぶように帰って行った。
Kizewashiku tsukue no ue o katazukete, tobu yō ni kaette itta.
He hurriedly straightened up his desk and then flew out the door.

kizukai 気遣い "*ki* handling"

1. anxiety, concern, fear, worry; (take) care (not to hurt someone's feelings), consideration, regard, solicitude

朝が早い母への気遣いから夜はテレビの音を小さくすることにしている。
Asa ga hayai haha e no kizukai kara yoru wa terebi no oto o chiisaku suru koto ni shite iru.
Out of consideration for my mother, who has to get up early in the morning, I'm keeping the TV turned down at night.

私の気遣いは彼にはまったく汲んでもらえなかった。
Watashi no kizukai wa kare ni wa mattaku kunde moraenakatta.
He didn't give any consideration to all the care I had taken on his behalf. / Nothing I did for him even registered.

2. [in the negative] no chance of, no risk of

この様子じゃ雨が降る気遣いはなさそうだな。
Kono yōsu ja ame ga furu kizukai wa nasasō da na.

By the looks of things, there's no danger of it raining, I guess.

あいつなら人に騙される気遣いはないさ。
Aitsu nara hito ni damasareru kizukai wa nai sa.
You don't have to worry about him ever getting taken in by anyone (having the wool pulled over his eyes).

✤ See note at *kikubari* 気配り for the distinction between it and *kizukai*.

☞ *kigane* 気兼ね, *kizukau* 気遣う

kizukare 気疲れ "tired *ki*"

mental fatigue, nervous exhaustion

転職してからこっち気疲れの連続で、少し酒の量が増えたかも知れないなあ。
Tenshoku shite kara kotchi kizukare no renzoku de, sukoshi sake no ryō ga fueta kamo shirenai nā.
It's just been one thing after another since I changed jobs, and I'm emotionally beat (drained). I may even be drinking a little more, too.

姉貴の結婚式の後、おふくろ気疲れで２、３日寝込んだんだ。
Aneki no kekkon-shiki no ato, ofukuro kizukare de ni-san-nichi nekonda n' da.
Mom was worn to a frazzle after my older sister's wedding and ended up in bed for a couple days.

あんまり張り切ると気疲れするんじゃないかい。
Anmari harikiru to kizukare suru n' ja nai kai.
Don't you think you ought to cool it a little bit? You're pretty wound up.

体は全然疲れてないのに、すっかり気疲れしちゃったみたい。
Karada wa zenzen tsukarete nai no ni, sukkari kizukare shichatta mitai.

I'm not a bit tired physically. I guess it's just nervous exhaustion.

↪ *kibone ga oreru* 気骨が折れる (see under *kikotsu* 気骨)

kizukau 気遣う "use *ki*"

be careful (not to hurt someone's feelings), be considerate, think of, think about, worry (about), have someone's best interests at heart

彼はいつも「君はどう思うの？」と、相手のことを気遣う。
Kare wa itsumo "Kimi wa dō omou no?" to, aite no koto o kizukau.
He's quite considerate of others, always asking, "What do you think?"

仕事も大切だろうが、もっと家族を気遣ってあげればいいのにね。
Shigoto mo taisetsu darō ga, motto kazoku o kizukatte agereba ii no ni ne.
Work's important, all right, but it'd be nice if he'd worry a little more about his family, too.

妊娠中は、体を気遣ってきちんと一日三食取らなければならない。
Ninshin-chū wa, karada o kizukatte kichin to ichinichi-sanshoku toranakereba naranai.
You've got to be careful to eat three meals a day and pay attention to your health when you're pregnant.

彼のことを気遣うあまりに他の人の気持ちに無神経だった。
Kare no koto o kizukau amari ni hoka no hito no kimochi ni mu-shinkei datta.
I was so wrapped up in him that I was oblivious to how other people felt.

気遣ったつもりで遠慮してかえって相手を傷つけてしまった。
Kizukatta tsumori de enryo shite kaette aite o kizutsukete shimatta.
I tried to take his feelings into consideration and not be pushy, but I ended him hurting him all the same.

がっかりしている父を気遣って母は努めて明るく振る舞っている。

Gakkari shite iru chichi o kizukatte haha wa tsutomete akaruku furumatte iru.

Dad is all bummed out, so Mom is doing what she can to cheer him up. / Mom is all smiles trying to cheer Dad up.

娘のことを気遣ってやったのにちっとも感謝しない。
Musume no koto o kizukatte yatta no ni chittomo kansha shinai.
I had my daughter's best interests at heart, but she doesn't show any gratitude at all.

※ *Kizukau* is used when closeness to and affection for others underlies one's concern. It is distinguished from *ki o kubaru*, which is the effort one undertakes more in response to another's perceived need than from any particular affection for that person. *Ki o tsukau*, on the other hand, is used of actions taken for another's benefit that do not come straight from the heart and therefore can easily become an emotional burden.

↪ *ki o tsukau* 気を使う, *ki o kubaru* 気を配る, *ki ni kakeru* 気にかける, *ki ni suru* 気にする, *kizukai* 気遣い

kizuku 気づく "attach *ki*"

be aware of, discover, find out, get wind of, occur to one, perceive, sense

そんなことぐらい気づくべきだよ。
Sonna koto gurai kizuku beki da yo.
You have to think of those kinds of things.

彼が気づくのを待った。
Kare ga kizuku no o matta.
I waited for him to recognize me.

煙に気づいた時はすでに遅かった。
Kemuri ni kizuita toki wa sude ni osokatta.
It was already too late when I noticed the smoke.

彼がどんなに大変か、誰も少しも気づかなかった。
Kare ga donna ni taihen ka, dare mo sukoshi mo kizukanakatta.
No one had the slightest inkling of what he was going through.

❦ Generally speaking, *ki ga tsuku* is somewhat more concrete and colloquial whereas *kizuku* is more abstract and literary.

☞ *ki ga tsuku* 気がつく

kizumari (na)　気詰まり（な）　"stuck *ki*"

awkward, ill at ease, tense, uncomfortable, uptight

彼女が義理でつきあってくれたのが見え見えで気詰まりだったよ。
Kanojo ga giri de tsukiatte kureta no ga miemie de kizumari datta yo.
It was really awkward for me since it was plain to see that she was just seeing me out of a sense of obligation.

喧嘩してから仲直りするまでの1週間はなんとも気詰まりな毎日だった。
Kenka shite kara nakanaori suru made no isshū-kan wa nan to mo kizumari na mainichi datta.
I was uptight as could be for the whole week after the argument until we finally made up.

あの人といるとあまり話すことがなくて気詰まりだ。
Ano hito to iru to amari hanasu koto ga nakute kizumari da.
I feel uneasy when I'm around him because we don't have much to talk about.

☞ *ki ga tsumaru* 気が詰まる; *heiki (na)* 平気(な), *kigaru (na)* 気軽(な)

kōgan-muchi 厚顔無恥 "a thick face and no shame"

impudent, shameless, brazen, cheeky, unscrupulous, barefaced

あんな厚顔無恥な奴とは思ってもみなかった。俺も人を見る目がないよ。
Anna kōgan-muchi na yatsu to wa omotte mo minakatta. Ore mo hito o miru me ga nai yo.
I would never have thought he was such an unscrupulous bastard. I'm obviously no great judge of character.

なんて図々しい！　厚顔無恥って、あの人のためにある言葉じゃないかしら。
Nante zūzūshii! Kōgan-muchi tte, ano hito no tame ni aru kotoba ja nai kashira.
What nerve! He's the sort of guy that the expression "barefaced cheek" was invented for.

koi こい（鯉）　carp, koi

We're talking major cultural differences here between the way this bottom feeder has been traditionally viewed in the East and West. While it seldom finds its way onto dining tables in the West where it is generally spurned as a garbage fish by anglers who inadvertently hook it, in Asia this esteemed denizen of slow-moving rivers, ponds, and lakes has long been raised for food or bred for the pleasure its variegated colors bring sedate viewers. Before modern times in Japan, the *koi* was even considered superior to the sea bream, or *tai*, and often served as the main course on auspicious or congratulatory occasions.

The fish's fabled spirit and strength have given rise to the custom of hanging large carp-shaped wind socks or streamers made of paper or cloth, one for each male child in a family, on and around Children's Day, May 5, to celebrate another year of growth and safety.

Carp are counted *ichio* 一尾 or *ippiki* 一匹.

⇨ *mataita no koi* まな板の鯉, *Tōryūmon* 登竜門

Koi no takinobori 鯉の滝登り "a carp's climb up a waterfall"
getting ahead; a quick rise to the top (of one's profession or field)

彼の人生はまさに鯉の滝登りであった。
Kare no jinsei wa masa ni koi no takinobori de atta.
His life was a case study of how to get ahead.

最近の若者は鯉の滝登りを夢見る者が少なくなった。
Saikin no wakamono wa koi no takinobori o yume miru mono ga sukunaku natta.
There are fewer and fewer in the younger generation who dream of making it big in (leaving their mark on) the world.

🐟 According to Chinese legend, the carp alone among all fishes was able to swim up a waterfall called the Dragon's Gate, *Tōryūmon* 登竜門, on the upper reaches of the Yellow River, and by so doing was transformed into a dragon itself. In a takeoff from this legend, the Japanese idiom *koi no takinobori* has come to express a quick rise to the top of one's profession, or getting ahead. See next entry.

---

koketsu ni irazunba koji o ezu 虎穴に入らずんば 虎児を得ず "You can't catch a tiger cub without going in the tiger's lair."

nothing ventured, nothing gained

「虎穴に入らずんば虎児を得ず」だ、思い切って彼女に気持ちを打ち明けてみたら。
"Koketsu ni irazunba koji o ezu" da, omoikitte kanojo ni kimochi o uchi-akete mitara.
You know what they say, nothing ventured, nothing gained. Why don't you just tell her how you feel about her?

「虎穴に入らずんば虎子を得ず」、あのスラム街に潜入して情報収集するしかない。
"Koketsu ni irazunba koji o ezu," ano suramu-gai ni sennyū shite jōhō-shūshū suru shika nai.
Sometimes you've got to take risks. I guess there's no way around it, I've got to just go into the slum to get the info I need.

kokimi-yoi 小気味よい "a little taste of *ki* is good"

clever, sharp, smart; delightful, happy

彼女の口からは小気味よいせりふがポンポン出てきた。
Kanojo no kuchi kara wa kokimi-yoi serifu ga ponpon dete kita.
She was spouting off all kinds of witty things.

お宅の自慢料理に小気味よいアクセントをつけるスパイスはいかがですか。
Otaku no jiman-ryōri ni kokimi-yoi akusento o tsukeru supaisu wa ikaga desu ka.
Wouldn't you like to try one of our spices on that special dish of yours for that extra-special little something? [a line that might be heard in a department store's food section]

✤ There is a *kokimi (ga) warui* 小気味(が)悪い, but it's not very common and it's not an antonym of *kokimi-yoi*. It means "a little creepy" or "kind of weird" and is less common than *usukimi ga warui*, which means the same thing.

komanezumi こま鼠 "a top mouse"

a hard (tireless) worker, a busy (eager) beaver, a busy bee

あの人は一日中こま鼠のようによく働く。
Ano hito wa ichinichi-jū komanezumi no yō ni yoku hataraku.
She works her tail off all day. / She keeps her nose to the grindstone all day.

こま鼠のように働いて、役に立たなくなったらクビなんてまっ
ぴら御免だ。
Komanezumi no yō ni hataraite, yaku ni tatanaku nattara kubi nante mappira gomen da.
No way I'm gonna spend my whole life with my nose to the grindstone only to be given my walking papers when I'm not needed anymore.

🐭 The idiomatic use of this expression derives from the unusual behavior of the mutant *komanezumi* (top mouse) or *mainezumi* (dancing mouse). Indigenous to Japan, the dancing mouse has a hereditary inner ear disorder resulting in an impaired sense of balance that causes it to chase its tail in a frenzied whirlwind of senseless activity. Perhaps some wry observer of the national work ethic found a parallel in this mouse's ceaseless spinning round and round like a top (hence, its name) with the way people work as though there were no more significant activity in life on the archipelago. In usage, there is apparently no nuance of "senseless, repetitive activity." Found almost exclusively followed by *no yō ni hataraku*.

kōmori こうもり（蝙蝠） bat

Although there are some twenty-five species of bats that can be found in Japan, this much maligned nocturnal mammal figures in but one idiom and a single picturesque description of an umbrella, now seldom seen. Shunned as much for their facial resemblance to rats as any imagined notion of nefariousness, bats can still be observed intercepting insects in midair in the night skies in certain areas of Tokyo.

Bats are counted *ippiki* 一匹 or *ichiwa* 一羽.

Kōmorigasa こうもり傘 "a bat umbrella"
a big black umbrella

> 最近ではこうもり傘を見かけなくなった。
> *Saikin de wa kōmorigasa o mikakenaku natta.*
> You don't see many big, black umbrellas around anymore.
>
> 当時の私の祖父はこうもり傘に黒マントといういでだちで町を歩いていたそうです。
> *Tōji no watashi no sofu wa kōmorigasa ni kuro-manto to iu idedachi de machi o aruite ita sō desu.*
> In those days my grandfather used to walk around in a cape and carry a big black umbrella.

❧ Also called just *kōmori*, these Western-style umbrellas, as opposed to traditional bamboo and paper Japanese umbrellas called *bangasa* 番傘, appear to be on the endangered list. Before umbrellas became fashion statements, most were black and, whether opened to expose the ribs underneath that appeared to resemble the wings of a bat when viewed from below, or folded as a bat might fold its wings, the umbrella evoked the image of a bat strongly enough to warrant its name. With the gradual decline of all-black umbrellas, the word is heard less and less today, although older Japanese still use it.

koshi 腰 waist, hips

Koshi is defined in dictionaries as the part of the body where the legs are attached to the trunk, wherever that might be. Hips is perhaps the most common translation of the word, but waist is also frequently used. When Japanese talk about it hurting, *koshi ga itai,* then it's safe to say that they mean their lower back.

It is considered in many oriental cultures to be the part of the body from which power comes, so idioms including *koshi* often refer to physical strength and willpower or their absence.

Koshi also refers to a certain elusive quality of noodles, rice cakes, *mochi* and even paper. Basically, to have it is good and not to have it is bad. It might best be described as firmness or chewiness when those qualities are desirable in a food.

Koshi ga hikui 腰が低い "have a low waist"
be courteous, humble, polite; have a low profile

あの店のおやじさんは本当に腰が低い。
Ano mise no oyaji-san wa hontō ni koshi ga hikui.
The old guy that works there is really courteous.

今日、とても腰の低いセールスマンが来た。
Kyō, totemo koshi no hikui sērusuman ga kita.
A very polite salesman came by today.

↔ *koshi ga takai* 腰が高い

Koshi ga nukeru / koshi o nukasu 腰が抜ける／腰を抜かす
"one's hips drop out"
be so surprised that one is unable to move

腰が抜けるほどびっくりした。
Koshi ga nukeru hodo bikkuri shita.
That surprised the heck out of me. / I was floored.

これから僕の話すことにびっくりして腰を抜かすなよ。

Kore kara boku no hanasu koto ni bikkuri shite koshi o nukasu na yo.
Now don't let what I'm going to say throw you for a loop.

↠ *kimo o hiyasu* 肝を冷やす, *kimo o tsubusu* 肝を潰す

Koshi ga omoi 腰が重い "be heavy-hipped"
be prone to stay somewhere a long time; have lead in one's pants, be nailed to the floor, be slow to act, sit on one's hands

---

官庁は腰が重い、とよく批判される。
Kanchō wa koshi ga omoi, to yoku hihan sareru.
Government agencies are notorious for being as slow as molasses in winter.

彼はやっと重い腰を上げる気になった。
Kare wa yatto omoi koshi o ageru ki ni natta.
He finally got off his duff (made a move).

Koshi ga takai 腰が高い "have a high waist"
be impolite, high-handed, arrogant, hoity-toity

あの店の主人は腰が高いので客が少ない。
Ano mise no shujin wa koshi ga takai no de kyaku ga sukunai.
The guy who runs that store is so snooty that he doesn't have many customers.

彼は名門の出ということが自慢で、とても腰が高い。
Kare wa meimon no de to iu koto ga jiman de, totemo koshi ga takai.
He is so stuck-up just because he graduated from some famous school.

↠ *koshi ga hikui* 腰が低い

Koshi ga tsuyoi 腰が強い "have strong hips"

(1) be determined, hang tough, unbending, resolute (2) (of food) chewy; (of paste or glue) sticky; (of a brush or paper) firm

(1) 彼は腰が強いので、いつでも自分の思い通りにする。
Kare wa koshi ga tsuyoi no de, itsu de mo jibun no omoidōri ni suru.
He's the strong-willed type who always does things his own way.

☞ *ki ga tsuyoi* 気が強い; *koshi ga yowai* 腰が弱い

(2) この餅は腰が強い。
Kono mochi wa koshi ga tsuyoi.
This *mochi* is nice and chewy.

☞ *koshi ga yowai* 腰が弱い

Koshi ga yowai 腰が弱い "have weak hips"

---

(1) be weak-kneed, give up quickly (2) (of food) not be chewy; (of paste or glue) not be very sticky; (of a brush or paper) be limp, weak

(1) あの男は腰が弱いので、交渉には向かないだろう。
Ano otoko wa koshi ga yowai no de, kōshō ni wa mukanai darō.
That guy's such a pushover that he wouldn't be much of a negotiator.

☞ *ki ga yowai* 気が弱い; *koshi ga tsuyoi* 腰が強い

(2) この紙は腰が弱いのですぐ破ける。
Kono kami wa koshi ga yowai no de sugu yabukeru.
This paper tears easily because there's not much to it.

☞ *koshi ga tsuyoi* 腰が強い

Koshi o ireru / hongoshi o ireru 腰を入れる／本腰を入れる
   "put one's (main) hips into something"
throw oneself into something, put one's shoulder to the wheel

息子がようやく商売に腰を入れ始めた。
Musuko ga yōyaku shōbai ni koshi o irehajimeta.
My son finally started to put his back into the business.

彼はコンクールに出品するために、本腰を入れて制作を始めた。
Kare wa konkūru ni shuppin suru tame ni, hongoshi o irete seisaku o hajimeta.
He threw himself into his work so he could enter a piece in the contest.

Koshi o kakeru 腰を掛ける "sit one's hips down"
sit down, take a load off one's feet

彼はベンチに腰を掛けて本を読んでいた。
Kare wa benchi ni koshi o kakete hon o yonde ita.
He was sitting on a bench, reading a book.

彼女はポーチに腰を掛けて空を眺めていた。
Kanojo wa pōchi ni koshi o kakete sora o nagamete ita.
She was sitting on the porch, looking up at the sky.

Also 腰掛ける *koshi-kakeru*.

kōtō-mukei 荒唐無稽 "pointless and groundless"

absurd, nonsensical, wild

そんな荒唐無稽な話を誰が信じるもんか。
Sonna kōtō-mukei na hanashi o dare ga shinjiru mon ka.
Who's ever going to believe a story as crazy as that?

かれらは本気であの荒唐無稽な説明を繰り返しているんだ。
Karera wa honki de ano kōtō-mukei na setsumei o kurikaeshite iru n' da.
They're sticking to that cock-and-bull story as if they really believed it.

SFは、合理的であるより荒唐無稽なくらいの方が面白いよ。
Esuefu wa, gōri-teki de aru yori kōtō-mukei na kurai no hō ga omoshiroi yo.
Science fiction that verges on the absurd is much more interesting than the rational (realistic) stuff.

kubi 首 neck

Kubi not only means "neck" as a part of the body, but like the English is also used to refer to the narrow part of a bottle. Since, unlike its literal English counterpart, *kubi* also means "head," *kubi o kiru* can mean either to cut someone's neck or to behead someone. Figuratively, it may also be used to mean one's life, since it is difficult to imagine life without a neck. Hence, if someone shouts at you *Kubi o yaru ze!*, it is best to take to your heels before he can get at your neck. Less threatening, but none the less unpleasant, is the threat *Omae wa kubi da!*, which you should recognize as a promise to have your head insofar as it means your job.

Kubi ga abunai 首が危ない "one's neck is in danger"
about to be get fired, on the verge of losing one's job

このプロジェクトが失敗したら私の首は危ない。
Kono purojekuto ga shippai shitara watashi no kubi wa abunai.
If I lay an egg on this project, they're going to want my head.

首が危なくなるようなことは止めた方がいいよ。
Kubi ga abunaku naru yō na koto wa yameta hō ga ii yo.
You'd better not do anything that'll put your head on the chopping block.

☞ *kubi ga tobu* 首が飛ぶ, *kubi o kiru* 首を切る, *kubi ni naru* 首になる

Kubi ga mawaranai 首が回らない "be unable to turn one's neck"
be deep in debt, be in hock

今月は借金が多くて首が回らない。
Kongetsu wa shakkin ga ōkute kubi ga mawaranai.
I'm up to my neck (ears, eyeballs) in debt this month. / I'm swimming in debt this month. / I'm really in the hole this month.

債務で首が回らなくなった企業が次々と倒産した。
Saimu de kubi ga mawaranaku natta kigyō ga tsugitsugi tōsan shita.
Debt-ridden companies went belly up one after another.

Kubi ga tobu 首が飛ぶ "one's neck (head) flies"
get fired, get canned, get one's walking papers

社長に知れたら首が飛ぶぞ。
Shachō ni shiretara kubi ga tobu zo.
If the boss finds out, heads are going to roll.

この事件が広まったら、僕の首はいっぺんに飛んでしまう。
Kono jiken ga hiromattara, boku no kubi wa ippen ni tonde shimau.
If this ever gets out, I'll be out on my ass real quick.

☞ *kubi ni naru / kubi ni suru* 首になる／首にする, *kubi o kiru* 首を切る

Kubi ga tsunagaru 首がつながる "one's neck is connected"
manage to hang on to (keep) one's job

彼のおかげで首がつながった。
Kare no okage de kubi ga tsunagatta.
Thanks to him, I managed to hold on to my job. / I didn't get fired because of him.

なんとか首がつながる方法はないだろうか。
Nan to ka kubi ga tsunagaru hōhō wa nai darō ka.
There must be something I can do to keep from getting fired.

Kubi ni naru / kubi ni suru 首になる／首にする "become a neck"
get fired, get the ax (the boot).

僕は首になる前に自分から会社を辞めた。
Boku wa kubi ni naru mae ni jibun kara kaisha o yameta.
I quit before I got fired. / I quit before they could give me my walking papers.

「君を首にすることなど簡単だ」と部長がおどした。
"Kimi o kubi ni suru koto nado kantan da" to buchō ga odoshita.
The manager threatened me by saying, "I can sack (can) you so fast it'll make your head spin."

☞ *kubi ga abunai* 首が危ない, *kubi ga tobu* 首が飛ぶ

Kubi o furu 首を振る "shake one's head"
[横に *yoko ni*] shake one's head [as if to say "no"]; [縦に *tate ni*] nod one's head [as if to say "yes"]

信じられない、というように彼は首を振るばかりだった。
Shinjirarenai, to iu yō ni kare wa kubi o furu bakari datta.
He just shook his head in disbelief.

彼はようやく首を縦に振った。
Kare wa yōyaku kubi o tate ni futta.
He finally nodded his head (said OK). / He gave me the thumbs up (the green light, the nod, the go-ahead) at last.

どんなに頼んでも、彼は首を横に振るだけだった。
Donna ni tanonde mo, kare wa kubi o yoko ni furu dake datta.
He just kept shaking his head (He wouldn't say yes) no matter what I said. / It was thumbs down no matter what I said.

Kubi o hineru 首をひねる "twist one's neck"
wonder, have some doubts (reservations) about; ponder, think hard

「本当かな」と彼は首をひねった。
"Hontō ka na" to kare wa kubi o hinetta.
"Really?" he wondered aloud.

出されたクイズに、回答者全員が首をひねった。
Dasareta kuizu ni, kaitō-sha zen'in ga kubi o hinetta.
All the panelists racked their brains trying to figure out the answer.

☞ *hanshin-hangi* 半信半疑

Kubi o kiru 首を切る "cut off someone's neck"
fire someone, let someone go, get rid of someone, lay someone off

会社側が理由もなく君の首を切るとは考えられない。
Kaisha-gawa ga riyū mo naku kimi no kubi o kiru to wa kangaerarenai.
I can't imagine them sacking you for no reason.

いきなり150人もの従業員が首を切られた。
Ikinari hyakugojū-nin mo no jūgyō-in ga kubi o kirareta.
A hundred and fifty workers were suddenly out on the street.

☞ *kubi ga abunai* 首が危ない, *kubi ni naru / kubi ni suru* 首になる／首にする

Kubi o tsukkomu 首を突っ込む "stick one's neck into something"

(1) get (jump, delve) into something (2) interfere, poke one's nose into, meddle

(1) 彼はなんにでもすぐ首を突っ込む。
Kare wa nanni de mo sugu kubi o tsukkomu.

No matter what it is, he always jumps in with both feet.

(2) 君には関係のないことだ。首を突っ込んでくるな。
Kimi ni wa kankei no nai koto da. Kubi o tsukkonde kuru na.
It's none of your business, so just keep your nose out of it (just butt out).

Kubittake 首ったけ "up to one's neck (head)"
be infatuated with someone

彼は彼女に首ったけだ。
Kare wa kanojo ni kubittake da.
He's head over heels in love with her. / He's nuts about (over) her.

女性からのネクタイのプレゼントは、「私はあたなに首ったけ」という意味なのだそうだ。
Josei kara no nekutai no purezento wa, "Watashi wa anata ni kubittake" to iu imi na no da sō da.
When a girl gives you a necktie, it's supposed to mean that she's crazy about (got a crush on) you.

kuchi 口 mouth

Kuchi has multiple meanings and appears as a suffix of sorts in numerous compounds as well. In addition to that part of the body into which we put food and various poisons, *kuchi* also means what we "say" and figures in many expressions related to both how, and how often, we say what we say. *Kuchikazu no sukunai otoko,* for example, is a man of few words, a sort of Gary Cooper type. *Kuchi* also means an opening resembling a mouth, such as the mouth of a jar as in *kuchi no hiroi bin*—a wide-mouth jar. It can mean a person when spoken of as a mouth to feed, a bite of food or a taste, and finally, a share of something or a "piece of the action," all of which are *hito-kuchi*. It appears in compounds (with the *k* sometimes changing to *g*) such as *tozan-guchi,* literally a mountain-climbing mouth, or trailhead, and often indicates the place where something begins, ends, or passes through. In a related sense, it appears in a compound indicating a job opening or *shūshoku-guchi*. But this is only the beginning—*jo no kuchi* also happens to be the lowest division of sumo wrestling.

Kuchi ga heranai 口が減らない "mouth doesn't decrease"
have diarrhea of the mouth, run off at the mouth, be a ratchet-mouth, a ratchet-jaw, long-winded

---

全く口の減らない奴だ。
Mattaku kuchi no heranai yatsu da.
You're a real motormouth. / You just go on and on. / It's hard to get a word in edgewise with you. / Don't you ever shut up?

ああ言えばこう言うで、全く口の減らない子だ。
Ā ieba kō iu de, mattaku kuchi no heranai ko da.
You've got an answer for everything, don't you, smarty-pants.

↪ *kuchi kara saki ni umareru* 口から先に生まれる

Kuchi ga karui 口が軽い "have a light mouth"
have loose lips, can't keep one's mouth shut, can't keep a secret

---

高橋さんは口が軽いので気をつけた方がいいよ。
Takahashi-San wa kuchi ga karui no de ki o tsuketa hō ga ii yo.
Takahashi can't keep anything to himself (Takahashi's got a big mouth), so you'd better be careful what you say (around him).

あの人に秘密を話したのが失敗だね。口が軽いので有名なんだから。
Ano hito ni himitsu o hanashita no ga shippai da ne. Kuchi ga karui no de yūmei nan da kara.
Telling the secret to him was a big mistake. The guy's a notorious blabbermouth.

↪ *kuchi ga katai* 口が固い

Kuchi ga katai 口が堅い "have a hard mouth"
be tight-lipped, closemouthed

彼はとても口が堅い。
Kare wa totemo kuchi ga katai.
He knows how to keep a secret (keep his mouth shut).

口が堅い君だからこそ、こんな話をしたのだ。
Kuchi ga katai kimi dakara koso, konna hanashi o shita no da.
I told you about it because I know you can keep your mouth shut.

☞ *kuchi ga karui* 口が軽い

Kuchi ga suberu / kuchi o suberaseru 口が滑る／口を滑らせる "let one's mouth slip"
blab something, let something slip

つい口が滑って秘密を話してしまった。
Tsui kuchi ga subette himitsu o hanashite shimatta.
I blurted out the secret before I could stop myself.

相手が口を滑らせて言ったことを、彼は聞き逃さなかった。
Aite ga kuchi o suberasete itta koto o, kare wa kikinogasanakatta.
He didn't miss a thing that the guy let slip out.

☞ *kuchi ga karui* 口が軽い

Kuchi ga sugiru 口が過ぎる "too much mouth"
say too much, go too far

「少し口が過ぎるぞ」と彼は私をたしなめた。
"Sukoshi kuchi ga sugiru zo" to kare wa watashi o tashinameta.
"You're out of line, saying that," he scolded.

おせっかいだと言ったのは、私も口が過ぎたと反省している。
Osekkai da to itta no wa, watashi mo kuchi ga sugita to hansei shite iru.
I think I went a little overboard myself when I said it was none of your business.

↪ *kuchi ni ki o tsukeru* 口に気をつける

Kuchi ga suppaku naru hodo 口がすっぱくなるほど "until one's mouth gets sour"
how many times have I told you; tell over and over

遅刻するな、と口がすっぱくなるほど言ったのに。
Chikoku suru na, to kuchi ga suppaku naru hodo itta no ni.
If I've told you once, I've told you a thousand times—don't be late.

口がすっぱくなるほど注意しても、あの子の言葉づかいはなおらない。
Kuchi ga suppaku naru hodo chūi shite mo, ano ko no kotobazukai wa naoranai.
I've told that child to watch his P's and Q's until I was blue in the face, but he hasn't changed one bit.

Kuchi ga umai 口がうまい "one's mouth is good"
be a slick talker, a smooth operator, honey-tongued

「口がうまいわね」と言いながらも、彼女は嬉しそうに笑った。
"Kuchi ga umai wa ne" to iinagara mo, kanojo wa ureshisō ni waratta.
She laughed happily and said, "You've got quite a line."

あの人は口がうますぎて、どうしても信用できない。
Ano hito wa kuchi ga umasugite, dō shite mo shin'yō dekinai.
He's just too smooth a talker to trust. / No way I'm going to trust him, the way he has with words.

Kuchi ga warui 口が悪い "have a bad mouth"
be a bad-mouth, be critical of everything

あいかわらず君は口が悪いね。
Aikawarazu kimi wa kuchi ga warui ne.
I see your tongue is as sharp as ever.

彼は口は悪いが、根はやさしい人だ。
Kare wa kuchi wa warui ga, ne wa yasashii hito da.
He's always trashing everything, but he's good at heart.

Kuchi kara saki ni umareru 口から先に生まれる "be born mouth first"
be a born talker, a motormouth, a windbag, not know when to shut up

---

子供の頃、口から先に生まれてきたのだろうとよく言われた。
Kodomo no koro, kuchi kara saki ni umarete kita no darō to yoku iwareta.
When I was little, people used to tell me that I must have been born with a big mouth.

あの人はおしゃべりで、口から先に生まれてきたような人だ。
Ano hito wa oshaberi de, kuchi kara saki ni umarete kita yō na hito da.
The guy talks so much you'd think he was born with the gift of gab.

☞ *kuchi ga heranai* 口が減らない

Kuchi ni au 口に合う "suit one's mouth"
suit one's taste

このくらいの甘さが私の口には合っている。
Kono kurai no amasa ga watashi no kuchi ni wa atte iru.
This is about as sweet as I like things.

お口に合うかどうかわかりませんが、食べてみてください。
Okuchi ni au ka dō ka wakarimasen ga, tabete mite kudasai.
I don't know if you'll find this to your taste, but please try it.

Kuchi ni ki o tsukeru 口に気をつける "be careful of one's mouth"
mind one's tongue, watch one's P's and Q's

少しは口に気をつけたまえ。

Sukoshi wa kuchi ni ki o tsuketamae.
Watch your tongue.

私がうそつきだとは失礼な。口に気をつけろ。
Watashi ga usotsuki da to wa shitsurei na. Kuchi ni ki o tsukero.
That's pretty rude, calling me a liar like that. You'd better watch what you say.

⇨ *kuchi ga sugiru* 口が過ぎる

Kuchi ni suru 口にする "make something into a mouth"

(1) eat, feed one's face (2) say, express

(1) 今日は、一日何も口にしていない。
Kyō wa, ichinichi nani mo kuchi ni shite inai.
I haven't had a thing to eat all day.

(2) 近ごろ、外交関係者はよく「管理貿易」という言葉を口にしますね。
Chikagoro, gaikō-kankeisha wa yoku "kanri bōeki" to iu kotoba o kuchi ni shimasu ne.
The latest buzzword in foreign-policy circles is "managed trade."

お金のことは、あまり口にしない方がいいと思う。
Okane no koto wa, amari kuchi ni shinai hō ga ii to omou.
I think it would be better if you didn't bring up money too much.

Kuchi o dasu / kuchi ga deru 口を出す／口が出る "put out one's mouth"
interfere

あの人のことを見ていると、つい心配で口を出してしまう。
Ano hito no koto o mite iru to, tsui shinpai de kuchi o dashite shimau.
I can't help putting in my two cents out of sheer worry when I see him doing something.

お金は出すが口は出さない。
Okane wa dasu ga kuchi wa dasanai.
He'll put up the money (for the project), but he won't interfere (in the way it's run).

↪ *kuchi o hasamu* 口を挟む

Kuchi o hasamu 口を挟む "stick one's mouth in"
get one's two cents worth in, chip in, butt in, cut in

私にも口を挟ませてもらえませんか。
Watashi ni mo kuchi o hasamasete moraemasen ka.
I'd like to say a word (put in my two cents) here if you don't mind.

私達の問題ですから、口を挟まないでください。
Watashi-tachi no mondai desu kara, kuchi o hasamanai de kudasai.
Since it's our problem, maybe you'd like to just stay out of it.

↪ *kuchi o dasu / kuchi ga deru* 口を出す／口が出る

Kuchi o kiku 口をきく "work one's mouth"
talk, say; talk to, put in a good word for

あの男とは二度と口をきくつもりはない。
Ano otoko to wa nido to kuchi o kiku tsumori wa nai.
I'm never going to talk to him again.

この会社に就職したいのなら、私が口をきいてあげましょう。
Kono kaisha ni shūshoku shitai no nara, watashi ga kuchi o kiite agemashō.
I'll put in a word for you if you think you'd like to work here (for this company).

kuchibiru 唇 lip(s)

There are no famous sensuous Japanese lips, no Marilyn Monroe and no Andy Warhol to immortalize her. From a culture only now warming to the lure of the public embrace, it is too much to ask that lips play a prominent role in love lore. This may account, if nothing else does, for the sparsity of idioms focusing on the lips.

By the way, Japanese chickens don't have them either.

Kuchibiru o kamu 唇をかむ "bite one's lip"
bite one's lip, be disappointed, be long-faced.

さよならホームランを打たれたピッチャーは、くやしそうに唇をかんだ。
Sayonara hōmuran o utareta pitchā wa, kuyashisō ni kuchibiru o kanda.
The pitcher bit his lip in disappointment after he gave up a game-winning homer.

個人投資家たちは株の大きな値下がりに思わず唇をかんだ。
Kojin tōshika-tachi wa kabu no ōki na ne-sagari ni omowazu kuchibiru o kanda.
The big drop in stock prices wiped the smiles right off the faces of many individual investors.

Kuchibiru o togarasu 唇をとがらす "sharpen one's lips"
complain, grumble; pout

「家事ばっかり」と家内は時々唇をとがらしているよ。
"Kaji bakkari" to kanai wa tokidoki kuchibiru o togarashite iru yo.
The wife moans and groans that all she ever does is housework.

彼女は少しでも気に入らないことがあると、唇をとがらして文句を言う。
Kanojo wa sukoshi de mo ki ni iranai koto ga aru to, kuchibiru o togarashite monku o iu.
She bitches about every little thing that doesn't suit her just right.

「お母さんは、妹ばかりかわいがる」とその男の子は唇をとがらした。

"Okāsan wa, imōto bakari kawaigaru" to sono otoko no ko wa kuchibiru o togarashita.
"You always pay more attention to Sis than me," the boy pouted.

You might run across the next expression in some romantic potboiler, but people in the real world don't use it all that much. I mean, after all, how many of us have ever actually done it—or had it done to us?

Kuchibiru o ubau　唇を奪う　"steal someone's lips"
steal a kiss

男は女の唇は奪ったが、心までは奪えなかった。
Otoko wa onna no kuchibiru wa ubatta ga, kokoro made wa ubaenakatta.
The man may have stolen a kiss from her, but winning her heart was another matter.

突然唇を奪われて、彼女はとても驚いた。
Totsuzen kuchibiru o ubawarete, kanojo wa totemo odoroita.
She was just floored when he kissed her all of a sudden.

kuike　食い気　"eating *ki*"

desire (to eat)

旅行の行き先を決めるのには景色の良さより食い気の方が優先する。
Ryokō no yukisaki o kimeru no ni wa keshiki no yosa yori kuike no hō ga yūsen suru.
I decide where I want to travel based on what the food is like rather than the scenery.

食い気の塊みたいなやつでさ、いつも 2 人前食うんだぜ。
Kuike no katamari mitai na yatsu de sa, itsumo ninin-mae kuu n' da ze.
Guy's a bottomless pit, man. Eats enough for two people every time he sits down at the table.

🐰 Not to be confused with the notion of appetite—something that can come and go—*kuike* is here to stay, a sort of personality trait. Consequently, there are no *kuike ga aru (nai, suru)* or *kuike o moyōsu (oboeru)* constructions.

↪ *iroke yori kuike* 色気より食い気

kumo 蜘蛛 spider

The species of these largely misunderstood arthropods found in Japan are despised there just there as they are elsewhere, though the shrieks and cries of Japanese arachnophobes seem somehow shriller. Bad boys of the insect kingdom, spiders fare poorly in folk wisdom, which dictates that nocturnal spiders are to be killed while diurnal spiders are spared. "Dirt Spider," or *tsuchigumo* 土蜘蛛, was a derogatory appelation given to a legendary race who refused to be subjugated by the early rulers of the Yamato court.

Some households in Japan still believe that a spider wrapped in tissue paper and placed in a closet will guarantee financial good fortune. Were it only so easy.

Spiders are counted *ippiki* 一匹.

---

kumo no ko o chirasu 蜘蛛の子を散らす "scatter baby spiders" scatter out, disperse

---

群衆は機動隊の催涙弾を受け蜘蛛の子を散らすように逃げた。
Gunshū wa kidō-tai no sairuidan o uke kumo no ko o chirasu yō ni nigeta.
The crowd lit out in all directions when the riot police lobbed in tear gas.

デモ隊は戦車の現れるのを見て蜘蛛の子を散らすように逃げた。
Demo-tai wa sensha no arawareru no o mite kumo no ko o chirasu yō ni nigeta.
Demonstrators took to their heels and scattered in all directions at the sight of the tanks moving in.

少年達はガラスの割れる音を聞いて蜘蛛の子を散らすように逃げた。
Shōnen-tachi wa garasu no wareru oto o kiite kumo no ko o chirasu yō ni nigeta.
The boys were all assholes and elbows when they heard the glass breaking.

✤ Used often, though not exclusively, with *yō ni nigeru*. From the observation that baby spiders rush out in all directions when a sack full of them is ripped open.

kusatte mo tai 腐っても鯛 "a rotten sea bream is still a sea bream"

once a winner, always a winner; an old eagle is better than a young crow; a diamond on a dunghill is still a diamond

「なんだベンツ買ったって、中古じゃないか。」
"Nan da bentsu katta tte, chūko ja nai ka."
"Thought you said you bought a Mercedes? But what's this, man, a used one?"

「腐っても鯛というじゃないか。」
"Kusatte mo tai to iu ja nai ka."
"Hey, it's still a Mercedes."

腐っても鯛、この桐のタンスは20年以上も使っているが少しもきしみがない。
Kusatte mo tai, kono kiri no tansu wa nijū-nen ijō mo tsukatte iru ga sukoshi mo kishimi ga nai.
There's no denying quality. Had this paulownia chest of drawers for over twenty years, and it's as solid as ever.

✤ From the notion that something superior remains so even in old age. The idiom arises from the fact that the flesh of the snapper is relatively fat-free, and the taste, therefore, does not decline significantly when not perfectly fresh.

kushin-santan 苦心惨憺 "take pains, trouble one's heart"

much hard work and effort; 〜する to take great pains, to go to a lot of trouble (to get something done), to struggle hard

苦心惨憺の結果、ようやくライフワークの『日本語方言大辞典』が完成した。
Kushin-santan no kekka, yōyaku raifuwāku no "Nihongo Hōgen Dai-jiten" ga kansei shita.
After much toil and effort she at last completed her lifework, *A Dictionary of Japanese Dialects*.

倉橋教授は何度も失敗して苦心惨憺したが、ついに新薬開発に成功した。
Kurahashi-kyōju wa nando mo shippai shite kushin-santan shita ga, tsui ni shin'yaku-kaihatsu ni seikō shita.
After a long hard struggle and many failures, Professor Kurahashi at last succeeded in developing the new drug.

まったく苦心惨憺させられたぜ、あいつには。
Mattaku kushin-santan saserareta ze, aitsu ni wa.
I was really put through the wringer on account of that jerk.

❀ *akusen-kutō* 悪戦苦闘, *shiku-hakku* 四苦八苦

kyōki 狂気 "crazy *ki*"

insanity, madness

弁護士は被告人の狂気を理由に無罪を主張した。
Bengo-shi wa hikoku-nin no kyōki o riyū ni muzai o shuchō shita.
The attorney for the accused pleaded not guilty by reason of insanity.

まるで狂気にとりつかれたような仕事ぶりじゃありませんか。
Marude kyōki ni toritsukareta yō na shigoto-buri ja arimasen ka.
You're really working like mad there, aren't you.

彼の狂気じみた言動には家族も困り果てているらしい。
Kare no kyōki-jimita gendō ni wa kazoku mo komarihatete iru rashii.
I heard his family is just about at its wit's end over his crazy (insane, outlandish) behavior.

☞ *kichigai* 気違い; *shōki* 正気

kyozetsu-hannō　拒絶反応　"refusal reaction"

rejection (of foreign tissue or organ); adverse reaction

移植手術は成功したが、拒絶反応が心配だ。
Ishoku-shujutsu wa seikō shita ga, kyozetsu-hannō ga shinpai da.
The transplant operation was a success, but we're still worried about possible rejection.

拒絶反応さえ抑えられれば、回復するんだが。
Kyozetsu-hannō sae osaerarereba, kaifuku suru n' da ga.
As long as we can keep the rejection symptoms under control, there's a good chance of recovery.

外国語と聞くと、拒絶反応を起こしてしまうようだよ。
Gaikoku-go to kiku to, kyozetsu-hannō o okoshite shimau yō da yo.
The words "foreign language" are enough to bring him out in a cold sweat.

原子力の利用には拒絶反応を起こす人が多い。
Genshi-ryoku no riyō ni wa kyozetsu-hannō o okosu hito ga ōi.
There are a lot of people who feel violently opposed to the use of nuclear power.

✣ A synonymous expression (when used in the figurative sense given in the last two examples) is 拒否反応 (*kyohi-hannō*).

kyōzon-kyōei 共存共栄 "living together, flourishing together"

coexistence and co-prosperity

下請けを利用するというのではなく、共存共栄して行くという考え方でなければだめさ。
Shitauke o riyō suru to iu no de wa naku, kyōzon-kyōei shite iku to iu kangaekata de nakereba dame sa.
We're not out to exploit our subcontractors; if we don't work together with them, none of us is gonna do well.

自国さえ繁栄すればよいのではなく、他の国々と共存共栄していきたい。
Jikoku sae han'ei sureba yoi no de wa naku, ta no kuniguni to kyōson-kyōei shite ikitai.
Just for our own country to be prosperous is not enough; we want to live and work together in harmony with all countries.

kyūshu 鳩首 "dove (or pigeon) necks"

get together to discuss something, put ones' heads together, huddle (up)

経営陣は不況対策で鳩首会議をしているところだ。
Keiei-jin wa fukyō-taisaku de kyūshu-kaigi o shite iru tokoro da.
The bigwigs are in the middle of a powwow, trying to figure out a way to cope with the recession.

首相のスキャンダル打開のため与党の幹部が鳩首密議を始めた。
Shushō no sukyandaru dakai no tame yotō no kanbu ga kyūshu-mitsugi o hajimeta.

Top-ranking members of the government (party in power) put their heads together to find a way out of the scandal swirling around the prime minister.

🕊 From the observation of the way pigeons congregate comes this expression for a number of people getting together to discuss something.

kyūso neko o kamu 窮鼠猫を噛む "a cornered rat will bite a cat"

a cornered rat can be dangerous; despair gives courage to a coward

窮鼠猫を噛むと言うぐらいだから誘拐犯との交渉にはくれぐれも気をつけてくれ。
Kyūso neko o kamu to iu gurai da kara yūkai-han to no kōshō ni wa kuregure mo ki o tsukete kure.
Remember that someone with his back to the wall will fight like hell. So watch your ass when you go in to negotiate with the kidnapper.

包囲された反乱軍はまさに窮鼠猫を噛むの言葉どおり猛反撃を開始した。
Hōi sareta hanran-gun wa masa ni kyūso neko o kamu no kotoba dōri mō-hangeki o kaishi shita.
With the desperation of a cornered rat, the surrounded rebels launched a vicious counterattack.

🐀 Those of us who have been there know the strength lurking deep within that allows even a weakling to stand up to someone of far superior strength. That fabled superhuman strength, both psychological as well as physical, that enables mothers to lift cars pinning their children is of a different ilk, at least in Japanese. It is called *kajiba no bakajikara*「火事場の馬鹿力」, or "the amazing strength (one displays) at the scene of a fire."

☞ *fukuro no (naka no) nezumi* 袋の(中の)鼠

kyūtai-izen 旧態依然 "(in the same) old style as ever"

the old school, things remain just as they have always been, a stick-in-the-mud, reactionary, fuddy-duddy, old-fashioned

若いのに、どうしてそんな旧態依然とした考え方しかできないの？
Wakai no ni, dōshite sonna kyūtai-izen to shita kangaekata shika dekinai no?
For somebody so young, how come you've got such a stick-in-the-mud attitude?

経営陣の頭が旧態依然のコチコチだから、もううちの社も長くないよ。
Keiei-jin no atama ga kyūtai-izen no kochikochi da kara, mō uchi no sha mo nagaku nai yo.
Our company's gonna go under soon; the guys at the top have got a mind-set so out-of-date it's almost Neanderthal.

mago ni mo ishō 馬子にも衣装 "clothes for even a (packhorse) driver"

(the) clothes make the man

馬子にも衣装っていうけど、本当に良く似合ってるよその服。
Mago ni mo ishō tte iu kedo, hontō ni yoku niatte 'ru yo sono fuku.
I know what they say about the clothes making the man, but you *really* look good in those duds.

スーツ新調して卒業パーティーに出たら、「馬子にも衣装」とかからかわれた。
Sūtsu shinchō shite sotsugyō pātī ni detara, "mago ni mo ishō" to karakawareta.

I got teased about clothes making the man when I went to our graduation party in a new suit.

🐾 Commonly used in Japan as a modest response to praise or jocularly among friends.

makeinu 負け犬 "defeated dog"

a loser, failure, down-and-outer, an also-ran; a nobody

おまえのような負け犬はこのチームにはいらない。
Omae no yō na makeinu wa kono chīmu ni wa iranai.
We don't need losers like you on the team.

負け犬になったらおしまいだよ。君のように上を狙っている奴がうようよしているんだから。
Makeinu ni nattara oshimai da yo. Kimi no yō ni ue o neratte iru yatsu ga uyouyo shite iru n' da kara.
If you tuck your tail between your legs and give up now, it's curtains for you. There are all kinds of people out there just like you who are trying to get on top.

🐾 This is not used of a person or team considered unlikely to compete successfully in a future event, someone referred to in English as an underdog. *Makeinu* is used of one who has already, often habitually, lost and has the air of failure about him. It comes from the image of a dog in full retreat, tail tucked between its legs, after losing a fight.

makeinu no tōboe 負け犬の遠吠え "the howling of a defeated dog"

a parting shot; an empty threat; (leave a person with) a few menacing words

加藤のせりふは負け犬の遠吠え以外の何ものでもなかった。
Katō no serifu wa makeinu no tōboe igai no nanimono de mo nakatta.
All that stuff Kato was saying was nothing but a bunch of sour grapes.

配置転換を批判する彼の言葉は負け犬の遠吠えに聞こえなくもない。
Haichi-tenkan o hihan suru kare no kotoba wa makeinu no tōboe ni kikoenaku mo nai.
His complaints about being transferred sound like so much whining.

❧ Of what people who have been defeated or humiliated say when they are unable to back up their words with action. From the observation that a dog defeated by another retreats, tail between its legs, to howl in the distance.

↪ *itachi no saigoppe* いたちの最後っぺ

man'in-densha 満員電車 "a full-of-people train"

a jam-packed train

毎日満員電車に乗って通勤するのが嫌で、田舎にUターンしたんだ。
Mainichi man'in-densha ni notte tsūkin suru no ga iya de, inaka ni yūtān shita n' da.
I couldn't stand the daily commute on a packed train, so I moved back to my hometown.

今朝、満員電車の中で、痴漢と間違えられて、思いっきり足踏まれた。

Kesa, man'in-densha no naka de, chikan to machigaerarete, omoikkiri ashi fumareta.
This morning, a woman on the rush-hour train thought I was molesting her and trod on my foot with all her might.

🐇 痴漢 (*chikan*) is a sexual molester (invariably a man) who often harasses women on the trains (hoping, one presumes, his victims will be unable to tell who their tormentor is and be unable to defend themselves, as the trains are so packed it is virtually impossible to move).

manaita no koi まな板の鯉 "a carp on the cutting board"

be resigned to one's fate, be ready to take one's punishment

いよいよ明日は試験ですね。勉強しなくていいの。
Iyoiyo ashita wa shiken desu ne. Benkyō shinakute ii no.
The test's tomorrow, isn't it? Hadn't you better be hitting the books?

まな板の鯉の心境だよ。
Manaita no koi no shinkyō da yo.
It's outa my hands now. I'll just have to take what's comin' to me.

裁判官の前に立ったときはまさにまな板の鯉になった。
Saiban-kan no mae ni tatta toki wa masa ni manaita no koi ni natta.
Standing there in front of the judge, I felt like I was just waiting for the axe to fall.

🐇 Of a situation over which one has no control and the likely unpleasant outcome, which one has no choice but to accept. From anthropomorphizing of a carp's imagined emotional state as it lies on the chef's cutting board awaiting beheading, disembowelment, and drawing and quartering in the service of culinary pleasure.

☞ *koi* 鯉, *Tōryūmon* 登竜門

mayu 眉 eyebrow(s), brow(s)

Most of the following idioms have to do with what lies behind the expression on someone's face: doubt, suspicion, concern, or worry.

Mayu ni tsuba o nuru 眉に唾をぬる "apply spit to one's eyebrows"
keep one's wits about one, be on one's guard, be wary, keep on one's toes

---

彼のもうけ話は眉に唾をぬって聞いた方がいい。
Kare no mōke-banashi wa mayu ni tsuba o nutte kiita hō ga ii.
You'd better take what he says about making a lot of money with a grain of salt.

その話はどうもうますぎるね。眉に唾をぬった方がよさそうだ。
Sono hanashi wa dō mo umasugiru ne. Mayu ni tsuba o nutta hō ga yosasō da.
You'd better watch your step. That sounds too good to be true.

Also 眉に唾を付ける *mayu ni tsuba o tsukeru.*

↔ *ki o tsukeru* 気をつける

Mayu o hisomeru 眉をひそめる "narrow one's brows"
knit one's brows, furrow one's brows, frown

車内の酔っぱらいに、みんなは眉をひそめた。
Shanai no yopparai ni, minna wa mayu o hisometa.
Everyone in the train was giving the drunk the bad eye.

彼は夜中でもボリュームを上げてロックを聞くので、近所の人は皆眉をひそめている。
Kare wa yonaka demo boryūmu o agete rokku o kiku no de, kinjo no hito wa mina mayu o hisomete iru.
The whole neighborhood is giving him dirty looks because he listens to rock music full-blast on his stereo late at night.

Also 眉を集める *mayu o atsumeru.*

me 目 eye   *me* 眼 eye

The importance of this part of the body is indicated by the number of expressions in which it figures. By my count, well over a hundred. Those selected for inclusion here reflect the wide range of meanings carried by the word. In addition to its basic reference to the seeing eye or eyeball itself, *me* includes the power of vision as exemplified most simply in the sentences *me ga warui* or *me ga ii,* which may mean to have bad or good eyesight respectively. By extension, *me* appears in many expressions concerning judgment or insight. It can also denote appearance or the way something looks, or an experience—usually bad. Although not exemplified in any of the idioms which follow, *me* also means the grain in a piece of wood, the pips on a die, or the points formed at the intersection of lines on a *go* board. Finally, one usage that you run into all the time is as a suffix after a number forming the Japanese equivalent of an English ordinal, as in *futatsume no mondai* (the second problem) or *shiri kara sanban-me* (third from the end or rear).

Me ga hanasenai 目が離せない "can't take one's eyes off"
can't take one's eyes off

最近の国際情勢には目が離せない。
Saikin no kokusai-jōsei ni wa me ga hanasenai.
You've really got to keep your eyes riveted on international developments these days.

ヨチヨチ歩きの赤ん坊だけに全く目が離せない。
Yochiyochi-aruki no akanbō dake ni mattaku me ga hanasenai.
He's just a toddler, so you can't take your eyes off him for even a moment.

☞ *ki o kubaru* 気を配る; *me o hanasu* 目を離す

Me ga kiku 眼が利く "one's eyes work"
know how to spot something good

彼女は、版画にはなかなか目が利く人です。
Kanojo wa, hanga ni wa nakanaka me ga kiku hito desu.
She's quite a connoisseur of woodblock prints. / She has good taste in (a good eye for) woodblock prints.

↪ *me ga takai* 目が高い, *me ga koeru* 目が肥える

Me ga koeru 目が肥える "one's eyes grow fat"
know a thing or two about something, be knowledgeable about something

彼女は骨董品屋の娘だけあって、古いものには目が肥えている。
Kanojo wa kottōhin-ya no musume dake atte, furui mono ni wa me ga koete iru.
Since her parents run an antique shop she really has a good eye for old things.

↪ *me ga kiku* 目が利く, *me ga takai* 目が高い

Me ga mawaru 目が回る "one's eyes go around"

(1) feel dizzy (2) be extremely busy

(1) おなかが空き過ぎて目が回りそうだ。
Onaka ga sukisugite me ga mawarisō da.
I'm so hungry I feel giddy (it feels like the room is going around).

(2) 歳末は目が回るほど忙しくなりそう。
Saimatsu wa me ga mawaru hodo isogashiku narisō.
It's really going to be hectic around the end of the year. / I bet my head is going to be spinning (I'm going to be up to my neck in things to do) around year-end.

↪ *ki o ushinau* 気を失う, *kizetsu suru* 気絶する

Me ga nai 目がない "have no eyes"

(1) be crazy about, like a lot (2) not know what one is doing

(1) 彼はすしに目がない。
Kare wa sushi ni me ga nai.
He's got quite a weakness for sushi.

日本人は外国製の高級品には目がないようだ。
Nihonjin wa gaikoku-sei no kōkyū-hin ni wa me ga nai yō da.
Japanese can't seem to get enough of foreign luxury goods.

(2) 君を採用しないなんて、あの会社の人事部は目がないね。
Kimi o saiyō shinai nante, ano kaisha no jinji-bu wa me ga nai ne.
Their personnel section must be totally blind (have its head up its ass) if they aren't going to hire you.

Me ga sameru 目が覚める "one's eyes wake up"

(1) wake up (2) come to one's senses, be enlightened (3) [used in the phrase ～ような *yō na*] amazing, startling

(1) 真夜中に大きな音がしたので目が覚めてしまった。
Ma-yonaka ni ōki na oto ga shita no de me ga samete shimatta.
A loud sound in the middle of the night woke me up.

(2) 親友の心からの忠告に、彼は目が覚めた。
Shinyū no kokoro kara no chūkoku ni, kare wa me ga sameta.
The heartfelt warning from his friend brought him to his senses (woke him up, made him see the light).

(3) 彼女は目の覚めるようなピンクのドレスを着て出かけた。
Kanojo wa me no sameru yō na pinku no doresu o kite dekaketa.
She went out wearing a startling (shocking) pink dress.

関東代表のチームは目の覚めるようなすばらしい試合をした。
Kantō-daihyō no chīmu wa me no sameru yō na subarashii shiai o shita.

The team representing the Kantō area played a spectacular game.

Me ga takai 目が高い "one's eyes are high"
know something backwards and forwards, know something inside and out

この絵を選ぶとは、さすが（お）目が高い。
Kono e o erabu to wa, sasuga (o)me ga takai.
You certainly have a sharp eye for paintings to have chosen this one.

☞ *me ga kiku* 目が利く, *me ga koeru* 目が肥える

Me ga todoku 目が届く "one's eyes reach"
keep an eye on something

1クラス40人に教師が1人では、なかなか生徒全員に目が届かない。
Hito-kurasu yonjū-nin ni kyōshi ga hitori de wa, nakanaka seito zen'in ni me ga todokanai.
With 40 students, it's pretty hard for one teacher to keep an eye on all of them.

監督の目が届かないところでさぼったりしないように。
Kantoku no me ga todokanai tokoro de sabottari shinai yō ni.
No goofing off when the manager's not watching.

Me ni amaru 目に余る "be too much for one's eyes"
be too much (a bit much), intolerable

あの男の横暴ぶりには目に余るものがある。
Ano otoko no ōbō-buri ni wa me ni amaru mono ga aru.
I've had just about enough of him acting so high and mighty. / There's something about his high-handedness that is really too much.

あの政治家の企業への癒着ぶりには目に余るものがある
Ano seiji-ka no kigyō e no yuchaku-buri ni wa me ni amaru mono ga aru.
That politician is much too cozy with business interests for me.

Me ni miete 目に見えて "can see it with one's eyes"
clearly, obviously

病人は目に見えて回復していった。
Byōnin wa me ni miete kaifuku shite itta.
The patient was improving right before our very eyes. / The patient's condition had clearly improved.

彼の権力は目に見えて衰えていった。
Kare no kenryoku wa me ni miete otoroete itta.
It was obvious to everyone that his power was waning.

彼らのたくらみが失敗するのは目に見えていた。
Karera no takurami ga shippai suru no wa me ni miete ita.
Everyone could see that their scheme was doomed to fail from the very beginning. / It was a foregone conclusion that their plot would end in failure.

↪ *ichimoku-ryōzen* 一目瞭然

Me ni suru 目にする "make something into an eye"
see

毛皮のコートを着ている人をよく目にするようになった。
Kegawa no kōto o kite iru hito o yoku me ni suru yō ni natta.
You run across more people wearing fur coats now than before.

「売り家あり」という張り紙を目にした。
"Uri-ya ari" to iu harigami o me ni shita.
I caught sight of a "house for sale" sign.

↪ *me o yaru* 目をやる

Me ni tomaru **目に留まる** "stop in one's eye"
get the attention of

彼女の演技がプロデューサーの目に留まった。
Kanojo no engi ga purodyūsā no me ni tomatta.
Her performance caught the attention of the producer.

花屋の店先で、ばらの鉢植えが目に留まった。
Hana-ya no misesaki de, bara no hachiue ga me ni tomatta.
Some potted roses in front of the flower shop caught my eye.

↬ *ki o hiku* 気を引く

Me ni tsuku **目につく** "stick on one's eye"
stick out, catch one's attention

派手なポスターが街のあちこちで目についた。
Hade na posutā ga machi no achikochi de me ni tsuita.
Colorful posters here and there throughout the city caught my eye.

背の高い彼女はどこへ行っても目につく。
Se no takai kanojo wa doko e itte mo me ni tsuku.
She is so tall that she stands out wherever she goes.

↬ *ki ni tomeru* 気に止める

Me ni ukabu **目に浮かぶ** "float into one's eyes"
can picture, visualize

彼女の慌てぶりが目に浮かぶ。
Kanojo no awate-buri ga me ni ukabu.
I can just imagine how excited she's going to be.

その情景が目に浮かんだ。
Sono jōkei ga me ni ukanda.

I could see the whole thing.

Me no doku 目の毒 "poison for the eyes"
the last thing one needs (wants) to see

ダイエット中の私に、おいしそうなケーキは目の毒だ。
Daietto-chū no watashi ni, oishisō na kēki wa me no doku da.
Being on a diet, mouth-watering cakes were the last thing I needed.

若い女性の水着姿は、中年男性には目の毒だ。
Wakai josei no mizugi-sugata wa, chūnen-dansei ni wa me no doku da.
It's tough for a middle-aged guy to have to look at all those young things in their swimsuits.

Me no kataki ni suru 目の敵にする "make someone an enemy of one's eyes"
don't like someone's looks, hate someone's guts, have it in for someone

---

どうも彼は外国人を目の敵にしているようだ。
Dō mo kare wa gaikoku-jin o me no kataki ni shite iru yō da.
You get the feeling that he hates the very sight of a foreigner.

なぜ共産主義者を目の敵にするのですか。
Naze kyōsan-shugisha o me no kataki ni suru no desu ka.
Why have you got it in for Communists?

Me no tama no kuroi uchi 目の玉の黒いうち "while one's eyes are black"
as long as one is alive and kicking; [in the negative] over my dead body

---

俺の目の玉の黒いうちは、お前の好きにはさせん。
Ore no me no tama no kuroi uchi wa, omae no suki ni wa sasen.
You're never going to get things your way as long as I'm around to see to it (if I've got anything to say about it).

私の目の玉の黒いうちは、この土地は絶対人手に渡さない。
Watashi no me no tama no kuroi uchi wa, kono tochi wa zettai hitode ni watasanai.
The only way anyone will ever get their hands on that property is over my dead body.

Also 目の黒いうち *me no kuroi uchi.*

Me no ue no (tan-)kobu 目の上の（たん）こぶ "a knot above one's eye"
someone who stands in one's way

彼にとっては、直属の上司が目の上のたんこぶだった。
Kare ni totte wa, chokuzoku no jōshi ga me no ue no tan-kobu datta.
His immediate superior was a real thorn in his side.

姉の存在が、彼女には目の上のこぶだった。
Ane no sonzai ga, kanojo ni wa me no ue no kobu datta.
Her elder sister stood in her way.

Me o hanasu 目を離す "take one's eyes off"
take one's eyes off

ちょっと目を離したすきに、盗まれたのです。
Chotto me o hanashita suki ni, nusumareta no desu.
Someone stole it when I looked the other way. / I just let it out of my sight for a moment, and someone stole it.

あの子は目を離すと、何をするかわからない。
Ano ko wa me o hanasu to, nani o suru ka wakaranai.
Take your eyes off that kid for a minute and she's up to something.

☞ *me ga hanasenai* 目が離せない

Me o hikarasu　**目を光らす**　"make one's eyes shine"
keep an eye on (as in surveillance), watch over someone's shoulder

> ガードマンが警備の目を光らせていた。
> *Gādoman ga keibi no me o hikarasete ita.*
> The rent-a-cop kept his eyes peeled.

> 刑事は容疑者の動きに目を光らせた。
> *Keiji wa yōgi-sha no ugoki ni me o hikaraseta.*
> The detective kept a close eye on the suspect's movements.

Me o hosomeru　**目を細める**　"narrow one's eyes"
beam, smile with one's eyes

> ベ母親は娘の踊る姿に目を細めていた。
> *Haha-oya wa musume no odoru sugata ni me o hosomete ita.*
> She beamed with delight (was bursting at the seams with pride) as she watched her daughter dance.

> ベビーカーの中を、老婆は目を細めてのぞき込んだ。
> *Bebīkā no naka o, rōba wa me o hosomete nozokikonda.*
> The old woman's eyes lit up when she peeked into the baby carriage.

Also 目を細くする *me o hosoku suru*.
↝ *kishoku-manmen* 喜色満面

Me o maruku suru　**目を丸くする**　"make one's eyes round"
be round-eyed, astounded; one's eyes get big

> 子供たちは目を丸くして子犬を見ていた。
> *Kodomo-tachi wa me o maruku shite ko-inu o mite ita.*
> The children watched the puppies with wide-eyed interest.

乱暴な娘の態度に母親は目を丸くした。
Ranbō na musume no taido ni haha-oya wa me o maruku shita.
She was flabbergasted at her daughter's violent behavior.

☞ *hato ga mamedeppo o kutta yō na* 鳩が豆鉄砲を食ったような

Me o mukeru 目を向ける "turn one's eyes toward"
look at, consider, look toward, turn to

細かいことばかりではなく、全体に目を向けたまえ。
Komakai koto bakari de wa naku, zentai ni me o muketamae.
Try not to get too caught up in the little things. Keep the big picture in mind.

経済援助をめぐって、第三世界はますます日本に目を向けるだろう。
Keizai-enjo o megutte, daisan-sekai wa masumasu Nihon ni me o mukeru darō.
In all likelihood, Third World countries will turn more and more to Japan for economic assistance.

Me o nusumu 目を盗む "steal someone's eyes"
avoid being seen by someone

子供たちは家の人の目を盗んでお酒を飲んだ。
Kodomo-tachi wa ie no hito no me o nusunde osake o nonda.
The kids sneaked a drink behind their family's back.

親の目を盗んでコソコソ男と会うとは何事だ。
Oya no me o nusunde kosokoso otoko to au to wa nanigoto da.
What do you think you're doing, slipping out and hanging around with guys without your parents knowing?

Me o samasu 目を覚ます "wake up one's eyes"

(1) wake up (2) know better, wake up

(1) 今朝、いつもより早く目を覚ました。
Kesa, itsu mo yori hayaku me o samashita.
I woke up earlier than usual this morning.

(2) いつまでバカなことをやっているんだ、いい加減に目を覚ませ！
Itsu made baka na koto o yatte irun da, ii kagen ni me o samase!
When are you ever going to learn? Get your act together!

☞ *me ga sameru* 目が覚める

Me o tōsu 目を通す "pass one's eyes over"
look at, look over

彼は毎朝新聞に目を通すことにしている。
Kare wa maiasa shinbun ni me o tōsu koto ni shite iru.
He's in the habit of skimming the newspaper every morning.

この原稿に目を通してください。
Kono genkō ni me o tōshite kudasai.
Take a look at (look over) this manuscript.

Me o tsuburu 目をつぶる "close one's eyes"
let something pass, wink at something

今回のことは目をつぶっておきましょう。
Konkai no koto wa me o tsubutte okimashō
I'm going to let it go this time. / I'm going to look the other way this once.

Me o tsukeru 目をつける "put one's eyes on something"
keep one's eye on, be interested in, check out

彼は警察から目をつけられている。
Kare wa keisatsu kara me o tsukerarete iru.
He's being watched by the police. / The police have zeroed in on him. / The police are onto him.

前からあの新型テレビに目をつけていたのだ。
Mae kara ano shingata-terebi ni me o tsukete ita no da.
I've had my eye on that new TV for a while.

Me o yaru 目をやる "give the eye"
look at

庭の桜の花に目をやった。
Niwa no sakura no hana ni me o yatta.
I looked at the cherry blossoms in the garden.

音のした方に目をやると、鳥が水浴びをしているところだった。
Oto no shita hō ni me o yaru to, tori ga mizuabi o shite iru tokoro datta.
When I looked in the direction the sound had come from, I saw some birds taking a bath.

Me to hana no saki 目と鼻の先 "right in front of one's eyes and nose"
right down the street, right over there; (of approaching events) impending, imminent

その店ならすぐそこ、目と鼻の先にありますよ。
Sono mise nara sugu soko, me to hana no saki ni arimasu yo.
Oh, that shop? It's just a stone's throw from here.

不況は目と鼻の先まで来ているようだ。

Fukyō wa me to hana no saki made kite iru yō da.
A recession appears to be at hand (right around the corner).

Ome ni kakaru お目にかかる "to be hung on the eyes"
meet

一度ゆっくりお目にかかって、お話を伺いたいと思っています。
Ichido yukkuri ome ni kakatte, ohanashi o ukagaitai to omotte imasu.
I hope to have the opportunity to speak with you at length sometime soon.

はじめてお目にかかります。私が山本です。
Hajimete ome ni kakarimasu. Watashi ga Yamamoto desu.
I believe this is the first time I've had the pleasure. Yamamoto is my name.

Shiroi me de miru 白い眼で見る "look at with white eyes"
look askance at, give someone a dirty look, look daggers at someone

---

容疑者の家族は皆から白い眼で見られた。
Yōgi-sha no kazoku wa mina kara shiroi me de mirareta.
The suspect's family was getting dirty looks from everyone.

老人は、彼女が未婚の母だというだけで、白い眼で見た。
Rōjin wa, kanojo ga mikon no haha da to iu dake de, shiroi me de mita.
The old man looked down on (looked down his nose at) her just because she was an unwed mother.

megitsune 牝狐 "a vixen"

bitch, witch; shrew, vixen

あの牝狐め、色仕掛けで秘密を探り出そうとしている。
Ano megitsune-me, irojikake de himitsu o saguridasō to shite iru.

That bitch is batting her eyelashes around trying to find out what's going on.

あの牝狐に引っかかったらどんな男もダメになる。
Ano megitsune ni hikkakattara donna otoko mo dame ni naru.
I don't care who you are, let that witch get her claws in you and that's all she wrote (you're done for).

☙ From the belief that foxes take the form of a woman to deceive people. Appears almost exclusively preceded by *ano*.

☞ *kitsune* 狐

messhi-hōkō 滅私奉公 "self-destruction, public service"

selfless service for the common good, to put the country's needs before one's own

今でもお役所では滅私奉公が要求されるみたいですね。
Ima de mo oyakusho de wa messhi-hōkō ga yōkyū sareru mitai desu ne.
Even today it seems that government offices demand that you sacrifice your personal life to your work.

東京にいた頃の僕は、典型的な滅私奉公の猛烈社員だったものだよ。
Tōkyō ni ita koro no boku wa, tenkei-teki na messhi-hōkō no mōretsu-shain datta mono da yo.
When I was in Tokyo I used to be a typical gung ho company employee, happy to put the company's needs before my own.

高度成長時代の日本のサラリーマンは、滅私奉公の精神で遮二無二働いた。
Kōdo-seichō jidai no Nihon no sararīman wa, messhi-hōkō no seishin de shani-muni hataraita.
During the postwar period of high economic growth Japanese white-collar

workers worked themselves to the bone in selfless sacrifice to rebuild the nation's wealth.

↣ *jiko-manzoku* 自己満足, *jiko-tōsui* 自己陶酔

mi ni amaru 身に余る "more than one's body"

more than one deserves

あなたからそのようなお言葉をいただくとは、身に余る光栄です。
Anata kara sono yō na okotoba o itadaku to wa, mi ni amaru kōei desu.
I hardly think I deserve such praise. / You are much too kind.

身に余る賞を贈られ、とても感謝しています。
Mi ni amaru shō o okurare, totemo kansha shite imasu.
I am deeply honored to be the recipient of such an award. / Thank you all so much for this most undeserved award.

↣ *karada* 体

mi ni naru 身になる "become someone's body"

put oneself in someone's place

少しは私の身になって考えてください。
Sukoshi wa watashi no mi ni natte kangaete kudasai.
Put yourself in my shoes for a minute.

親の身になって考えてみれば、そんなにわがままばかり言えないはずだ。
Oya no mi ni natte kangaete mireba, sonna ni wagamama bakari ienai hazu da.
If he ever looked at things from his parents' standpoint, he wouldn't be saying selfish things like that.

☞ *karada* 体

mi ni oboe ga aru 身に覚えがある "one's body remembers"

know about, have actually done something

君にも身に覚えがあるだろう。
Kimi ni mo mi ni oboe ga aru darō.
You know what this is all about, don't you? / What I'm saying rings a bell, doesn't it?

彼は、身に覚えのない罪で逮捕された。
Kare wa, mi ni oboe no nai tsumi de taiho sareta.
He was picked up for a crime that he knew nothing about (that he was completely in the dark about, had nothing to do with, hadn't committed).

☞ *karada* 体

mi ni shimiru 身にしみる "seep into one's body"

(1) to the bone (2) be deeply impressed by something or someone, make a lasting impression on one, sink in

(1) 夜風が身にしみる。
Yokaze ga mi ni shimiru.
The night wind is cutting (chilling) me to the bone.

(2) 旅先での人の親切が身にしみた。
Tabisaki de no hito no shinsetsu ga mi ni shimita.
I was struck by the kindness people showed me on my trip.

☞ *karada* 体

mi ni tsukeru 身に付ける "attach to one's body"

(1) wear, put on (2) learn, acquire (a skill)

(1) 彼は、いつも身に付けるものに気を配っている。
Kare wa, itsu mo mi ni tsukeru mono ni ki o kubatte iru.
He pays close attention to what he wears.

(2) 再就職するために、何か技術を身につけておこうと思う。
Sai-shūshoku suru tame ni, nani ka gijutsu o mi ni tsukete okō to omou.
I'm going to learn a skill before I go back into the job market.

☞ *karada* 体

mi o hiku 身を引く "pull one's body (away)"

get out, back out; back off; retire

社長は、来年身を引くと言っている。
Shachō wa, rainen mi o hiku to itte iru.
The president is talking about stepping down next year.

身を引く時期が来た。
Mi o hiku jiki ga kita.
The time has come to pull out.

彼女の将来を考えて、彼は身を引いた。
Kanojo no shōrai o kangaete, kare wa mi o hiita.
He decided it would be in her best interests to remove himself from the picture.

☞ *karada* 体

mi o ireru　身を入れる　"put one's body into something"

throw oneself into something

少しは勉強に身を入れなさい。
Sukoshi wa benkyō ni mi o irenasai.
It won't hurt you to study a little bit.

☞ *honki de ~ o suru* 本気で〜をする, *honki ni naru* 本気になる, *karada* 体, *ki o ireru* 気を入れる

mi o katameru　身を固める　"harden one's body"

(1) (get married and) settle down (2) bundle up

(1) 僕もそろそろ身を固めようと思います。
Boku mo sorosoro mi o katameyō to omoimasu.
I'm about ready to settle down and start a family myself.

(2) 防寒具に身を固めて、冬山を登った。
Bōkangu ni mi o katamete, fuyuyama o nobotta.
I bundled up in warm clothes and climbed the snowy mountain.

☞ *karada* 体

mi o ko ni suru　身を粉にする　"make powder out of one's body"

work like crazy, work until one drops, bust ass, bust one's buns

彼は借金を返すために、朝から晩まで身を粉にして働いた。
Kare wa shakkin o kaesu tame ni, asa kara ban made mi o ko ni shite hataraita.
He worked his fingers to the bone day in and day out to repay the loan.

身を粉にして働く毎日だった。
Mi o ko ni shite hataraku mainichi datta.
I was working like a dog back then.

Also 体を粉にする *karada o ko ni suru* and 身を砕く *mi o kudaku*.
☞ *isshō-kenmei* 一生懸命, *karada* 体

mi o makaseru 身を任せる "entrust one's body (to someone)"

(1) throw oneself on the mercy of someone (2) give oneself to someone, go to bed with a man

(1) 運命に身を任せることにした。
Unmei ni mi o makaseru koto ni shita.
I cast my fate to the wind.

(2) その夜、彼女は彼に身を任せた。
Sono yoru, kanojo wa kare ni mi o makaseta.
She gave herself to him that night.

☞ *hada o yurusu* 肌を許す, *karada* 体

mikka-bōzu 三日坊主 "a three-day priest"

someone who starts something only to give it up at once, someone with no staying power, (he) won't keep it up for long, (he) never sticks to anything for very long, it won't last

今年も日記帳を買ったが、三日坊主だからいつまで続くことやら。
Kotoshi mo nikki-chō o katta ga, mikka-bōzu da kara itsu made tsuzuku koto yara.
I bought a diary again this year, but with my usual lack of stick-to-itive-ness, who knows how long I'll keep it up.

姉のダイエットは、今回も三日坊主に終わった。
Ane no daietto wa, konkai mo mikka-bōzu ni owatta.
My big sister went on a diet again, but as usual she soon gave it up.

結果は三日坊主だったけど、一度はやる気になっただけいいじゃないか。
Kekka wa mikka-bōzu datta kedo, ichido wa yaru-ki ni natta dake ii ja nai ka.
It didn't last very long, but at least you had the gumption to give it a try.

✂ Here "three days" simply means "a short period of time," not necessarily 72 hours.

☞ *ki ga kawaru* 気が変わる

mikka-tenka 三日天下 "three days' reign"

a short-lived reign, a very brief reign, to be in power for a very short time

権力闘争の末、やっと首相になったが、女性問題のスキャンダルで三日天下に終わった。
Kenryoku-tōsō no sue, yatto shushō ni natta ga, josei-mondai no sukyan-daru de mikka-tenka ni owatta.

At the end of a power struggle he at last became prime minister, but his premiership was shortlived after he was caught having an extramarital affair.

重役会の造反で、新社長は退任に追込まれ、三日天下だった。
Jūyaku-kai no zōhan de, shin-shachō wa tainin ni oikomare, mikka-tenka datta.
The new president got caught up in a revolt by the board of directors and soon found himself out of a job (ousted from office).

※ The origin of this expression dates from the Sengoku era (1467–1568), when Akechi Mitsuhide made a surprise attack on Oda Nobunaga at Honnō-ji in Kyoto and wrested power from him, only to lose it to Toyotomi Hideyoshi almost immediately.

mimi 耳 ear

In addition to the external ear on humans and other animals, *mimi* means the power of hearing. Relatedly, it indicates a good ear for something, as for music. *Mimi* can also refer to one of usually a pair of earlike protuberances, such as a lug or a handle, the edge of a sheet of paper, or the crust of a piece of bread. *Mimi* may be the heel of a loaf of bread, though this usage may cause confusion due to the fact that it more commonly means the crust in general. *Mimi* appears in many compounds, one of which, *mimi-gakumon* or "ear learning," means "hearsay."

Mimi ga hayai **耳が早い** "have fast ears"
have one's ear to the ground

いつも井戸端会議をしている母は隣近所のことには耳が早い。
Itsu mo idobata-kaigi o shite iru haha wa tonari-kinjo no koto ni wa mimi ga hayai.

My mom's always gossiping with the women in the neighborhood, so she's always up on the latest news (skinny).

Mimi ga itai 耳が痛い "one's ears hurt"
hit a sore spot, hit where it hurts

彼の失敗談には耳が痛かった。
Kare no shippai-dan ni wa mimi ga itakatta.
My ears really burned when I heard him talk about how he had screwed things up.

彼の話は、遅刻常習犯の私には耳が痛い。
Kare no hanashi wa, chikoku-jōshūhan no watashi ni wa mimi ga itai.
It really makes me feel guilty listening to him talk about being punctual because I'm the kind of guy who'd be late to his own funeral.

☞ *mi ni oboe ga aru* 身に覚えがある

Mimi ga tōi 耳が遠い "one's ears are far away"
be hard of hearing, be deaf

私は耳が遠いので大きな声で話してください。
Watashi wa mimi ga tōi no de ōki na koe de hanashite kudasai.
I'm a little hard of hearing, so would you mind speaking in a loud voice.

祖母は最近耳が遠くなってきたようだ。
Sobo wa saikin mimi ga tōku natte kita yō da.
I think my grandmother's starting to lose her hearing.

Mimi ni hairu 耳に入る "go in one's ear"
hear of

株価暴落の噂が耳に入った。
Kabuka-bōraku no uwasa ga mimi ni haitta.
I got wind of a rumor that the stock market was crashing.

彼については、悪いことばかりが私の耳に入る。
Kare ni tsuite wa, warui koto bakari ga watashi no mimi ni hairu.
Everything I ever hear about him is bad.

Mimi ni suru **耳にする** "make something into an ear"
hear, get wind of, find out about

環境問題について、よく耳にするようになった。
Kankyō-mondai ni tsuite, yoku mimi ni suru yō ni natta.
You hear about the environment all the time now.

彼の悪い噂を耳にすることが多いが事実なのだろうか。
Kare no warui uwasa o mimi ni suru koto ga ōi ga jijitsu na no darō ka.
I get wind of a lot of bad rumors about him, but I wonder if there is any truth to them.

Mimi ni tako ga dekiru **耳にたこができる** "get calluses on one's ears"
have heard about all one wants to hear of something

その話なら耳にたこができるほど聞かされた。
Sono hanashi nara mimi ni tako ga dekiru hodo kikasareta.
I've heard that story so many times that I could tell it backwards.

車に気をつけるように毎朝言われて、耳にたこができちゃったよ。
Kuruma ni ki o tsukeru yō ni maiasa iwarete, mimi ni tako ga dekichatta yo.
I'm sick and tired of being told to watch out for cars every morning.

Mimi o kasu **耳を貸す** "lend an ear"
listen to, give an ear to

くだらない噂話に耳を貸す気はない。
Kudaranai uwasabanashi ni mimi o kasu ki wa nai.

I have no intention of listening to a bunch of ridiculous gossip.

政府は消費者の不満の声に全く耳を貸さなかった。
Seifu wa shōhi-sha no fuman no koe ni mattaku mimi o kasanakatta.
The government turned a deaf ear to complaints from consumers.

↪ *mimi o katamukeru* 耳を傾ける

Mimi o katamukeru 耳を傾ける "incline one's ears"
listen to, lend an ear to

少しは他人の意見に耳を傾けたらどうですか。
Sukoshi wa tanin no iken ni mimi o katamuketara dō desu ka.
Why don't you try paying a little attention to what other people have to say?

国民の声に耳を傾ける政治家こそ必要だ。
Kokumin no koe ni mimi o katamukeru seiji-ka koso hitsuyō da.
What we really need are politicians who will listen to the people.

↪ *mimi o kasu* 耳を貸す

Mimi o utagau 耳を疑う "doubt one's ears"
be unable to believe one's rears

突然の別れ言葉に彼は自分の耳を疑った。
Totsuzen no wakare-kotoba ni kare wa jibun no mimi o utagatta.
He couldn't believe he was hearing her say that this was the end.

あんな乱暴な言葉が、あの人の口から出るなんて、私は思わず耳を疑った。
Anna ranbō na kotoba ga, ano hito no kuchi kara deru nante, watashi wa omowazu mimi o utagatta.
I couldn't believe my ears when I heard him using such rough language.

mimizu みみず (蚯蚓) earthworm

Our annelid little buddies have hardly wormed their way into the Japanese lexicon. About all the use they get is as fish bait. But now they're in the news with recent discoveries that, in some areas of Japan, the use of chemical fertilizers, pesticides, and herbicides has been so extensive that the birds eating the beneficial little fellas are starting to drop out of the sky from some kind of poisoning. Some of the more interesting kanji compounds that have been used to write this word include 歌女, or songstress, 地竜, or earth dragon, and 土竜, or dirt dragon. Visions of *Dune*? Earthworms are counted *ippiki* 一匹.

Mimizu no nutakutta yō na ji **みみずのぬたくったような字** "letters (handwriting) like an earthworm had crawled and squirmed"
one's calligraphy (handwriting) is like hen scratches

このみみずのぬたくったような字はあの人に違いない。
Kono mimizu no nutakutta yō na ji wa ano hito ni chigainai.
This scribbling has gotta be hers.

手紙の字はみみずがぬたくったようだったので、彼女は何が書いてあるのか読めなかった。
Tegami no ji wa mimizu ga nutakutta yō datta no de, kanojo wa nani ga kaite aru no ka yomenakatta.
The handwriting in the letter was so squiggly she couldn't make it out.

Mimizubare **みみず腫れ** "an earthworm swelling"
welt, weal, wheal, wale (or the result of being whaled on); blister

---

どうしたのその腕のみみず腫れ？
Dō shita no sono ude no mimizubare?
How'd ya get that weal on your arm?

捕虜の背中は一面みみず腫れだった。
Horyo no senaka wa ichimen mimizubare datta.

The prisoner of war's back was a mass of welts.

※ From the resemblance of a wound or blister containing watery matter to the shape of an earthworm.

mizu o eta uo 水を得た魚 "a fish (back) in water"

back in one's element

> 転職して、いまの彼女は水を得た魚だね。
> *Tenshoku shite, ima no kanojo wa mizu o eta uo da ne.*
> Changing jobs has done wonders for her.

> 彼は水を得た魚のように、元の部署に戻ってからはその能力を発揮した。
> *Kare wa mizu o eta uo no yō ni, moto no busho ni modotte kara wa sono nōryoku o hakki shita.*
> Upon returning to his former section, he was back in his element and soon showing what he could do.

※ The opposite of the English "like a fish out of water," this idiom describes a change in surroundings that breathe new life into someone who has previously suffered.

↪ *mizu o hanareta uo* 水を離れた魚

mizu o hanareta uo 水を離れた魚 "a fish away from water"

(be) like a fish out of water, out of one's element

> 父は定年退職してまるで水を離れた魚状態になってしまった。

Chichi wa teinen-taishoku shite maru de mizu o hanareta uo jōtai ni natte shimatta.
Dad was just like a fish out of water when he retired.

人事移動で営業をはずされた彼は水を離れた魚のようになってしまった。
Jinji-idō de eigyō o hazusareta kare wa mizu o hanareta uo no yō ni natte shimatta.
Reassignment within the company left him high and dry, his connections to the sales department severed.

🐇 Also (though less commonly) used in the reshuffled form *uo no mizu ni hanareta yō* 魚の水に離れたよう.

↪ *mizu o eta uo* 水を得た魚

mogura モグラ mole

Bigger than earthworms maybe, but no worthier of being hailed as earth dragons (土竜, which is one kanji-fication of their name), these little mammals have finally burrowed their way into the language in the form of at least one fairly recent, but widely heard, idiom that you'll have to dig to find in Japanese dictionaries. But more about that later. First, the name *mogura* has a history as intricate as any tunnel a mole might dig. It derives, according to one source, from the verb *uguromotsu,* which means "to mound dirt," something readers who know anything about ancient Japan will recognize as an activity that bordered on becoming a national obsession for three or four centuries some fifteen hundred years ago, at least for the rich and famous. Anyway, for those who are still with us, there's a noun, *uguromochi*—presumably having something to do with the mounding of dirt and, not surprisingly, another name for a mole—that underwent a transformation to become *muguromochi*, and was shaken up again and abbreviated to give us the word we all can now appropriately appreciate, *mogura*. Now if you think this is making a mountain out of a molehill, well, you're right. But you'll have to find another way to say that in Japanese, because that's one idiom that doesn't come out the same. Moles are counted *ippiki* 一匹.

Mogura-tataki もぐらたたき "mole pounding"
an endless battle

週末の暴走族取締まりはもぐらたたきと同じだ。
Shūmatsu no bōsōzoku-torishimari wa mogura-tataki to onaji da.
Trying to round up motorcycle gangs on the weekends is an endless battle.

電話ボックスに張り付けてあるカードに、警察は摘発に乗り出しているが、まるでもぐらたたき状態である。
Denwa-bokkusu ni haritsukete aru kādo ni, keisatsu wa tekihatsu ni noridashite iru ga, maru de mogura-tataki jōtai de aru.
The police are trying to do something about the stickers that are pasted all over phone booths, but the minute one place is cleared out they go up someplace else.

꽃 From the popular game found in many arcades in Japan. Put your money in, stand in front of a waist-high platform full of holes, and wait for the moles (*mogura*) to start popping their heads up. The idea is to whack (*tataku*) as many of them as you can in the allotted time with a large plastic mallet. Great fun for the intellectually challenged. By extension, the idiom is used to describe attempts to eradicate crime or antisocial behavior, like having a good time, only to find that the behavior resurfaces somewhere else soon thereafter.

☞ *itachigokko* いたちごっこ

mōretsu-shain 猛烈社員 "a zealous employee"
an eager-beaver employee, hard worker, tireless worker, workaholic

猛烈社員として働いて、やっと管理職になった途端に、リストラの対象にされた。
Mōretsu-shain toshite hataraite, yatto kanri-shoku ni natta totan ni, risutora no taishō ni sareta.
I worked my butt off as an eager-beaver employee, and then the minute I finally get a management position, I'm targeted in the company's restructuring.

主人は日曜日も会社へ行くような猛烈社員なので、過労死が心配なんです。
Shujin wa nichiyōbi mo kaisha e iku yō na mōretsu-shain na no de, karōshi ga shinpai nan desu.
My husband's the kind of tireless worker who goes into the office even on Sundays, and I'm worried he's going to work himself to death.

mubyō-sokusai 無病息災 "without sickness, stopping devastation"

as fit as a fiddle, hale and hearty, in sound (good) health

お金よりも地位よりも、無病息災が何よりですね。
Okane yori mo chii yori mo, mubyō-sokusai ga nani yori desu ne.
Health and fitness are what's important, not money and position.

初詣で、今年一年の家族の無病息災を祈ってきた。
Hatsumōde de, kotoshi ichinen no kazoku no mubyō-sokusai o inotte kita.
When I visited the shrine at the New Year, I prayed that my family would remain hale and hearty for the coming twelve months.

※ Everyone wants to be healthy, but many Japanese believe that in middle age it is better to have some minor ailment since then we are more likely to pay closer attention to our physical condition. This idea of one ailment keeping us on our toes, vigilant as to our health, is expressed as 一病息災 (*ichibyō-sokusai*, "One ailment keeps you healthy").

muga-muchū 無我夢中 "selfless absorption"

to lose oneself in, to be totally absorbed (immersed, engrossed, wrapped up) in, to forget oneself

当時は無我夢中だったから何とも思わなかったが、今考えるとよくあんなことに耐えられたと我ながら感心する。
Tōji wa muga-muchū datta kara nan to mo omowanakatta ga, ima kangaeru to yoku anna koto ni taerareta to warenagara kanshin suru.
At the time I was totally absorbed in what I was doing so I didn't think much about it, but looking back now, I'm amazed how I managed to get through it all.

無我夢中でプラモデル組み立ててるから、今は何を言っても聞こえませんよ。
Muga-muchū de puramoderu kumitatete 'ru kara, ima wa nani o itte mo kikoemasen yo.
He's putting a plastic model together and lost to the world, so he won't hear a word you say.

↪ *isshō-kenmei* 一生懸命

mugei-taishoku 無芸大食 "a talentless big eater"

someone whose only talent is eating

お恥ずかしいんですが無芸大食で、カラオケもてんでだめなんですよ、勘弁してください。
Ohazukashii n' desu ga mugei-taishoku de, karaoke mo tende dame nan desu yo, kanben shite kudasai.
I hate to admit it (to be a party pooper), but all I'm good at is eating. I'm terrible at karaoke, so I'll have to pass on this one.

彼が自分は無芸大食だって言うのは、謙遜じゃなくて本当なんだよ。

Kare ga jibun wa mugei-taishoku datte iu no wa, kenson ja nakute hontō nan da yo.

When he says he doesn't have a talent to his name but filling his face, he's not being modest—it's the truth.

mujina むじな(狢) badger

Also called a hole bear, or *anaguma* 穴熊, and often confused with the raccoon dog, or *tanuki* 狸, the badger shares an image of persistence with its Western counterpart, although such has not found its way into idiomatic usage. Still, this member of the weasel family comes off little better in Japanese than in English, figuring in a single idiom, and that with negative connotations. Badgers are counted *ippiki* 一匹.

Onaji ana no mujina 同じ穴のむじな "badgers from the same den" birds of a feather, (be) just like (no different/no better than) the others

---

今だからお前善人面しているが、元はヤクザ俺とは同じ穴のむじなだ。

Ima da kara omae zennin-zura shite iru ga, moto wa yakuza ore to wa onaji ana no mujina da.

You can play Mr. Nice Guy now, but you've got a past just like I do.

今の日本はどこの政党が政権をとっても変わりなし、政治家は皆同じ穴のむじな。

Ima no Nihon wa doko no seitō ga seiken o totte mo kawari nashi, seijika wa mina onaji ana no mujina.

It doesn't make a bit of difference which party is in power in Japan today, politicians are all the same, you can't tell one from another.

mumi-kansō 無味乾燥 "tasteless and dry"

dull, tasteless, bland, uninteresting, boring, insipid, vapid, prosaic

今日の主賓のスピーチは、なんとも面白みがなくて無味乾燥だったね。
Kyō no shuhin no supīchi wa, nan to mo omoshiromi ga nakute mumi-kansō datta ne.
The speech by the guest of honor today was not only uninteresting but downright inane.

誰が書いたか知らないけど、すいぶんと無味乾燥な挨拶状だ。
Dare ga kaita ka shiranai kedo, zuibun to mumi-kansō na aisatsu-jō da.
I don't know who wrote this, but it's a pretty insipid greeting card.

mune 胸 chest, breast

Besides meaning chest or breast, *mune* can also mean one's mind or feelings, the lungs, the stomach, or the heart, either as an organ or as the seat of the emotions. In Japan, as in the West, the breast has long been considered the seat of the emotions. So it should come as no surprise that feelings of joy, excitement, and anticipation as well as those of sorrow and disappointment, which might be expressed in English by referring to the heart, are often conveyed in Japanese by idioms including *mune.*

When used in a compound, *mune* may be pronounced *muna,* as in *munayake* (or, also, *muneyake*) which literally means that one's heart is on fire, but actually that one has "heartburn." Similarly, to figure or count on something happening is expressed in the Japanese phrase *munazan'yō o suru,* which literally means to "count something in one's chest."

Mune ga ippai ni naru **胸がいっぱいになる** "one's chest becomes full"
get a lump in one's throat, one's heart is filled with something [like joy], have one's heart in one's mouth

故郷の写真を見ていたら、なつかしさで胸がいっぱいになった。
Kokyō no shashin o mite itara, natsukashisa de mune ga ippai ni natta.
I got all choked up with nostalgia when I looked at the pictures of my hometown.

思いがけない誕生日プレゼントに、彼女はうれしさで胸がいっぱいになった。
Omoigakenai tanjōbi-purezento ni, kanojo wa ureshisa de mune ga ippai ni natta.
Her heart was filled with happiness when she was given an unexpected birthday present.

Mune ga itamu / mune o itameru **胸が痛む／胸を痛める** "one's chest hurts"
painful, pitiful, heartrending, heartbreaking, gut-wretching

母の病気がとても重いことを知って、私の胸は痛んだ。
Haha no byōki ga totemo omoi koto o shitte, watashi no mune wa itanda.
My heart sank when I found out how sick my mother really was.

自分の不注意で花を枯らしてしまい、彼女は胸を痛めた。
Jibun no fuchūi de hana o karashite shimai, kanojo wa mune o itameta.
She was heartsick because it was due to her own carelessness that the flowers died.

Mune ga sawagu / munasawagi ga suru **胸が騒ぐ／胸騒ぎがする** "one's chest clamors"
be excited, be worried

息子が事故にあったその日は、朝から胸が騒いでどうしようもなかった。
Musuko ga jiko ni atta sono hi wa, asa kara mune ga sawaide dō shiyō mo nakatta.
The day my son had his accident I woke up in the morning feeling very uneasy (with a feeling that something bad was going to happen).

夫の出張先でテロ事件が起きたことを知り、急に胸騒ぎがした。
Otto no shutchō-saki de tero-jiken ga okita koto o shiri, kyū ni munasawagi ga shita.
She was worried sick when she heard that a terrorist attack had occurred where her husband was posted overseas.

Mune ga suku 胸がすく "one's chest is emptied"
be a load off one's mind, get something off one's chest

単刀直入な彼の発言に、胸がすく思いがした。
Tantō-chokunyū na kare no hatsugen ni, mune ga suku omoi ga shita.
It was a real relief when he just spoke his mind.

その映画には、胸のすくようなラストシーンが用意されていた。
Sono eiga ni wa, mune no suku yō na rasutoshīn ga yōi sarete ita.
The movie had a last scene that left you feeling like a million dollars. / The movie ended with a cathartic scene.

Mune ga tsubureru 胸がつぶれる "one's chest is crushed"

---

(1) be scared to death (2) be choked with sorrow, all choked up

(1) ああ、びっくりした。胸がつぶれるかと思った。
Ā, bikkuri shita. Mune ga tsubureru ka to omotta.
Jesus, you nearly scared the pants off me.

(2) 突然会社をクビになった友人の気持ちを考えると、胸がつぶれて何も言えなかった。

Totsuzen kaisha o kubi ni natta yūjin no kimochi o kangaeru to, mune ga tsuburete nani mo ienakatta.
I felt so bad when I heard that a friend of mine had lost his job that I couldn't think of anything to say.

Mune ga warui **胸が悪い** "one's chest is bad"
be sick to one's stomach; sickening, revolting, disgusting

不潔な調理場を見たら、胸が悪くなった。
Fuketsu na chōriba o mitara, mune ga waruku natta.
When I noticed how filthy the restaurant's kitchen was, I thought I was going to barf.

あの男の名前を聞いただけでも胸が悪くなる。
Ano otoko no namae o kiita dake de mo mune ga waruku naru.
Just hearing his name makes me want to puke.

☞ *kimochi ga warui* 気持ちが悪い

Mune ni egaku **胸に描く** "picture in one's chest"
imagine, see in one's mind

彼女は楽しい学園生活を胸に描いていた。
Kanojo wa tanoshii gakuen-seikatsu o mune ni egaite ita.
She pictured living a carefree life at school.

あなたは子供の頃、どのような将来を胸に描いていましたか。
Anata wa kodomo no koro, dono yō na shōrai o mune ni egaite imashita ka.
When you were a kid, what did you see yourself doing when you grew up?

Mune ni kiku **胸に聞く** "ask one's chest"
ask one's heart; follow one's heart, let one's conscience be one's guide

なぜそんなことになったのか、よく自分の胸に聞いてみなさい。
Naze sonna koto ni natta no ka, yoku jibun no mune ni kiite minasai,.
Ask yourself why things ended up the way they did.

何度自分の胸に聞いてみても、やってないものはやってないのです。
Nando jibun no mune ni kiite mite mo, yatte nai mono wa yatte nai no desu.
I've done a lot of soul-searching, but I swear that I just didn't do anything wrong.

Mune ni kotaeru **胸に応える** "affect one's chest"
cut one to the quick, tug at one's heartstrings

彼女の批判は、当たっているだけに、胸に応えた。
Kanojo no hihan wa, atatte iru dake ni, mune ni kotaeta.
Her criticisms of me really hit home.

娘から「酔っぱらいは嫌い」と言われて胸に応えた。
Musume kara "yopparai wa kirai" to iwarete mune ni kotaeta.
It really cut me to the quick when my daughter said, "I just hate drunks."

Mune ni semaru **胸に迫る** "press on one's chest"
be moving, be touching; leave a strong impression

この自画像は、何か胸に迫るものがある。
Kono jiga-zō wa, nani ka mune ni semaru mono ga aru.
There's something about this self-portrait that I just can't get off my mind.

彼のジャングルでの体験談には胸に迫るものがある。
Kare no janguru de no taiken-dan ni wa mune ni semaru mono ga aru.
His stories about his experiences in the jungle are stirring.

Mune o fukuramaseru / mune ga fukuramu **胸をふくらませる／胸がふくらむ** "expand one's chest"
be full of hope, be upbeat

来月からカナダでホームステイすることになり、彼は期待に胸をふくらませている。
Raigetsu kara Kanada de hōmusutei suru koto ni nari, kare wa kitai ni mune o fukuramasete iru.
He is high on going to Canada next month for a home-stay.

新婚生活への希望に、彼女の胸はふくらんだ。
Shinkon-seikatsu e no kibō ni, kanojo no mune wa fukuranda.
Her heart filled with hope as she began a new life as a married woman.

Mune o haru **胸を張る** "stretch one's chest"
brag, be proud of, throw out one's chest, puff up one's chest

我が社の製品には個性がある、と社長は胸を張った。
Waga-sha no seihin ni wa kosei ga aru, to shachō wa mune o hatta.
The president of the company proudly told us that each of his company's products was distinctive.

自分で正しいと思うなら、噂など気にせず胸を張っていなさい。
Jibun de tadashii to omou nara, uwasa nado ki ni sezu mune o hatte inasai.
If you think you're right, then just stand tall and don't pay any attention to rumors.

Mune o kasu / Mune o kariru **胸を貸す／胸を借りる** "lend someone one's chest"
give someone a workout

横綱が弟子たちに胸を貸して、稽古をつけていた。
Yokozana ga deshi-tachi ni mune o kashite, keiko o tsukete ita.

The yokozuna gave the lower-ranking wrestlers in his stable a chance to try their skill against him.

今日の対戦相手は、とても君たちの歯のたつチームではないが、胸を借りるつもりでがんばりなさい。
Kyō no taisen-aite wa, totemo kimi-tachi no ha no tatsu chīmu de wa nai ga, mune o kariru tsumori de ganbarinasai.
The team you're up against today is a lot better than you are, but think of it as good experience and give it your best shot.

Mune o nadeorosu 胸をなで下ろす "rub one's chest downward"
be a great relief, a load off one's mind, reassuring; take comfort from

---

救急車のサイレンに胸騒ぎを覚えたが、家族全員無事だったので、ほっと胸をなで下ろした。
Kyūkyū-sha no sairen ni munasawagi o oboeta ga, kazoku zen'in buji datta no de, hotto mune o nadeoroshita.
The ambulance siren sent a shudder through me, so it was a load off my mind when I found my family safe.

彼は、検査の結果がんではなかったので、胸をなで下ろした。
Kare wa, kensa no kekka gan de wa nakatta no de, mune o nadeoroshita.
He heaved a sigh of relief when the cancer tests came back negative.

Mune o utsu / mune o utareru 胸を打つ／胸を打たれる "strike one's chest"
touch, move, impress

彼女の小説は、うまくはないが人の胸を打つものがあった。
Kanojo no shōsetsu wa, umaku wa nai ga hito no mune o utsu mono ga atta.
Her novel isn't much to get excited about, but there is something about it that really grabs you.

彼の言葉に、聴衆は胸を打たれた。

Kare no kotoba ni, chōshū wa mune o utareta.
The audience was moved by what he said.

mushi 虫 bug or insect

This is more than a generic term for the whole swarming, buzzing bunch of little critters that crawl on your screen door or splatter on your windshield. It is also the name for internal parasites that inhabit the bodies of animals, and, perhaps by extension and in the absence of any verifiable source of trouble, for the nebulous alien inside us all that has been attributed with the ability to move us to like or dislike, be angry or mollified. It is also believed to be the source of childhood irritability and other minor nervous disorders. Insofar as it affects others, attributing responsibility to its peevishness is a way to avoid ascribing responsibility to a person's actions or decisions. It is used in much the same way as the English "seven year itch" to describe a person's inexplicable desire to cheat on a spouse or lover. In Japanese you awaken the "cheating bug" *uwaki no mushi o okosu* 浮気の虫を起こす. The idioms in which *mushi* appear have been loosely organized into several catagories to expedite understanding.

A. Things the source of which remains uncertain and ascribed to some "bug."

Kan no mushi **かんの虫** "the childhood sickness bug"
a source of peevishness

この薬は赤ちゃんのかんの虫によく効きます。
Kono kusuri wa aka-chan no kan no mushi ni yoku kikimasu.
This medicine does wonders for a baby that's always fretting.

この子はよく泣くけど、かんの虫でも悪いのだろうか？
Kono ko wa yoku naku kedo, kan no mushi de mo warui no darō ka?

Little thing's always crying. I wonder if maybe she's not just sensitive?

🐛 Actually a kind of childhood nervous disorder, when all else fails you can blame just about any problem an infant might have which leads to crying on this "bug," supposedly inside its tiny body. Hunger, pain, unpleasantness, unease, and diaper rash, all—well almost all—qualify.

(Hara no) mushi ga osamaru （腹の）虫が納まる "the (stomach) bug settles down"

be satisfied (mollified, placated), cool down, settle down, have one's ruffled feathers smoothed

---

彼が直接謝りに来ない限り虫が納まらない。
Kare ga chokusetsu ayamari ni konai kagiri mushi ga osamaranai.
I'm not going to be satisfied (happy) until he apologizes directly to me.

あいつが部長になるのは虫が納まらない。
Aitsu ga buchō ni naru no wa mushi ga osamaranai.
I can't stomach the idea of him (It really gripes me that he's) being promoted to department head.

違法駐車で悩まされていた住人は、警察の一斉取締まりにやっと腹の虫が納まった。
Ihō-chūsha de nayamasarete ita jūnin wa, keisatsu no issei-torishimari ni yatto hara no mushi ga osamatta.
Long troubled by people parking illegally in their neighborhood, residents finally got some relief when the police cracked down. / The police crackdown on illegal parking finally smoothed the local residents' ruffled feathers.

🐛 Whatever the source of the complaint, it's that thing inside that's bugging you that has to be mollified.

☞ *ki ga sumu* 気が済む

Mushi no idokoro ga warui 虫の居所が悪い "the bug's in a bad place"

be in a bad mood, be in bad humor, be grumpy, be bent (out of shape), be out of sorts; get up on the wrong side of the bed in the morning

---

あいつ彼女とでももめて虫の居所が悪いようだ。
Aitsu kanojo to de mo momete mushi no idokoro ga warui yō da.
He musta got into it with his girlfriend or somethin', the way he's all bent out of shape.

俺のおふくろは虫の居所が悪いとすぐ八つ当たりするんだ。
Ore no ofukuro wa mushi no idokoro ga warui to sugu yatsuatari suru n' da.
My old lady takes it out on everybody when she's feeling out of sorts.

ジョンは虫の居所でも悪いんだろう、あんなに怒鳴り散らしてるよ。
Jon wa mushi no idokoro de mo warui n' darō, anna ni donarichirashite 'ru yo.
I wonder what's bugging John, the way he's dumping on everybody.

🐛 The source of the problem is not ascertainable.

Mushi no shirase / mushi ga shiraseru 虫の知らせ／虫が知らせる "the bug lets you know"

(have) a hunch, premonition, funny feeling; just know (something is wrong); feel (something) in one's bones

---

虫の知らせで実家に電話したら、祖父が入院したと言うことだった。
Mushi no shirase de jikka ni denwa shitara, sofu ga nyūin shita to iu koto datta.
I called home on a hunch and sure enough my grandfather had been hospitalized. / Something told me to call home, and when I did I discovered that grandpa was sick in the hospital.

虫が知らせたのか、事故を起こした便には乗らずに電車で帰ったので命拾いした。
Mushi ga shiraseta no ka, jiko o okoshita bin ni wa norazu ni densha de kaetta no de inochibiroi shita.
I got this strange feeling and took the train instead of that plane that crashed. I really lucked out.

✣ What native speakers of English feel in their bones, Japanese hear from a bug in their heart. And what they hear is usually bad.

Mushi ga sukanai 虫が好かない "the bug doesn't like (it)"
dislike for some reason, just don't like, get bad vibes from, the chemistry's wrong (not there)

虫が好かないんだよなあ、あいつは。
Mushi ga sukanai n' da yo nā, aitsu wa.
There's just something about him that bugs me. / He just rubs me the wrong way.

あの人の言うことはわかるけど、虫が好かないんだよあの言い方が。
Ano hito no iu koto wa wakaru kedo, mushi ga sukanai n' da yo ano iikata ga.
I understand what she's saying, but it's the way she says it that gets me.

あのカフェちょっと気取りすぎて虫が好かないなあ。
Ano kafe chotto kidorisugite mushi ga sukanai nā.
That cafe is a little too hoity-toity for my tastes. I can't get into going there.

✣ We've got a near match here with the word bug, as in "Don't bug me," which you can still hear occasionally. The Japanese idiom is always encountered in the negative, always of a vague source of dislike, one the speaker can't seem to pin down.

☞ *uma ga au* 馬が合う

Nakimushi 泣き虫 "a crying insect"
a crybaby, a whiner, a big baby; a weenie, pussy, wuss, wimp

彼がそんな泣き虫だなんて、人は見かけによらないものだ。
Kare ga sonna nakimushi da nante, hito wa mikake ni yoranai mono da.
Who would have ever thought he was such a big baby. Guess you just can't tell from the way a guy looks.

彼女は飲むと、泣き虫になる。
Kanojo wa nomu to, nakimushi ni naru.
She gets on these crying jags whenever she ties one on.

🐛 Used of a person who cries often or quickly.

↪ *yowamushi* 弱虫

Yowamushi 弱虫 "a weak insect"
a baby, coward; sissy, pussy, weakling, weenie, wuss, wimp, candy ass; (of a boy) a momma's boy, a girl

弱虫、毛虫、はさんで捨てろ。
Yowamushi, kemushi, hasande sutero.
Cry baby! Cry baby!

そんな弱虫でどうする。
Sonna yowamushi de dō suru.
You're a big sissy, aren't ya!

～ *no mushi* ～の虫 "a bug about (over) something"
be into (something), be fanatical (wild/crazy about something), be a fan (of something), live and breathe (something), live (for something / to do something)

彼は本の虫だ。
Kare wa hon no mushi da.
He's a bookworm.

彼女は勉強の虫だ。
Kanojo wa benkyō no mushi da.
She's a grind (powertool). / She's into studying.

子供は遊びの虫だ。
Kodomo wa asobi no mushi da.
Kids love to play. / Kids could play all day. / Kids live to play.

✌ Used of someone engrossed in one particular activity.

B. Metaphoric use deriving from some characteristically "buggy" trait.

Mushikui 虫食い "insect-eaten"

---

1. (literally) insect- (worm-, moth-, etc.) eaten

   この古文書は虫食い状態で発見された。
   Kono komonjo wa mushikui jōtai de hakken sareta.
   This old manuscript was discovered in a worm-eaten condition.

   このセーターは虫食いがひどいので捨てるしかない。
   Kono sētā wa mushikui ga hidoi no de suteru shika nai.
   This sweater's so moth-eaten there's nothing to do but throw it out.

2. (metaphorically) partial; broken

   用地買収がままならないため、新新幹線ルートは虫食い着工を余儀なくされた。
   Yōchi-baishū ga mama naranai tame, shin-shinkansen rūto wa mushikui chakkō o yogi naku sareta.
   With procurement of land for new Shinkansen routes not going as well as hoped, the railroad was forced to undertake the construction piecemeal.

工事は今のところ虫食い状態で、いつになったらこの高速が開通するのかまったくわかりませんね。

Kōji wa ima no tokoro mushikui jōtai de, itsu ni nattara kono kōsoku ga kaitsū suru no ka mattaku wakarimasen ne.

At present, with construction proceeding in fits and starts, there is no telling when the highway will open to traffic.

🐛 Used metaphorically of something that proceeds intermittently or is completed in segments that remain disconnected for some time.

☞ *chūto-hanpa* 中途半端, *shirikire-tonbo* 尻切れとんぼ

Mushi no iki 虫の息 "an insect's breath"
(literally) faint (shallow) breathing; (metaphorically) be (knocking) at death's door, be on one's last legs, have had it, be curtains, be all over

---

家族が駆けつけたとき、彼女はすでに虫の息だった。
Kazoku ga kaketsuketa toki, kanojo wa sude ni mushi no iki datta.
She was at death's door when the family rushed in.

暫定政権はほとんど機能しておらず、もう虫の息だ。
Zantei-seiken wa hotondo kinō shite orazu, mō mushi no iki da.
The provisional government is on its last legs. / It's all over for the provisional government.

彼は虫の息だったが、医者の懸命の努力で奇跡的に命は取り留めた。
Kare wa mushi no iki datta ga, isha no kenmei no doryoku de kiseki-teki ni inochi wa toritometa.
He had one foot in the grave (He was hardly breathing), but the doctor's heroic efforts saved his life.

🐛 Used to mean both that one's breathing has all but stopped and that one is close to death for reasons other than those respiratory-related.

C. Idioms that don't fit in the other categories.

Nigamushi 苦虫 "a bitter insect"
(*~ o (kami)tsubushita yō na kao o suru*) make a sour face; scowl

その議員は不正の証拠を突きつけられ、苦虫を噛みつぶしたような顔を隠せなかった。
Sono giin wa fusei no shōko o tsukitsukerare, nigamushi o kamitsubushita yō na kao o kakusenakatta.
The Diet member couldn't help grimacing (couldn't hide his displeasure) when presented with the proof of his malfeasance.

言葉につまり、彼は苦虫をつぶした顔をしていた。
Kotoba ni tsumari, kare wa nigamushi o tsubushita kao o shite ita.
Stumped (At a loss for what to say), he got a sour look on his face.

警察官の不祥事に、県警の幹部は釈明の記者会見で終始苦虫をつぶした表情を見せていた。
Keisatsu-kan no fu-shōji ni, kenkei no kanbu wa shakumei no kisha-kaiken de shūshi nigamushi o tsubushita hyōjō o misete ita.
Prefectural police officials, explaining the scandal involving cops under their command, openly showed their distaste for the task throughout the press conference.

彼は過去の失敗を問題にされて苦虫を噛んだ。
Kare wa kako no shippai o mondai ni sarete nigamushi o kanda.
He had to just grin and bear it when someone brought up his past mistakes.

🐛 Used of people who are painfully aware their situation is worsening and who find themselves at a loss for words to respond to accusations or the like. The "bitter bug" is chimerical, though almost any insect would probably be sufficiently disgusting to warrant a sour face. The last example features an abbreviated form.

(Warui) mushi ga tsuku （悪い）虫がつく "a bad bug attaches (itself)"
have (get) a boyfriend (lover)

彼女は、箱入り娘だから虫がつかないように親がいつも目を光らせている。
Kanojo wa, hakoiri-musume da kara mushi ga tsukanai yō ni oya ga itsumo me o hikarasete iru.
She's led a sheltered life, her parents always making sure there're no guys sniffing around her (that she doesn't get mixed up with some guy).

悪い虫でもついたのか、最近彼女帰りが遅いらしいのよ。
Warui mushi de mo tsuita no ka, saikin kanojo kaeri ga osoi rashii no yo.
Maybe she's got a boyfriend. Seems like she's been getting home later and later.

🥀 Used almost exclusively about women, particularly unmarried or widowed ones. Less commonly used of married women who are having an affair. *Warui* appears with the idiom with great regularity.

Mushi no ii 虫のいい "bug well"
take too much for granted, be asking too much; be all me, my, mine

---

そんな虫のいい話どこにもないよ。
Sonna mushi no ii hanashi doko ni mo nai yo.
You're asking an awful lot there.

そんな虫のいいことをいって、自分の立場を考えなさい。
Sonna mushi no ii koto o itte, jibun no tachiba o kangaenasai.
You sound like you're taking a lot for granted, but are you really in a position to get all that? / That's all very nice for you, but I mean, who do you think you are?

旅行費を出してもらってその上小遣いまでせびるとは虫がよすぎる。
Ryokō-hi o dashite moratte sono ue kozukai made sebiru to wa mushi ga yosugiru.
You're dreamin' if you think we're gonna pay your travel expenses *and* shell out spending money on top of that. / You think we're paying for your trip and giving you pocket money? You've got another think coming.

Mushi mo korosanai 虫も殺さない "wouldn't kill a bug"
innocent-looking; look as if one could not kill (hurt, harm) a fly (flea)

> あの人は取っつきにくいけど、実は虫も殺さないほど優しい人だよ。
> *Ano hito wa tottsukinikui kedo, jitsu wa mushi mo korosanai hodo yasashii hito da yo.*
> He's a little hard to get to know, but deep down inside he's a big softy (got a heart of gold).

> あいつは虫も殺さない顔して、陰でやることは卑劣なんだから、まあ畳の上では死ねないな。
> *Aitsu wa mushi mo korosanai kao shite, kage de yaru koto wa hiretsu nan da kara, mā tatami no ue de wa shinenai na.*
> He's got this innocent look, but the way he's up to no good every chance he gets, the guy's not gonna die a natural death.

> あの殺人犯、近所の人の話では、虫も殺さないような人に見えたらしい。
> *Ano satsujin-han, kinjo no hito no hanashi de wa, mushi mo korosanai yō na hito ni mieta rashii.*
> The murderer looked like he wouldn't hurt a fly, according to what his neighbors were saying.

🌣 Looks are deceptive. That's often the point Japanese want to make about someone when they begin a sentence with this idiom. Whoever it is they are talking about is usually not nearly as nice as he makes out to be. *Mushi mo korosanai kao* 虫も殺さない顔, *mushi mo korosanai yō na hito* 虫も殺さないような人, and *mushi mo korosanai yō na koto o iu* 虫も殺さないようなことを言う are all either followed by a comment negating that image or it is understood by the context that such feelings exist.

↪ *ki ga yasashii* 気が優しい

Tonde hi ni iru natsu no mushi 飛んで火に入る夏の虫 "a summer insect that has flown into the flames"

(like) a moth drawn to flame, self-destructive; ask for trouble, ask for it

彼の行動はまさに「飛んで火に入る夏の虫」であった。
Kare no kōdō wa masa ni "Tonde hi ni iru natsu no mushi" de atta.
He was just asking for trouble the way he was acting.

まさか本人が来るとは「飛んで火に入る夏の虫」だな。
Masaka honnin ga kuru to wa "Tonde hi ni iru natsu no mushi" da na.
Who would have ever thought she'd show her face here. She must have some kind of death wish.

From the observation that insects drawn to the flame die.

nakitsura ni hachi 泣き面に蜂 "a bee(sting) on a crying face"

misfortunes seldom come alone; rubbing salt into the wound; adding insult to injury; when it rains, it pours

上司に小言を言われ、おまけに帰りに財布を落とすとは泣き面に蜂もいいところだ。
Jōshi ni kogoto o iware, omake ni kaeri ni saifu o otosu to wa nakitsura ni hachi mo ii tokoro da.
Like getting chewed out by my boss wasn't enough, then I had to go and lose my wallet on my way home to boot. Some days you just can't win.

仕事は増えるは、給料は下がるはで、泣きっ面に蜂だもうこりゃ。
Shigoto wa fueru wa, kyūryō wa sagaru wa de, nakittsura ni hachi da mō korya.
More work and less pay. Jeez, this is like adding insult to injury.

今度の円高は日本にとって泣き面に蜂みたいなもんだ。
Kondo no endaka wa Nihon ni totte nakitsura ni hachi mitai na mon da.
The most recent rise in the yen rate is like rubbing salt into the wound for Japan.

🐝 From the notion that someone who is crying is probably already unhappy, and getting stung by a bee on top of that is about as bad as it can get.

☞ *kaeru no tsura ni shōben* 蛙の面に小便

naku neko (wa) nezumi o toranu 鳴く猫（は）鼠をとらぬ "a meowing cat catches no rats"

talk a good show, (be) all talk, talk big but be unable to produce

鳴く猫鼠をとらぬ、彼女は辞めないよ。
Naku neko nezumi o toranu, kanojo wa yamenai yo.
She's full of hot air. She's never going to quit her job.

「鳴く猫は鼠をとらぬ」というが、あの人本当に事業始めるのかなあ。
"Naku neko wa nezumi o toranu" to iu ga, ano hito hontō ni jigyō hajimeru no ka nā.
The way he tends to be all talk and no action makes me wonder if he'll ever go into business for himself.

☞ *neko* 猫

namaiki (na) 生意気（な） "fresh *ki*"

cheeky, fresh, impertinent, insolent

新入りのくせに生意気なことを言うな。
Shin'iri no kuse ni namaiki na koto o iu na.
For a new guy you're a real smart ass.

息子は近ごろ生意気になって口答えばかりするんですよ。
Musuko wa chikagoro namaiki ni natte kuchigotae bakari suru n' desu yo.
My son's become a little wise guy, always talking back.

nanige nai 何気ない "no *ki* at all"

casual, cool, indifferent, nonchalant

何気ない仕草の端々に品のよさが感じられる人ですね。
Nanige nai shigusa no hashibashi ni hin no yosa ga kanjirareru hito desu ne.
She's a woman whose excellect upbringing shows in all the nonchalant little gestures she makes.

彼の何気ない一言がヒントになったよ。
Kare no nanige nai hitokoto ga hinto ni natta yo.
Some casual comment he made gave me a hint.

↪ *nanige naku* 何気なく

nanige naku 何気なく "without *ki*"

as though it were nothing, coolly, indifferently, nonchalantly; thoughtlessly, without thinking

何気なく窓の外を見ると夕焼けがきれいだった。
Nanige naku mado no soto o miru to yūyake ga kirei datta.
I kinda just looked outside, and boy was there a beautiful sunset.

何気なく言ったことが彼女を傷つけてしまったらしいんだよ。
Nanige naku itta koto ga kanojo o kizutsukete shimatta rashii n' da yo.
Some offhand comment I made seems to have hurt her.

☞ *nanige nai* 何気ない

neko ねこ（猫） cat

Despite being one of the most common animals in and around human habitations—this is especially true of urban Japan, where clowders form at shrines in the early hours of evening to preen and perhaps boast of the day's adventures—and although they are held to be smart, cunning, and mysterious, cats failed to make the Chinese zodiac menagerie. According to one account, this is due to the fact that the cat alone among all animals did not show up at a meeting called by one of the gods. This handy anecdote also accounts for the reason why cats chase mice, for it was the mouse who is said to have wrongly informed the cat of the date for the meeting. Often appearing in Japanese ghost stories where they take the forms of monsters, cats were also believed to harm people.

In the early 1990s, cats figured in several short-lived idioms that burst on the linguistic scene only to all but disappear within a few years. *Nekobaba genshō* 猫ババ現象 (cats and grandmothers phenomenon), a homonym for *nekobaba* 猫ばば (an idiom included in this book), apparently started when some waggish door-to-door salesmen found no one home but cats (*neko*) and grandmothers (*baba*) when they came calling, Japanese housewives having discovered the joys of part-time work, health clubs, culture centers, lovers' trysts, and the freedom of two-income families.

A second linguistic flash in the pan in the nineties involving cats also illustrated the changing times. *Nekogata shain,* ネコ型社員 (cat-type employees), were singled out for criticism for their self-centeredness. These willful workers were said to launch enthusiastically into tasks they found interesting, but be almost catlike in their utter disinterest in anything else. Employers and social commentators alike bemoaned the changes in society that allowed a worker, heaven forbid, to have an opinion or an abiding interest in something beyond the corporate weal.

Not to be outdone by their canine competition, and perhaps hoping to reverse feline fortunes, Japanese cat lovers took a hint from some Belgian festival and designated February 22, 1988, as the first Cat Day, or *Neko no Hi* 猫の日. The date was set by playing on the cat's meow, *nyā-nyā*, "two" being pronounced *ni*—hey, it's only a slight stretch—and the date having all those twos in it.

The cat's meow, literally, is *nyānyā* ニャーニャー. They are counted *ippiki* 一匹.

Karite kita neko **借りてきた猫** "a borrowed cat"
be a pussycat; (uncharacteristically) quiet or well mannered; be lamblike

---

花子は叔父さんの家に行くのが初めてだったので、借りてきた猫のようだった。
Hanako wa ojisan no ie ni iku no ga hajimete datta no de, karite kita neko no yō datta.
Hanako was uncharacteristically well behaved because it was the first time she visited her uncle.

毒舌の彼も奥さんの前では借りてきた猫だ。
Dokuzetsu no kare mo okusan no mae de wa karite kita neko da.
He's usually pretty poison-tongued, but he's a regular pussycat around his wife.

🐱 One of my personal all-time favorites. From the observation that a cat in unfamiliar surroundings, subdued and uncertain, appears well behaved. But put his rambunctious self on home turf and you've got a horse of a different color, so to speak. Often followed by *no yō* or *mitai*.

Naku neko (wa) nezumi o toranu 鳴く猫（は）鼠をとらぬ "a meowing cat catches no rats"
talk a good show, (be) all talk, talk big but be unable to produce

鳴く猫鼠をとらぬ、彼女は辞めないよ。
Naku neko nezumi o toranu, kanojo wa yamenai yo.
She's full of hot air. She's never going to quit her job.

「鳴く猫は鼠をとらぬ」というが、あの人本当に事業始めるのかなあ。
"Naku neko wa nezumi o toranu" to iu ga, ano hito hontō ni jigyō hajimeru no ka nā.
The way he tends to be all talk and no action makes me wonder if he'll ever go into business for himself.

Neko mo shakushi mo 猫もしゃくしも "cats and ladles too"
everybody (and his brother), every mother's son, all the world, every Tom, Dick, and Harry; (of men) every swinging dick, every dog and his brother

日本では冬になると、猫もしゃくしもスキーに出かける。
Nihon de wa fuyu ni naru to, neko mo shakushi mo sukī ni dekakeru.
Everybody and his brother hit the slopes in Japan during the winter.

ミニスカートが流行るのはいいけど、猫もしゃくしもとなるとどうもね。
Minisukāto ga hayaru no wa ii kedo, neko mo shakushi mo to naru to dōmo ne.
It's great when miniskirts are in style, but it's a bit much when everybody's gotta be wearing one.

✺ *Shakushi* is another word for the more common *shamoji*, the wooden ladle used in Japanese homes to scoop rice from a rice cooker and into bowls. The expression comes from the fact that cats and ladles were common in all homes.

Neko ni katsuobushi (o azukeru) 猫に鰹節（を預ける） "entrusting a cat with a dried bonito"
trust a wolf to watch over sheep, leave a fox to guard the henhouse

借金で首が回らなくなっている彼にそんな大金を預けるなんて、猫に鰹節を預けるようなものだ。
Shakkin de kubi ga mawaranaku natte iru kare ni sonna taikin o azukeru nante, neko ni katsuobushi o azukeru yō na mono da.
Entrusting a guy like that, up to his ears in debt, with all that money is asking for trouble.

そんな学生の目の届くところに試験の原稿を置くなんて、猫に鰹節じゃないか。
Sonna gakusei no me no todoku tokoro ni shiken no genkō o oku nante, neko ni katsuobushi ja nai ka.
Don't you think you're inviting trouble by leaving the test questions lying around where students can see them?

Neko ni koban 猫に小判 "gold coins to a cat"
like casting pearls before swine

そんな小さな子にコンピュータを買い与えるなんて、猫に小判だ。
Sonna chiisana ko ni konpyūta o kaiataeru nante, neko ni koban da.
Buying a computer for a small child like that is simply a waste.

彼にそんな高級なゴルフクラブは猫に小判だ。
Kare ni sonna kōkyū na gorufu-kurabu wa neko ni koban da.
A guy like that with expensive golf clubs! What a terrible waste!

❦ From the fact that a cat cannot appreciate the value of a gold coin, *neko ni koban* expresses the futility of an unappreciative person possessing something of value. Seldom if ever used of abstractions, including ideas or emotions.

☞ *buta ni shinjū* 豚に真珠, *uma (no mimi) ni nenbutsu* 馬（の耳）に念仏

Neko ni matatabi 猫にまたたび "catnip to a cat"
sure to produce the desired effect; a cure all

> 猫にまたたび、うちの子供にはテレビゲーム。
> *Neko ni matatabi, uchi no kodomo ni wa terebi-gēmu.*
> Turning my kids loose with a Nintendo will do the trick every time.

> うちの亭主は酒の肴にピーナッツを出しておけば猫にまたたびだから楽よ。
> *Uchi no teishu wa sake no sakana ni pīnattsu o dashite okeba neko ni matatabi da kara raku yo.*
> All you have to do is give my husband his sake and some peanuts, and he gets quiet as a mouse.

Neko no hitai (hodo no) 猫の額（程の） "(about as big as) a cat's forehead"
a tiny plot of land, postage stamp-size piece of ground; a hole in the wall, cubbyhole

> 東京では、猫の額ほどの土地が何千万円もする。
> *Tokyo de wa, neko no hitai hodo no tochi ga nanzenman-en mo suru.*
> A piece of ground so small you can't even swing a cat can cost tens of millions of yen in Tokyo.

> その居酒屋は猫の額ほどの広さで、細々と商売している。
> *Sono izakaya wa neko no hitai hodo no hirosa de, hosoboso to shōbai shite iru.*
> That hole-in-the-wall tavern is just scraping by.

❧ Quick, find a cat and check out its forehead. If you can find it, that is. It's about the same situation with space in Japan; there's just not a lot of it to go around. Although this colorful expression is most commonly used about land, as the second example illustrates it may also be used to describe a small indoor space as well. It is commonly followed by *hodo no*. Though rare, there is also a shortened form, *nekobitai* 猫額.

Neko no ko ippiki inai 猫の子一匹いない "not even a kitten around"
abandoned, no sign of life

警察が現場に到着したときには猫の子一匹いなかった。
Keisatsu ga genba ni tōchaku shita toki ni wa neko no ko ippiki inakatta.
There wasn't a soul around when the police arrived at the scene.

こんな猫の子一匹いない場所に呼び出して、いったい何の用だ？
Konna neko no ko ippiki inai basho ni yobidashite, ittai nan no yō da?
What do you want with me out here in the middle of nowhere?

🐾 From the observation that cats have lots of kittens. The reasoning is that if there isn't even a kitten around, the place must really be forlorn. Always in the negative, *neko no ko ippiki inai* is used of a place where there are no signs of life.

Neko no me no yō ni kawaru 猫の目のように変わる "change like a cat's eye"
be in flux, change rapidly (in the twinkle of an eye); (of one's ideas or what one says) be fickle, flip-flop, sing a different tune

---

彼の言うことは猫の目のように変わるから、信じない方がいいよ。
Kare no iu koto wa neko no me no yō ni kawaru kara, shinjinai hō ga ii yo.
He's always changing what he says, so you'd better not believe him.

原油価格が猫の目のように変わっている現在ではガソリンの末端価格設定も難しい。
Genyū-kakaku ga neko no me no yō ni kawatte iru genzai de wa gasorin no mattan kakaku-settei mo muzukashii.
Setting gasoline prices at the pumps is difficult at times like this when the price of crude is fluctuating.

ここ数年、東欧の政治情勢は猫の目のように変わっている。
Koko sūnen, tōō no seiji-jōsei wa neko no me no yō ni kawatte iru.

The political situation in Eastern Europe has been in flux over the past few years.

🐾 From the quick reaction of a cat's pupil to small changes in light, this often unflattering expression can be used about change of all kinds but is most commonly used about a person's attitude, mood or opinion.

Neko no te mo karitai 猫の手も借りたい "want to borrow a cat's paw"
(be) swamped, overloaded, up to one's ass (in work), be shorthanded

---

今日は猫の手も借りたいほど忙しい。
Kyō wa neko no te mo karitai hodo isogashii.
We're up to our ass in work today. / We're busier than a bunch of one-armed paperhangers today.

店は猫の手も借りたいほどなのに、お前は遊びに行くつもりなのか。
Mise wa neko no te mo karitai hodo na no ni, omae wa asobi ni iku tsumori na no ka.
We need every warm body we can get at the shop, and you think you're going out?

🐾 Unlike dogs, cats are a notoriously good-for-nothing bunch in Japan. This idiom expresses just how close the speaker is to scraping the bottom of the barrel for help. *Mo* often replaces *o*, and *hodo* or *gurai* follows the whole to emphasize how busy one is.

Neko o kaburu 猫をかぶる "put on the cat"
dissemble, feign (put on an act of) ignorance or innocence; be a wolf in sheep's clothing

---

入学直後は猫をかぶっている学生が多い。

Nyūgaku-chokugo wa neko o kabutte iru gakusei ga ōi.
A lot of students watch their P's and Q's (are on their best behavior) at the beginning of the academic year.

真智子は叔父さんの家で一日中猫をかぶっていた。
Machiko wa ojisan no ie de, ichinichi-jū neko o kabbute ita.
Little Machiko put on her best behavior all day long at her uncle's house.

無理を承知で頼むのだから、何を言われても猫をかぶって紳士でとおせ。
Muri o shōchi de tanomu no da kara, nani o iwarete mo neko o kabutte shinshi de tōse.
We're asking a lot of them, so no matter what they say to you just handle it as gentlemanly as you can.

❧ The point here is that a person about whom this idiom is used is concealing his real personality and *acting* well behaved or demure. The noun form is *nekokaburi* 猫かぶり, meaning hypocrite, or a put-on.

Neko-kawaigari suru **猫かわいがりする** " indulge a cat" dote on

山田さん夫婦は娘を猫かわいがりしている。
Yamada-san fūfu wa musume o neko-kawaigari shite iru.
The Yamadas really dote on their daughter.

先生は、一番弟子の山本さんばかり猫かわいがりするので、ほかの弟子はやめていってしまう。
Sensei wa, ichiban-deshi no Yamamoto-san bakari neko-kawaigari suru no de, hoka no deshi wa yamete itte shimau.
The prof's always paying so much attention to Yamamoto, her favorite student, that the others stop coming.

❧ This expression of extreme care and attention comes from the idea that cat lovers seem to think their cat is the cat's pajamas.

Nekobaba suru 猫ばば（ババ）する "cat poop"
pocket, find and keep

目を離している間に、うちの猫に焼き魚を猫ばばされた。
Me o hanashite iru aida ni, uchi no neko ni yakizakana o nekobaba sareta.
When I wasn't looking, the cat made off with the fish I was broiling.

次郎は母親の財布から1,000円猫ばばした。
Jiro wa haha-oya no saifu kara sen-en nekobaba shita.
Jiro filched (pocketed) one thousand yen from his mother's wallet.

彼女は拾った財布を猫ばばした。
Kanojo wa hirotta saifu o nekobaba shita.
She pocketed the wallet that she picked up on the street.

❦ Always a verb, this often-heard expression comes from a cat's sanitary practice of covering its toilet with soil. The underlying notion here though is not one of cleaning up after oneself, but of hiding something and then acting innocent. It is most commonly used of something found and kept rather than returned, a wallet on the street or an umbrella in the train. *Baba* is baby talk for a bowel movement, something like "number two" or "pooh-pooh" in American English.

Nekojita 猫舌 "cat's tongue"
(a person who) can't eat or drink hot things

私は猫舌です。
Watashi wa nekojita desu.
I don't like hot things.

これは猫舌の人にはすぐ食べられない料理かも知れない。
Kore wa nekojita no hito ni wa sugu taberarenai ryōri kamo shirenai.
This is probably too hot for you if you burn your tongue easily.

🐇 From the fact that cats are prone to throwing catfits when they try to lap up food or milk heated by well-meaning doters. This is what you've got if a layer of skin comes off the roof of your mouth when you try to get that hot coffee down. Many foreigners come off looking like they have a terminal case of cat's tongue when they eat *ramen* or *udon* without slurping it down and end up burning their tongue or throat. The secret is to suck a lot of air in with the noodles to cool them as they go down. It's your one chance in Japan to make noise when you're eating, without being scolded. Be aware, this expression cannot be applied to those who do not like spicey foods.

Nekokke 猫っ毛 "cat hair"
soft, fine hair [on one's head]

私、猫っ毛なのよ。
Watashi, nekokke na no yo.
I've got fine hair.

猫っ毛で薄いから、雨なんかに濡れると最悪よ。
Nekokke de usui kara, ame nanka ni nureru to saiaku yo.
I've got this thin, fine hair so it's the pits when it gets wet in the rain.

🐇 From the resemblance of such hair to a cat's soft fur.

Nekomatagi 猫またぎ "cat straddling"
a fish that tastes so bad even a cat would turn its nose up at it

---

なんだこの魚、猫またぎだなあ。
Nan da kono sakana, nekomatagi da nā.
What's this fish? No self-respecting cat would touch it!

こんな猫またぎよく食べれるなあ。
Konna nekomatagi yoku tabereru nā.
How can you eat this crap?

🐾 From the notion that even a fish-loving animal like a cat would step over and pass by a fish if it tasted bad enough. Not used about other foods.

Nekonade-goe　猫撫で声　"a cat-cajoling voice"
a coaxing (wheedling, flattering) (tone of) voice

洋子は猫撫で声で母親にそのドレスをねだった。
Yōko wa nekonade-goe de haha-oya ni sono doresu o nedatta.
Yoko begged her mother in a coaxing voice to buy the dress.

何だその猫撫で声は、今度は何が欲しいんだ？
Nan da sono nekonade-goe wa, kondo wa nani ga hoshii n' da?
What do you want now, talking sweet like that?

🐾 Studies, by the way, show that many cat lovers unconsciously raise their voice an octave or two when talking to their pets. Maybe there is something to this idiom besides fancy.

Nekoze　猫背　"a cat's back"
a slight stoop, rounded shoulders

本を読むときはもっと姿勢よくしなさい、猫背になっちゃうよ。
Hon o yomu toki wa motto shisei yoku shinasai, nekoze ni natchau yo.
Sit up straight (don't slouch) when you're reading or you'll end up having a stoop.

スキーの基本姿勢のこつは猫背を保つことです。
Sukī no kihon-shisei no kotsu wa nekoze o tamotsu koto desu.
The secret to the proper skiing position is to keep your shoulders hunched over.

🐾 From the similarity between such a posture and that of a cat when it has hunched up its back in a stretch or a threat. It is definitely not complimentary.

nemuke 眠気 "sleepy *ki*"

drowsiness, sleepiness

丘の上から見たその村の風景は眠気を誘うように穏やかだった。
Oka no ue kara mita sono mura no fūkei wa nemuke o sasou yō ni odayaka datta.
The view of the sleepy village from the top of the hill was so peaceful.

映画の途中で急に眠気に襲われて居眠りしちまったよ。
Eiga no tochū de kyū ni nemuke ni osowarete inemuri shichimatta yo.
I got so sleepy (I just couldn't keep my eyes open) during the movie and ended up nodding off in the middle of it.

運転中眠気を催したら、無理せず、車を止めて仮眠するとよい。
Unten-chū nemuke o moyōshitara, muri sezu, kuruma o tomete kamin suru to yoi.
If you get drowsy (get sleepy, start nodding off) when you're on the road, you ought to just pull over and take a nap.

その知らせを聞いて眠気もすっ飛んだ。
Sono shirase o kiite nemuke mo suttonda.
I woke right up when I heard the news.

起きて2時間にもなるのにまだ眠気が覚めないよ。
Okite niji-kan ni mo naru no ni mada nemuke ga samenai yo.
I've been up for two hours and I'm still half asleep.

眠気を覚ますには冷たいシャワーが一番さ。
Nemuke o samasu ni wa tsumetai shawā ga ichiban sa.
Nothing like a cold shower to wake you right up.

☞ *nemukezamashi* 眠気覚まし

nemukezamashi 眠気覚まし "a sleepy *ki* wake-up"

1. waking up; something used to wake one up

    まだボートしてるんでしょ。眠気覚ましにコーヒーをどうぞ。
    Mada bōtto shite 'ru n' desho. Nemukezamashi ni kōhī o dōzo.
    Hey, sleepyhead, how about a little coffee to wake you up?

    ついうとうとしちゃうよ。眠気覚ましにちょっと散歩して来よう。
    Tsui uto-uto shichau yo. Nemukezamashi ni chotto sanpo shite koyō.
    I'm falling asleep here. Think I'll go for a walk to wake up.

2. [as *nemukezamashi mitai na mon (koto)*] child's play; a cinch, cakewalk, picnic, piece of cake, snap

    この程度の仕事は彼にとっては眠気覚ましみたいなものさ。
    Kono teido no shigoto wa kare ni totte wa nemukezamashi mitai na mono sa.
    A little job like this is a piece of cake for him.

☞ *nemuke* 眠気

nenkō-joretsu 年功序列 "years of long service (determine one's) rank"

seniority; the seniority system where rank and position are determined by age and the number of years spent working in the company

日本の雇用制度の特徴と言われてきた終身雇用と年功序列は、いまや崩れつつある。
Nihon no koyō-seido no tokuchō to iwarete kita shūshin-koyō to nenkō-joretsu wa, imaya kuzuretsutsu aru.

給与も出世も年功序列で決まるのが当然と思っていたサラリーマンは、能力給の導入に戸惑っている。
Kyūyo mo shusse mo nenkō-joretsu de kimaru no ga tōzen to omotte ita sararīman wa, nōryoku-kyū no dōnyū ni tomadotte iru.
To white-collar workers used to salary and promotion being determined by the number of years of service, the introduction of salary levels based on ability is causing bewilderment.

いくら年功序列でも、あんなトロイ人が課長じゃ、我々ははっきり言って迷惑ですよ。
Ikura nenkō-joretsu de mo, anna toroi hito ga kachō ja, wareware wa hakkiri itte meiwaku desu yo.
I don't care how long he's been with the company; with a section chief as stupid as that our life's being made simply impossible.

nenrei-fushō 年齢不詳 "age unknown"

of uncertain age; it's impossible to tell one's age

女優には若いんだか老けてるのか分からない人が多いけど、中でもこの人は年齢不詳だね。
Joyū ni wa wakai n' da ka fukete 'ru no ka wakaranai hito ga ōi kedo, naka de mo kono hito wa nenrei-fushō da ne.
With many actresses you can't tell if they're young or old, but with her it's simply impossible to guess her age.

うちの母はまだ20代の体形で、白髪も全然ないから、人からよく年齢不詳だと言われる。
Uchi no haha wa mada nijū-dai no taikei de, shiraga mo zenzen nai kara, hito kara yoku nenrei-fushō da to iwareru.
My mother's got the body of a woman in her twenties and doesn't have a grey hair on her head, so people always say it's impossible to tell her age.

nezumi ねずみ（鼠） rat, mouse

There is no linguistic distinction in Japanese between rats and mice—they are both just plain ol' *nezumi*. And they are numerous and common, facts that probably have given rise to many of the idioms that follow. While rats and mice have been held responsible for everything from ravaging granaries to spreading plague, it is important to note that at one time they were also believed to be the messengers of *Daikokuten,* a god of luck associated with wealth. This ambivalence toward rats and mice is manifest in the idioms that follow.

One interesting proverb featuring mice, *taizan-meidō shite nezumi ippiki* 大（泰）山鳴動して鼠一匹, is used to describe a situation in which there was a lot of smoke but little fire, a terrible ruckus but little to show for it, as though the mountains had labored mightily only to bring forth a mouse.

The onomatopoeic cry of rats and mice is *chūchū* チュウチュウ. They are counted *ippiki* 一匹. When appearing as the first sign of the Chinese zodiac, *nezumi* is written 子.

☞ *atama no kuroi nezumi* 頭の黒い鼠, *dobunezumi* どぶ鼠, *fukuro no (naka no) nezumi* 袋の(中の)鼠, *komanezumi* こま鼠, *kyūso neko o kamu* 窮鼠猫を噛む

Nezumi ni hikaresō **鼠に引かれそう** "ready to be led away by a mouse"
(home alone and) feeling lonely; all by one's lonesome

夜一人で残業してると、鼠に引かれそうになるわ。
Yoru hitori de zangyō shite 'ru to, nezumi ni hikaresō ni naru wa.
I really get lonely sometimes when I'm working late in the office all by myself.

えー、あなたが一人暮らし始めたの。夜、鼠に引かれないように ね。
Ē, anata ga hitorigurashi hajimeta no. Yoru, nezumi ni hikarenai yō ni ne.

Wow, you're living by yourself now! Don't let being alone at night get you down.

🐭 We're talking real lonely here, folks, so lonely that you'd let a rat come and take you away.

Nezumikō **ねずみ講** "a rat association"
a pyramid scheme

ねずみ講はマルチ商法と呼ばれ、日本では厳しく規制されている。
Nezumikō wa maruchi-shōhō to yobare, Nihon de wa kibishiku kisei sarete iru.
A kind of multilevel marketing plan, pyramid schemes are strictly regulated in Japan.

ねずみ講は姿を変え形を変え騙される消費者は後を絶たない。
Nezumikō wa sugata o kae katachi o kae damasareru shōhi-sha wa ato o tatanai.
The list of consumers taken in by pyramid schemes, which keep popping up in all shapes and forms, continues to grow.

🐭 The idiom arises from the use in Japanese math classes of examples of rats having babies and the babies having babies ad infinitim to illustrate geometrical progression. See the second entry after this one. One thing about these kinds of schemes in Japan, America, or anywhere else is that you can be sure to find a rat in the works somewhere.

Nezumitori **ねずみ捕り** "mousetrap"
a (police) speed trap, radar trap

こんなところでねずみ捕りなんかしやがって。
Konna tokoro de nezumitori nanka shiyagatte.
It pisses me off the way they put up speed traps in places like this.

この辺はよくねずみ捕りやっているから気をつけろよ。
Kono hen wa yoku nezumitori yatte iru kara ki o tsukero yo.
The cops love to set up radar traps around here, so watch out.

この間ねずみ捕りにやられて、反則金5万円払ったよ。
Kono aida nezumitori ni yararete, hansoku-kin goman-en haratta yo.
I got caught in a police speed trap the other day and paid a fine of fifty thousand yen.

🐭 Slang. The Japanese police version of this universally denounced misuse of power, in keeping with many other Japanese practices, is employed when least likely to interrupt the conduct of business and most likely to infringe on the general population's right to enjoy what little free time they have; that is, on weekends and holidays, when the only people on the roads are out trying to relax and maybe go a little faster than the snail's pace that traffic and a national highway speed limit of 60 kph (36 mph) requires. The literal meaning, of which no examples are included here, is mousetrap.

Nezumizan **ねずみ算** "count rats"
a pyramid, geometrical (exponential) increase

コンビニがねずみ算のようにあっという間に増えた。
Konbini ga nezumizan no yō ni atto iu ma ni fueta.
Convenience stores sprang up like mushrooms (multiplied like rabbits) overnight.

彼女の借金はねずみ算式に増えていった。
Kanojo no shakkin wa nezumizan-shiki ni fuete itta.
Her debts were growing by leaps and bounds.

🐭 As the second example indicates, the idiom commonly appears with the suffix *-shiki,* meaning way or fashion. Common verbs accompanying it include *fueru* and *zōka suru,* both of which mean "increase." A possible translation for such usage might be "multiply like rabbits," although use would be limited to living things. The typical example given for teaching geometrical increase in "Japanese mathematics"—whatever that is—is that in January a pair of rats have twelve little ratlets. Rats being rats, a month later the twelve second-generation rats find an incestuous mate among themselves and together with the first generation rats have a bunch more little beady-eyed beasts. How many rats will there be in December? Well, there'll be a whole lot more than the neighborhood tabby can tolerate. Would you believe something like 2×7^{12} or about 27,600,000,000?

Nurenezumi ぬれ鼠 "a wet rat"
(figuratively) a drowned rat, a person soaked to the bone

彼は雨のふる街をあてもなく歩き回りぬれ鼠になった。
Kare wa ame no furu machi o ate mo naku arukimawari nurenezumi ni natta.
He got soaking (dripping) wet wandering around the city in the rain.

全身ぬれ鼠で僕の部屋の前に立っていた彼女を見たときは一瞬お化けかと思ったよ。
Zenshin nurenezumi de boku no heya no mae ni tatte ita kanojo o mita toki wa isshun obake ka to omotta yo.
For a second I thought she was a ghost or something when I saw her standing outside my apartment soaked to the bone.

🐭 Used to describe a person who looks pitiful and, of course, very wet, *nurenezumi* is used of a person who is fully clothed.

ni-no-ashi o fumu 二の足を踏む "put one's second foot down"

hesitate, have misgivings

あまりにも高くて、彼は二の足を踏んだ。
Amari ni mo takakute, kare wa ni-no-ashi o funda.

It was so expensive that he thought better of buying it.

近ごろ、彼は企業買収に対して、二の足を踏むようになった。
Chikagono, kare wa kigyō-baishū ni taishite, ni-no-ashi o fumu yō ni natta.
He has recently come to think twice about takeovers.

nichijō-sahan 日常茶飯 "everyday tea and rice"

an everyday occurrence (affair), a daily (common, commonplace, ordinary) occurrence, a common or garden-variety event, no big deal, ten a penny

今の高校生にとっては、こんなことは日常茶飯だよ。知らないのは親ばかりさ。
Ima no kōkō-sei ni totte wa, konna koto wa nichijō-sahan da yo. Shiranai no wa oya bakari sa.
For today's high-school students something like this is no big deal. The only ones who don't know about it are their parents.

この程度の事故は、このカーブじゃ日常茶飯事なんですよ。
Kono teido no jiko wa, kono kābu ja nichijō-sahan-ji nan desu yo.
Accidents like that are ten a penny on this corner.

🖋 Literally 日常茶飯 means "everyday tea and rice"; the expression is usually followed by the character 事, in which case the meaning is "an everyday occurrence." The character for rice 飯 is also used in the expression 朝飯前 (*asameshi-mae*), which literally means "before breakfast," and is used to refer to something that is easy to do, e.g., 俺ならこんな仕事は朝飯前だ (*Ore nara konna shigoto wa asameshi-mae da*, "A job like that I could do with my eyes closed"). A synonymous expression is お茶の子さいさい (*ocha no ko saisai*). お茶の子 is a small Japanese sweet eaten when drinking green tea, and might be suitably translated as "a piece of cake," as in the following example:

任しといて下さい。お茶の子さいさいです。
Makashitoite kudasai. Ocha no ko saisai desu.
Leave it to me. It's a piece of cake.

nichiyō-daiku 日曜大工 "Sunday carpenter"

a DIY (do-it-yourself) fanatic

クロも大きくなってきたから、今度の休みにはお父さんが日曜大工で犬小屋を作ってやろう。
Kuro mo ōkiku natte kita kara, kondo no yasumi ni wa otōsan ga nichiyō-daiku de inugoya o tsukutte yarō.
Blackie's now got to be quite a big dog, so Daddy's going to make him a nice kennel, come Sunday.

あの棚は主人の日曜大工の作品で、ちょっと格好は悪いけど、便利で重宝してるのよ。
Ano tana wa shujin no nichiyō-daiku no sakuhin de, chotto kakkō wa warui kedo, benri de chōhō shite 'ru no yo.
Those shelves are ones my husband knocked up himself. They look a bit naff (ugly), but they come in handy and I couldn't do without them.

nigamushi 苦虫 "a bitter insect"

(~ *o (kami)tsubushita yō na kao o suru*) make a sour face; scowl

その議員は不正の証拠を突きつけられ、苦虫を噛みつぶしたような顔を隠せなかった。
Sono giin wa fusei no shōko o tsukitsukerare, nigamushi o kamitsubushita yō na kao o kakusenakatta.
The Diet member couldn't help grimacing (couldn't hide his displeasure) when presented with the proof of his malfeasance.

言葉につまり、彼は苦虫をつぶした顔をしていた。
Kotoba ni tsumari, kare wa nigamushi o tsubushita kao o shite ita.
Stumped (At a loss for what to say), he got a sour look on his face.

警察官の不祥事に、県警の幹部は釈明の記者会見で終始苦虫をつぶした表情を見せていた。
Keisatsu-kan no fu-shōji ni, kenkei no kanbu wa shakumei no kisha-kaiken de shūshi nigamushi o tsubushita hyōjō o misete ita.
Prefectural police officials, explaining the scandal involving cops under their command, openly showed their distaste for the task throughout the press conference.

彼は過去の失敗を問題にされて苦虫を噛んだ。
Kare wa kako no shippai o mondai ni sarete nigamushi o kanda.
He had to just grin and bear it when someone brought up his past mistakes.

🐞 Used of people who are painfully aware their situation is worsening and who find themselves at a loss for words to respond to accusations or the like. The "bitter bug" is chimerical, though almost any insect would probably be sufficiently disgusting to warrant a sour face. The last example features an abbreviated form.

↪ *mushi* 虫

nigashita sakana wa ōkii 逃がした魚は大きい
"the uncaught fish is big"

the one that got away, it's always the biggest fish that gets away

逃がした魚は大きいと言うが、別れて初めて彼女のすばらしさに気づいたよ。
Nigashita sakana wa ookii to iu ga, wakarete hajimete kanojo no subarashisa ni kizuita yo.
They say the biggest one always gets away, and it was only after we had broken up that I realized what a wonderful person she is.

あの人の自慢話は大分差し引いて聞かなければいけない「逃がした魚は大きい」というでしょう。
Ano hito no jiman-banashi wa daibu sashihiite kikanakereba ikenai "Nigashita sakana wa ookii" to iu deshō.
You have to take everything he says with a grain of salt. It's always "the big one got away" with him.

nijū-jinkaku 二重人格 "a double personality"

a split personality, a double (dual) personality, a Jekyll and Hyde

彼の場合は、内弁慶なんて生やさしいものじゃない。完全な二重人格だ。
Kare no bāi wa, uchi-benkei nante nama-yasashii mono ja nai. Kanzen na nijū-jinkaku da.
It's not just that he's difficult (a handful) at home but as good as gold elsewhere. He's a downright Jekyll and Hyde.

この本の著者によると、凶悪犯罪の犯人には二重人格者が多いらしい。
Kono hon no chosha ni yoru to, kyōaku-hanzai no hannin ni wa nijū-jinkaku-sha ga ōi rashii.
According to the author of this book, many criminals who commit violent crimes seem to have split personalities.

二重人格どころか、多重人格という症例もあるそうだ。
Nijū-jinkaku dokoro ka, tajū-jinkaku to iu shōrei mo aru sō da.
They say there are cases where the personality is not simply dual but actually multiple.

ninin-sankyaku 二人三脚 "two people, three legs"

a three-legged race, cooperating with singleness of purpose, working together to achieve the same goal

小学校の運動会というと、二人三脚とスプーンレースを思い出すなあ。
Shōgakkō no undō-kai to iu to, ninin-sankyaku to supūn-rēsu o omoidasu nā.
Talking of elementary school sports days reminds me of three-legged races and egg-and-spoon contests.

今日からは新郎新婦力を合わせて、仲良く二人三脚の人生をお送り下さい。
Kyō kara wa shinrō-shinpu chikara o awasete, naka-yoku ninin-sankyaku no jinsei o ookuri kudasai.
To the bride and groom I say, please join forces to live in happy harmony from this day on.

ninki 人気 "people's *ki*"

popularity, [〜の] fashionable, in, in vogue, popular, trendy

あの新人候補は人気だけでトップ当選した。
Ano shinjin-kōho wa ninki dake de toppu-tōsen shita.
That new candidate got the most votes during the election on the sole strength of her popularity.

このゲームの爆発的人気の理由は何だろうか。
Kono gēmu no bakuhatsu-teki ninki no riyū wa nan darō ka.
What do you suppose is behind this game's explosive popularity?

人気のランチスペシャルは試してみる価値があるよ。
Ninki no ranchi-supesharu wa tameshite miru kachi ga aru yo.

The popular lunch special is well worth a try.

若い人の間で人気のディスコが近くにあるけど、行ってみる？
Wakai hito no aida de ninki no disuko ga chikaku ni aru kedo, itte miru?
There's a disco nearby that's popular (that's in) with the young crowd. Wanna check it out?

ボディ・ピアスは最近急に人気が出てきた。
Bodī-piasu wa saikin kyū ni ninki ga dete kita.
Body piercing is suddenly all the rage.

最近また和服の人気が出てきたそうだ。
Saikin mata wafuku no ninki ga dete kita sō da.
Recently, they're saying kimonos are getting popular again.

いつまでも今の人気が続くとは思えない。
Itsu made mo ima no ninki ga tsuzuku to wa omoenai.
I can't see it staying as popular as it is now forever.

恐竜は子供の間でいつの時代も変わらない人気を保ち続けている。
Kyōryū wa kodomo-tachi no aida de itsu no jidai mo kawaranai ninki o tamochitsuzukete iru.
Dinosaurs have continued to maintain their popularity with kids over the years.

芸名を変えたとたんに人気が落ちちゃった。
Geimei o kaeta totan ni ninki ga ochichatta.
His popularity plummeted the instant he changed his stage name.

クリスティの『ねずみとり』は初演以来大人気で、これまで40年以上連続公演されている。
Kurisutī no "Nezumi-tori" wa shoen irai dai-ninki de, kore made yonjū-nen ijō renzoku kōen sarete iru.
Agatha Christie's *Mousetrap* has been a big hit, performed continuously since its opening more than forty years ago.

Ｊリーグが発足してサッカーは大人気だから、試合の切符がなかなか手に入らない。

Jē-rīgu ga hossoku shite sakkā wa dai-ninki da kara, shiai no kippu ga nakanaka te ni hairanai.
Soccer's taken the nation by storm since the J-League started up, so tickets are nearly impossible to come by.

↪ *ninki + noun* 人気＋名詞, *ninki ga aru* 人気がある, *ninki ga nai* 人気がない

ninki + noun 人気＋名詞

popular

うちの祐二はクラスの人気者だ。
Uchi no Yūji wa kurasu no ninki-mono da.
My Yuji's one of the most popular kids in his class.

この動物園の人気者はなんといってもパンダとラッコでしょう。
Kono dōbutsu-en no ninki-mono wa nan to itte mo panda to rakko deshō.
Two of the most popular animals in the zoo are almost certainly the panda and the otter.

処女作を発表してすぐ人気作家になった。
Shojo-saku o happyō shite sugu ninki-sakka ni natta.
He became a best-selling author soon after publishing his first book.

週刊誌はまたも人気力士と人気女優の婚約の話題でもちきりだ。
Shūkan-shi wa mata mo ninki-rikishi to ninki-joyū no kon'yaku no wadai de mochikiri da.
Once again the weeklies are full of stories about another engagement between a popular sumo wrestler and a popular actress.

人気選手が必ずしもチームにいちばん貢献しているわけではない。
Ninki-senshu ga kanarazushimo chīmu ni ichiban kōken shite iru wake de wa nai.
The popular ball players aren't necessarily the ones who contribute the most to the team.

この歌は人気ドラマの主題歌として有名になった。
Kono uta wa ninki-dorama no shudai-ka toshite yūmei ni natta.
This song became famous as the theme song for a popular TV soap.

冷やし中華は夏の人気メニューだ。
Hiyashi-chūka wa natsu no ninki-menyū da.
Cold Chinese-style noodles are a popular summer dish.

༅ How do you read 人気? Well, you know there have to be at least two ways for us to ask the question, right? And since you've read the entry to here, you probably know how to use the first and most common, *ninki* (popularity). The key to figuring out whether it's that reading or the other, *hitoke* (a sign or sense of someone being around), is, of course, the context and, more helpfully, the phrase in which it appears. *Ninki* is the only reading when the word is followed by ~ *ga deru,* ~ *ga ochiru,* ~ *ga ochime,* and ~ *ga takai,* most of which are exemplified above, or preceded by the likes of *sugoi , batsugun no, saikō no,* and *takai*. *Hitoke,* on the other hand, does not appear outside a very limited number of expressions: ~ *ga (no, mo) aru,* ~ *ga (no, mo) nai,* ~ *ga (no) ōi* and ~ *ga (no) sukunai*.

Those slightly ahead of the game will wonder about the several situations in which either reading is possible, namely ~ *ga (no, mo) aru* and ~ *ga (no, mo) nai*. The short answer is, "good luck," because it all depends on what is being discussed. Take 人気のない寂しい裏通り (~ *no nai sabishii uradōri*), for example. It could be *ninki*, I guess, but why would anyone be talking about whether a back alley was popular or not? And why would they use the adjective *sabishii* (lonesome or empty) about it? No, it's *hitoke*. Of course, the contrarians among us will be quick to point out that if it's not popular, *ninki ga nai,* then there sure won't be any people milling around (*hitoke ga nai*) and likewise if there's no sign of anyone being around, well then it certainly isn't a popular place, not at that moment at least.

One final note, in case you haven't realized it, 大人気 also has two unrelated readings. One, *dai-ninki,* shows up in two examples under *ninki*; the other, *otonage,* is embedded in the entry *otonage (ga) nai,* to which an explanatory note similar to this one is attached.

༄ *ninki* 人気, *ninki ga aru* 人気がある, *ninki ga nai* 人気がない

ninki ga aru 人気がある

be all the rage, in, popular; enjoy popularity

この雑誌はもともと若い人向けだったが、今ではむしろ中年の人の間で人気がある。
Kono zasshi wa motomoto wakai hito muke datta ga, ima de wa mushiro chūnen no hito no aida de ninki ga aru.
This magazine originally targeted younger readers, but has ended up being popular among middle-aged people instead.

人気のある時はいいが、落ち目になったらみじめだよ。
Ninki no aru toki wa ii ga, ochime ni nattara mijime da yo.
Everything's hunky-dory when you're hot, but it's really the pits when you start going downhill.

少し人気があると思って天狗になっているんじゃないか。
Sukoshi ninki ga aru to omotte tengu ni natte irun ja nai ka.
Look at you! Get the least bit popular, and it goes straight to your head.

⇨ *ninki* 人気, *ninki* + *noun* 人気＋名詞, *ninki ga nai* 人気がない

ninki ga nai 人気がない

be out, unpopular

どこといって悪いところはないのになぜか人気がない。
Doko to itte warui tokoro wa nai no ni naze ka ninki ga nai.
There's nothing in particular that's wrong with him, but for some reason no one seems to like him.

売り場面積が狭いので、人気のない商品はどんどん入れ換えている。
Uriba-menseki ga semai no de, ninki no nai shōhin wa dondon irekaete iru.
The shop's floor space is limited, so we're always changing the displays to get rid of products that don't sell (aren't moving, popular).

↪ *ninki* 人気, *ninki* + *noun* 人気 + 名詞, *ninki ga aru* 人気がある

nisoku-sanmon 二束三文 "two bundles for three mon"

dirt cheap, at bargain-basement prices, for peanuts, for a song, for chicken feed, for next to nothing

売り急いでいたので、やむをえず二束三文で処分した。
Uriisoide ita no de, yamu o ezu nisoku-sanmon de shobun shita.
I was in a rush to sell, which unavoidably meant I got rid of them dirt cheap (at throwaway prices).

思い出の品だったが、二束三文にしかならなかった。
Omoide no shina datta ga, nisoku-sanmon ni shika naranakatta.
It had a lot of sentimental value, but it ended up going for peanuts.

✤ A *mon* was the smallest unit of monetary value in the Edo era (1600–1868). Originally this expression was written with the character for "foot" 足 (which is also the counter used for pairs of shoes), as in Edo Japan you could buy two pairs of rush sandals for three *mon*. Thereafter the character for "bundle" was used and the expression took on its present meaning.

nisshin-geppo 日進月歩 "progress by days and months"

steady advance, rapid progress; 〜する to advance by leaps and bounds, to make rapid progress

パソコンは日進月歩の業界だから、新製品も半年も経つと安く買えるよ。
Pasokon wa nisshin-geppo no gyōkai da kara, shin-seihin mo hantoshi mo tatsu to yasuku kaeru yo.

Advancements in personal computers are happening so fast that new products are discounted after only six months on the market.

医療技術は日進月歩しているけれど、患者の心のケアの方はあまり進んでいない。
Iryō-gijutsu wa nisshin-geppo shite iru keredo, kanja no kokoro no kea no hō wa amari susunde inai.
Although medical technology is advancing by leaps and bounds, there has been very little progress in dealing with patients' spiritual well-being.

nō aru taka wa tsume o kakusu 能ある鷹は爪を隠す "a powerful hawk hides its talons"

an able person does not show off his skills; tell not all you know, all you have, or all you can do

能ある鷹は爪を隠す、ちょっとピアノが弾けるからって自慢するもんじゃないよ。
Nō aru taka wa tsume o kakusu, chotto piano ga hikeru kara tte jiman suru mon ja nai yo.
Don't toot your horn because you can play the piano a little. If you're good, people will discover it for themselves.

能ある鷹は爪を隠すと言うけど、あの人がコンピュータプログラムが出来るとは知らなかった。
Nō aru taka wa tsume o kakusu to iu kedo, ano hito ga konpyūta puroguramu ga dekiru to wa shiranakatta.
I know what they say about ability being its own best advertisement, but what a surprise it was to find out that he knows how to program computers.

❧ The opposite being equally true, it is to those who seek approbation for their modest abilities that this maxim is most often directed.

nodo のど throat

There aren't many variations on the meaning of *nodo*. Besides "throat," it can mean one's singing voice, hence the *nodo jiman* or "proud throat" contests and programs that choke Japanese television year in and year out. Another more arcane meaning comes from the printing world and refers to the white space between the facing pages of an open book that collects dust and cookie crumbs and is equally interestingly called a "gutter" in English.

Nodo ga naru / nodo o narasu のどが鳴る／のどを鳴らす
"one's throat cries"
one's mouth is watering, lick one's chops

手作りケーキに、思わずどのが鳴った。
Tezukuri kēki ni, omowazu nodo ga natta.
My mouth started watering when I saw the homemade cake.

サラリーマンたちは仕事の後のビールにのどを鳴らした。
Sararīman-tachi wa shigoto no ato no bīru ni nodo o narashita.
The businessmen were smacking their lips as they gulped down their beers after a hard day at the office.

Nodo kara te ga deru のどから手が出る "a hand comes out of one's throat"
really want, desperately need

のどから手が出るほどあの車が欲しい。
Nodo kara te ga deru hodo ano kuruma ga hoshii.
I want that car so bad I can taste it. / I'm just dying to have that car. / I'd give anything to have that car.

いま彼がのどから手の出るほど欲しいものは、お金ではなく名前だろう。

Ima kare ga nodo kara te no deru hodo hoshii mono wa, okane de wa naku namae darō.
What he wants more than anything now is to be known, not to be rich.

nomi 蚤 flea

Not on anybody's top-ten list of favorite insects, fleas figure in four idioms included here, all of which play on its diminutive size rather than its notorious ability to drive both animals and people crazy, as well as deprive them of sleep. Fleas are counted *ippiki* 一匹, when you can find them.

Nomi no fūfu 蚤の夫婦 "husband and wife fleas"
a little husband and a big wife, Jack Sprat and his wife

中村さんは蚤の夫婦で知られている。
Nakamura-san wa nomi no fūfu de shirarete iru.
The Nakamuras are one of those couples where the wife is bigger than her husband.

あの人と結婚したら、蚤の夫婦になっちゃうから二の足踏んじゃうのよね。
Ano hito to kekkon shitara, nomi no fūfu ni natchau kara ni no ashi funjau no yo ne.
I can't see myself getting married to a guy like him who's so much smaller than me.

🦟 From the observation that the female flea is larger than the male. You probably don't want to say it in front of a couple who fit the description. Who knows, the woman might take offense and stomp you.

Nomi no shinzō 蚤の心臓 "a flea's heart"
chickenheartedness, faintheartedness, mousiness, timidity

きみの蚤の心臓を鍛えるために肝試しをやろう。
Kimi no nomi no shinzō o kitaeru tame ni kimodameshi o yarō.
Let's see if we can't do something about that yellow belly (candy ass) of yours by playing a little game of chicken.

蚤の心臓の持ち主の山田さんが直接社長に抗議したとは大したものだ。
Nomi no shinzō no mochinushi no Yamada-san ga chokusetsu shachō ni kōgi shita to wa taishita mono da.
For someone as lily-livered as Yamada to have complained to the boss must have taken a lot of guts.

꽁 From the notion that a flea's heart, presuming they have one, has got to be miniscule, and the general belief that the size of one's heart is directly related to one's courage. To have the heart of a flea is to be a weenie or a wimp.

☞ *ki ga chiisai* 気が小さい, *ki ga yowai* 気が弱い, *shinzō ga yowai* 心臓が弱い, *shōshin-yokuyoku* 小心翼々; *ki ga tsuyoi* 気が強い

nonki (na) 呑気(な), 暢気(な) "loose *ki*"

carefree, easygoing, laid-back, relaxed

まったく何考えてるのか。呑気なんだから。
Mattaku nani kangaete 'ru no ka. Nonki nan da kara.
What are you thinking? Jeez, you're so happy-go-lucky!

こっちは貧乏暇なしなのに、お前は呑気な身分で羨ましいよ。
Kotchi wa binbō hima nashi na no ni, omae wa nonki na mibun de urayamashii yo.
I sure envy you. Here I am working my buns off for peanuts while you kick back and take it all in.

꽁 Bear in mind that in a society that so respects and encourages industriousness, it is not always complimentary to be considered *nonki*.

⇨ *ki ga raku ni naru* 気が楽になる, *kiraku (na)* 気楽(な)

noriki (na) 乗り気(な) "mounted *ki*"

eagerness, enthusiasm (for)

先方は乗り気ですから、気が変わらないうちに契約してしまいましょう。
Senpō wa noriki desu kara, ki ga kawaranai uchi ni keiyaku shite shimaimashō.
The other party's interested, so let's get the contract signed before they change their minds.

僕は乗り気だったんだが、女房がどうしてもいやだと言い張ってね。
Boku wa noriki datta n' da ga, nyōbō ga dōshite mo iya da to iihatte ne.
I was all ready to go ahead with it, but the wife wouldn't hear of it. / I thought it sounded great, but the better half wouldn't have anything to do with it.

今度の話にはずいぶん乗り気になっているようですね。
Kondo no hanashi ni wa zuibun noriki ni natte iru yō desu ne.
You really seem to be high on (up for) the project this time.

せっかく乗り気になっていたら、向こうから断わられてしまった。
Sekkaku noriki ni natte itara, mukō kara kotowararete shimatta.
They pulled the plug [on the project] just when I was getting into it.

三時間ぐらいねばって説明したら、やっと乗り気になってくれましたよ。
Sanji-kan gurai nebatte setsumei shitara, yatto noriki ni natte kuremashita yo.
They finally showed some interest after I explained things for about three hours. / It took around three hours of explaining, but they finally came around (warmed up to it).

ぜんぜん乗り気じゃなかったから、断られてむしろ幸いだった。

Zenzen noriki ja nakatta kara, kotowararete mushiro saiwai datta.
I wasn't into it at all, so I was actually glad when it fell through.

☞ *ki ga noru* 気が乗る, *kinori (ga) suru* 気乗り(が)する, *ki ga muku* 気が向く; *kinori-usu (na)* 気乗り薄(な)

nyonin-kinsei 女人禁制 "no females allowed"

off limits to women, no admittance to women, out-of-bounds to women

昔、高野山は女人禁制だったから、女性は室生寺に参りました。室生寺が女人高野と呼ばれるのは、そのためです。
Mukashi, Kōya-san wa nyonin-kinsei datta kara, josei wa Murōji ni mairimashita. Murōji ga Nyonin Kōya to yobareru no wa, sono tame desu.
In the old days Mount Kōya was strictly out-of-bounds to women, who instead went to pray at Murō-ji. For that reason Murō-ji is known as "the women's Mount Kōya."

❧ 高野山 (Kōya-san) is a mountain temple in Wakayama Prefecture, famous as a place of pilgrimage. Long ago only men were able to visit it, and women were forced to seek spiritual salvation elsewhere. Murō-ji is a temple in Nara.

女人禁制だった山が多いのは、山の神様が女性だと考えられていたかららしい。
Nyonin-kinsei datta yama ga ōi no wa, yama no kamisama ga josei da to kangaerarete ita kara rashii.
So many mountains used to be off limits to women because it was thought the mountain god was a goddess.

現在でも土俵は女人禁制で、文部大臣ですら女性は土俵には上がれません。
Genzai de mo dohyō wa nyonin-kinsei de, monbu-daijin de sura josei wa dohyō ni wa agaremasen.

> Even today women are not allowed to set foot inside the sumo wrestling ring, even if they happen to be the Minister of Education.

🍂 At the end of every sumo competition, the champion wrestler is presented with prizes given by various organizations such as foreign embassies, companies, and even the Japanese Education Ministry. In the early 1990s two successive Ministers of Education were women (Mayumi Moriyama and Ryoko Akamatsu). They should have presented the prizes but were prevented from doing so by the sumo authorities, who would not allow them to sully the sacred soil of the sumo ring (where the prize-giving ceremony always takes place). In their place a male underling was sent along from the ministry to hand over the awards instead. Even though this caused a storm of publicity at the time, nothing has changed, and the sumo ring is still a distinctly all-male preserve.

Some older men use the expression 山の神 (*yama no kami*, "the god of the mountain") to refer to their wife (a British equivalent might be "She who must be obeyed"). Perhaps the reason for this is that the said deity was in fact a goddess and not a god, and one with a fearsome reputation for wild pangs of jealousy and anger if any woman should dare to encroach on her domain.

☞ *danson-johi* 男尊女卑

ōkami おおかみ（狼） wolf

Now considered extinct, the last known *Nihon ōkami* was shot and killed in 1905. And, no, public opinion is not divided by government plans to reintroduce these widely misunderstood canine carnivores into the nation's national parks. There are no such plans, not yet at least.

It was previously believed that the wolf was a divine creature capable of protecting humans from a variety of misfortunes. Folk practices related to this belief included use of a wolf's skull to guard against a form of mental illness known as fox possession, possibly from the fact that the wolf was a natural enemy of the fox.

Folk beliefs evoking wolves are often related to childbirth, since the mountain god, whom some folk tales depict as changing into a wolf, was also held to be the guardian god of childbirth.

In addition, the indigenous people of Japan's northernmost island Hokkaido, the Ainu, worshiped wolves and claim one as the father of the clan.

The wolf's howl is *uō-uō.* Wolves are counted *ippiki* 一匹 or *ittō* 一頭.

Ippiki ōkami　**一匹狼**　"a single wolf"
a lone wolf, loner, maverick

彼は出版業界の一匹狼で通っている。
Kare wa shuppan-gyōkai no ippiki ōkami de tōtte iru.
He's known in the publishing industry as a maverick.

一匹狼だったその男の居所を知る者はいない。
Ippiki ōkami datta sono otoko no idokoro o shiru mono wa inai.
Nobody knows the whereabouts of that loner.

Ōkami shōnen　**狼少年**　"a wolf-boy"
the boy who cried wolf (once too often); a habitual liar

そんないい加減なこと言ってると、狼少年になっちゃうよ。
Sonna ii kagen na koto itte 'ru to, ōkami shōnen ni natchau yo.
Nobody's going to believe you anymore if you keep crying wolf (bullshiting) all the time.

ダメだよ、あんな奴のこと信じちゃ、狼少年ってみんなに言われてるんだから。
Dame da yo, anna yatsu no koto shinjicha, ōkami shōnen tte minna ni iwarete 'ru n' da kara.
You can't believe that dude. Everyone says he's full of it (full of hot air, beans).

🐾 From *Aesop's Fables*.

Okuri ōkami 送り狼 "a see-you-home wolf"
a man professing to be a gentleman who escorts his date to her home, only to try to force her to have sex with him once he's in the door

「彼ったら、『京子さん、ぼくがアパートまで送って行きましょう』って言うのよ。」
"Kare ttara, 'Kyoko-san, boku ga apāto made okutte ikimashō' tte iu no yo."
"Then he ups and says, 'Kyoko, can I give you a lift home?'"
「せいぜい送り狼には気をつけてね。」
"Seizei okuri ōkami ni wa ki o tsukete ne."
"I'd watch out if I were you. He may not be as innocent as he seems."

酒に弱い宏君は送り狼になるどころか、女友達に家まで送ってもらうことの方が多い。
Sake ni yowai Hiroshi-kun wa okuri ōkami ni naru dokoro ka, onna tomodachi ni ie made okutte morau koto no hō ga ōi.
Far from being a wolf on the prowl, Hiroshi usually ends up having to get a lift home with one of his girlfriends because he's so drunk.

❦ From a former belief that there were wolves in Japan who followed travelers along lonely mountain roads either to protect them from other roving packs of wolves or attack them should the travelers ever look back to see if they were being followed (or stumble and fall, according to other versions).

okera おけら（螻蛄） mole cricket

Built for digging, this inch-long subterranean can sometimes be found under stones or down wood. In the fall its cry—*jī* ジー—is commonly said to be the cry of earthworms. Mole crickets are counted *ippiki* 一匹.

Okera (or *kera*) **おけら（螻蛄）** "mole cricket"
be (flat) broke, cleaned out, penniless, tapped (out), wiped out

彼女は競馬にボーナス全部つぎ込んで結局おけらになった。
Kanojo wa keiba ni bōnasu zenbu tsugikonde kekkyoku okera ni natta.
She blew her whole bonus on the ponies and now she's flat-ass broke.

おけらだと言っていた彼がどうやって海外旅行なんか行けたのだろう？
Okera da to itte ita kare ga dō yatte kaigai-ryokō nanka iketa no darō?
How'd that dude ever afford to travel abroad when he was just saying he was tapped out and all?

✌ Idiomatic use apparently derives from the association of the Japanese body language for being broke, both arms extended over one's head as in a "banzai" gesture, with the appearance of the mole cricket. Whoever said the Japanese weren't creative? Originally gamblers' and pickpockets' argot, it is usually written in katakana.

ōki na kao o suru 大きな顔をする "have a big face"

be proud of oneself, be cocky, lord it over someone

新人のくせに大きな顔をするんじゃない。
Shinjin no kuse ni ōki na kao o surun ja nai.
I wouldn't be acting so big if I were a new guy like you.

一度世話をしてくれたからといってそんなに大きな顔をされても困る。
Ichido sewa o shite kureta kara to itte sonna ni ōki na kao o sarete mo komaru.
Just because you helped me out once doesn't give you the right to act so high and mighty.

Also 大きい顔をする *ōkii kao o suru.*

oki ni mesu お気に召す "take into *one's ki*"

favor, like, look favorably upon

お気に召す品がございましたか。
Oki ni mesu shina ga gozaimashita ka.
Were you able to find anything you liked?

お気に召したらいくつでもどうぞ。
Oki ni meshitara ikutsu de mo dōzo.
If you find them to your liking, please feel free to take as many as you want.

鈴木さんはこの春の人事異動で田中さんが先に部長になったのがお気に召さないらしい。
Suzuki-san wa kono haru no jinji-idō de Tanaka-san ga saki ni buchō ni natta no ga oki ni mesanai rashii.
Suzuki isn't exactly jumping for joy now that Tanaka has been promoted ahead of him as a department head in this spring's reshuffling of personnel.

「お気に召すまま」見に行かない？ 新しい演出だって。
"Oki ni mesu mama" mi ni ikanai? Atarashii enshutsu datte.
Do you want to go see *As You Like It*? It's supposed to be a new interpretation.

✻ *Oki ni mesu* is the honorific form of *ki ni iru*.

↝ *ki ni iru* 気に入る, *oki-ni-iri* お気に入り

oki-ni-iri お気に入り

favorite, pet, the apple of one's eye

あいつは先生のお気に入りだから、さぼっても大丈夫さ。
Aitsu wa sensei no oki-ni-iri da kara, sabotte mo daijōbu sa.
Since he's the teacher's pet he can get away with cutting class.

これが彼女のお気に入りの香水らしい。
Kore ga kanojo no oki-ni-iri no kōsui rashii.
This seems to be her favorite perfume.

🐾 Compared with *suki na*, *ki ni itta*, or *ki ni itte iru*, *oki-ni-iri* generally expresses a stronger sense of liking—something akin to "loving" perhaps. When casting about for an appropriate way to say "my favorite . . ." in Japanese, it is usually safer to go with "*watakushi no suki na . . .*" or "*watakushi no ki ni itte iru . . .*," for although "*watakushi no oki-ni-iri . . .*" is not always inappropriate, it has a childish ring for many Japanese.

↪ *ki ni iru* 気に入る, *oki ni mesu* お気に召す; *ki ni kuwanai* 気に食わない

okuri ōkami 送り狼 "a see-you-home wolf"

a man professing to be a gentleman who escorts his date to her home, only to try to force her to have sex with him once he's in the door

「彼ったら、『京子さん、ぼくがアパートまで送って行きましょう』って言うのよ。」
"Kare ttara 'Kyoko-san, boku ga apāto made okutte ikimashō' tte iu no yo."
"Then he ups and says, 'Kyoko, can I give you a lift home?'"
「せいぜい送り狼には気をつけてね。」
"Seizei okuri ōkami ni wa ki o tsukete ne."

"I'd watch out if I were you. He may not be as innocent as he seems."

酒に弱い宏君は送り狼になるどころか、女友達に家まで送ってもらうことの方が多い。
Sake ni yowai Hiroshi-kun wa okuri ōkami ni naru dokoro ka, onna tomodachi ni ie made okutte morau koto no hō ga ōi.
Far from being a wolf on the prowl, Hiroshi usually ends up having to get a lift home with one of his girlfriends because he's so drunk.

※ From a former belief that there were wolves in Japan who followed travelers along lonely mountain roads either to protect them from other roving packs of wolves or attack them should the travelers ever look back to see if they were being followed (or stumble and fall, according to other versions).

↪ *ōkami* 狼

ome ni kakaru お目にかかる "to be hung on the eyes"

meet

一度ゆっくりお目にかかって、お話を伺いたいと思っています。
Ichido yukkuri ome ni kakatte, ohanashi o ukagaitai to omotte imasu.
I hope to have the opportunity to speak with you at length sometime soon.

はじめてお目にかかります。私が山本です。
Hajimete ome ni kakarimasu. Watashi ga Yamamoto desu.
I believe this is the first time I've had the pleasure. Yamamoto is my name.

↪ *me* 目

ōmu おうむ (鸚鵡) parrot

Although this import's ability to mimic sounds, particularly the human voice, is its only quality worthy of linguistic mention, the sky above Japanese urban parks (as exaggerated reports would have it) is darkened by flocks of parrots that have escaped the wire and wicker confines of their cramped cages and banded together in the few remaining natural areas in the cities to live in freedom, eking out a subsistence among the concrete edifices that loom above them. Yeah, well. While it may be true that parrots occasionally escape from their cages—sightings of small flocks have been documented in Tokyo's parks—the "problem" is undoubtedly overstated. Having said that, it must be remarked that psittacosis, or parrot fever, a disease that can infect humans, is fairly common among the nation's imported birds, and as early as ten years ago it had spread to nearly half the dogs and 10 percent of the cats brought into Tokyo's pet shelters. It sounds like the makings of a B movie, *Revenge of the Parrots.*

At this writing, the first thing that comes to mind for most Japanese upon hearing the word *ōmu* is the discredited religious sect of Shoko Asahara, whose Aum Shinrikyo appears ("appears" added by my timorous editor!) to have been behind the poison gas attacks in Tokyo's subways in early 1995 as well as numerous other murders, extortions, and, on a lighter note, one of the most entertaining political campaigns in recent memory, during which dozens of followers donned papier-mâché heads modeled after Asahara's dour phiz and "parroted" ridiculous ditties. But this *ōmu* is not of the natural world, deriving instead from the two phonemes that comprise the universal mantra written "om" in the roman alphabet and *aun* in Japanese.

Parrots are counted *ichiwa* 一羽.

Ōmugaeshi **おうむ返し** "a parrot's refrain"
parrot, regurgitate, echo (what someone says)

彼女は緊張のあまり、面接官の質問をオウム返しするばかりだった。

Kanojo wa kinchō no amari, mensetsu-kan no shitsumon o ōmugaeshi suru bakari datta.
She was so nervous all she could do was repeat the interviewer's questions.

うちの娘は親の言うことをオウム返しするので下手なこと言えない。
Uchi no musume wa oya no iu koto o ōmugaeshi suru no de heta na koto ienai.
My daughter parrots everything she hears at home, so we have to watch what we say.

onaji ana no mujina 同じ穴のむじな "badgers from the same den"

birds of a feather, (be) just like (no different/no better than) the others

今だからお前善人面しているが、元はヤクザ俺とは同じ穴のむじなだ。
Ima da kara omae zennin-zura shite iru ga, moto wa yakuza ore to wa onaji ana no mujina da.
You can play Mr. Nice Guy now, but you've got a past just like I do.

今の日本はどこの政党が政権をとっても変わりなし、政治家は皆同じ穴のむじな。
Ima no Nihon wa doko no seitō ga seiken o totte mo kawari nashi, seiji-ka wa mina onaji ana no mujina.
It doesn't make a bit of difference which party is in power in Japan today, politicians are all the same, you can't tell one from another.

onko-chishin 温故知新 "visit the past to know the new" (*in old Japanese* 温 *means "to visit"*)

a study of the classics is the springboard for new research

情報の氾濫する現代だからこそ、温故知新の精神を忘れてはいけないと思うよ。
Jōhō no hanran suru gendai da kara koso, onko-chishin no seishin o wasurete wa ikenai to omou yo.
It is precisely because we find ourselves living in an age deluged with information that we must not forget the importance of a thorough grounding in the classics.

温故知新のために、世界中の古典を読破したい。
Onko-chishin no tame ni, sekai-jū no koten o dokuha shitai.
To help me pursue my research, I first want to read the classics of world literature to get acquainted with what's gone before.

onnakke 女っ気 "woman's *ki*"

1. (of an object or place) a woman's touch

若い女の部屋にしては女っ気がないなあ。
Wakai onna no heya ni shite wa onnakke ga nai nā.
For a young woman's room, this place sure lacks a feminine touch.

わが家は全く女っ気がなくて殺風景だね。
Wagaya wa mattaku onnakke ga nakute sappūkei da ne.
The old place is kind of stark now, without any of the warmth a woman would give it.

2. (of a man) a sign, feeling or sense that someone has a girlfriend or wife

あの人のまわりには全く女っ気がない。
Ano hito no mawari ni wa mattaku onnakke ga nai.
There's no sign at all that he's got a girlfriend (wife, woman).

真面目な息子だが、あまりに女っ気がないのも親としては気がかりだ。

Majime na musuko da ga, amari ni onnakke ga nai no mo oya toshite wa kigakari da.
My son's serious enough, but as a parent I'm a little worried that there don't seem to be any women in his life.

🌶 The good news is that the word itself is not particularly sexist, characterizing women as meek and subservient. The bad news is that it is used almost exclusively in the phrase *onnakke ga nai* as something seen as absent, especially in the lives of men. Oh, and yes, Virginia, there is a masculine equivalent, *mutatis mutandis*, replete with all the loathsome sociocultural accoutrements of a male-dominated society. Check out *otokogi* 男気.

Also 女気 *onnagi*, 女気 *onnake*.
☞ *iroke* 色気 (#2)

onshin-futsū 音信不通 "correspondence interrupted"

to lose touch with someone, to be no longer in contact with someone

何年かは年賀状をやりとりしていたが、今は音信不通だ。
Nannen ka wa nenga-jō o yaritori shite ita ga, ima wa onshin-futsū da.
For many years we sent each other New Year's cards, but now we've lost touch.

長い間音信不通になっていた嵯峨さんの消息が分かったよ。
Nagai aida onshin-futsū ni natte ita Saga-san no shōsoku ga wakatta yo.
I got news of ol' Saga the other day; I hadn't heard from him in donkey's years.

oshidori おしどり（鴛鴦）mandarin duck

Often seen in pairs, especially during the winter in Japan, this beautiful crested Asian duck is considered a symbol of conjugal affection, harmony, and fidelity in China as well as Japan, where it is common in shady ponds and lakes. In truth, however, these ducks change partners every year, only slightly less often than daytime Japanese TV would have contemporary housewives slip under the sheets with hard-working hubby's friends.

Mandarin ducks are counted *ichiwa* 一羽.

Oshidori-fūfu **おしどり夫婦** "mandarin duck man and wife"

a happily married couple, a couple of (married) lovebirds, two people whose marriage was made in heaven

---

佐々木さんはおしどり夫婦で有名だ。
Sasaki-san wa oshidori-fūfu de yūmei da.
The Sasakis are notorious as a happily married couple.

おしどり夫婦で通っていたあのタレント夫婦の突然の離婚で、芸能雑誌が騒いでいる。
Oshidori-fūfu de tōtte ita ano tarento-fūfu no totsuzen no rikon de, geinō-zasshi ga sawaide iru.
The tabloids are going crazy now, what with the marriage of those two stars on the rocks, when everyone thought they were a couple of lovebirds.

✌ From the mistaken belief that mandarin ducks mate for life.

oshige mo naku 惜し気もなく "with no regretful *ki*"

freely, generously, openhandedly; without regret, without a second thought, without looking back

あのミュージシャンはコンサート収益の大部分を惜し気もなく自然保護団体に寄付するんだって。

Ano myūjishan wa konsāto shūeki no dai-bubun o oshige mo naku shizenhogo-dantai ni kifu suru n' datte.
They say that that musician generously donates most of the proceeds from his concerts to environmental organizations.

彼女は惜し気もなく湯水のように金を使いますよ。
Kanojo wa oshige mo naku yumizu no yō ni kane o tsukaimasu yo.
She's such a spendthrift, she goes through money like it grew on trees.

✌ *yumizu no yō ni tsukau*: literally, "use like hot water" (a set phrase).

もう10年も使って古くなったから、惜し気もなく捨てられるさ。
Mō jūnen mo tsukatte furuku natta kara, oshige mo naku suterareru sa.
Ten years I used that old sucker. I won't even think twice about getting rid of it.

✌ Found under its noun form (*oshige*) in traditional dictionaries, *oshige mo naku* is included here as an idiom since *oshige* is encountered almost exclusively in this form in both written and spoken Japanese.

↝ *kimae* (*yoku*) 気前(よく) (in the sense of "giving freely")

otamajakushi おたまじゃくし "tadpole"

1. a musical note; music

俺おたまじゃくしに弱いんだよね。
Ore otamajakushi ni yowai n' da yo ne.
I wish I could read music.

✌ From a pollywog's chimerical resemblance to a musical note.

2. a ladle

ちょっとそこのおたまじゃくし取って。
Chotto soko no otamajakushi totte.
Get that ladle for me, would you?

🕊 From the physical resemblance of the shape of a ladle to that of a pollywog.

otokogi 男気 "manly *ki*"

machismo, manliness, masculinity; bravery; chivalry, gallantry

「男女」みたいな人ばっかりだと思ってたけど、まだあんな男気がある人もいたのねえ。
"Otoko-onna" mitai na hito bakkari da to omotte 'ta kedo, mada anna otokogi ga aru hito mo ita no nē.
This he-man appeared just when I figured all that was left were a bunch of pansies. / Here I was thinking there weren't any real men left and then, look, here's Mr. Macho himself.

🕊 *otoko-onna*: an effeminate man or a masculine woman.

ここは一つ男気を出して、「うん」と言って下さいよ。
Koko wa hitotsu otokogi o dashite, "Un" to itte kudasai yo.
Now's the time to be a man and just say you'll do it.

🕊 Variously defined as "the self-sacrificial nature [of men] which lends itself to the service of the weak or less fortunate" and "a temperament free from self-interest and willing to help the weak," this prime candidate for politically correct revisionist exclusion from the language is much more clearly—and positively—defined than its feminine counterpart *onnakke* 女っ気, which, by the way, has little to do with the qualities thought to be common to women except as homemakers.

otonage (ga) nai 大人気(が)ない "no adult *ki*"

childish, infantile, juvenile, puerile, sophomoric

いい年をしてそんな大人気ないことを言うもんじゃない。
Ii toshi o shite sonna otonage nai koto o iu mon ja nai.
Why don't you start acting your age and stop being such a baby.

✌ *ii toshi*: advanced in years or, simply, old enough to know better.

まさかあんな大人気ない行動をとる人とは思わなかったよ。
Masaka anna otonage nai kōdō o toru hito to wa omowanakatta yo.
Who would have thought he could ever behave so childishly?

✌ Of an adult's, not a child's, attitude, behavior, speech, or way of doing something. Incidentally, the kanji 大人気 can be read two ways, rendering entirely different meanings. Happily, the subject of this entry, *otonage (ga) nai,* appears in only that phrase and is often written 大人げ, making it quite easy to spot. The other reading, *dai-ninki*, is a simple superlative, appearing in many of the same phrases as does *ninki*.

reikyaku-kikan 冷却期間 "cooling period"

cooling-off period

今は頭に血が上ってるから、何を言ってもだめですよ。冷却期間を置いて、また話しましょう。
Ima wa atama ni chi ga nobotte 'ru kara, nani o itte mo dame desu yo. Reikyaku-kikan o oite, mata hanashimashō.
They're mad as hell right now, so whatever you say it won't do any good. Let's talk to them again after they've cooled down.

少しの間会わない、冷却期間があった方がいいと思うんだ。

Sukoshi no aida awanai, reikyaku-kikan ga atta hō ga ii to omou n' da.
Why don't we have a cooling-off period and not see each other for a while?

reisei-chinchaku 冷静沈着 "cool quietude, calm composure"

cool; calm and collected; as cool as a cucumber

あわや暗殺されるところだったのに、大統領の態度は驚くほど冷静沈着だった。
Awaya ansatsu sareru tokoro datta no ni, daitōryō no taido wa odoroku hodo reisei-chinchaku datta.
Although he had just escaped assassination by a hair's breadth, the president astonished everyone with his cool, calm composure.

いざとなると、避難訓練通り冷静沈着に行動するのは無理だろう。
Iza to naru to, hinan-kunren dōri reisei-chinchaku ni kōdō suru no wa muri darō.
When it comes to the real thing, there's no way everyone's going to act as calm and collected as they do during a routine evacuation drill.

rensa-hannō 連鎖反応 "link chain response"

chain reaction

一人が辞表を出すと、連鎖反応で次々に辞める人が出てきた。
Hitori ga jihyō o dasu to, rensa-hannō de tsugitsugi ni yameru hito ga dete kita.
When one guy handed in his resignation, others began to quit in a chain reaction.

笑い声は連鎖反応を起こして、さざなみのように広がって行った。
Waraigoe wa rensa-hannō o okoshite, sazanami no yō ni hirogatte itta.

Her laughter started off a chain reaction and spread like ripples on a pond.

rinki-ōhen 臨機応変 "adapting to circumstances"

extemporaneously, impromptu; flexibility, adapting to circumstances as they arise (on an ad hoc basis)

二言目には規則、規則って言わないで、もっと臨機応変に考えてもらえませんかね。
Futakoto-me ni wa kisoku, kisoku tte iwanai de, motto rinki-ōhen ni kangaete moraemasen ka ne.
Can't you open your mouth without talking about rules and regulations for once? It'd be nice if we could see a little more flexibility.

担当者の臨機応変の対応が望まれる。
Tantō-sha no rinki-ōhen no taiō ga nozomareru.
It is to be hoped that those in charge will show some flexibility in their response.

risshin-shusse 立身出世 "going up in the world"

success in life, getting ahead, getting on in the world, making a success of oneself, going out into the world and making a name for oneself

明治時代の日本では、大学さえ出ていれば立身出世の道が開けていた。
Meiji-jidai no Nihon de wa, daigaku sae dete ireba risshin-shusse no michi ga hirakete ita.
In Meiji Japan, as long as you had a university education the road to success was assured.

立身出世だけが人生の目的じゃないだろう。

Risshin-shusse dake ga jinsei no mokuteki ja nai darō.
Getting ahead in the world isn't the only purpose in life, you know.

若くして立身出世しただけに、かなり無理もしたらしいよ。
Wakaku shite risshin-shusse shita dake ni, kanari muri mo shita rashii yo.
He's done well, making a name for himself in the world while still a young man, but it appears to have taken its toll.

roba ろば (驢馬) donkey

As rare as this hardworking little beast is in the land, it is even rarer in the language. Its fabled stubbornness is not enough to warrant its inclusion in any idioms, but those ears seem to have done the trick. In fact, a second name for the donkey in Japanese derives from its oversized audio equipment, *usagiuma* 兎馬, or literally "rabbit horse." Whatever they are called, they are counted *ippiki* 一匹 or *ittō* 一頭.

---

roba no mimi ろばの耳 "donkey ears"
(be) all ears

先生達がひそひそ話してたから、思わずろばの耳になった。
Sensei-tachi ga hisohiso hanashite 'ta kara, omowazu roba no mimi ni natta.
I couldn't help pricking up my ears to hear what the teachers were whispering about.

電車の中で私のこと噂している高校のときの友達がいて、ろばの耳になっちゃったよ。
Densha no naka de watashi no koto uwasa shite iru kōkō no toki no tomodachi ga ite, roba no mimi ni natchatta yo.
I was all ears when some of my friends from high school were talking about me in the train.

🕯 Used jocularly of people trying so hard to hear something that they could benefit from larger ears than the gods gave them. Appears most commonly followed by *ni naru*.

☞ *mimi ga hayai* 耳が早い

rōnyaku-nannyo 老若男女 "the old, the young, men and women"

people of all ages and both sexes, men and women of all ages, everybody (irrespective of age or sex)

老若男女のどなたでも、それぞれに楽しめる施設が整ったお宿です。
Rōnyaku-nannyo no donata de mo, sorezore ni tanoshimeru shisetsu ga totonotta oyado desu.
This inn is fully equipped with facilities that can be enjoyed by anyone of any age.

広場に集まった人々は、老若男女を問わず盆踊りを楽しんでいた。
Hiroba ni atsumatta hitobito wa, rōnyaku-nannyo o towazu bon-odori o tanoshinde ita.
People of all ages were gathered together in the square enjoying the Bon Festival dance.

ryōsai-kenbo 良妻賢母 "a good wife and wise mother"

a model wife and mother

本校は創立以来、良妻賢母教育をその柱としております。
Honkō wa sōritsu irai, ryōsai-kenbo-kyōiku o sono hashira to shite orimasu.
Since the school's foundation its ethos has been to educate young girls to become model wives and mothers.

良妻賢母の鑑のようだったお隣の奥さんが、年下の男の人と駆け落ちしたそうですよ。
Ryōsai-kenbo no kagami no yō datta otonari no oku-san ga, toshishita no otoko no hito to kakeochi shita sō desu yo.
Our neighbor's wife seemed to be the perfect wife and mother, but now I hear she's run off with a younger man.

ryūgen-higo 流言飛語 "flowing speech, flying words"

wild (unfounded) rumors

皆さん、流言飛語に惑わされないでください。
Mina-san, ryūgen-higo ni madowasarenai de kudasai.
Please do not let yourselves be led astray by all the rumors that are flying around.

大震災の後、流言飛語が広がり、たくさんの被災者がパニックに陥った。
Dai-shinsai no ato, ryūgen-higo ga hirogari, takusan no hisai-sha ga panikku ni ochiitta.
Wild rumors started to spread after the big earthquake, and many of the victims were thrown into panic.

無責任な流言飛語が引き金になって、悲惨な事件が起きてしまった。
Mu-sekinin na ryūgen-higo ga hikigane ni natte, hisan na jiken ga okite shimatta.
Irresponsible rumors were the trigger that led to a tragic event.

政府は流言飛語を打ち消そうと躍起になっているが、うまくいかない。
Seifu wa ryūgen-higo o uchikesō to yakki ni natte iru ga, umaku ikanai.
The government is doing its utmost to quash the wild rumors but without much success.

ryūtō-dabi 竜頭蛇尾 "a dragon's head, a snake's tail"

a fast start and a slow finish, a tame ending; ending in an anticlimax, dwindling out; petering out, fizzling out; to start well but fade badly, to fail miserably after a good start

社運を懸けたプロジェクトのはずだったけど、竜頭蛇尾に終わってしまった。
Shaun o kaketa purojekuto no hazu datta kedo, ryūtō-dabi ni owatte shimatta.
It was supposed to be the project that decided the company's future, but it ended not with a bang but a whimper.

この本、初めのほうはおもしろかったけど結末は竜頭蛇尾で、読んで損したよ。
Kono hon, hajime no hō wa omoshirokatta kedo ketsumatsu wa ryūtō-dabi de, yonde son shita yo.
The book started strong but petered out at the end. It was a waste of my time.

都市計画はバブル崩壊で竜頭蛇尾に終わる恐れが出てきた。
Toshi-keikaku wa baburu hōkai de ryūtō-dabi ni owaru osore ga dete kita.
There's a good possibility that the urban renewal plan will peter out now that the economic bubble has burst.

政府の所得倍増計画は竜頭蛇尾に終わった。
Seifu no shotoku-baizō-keikaku wa ryūtōdabi ni owatta.
The government's plans for doubling income started with a fanfare but ended in a fizzle.

🐍 This colorful expression stems from the observation that things that start off with a bang seldom end with such great fanfare. The expression is most commonly accompanied by the verb *owaru* 終わる.

saba さば（鯖） mackerel

This common saltwater fish has long been caught and eaten in great numbers in Japan, and is becoming increasingly prized in the autumn for its oily flesh, now that other species have been overfished throughout the world.

The mackerel is also known in Japan for the speed with which it rots from within while remaining apparently fresh on the outside. This is due to the presence of histidine, a crystalline basic amino acid, in its flesh. After the fish's death, the histidine is rapidly transformed into histimine, which can cause allergic rashes.

Mackerel are counted *ichio* 一尾 or *ippiki* 一匹 when alive or uncleaned, and *ichimai* 一枚 when they have been filleted or butterflied.

Saba o yomu さばを読む "read mackerel"
fudge, miscount, cheat on (fudge) the count

パーティーの参加人数を幹事がさばを読んで、儲けたらしいぞ。
Pātī no sanka-ninzū o kanji ga saba o yonde, mōketa rashii zo.
It looks like the guy who was in charge of the party padded the number of people coming and pocketed the difference (between that number and the amount received from his office for the party based on his padded figures).

24歳だって、ちょっとさば読んでるんじゃないの、あの人。
Nijū-yon-sai datte, chotto saba yonde 'ru n' ja nai no, ano hito.
Says she's twenty-four? I'll bet she's fudging it a little bit.

🐟 Sources differ slightly on the origin of this idiom, but seem to agree that the practice of counting mackerel (some say by twos because so many of them are caught at one time) very fast at fish markets is done intentionally in hopes of adding to or subtracting from the actual number, whichever is in the counter's favor. The *"o"* is often dropped, especially in spoken Japanese. Also *saba yomi* 鯖読み.

sagi さぎ (鷺) (snowy) heron

These medium-sized water birds were formerly thought to be the cause of "balls of fire" seen flying through the night skies, and in a way they were. While they were not exactly breathing fire (some were actually called *hifukidori* 火吹き鳥, or "fire-breathing birds"), a certain species of heron was later discovered to have feathers that shine in the darkness. In this way, yet another of nature's wonderful mysteries was solved at the expense of our ability to marvel at the unknown.

Herons are counted *ichiwa* 一羽.

Sagi o karasu to iikurumeru 鷺を烏と言いくるめる "to insist that a heron is a crow"
talk black into white, twist everything to suit oneself

そういう鷺を烏と言いくるめるようなことを言っているから商売にならないんだよ。
Sō iu sagi o karasu to iikurumeru yō na koto o itte iru kara shōbai ni naranai n' da yo.
You're never going to make a go of it by saying things that fly in the face of reason.

彼女は鷺を烏と言いくるめる性格だから、困ったものだ。
Kanojo wa sagi o karasu to iikurumeru seikaku da kara, komatta mono da.
The way she looks you straight in the eye and says that black is white without cracking a smile is just too much.

🐦 From the obviously opposite colors and characteristics of the two birds and the fact that the heron is held in higher esteem.

saishoku-kenbi 才色兼備 "equipped with both brains and beauty"

blessed (gifted, endowed) with both brains and beauty (mostly in reference to women)

結婚式のスピーチでは、どんな人でも才色兼備になっちゃうんだよね。
Kekkon-shiki no supīchi de wa, donna hito de mo saishoku-kenbi ni natchau n' da yo ne.
In wedding speeches, no matter what the bride is like, she is said to be blessed with both brains and beauty.

彼女みたいに才色兼備でしかも家が金持ちって人見ると、神様は不公平だと思うわ。
Kanojo mitai ni saishoku-kenbi de shikamo uchi ga kanemochi tte hito miru to, kamisama wa fu-kōhei da to omou wa.
When I see people like her who are intelligent, beautiful, and from a wealthy background, I can't help thinking God isn't quite fair.

same さめ (鮫) shark

You'd think that with a hundred or so species in the oceans around Japan and the Japanese dependence upon the seas for food that there would have been sufficient contact over the centuries with these killers to produce a few idioms about aggressiveness or bloodthirstyness, but no, this fish is oddly missing from the lexicon. Basically all that can be said about its importance, linguistic or otherwise, is that its flesh is an important ingredient in fish paste, or *kamaboko*.

Samehada 鮫肌 "sharkskin"
rough skin

彼女可愛いんだけど、鮫肌だよね。
Kanojo kawaii n' da kedo, samehada da yo ne.
She's cute all right, but her skin's like sandpaper.

この生地は一見滑らかそうに見えるが触ってみるとちょうど鮫肌のようです。
Kono kiji wa ikken namerakasō ni mieru ga sawatte miru to chōdo samehada no yō desu.
At first glance this material appears to be smooth, but feel it for yourself and you'll see how rough it is.

❦ Dictionaries indicate usage limited to descriptions of human skin, but experience reveals that its appearance with *no yō da* indicates a broader sense. No relation to the fabric by the same name in English long associated with fashion criminals.

samuke 寒気 "cold *ki*"

a chill, shudder; the chills, shivers

寒気がするから、今日は風邪薬飲んで早く寝よう。
Samuke ga suru kara, kyō wa kaze-gusuri nonde hayaku neyō.
I've got the chills, so I think I'll take some cold medicine and get to bed early.

少し熱でもあるらしく、寒気を覚えた。
Sukoshi netsu de mo aru rashiku, samuke o oboeta.
I think I might have come down with a bit of a fever. I've got the shivers.

そんな恐ろしいこと思っただけでも寒気がするよ。
Sonna osoroshii koto omotta dake de mo samuke ga suru yo.
It's so horrible it makes me shudder just to think of it.

samukedatsu 寒気立つ "cold *ki* stands"

get a chill, shudder

その事件の全貌が明らかになるにつれ、同じ年頃の子を持つ親は寒気立ったに違いない。
Sono jiken no zenbō ga akiraka ni naru ni tsure, onaji toshigoro no ko o motsu oya wa samukedatta ni chigai nai.
Parents with children around the same age must have felt a cold chill (gotten a scare) as the details of the crime took shape.

暖かい日が続いてたが、今朝は久々に寒気立つなあ。
Atatakai hi ga tsuzuite ita ga, kesa wa hisabisa ni samukedatsu nā.
We've had a little warm spell here lately, but it's a bit chilly (there's a chill in the air) this morning.

🦢 Another of those pesky multiple readings/meanings. The characters 寒気 can also be read *kanki*, which is strictly a meteorological term for "cold air."

日本列島はすっぽり寒気に覆われていて、今日も寒い一日になりそうです。
Nihon-rettō wa suppori kanki ni ōwarete ite, kyō mo samui ichinichi ni narisō desu.
Japan (the Japanese archipelago) is covered by a cold air mass, so we can look forward to yet another cold day today.

sanba-garasu 三羽がらす "three crows"

three people of ability; a triumvirate; the Big Three (of something)

三人はわが校、卓球部の三羽がらすと呼ばれている。
Sannin wa wagakō, takkyū-bu no sanba-garasu to yobarete iru.
They are known as the "Big Three" of our school's table tennis team.

陸上界の三羽がらすの一人と言われた彼女もその後は記録が伸びなかった。

Rikujō-kai no sanba-garasu no hitori to iwareta kanojo mo sono go wa kiroku ga nobinakatta.

Heralded as one of the top three stars of the track and field world, she was unable thereafter to break her own record.

sankaku-kankei 三角関係 "a triangular relationship"

a love triangle

三角関係のもつれから、男が妻の愛人を殺すという事件が起こった。

Sankaku-kankei no motsure kara, otoko ga tsuma no aijin o korosu to iu jiken ga okotta.

There was a case (recently) of a guy killing his wife's lover after they got involved in a love triangle.

親友の彼氏と付き合い始めちゃって、今どろどろの三角関係なんだよね。

Shin'yū no kareshi to tsukiaihajimechatte, ima dorodoro no sankaku-kankei nan da yo ne.

I started going out with my best friend's boyfriend, and now we're involved in this messy triangular relationship.

そろそろ三角関係を清算しなくちゃと思うんだが、二人ともいいところがあって捨て難いんだ。

Sorosoro sankaku-kankei o seisan shinakucha to omou n' da ga, futari tomo ii tokoro ga atte sutegatai n' da.

Pretty soon I'm gonna have to put a end to this triangular relationship. The thing is, they both have good points and I hate to chuck either one of them.

sankan-shion 三寒四温 "three cold days (followed by) four warm days"

a cycle of three cold days and four warm days

立春も過ぎ、三寒四温のすごしやすい季節となりましたが、お元気ですか。
Risshun mo sugi, sankan-shion no sugoshiyasui kisetsu to narimashita ga, ogenki desu ka.
The vernal equinox has come and gone. Winter's chill is slowly giving way to the warmth of spring, as we enter this most pleasant time of the year. How are you keeping? (This is a traditional greeting in letters written toward the end of February.)

三寒四温のこのころが、一年中で一番好きだよ。
Sankan-shion no kono koro ga, ichinen-jū de ichiban suki da yo.
This is my favorite time of year, as the cold days of winter gradually recede to be replaced by the warmth of spring.

sanpai-kyūhai 三拝九拝 "three bows, nine bows"

to bow many times, to kowtow, (to ask a favor) on bended knee, to bow and scrape, to fall on one's knees

彼女のおやじさんに三拝九拝して、やっと結婚を許してもらった。
Kanojo no oyaji-san ni sanpai-kyūhai shite, yatto kekkon o yurushite moratta.
After I begged on bended knee, my girlfriend's father finally consented to our marriage.

三拝九拝して、せっかくもらってきた注文なのに、在庫がないなんてついてないよ。
Sanpai-kyūhai shite, sekkaku moratte kita chūmon na no ni, zaiko ga nai nante tsuite 'nai yo.

After a lot of bowing and scraping I finally get the order and what happens? We're out of stock. It's just not my day.

saru さる（猿） monkey

Where would these little primates be if it weren't for Charles Darwin? Not in the schools as living proof that we too once had prehensile tails and funny looking butts, that's for sure. They suffer by comparison to humans, a relief to those of us who need to know we're not at the bottom of the heap, and although they figure in several idioms touting intelligence, Japanese monkeys never quite measure up to human standards and usually end up with the short end of the stick in folk tales. In general, they are considered to be resourceful, quick, fidgety, and, yes, stupid.

The monkey's cry is *kīkī* キーキー or *kya'-kya'* キャッキャッ. They are counted *ippiki* 一匹 or *ittō* 一頭. Written 申, the monkey is the ninth of the twelve signs of the Chinese zodiac.

Mizaru kikazaru iwazaru　**見猿聞か猿言わ猿**　"see monkey, hear monkey, speak monkey"
see no evil, hear no evil, and speak no evil

こんな厄介なことごめんだ、見猿聞か猿言わ猿でいこう。
Konna yakkai na koto gomen da, mizaru kikazaru iwazaru de ikō.
I don't want to have anything to do with this hassle; I'm just gonna keep my distance.

夫婦の問題にお節介は禁物だよ、こういうことは見猿聞か猿言わ猿が一番いいんだよ。
Fūfu no mondai ni osekkai wa kinmotsu da yo, kō iu koto wa mizaru kikazaru iwazaru ga ichiban ii n' da yo.

You've got to stay away from domestic quarrels like the plague. The best policy is just not to see anything, hear anything, or say anything.

🐵 Yeah, it *is* the same three monkeys we've all seen somewhere advising us, by covering their eyes, ears and mouth, to butt out of other people's business and to protect our own interests. The ~*zaru* ~猿 is a play on the homonymic Japanese negative-verb ending ~*zaru* ~ざる. Hence, *mizaru* means "not see," etc.

Saru mo ki kara ochiru 猿も木から落ちる "even a monkey can fall out of a tree"
even Homer sometimes nods, anybody can make a mistake, nobody's perfect

---

彼がそんな単純なミスを犯すなんて、猿も木から落ちるんだな。
Kare ga sonna tanjun na misu o okasu nante, saru mo ki kara ochiru n' da na.
For him to make such a simple mistake makes you realize that it can happen to the best of us.

「猿も木から落ちる … か。」
"Saru mo ki kara ochiru . . . ka."
"I guess nobody's perfect."

「え？」
"E?"
"Come again."

「あのF1ドライバー首都高でおかまほったらしいよ。」
"Ano F-1 doraibā shutokō de okama hotta rashii yo."
"It looks like that F-l racer rammed into the back of some car on the Tokyo freeway."

Sarugutsuwa 猿ぐつわ "a monkey bit"
a gag

猿ぐつわをかまされていたので助けを呼ぶことが出来なかった。
Sarugutsuwa o kamasarete ita no de tasuke o yobu koto ga dekinakatta.
I couldn't call out for help, because they had me gagged.

目隠しと猿ぐつわをされていたので、どこをどうやって連れて
こられたのかかいもく見当がつかない。
Mekakushi to sarugutsuwa o sarete ita no de, doko o dō yatte tsurete korareta no ka kaimoku kentō ga tsukanai.
I don't have the slightest idea where they took me because I was gagged and blindfolded.

🐵 From the fact that *saru* is the name of a small, usually wooden, sliding block used to lock shutters from the inside. The connection between the animal and the sliding block is unclear. The connection between the sliding block that slides into a hole in the window, door frame, or lintel (which, by the way, is a "duck place" 鴨居 another story) and the expression *sarugutsuwa* is clearer, the point being to stuff a hole—one's mouth, for example—with something.

Sarujie 猿知恵 "monkey wisdom"
shallow cunning

猿知恵のはたらく奴だな、お前は。
Sarujie no hataraku yatsu da na, omae wa.
You may think you're smart, but you're not.

そんな猿知恵すぐ見破られるぞ。
Sonna sarujie sugu miyaburareru zo.
They're gonna see right through an asinine stunt like that.

🐵 Monkeys have long been compared with humans. One popular ancient belief appears to have been that they were just three hairs short of being human, *saru wa ningen yori ke ga sanbon tarinai* 猿は人間より毛が三本足りない. The expression can be used to convey the belief that monkeys fall slightly short of human wisdom.

Sarumane 猿真似 "monkey mimicking"
apery, copycatting, mimicry, mockery; monkey see, monkey do; a copy, fake, crib, knock off

---

この作品は単なる猿真似だ。
Kono sakuhin wa tan naru sarumane da.
The work is nothing more than a copy.

しょせん猿真似は猿真似。本物にはかなわない。
Shosen sarumane wa sarumane. Honmono ni wa kanawanai.
When all is said and done, it's still just a fake. It's not even close to the original.

🐵 From the observation that monkeys often ape humans, and the happy discovery that they never quite pull it off.

Sarushibai 猿芝居 "a monkey (mime) show"

---

1. (of a dramatic production) a bad play, a joke

この前小さな劇団の公演見たけど、猿芝居もいいとこだったよ。
Kono mae chiisana gekidan no kōen mita kedo, sarushibai mo ii toko datta yo.
The other day I went to a play put on by a small troupe, but it was really amateurish.

2. (of extremely stupid behavior or a transparent scheme or plot) monkey business, a sham, mumbo jumbo

へたな猿芝居はやめろ。
Heta na sarushibai wa yamero.
Cut out the mumbo jumbo, man.

そんな猿芝居すぐばれてしまうぞ。
Sonna sarushibai sugu barete shimau zo.
You're not fooling anyone with that monkey business.

🐒 From this rudimental form of entertainment in which a trained monkey is made to act out a play, this idiom is used to describe a poorly produced play or some shallow, ill-conceived deception or otherwise ridiculous behavior.

Yamazaru 山猿 "mountain monkey"
a rustic; a clodhopper, a boor

あんな山猿に会社を乗っ取られてたまるもんか。
Anna yamazaru ni kaisha o nottorarete tamaru mon ka.
If you think I'm going to stand by while some hick takes over the company, you've got another think coming.

若い頃は山猿と馬鹿にされていた彼も、今では売れ子の詩人になった。
Wakai koro wa yamazaru to baka ni sarete ita kare mo, ima de wa ureko no shijin ni natta.
Once treated like a country bumpkin, he's a best-selling poet now.

🐒 The original meaning is a wild mountain monkey. No surprises there, huh. Metaphorically it became a derisive term for an unschooled person from the country, untutored in the niceties of urban life.

se 背 back

In addition to that part of the human anatomy which we all love to have scratched, meanings of *se* also include heights of things both animate and inanimate, as exemplified in the first few expressions that follow. If you ever go hiking in Japan, you'll soon become all too familiar with that part of a mountain range that this word refers to, the backbone or ridge, because few hiking trails in Japan follow the contours, favoring instead the grueling ridge route. Finally, *se* also means that part of a book that those of us interested in appearances often crack, even though we don't actually read the book. That's right, the spine.

Se ga hikui **背が低い** "have a low back"
short, squat, low

私は父に似て背が低い。
Watashi wa chichi ni nite se ga hikui.
I'm short like my father.

背の低い家が道の両側に並んでいる。
Se no hikui ie ga michi no ryōgawa ni narande iru.
Low houses line both sides of the road.

Se ga takai **背が高い** "have a high back"
tall, high

女性は、背が高い男性が好きですね。
Josei wa, se ga takai dansei ga suki desu ne.
Women like tall men.

最近背の高いビルがたくさん建ち始めた。
Saikin se no takai biru ga takusan tachihajimeta.
A lot of tall buildings are starting to go up.

Se ni hara wa kaerarenai **背に腹はかえられない** "one can't turn one's stomach into a back"

endure or do something because one doesn't have any other choice, there's no way around it

背に腹はかえられない、と彼は条件の悪いその仕事を引き受けた。
Se ni hara wa kaerarenai, to kare wa jōken no warui sono shigoto o hiki-uketa.
He had no choice but to take the job, even though the conditions weren't good. / It wasn't a very good job, but he figured he'd just have to tough it out and take it.

Se ni suru **背にする** "make into a back"

(1) carry, shoulder (2) put (leave) something behind one (3) put one's back to something

(1) 青年は大きなリュックを背にして山道を登って行った。
Seinen wa ōki na ryukku o se ni shite yamamichi o nobotte itta.
The boy climbed up the trail with a big backpack on.

(2) 村の人達の別れの言葉を背に(して)、彼は旅に出た。
Mura no hitotachi no wakare no kotoba o se ni (shite), kare wa tabi ni deta.
He started out on his journey, leaving the well-wishers from the village behind.

(3) 父は床の間を背にして座っていた。
Chichi wa tokonoma o se ni shite suwatte ita.
My father was sitting with his back to the tokonoma.

富士山を背に写真を撮りましょう。
Fuji-san o se ni shashin o torimashō.
Let's take a picture with Mt. Fuji in the background.

Se o mukeru 背を向ける "turn one's back to or on"
turn one's back on something or someone, reject

「さようなら」と言って彼女は彼に背を向けた。
"Sayōnara" to itte kanojo wa kare ni se o muketa.
"Goodbye," she said, and turned to walk away.

東欧諸国はマルクス主義に背を向けた。
Tōō-shokoku wa marukusu-shugi ni se o muketa.
The countries of Eastern Europe have turned their backs on Marxism.

seiren-keppaku 清廉潔白 "honest and pure"

(a person of) integrity; (a person with) an unblemished record; totally blameless, beyond reproach, as straight as a die

私は賄賂なんかもらってない。清廉潔白だ。
Watashi wa wairo nanka moratte 'nai. Seiren-keppaku da.
There's no way I've taken any bribes. I'm as straight as a die.

あの人のように誠実で清廉潔白な政治家はもう出て来ないだろうな。
Ano hito no yō ni seijitsu de seiren-keppaku na seiji-ka wa mō dete konai darō na.
I don't suppose we'll ever see any politicians as honest and as upright as him again.

↝ *hara ga kuroi / haraguroi* 腹が黒い／腹黒い

seisei-dōdō 正々堂々 "true and noble"

fair and square; open and aboveboard; on the level; openly and fairly

正々堂々と胸を張った生き方がしたいんです。
Seisei-dōdō to mune o hatta ikikata ga shitai n' desu.
I want to live life fair and square, with my head held high.

自分にやましいところがないなら、もっと正々堂々としていなさい。
Jibun ni yamashii tokoro ga nai nara, motto seisei-dōdō to shite inasai.
If you've got nothing to be ashamed of, then stop acting as if you've got something to hide.

意見があるなら、陰口じゃなくて正々堂々と会議の場で言いたまえ。
Iken ga aru nara, kageguchi ja nakute seisei-dōdō to kaigi no ba de iitamae.
Don't talk behind people's backs. If you've got something to say, say it loud and clear at a meeting.

seishin-seii 誠心誠意 "sincere mind, sincere intention"

sincerely, faithfully, wholeheartedly

採用していただければ、誠心誠意会社のために働きます。
Saiyō shite itadakereba, seishin-seii kaisha no tame ni hatarakimasu.
If you hire me, I will be a faithful and devoted employee.

説得しようと誠心誠意話してみたが、とりつく島もなかったよ。
Settoku shiyō to seishin-seii hanashite mita ga, toritsuku shima mo nakatta yo.
I tried with the best will in the world to persuade him, but I just couldn't get through.

彼の誠心誠意の態度には、打たれますね。
Kare no seishin-seii no taido ni wa, utaremasu ne.
I'm really impressed by his sincere attitude.

senbazuru 千羽鶴 "a thousand cranes"

a thousand folded-paper cranes (on a string)

則男君のお見舞いにみんなで千羽鶴を折りましょう。
Norio-kun no omimai ni minna de senbazuru o orimashō.
Let's all make a chain of paper cranes for when we go to see Norio in the hospital.

千羽鶴は折り紙の中で一番ポピュラーだと思うよ。
Senbazuru wa origami no naka de ichiban popyurā da to omou yo.
Crane chains are the most popular type of origami, I'd say.

※ As can be seen from the examples, *senbazuru* are folded and attached to a string to express one's hopes for success in a specific endeavor or the speedy recovery of an ill or injured person. They are sent or given directly to the person to whom one's good wishes are directed or may be hung at Shinto shrines, where they represent the earnest prayers of the makers.

senkyaku-banrai 千客万来 "a thousand customers (guests) coming ten thousand times"

to have one visitor after another, to have an interminable succession of visitors, to be pulling in the crowds

今日は千客万来で、すごく忙しい。
Kyō wa senkyaku-banrai de, sugoku isogashii.
We've been rushed off our feet today with all the customers we've had.

千客万来の一日で、たまってた仕事が全然かたづかなかったよ。
Senkyaku-banrai no ichinichi de, tamatte 'ta shigoto ga zenzen katazuka-nakatta yo.
I had so many visitors today that I couldn't get around to all the work that's piled up.

sensen-kyōkyō 戦々恐々 "trembling and frightened"

timidly, with fear and trembling, in great fear, nervously, gingerly, on tenterhooks

まだ余震が来るかも知れないので、戦々恐々の毎日ですよ。
Mada yoshin ga kuru ka mo shirenai no de, sensen-kyōkyō no mainichi desu yo.
There's still a chance of after-shocks, so everyday we're on tenterhooks.

いつわが社にも捜査のメスが入るか、戦々恐々としている。
Itsu wagasha ni mo sōsa no mesu ga hairu ka, sensen-kyōkyō to shite iru.
We are all practically quaking in our boots, wondering when they are going to probe into our company, too.

☞ *ki ga ki ja nai* 気が気じゃない

sente-hisshō 先手必勝 "The first hand (is) sure to win."

the player who makes the first move in a game is sure to win, to make the first strike, to seize the initiative, to take the game by the scruff of the neck

このゲームは先手必勝だからね。とにかく攻めの一手だよ。

Kono gēmu wa sente-hisshō da kara ne. Tonikaku seme no itte da yo.
Whoever seizes the initiative in this game is going to win it. We've got to go out there and attack.

先手必勝で行こうと思ってはいたんだが、つい守りにまわってしまった。
Sente-hisshō de ikō to omotte wa ita n' da ga, tsui mamori ni mawatte shimatta.
We went out there determined to attack from the start, but before we knew it, we found ourselves pushed back on the defensive.

senzai-ichigū 千載一遇 "meeting once in a thousand years"

once in a lifetime

こんな千載一遇のチャンスを逃す手はないよ。
Konna senzai-ichigū no chansu o nogasu te wa nai yo.
There's no way you're going to let slip this chance of a lifetime.

千載一遇の投資の機会だと勧められて、話にのったのが間違いだった。
Senzai-ichigū no tōshi no kikai da to susumerarete, hanashi ni notta no ga machigai datta.
It was presented as the investment chance of a lifetime, so I went along with it. Was that a mistake!

sessa-takuma 切磋琢磨 "cut, plane, fashion, and polish"

to strive to improve oneself intellectually or morally; to strive together with others for such improvement

彼らはお互いに切磋琢磨するより、いかに相手に勝つかばかり
考えているようだ。
Karera wa otagai ni sessa-takuma suru yori, ika ni aite ni katsu ka bakari kangaete iru yō da.
Instead of trying to learn from each other and improve themselves, all they seem to think about is how they can beat the other guy.

新入社員諸君は、この研修期間に切磋琢磨しあって、おおいに
実力をつけてもらいたい。
Shinnyū-shain shokun wa, kono kenshū-kikan ni sessa-takuma shiatte, ōi ni jitsuryoku o tsukete moraitai.
What we want from all you new recruits during this induction period is for you to work hard together at developing your abilities.

🐌 Just as in former times an artisan would cut (切), then file and plane (磋), then form the shape (琢), and finally polish (磨) a piece of ivory or horn to make a gorgeous piece of jewelry, so we too must work hard to improve ourselves.

shichiten-battō 七転八倒 "falling over seven times, collapsing eight times"

writhing in agony, to be in excruciating pain

急に胸が痛くなって、病院に運ばれるまで七転八倒の苦しみだ
った。
Kyū ni mune ga itaku natte, byōin ni hakobareru made shichiten-battō no kurushimi datta.
I felt this sudden pain in my chest and until they got me to the hospital, I was in excruciating agony.

畳の上で脂汗を流しながら七転八倒しているところへ、家内が
帰って来てくれてね。
Tatami no ue de abura-ase o nagashinagara shichiten-battō shite iru tokoro e, kanai ga kaette kite kurete ne.

Luckily my wife came home when she did; she found me writhing in agony on the floor, covered in sweat.

患者は鎮痛剤が切れて、七転八倒の苦しみようだった。
Kanja wa chintsū-zai ga kirete, shichiten-battō no kurushimi yō datta.
Once the anesthetic had worn off, the patient was in real agony.

shihō-happō 四方八方 "four directions, eight directions"

in all directions, in every direction, far and wide, every which way, (from) all quarters, (from) all over

発表と同時に四方八方から引き合いが来て、嬉しい悲鳴を上げてるんだ。
Happyō to dōji ni shihō-happō kara hikiai ga kite, ureshii himei o agete 'ru n' da.
Since the announcement was made, we have been inundated with inquiries and positively overwhelmed by the response.

娘が家出して以来、四方八方手を尽くして探してるんだが、全く行方が知れない。
Musume ga iede shite irai, shihō-happō te o tsukushite sagashite 'ru n' da ga, mattaku yukue ga shirenai.
We've left no stone unturned, but still we have no idea of my daughter's whereabouts since she ran away from home.

※ The four directions referred to in the first half of this four-character compound—四—are the four points of the compass. Add northeast, northwest, southeast, and southwest, and you end up with a total of eight different directions—八方.

shikō-sakugo 試行錯誤 "trial undertaking, confused failure"

trial and error

前例もないし、今はまだ試行錯誤の段階ですよ。
Zenrei mo nai shi, ima wa mada shikō-sakugo no dankai desu yo.
There's no precedent to help us, so for the moment we're still at the trial-and-error stage.

試行錯誤を繰り返して、やっと自分にあったやり方がわかってきたような気がします。
Shikō-sakugo o kurikaeshite, yatto jibun ni atta yarikata ga wakatte kita yō na ki ga shimasu.
After repeated trial and error, I finally feel that I've found the method that suits me best.

shiku-hakku 四苦八苦 "four pains, eight pains"

to writhe in agony, to be in dire distress, to sweat blood

好きな作家の新作が出たんだけど、まだ翻訳がないから、読み終えるのに四苦八苦したよ。
Suki na sakka no shinsaku ga deta n' da kedo, mada hon'yaku ga nai kara, yomioeru no ni shiku-hakku shita yo.
One of my favorite authors came out with a new book, but since there's no translation yet, I had to sweat blood to get through it.

中年サラリーマンの多くが、マイホームのローンと子供の教育費に四苦八苦している。
Chūnen-sararīman no ōku ga, maihōmu no rōn to kodomo no kyōiku-hi ni shiku-hakku shite iru.
A lot of middle-aged white-collar workers have a devil of a time paying for the mortgage and the kids' education.

🦑 In Buddhism the four types of pain that are considered to be the root causes of human suffering are (1) the pain of birth, (2) the pain of sickness and ill health, (3) the pain of old age, (4) the pain of death. In addition, there are four further types of pain, which are (1) 愛別離苦 (*aibetsu-riku*) the pain of being away from the ones you love, (2) 怨憎会苦 (*onzō-eku*) the pain of meeting with things you dislike, (3) 求不得苦 (*gufu-tokuku*) the pain of not getting what you want, (4) 五陰盛苦 (*goon-jōku*) mental and physical pain. These eight types of pain are the 八苦 referred to in this four-character compound.

↪ *akusen-kutō* 悪戦苦闘

shimaguni-konjō 島国根性 "island country mentality"

an island-nation mentality, insularism, insularity

イギリス人と日本人の国民性はずいぶん違うけど、一つ共通してるのは島国根性だね。
Igirisu-jin to nihon-jin no kokumin-sei wa zuibun chigau kedo, hitotsu kyōtsū shite 'ru no wa shimaguni-konjō da ne.
The British and the Japanese have quite different national characteristics, but one thing they do have in common is their insular mentality.

経済的に大国になったのに、いつまでたっても島国根性が抜けないでいる。
Keizai-teki ni taikoku ni natta no ni, itsu made tatte mo shimaguni-konjō ga nukenai de iru.
Even though Japan has become an economic superpower, we just can't seem to free ourselves of our insularity.

🦑 The opposite to this is 大陸的な (*tairiku-teki na*), which literally means "continental" and refers to peoples who are generous of spirit and who do not fuss about trifles.

shimen-soka 四面楚歌 "(on) all four sides (can be heard) the So song"

surrounded on all sides by one's enemies, without a friend in the world, all alone without a single ally (in sight), under siege, besieged

会議の席で上司を非難してしまい、四面楚歌の立場に追い込まれてしまった。
Kaigi no seki de jōshi o hinan shite shimai, shimen-soka no tachiba ni oikomarete shimatta.
After criticizing the boss at the meeting I found myself being cold-shouldered by everyone in the office.

女房も子供もおふくろも、皆俺のせいだって言うんだ。まったく四面楚歌だよ。
Nyōbō mo kodomo mo ofukuro mo, minna ore no sei datte iu n' da. Mattaku shimen-soka da yo.
The wife and kids and even my own Mom are all convinced it's my fault; no one's taking my side at all.

🕯 In ancient China Ryuho (the founder of the Kan dynasty) and his arch-rival Kō, a mighty warrior of great strength and the warlord of the So region, were locked in a bitter power struggle to become emperor. By 202 BC the balance of power was in Ryuho's favor, and Kō found himself facing severe difficulties.

Kō was surrounded in his garrison at Gaika (in An Hui province in present-day China) by Kan troops under the command of Kanshin, one of Ryuho's most able generals. One evening Kanshin thought up a plan to break the will of his still powerful enemy. He got his men to sing a So folk song in a sad and mournful way. When Kō heard this, he immediately assumed that Ryuho had overrun the So region and taken all Kō's followers prisoner, and that it was they who were singing. Convinced that he had lost his power base and the war was as good as over, Kō committed suicide.

shinki-itten 心機一転 "a complete change of heart"

a change of mind, a change of heart, turning over a new leaf, making a fresh start in life, taking a new lease on life

入院をきっかけに心機一転し、体をもっと大切にしようと決心した。
Nyūin o kikkake ni shinki-itten shi, karada o motto taisetsu ni shiyō to kesshin shita.
Being hospitalized really changed me (gave me a new perspective on life). I've decided to be a lot more careful about my health.

彼女は香港への転勤で心機一転、人生の再出発を決意した。
Kanojo wa Honkon e no tenkin de shinki-itten, jinsei no sai-shuppatsu o ketsui shita.
She saw her transfer to Hong Kong as an ideal chance to turn over a new leaf and make a fresh start in life.

shinryo-enbō 深慮遠謀 "thoughtfulness and foresight"

carefully laid plans for the future; farsighted; meticulous in one's planning

今回の作戦は、彼の深慮遠謀の結果だった。
Konkai no sakusen wa, kare no shinryo-enbō no kekka datta.
Our strategy this time is the result of his meticulous planning.

あいつは行きあたりばったりで、深慮遠謀には縁がない。
Aitsu wa yukiatari-battari de, shinryo-enbō ni wa en ga nai.
Always leaving things to chance the way he does, he can hardly be called meticulous in his planning.

自分は決して表に出ないのが、この政治家の深慮遠謀だよ。
Jibun wa kesshite omote ni denai no ga, kono seiji-ka no shinryo-enbō da yo.
That politician always carefully plans it so that he stays well out of the public eye.

❧ The phrase can also be written as 深謀遠慮 (*shinbō-enryo*); here the meaning of *enryo* is not "to refrain from doing something," but "to look to the future."

shinshin-kiei 新進気鋭 "new and sharp"

up-and-coming; someone to watch

君のような新進気鋭の医者に来てもらえれば、うちの病院も鬼に金棒だよ。
Kimi no yō na shinshin-kiei no isha ni kite moraereba, uchi no byōin mo oni ni kanabō da yo.
If we could get an up-and-coming doctor such as yourself to work at our hospital, we would make an unbeatable team.

これは、この間賞をとった新進気鋭の作家の作品ですね。
Kore wa, kono aida shō o totta shinshin-kiei no sakka no sakuhin desu ne.
This is a book by that up-and-coming writer who won that award the other day.

shinshō-bōdai 針小棒大 "(to make something) as small as a needle, as big as a stick"

making a mountain out of a molehill; exaggerating

彼女はいつも物事を針小棒大に言うから、少し割引きして聞いたほうがいいよ。

Kanojo wa itsumo monogoto o shinshō-bōdai ni iu kara, sukoshi waribiki shite kiita hō ga ii yo.
She always makes a mountain out of a molehill, so I'd take it all with a pinch of salt if I were you.

スポーツ新聞の見出しは針小棒大のことが多くて、見出しにひかれて買ってしまってから後悔する。
Supōtsu-shinbun no midashi wa shinshō-bōdai no koto ga ōkute, midashi ni hikarete katte shimatte kara kōkai suru.
The headlines in sports newspapers are often wildly sensational. Your eye gets caught by these headlines, but after you've bought the paper you regret it.

shinshutsu-kibotsu 神出鬼没 "god comes out, the devil sinks (disappears)"

elusive, (as) slippery (as an eel); here one minute, gone the next; (gone) like a ghost in the night

さっきまでここにいたのに、まったく彼は神出鬼没だね。
Sakki made koko ni ita no ni, mattaku kare wa shinshutsu-kibotsu da ne.
He was here just a second ago. That's just like him—here one minute, gone the next.

神出鬼没の泥棒は、必死の捜査にもかかわらずなかなか捕まらない。
Shinshutsu-kibotsu no dorobō wa, hisshi no sōsa ni mo kakawarazu nakanaka tsukamaranai.
In spite of an exhaustive manhunt by the police, the burglar has managed to slip like a phantom through their fingers.

shinzō 心臓 heart

The several figurative meanings of *shinzō* derive both from its function as the organ that sustains life and from notions of the heart as the seat of the emotions. Hence a strong *shinzō* emboldens, a weak one enervates. As with "heart," *shinzō* can also be used to mean the center or most important part of, say, a factory or organization. Note that the first two idioms also carry the literal physiological meanings expressed.

Shinzō should not be confused with *kokoro,* which has no anatomical referent. Both may be translated as "heart," but the latter is not an organ.

Shinzō ga tsuyoi **心臓が強い** "have a strong heart"
have nerve, chutzpa, brass balls, heart; be brazen, be gutsy; have guts

---

デパートで値切るとは、彼も心臓が強いね。
Depāto de negiru to wa, kare mo shinzō ga tsuyoi ne.
The guy's got a lot of cheek, bargaining in a department store.

私は心臓が強いらしく、どんなに大勢の人の前でも、あがらずにスピーチができる。
Watashi wa shinzō ga tsuyoi rashiku, donna ni ōzei no hito no mae de mo, agarazu ni supīchi ga dekiru.
I must be pretty nervy, the way I can give a speech in front of a lot of people without getting nervous.

Shinzō ga yowai **心臓が弱い** "have a weak heart"
be timid, shy, bashful; be a pussy, a wimp

僕は心臓が弱いから、あまり脅かさないでくれよ。
Boku wa shinzō ga yowai kara, amari odokasanai de kure yo.
Don't scare me like that. I can't take that kind of stuff.

彼は心臓が弱いので、仕事で小さなミスをする度に、首になるのではないかとビクビクしている。

Kare wa shinzō ga yowai no de, shigoto de chiisa na misu o suru tabi ni, kubi ni naru no de wa nai ka to bikubiku shite iru.
He's such a weenie that every little mistake he makes at work has him fretting about getting fired.

☞ *ki ga chiisai* 気が小さい, *ki ga yowai* 気が弱い, *nomi no shinzō* 蚤の心臓

Shinzō ni ke ga haete iru　**心臓に毛が生えている**　"have hair on one's heart"
be brazen, a wise-ass, a smart aleck, cocky

彼ほど図々しくて心臓に毛が生えてるような男は見たことがない。
Kare hodo zūzūshikute shinzō ni ke ga haete iru yō na otoko wa mita koto ga nai.
I've never seen anyone that's such a wise guy.

彼は心臓に毛が生えているから、何を言われても少しも応えない。
Kare wa shinzō ni ke ga haete iru kara, nani o iwarete mo sukoshi mo kotaenai.
He's such a smart aleck that nothing you say to him makes any difference.

☞ *heiki no heiza* 平気の平左

shirami 虱 louse

Like other diminutive bloodsucking parasites, lice generally figure in unflattering expressions and maxims. Their tiny size also lends itself to comments regarding minutiae. Lice are counted *ippiki* 一匹, and move around so quickly that the same one is often counted more than once.

Shirami tsubushi (ni) 虱つぶし（に）"lice crushing"
comb (a place for), search (go through/over) with a fine-tooth comb; check out every lead one by one

部屋中虱つぶしに捜したが、結局その書類は見つからなかった。
Heya-jū shirami tsubushi ni sagashita ga, kekkyoku sono shorui wa mitsukaranakatta.
I went through the house with a fine-tooth comb but couldn't locate the papers.

警察は犯人の手がかりがないかどうか犯行現場一帯を虱つぶしにした。
Keisatsu wa hannin no tegakari ga nai ka dō ka, hankō-genba ittai o shirami tsubushi ni shita.
In hopes of finding clues that would help identify the perpetrator, police investigators conducted a thorough search of the crime scene.

❧ The word *shirami* is often written in katakana, presumably because the kanji is difficult to read and not included in the government's *Jōyō Kanji* list. It almost always appears in the form *o shirami tsubushi ni suru,* where the verb has to do with searching or investigation possibilities. It derives from the image of someone crushing lice one by one, hence being very thorough. Unfortunately, "nit pick" is a false friend, for the Japanese lacks any sense of niggling or criticism, which is inherent in the English.

shirauo no yō na yubi 白魚のような指 "fingers like white fish"

delicate white fingers

彼女は白魚のような指をしていた。
Kanojo wa shirauo no yō na yubi o shite ita.
She had delicate white fingers.

白魚のような指の彼女には、真珠の指輪がぴったりだ。
Shirauo no yō na yubi no kanojo ni wa, shinju no yubiwa ga pittari da.
A pearl ring is perfect for a woman like her with beautiful, long white fingers.

☙ This colorless, semitransparent fish is about four inches in length and, unlike fingers, is eaten in Japan. Idiomatic usage derives from the fish's fanciful resemblance to a finger and the traditional Japanese aesthetic which dictates that white skin, especially on women, is desirable.

shiri 尻 **rear, buttocks**

Shiri, often preceded by *o,* is like saying "posterior," rear end," or "bottom." It may also be used to refer to the tail or rear end of something, as a sentence or vehicle. The man who thinks of nothing but sex, the one chasing women all the time, is said to "chase bottom" in Japanese, *onna no shiri bakari ou.*

Shiri can mean the last part of something, as in *shiri kara niban-me,* or second from the last. It may also refer to the seat of one's pants or the bottom of a pan—seen from the outside. *Ketsu,* a much less formal word for *shiri,* might best be translated as butt, buns, or ass.

Ketsu no ana ga chiisai けつの穴が小さい "have a small asshole"
be a tightwad, stingy, a cheapskate, a piker, small-minded

開店サービスが先着5名にコーヒー半額だなんて、けつの穴が小さいなぁ。
Kaiten sābisu ga senchaku go-mei ni kōhī hangaku da nante, ketsu no ana ga chiisai nā.
Half-price coffee for the first five customers at opening! How tightfisted can you get?

けつの穴が小さい男は出世できないぞ。
Ketsu no ana no chiisai otoko wa shusse dekinai zo.
If you don't stop being so small-minded, you'll never get anywhere.

Shiri ga aoi 尻が青い "have a blue butt"
[from the fact that Japanese babies have a blue spot on their butt for a short time after birth] be green, wet behind the ears

---

まだ尻が青いくせに、親に対して偉そうなことを言うんじゃない。
Mada shiri ga aoi kuse ni, oya ni taishite erashō na koto o iun ja nai.
You'd better show a little more respect for your parents there, young fella.

まだ尻が青い新任社長の下では働きたくない。
Mada shiri ga aoi shinnin shachō no shita de wa hatarakitaku nai.
I'm not into working for some greenhorn that's just been kicked upstairs.

Shiri ga karui 尻が軽い "have a light butt"

(1) (of a woman) put out, sleep around, be an easy lay, be loose. (2) be flighty, rash

彼女は尻が軽い。
Kanojo wa shiri ga karui.
She puts out./ She can be had.

彼は尻が軽いので、ときどき仕事で失敗する。
Kare wa shiri ga karui no de, tokidoki shigoto de shippai suru.
He's a little flighty, so he screws things up once in a while.

Shiri ga omoi 尻が重い "have a heavy butt"
be slow, reluctant to start anything

彼は尻が重くて、なかなか行動に移らない。
Kare wa shiri ga omokute, nakanaka kōdō ni utsuranai.
You'd think he had lead in his pants, slow as he is to get off his duff.

年をとるとともに、尻が重くなってきた。
Toshi o toru to tomo ni, shiri ga omoku natte kita.
The older I get, the more difficult it is for me to get started on anything.

Shiri ni hi ga tsuku 尻に火がつく "a fire is lit on one's butt"
have a fire lit under one

明日が原稿の締め切りなので、尻に火がついているのだよ。
Ashita ga genkō no shimekiri na no de, shiri ni hi ga tsuite iru no da yo.
Tomorrow's the deadline to turn in the manuscript, so I've really got to get a move on.

大都市の住宅問題は、とっくに尻に火がついているのに、解決策のないままである。
Dai-toshi no jūtaku-mondai wa, tokku ni shiri ni hi ga tsuite iru no ni, kaiketsusaku no nai mama de aru.
The big-city housing situation has been a pressing problem for some time now, but no one has come up with a solution yet.

Shiri ni shiku 尻に敷く "spread on one's butt"
have someone under one's thumb; [with 〜しかれて *shikarete*] be tied to someone's apron strings

---

彼は、会社ではいばっているが、家では奥さんの尻に敷かれているそうだ。
Kare wa, kaisha de wa ibatte iru ga, ie de wa okusan no shiri ni shikarete iru sō da.
He acts like he rules the roost around the office, but I hear he's henpecked.

彼女は結婚したらだんなを尻に敷くタイプだ。
Kanojo wa kekkon shitara danna o shiri ni shiku taipu da.

She's the type that'll want to wear the pants in the family when she gets married.

Shiri o nuguu 尻をぬぐう "wipe someone's butt"
clean up after someone, clean up someone's mess

もうこれ以上、上司の尻をぬぐうのは御免だ。
Mō kore ijō, jōshi no shiri o nuguu no wa gomen da.
I've had enough of straightening things out after the big weenies screw up.

私は幼い時から、弟の尻をぬぐってきた。
Watashi wa osanai toki kara, otōto no shiri o nugutte kita.
I've been picking up after my younger brother ever since I was a kid.

Also 尻ぬぐいをする *shiri-nugui o suru.*

---

shiri-metsuretsu 支離滅裂 "support (taken) away (leads to) ruin and destruction"

incoherence, inconsistency, disruption, chaos, utter confusion, gobbledegook

まだ熱が高くて、言うことも支離滅裂なんだよ。
Mada netsu ga takakute, iu koto mo shiri-metsuretsu nan da yo.
He's still running a high temperature and is making no sense whatsoever (you can't make out a word of what he's saying).

こんな支離滅裂なことを書いて来て、どういうつもりかね。
Konna shiri-metsuretsu na koto o kaite kite, dō iu tsumori ka ne.
What do you mean by bringing me this incoherent mess?

shiri-shiyoku 私利私欲 "one's own interests, one's own desires"

self-interest, personal gain, feathering one's own nest, lining one's own pockets

残念ながら、わが国の政治家には国民のためというより、私利私欲のために行動している人が多い。
Zannen nagara, wagakuni no seiji-ka ni wa kokumin no tame to iu yori, shiri-shiyoku no tame ni kōdō shite iru hito ga ōi.
Sadly, most politicians in this country are more intent on feathering their own nests than working on behalf of the people.

私利私欲に駆られて、他人をけおとしてきた自分が、今ではむなしいよ。
Shiri-shiyoku ni kararete, tanin o keotoshite kita jibun ga, ima de wa munashii yo.
Driven by blind self-interest, I've gotten ahead by pushing others aside. What a wasted life it's been.

↪ *gaden-insui* 我田引水, *jiga-jisan* 自画自賛

shirikire-tonbo 尻切れとんぼ "a dragonfly with its tail broken off"

unfinished, half-finished, half-done; fizzle out, sputter; start with a bang and end with a whimper; (of negotiations or discussions) be abruptly broken off

おまえの話はいつも尻切れとんぼだ。
Omae no hanashi wa itsumo shirikire-tonbo da.
You never finish what you start out to say.

交渉は2時間以上も続いたにもかかわらず尻切れとんぼに終わった。

Kōshō wa niji-kan ijō mo tsuzuita ni mo kakawarazu shirikire-tonbo ni owatta.
Negotiations continued for more than two hours before being broken off.

☞ *chūto-hanpa* 中途半端, *shirikire-tonbo* 尻切れとんぼ

shiriuma ni noru 尻馬に乗る "ride on the rear of a horse"

ride in on someone's coattails; jump on the bandwagon; go along uncritically with something

あんな奴の尻馬に乗るな。
Anna yatsu no shiriuma ni noru na.
I wouldn't go along with him (what he says) if I were you.

あいつの尻馬に乗ってそんな壺につぎ込んでいると身の破滅だぞ。
Aitsu no shiriuma ni notte sonna tsubo ni tsugikonde iru to mi no hametsu da zo.
You'll end up signing your own death warrant if you believe everything he tells you. / Jump on that bandwagon, and it'll lead to your downfall.

あの人の尻馬に付くような言動を続けていると、誰にも相手にされなくなるよ。
Ano hito no shiriuma ni tsuku yō na gendō o tsuzukete iru to, dare ni mo aite ni sarenaku naru yo.
If you keep following him around blindly like you are, nobody's going to pay any attention to you any more.

🐎 Originally *shiriuma* meant the rear of a horse with mounted rider, and then, by extension, to ride on the back of a horse behind someone else, i.e., ride on the horse's rump, as opposed to its back; hence, to go along with something or someone without exercising control of the direction events take or adhering to specific principles.

shiroi me de miru 白い眼で見る "look at with white eyes"

look askance at, give someone a dirty look, look daggers at someone

容疑者の家族は皆から白い眼で見られた。
Yōgi-sha no kazoku wa mina kara shiroi me de mirareta.
The suspect's family was getting dirty looks from everyone.

老人は、彼女が未婚の母だというだけで、白い眼で見た。
Rōjin wa, kanojo ga mikon no haha da to iu dake de, shiroi me de mita.
The old man looked down on (looked down his nose at) her just because she was an unwed mother.

☞ *me* 目

shisha-gonyū 四捨五入 "throw away the fours, put in the fives"

to round to the nearest whole number, dropping anything below five

若いつもりでいててももう25、四捨五入したら30だもんね。
Wakai tsumori de ite mo mō nijū-go, shisha-gonyū shitara sanjū da mon ne.
At twenty-five I like to think of myself as still being young, but rounded off it comes to thirty.

100円以下は切り捨てますか、切り上げますか、それとも四捨五入しますか。
Hyaku-en ika wa kirisutemasu ka, kiriagemasu ka, sore tomo shisha-gonyū shimasu ka.
Are we going to round down amounts of less than one hundred yen, or round them up? Or are we going to round up anything over fifty and round down the rest?

shita 舌 tongue

As an organ essential to both digestion and speech, *shita* figures in numerous idioms about ingestion and articulation. It appears in interesting compounds such as *nekojita*—a "cat's tongue"—to describe someone who cannot drink their coffee or eat their potatoes too hot, and *zessen,* which means a "tongue battle" or more naturally, a war of words. In this combination, *shita* is pronounced *zetsu.*

Tongues are standard equipment in Japan, but some politicians opt for the double model or *nimai-jita.* In other words, they come forked in Japan, too.

Bero is a more colloquial word for tongue, *berobero* an onomatopoeic word for licking.

Shita ga mawaru 舌が回る "one's tongue goes around (revolves)" be able to talk (very well or fast), be a real talker

---

あのアナウンサーはよく舌が回るね。
Ano anaunsā wa yoku shita ga mawaru ne.
That announcer can really rattle off the news.

女の子の方が、男の子よりも舌が回るようだ。
Onna no ko no hō ga, otoko no ko yori mo shita ga mawaru yō da
It appears that little girls are a lot more talkative than little boys.

Shita o dasu 舌を出す "stick out one's tongue"

---

(1) be playfully disturbed at something (2) thumb one's nose at someone

(1) 彼は英単語の発音を何度も間違えて、舌を出した。
Kare wa Ei-tango no hatsuon o nando mo machigaete, shita o dashita.
He stuck his tongue out in frustration when he repeatedly mispronounced the same English words.

(2) 彼は口では同情していたが、心の中では舌を出していたのだろう。

Kare wa kuchi de wa dōjō shite ita ga, kokoro no naka de wa shita o dashite ita no darō.

He may have said that he sympathized, but secretly he was probably thumbing his nose at you.

Shita o maku **舌を巻く** "roll up one's tongue"
be taken aback, blown away, thunderstruck

その投手の速球には、ホームラン王も舌を巻くほどだった。
Sono tōshu no sokkyū ni wa, hōmuran-ō mo shita o maku hodo datta.
The pitcher had a fastball that even had the other team's big gun rolling his eyes.

少女のピアノ演奏に会場の人々は皆舌を巻いた。
Shōjo no piano ensō ni kaijō no hitobito wa mina shita o maita.
The young girl played the piano so well that the audience was all agog.

shitta-gekirei 叱咤激励 "scolding, encouraging (encouragement with a berating voice)"

〜する to give somebody a pep talk, to psyche them up, to fire them up, to get them going, to put some fire in their belly

監督は声を張り上げて、選手たちを叱咤激励した。
Kantoku wa koe o hariagete, senshu-tachi o shitta-gekirei shita.
The manager screamed his head off, trying to get his team psyched up.

皆様から叱咤激励をいただいて頑張りたいと思います。
Minasama kara shitta-gekirei o itadaite ganbaritai to omoimasu.
With everyone's encouragement and advice, I will endeavor to do the very best I can.

若い人を叱咤激励して、やる気にさせるのもなかなか大変だよ。
Wakai hito o shitta-gekirei shite, yaru ki ni saseru no mo nakanaka taihen da yo.
Trying to encourage young people to get up and do something is no piece of cake.

自分で自分を叱咤激励しながら、今日までやって来ました。
Jibun de jibun o shitta-gekirei shinagara, kyō made yatte kimashita.
I got where I am today by spurring myself on all along the way.

shiyō-massetsu 枝葉末節 "branch, leaves, end joints"

trivial details, unimportant details, trifling details, trifles, matters of extremely minor importance

君は枝葉末節にこだわり過ぎるよ。もっと大きな視点から、物事を見られないかね。
Kimi wa shiyō-massetsu ni kodawarisugiru yo. Motto ōkina shiten kara, monogoto o mirarenai ka ne.
You pay too much attention to trivial details. You're gonna have to start seeing things as part of a bigger picture.

枝葉末節にとらわれていると、大切なことを見逃してしまうよ。
Shiyō-massetsu ni torawarete iru to, taisetsu na koto o minogashite shimau yo.
If you let yourself get caught up in trifling details, you'll end up missing what's important.

shōbai-hanjō 商売繁盛 "business is flourishing"

business is booming, business is on the up and up, doing a roaring trade, doing good business

ご商売繁盛で結構ですねえ。
Go-shōbai-hanjō de kekkō desu nē.
So business is booming. That's nice.

はごいた市は、商売繁盛を願って縁起物の羽子板を買いに来た人たちで一杯だ。
Hagoita-ichi wa, shōbai-hanjō o negatte engi-mono no hagoita o kai ni kita hito-tachi de ippai da.
The battledore market is full of people who have come to buy battledore charms to bring prosperity to their business.

❧ 羽子板 (*hagoita*) is a wooden bat (a bit larger than a table-tennis paddle in size) on which a picture is usually painted. At New Year children traditionally play *hanetsuki*, a game not dissimilar to badminton, using the bats and a *hane* (a kind of shuttlecock). In addition, many people buy the bats as talismans (*engi-mono*), which they hang up on the walls of their home. It is this custom that is being alluded to in the above example.

この神社は商売繁盛の神様をまつっているんだよ。
Kono jinja wa shōbai-hanjō no kamisama o matsutte iru n' da yo.
This shrine is dedicated to the god of prosperous business.

shōki 正気 "right *ki*"

1. sanity, right-mindedness, all there

心配するな。俺は正気だ。
Shinpai suru na. Ore wa shōki da.
Don't worry. I know what I'm doing.

自分で正気だという奴に限って正気じゃないそうだよ。
Jibun de shōki da to iu yatsu ni kagitte shōki ja nai sō da yo.
I've heard that it's the guys who think they're all there that really aren't (who are really out of their senses).

麻薬で一時的に正気を失っていたということだ。
Mayaku de ichiji-teki ni shōki o ushinatte ita to iu koto da.
It's a case of someone flipping out for a while because he's on drugs.

兄貴のやってることはとても正気の沙汰じゃない。
Aniki no yatte 'ru koto wa totemo shōki no sata ja nai.
You've gone completely off the deep end.

お前あの女に騙されてるんだぞ。正気に返れ。
Omae ano onna ni damasarete 'ru n' da zo. Shōki ni kaere.
You'd better come to your senses (wake up); the girl's sleeping around on you.

正気を取り戻すまでは誰が何を言っても聞く耳は持たんでしょう。
Shōki o torimodosu made wa dare ga nani o itte mo kiku mimi wa motan deshō.
He's not going to listen to anything anybody says until he's regained his senses.

正気になって考えると、どうしてあんなインチキ話にひっかかったのか自分でも不思議さ。
Shōki ni natte kangaeru to, dōshite anna inchiki-banashi ni hikkakatta no ka jibun de mo fushigi sa.
When I came to my senses and thought about it, I couldn't understand how I could have ever fallen for such a lame-brain scheme.

↪ *ki ga tashika (na)* 気が確か(な); *ki ga chigau* 気が違う, *ki ga fureru* 気がふれる, *ki ga hen ni naru* 気が変になる, *ki ga kuruu* 気が狂う, *kyōki* 狂気

2. consciousness

正気に返ったら、財布も時計もなくなってたんです。
Shōki ni kaettara, saifu mo tokei mo nakunatte 'ta n' desu.
When I came to (around), my wallet and watch were both gone.

事故から丸一日たってやっと正気を取り戻したんだ。

Jiko kara maru-ichinichi tatte yatto shōki o torimodoshita n' da.
It took him a full day to regain consciousness after the accident.

shokubutsu-ningen 植物人間 "vegetable human being"

a (human) vegetable

妻が手術中の事故で植物人間になってしまったので、夫は病院と医師を訴えた。
Tsuma ga shujutsu-chū no jiko de shokubutsu-ningen ni natte shimatta no de, otto wa byōin to ishi o uttaeta.
His wife ended up a vegetable as a result of a botched operation, so he sued the hospital and the surgeon responsible.

もしも私が植物人間になったら、延命治療はしないでほしい。
Moshimo watashi ga shokubutsu-ningen ni nattara, enmei-chiryō wa shinai de hoshii.
If I should ever end up a human vegetable, I don't want to receive treatment to prolong my life.

shokunin-katagi or *shokunin-kishitsu* 職人気質 "the artisan spirit"

craftsmanship, attention and devotion to quality

昔のような職人気質の大工さんは、このごろでは見られなくなったね。
Mukashi no yō na shokunin-katagi (shokunin-kishitsu) no daiku-san wa, konogoro de wa mirarenaku natta ne.
Nowadays you no longer see carpenters who are really devoted to their craft the way they used to be.

いろんな物が機械で大量生産されている時代だからこそ、職人気質を忘れないで、手作りにこだわりたいんですよ。
Ironna mono ga kikai de tairyō-seisan sarete iru jidai da kara koso, shokunin-katagi (shokunin-kishitsu) o wasurenai de, tezukuri ni kodawaritai n' desu yo.
It's precisely because we're living in an age when all sorts of things are mass-produced by machines that I want to stick to handicrafts and keep alive the artisan spirit.

shōshin-shōmei 正真正銘 "genuine article, authentic signature"

the real McCoy, the genuine article, authentic, the real thing

「スコッチウイスキー」は山ほどあるが、正真正銘のものは少ない。
"Sukotchi uisukī" wa yama hodo aru ga, shōshin-shōmei no mono wa sukunai.
There are plenty of "Scotch" whiskies around, but very few of them are the real McCoy.

これは間違いなく、正真正銘のダリですよ。
Kore wa machigai naku, shōshin-shōmei no Dari desu yo.
Without any doubt, this is a genuine Dali.

shōshin-yokuyoku 小心翼々 "small heart, many feathers"

cowardly, fainthearted, (over-)cautious, timid, spineless, wimpish, weak-kneed, namby-pamby

そんな小心翼々としたことでどうするんだ。もっと堂々としていなさい。

Sonna shōshin-yokuyoku to shita koto de dō suru n' da. Motto dōdō to shite inasai.
Why are you acting as though you're afraid of your own shadow? Let's see a little more backbone!

あいつ意外と小心翼々としてるんだよな、今度のことでよく分かったよ。
Aitsu igai to shōshin-yokuyoku to shite 'ru n' da yo na, kondo no koto de yoku wakatta yo.
I just realized it from what happened the other day, but he's a surprisingly timid guy.

※ Originally this expression was used to mean "scrupulously and with great attention to detail," but in later years it came to take on the pejorative meanings listed above.

☞ *ki ga chiisai* 気が小さい, *nomi no shinzō* 蚤の心臓

shōsō-kiei 少壮気鋭 "young and sharp-spirited"

young and enthusiastic, up-and-coming, young and energetic, full of youthful talent and spirit, young and keen, young and full of vim and vigor, a bright-faced go-getter

林教授は少壮気鋭の学者だ。
Hayashi-kyōju wa shōsō-kiei no gakusha da.
Professor Hayashi is a gifted young scholar (an up-and-coming scholar full of talent).

こちらが少壮気鋭の翻訳家、滝本さんです。
Kochira ga shōsō-kiei no hon'yaku-ka, Takimoto-san desu.
May I introduce Mr. Takimoto, an up-and-coming translator worth watching out for.

※ The expression 新進気鋭 (*shinshin-kiei*) is virtually synonymous. While

少壮気鋭 is used to describe people in their twenties and thirties who are full of dynamism and pep, 新進気鋭 is used to describe people who are new on the scene or new to a certain field of activity. People entering into new fields of endeavor are generally young (especially, in Japan). However, if (for example) you were talking about an office worker in his fifties who had quit his job and become a successful writer, you could only use 新進気鋭.

shōsū-seiei 少数精鋭 "small number, sharp spirits"

an elite corps; a select few; the cream of the crop; the crème de la crème

もう人海戦術は古い。これからは少数精鋭主義で行かなくちゃ。
Mō jinkai-senjutsu wa furui. Kore kara wa shōsū-seiei-shugi de ika-nakucha.
Trying to solve problems by throwing more and more people into the fray is out-of-date. From now on we've got to slim down our operation and make ourselves into an elite corps.

この部隊は、自衛隊きっての少数精鋭、つまりエリート部隊なんだ。
Kono butai wa, jiei-tai kitte no shōsū-seiei, tsumari erīto-butai nan da.
This unit is the Self-Defense Force's crack outfit. They are, in other words, the elite troops.

☞ *ugō no shū* 烏合の衆

shusha-sentaku 取捨選択 "selecting and choosing"

selection or rejection, choice

大掃除のときはいつも、何を捨てるかの取捨選択に丸一日かかってしまうんだ。

Ōsōji no toki wa itsumo, nani o suteru ka no shusha-sentaku ni maru-ichinichi kakatte shimau n' da.

Every time I do spring cleaning, I end up spending the whole day deciding what to keep and what to throw away.

手当たり次第にやってみるのも一つのやり方だと思うけど、ある程度は取捨選択した方がいいよ。

Teatari-shidai ni yatte miru no mo hitotsu no yarikata da to omou kedo, aru teido wa shusha-sentaku shita hō ga ii yo.

Doing whatever comes to hand is one way of doing things, but you really ought to pick and choose a bit.

shutsuba (suru) 出馬（する） "entering a horse"

run (stand) for (election/office)

沢田さんは今度の選挙の出馬を決意した。
Sawada-san wa kondo no senkyo no shutsuba o ketsui shita.
Ms. Sawada made up her mind to run for office in the next election.

あの議員は今度出馬してもチャンスはないだろう。
Ano giin wa kondo shutsuba shite mo chansu wa nai darō.
Even if that representative runs in the next election, he doesn't stand much of a chance.

❦ From the former practice of high-ranking warriors going to battle on horseback.

sonna ki そんな気 "that (kind of) *ki*"

that feeling, (feel) that way, feel like

そんな気はなかったんだが、どうも誤解されちゃったみたいなんだよ。
Sonna ki wa nakatta n' da ga, dōmo gokai sarechatta mitai nan da yo.
That's not what I had in mind at all. It looks like they took it the wrong way.

そう言われればそんな気もする。
Sō iwarereba sonna ki mo suru.
Now that you mention it, that's probably right.

パーティーに誘われたけど、とてもそんな気になれないよ。
Pātī ni sasowareta kedo, totemo sonna ki ni narenai yo.
I was invited to a party, but I'm not in the mood (in the party mode) at all.

As with *sono ki,* its linguistic cousin, *sonna ki* fits the same mold as a class of entry—#2—listed under the ~ *ki da* heading, with *sonna* replacing the part of speech normally in that position, often to avoid repeating it (see the note under ~ *ki da*). Although the expression itself is ambiguous, its meaning is usually clear from the context. See the examples below to get a clearer picture of the difference between the two expressions in the same context.

そちらがその気なら、こちらにも考えがある。
Sochira ga sono ki nara, kochira ni mo kangae ga aru.
If that's what you're up to, I've got a little something up my sleeve as well.
そちらがそんな気なら、こちらにも考えがある。
Sochira ga sonna ki nara, kochira ni mo kangae ga aru.
If that's the way you feel, don't expect much help from me.

sono ki その気 "that ki"

the mood, feeling

一度はその気になったんだが、結局気が変わった。

Ichido wa sono ki ni natta n' da ga, kekkyoku ki ga kawatta.
I was ready to do it at one time, but I've changed my mind.

若い頃は政治家になる気はなかったが、中年になってその気になった。
Wakai koro wa seiji-ka ni naru ki wa nakatta ga, chūnen ni natte sono ki ni natta.
I had no thought of going into politics when I was young, but middle age changed all that.

一杯やって行こうと誘われたが、今日はその気にならなかった。
Ippai yatte ikō to sasowareta ga, kyō wa sono ki ni naranakatta.
They invited me to go out with them for a drink, but today I just didn't feel like it.

その気があるのなら早く言った方がいいよ。
Sono ki ga aru no nara hayaku itta hō ga ii yo.
If that's the way you feel, you'd better go ahead and say so.

前々から言われてはいるが、まだその気はない。
Maemae kara iwarete wa iru ga, mada sono ki wa nai.
Everybody's been trying to talk me into it, but I just don't feel like doing it.

彼はいつもその気だ。
Kare wa itsumo sono ki da.
He's horny all the time. / He's always ready to go.

その気にさせておいて、今になって逃げるなんてひどいよ。
Sono ki ni sasete oite, ima ni natte nigeru nante hidoi yo.
How can you get me in the mood like that and then just up and take off?

֍ Ambiguity at its best. Structurally, *sono ki* fits the same mold as the entries listed under section one of the ~ *ki da* heading, *sono* replacing the verb normally in that position, often to avoid repeating it (see the note under ~ *ki da*). Although the expresson itself is ambiguous, just what the *sono* means is usually clear from the context, especially from what has preceded. Of all the possible meanings, however, the one most readily understood without reference to context is euphemistic mention of sexual excitement. *Sono ki* is the kind of expression likely to be picked up and commented upon, often with a wink and a nudge, even when the speaker intends no sexual innuendo. Relatedly—broadly speaking—*sono ke* is another pronunciation of the term, which in context is a slang term describing someone of abnormal or unusual sexual tendencies.

お前その気があるんじゃないか。
Omae sono ke ga aru n' ja nai ka.
What are you, queer or what?

あの人その気があるみたいよ。
Ano hito sono ke ga aru mitai yo.
You can tell he's into S&M.

sōshi-sōai 相思相愛 "think of each other, love each other"

mutual love, reciprocal affection, to be in love with one another

相思相愛で結ばれたはずが、1年もしないうちに別れちゃった。
Sōshi-sōai de musubareta hazu ga, ichinen mo shinai uchi ni wakarechatta.
They were supposed to be madly in love, but within a year they'd split up.

そのうち、あなたにも相思相愛の相手が現れるよ。
Sono uchi, anata ni mo sōshi-sōai no aite ga arawareru yo.
It won't be long before you too have someone of your own to love and cherish.

あいつら相思相愛だからさあ、一緒にいるとあてられっぱなしだよ。
Aitsura sōshi-sōai da kara sā, issho ni iru to aterareppanashi da yo.
They're just a couple of lovebirds, and they're always flaunting it when you're with them.

☞ *awabi no kataomoi* 鮑の片思い

sune すね shin

The front part of the leg from the knee to the ankle is all *sune* means. Japanese college students tend to chew on their parent's shins so much, though, that you'd think there would be little left for locomotion.

Sune ni kizu o motsu **すねに傷を持つ** "have an injury on one's shin"
have a skeleton in the closet, have a (shady) past

すねに傷を持つ身では、まともな職業にはつけないだろう。
Sune ni kizu o motsu mi de wa, matomo na shokugyō ni wa tsukenai darō.
With a skeleton in the closet like that, you're going to have trouble landing a decent job.

その飲み屋の客には、すねに傷を持つ者が多かった。
Sono nomi-ya no kyaku ni wa, sune ni kizu o motsu mono ga ōkatta.
A lot of the bar's customers had something to hide.

Sune o kajiru **すねをかじる** "chew on someone's shin"
sponge off (one's parents), be a mooch, freeload

お前はいつまで親のすねをかじっているつもりだ。
Omae wa itsu made oya no sune o kajitte iru tsumori da.
Just how long do you think you're gonna keep mooching off your parents?

結婚後も親のすねをかじっていて、恥ずかしくないのだろうか。
Kekkon-go mo oya no sune o kajitte ite, hazukashiku nai no darō ka.
Doesn't it bother you at all to still be sponging off your parents even though you're married?

suppon すっぽん soft-shelled turtle

In Japan the lowly mud turtle figures in a few expressions that will give you a pretty clear idea of the esteem in which this freshwater terrapin is held. *Suppon* is also slang for "dick," as in "purple turkey neck," "one-eyed trouser mouse," or any of the hundreds of English words for the penis, from some physical resemblance between the male member and the turtle's head and neck. Coming off better in questions of the palate, its meat, the soft-shelled turtle's that is, is prized for use in porridge, especially during the winter months.

Soft-shelled turtles are counted *ippiki* 一匹.

Suppon **すっぽん** "soft-shelled turtle"
a persistent person, bulldog, badger

あの刑事は俗に「すっぽん」と呼ばれている。
Ano keiji wa zoku ni "suppon" to yabarete iru.
That dick is known on the street as the bulldog.

芸能レポーターはすっぽんのようにその俳優を追い回した。
Geinō-repōtā wa suppon no yō ni sono haiyū o oimawashita.
Reporters on the celebrity beat were badgering that actor everyplace he went.

🦴 From the observation that soft-shelled turtles have strong jaws, and once they glom onto prey or fingers they never let go.

Tsuki to suppon **月とすっぽん** "the moon and a soft-shelled turtle"
as different as night and day (chalk from cheese), a whale of a difference

---

一番弟子といってもやっぱり先生と比べたら月とすっぽんだよ。
Ichiban-deshi to itte mo yappari sensei to kurabetara tsuki to suppon da yo.
She may be the professor's protégée, but there's a world of difference between them.

さすがここのケーキおいしいわ、あの新宿のケーキと比べたら月とすっぽんね。
Sasuga koko no kēki oishii wa, ano Shinjuku no kēki to kurabetara tsuki to suppon ne.
The pastries here are truly sublime, so much better than those we had in Shinjuku the other day.

❦ From the observation that although the round shape of a soft-shelled turtle's carapace may resemble the moon, the two are vastly different (and the latter much more esteemed for its beauty).

suzume すずめ (雀) sparrow

They're everywhere, including some Japanese dinner tables. Not that nouvelle cuisine is in, or dieting all the rage. No, they just eat sparrows butterflied and cooked over charcoal at some upscale eateries and at some definitely downtown *yakitori-ya*s. If you can't manage to finish off a Cornish game hen, then maybe a sparrow is right down your alley. As a bonus, they are served head intact.

Sparrows figure in the language as metaphors for small things (some diminutive or relatively small grasses and insects, for example, include the character for "sparrow" in their names, usually indicating it is smaller than other such species; the sparrow pea is smaller than the crow pea). In yet another equally fascinating bit of trivia, a person who is always chattering away is called a "sparrow," as is a person who has the inside dope on something and is not shy about sharing it. Such a chatterbox is called a *gakuya suzume* 楽屋雀, or a backstage sparrow, from the term's origin in the dressing rooms of Japanese theaters, where gossips insinuated themselves and lived to tell all they had discovered about actors and actresses.

The sparrow's chirp is *chunchun* チュンチュン, and when there are a lot of them going at it full blast in the trees, we have a *suzume-gassen* 雀合戦, or a sparrow battle. When they sit still enough for a roll call, which is rare, sparrows can be counted *ichiwa* 一羽 or *ippiki* 一匹.

Suzume hyaku made odori wasurezu **雀百まで踊り忘れず** "a sparrow can live to be a hundred and it won't forget how to dance"
old (bad) habits die hard; what is learned in the cradle is carried to the grave

---

「雀百まで踊り忘れず」とよく言ったもので、この年になってもまだ部屋を暗くすると眠れません。
"Suzume hyaku made odori wasurezu" to yoku itta mono de, kono toshi ni natte mo mada heya o kuraku suru to nemuremasen.
They say old habits die hard, but I still can't get to sleep without having a light on, even at my age.

私の息子は50歳にもなるのに、いまだになんでもやりっぱなし、「雀百まで踊り忘れず」ですよ。
Watakushi no musuko wa gojū-sai ni mo naru no ni, imada ni nan de mo yarippanashi, "suzume hyaku made odori wasurezu" desu yo.
My son's going on fifty and he's still not acting his age (running wild). I guess it's true what they say about old habits dying hard.

❦ The dancing here refers to the sparrow's proclivity to hop around, something it presumably does to the bitter end. The expression is primarily used of the bad habits one learns to enjoy early in life, often those born of a dissipated life of pleasure; wine, women (or men), and song.

Suzume no namida **雀の涙** "a sparrow's tear"
a very small amount (of money), a piddling sum, a drop in the bucket, next to nothing

一日炎天下で働いて、報酬は雀の涙だった。
Ichinichi enten-ka de hataraite, hōshū wa suzume no namida datta.
Sweated my ass off in the hot sun all day for next to nothing.

今どき、そんな雀の涙のようなバイト料で働く奴いないよ。
Imadoki, sonna suzume no namida no yō na baito-ryō de hataraku yatsu inai yo.
Nobody's going to take a part-time job these days for a piddling sum like that.

✌ Used exclusively of money.

☞ *ka no namida* 蚊の涙

tai たい（鯛） sea bream / red snapper

Why is snapper served as the main course on many joyous occasions in Japan? The kanji for *tai* is written with two components, the fish radical and the element for vicinity, suggesting that the fish has long been plentiful in the seas surrounding the archipelago. This inference is supported by the mention of the fish in Japan's oldest extant poetry compendium, the *Man'yoshū*, which is thought to have been compiled around the end of the Nara period (710–784). Having said that, the more immediate reason seems to be a simple play on words, since the Japanese for happy or joyous is *medetai*, leading one to speculate that either some ancient wag or person with a vested interest in the sale of the fish contrived a linguistic inducement to its consumption.

Kusatte mo tai 腐っても鯛 "a rotten sea bream is still a sea bream" once a winner, always a winner; an old eagle is better than a young crow; a diamond on a dunghill is still a diamond

---

「なんだベンツ買ったって、中古じゃないか。」

"Nan da bentsu katta tte, chūko ja nai ka."
"Thought you said you bought a Mercedes? But what's this, man, a used one?"

「腐っても鯛というじゃないか。」
"Kusatte mo tai to iu ja nai ka."
"Hey, it's still a Mercedes."

腐っても鯛、この桐のタンスは20年以上も使っているが少しもきしみがない。
Kusatte mo tai, kono kiri no tansu wa nijū-nen ijō mo tsukatte iru ga sukoshi mo kishimi ga nai.
There's no denying quality. Had this paulownia chest of drawers for over twenty years, and it's as solid as ever.

✀ From the notion that something superior remains so even in old age. The idiom arises from the fact that the flesh of the snapper is relatively fat-free, and the taste, therefore, does not decline significantly when not perfectly fresh.

taigen-sōgo 大言壮語 "big talk, brave language"

big (tall) talk, bragging, boasting, swaggering

あんな大言壮語して、大丈夫なのかね。
Anna taigen-sōgo shite, daijōbu na no ka ne.
I wonder if he ought to be bragging quite so much.

君の大言壮語は聞きあきたよ。そろそろ結果を見せてくれ。
Kimi no taigen-sōgo wa kikiakita yo. Sorosoro kekka o misete kure.
I'm fed up with you and your big mouth. How about showing us some results one of these days.

taiki-bansei 大器晩成 "Great talents mature late."

to achieve greatness late in life; great talents are slow in maturing; to be a late (slow) developer, a late bloomer; to bloom (hit one's peak) late in life

この子のんびり屋でちょっと心配なんだけど、みんなは大器晩成だって言ってくれるのよ。
Kono ko nonbiri-ya de chotto shinpai nan da kedo, minna wa taiki-bansei datte itte kureru no yo.
Our kid's so laid back it worries me sometimes, but everyone tells me he's just a late developer.

大器晩成と言われ続けて、還暦を迎えてしまった。
Taiki-bansei to iwaretsuzukete, kanreki o mukaete shimatta.
All my life people have told me I'm a late developer, but here I am turning sixty!

taikōba 対抗馬 "an opposing horse"

a strong opponent, a contender, someone (usually a candidate) who will give someone a run for his/her money

次期首相の本命の対抗馬として3人が出馬を表明した。
Jiki-shushō no honmei no taikōba toshite sannin ga shutsuba o hyōmei shita.
Three strong candidates threw their hats in the ring to oppose the frontrunner for the prime ministership.

あいつは対抗馬としてはたいしたことないな。
Aitsu wa taikōba toshite wa taishita koto nai na.
I'm not gonna lose any sleep over running against somebody like him.

🐎 From horse racing, of a horse considered capable of giving the favorite a run for the money, *taikōba* is now widely used in the political arena as well.

taizen-jijaku 泰然自若 "calm and composed"

imperturbable; with great presence of mind; cool, calm and collected; as cool as a cucumber; (to keep) a cool head; a model of composure

ここまで来るともう覚悟ができたらしく、泰然自若としている。
Koko made kuru to mō kakugo ga dekita rashiku, taizen-jijaku to shite iru.
Having gotten this far, he seems prepared for anything; he's as cool as a cucumber.

さっきまで泰然自若としていたが、急にそわそわし始めた。
Sakki made taizen-jijaku to shite ita ga, kyū ni sowasowa shihajimeta.
Up until a minute ago he was a model of composure, but all of a sudden he's begun to get on edge.

🕸 The difference between 泰然自若 and 冷静沈着 (*reisei-chinchaku*), although they are similar, is that, first, the former is accompanied by *to shite iru* while the latter is followed by *na* or *da*; secondly, in terms of meaning the former suggests leisurely body movement (or action) as a result of mental composure; on the other hand, the latter doesn't necessarily entail any degree of leisureliness. Thus, 冷静沈着に素早く行動する (*Reisei-chinchaku ni subayaku kōdō suru*, to act quickly and calmly) is possible, but you cannot use 泰然自若 here.

↪ *reisei-chinchaku* 冷静沈着

taka たか (鷹) hawk

Hawking and falconry have both been practiced in Japan since ancient times, when the sport was brought from Korea. Bravery, grace, and integrity, all positive characteristics, are associated with hawks. Yes, intransigent hardliners and warmongers are hawks in Japanese too, as in *taka-ha* 鷹派, or "hawk faction."

Hawks are counted *ichiwa* 一羽.

Nō aru taka wa tsume o kakusu　**能ある鷹は爪を隠す**　"a powerful hawk hides its talons"

an able person does not show off his skills; tell not all you know, all you have, or all you can do

---

> 能ある鷹は爪を隠す、ちょっとピアノが弾けるからって自慢するもんじゃないよ。
>
> *Nō aru taka wa tsume o kakusu, chotto piano ga hikeru kara tte jiman suru mon ja nai yo.*
>
> Don't toot your horn because you can play the piano a little. If you're good, people will discover it for themselves.

> 能ある鷹は爪を隠すと言うけど、あの人がコンピュータプログラムが出来るとは知らなかった。
>
> *Nō aru taka wa tsume o kakusu to iu kedo, ano hito ga konpyūta puroguramu ga dekiru to wa shiranakatta.*
>
> I know what they say about ability being its own best advertisement, but what a surprise it was to find out that he knows how to program computers.

🦅 The opposite being equally true, it is to those who seek approbation for their modest abilities that this maxim is most often directed.

---

tako たこ（蛸）　octopus

Although this mollusk dwells at the bottom of the sea, it surfaces regularly in the lexicon through a broad variety of idioms and expressions that draw from such things as the unique octopodous configuration of its arms (legs, really) and the reversal of the relative position of body parts, with the trunk sitting atop the head to which the legs appear to be directly attached. There is even a financial term, *tako-haitō* 蛸配当, describing a bogus dividend paid from a corporation's assets to investors even though the bottom line fails to show a profit. This derives from the superstitious belief that starvation drives the octopus to the ultimately suicidal practice of devouring its own legs in order to survive. The earthenware jar used to catch octopi, *takotsubo* 蛸壷, has lent its name to the Japanese military's equivalent of our "foxhole," a shallow one- or two-man trench dug to protect soldiers from enemy fire.

Unlike in the West, where its demonization has led to its being called a "devilfish," with one American naturalist, Frank Norris, even entitling his great novel depicting the Southern Pacific Railroad and its far-reaching control of California wheat farmers, *The Octopus*; and notwithstanding recent slang coinages, such as the first entry below indicating that its image is not one of uniform popularity, this cephalopod is generally held in Japan to be friendly toward man and is often depicted as intelligent and mischievous.

Octopuses are counted *ippiki* 一匹 and, less commonly, *ippai* 一杯 (because of the shape of the pot, perhaps), unless they are gutted, flattened, and hung out to dry, when they are counted *ichiren* 一連.

Tako **タコ** "octopus"
birdbrain, bunhead, dope, dummy, fool, idiot, imbecile, ninny, stupid

あっ！映画のチケット忘れたじゃないか、このタコ。
A! Eiga no chiketto wasureta ja nai ka, kono tako.
Duh, you didn't forget to bring the tickets for the movie, did you, numbnuts?

「タコ！」
"Tako!"
"Boy am I dumb! / Fuck me!"

「どうしたの。」
"Dōshita no."

"What's wrong?"

「財布落とした。」
"Saifu otoshita."
"Oh, I lost my wallet somewhere."

🥀 As exemplified above, this recent addition to the language of youth can be used of others or the speaker, and may become the modern equivalent of the more common *baka*.

Tako-beya たこ部屋 "an octopus room"
a pigsty, pit, dump

不法入国した労働者はたこ部屋のようなところに押し込められていた。

Fuhō-nyūkoku shita rōdō-sha wa tako-beya no yō na tokoro ni oshi-komerarete ita.

Illegal immigrant laborers were herded into disgusting labor camps like so many cattle.

その旅館の部屋はまるでたこ部屋のようで、雑魚寝する貧乏旅行者でいっぱいだった。

Sono ryokan no heya wa maru de tako-beya no yō de, zako-ne suru binbō-ryokō-sha de ippai datta.

The inn was a veritable pigsty, with down-at-the-heel travelers sprawled all over the floor.

🥀 From their resemblance to the masonry jars used to catch octopuses and the difficulty the animal has escaping once it has entered, this term was originally used of the forced labor camps at the mines of Hokkaido prior to World War II, where squalid living conditions prevailed and from which escape was all but impossible.

↪ *butagoya* 豚小屋, *unagi no nedoko* 鰻の寝床, *unagigoya* 鰻小屋

Tako-nyūdō **たこ入道** "a tonsured octopus"
a bald person, baldy, cue ball, egghead, skinhead

山田先生は生徒の間でたこ入道と呼ばれている。
Yamada-sensei wa seito no aida de tako-nyūdō to yobarete iru.
His students call Mr. Yamada "cue ball."

あのたこ入道みたいな俳優なんていったけ？
Ano tako-nyūdō mitai na haiyū nante itta ke?
What was that bald actor's name?

❧ Jocular reference to a bald person. From the resemblance of the octopus's trunk, which sits where its head *should* be, to a bald pate.

Takoashi-haisen **たこ足配線** "electrical cords (like) octopus legs"
an overloaded electrical outlet; a scramble of electrical cords

こんなたこ足配線してたら、火事になるよ。
Konna takoashi-haisen shite 'tara, kaji ni naru yo.
You're going to cause a fire by overloading an outlet like this.

彼の部屋はたこ足配線で足の踏み場に困った。
Kare no heya wa takoashi-haisen de ashi no fumiba ni komatta.
His room was so cluttered with electrical cords running here and there that you could hardly find a place to stand.

❧ From the resemblance of the many cords trailing out from an overloaded electrical outlet to the eight legs of the octopus.

tamamushi 玉虫 jewel beetle

This iridescent beetle's greenish wings and reddish gold striped body reflect light beautifully. It has given its name to a type of weaving, *tamamushi-ori,* that incorporates threads of different colors in the warp and woof so as to reflect light in a rainbow of colors, depending upon the angle from which it is viewed.

Jewel beetles are counted *ippiki* 一匹.

Tamamushi-iro 玉虫色 "jewel-beetle colored"
ambiguous, equivocal, obscure, enigmatic, weasel-worded; open for interpretation; clear as mud

---

今度の調停案はまさに玉虫色だ。
Kondo no chōtei-an wa masa ni tamamushi-iro da.
The compromise proposal is about as clear as mud. / It's anybody's guess what the compromise plan actually means.

会長の説明はまったく玉虫色で会社が潰れる恐れもあるぞ。
Kaichō no setsumei wa mattaku tamamushi-iro de kaisha ga tsubureru osore mo aru zo.
The chairperson's explanation was so weasel-worded that I wouldn't be surprised to see the company go belly up.

記者会見での代表の見解は玉虫色の表現ばかりであった。
Kisha-kaiken de no daihyō no kenkai wa tamamushi-iro no hyōgen bakari de atta.
The explanation offered by the rep at the press conference was just a lot of smoke and mirrors.

🐇 Of decisions, explanations, wording, and the like that can be interpreted in various ways depending on how they are viewed.

↪ *biji-reiku* 美辞麗句, *gaikō-jirei* 外交辞令

tanin-gyōgi 他人行儀 "act as if you were strangers"

stand on formality, stand on ceremony, act like a stranger

そんな他人行儀なこと、おっしゃらないで下さいな。
Sonna tanin-gyōgi na koto, ossharanai de kudasai na.
Please don't stand on ceremony.

松井さんとは知り合ってもう何年にもなるのに、いつまでたっても他人行儀なんだ。
Matsui-san to wa shiriatte mō nan-nen ni mo naru no ni, itsu made tatte mo tanin-gyōgi nan da.
Even though I've known Matsui for years, he always stands on formality.

tanjun-meikai 単純明快 "simple and clear"

as clear as day, plain and simple, pellucid

これほど単純明快な話はないよ。
Kore hodo tanjun-meikai na hanashi wa nai yo.
There couldn't be anything simpler than this.

こんな単純明快な理屈も分からないのかい？
Konna tanjun-meikai na rikutsu mo wakaranai no kai?
Can't you follow a line of reasoning as clear and as simple as that?

tanki 短気 "a short *ki*"

a quick temper, short temper, a short fuse; [~ *o okosu*] get angry (mad), explode, blow up

ここで短気を起こしたら今までの苦労が水の泡じゃないか。
Koko de tanki o okoshitara ima made no kurō ga mizu no awa ja nai ka.
Blow a fuse now and everything you've worked so hard for will go up in smoke.

🌱 *mizu no awa*: literally, "water bubbles"; from the sense of "short/ephemeral" comes, by extension, "useless, wasted."

☞ *ki ga mijikai* 気が短い

tanki (na) 短気(な) "short *ki*"

explosive, short-tempered, have a short fuse

津山は短気な男だが機嫌を直すのも早いよ。
Tsuyama wa tanki na otoko da ga kigen o naosu no mo hayai yo.
Tsuyama's pretty short-tempered, but he cools down fast, too.

彼はいいやつだが短気で怒りっぽいのがたまにきずだ。
Kare wa ii yatsu da ga tanki de okorippoi no ga tama ni kizu da.
He's a good enough guy, but that short temper he's got is his one fault.

家の子は誰に似てあんなに短気なんだろう。
Uchi no ko wa dare ni nite anna ni tanki nan darō.
Sometimes I wonder where that son of mine got such a short temper.

Also 気短(な) *kimijika (na)*.
☞ *ki ga mijikai* 気が短い

tanki wa miren no moto 短気は未練の元 "a short *ki* is a source of regret."

get mad and you'll live to regret it

「短気は未練の元」って知らない？　後悔するかもよ。
"Tanki wa miren no moto" tte shiranai? Kōkai suru kamo yo.
You've heard the axiom "anger causes regret," right? Well, you might be sorry later on [if you lose your temper now].

🙠 Similar in meaning and usage to *tanki wa sonki*.

☞ *ki ga mijikai* 気が短い

tanki wa sonki 短気は損気　"a short *ki* is a losing *ki*."

impatience can be expensive; a short temper is costly

「短気は損気」と思って我慢してきたけど、もう嫌だ。
"Tanki wa sonki" to omotte gaman shite kita kedo, mō iya da.
I've told myself all along that getting pissed off would only cost me in the end, but now I've had it up to here.

ここはぐっと我慢しなさい。「短気は損気」だよ。
Koko wa gutto gaman shinasai. "Tanki wa sonki" da yo.
Now's the time you've got to stand there and take it. Get impatient now and it'll cost you. / Hang in there (Tough it out). Fly off the handle now and you'll regret it later.

「短気は損気」と言うだろう。言い過ぎたら取り返しがつかないよ。
"Tanki wa sonki" to iu darō. Iisugitara torikaeshi ga tsukanai yo.
You know what they say about losing your temper and being sorry later. Go too far now, and you'll never be able to take it back.

🙠 Used exclusively to admonish someone about the dangers of losing his temper or growing impatient. *Sonki* is a term created solely to rhyme with *tanki*, and is not seen outside this aphorism.

☞ *ki ga mijikai* 気が短い

tanki wa tanmei 短気は短命 "a short *ki* is a short life."

a short temper shortens life

カッカしてる親父に「『短気は短命』だよ」と言ったら、ますます怒った。
Kakka shite 'ru oyaji ni "'Tanki wa tanmei' da yo" to ittara, masumasu okotta.
When I told my dad, "That temper of yours will be the death of you," he just got madder.

🖋 Used to encourage patience in someone or advise them not to get angry.

☞ *ki ga mijikai* 気が短い

tanshin-funin 単身赴任 "a solitary posting"

going to a new post by oneself (without one's spouse and children)

単身赴任も長くなると、問題が多くなるらしいね。
Tanshin-funin mo nagaku naru to, mondai ga ōku naru rashii ne.
It seems the longer a post keeps you away from home and loved ones, the more problems arise.

父は京都へ単身赴任中だが、週末には必ず帰ってくるよ。
Chichi wa Kyōto e tanshin-funin-chū da ga, shūmatsu ni wa kanarazu kaette kuru yo.
Dad's away in Kyoto where he's been posted by his company, but he always comes home on weekends.

🖋 This refers to a company posting where an employee (usually a man) is sent to work far away from home, and decides to go alone so as not to disrupt his children's education.

tantō-chokunyū 単刀直入 "(with) a single sword (charge) straight in"

without preamble, without mincing words, without beating about the bush, bluntly, directly, frankly

単刀直入に言うと、君はこの仕事には適性がないんだ。
Tantō-chokunyū ni iu to, kimi wa kono shigoto ni wa tekisei ga nai n' da.
To be perfectly frank with you, you're simply not cut out for this job.

失礼ながら、単刀直入におうかがいしますが、業績が上がる見通しがあるのですか。
Shitsurei nagara, tantō-chokunyū ni oukagai shimasu ga, gyōseki ga agaru mitōshi ga aru no desu ka.
Excuse me for asking quite so bluntly, but are there any prospects of your business improving?

tanuki たぬき（狸） raccoon dog

When found in idioms describing people, this is basically the male equivalent of *kitsune,* or fox, which is used primarily of women. Both animals were thought capable of bewitching humans. The raccoon dog has large, round eyes, which make it, unlike the fox, a lovable creature. But the *tanuki* was also believed to possess humans, making their appetites become uncontrollable and their stomachs distend as they grew listless and weak and eventually died. *Tanuki* are the animals immortalized in porcelain outside many Japanese taverns and pubs. Characteristically, they have scrotums about half the size of their diminutive bodies, about which ditties have been written and idioms created. According to one such idiom, the *tanuki*'s scrotum spreads out over eight tatami mats (*tanuki no kintama hachi-jō jiki* 狸のきん玉八畳敷).

Tanuki are counted *ippiki* 一匹. They are too small to warrant being counted *ittō* 一頭.

Furudanuki 古狸 "an old raccoon dog"
a sly old fox, a wily (crafty) old dog

あの古狸また新入社員をいびってるらしいぞ。
Ano furudanuki mata shinnyū-shain o ibitte'ru rashii zo.
That wily old dog is at it again, giving the new employees a hard time.

あの人は古狸だからうかつなこと言うな。
Ano hito wa furudanuki da kara ukatsu na koto iu na.
Watch what you say around him, he's a sly old fox.

✥ Used exclusively of older men.

↪ *furugitsune* 古狐 (of older women)

Tanuki 狸 "raccoon dog"
a cunning person, sly (crafty) fellow, an old fox (coon); nobody's fool

あの人はなかなかの狸だよね。
Ano hito wa nakanaka no tanuki da yo ne.
That guy's crazy (dumb) like a fox. / There're no flies on him. / He's a foxy (cagey) fellow.

政治家なんて狸じゃなきゃやってけないよ。
Seiji-ka nante tanuki ja nakya yatte 'ke nai yo.
You've got to be wily (crafty) to make it as a politician.

相手は相当な狸おやじだから気をつけろよ。
Aite wa sōtō na tanuki oyaji da kara ki o tsukero yo.
Better watch yourself, the guy you'll be dealing with is an old sharpie.

✥ Used primarily of men on the distant side of forty. When followed by *oyaji* it is reserved exclusively for males. Although rarely, *tanuki* can be used of both sexes. As the examples indicate, by convention the expression is often preceded by a qualifier like *sōtō na* or *nakanaka no*.

Tanuki-neiri たぬき寝入り "a raccoon dog sleeping"
playing possum, pretending to be asleep

彼は分が悪くなったのでたぬき寝入りを決め込んだ。
Kare wa bu ga waruku natta no de tanuki-neiri o kimekonda.
He made up his mind to play possum when things started going against him.

ちょっと、たぬき寝入りなんかしないで、私の話を聞いてよ。
Chotto, tanuki-neiri nanka shinai de, watashi no hanashi o kiite yo.
Come on now, don't pretend to be asleep. Listen to what I'm saying.

席をゆずるのが面倒だから、電車ではたぬき寝入りをするという人がけっこういるよ。
Seki o yuzuru no ga mendō da kara, densha de wa tanuki-neiri o suru to iu hito ga kekkō iru yo.
There are lots of people who don't want to give up their seats on the train, so they pretend to be asleep.

🐾 Said to have its origin in the days when no distinction was made between the *tanuki* and the *mujina* 狢 or badger, and the latter was believed to have been unable to see or hear during the daytime and therefore likely to just sit tight and try not to attract too much attention to itself. Today the most common place to find people playing possum is in crowded commuter trains and subways, where younger people lucky enough to have found seats feign sleep to avoid making eye contact with elderly commuters to whom social convention dictates they give up their seat. Along with both its less common variations, *tanuki* 狸 and *tanuki-ne* 狸寝, the idiom is not used—as it's English equivalent "play possum" is—to mean "feign ignorance."

Toranu tanuki no kawazan'yō 捕らぬ狸の皮算用 "counting the pelts of untrapped raccoon dogs"
counting one's chickens before they hatch

「この計算でいけば、10カ月で100万儲かるよ。」

"Kono keisan de ikeba, jukkagetsu de hyaku-man mōkaru yo."
"The way I've got it figured, we're gonna make a million yen in ten months."

「捕らぬ狸の皮算用にならなければいいけど。」
"Toranu tanuki no kawazan'yō ni naranakereba ii kedo."
"Let's just hope we're not counting our chickens before they hatch."

あいつはいつも捕らぬ狸の皮算用ばかりで、言ったとおりになったことがない。
Aitsu wa itsumo toranu tanuki no kawazan'yō bakari de, itta tōri ni natta koto ga nai.
She's always counting her chickens before they hatch; nothing ever turns out the way she says it will.

※ In addition to the usual explanation of overeagerness, another theory regarding this idiom relates to the *tanuki*'s ability to possess a human. In this somewhat farfetched view, the number of *tanuki* pelts actually taken differs from the count because the wily animal has somehow deceived the trapper.

tariki-hongan 他力本願 "fulfill one's wish depending on others' power"

reliance upon others, to get others to do your work for you, to always turn to others for help

あいつは他力本願でいけないな。自分では何もしないで、いつも人を当てにしてる。
Aitsu wa tariki-hongan de ikenai na. Jibun de wa nani mo shinai de, itsumo hito o ate ni shite 'ru.
He'll never get anywhere, always relying on others and never doing anything himself.

会社の危機なのに上層部は他力本願で、互いに誰かがなんとかしてくれるのを期待している様子だ。
Kaisha no kiki na no ni jōsō-bu wa tariki-hongan de, tagai ni dare ka ga nan to ka shite kureru no o kitai shite iru yōsu da.

Even though the company's in a crisis, the upper echelons all seem to be hoping that somebody will come along and save the situation, without doing anything themselves.

🦋 This four-character compound is originally a Buddhist term meaning "salvation by faith through the benevolence of Amida Buddha." It is the Buddhist belief that your deeds in this life will determine what you become in your next life (when you are reincarnated). If you are noble and honest, perhaps you will return as an eagle. If not, perhaps you will return as a rat. The process of reincarnation itself, however, is seen as a painful cycle of birth and death, from which it is difficult to escape. There are two ways to achieve one's 本願 (the desire to break out of the reincarnation cycle and attain eternal bliss, being reborn on a lotus leaf in Buddhist heaven): the first, called 他力本願 (*tariki-hongan*), is by putting oneself in Buddha's hands. The second, called 自力本願 (*jiriki-hongan*), meaning "trying to seek salvation relying on one's own strength," is by practising asceticism.

↩ *dokuritsu-doppo* 独立独歩

tatsu tori ato o nigosazu 立つ鳥跡を濁さず
"birds taking to flight leave nothing sullied behind"

clean up a place before one leaves, leave a place like one found it

ちゃんと掃除してから帰りなさい、立つ鳥跡を濁さずと言うでしょう。
Chanto sōji shite kara kaerinasai, tatsu tori ato o nigosazu to iu deshō.
Clean up before you leave. You know what they say about leaving a place like you found it.

花見の季節の上野公園のゴミは十数トンにのぼる、立つ鳥跡を濁さずは鳥の世界だけのものになってしまった。
Hanami no kisetsu no Ueno-kōen no gomi wa jūsū ton ni noboru, tatsu tori ato o nigosazu wa tori no sekai dake no mono ni natte shimatta.
The way they have to collect more than a dozen tons of garbage in Ueno Park when the cherry blossom viewing season winds down, it makes you think

that the old adage about cleaning up after yourself has gone out the window.

❦ From the notion that waterfowl do not leave the water befowled upon flying off. Used as an exhortation to leave a place the way one found it.

te 手 hand, arm

Sure, we say "tongues of flame" in English, but just because they lick at the walls doesn't mean they can't be called hands. That's what they are in Japanese, "hands of flame," *hi no te*. Unlike *ude* which only means arm, *te* can mean either hand or arm. It can mean paw, too, for that matter. In fact, there's a neat expression about being so busy that you want to borrow a cat's paw: *neko no te mo karitai-gurai isogashii*.

Second only to *me* in the number of idioms in which it appears, *te* has many other meanings, including, for example, that thing you grab to lift a pot or pan, its handle; a worker or "hand"; someone's handwriting or their "hand"; a move as in chess or negotiations, or a particular way of doing something.

Te ga aku 手が空く "one's hand becomes empty"
be free, caught up (with one's work), have a minute

斎藤君、手が空いたら私の部屋に来てください。
Saitō-kun, te ga aitara watashi no heya ni kite kudasai.
Saito, come into my office when you've got a minute (you're not busy).

今はとても忙しいので、夕方手が空く頃また来て下さい。
Ima wa totemo isogashii no de, yūgata te ga aku koro mata kite kudasai.
I'm swamped right now, but I should be caught up this evening. Come around again then.

Also 手がすく *te ga suku*.

Te ga denai 手が出ない "one's hand doesn't go out"

(1) be too expensive for one (2) be too difficult for one

(1) あまりにも高くて手が出ない。
Amari ni mo takakute te ga denai.
It's way out of my range. / I could never afford that.

(2) 厄介な問題で私には手が出ない。
Yakkai na mondai de watashi ni wa te ga denai.
This is one tough puppy. I don't even know where to start.

Te ga hayai 手が早い "the hands are fast"

(1) be fast to put the make on a woman (2) be quick to fight

(1) あの男は女に手が早い。
Ano otoko wa onna ni te ga hayai.
He's a fast worker. / That dude moves quick. / He's a lady's man.

(2) あの男は口よりも手の方が早い。
Ano otoko wa kuchi yori mo te no hō ga hayai.
That guy doesn't waste time talking; he goes right into action (comes out fighting). / He shoots first and asks questions later.

Te ga kakaru 手がかかる "take (occupy) hands"
take time, be a hassle, be a big job

有機栽培は手がかかるそうだ。
Yūki-saibai wa te ga kakaru sō da.
They say that organic farming is quite a lot of work.

失恋のひとつやふたつで生きるの死ぬのと大騒ぎして、全く手のかかる奴だ。

Shitsuren no hitotsu ya futatsu de ikiru no shinu no to ōsawagi shite, mattaku te no kakaru yatsu da.

The guy's a real hassle, man. Gets dumped once or twice and goes off the deep end thinking it's the end of the world.

Te ga tarinai 手が足りない "not have enough hands"
not have enough help

年末は特に手が足りなくて困っている。
Nenmatsu wa toku ni te ga tarinakute komatte iru.
We're especially shorthanded around the end of the year.

肉体労働を嫌がる人が増えて、どこの工事現場でも手が足りないそうだ。
Nikutai-rōdō o iyagaru hito ga fuete, doko no kōji-genba de mo te ga tarinai sō da.
With fewer and fewer people willing to do manual labor, construction sites everywhere are suffering from a shortage of workers.

Te ga todoku 手が届く "one's hand reaches"

---

(1) [usually in the negative] reach, realize (2) painstaking, meticulous (3) almost [a certain age]

(1) 都心の庭付き一軒家なんて、一生働いても手が届かない。
Toshin no niwa-tsuki ikkenya nante, isshō hataraite mo te ga todokanai.
There's no way in hell I will ever be able to afford a house with a yard in the middle of town.

その主人公は、もう少しで願いに手が届くというところで死んだ。
Sono shujinkō wa, mō sukoshi de negai ni te ga todoku to iu tokoro de shinda.
The hero died just when his goal was within reach.

(2) 痒いところに手が届くようなもてなしをしてくれた。
Kayui tokoro ni te ga todoku yō na motenashi o shite kureta.
They saw to my every need. / The service there left nothing to be desired. / They catered to may every whim.

(3) 彼女のお父さんなら、60に手が届くか届かないかというところだろうか。
Kanojo no otōsan nara, rokujū ni te ga todoku ka todokanai ka to iu tokoro darō ka.
Her dad? He must be pushing sixty or so, I'd say.

Te ga tsukerarenai 手がつけられない "can't put one's hand on something"
be cut of control, running wild

彼は夕べから荒れ狂って、全く手がつけられない。
Kare wa yūbe kara arekurutte, mattaku te ga tsukerarenai.
He went bananas last night and has been completely out of control ever since.

彼女は昔、手のつけられないあばずれだった。
Kanojo wa mukashi, te no tsukerarenai abazure datta.
She really used to be a wild bitch.

よくもこんな手がつけられないほど散らかっている部屋に住めるね。
Yoku mo konna te ga tsukerarenai hodo chirakatte iru heya ni sumeru ne.
How can you stand to live in a room like this? It looks like a tornado just went through.

Te mo ashi mo denai 手も足も出ない "neither hands nor feet will move out"
be unable to do something, can't handle, can't get to first base

---

柔道3段の田中さんが相手では手も足も出ない。

Jūdō san-dan no Tanaka-san ga aite de wa te mo ashi mo denai.
I don't have a snowball's chance in hell up against a guy like Tanaka, who's got a third-degree black belt in Jūdō.

数学の試験問題は難しくて手も足も出なかった。
Sūgaku no shiken-mondai wa muzukashikute te mo ashi mo denakatta.
The problems on the math test were so difficult that I didn't even know where to start (knew I was in over my head).

Te ni ireru 手に入れる "get something in one's hand"
get hold of, land

ずっと欲しかった人形をやっとの思いで手に入れた。
Zutto hoshikatta ningyō o yatto no omoi de te ni ireta.
I finally got the doll I had wanted for so long.

この壺は知人に頼んで手に入れたものです。
Kono tsubo wa chijin ni tanonde te ni ireta mono desu.
This pot is one that I had a friend of mine pick up for me.

Te ni noru 手に乗る "ride someone's hand"
[in the negative] not fall for, not bite

どんなにおだてても、その手には乗らないよ。
Donna ni odatete mo, sono te ni wa noranai yo.
You can soft-soap me all you want, but there's no way I'm going to fall for it.

泣いても、今度はその手には乗らない。
Naite mo, kondo wa sono te ni wa noranai.
Cry all you want. I'm not buying it, not this time.

Te ni oenai 手に負えない "the hands can't take on"
be out of one's control, have one's hands full with something

---

事態は手に負えなくなった。
Jitai wa te ni oenaku natta.
The situation got out of hand.

今度の仕事は私一人では手に負えません。
Kondo no shigoto wa watashi hitori de wa te ni oemasen.
This is one job I can't handle alone.

↪ *te o yaku* 手を焼く

Te ni suru 手にする "make into a hand"
gain, get, acquire, win

こんな高価な物を手にするのは初めてだ。
Konna kōka na mono o te ni suru no wa hajimete da.
This is the first time I've ever had anything this expensive.

彼女は努力の末今の幸せを手にした。
Kanojo wa doryoku no sue ima no shiawase o te ni shita.
She kept plugging away and finally found happiness.

現役の議員が勝利を手にすることはなかった。
Gen'eki no giin ga shōri o te ni suru koto wa nakatta.
The incumbent congressman couldn't pull the election off (came up a loser).

Te ni toru yō 手に取るよう "as if one could almost take something in hand"
perfectly, clearly

彼の考えていることが手に取るようにわかった。
Kare no kangaete iru koto ga te ni toru yō ni wakatta.
I could read his thoughts like a book. / I knew exactly what he was thinking.

窓の下を通る人の話し声が、手に取るように聞こえた。

Mado no shita o tōru hito no hanashi-goe ga, te ni toru yō ni kikoeta.
I could hear people talking as clear as a bell as they passed below the window.

Te ni tsukanai 手につかない "won't stick to one's hand"
can't get down to, can't concentrate on

宝くじの当選発表が気になって、仕事が手につかない。
Takarakuji no tōsen-happyō ga ki ni natte, shigoto ga te ni tsukanai.
I just can't seem to get down to work because I'm thinking all the time about who's going to win the lottery.

テレビの音がうるさくて試験勉強が手につかない。
Terebi no oto ga urusakute shiken-benkyō ga te ni tsukanai.
The TV is so loud that it's keeping me from studying for the test.

Te ni wataru 手に渡る "cross into one's hand"
be passed on to

権力はタカ派の手に渡った。
Kenryoku wa taka-ha no te ni watatta.
Power was passed on to the hawks.

宝物のありかを書いた地図が、盗賊の手に渡ってしまった。
Takaramono no arika o kaita chizu ga, tōzoku no te ni watatte shimatta.
The map showing the location of the hidden treasure fell into the hands of some robbers.

Te no uchi o yomu 手の内を読む "read someone's palm"
read, see through

相手チームにすっかり手の内を読まれてしまった。
Aite-chīmu ni sukkari te no uchi o yomarete shimatta.

The other team saw right through us. / The other team read our every move.

相手の手の内を先に読んだ方が勝ちだ。
Aite no te no uchi o saki ni yonda hō ga kachi da.
Whichever side is first to figure out what the other side is up to is going to win.

Te o dasu 手を出す "stick out one's hand"

(1) throw a punch (2) get involved in (3) put the make on, hit on

(1) あのデブが先に手を出したんだ。
Ano debu ga saki ni te o dashitan da.
That fat mother threw the first punch (started it).

(2) 競馬に手を出すべきではなかった。
Keiba ni te o dasu beki de wa nakatta.
I should have never started playing the ponies.

(3) 俺の女に手を出すな。
Ore no onna ni te o dasu na.
Keep your mitts off my woman. / You best not be trying to put a move on (hit on) my woman, Jack.

Te o hiku 手を引く "pull one's hand"
leave, get out, back out, drop out, give something up

政治情勢は不安定だが、アメリカの企業はそれだけでその国から手を引くことはないだろう。
Seiji-jōsei wa fu-antei da ga, Amerika no kigyō wa sore dake de sono kuni kara te o hiku koto wa nai darō.
American businesses are not going to pull up stakes just because the political situation in the country is unstable.

私はこの計画から手を引かせてもらう。

Watashi wa kono keikaku kara te o hikasete morau.
I'm pulling out of this project.

Te o hirogeru 手を広げる "spread out one's hands"
expand, diversify

彼はホテル経営にまで手を広げた。
Kare wa hoteru-keiei ni made te o hirogeta.
He expanded into the hotel business.

会社は手を広げすぎて倒産した。
Kaisha wa te o hirogesugite tōsan shita.
The company overextended itself and went under.

Te o kae shina o kae 手を変え品を変え "change hands and change products"
every possible means, every trick in the book, the whole bag of tricks

---

彼は手を変え品を変え、彼女の機嫌を取ろうとしていた。
Kare wa te o kae shina o kae, kanojo no kigen o torō to shite ita.
He tried everything under the sun to get on her good side.

セールスマンは手を変え品を変え、商品を売りつけようとした。
Sērusuman wa te o kae shina o kae, shōhin o uritsukeyō to shita.
This salesman tried more ways than you could shake a stick at to get me to buy something.

Also あの手この手（を使う）*ano te kono te (o tsukau).*

Te o kasu 手を貸す "lend a hand"
lend a hand

ちょっと手を貸してもらえませんか。
Chotto te o kashite moraemasen ka.
Would you mind giving me a hand for a second?

山崎は、自分の兄弟を殺す謀略に手を貸した。
Yamasaki wa, jibun no kyōdai o korosu bōryaku ni te o kashita.
Yamazaki helped engineer a scheme to kill his own brother.

Te o kiru 手を切る "cut one's hand"
be through with something, cut something loose

「この仕事を最後に、あの連中とは手を切る」と彼は言った。
"Kono shigoto o saigo ni, ano renchū to wa te o kiru" to kare wa itta.
He said, "This is the last job I'm doing with those scumbags. I'm calling it quits."

See also 足を洗う *ashi o arau.*

Te o nuku 手を抜く "pull one's hand out"
cut corners, skate

彼は最近仕事の手を抜いている。
Kare wa saikin shigoto no te o nuite iru.
Recently he's been skating on the job.

あの業者は工事の手を抜いて訴えられた。
Ano gyōsha wa kōji no te o nuite uttaerareta.
The contractor was sued for cutting corners on his buildings (for shoddy construction practices).

Te o someru 手を染める "dye one's hand"
start, begin, get involved

彼は悪事に手を染めてしまった。
Kare wa akuji ni te o somete shimatta.
He went bad. / He got mixed up with the wrong people.

株に手を染めて大失敗した。
Kabu ni te o somete dai-shippai shita.
He tried his hand at the stock market and fell flat on his face.

Te o tsukau **手を使う** "use a hand"
use some way, use some means

彼は不正な手を使って、その土地をものにした。
Kare wa fusei na te o tsukatte, sono tochi o mono ni shita.
He got that land in an underhanded way.

どんな手を使っても、この計画は成功させる。
Donna te o tsukatte mo, kono keikaku wa seikō saseru.
I don't care how I do it, but I'm going to see that this project makes it.

Te o tsukeru **手をつける** "put one's hand on"

---

(1) start, begin (2) screw, lay (a woman) (3) embezzle money

(1) そろそろ次の仕事に手をつけよう。
Sorosoro tsugi no shigoto ni te o tsukeyō.
I guess I'm about ready to get started on something else.

片づけたくても、散らかり過ぎて、どこから手をつけたらいいのかわからない。
Katazuketakute mo, chirakarisugite, doko kara te o tsuketara ii no ka wakaranai.
I'd really like to straighten up the place, but it's so cluttered I don't know where to begin.

(2) あの教師は、生徒に手をつけて学校を首になった。
Ano kyōshi wa, seito ni te o tsukete gakkō o kubi ni natta.
That teacher got fired for poking (fooling around with) one of the students.

(3) 彼は、会社の金に手をつけてとうとう首になった。
Kare wa, kaisha no kane ni te o tsukete tōtō kubi ni natta.
He was caught with his hand in the till and ended up getting fired.

Te o tsukusu 手を尽くす "use up all one's hands"
try everything, do one's best

彼女の行方を八方手を尽くして捜した。
Kanojo no yukue o happō te o tsukushite sagashita.
I did my level best to find her.

医者は、出来るかぎりの手は尽くしたが、患者はやはり手遅れだった。
Isha wa, dekiru kagiri no te wa tsukushita ga, kanja wa yahari teokure datta.
The doctors did everything they could, but the patient was too far gone.

Te o utsu 手を打つ "hit one's hand"

---

(1) do something (about), make a move (2) shake (hands) on it

(1) 冗談を言うほかには、手の打ちようがなかった。
Jōdan o iu hoka ni wa, te no uchiyō ga nakatta.
I'm afraid there wasn't much we could do except laugh it off.

今すぐ手を打たなければ、環境は破壊される。
Ima sugu te o utanakereba, kankyō wa hakai sareru.
If we don't do something right away, the environment will be destroyed.

(2) 仕方がない、500万円で手を打ちましょう。
Shikata ga nai, gohyaku-man-en de te o uchimashō.
Well, all right, five million yen it is. Let's shake on it.

Te o yaku 手を焼く "burn one's hand"
have one's hands full

あの子供には手を焼くよ。
Ano kodomo ni wa te o yaku yo.
That kid is a real handful.
メーカーは電気自動車の設計に手を焼いている。
Mēkā wa denki-jidōsha no sekkei ni te o yaite iru.
Automobile manufacturers are having trouble designing an electric car.

↝ *te ni oenai* 手に負えない

Te o yasumeru 手を休める "give one's hand a rest"
take a break, stop doing something

お姉さん、ちょっと手を休めてテレビゲームでもやろうよ。
Onē-san, chotto te o yasumete terebi-gēmu de mo yarō yo.
Come on, Sis, put down what you're doing and let's play a video game or something.

母は編み物の手を休めて、テレビを見た。
Haha wa amimono no te o yasumete, terebi o mita.
Mom put down her knitting to watch TV for a while.

teishu-kanpaku 亭主関白 "husband and Chief Adviser to the Emperor"

a tyrant in his own home, a despotic husband, a husband who lords it over his wife

彼は会社じゃおとなしいけど、家じゃすごい亭主関白らしいよ。
Kare wa kaisha ja otonashii kedo, uchi ja sugoi teishu-kanpaku rashii yo.

At the office he's as quiet as a mouse, but at home he's a right little Hitler, it seems.

うちは蚤の夫婦だから、かかあ天下に見えるけど、実は亭主関白なの。
Uchi wa nomi no fūfu da kara, kakā-denka ni mieru kedo, jitsu wa teishu-kanpaku na no.
I'm much bigger than my husband, so people often think I wear the pants at home. In fact, it's him who's the boss.

🐾 かかあ天下 (*kakā-denka*) refers to a wife who wears the pants in the family. 蚤の夫婦 (*nomi no fūfu*) refers to a married couple where the wife is big and fat, and the husband small and thin. In Japanese it is "Mr. and Mrs. Flea," while in English we might say "Jack Sprat and his wife."

tekizai-tekisho 適材適所 "the appropriate material (in) the appropriate place"

the right person in the right place; the right person for the right job; just the person we need; just the ticket; well suited for the job (role)

適材適所と言いながら、実は情実人事が横行している。
Tekizai-tekisho to iinagara, jitsu wa jōjitsu-jinji ga ōkō shite iru.
They're always talking about choosing the best man for the job, but the fact is that favoritism rules the day.

優秀な人材を適材適所で使っていかなければ駄目だよ。
Yūshū na jinzai o tekizai-tekisho de tsukatte ikanakereba dame da yo.
You've got to use the best people you have effectively, putting the right people in the right places.

年功序列にこだわらず、適材適所の精神で、若い人をどんどん活用していきたいんだ。
Nenkō-joretsu ni kodawarazu, tekizai-tekisho no seishin de, wakai hito o dondon katsuyō shite ikitai n' da.

We want to make full use of our younger staff, putting them in jobs best suited to their abilities, without worrying about questions of seniority.

ten'i-muhō 天衣無縫 "heavenly garments without a stitch (showing)"

perfect, flawless; (a person of) artless and unaffected character; without artifice (airs and graces)

この書家の天衣無縫な作風は誰にも真似が出来ない。
Kono shoka no ten'i-muhō na sakufū wa dare ni mo mane ga dekinai.
Nobody could possibly emulate this calligrapher's free and easy style.

彼は天才肌の優秀な男だが、天衣無縫過ぎたのが裏目に出た。
Kare wa tensai-hada no yūshū na otoko da ga, ten'i-muhō sugita no ga urame ni deta.
He is touched with genius, but his lack of guile has turned to his disadvantage.

※ The literal meaning of 天衣無縫 is that angels' clothes show no trace of human handicraft (of having been sewn by the human hand). Their garments are so immaculate, there isn't a stitch showing. From this came the figurative meaning of something being very natural and beautiful, and it was often used to describe poetry or prose that was of impeccable style. Nowadays this meaning is no longer current; instead 天衣無縫 is now used as a synonym for 天真爛漫 (*tenshin-ranman*; see below); it is used to describe someone who doesn't worry too much about what other people think, who says what he thinks and does what he wants, but who has no malice in him and so is usually not thought ill of.

tenka-ippin 天下一品 "only one under the sky"

be unrivalled, second to none, be tops, be out of this world

うちの兄貴のスピーチは天下一品だよ。どこであんなに上手になったんだろう。
Uchi no aniki no supīchi wa tenka-ippin da yo. Doko de anna ni jōzu ni natta n' darō.
My big brother's speeches are really something else. I wonder where he got to be so good.

玲子さんのお料理は天下一品ね。
Reiko-san no oryōri wa tenka-ippin ne.
Reiko's cooking is really out of this world.

tenshin-ranman 天真爛漫 "heavenly purity overflowing"

naivety, simplicity, innocence

天真爛漫な子供の笑顔を見ていると、嫌なことも忘れられます。
Tenshin-ranman na kodomo no egao o mite iru to, iya na koto mo wasureraremasu.
Just seeing a child's innocent smiling face makes us forget all the bad in the world.

うちのおばあちゃんはまるで子供のように天真爛漫で、誰にでも好かれるんだ。
Uchi no obāchan wa marude kodomo no yō ni tenshin-ranman de, dare ni de mo sukareru n' da.
My grandmother has a child's innocent naivety and is loved by everyone.

監督の天真爛漫な人柄のせいでチームの人気はうなぎ上りだ。
Kantoku no tenshin-ranman na hitogara no sei de chīmu no ninki wa unaginobori da.
Thanks to our manager's open, forthright nature, our team's popularity is skyrocketing.

to(n)bi とび／とんび（鳶） kite

As may be garnered from one of the entries included below, these slender, graceful hawks are one rung down on the linguistic ledger from their usually larger cousins. They make their homes near human habitations or the ocean and circle high above, searching for the carrion upon which they often feed.

Their high-pitched cry is *pīhyororo* ピーヒョロロ. They are counted *ichiwa* 一羽.

To(n)bi ni aburaage o sarawareru **鳶に油揚げをさらわれる**
  "to have the deep-fried bean curd carried off by a kite"
have something stolen that was almost in one's hand, have one's share snatched away at the last moment

---

鳶に油揚げをさらわれるというけどまさか親友に彼女を取られるとは思わなかった。
Tonbi ni aburaage o sarawareru to iu kedo masaka shin'yū ni kanojo o torareru to wa omowanakatta.
Who would have ever thought that such a close friend would up and steal my girl.

ダントツで首位だったドライバーが最終周でエンジントラブル、2位が優勝して、鳶に油揚げをさらわれた形になった。
Dantotsu de shui datta doraibā ga saishū-shū de enjin toraburu, nii ga yūshō shite, tonbi ni aburaage o sarawareta katachi ni natta.
After being way out in front, he snatched defeat from the jaws of victory by losing to the number two car when engine trouble forced him to drop out on the last lap.

Of things, thought to have been uncontestably one's own, being stolen by someone else, usually at the last minute.

Tobi (tonbi) ga taka o umu 鳶が鷹を生む "a kite gives birth to a hawk"

parents may have children who are much better than they are

> あの人の子が東大に入るなんて、鳶が鷹を生んだんだよそれは。
> *Ano hito no ko ga Tōdai ni hairu nante, tonbi ga taka o unda n' da yo sore wa.*
> His kid's getting into Tokyo University shows that anybody can have a genius in the family.
>
> 鳶が鷹を生むっていうけど、あの八百屋の娘はまさにそれだ。
> *Tonbi ga taka o umu tte iu kedo, ano yaoya no musume wa masani sore da.*
> That greengrocer's daughter is living proof that kids can turn out better than their parents.

🦅 From the notion that a kite is lesser than other hawks comes this notion that an ordinary couple can have extraordinary children.

↪ *kaeru no ko wa kaeru* 蛙の子は蛙

Tobishoku 鳶職 "kite work"

construction work; a construction worker, a hardhat, (especially) a steeplejack

> 俺の親父は鳶職で、若い頃に一度大けがして命拾いしてるんだ。
> *Ore no oyaji wa tobishoku de, wakai koro ni ichido ōkega shite inochi-biroi shiteru n' da.*
> My old man's a hardhat, and once he almost got killed on the job.
>
> 最近は3Kなどといわれて、鳶職が少なくなっている。
> *Saikin wa san-kei nado to iwarete, tobishoku ga sukunaku natte iru.*
> With the aversion lately for difficult, dangerous, and dirty work, there are fewer and fewer people willing to work high up in scaffolding.

🐦 Of construction workers, especially when their duties take them high up on scaffolding. Also *tobi no mono* 鳶の者 or simply *tobi* 鳶. Formerly of firemen, men involved in the moving of logs, as well as construction workers, the appellation arises from the fact that men doing such work carried pikelike fire hooks or other sharply hooked poles that resembled the kite's beak.

tobu tori o otosu ikioi 飛ぶ鳥を落とす勢い
"powerful enough to bring down a bird in flight"

high-flying, very energetic, vigorous; powerful; influential

彼は飛ぶ鳥を落とす勢いで出世した。
Kare wa tobu tori o otosu ikioi de shusse shita.
He practically shot to the top. / He got on the fast track and went right to the top.

飛ぶ鳥を落とす勢いだった日本車の輸出も今では昔話になりつつある。
Tobu tori o otosu ikioi datta Nihonsha no yushutsu mo ima de wa mukashibanashi ni naritsutsu aru.
The Japanese auto export juggernaut is well on its way to being a thing of the past.

🐦 Perhaps from the notion that it requires a great deal of speed for a projectile to hit and kill a bird on the wing.

todo とど (鯔) (a grown) mullet

A common food fish found throughout the warm waters of the world, the mullet lends its name, at least one of its names, to a single idiom.

Todo no tsumari **とどのつまり** "the end mullet"
in the end, finally, eventually; when all is said and done, in the final analysis

---

とどのつまり、彼は女にだまされたということだよ。
Todo no tsumari, kare wa onna ni damasareta to iu koto da yo.
He ended up getting taken in by some woman.

とどのつまり、マスコミが騒いだだけに終わった。
Todo no tsumari, masukomi ga sawaida dake ni owatta.
When all was said and done, it was nothing but media hype.

🐟 This idiom comes from the fact that this fish goes through so many name changes as it grows that it must suffer an identity crisis. Called *oboko, subashiri, ina, bora*, and the final one from which this idiom is derived, *todo*; hence the meaning "eventually" or "finally."

tokage とかげ (蜥蜴) lizard

Like other reptiles, the lizard doesn't have much of a following—there are no Lizard Days in Japan. There was a bit of excitement in the late 1980s when Japanese TV viewers were introduced to the frilled lizard by Japan's ad industry in a Mitsubishi Motors commercial for its Mirage model. But that has all died down at the time of this writing, and the little scamps are probably running around happily in the natural light of the Australian desert again (at least those that survived the rigors of commercial film making).

   Lizards are counted *ippiki* 一匹.

Tokage no shippo-kiri **とかげのしっぽ切り** "breaking off a lizard's tail"

pass the buck to one's subordinate; save one's ass by sacrificing an underling, throw someone to the lions (wolves)

市役所の汚職事件の処罰はとかげのしっぽ切りで終わってしまった。
Shi-yakusho no oshoku-jiken no shobatsu wa tokage no shippo-kiri de owatte shimatta.
The corruption scandal at city hall ended with subordinates taking the rap (being the fall guys/patsies) for the bigwigs.

オウム真理教のら致事件はとかげのしっぽ切りで終わらないだろう。
Ōmu Shinri-kyō no rachi-jiken wa tokage no shippo-kiri de owaranai darō.
The Supreme Truth Sect abductions won't end with the underlings being thrown to the lions (going to the gallows for the real criminals).

✌ From a lizard's ability to detach its tail and regenerate another when pursued by children or other less rapacious predators.

tokui-manmen 得意満面 "a face full of pride"

looking pleased with yourself, looking smug, strutting about like a peacock, be as proud as a peacock

息子は第1志望校に合格して、得意満面だよ。
Musuko wa daiichi-shibōkō ni gōkaku shite, tokui-manmen da yo.
When our son got into his first-choice university, he went round looking as proud as a peacock.

あいつ、ちょっとほめられたと思って、得意満面になってるぜ。
Aitsu, chotto homerareta to omotte, tokui-manmen ni natte 'ru ze.
He thinks he's the cat's whiskers just because he got a pat on the back.

※ 喜色満面 (*kishoku-manmen*) is a neutral expression used to describe someone who looks happy. However 得意満面 is used pejoratively to imply that the person is a bit too pleased. It is often used when criticizing or simply teasing someone.

tonbo とんぼ（蜻蛉） **dragonfly**

These delightful creatures formerly numbered in the zillions in Japan, where around two hundred species have been identified. Although numbers have decreased with urbanization, they remain a national favorite. Early texts recounting the mythological creation of the Japanese archipelago refer to the largest island with a word now thought by scholars to mean dragonfly. They were also formerly regarded as the embodied spirit of the rice plant (and harbinger of abundant harvests) or, in some regions, as the god of the paddy fields. The red dragonfly in particular was regarded as transporter of the spirits of departed souls. Children are especially discouraged from pulling off the wings of this insect. Dragonflies are counted *ippiki* 一匹.

Shirikire-tonbo 尻切れとんぼ "a dragonfly with its tail broken off"

unfinished, half-finished, half-done; fizzle out, sputter; start with a bang and end with a whimper; (of negotiations or discussions) be abruptly broken off

---

おまえの話はいつも尻切れとんぼだ。
Omae no hanashi wa itsumo shirikire-tonbo da.
You never finish what you start out to say.

交渉は2時間以上も続いたにもかかわらず尻切れとんぼに終わった。

Kōshō wa niji-kan ijō mo tsuzuita ni mo kakawarazu shirikire-tonbo ni owatta.
Negotiations continued for more than two hours before being broken off.

↪ *chūto-hanpa* 中途半端

Tonbo-megane とんぼ眼鏡 "dragonfly eyeglasses"
big, round glasses (sunglasses)

これ若い頃に買ったとんぼ眼鏡、結構流行ったんだけど。
Kore wakai koro ni katta tonbo-megane, kekkō hayatta n' da kedo.
These are a pair of those great big sunglasses that used to be in when I was young.

とんぼ眼鏡がトレードマークだった女優最近テレビに出なくなったね。
Tonbo-megane ga torēdomāku datta joyū saikin terebi ni denaku natta ne.
That actress whose trademark was those great big glasses hasn't been on TV much lately, has she?

🐞 From the resemblance of the large size and round shape of the glasses to the eyes of a dragonfly.

Tonbogaeri とんぼ返り "a dragonfly turnaround"

---

1. (in acrobatics) a midair somersault; (in swimming) a somersault turn

彼はとんぼ返りが得意な役者だ。
Kare wa tonbogaeri ga tokui na yakusha da.
That actor's good at doing midair somersaults.

さあ今日はクロールととんぼ返りを練習しましょう。
Sā kyō wa kurōru to tonbogaeri o renshū shimashō.
OK, today we're going to practice the crawl and somersault turns.

2. (of a journey) a quick return (without a layover)

今日は東京と札幌のとんぼ返りの出張だった。
Kyō wa Tokyo to Sapporo no tonbogaeri no shutchō datta.
I had to go from Tokyo to Sapporo and back on business today.

香港に到着したとたん会社からの連絡で、休む暇もなくとんぼ返りさせられた。
Honkon ni tōchaku shita totan kaisha kara no renraku de, yasumu hima mo naku tonbogaeri saserareta.
No sooner had I arrived in Hong Kong than a message from the office had me turning around to head back without a moment's rest.

⚜ Of a quick trip from one place to another in which little time is spent at the destination, and the return is to the point of origin. From the dragonfly's ability to change direction quickly in flight.

tonde hi ni iru natsu no mushi 飛んで火に入る夏の虫 "a summer insect that has flown into the flames"

(like) a moth drawn to flame, self-destructive; ask for trouble, ask for it

彼の行動はまさに「飛んで火に入る夏の虫」であった。
Kare no kōdō wa masa ni "Tonde hi ni iru natsu no mushi" de atta.
He was just asking for trouble the way he was acting.

まさか本人が来るとは「飛んで火に入る夏の虫」だな。
Masaka honnin ga kuru to wa "Tonde hi ni iru natsu no mushi" da na.
Who would have ever thought she'd show her face here. She must have some kind of death wish.

⚜ From the observation that insects drawn to the flame die.

☞ *mushi* 虫

tonikaku とにかく（兎に角） "horns on a rabbit"

anyway, anyhow, in any case, at any rate, either way, even so, be that as it may

とにかく、彼に尋ねてみよう。
Tonikaku, kare ni tazunete miyō.
Anyway, I'll just ask him and see what's up.

とにかく、これ食べてごらんよ、美味しいから。
Tonikaku, kore tabete goran yo, oishii kara.
Don't give me that, just try it. It's really good.

とにかく、彼女は強情だ。
Tonikaku, kanojo wa gōjō da.
At any rate, she's one hardheaded woman.

※ The characters for rabbit and horn are said to be merely phonetic equivalents, though it is not a great leap to the notion that even in the unlikely event that rabbits were found to have horns, the speaker would still hold such-and-such to be the case, i.e., anyhow. But this is idle speculation.

tonma とん馬 "a stupid horse"

(of a person) an ass, airhead, idiot, a complete fool, zero, nitwit; (of what such a person does or says) stupidity, foolishness

財布を忘れるなんてとん馬だなあ。
Saifu o wasureru nante tonma da nā.
What a dumbfuck, losing your wallet like that.

入社式の日から遅刻するとはとん馬なやつだよ。
Nyūsha-shiki no hi kara chikoku suru to wa tonma na yatsu da yo.
Guy's got to be a certified zero to start a new job by arriving late to the welcoming ceremony for new employees.

⚐ No evidence that this expression ever meant "a stupid horse."

tora とら（虎） tiger

The king of beasts to most Japanese, perhaps because unlike the African lion it is close to home; indigenous to neighboring China and Korea and figuring in numerous folk tales and stories in the region. Widely feared for its ferocity and fabled predilection for attacking humans, the tiger was targeted by Japanese who traveled to the then distant Korean peninsula to eradicate them. While tigers survived that onslaught, they have not fared so well in modern times as their habitat is gradually being destroyed by ever expanding Asian populations and economies.

Tigers are counted any way they want to be, but *ippiki* 一匹 or *ittō* 一頭 are both safe.

When used as the third sign of the Chinese zodiac, *tora* is written 寅.

Koketsu ni irazunba koji o ezu 虎穴に入らずんば虎児を得ず
"You can't catch a tiger cub without going in the tiger's lair."
nothing ventured, nothing gained

「虎穴に入らずんば虎児を得ず」だ、思い切って彼女に気持ちを打ち明けてみたら。
"Koketsu ni irazunba koji o ezu" da, omoikitte kanojo ni kimochi o uchiakete mitara.
You know what they say, nothing ventured, nothing gained. Why don't you just tell her how you feel about her?

「虎穴に入らずんば虎子を得ず」、あのスラム街に潜入して情報収集するしかない。
"Koketsu ni irazunba koji o ezu," ano suramu-gai ni sennyū shite jōhō-shūshū suru shika nai.

Sometimes you've got to take risks. I guess there's no way around it, I've got to just go into the slum to get the info I need.

Tora ni naru　虎になる　"become a tiger"

a bad (violent, uncontrollable) drunk; get Dutch [drunken] courage; get shitfaced, falling-down drunk, bombed, blotto, tanked, dead drunk, drunk as a skunk, potted, smashed, embalmed, pissed, bent, potted

---

あの人は飲むと虎になるから一緒に飲むのはやめたよ。
Ano hito wa nomu to tora ni naru kara issho ni nomu no wa yameta yo.
He gets a mean streak whenever he ties one on, so I quit drinking with him.

昨日は久々に虎になったよ。
Kinō wa hisabisa ni tora ni natta yo.
I got wiped out yesterday for the first time in quite a while.

🥃 The association of tigers and alcohol is from the figurative reference to alcohol as *chikuyō* 竹葉 or *take no ha* 竹の葉, literally "bamboo leaves," and the belief that tigers lurk in bamboo groves. The association of tigers with alcohol is not uniquely Japanese. In American slang, for example, cheap or inferior liquor is called tiger piss or tiger sweat, and a strong alcoholic drink is known as tiger juice.

Tora no i o karu kitsune　虎の威を借る狐　"a fox borrowing the prestige of a lion"

an otherwise powerless person strutting about or throwing his weight around because of the power of the person he works for; an ass in a lion's skin; a nobody acting big because of his superior's power

---

あいつは社長の息子だと思って虎の威を借る狐になっているんだ。
Aitsu wa shachō no musuko da to omotte tora no i o karu kitsune ni natte iru n' da.

He thinks he can throw his weight around just because he's the president's son.

あんな虎の威を借る狐は相手にしなくて大丈夫だよ。
Anna tora no i o karu kitsune wa aite ni shinakute daijōbu da yo.
He's just acting big because he's got some guy upstairs behind him. You don't have to pay any attention to him.

Tora no ko　**虎の子**　"tiger cub"
one's treasure; (of money) one's nest egg

彼は虎の子の貯金をはたいたが事業に失敗した。
Kare wa tora no ko no chokin o hataita ga jigyō ni shippai shita.
He put up all his savings, but the business failed.

全日本は虎の子の1点を守り切れず、引き分けてしまった。
Zen-Nippon wa tora no ko no itten o mamorikirezu, hikiwakete shimatta.
The All-Japan team couldn't hold on to its hard-earned one-point lead, and the game ended in a tie.

彼女は長年かけて貯めた虎の子の金を男に騙し取られた。
Kanojo wa naganen kakete tameta tora no ko no kane o otoko ni damashitorareta.
She had the nest egg she'd saved up for years ripped off by some guy.

🐾 From the belief that a tiger takes very good care of its cubs. By convention this expression is used most commonly upon the loss of something treasured.

Tora no maki　**虎の巻**　"a tiger-tome"
a crib, a pony, a study guide; a book of secret teachings

その虎の巻どこで手に入れたの。
Sono tora no maki doko de te ni ireta no.
Where'd you get ahold of that pony?

この虎の巻を使って勉強すれば試験はバッチリだ。
Kono tora no maki o tsukatte benkyō sureba shiken wa batchiri da.
With this crib, the test'll be a breeze.

この虎の巻さえあれば、鬼に金棒だ。
Kono tora no maki sae areba, oni ni kanabō da.
There'll be no stopping you with this pony in your arsenal.

これが伊賀忍者の虎の巻です。
Kore ga Iga-ninja no tora no maki desu.
This contains the secret teachings of the Iga ninja.

🐰 From an ancient Chinese text expounding secret military strategies. As the last example illustrates, it also means a text that encapsulates the secrets of an artistic or martial tradition or its practices. In the sense of "crib" it is also called *torakan* 虎巻 or *anchoko* アンチョコ, the latter said to be a corruption of *anchoku* 安直, which in addition to meaning cheap or inexpensive, also means easy or simple.

toranu tanuki no kawazan'yō 捕らぬ狸の皮算用
"counting the pelts of untrapped raccoon dogs"

counting one's chickens before they hatch

「この計算でいけば、10カ月で100万儲かるよ。」
"Kono keisan de ikeba, jukkagetsu de hyaku-man mōkaru yo."
"The way I've got it figured, we're gonna make a million yen in ten months."
「捕らぬ狸の皮算用にならなければいいけど。」
"Toranu tanuki no kawazan'yō ni naranakereba ii kedo."
"Let's just hope we're not counting our chickens before they hatch."

あいつはいつも捕らぬ狸の皮算用ばかりで、言ったとおりになったことがない。
Aitsu wa itsumo toranu tanuki no kawazan'yō bakari de, itta tōri ni natta koto ga nai.

She's always counting her chickens before they hatch; nothing ever turns out the way she says it will.

🦝 In addition to the usual explanation of overeagerness, another theory regarding this idiom relates to the *tanuki*'s ability to possess a human. In this somewhat farfetched view, the number of *tanuki* pelts actually taken differs from the count because the wily animal has somehow deceived the trapper.

tori とり（鳥） bird

The generic word for feathered fellows of all kinds, *tori* is also used to mean chicken or pheasant, and *toriniku* 鳥肉 is the word for "chicken," as in "meat" or "fowl."

Tatsu tori ato o nigosazu 立つ鳥跡を濁さず "Birds taking to flight leave nothing sullied behind."
clean up a place before one leaves, leave a place like one found it

---

ちゃんと掃除してから帰りなさい、立つ鳥跡を濁さずと言うでしょう。
Chanto sōji shite kara kaerinasai, tatsu tori ato o nigosazu to iu deshō.
Clean up before you leave. You know what they say about leaving a place like you found it.

花見の季節の上野公園のゴミは十数トンにのぼる、立つ鳥跡を濁さずは鳥の世界だけのものになってしまった。
Hanami no kisetsu no Ueno-kōen no gomi wa jūsū ton ni noboru, tatsu tori ato o nigosazu wa tori no sekai dake no mono ni natte shimatta.
The way they have to collect more than a dozen tons of garbage in Ueno Park when the cherry blossom viewing season winds down, it makes you think that the old adage about cleaning up after yourself has gone out the window.

✌ From the notion that waterfowl do not leave the water befowled upon flying off. Used as an exhortation to leave a place the way one found it.

Tobu tori o otosu ikioi **飛ぶ鳥を落とす勢い** "powerful enough to bring down a bird in flight"
high-flying, very energetic, vigorous; powerful; influential

彼は飛ぶ鳥を落とす勢いで出世した。
Kare wa tobu tori o otosu ikioi de shusse shita.
He practically shot to the top. / He got on the fast track and went right to the top.

飛ぶ鳥を落とす勢いだった日本車の輸出も今では昔話になりつつある。
Tobu tori o otosu ikioi datta Nihonsha no yushutsu mo ima de wa mukashibanashi ni naritsutsu aru.
The Japanese auto export juggernaut is well on its way to being a thing of the past.

✌ Perhaps from the notion that it requires a great deal of speed for a projectile to hit and kill a bird on the wing.

Tori mo kayowanu **鳥も通わぬ** "even birds don't frequent"
isolated, remote, deserted

その寺は鳥も通わぬ山奥にあった。
Sono tera wa tori mo kayowanu yamaoku ni atta.
The remote temple was situated deep in the mountains.

人との接触を嫌ったその老人は鳥も通わぬ離れ小島で余生を送った。
Hito to no sesshoku o kiratta sono rōjin wa tori mo kayowanu hanarekojima de yosei o okutta.

Wanting nothing to do with human beings, the old man spent his remaining years on an isolated outlying island.

⚜ From the notion that if not even birds, which seem to be just about everywhere, aren't around, a place must be way out in the sticks. It is used adjectivally of remote places.

Torihada ga tatsu　鳥肌が立つ　"chicken skin stands"
get goose bumps (goose pimples, gooseflesh)

寒いな、ほら見てよ、鳥肌が立ってるよ。
Samui na, hora mite yo, torihada ga tatte 'ru yo.
Burr, it's cold. Just look, I've got goose bumps all over.

昨夜のコンサートは鳥肌が立つほど感動した。
Sakuya no konsāto wa torihada ga tatsu hodo kandō shita.
Last night's concert was so great that it actually gave me goose pimples.

⚜ Metaphoric use about how cold, fearful, or exciting something may be; usually expressed by adding 〜ような. Examples of this use follow.

Torihada ga tatsu yō na　鳥肌が立つような　"enough to make chicken skin stand"
cold (frightening, exciting) enough to give one goose bumps

鳥肌が立つようなぞっとする光景を目の当たりにして、彼は身動きひとつできなかった。
Torihada ga tatsu yō na zotto suru kōkei o ma no atari ni shite, kare wa miugoki hitotsu dekinakatta.
He stood there unable to move as the horrific sight unfolded before him.

今日は鳥肌が立つような寒さだなあ。
Kyō wa torihada ga tatsu yō na samusa da nā.
Jeez, it's cold enough to give you goose pimples today.

Torime 鳥目 "bird eyes"
night blindness, nyctalopia; a night-blind person

> 私は鳥目です。
> *Watashi wa torime desu.*
> I am night blind. / I can't see at night.

> 鳥目の彼女は交差点の向こうにいるボーイフレンドに気づかなかった。
> *Torime no kanojo wa kōsaten no mukō ni iru bōifurendo ni kizukanakatta.*
> She was so night blind that she couldn't even make out her boyfriend, who was just across the intersection.

☙ From the observation that the majority of birds do not see well at night, this slang term for the medical condition is most commonly used of people who just have trouble seeing in the dark. Jocular, it is rarely used for the actual medical condition.

↪ *tori / niwatori* とり／にわとり(鶏)

tori / niwatori とり／にわとり（鶏） chicken

This common barnyard fowl figures in few idioms, none of which indicate it is held in any particular esteem in Japan. In general, compounds incorporating the character for chicken display the disdain in which this lowly yardbird is held. *Keikan* 鶏姦, literally "chicken rape," is a literary term for sodomy or pederasty, presumably from this barnyard fowl's indiscriminate amorousness. *Keigun* 鶏群, literally "a flock of chickens," is another literary term for a bunch of people raising a ruckus over nothing. From this term comes the idiom *keigun no ikkaku* 鶏群の一鶴, literally "a crane among chickens," that describes a person of superior qualities who stands out among surrounding pedestrian types. *Keikō* 鶏口, or "chicken mouth," is a term to describe the head of a small group. It figures in the idiom *keikō to naru mo gyūgo to naru nakare* 鶏口となるも牛後となる勿れ, literally "become a chicken's mouth, not a cow's butt." Loosely translated it means something like "better a big fish in a small pond than a small fish in a big one," though it is more accurately rendered as "better to lead a small group than follow in a large one." And finally, *keiroku* 鶏肋, "a chicken's breastbone," plays on the notion that while the amount of meat on a breastbone may not be much, it is just enough to make it difficult to throw away, and produces the metaphorical meaning of something or someone that is not particularly useful but doesn't quite warrant being gotten rid of. It can also mean a small, weak body.

Kazamidori　**風見鶏**　"a bird that looks at the wind"
a weathercock, an opportunist, an unprincipled person who follows the majority

---

あいつは風見鶏だから同僚からは信頼されていない。
Aitsu wa kazamidori da kara dōryō kara wa shinrai sarete inai.
The guy's such an opportunist that none of his co-workers trust him.

昔風見鶏と言われた日本の首相がいたが、その後政治スキャンダルで辞任した。
Mukashi kazamidori to iwareta Nihon no shushō ga ita ga, sono go seiji sukyandaru de jinin shita.
A long time ago there used to be a Japanese prime minister that everybody called the weathercock, but he resigned because of some political scandal.

🐦 This bird (*tori*) is really a chicken (*niwatori*). But the character can be pronounced *tori,* and is, in fact, so pronounced at meat markets all around the country. Ask for *toriniku*, or "bird meat," and you'll get chicken and not sparrow or pheasant. The weathervane usage is similar to the English and derives from the similarity of such a person to the erratic gyrations of the figurine atop buildings. Roosters make the sound *kokekokkō* コケコッコウ.

↪ *tori* とり(鳥)

Tōryūmon 登竜門 "climb the Dragon's Gate"

pass muster, get over an important hurdle

この文学賞は若手作家の登竜門と呼ばれている。
Kono bungaku-shō wa wakate-sakka no Tōryūmon to yobarete iru.
This literary prize is considered to guarantee (be the gateway to) success as an author.

君にとってこのプロジェクトは重役への登竜門だ。
Kimi ni totte kono purojekuto wa jūyaku e no Tōryūmon da.
Success (or failure) on this project will seal your fate as a future director with the company.

※ See note under *koi no takinobori* 鯉の滝登り for explanation.

↪ *koi* 鯉, *manaita no koi* まな板の鯉

tsubame つばめ (燕) swallow

This auspicious migratory bird comes to Japan each spring from Southeast Asia, and most return when the weather turns cold. Swallows are considered to herald the arrival of spring, where many consider a swallow's nest under the eaves of their home a sign that the household will prosper. In appreciation for having one's house selected by swallows as a nesting place, some families even place small shell amulets in the nest, believing that they will guarantee the safe birth of children. Swallows are counted *ichiwa* 一羽.

Wakai tsubame 若い燕 "a young swallow"
a young male lover, a gigilo

あの中年女優は若い燕と同棲している。
Ano chūnen-joyū wa wakai tsubame to dōsei shite iru.
That middle-aged actress is shacking up with some young stud.

京子最近若い燕ができたらしいわよ。
Kyōko saikin wakai tsubame ga dekita rashii wa yo.
It looks like Kyoko's found herself a young bohunk.

🕊 Of a young man who has attached himself to an older woman and is usually kept by her as a lover. Said to have originated during the Meiji period (1868–1912) when a famous woman's rights activist received a letter written by a painter (to whom she was later married by common law), in which he referred to himself as a *wakai tsubame*.

tsukeuma 付け馬 "an attached horse"

1. a person who goes home from a bar or cabaret with a customer to collect money he owes, a collector, enforcer

付け馬をつけるとは、あの店もやるねえ。
Tsukeuma o tsukeru to wa, ano mise mo yaru nē.
That place has got some nerve. Imagine sending someone home with a customer to put the squeeze on him.

あの人は一度飲み始めると付け馬を引くほど飲む。
Ano hito wa ichido nomihajimeru to tsukeuma o hiku hodo nomu.
That guy starts drinking and it never fails; he's always got to go home with some guy from the bar to get the money to pay up.

今どき付け馬を連れて帰る人など山田さん以外いないな。
Imadoki tsukeuma o tsurete kaeru hito nado Yamada-san igai inai na.
Yamada's the only guy I know who still gets followed home from bars by dunners.

❧ From the practice of sending someone home with a patron to collect the money for his bar or brothel bill. Based on its reported relation to *uma-tsunagi* 馬繋ぎ, "hitching post," or the act of tying up a horse to such an object, we may speculate that use of the expression derives from such tethering of a horse in order to prevent it from wandering away. Hence, although it remains unclear whether it is from the patron tethered to the collector (*tsukeuma o tsukeru* or *hiku*) or from the collector tethered to the drinking establishment (*tsukeuma*) that the idiom arises, its origin is clearly to be found in keeping a horse tied up.

2. (criminal argot) a (police) tail

おまえ付け馬されてるぞ。
Omae tsukeuma sarete 'ru zo.
You're being tailed, man.

tsume 爪 fingernail, claw

This is one of those words that you can use for several similar things that require different words in English. People have fingernails, cats claws, and birds of prey talons, but in Japanese they all simply have *tsume*. Other meanings of the word include picks or plectrums, the prongs or claws that hold a gemstone in the setting of a ring, and other such devices that hold things in place. *Tsume* is also used to mean an extremely small amount of something.

Lighting your fingernail instead of a candle is certainly one way to cut back on expenses, I suppose. The first expression below evokes an interesting image that should make it easy to remember. In English, a person so inclined is nothing other than a skinflint!

Tsume ni hi o tomosu　**爪に火をともす**　"light one's fingernail"
be very frugal, tightfisted

この100万円は、爪に火をともすようにして貯めたお金です。
Kono hyaku-man-en wa, tsume ni hi o tomosu yō ni shite tameta okane desu.
I pinched pennies to save up this million yen.

私が爪に火をともすようにして貯めたお金を、彼は博打で一晩
のうちになくしてしまった。
Watashi ga tsume ni hi o tomosu yō ni shite tameta okane o, kare wa bakuchi de hitoban no uchi ni nakushite shimatta.
In one night at the tables he blew all the money I had scrimped and saved to get.

Tsume no aka o senjite nomu　**爪の垢をせんじて飲む**　"boil the dirt from someone's nails and drink it"
emulate someone, try to be like someone

僕も頭がよくなるように、君の爪の垢をせんじて飲ませてくれ。
Boku mo atama ga yoku naru yō ni, kimi no tsume no aka o senjite nomasete kure.
I just want to be smart like you. Tell me what I should do.

田中さんの爪の垢をせんじて飲みなさい。
Tanaka-san no tsume no aka o senjite nominasai.
You ought to take a lesson from Tanaka.

Tsume o togu　**爪を研ぐ**　"sharpen one's claws"
wait for an opportunity to do something

彼は、逆転ホームランを打つチャンスを、爪を研いで狙っていた。
Kare wa, gyakuten-hōmuran o utsu chance o, tsume o toide neratte ita.
He was licking his chops at the chance to hit a homer that would turn the game around.

彼は長い間、復讐の爪を研いできた。
Kare wa nagai aida, fukushū no tsume o toide kita.
He waited a long time for a chance to get even.

tsuru つる(鶴) **crane**

Known for its grace and beauty, the crane has long been revered in Japan as a sacred bird that embodied a divine spirit and transported it to Japan's shores from distant lands. Folk legend throughout Japan has the crane bringing rice cultivation to Japan from the north, and the bird's yearly arrival in winter is a newsworthy event that prompts television reports and specials even today.

Japanese folk legend also associates the crane with the weather. It is thought that the bird, craning its neck upward with a whoop, signals blue skies ahead, and looking down, conversely, rain.

Finally, as can be seen from the phrase *tsuru wa sennen kame wa mannen* 鶴は千年亀は万年, cranes, like turtles, are thought to have extremely long life-spans, and dreaming of them, therefore, is believed to guarantee that the dreamer will enjoy a long life.

Cranes are counted *ichiwa* 一羽.

Senbazuru **千羽鶴** "a thousand cranes"
a thousand folded-paper cranes (on a string)

則男君のお見舞いにみんなで千羽鶴を折りましょう。
Norio-kun no omimai ni minna de senbazuru o orimashō.
Let's all make a chain of paper cranes for when we go to see Norio in the hospital.

千羽鶴は折り紙の中で一番ポピュラーだと思うよ。
Senbazuru wa origami no naka de ichiban popyurā da to omou yo.
Crane chains are the most popular type of origami, I'd say.

❦ As can be seen from the examples, *senbazuru* are folded and attached to a string to express one's hopes for success in a specific endeavor or the speedy recovery of an ill or injured person. They are sent or given directly to the person to whom one's good wishes are directed or may be hung at Shinto shrines, where they represent the earnest prayers of the makers.

Tsuru no hitokoe 鶴の一声 "the single cry of a crane"
a word from on high, the voice of authority; one's word is law

---

社長の鶴の一声でその計画は実行に移った。
Shachō no tsuru no hitokoe de sono keikaku wa jikkō ni utsutta.
One word from the boss and the plan was implemented.

やっぱりお前の鶴の一声がないとみんな動かないよ。
Yappari omae no tsuru no hitokoe ga nai to minna ugokanai yo.
You know, nobody's going to make a move until you give the go-ahead.

❦ In Japan, authority has the last word, especially when the small fry are at loggerheads over how to proceed or in an otherwise confused state. The logjam is broken when someone whose word is law finally speaks.

tsuyoki (na) 強気(な) "strong *ki*"

aggressive, firm, hard-nosed, tough; (of the stock market) bullish

ずいぶん強気な発言だな。
Zuibun tsuyoki na hatsugen da na.
You don't mince words, do you. / You seem pretty confident.

いつもながら強気な人だな。
Itsumo-nagara tsuyoki na hito da na.
He's his usual pushy (in-your-face) self.

あの人が相手なら強気に出た方が成功するだろう。
Ano hito ga aite nara tsuyoki ni deta hō ga seikō suru darō.
You'd better play hardball when you're dealing with him. You're more
   likely to succeed that way.

☞ *kachiki (na)* 勝ち気(な), *ki ga tsuyoi* 気が強い, *ki o tsuyoku motsu* 気
を強く持つ; *ki ga yowai* 気が弱い; *yowaki (na)* 弱気(な)

u う (鵜) cormorant

Fables in the *Nihon Shoki* and the *Kojiki* depict the thatching of special maternity huts with cormorant feathers. They describe women in labor within these huts as holding a cormorant feather in the belief that doing so would guarantee a safe birth, probably from the observation that the bird is capable of disgorging intact fish it has swallowed whole. Another folk belief held that intoning *u no nodo* 鵜の喉 or *u no tori* 鵜の鳥 would dislodge a fish bone caught in one's throat. The cormorant is still used to fish in Japan, with a rope tied around its neck to prevent it from swallowing before it has been forced to disgorge the fish it has captured. Thought in the West to be gluttonous, and lending its name to a person so viewed, this cousin of the pelican has no such reputation in Japan.

   Cormorants are counted *ichiwa* 一羽.

U no me taka no me　鵜の目鷹の目　"a cormorant's eye, a hawk's
   eye"
scrutinize, pour over, look over carefully; keep one's eyes peeled (for)

私の姑は鵜の目鷹の目で私のあらを探している。
Watashi no shūtome wa u no me taka no me de watashi no ara o sagashite iru.

My mother-in-law's always on the lookout for any little fault she can find in me.

会社が倒産しそうなので、鵜の目鷹の目で彼は転職先を探している。
Kaisha ga tōsan shisō na no de, u no me taka no me de kare wa tenshoku-saki o sagashite iru.
He is keeping his eyes peeled for a new job because the company he's with now is on the ropes.

✌ From the fact that both the cormorant and the hawk are sharp-eyed.

U-nomi 鵜呑み "swallow (whole) like a cormorant"
swallow (something) whole; swallow a story hook, line, and sinker; be gullible

---

何でもかんでも鵜呑みはよくない。
Nandemo-kandemo u-nomi wa yoku nai.
You can't go around believing everything you hear. / Don't be so gullible.

鵜呑みは禁物だ、この件に関してはほかの人の意見も参考にしよう。
U-nomi wa kinmotsu da, kono ken ni kanshite wa hoka no hito no iken mo sankō ni shiyō.
Can't take things at face value. Better get another opinion of what's coming down here.

彼のいうことを鵜呑みにするのは危険だ。
Kare no iu koto o u-nomi ni suru no wa kiken da.
You're just asking for trouble if you take him at his word. / You've got to take what he says with a grain of salt or you'll be sorry.

あなたのいうことをそのまま鵜呑みにするわけにはいかない。
Anata no iu koto o sono mama u-nomi ni suru wake ni wa ikanai.
You can't really expect me to take your word for it.

✌ From the way a cormorant swallows fish whole to be digested in its stomach.

uchiki (na) 内気（な） "inner *ki*"

private, keep to oneself, not outgoing, not very sociable, reserved, shy

友成くんは内気なので営業には向かない。
Tomonari-kun wa uchiki na no de eigyō ni wa mukanai.
Tomonari's so shy that he's just not cut out for sales. / Tomonari's not outgoing enough to make it as a salesman.

幸子さんは内気だからか美人なのに男の友だちがいない。
Sachiko-san wa uchiki da kara ka bijin na no ni otoko no tomodachi ga inai.
Maybe the reason Sachiko doesn't have any boyfriends, even though she's really pretty, is that she's not very social.

↔ *gaijū-naigō* 外柔内剛

ude 腕 arm

In modern speech, *ude* refers to the whole arm, from the shoulder to the wrist. Previously, it referred only to the forearm, and *kaina,* a word no longer in general use, indicated the arm. Common compounds with *ude* include *ude-dokei* or wristwatch, *udezumo* or arm wrestling, and *udemae* or skill.

A guy's right-hand man is his *migi-ude,* or "right arm," but forget trying to figure out a catchy word for main squeeze. *Aibō,* an old word still in use by men today, originally referred to the guy on "the other end of the pole" supporting a palanquin. This is about as close as you can get in Japanese.

The idioms below are almost exclusively about skill—getting it, proving it, improving it, and showing it off.

Ude ga agaru / ude o ageru 腕が上がる／腕を上げる "one's arm rises."
get better, improve

君は、将棋の腕が上がったね。
Kimi wa, shōgi no ude ga agatta ne.
Your shōgi game is coming around (along).

ゴルフの腕を上げたければ、毎日の練習は欠かせない。
Gorufu no ude o agetakereba, mainichi no renshū wa kakasenai.
If you want to see some improvement in your golf game, daily practice is the ticket.

Ude ga ii 腕がいい "one's arm is good"
be skilled, good at, quite a hand at

この店の板前さんは腕がいい。
Kono mise no itamae-san wa ude ga ii.
The chef here really knows his stuff. / They've got a great chef here.

腕のいい仕立て屋さんを知りませんか。
Ude no ii shitateya-san o shirimasen ka.
I was wondering if you happened to know a good tailor?

Ude ni oboe ga aru 腕に覚えがある "one's arm remembers"
be good at something, be able to hold one's own at

私はスキーならば、少しは腕に覚えがある。
Watashi wa sukī naraba, sukoshi wa ude ni oboe ga aru.

I can handle myself all right on the slopes. / I know a little something about skiing.

この老人ホームには、将棋なら腕に覚えがあるというお年寄りが多い。
Kono rōjin-hōmu ni wa, shōgi nara ude ni oboe ga aru to iu otoshiyori ga ōi.
Quite a few of the old folks here in this rest home say they are pretty good shōgi players.

Ude no mise-dokoro **腕の見せどころ** "the time to show one's arm"

time to show one's stuff, a chance to show what one can do

彼は、ここが腕の見せどころ、とばかり張り切っていた。
Kare wa, koko ga ude no mise-dokoro, to bakari harikitte ita.
He was really up because he knew it was his big chance to strut his stuff.

お前の番だ。腕の見せどころだからがんばって来い。
Omae no ban da. Ude no mise-dokoro da kara ganbatte koi.
OK, it's your turn, kiddo. Get out there and show 'em what you've got (do your thing).

Don't be tempted to experiment too much with the following expression. It is used almost exclusively about cooking.

Ude o furuu **腕を振るう** "shake one's arm"
show one's skill, go to town doing something

パーティーのために、腕を振るって料理を作った。
Pātī no tame ni, ude o furutte ryōri o tsukutta.
I cooked up a storm for the party.

彼女は隣の家族を夕食に誘い、自慢の腕を振るった。
Kanojo wa tonari no kazoku o yūshoku ni sasoi, jiman no ude o furutta.

She invited the next-door neighbors over for dinner and laid out quite a spread.

Ude o migaku 腕を磨く "polish one's arm"
practice, brush up

彼はゴルフの腕を磨くために、練習場に通っている。
Kare wa gorufu no ude o migaku tame ni, renshū-jō ni kayotte iru.
He goes to a driving range to improve his golf game.

お前の負けだ。腕を磨いて出直してこい。
Omae no make da. Ude o migaite denaoshite koi.
You lose. Come back and try again when you've done a little more practicing.

ugō no shū 烏合の衆 "flock of crows"
a disorderly crowd, a gaggle, a herd of cats

人数ばかり多くても烏合の衆では役に立たないよ。
Ninzū bakari ōkute mo ugō no shū de wa yaku ni tatanai yo.
No matter how many people you've got, they're useless if they're just a milling crowd.

あんな弱いチームに負けたんじゃ、単なる烏合の衆といわれてもしかたがないよ。
Anna yowai chīmu ni maketa n' ja, tan-naru ugō no shū to iwarete mo shikata ga nai yo.
If we can't beat a team as weak as that, we can't complain if we're called a passel of good-for-nothings.

わが軍は単なる烏合の衆だ。
Wagagun wa tan-naru ugō no shū da.
Our army is nothing more than a ragtag bunch of rowdies.

❦ From the observation that crows are an unruly bunch.

↝ *shōsū-seiei* 少数精鋭

uguisu うぐいす（鶯） bush warbler

Intimately associated with the early-blooming plum in traditional poetry and painting, the arrival of this melodious harbinger of spring to the garden remains an annual event commented upon to neighbors and friends by many suburban Japanese. So closely is this songster linked with the plum, that the two are sometimes paired together in the metaphoric description of a perfect match. Although keeping the bird caged to enjoy its song now requires legal authorization, the practice was once common, with competitions called *uguisu-awase*, literally "the bringing together of bush warblers," held to judge the most beautiful warble. (The bird's song is so highly esteemed that the word *uguisu* has become a metaphor for a woman with a beautiful voice.) So-called nightingale floors—only a slight misnomer—have even been designed to squeak—er, that is, sing—like the warbler and, the explanation goes, forewarn wary military leaders of the late-night approach of assassins. In one practice, thankfully no longer common, the warbler's excrement was mixed with rice bran and used as a scrub for the skin.

The bush warbler's song is *hōhokekyo* ホーホケキョ. It is counted *ippiki* 一匹 or *ichiwa* 一羽.

Uguisu nakaseta koto mo aru 鶯鳴かせたこともある "has even made the bush warbler sing"
used to be quite a looker, used to have men wrapped around her little finger

---

うちのおばあちゃん鶯鳴かせたこともあるほど可愛かったらしいわよ。

> *Uchi no obāchan uguisu nakaseta koto mo aru hodo kawaikatta rashii wa yo.*
>
> My grandmother used to have to beat men off with a stick, she was so good-looking.

> そこの角のタバコ屋のおばさん、若いときはちょっとしたもので鶯鳴かせたこともあるらしいわよ。
>
> *Soko no kado no tabakoya no obasan, wakai toki wa chotto shita mono de uguisu nakaseta koto mo aru rashii wa yo.*
>
> From what I hear, the woman who runs that cigarette shop on the corner used to be quite the talk of the town.

🍃 In a male/female role reversal, this idiom equates a woman with a plum tree and a man with a warbler so attracted to the tree's beautiful blossoms that it breaks out in song. The thinking here is from the observation that warblers are often seen singing among the spring blossoms of the plum, and that even a wizened old plum tree was once young and had beautiful blossoms that attracted bush warblers; hence, while a woman may no longer be young and beautiful, she once had her pick of men.

Uguisu-jō うぐいす嬢 "a young woman warbler"
a woman, usually young, who sings or speaks with a beautiful voice; woman announcer over a PA system

---

> 彼女の声はうぐいす嬢にピッタリだ。
> *Kanojo no koe wa uguisu-jō ni pittari da.*
> Her voice is perfect (just right) for a PA announcer.

> 選挙の時のうぐいす嬢はいいアルバイトになるそうだ。
> *Senkyo no toki no uguisu-jō wa ii arubaito ni naru sō da.*
> They say that elections are a great time for young female PA announcers to get well-paying part-time jobs.

> うぐいす嬢の声は、バッターボックスに立ったイチローへの歓声にかき消された。

Uguisu-jō no koe wa, battā bokkusu ni tatta Ichirō e no kansei ni kakike-sareta.

When Ichirō stood in the batter's box, the female announcer's voice was drowned out by the cheering.

🌣 Use of this expression seems to be limited to women announcing sporting events in a stadium, standing in the front of buses explaining inane facts about bad architecture and obscure personages, or riding around in sound cars bristling with loudspeakers mindlessly waving their white-gloved hands at anyone who happens to look up, and repeating a few rote expressions that have absolutely nothing to do with the political candidate for whose campaign they have been optimistically hired to lend an air of freshness—an all but impossible task in contemporary Japan.

ukanai kao o suru / ukanu kao o suru 浮かない顔をする／浮かぬ顔をする "make a non-floating face"

have a glum face, have a sad face

どうしたの、浮かない顔をして。
Dō shita no, ukanai kao o shite.
Why do you have such a long face? / What's the long face all about?

彼は一日中浮かぬ顔をしていた。
Kare wa ichinichi-jū ukanu kao o shite ita.
He was down in the mouth all day long. / He was moping around all day.

uma ga au 馬が合う "the horse fits"

get along (get on) well (with each other), be on the same wavelength, click

俺、馬が合うんだよあの人とは。
Ore, uma ga au n' da yo ano hito to wa.
I get along great with him.

最初から馬が合ったその二人はトントン拍子で結婚した。
Saisho kara uma ga atta sono futari wa tonton byōshi de kekkon shita.
The two of them hit it off right from the start and sailed straight into marriage.

山川部長と社長はどうも馬が合わないようだ。
Yamakawa buchō to shachō wa dōmo uma ga awanai yō da.
Department head Yamakawa and the CEO just don't seem to be on the same wavelength.

In the negative form, *uma ga awanai,* this expression is similiar to *mushi ga sukanai* 虫が好かない. Care should be taken, however, in distinguishing the two, for while the former can be used by the speaker about two third-parties who do not get along, use of the latter is limited to the relationship between the speaker and a third party and is not used to describe how others feel toward one another. Insofar as it expresses feelings of incompatibility, *uma ga awanai* shares common ground with *inusaru no naka* 犬猿の仲, another expression included in this book.

☞ *hada ga au* 肌が合う, *ki ga au* 気が合う

uma no hone 馬の骨 "horse bones"

a mystery man, (rarely and not within the context of marriage) a mystery woman; a person from nowhere, a nobody

どこの馬の骨だ、お前と結婚したいと言っているのは。
Doko no uma no hone da, omae to kekkon shitai to itte iru no wa.
So exactly who is this character who says he wants to marry you?

どこの馬の骨ともわからない奴に娘をやるぐらいなら一生俺が面倒見てやる。
Doko no uma no hone tomo wakaranai yatsu ni musume o yaru gurai nara isshō ore ga mendō mite yaru.
I'd rather look after my daughter for the rest of my life than see her married off to some Joe Schmo.

どこの馬の骨ともわからない奴に会社を乗っ取られてたまるか。
Doko no uma no hone to mo wakaranai yatsu ni kaisha o nottorarete tamaru ka.
I'm not putting up with some guy outa' nowhere coming in and taking over the company!

🦥 Often immediately preceded by *doko no*, this idiom is most commonly wielded by irate fathers about to lose their beloved daughters to suitors whom they are unwilling to recognize. Pejorative reference to the unknown origin or parentage of the male suitor. It is this sense of "suitor" that makes the final example possible.

uma no mimi ni nenbutsu 馬の耳に念仏 "(chanting) the prayer to Amida Buddha in a horse's ear"

(like) preaching to the wind, preaching to deaf ears; (like) water off a duck's back, whistling in the wind

もうけ主義の会社に、資源保護を訴えても、馬の耳に念仏だ。
Mōke-shugi no kaisha ni, shigen-hogo o uttaete mo, uma no mimi ni nenbutsu da.
Appealing for environmental protection measures to corporations bent on maximizing profits is like preaching to the wind.

暴走族に騒音防止を唱えても、それこそ馬の耳に念仏じゃないか。
Bosō-zoku ni sōon-bōshi o tonaete mo, sore koso uma no mimi ni nenbutsu ja nai ka.

Talking to motorcycle gangs about reducing the noise level is a waste of breath, if you ask me.

🐎 From the notion that a horse, being a horse, will never understand or appreciate the prayer to Amida Buddha.

↝ *baji-tōfu* 馬耳東風

uma o shika to iu 馬を鹿と言う "call a horse a deer"

call black white; try to pull the wool over someone's eyes

それじゃあ、馬を鹿と言うのと同じじゃないか。
Sore jā, uma o shika to iu no to onaji ja nai ka.
You're full of it. / Who are you trying to kid?

あの人は馬を鹿と言う性格だから部下に慕われないんだよ。
Ano hito wa uma o shika to iu seikaku da kara buka ni shitawarenai n' da yo.
He's the kind of guy who's got to have his own way, right or wrong, so nobody really wants to work for him.

お前のその馬を鹿と言う性格は誰に似たんだ。
Omae no sono uma o shika to iu seikaku wa dare ni nita n' da.
Which side of the family did you get that contrariness from?

🐎 Used to describe intentional misrepresentation of something or to say something that flies in the face of facts for one's own purposes.

umazura 馬面 "a horseface"

a horseface, (literally) a long face

彼は馬面だ。
Kare wa umazura da.
He has a face like a horse. / He's horse-faced.

あの役者は馬面だから舞台映えする。
Ano yakusha wa umazura da kara butai-bae suru.
Guy's got one big ol' face; just right for the stage.

※ Used exclusively to describe or mock an elongated face, not to describe one as appearing unhappy.

umisen-yamasen 海千山千 "a thousand (years) in the sea and a thousand (years) in the mountains"

a sly old dog, a crafty old fox

彼女おとなしそうにしてたけど、結構海千山千だぜ。
Kanojo otonashisō ni shite 'ta kedo, kekkō umisen-yamasen da ze.
She acted all shy and quiet, but she ain't nobody's fool.

私のような海千山千の女は、これぐらいのことじゃ驚きませんよ。
Watashi no yō na umisen-yamasen no onna wa, kore gurai no koto ja odorokimasen yo.
Don't think you're gonna shock a woman like me with something like that.

先方は海千山千の強者だから、気をつけろよ。
Senpō wa umisen-yamasen no tsuwamono da kara, ki o tsukero yo.
The other guy's crafty as a fox and a real go-getter, so watch your step.

あの海千山千がそんな脅しぐらいでびびるもんか。
Ano umisen-yamasen ga sonna odoshi gurai de bibiru mon ka.
Do you really think a threat like that's going to make him quake in his boots? He's seen it all before.

※ This four-character compound has its origins in the folk belief that a snake will turn into a dragon after living a thousand years in the sea and a thousand years in the mountains.

☞ *furudanuki* 古狸, *furugitsune* 古狐

unagi（うなぎ）鰻 eel

Though its fry are born in the ocean, the Japanese eel is considered a freshwater fish because it swims up streams and rivers to live. Eels have long been considered nutritious and are eaten on the eighteenth day of July by many Japanese in the hope that doing so will protect them from getting sick during the summer. Eels are counted *ippiki* 一匹 or *ippon* 一本.

Unagi no nedoko 鰻の寝床 "an eel's bed"
a long, narrow place to sleep or live; a sliver of land

派手な生活をしている中村さんも家に帰れば鰻の寝床のようなボロ家住まいだ。
Hade na seikatsu o shite iru Nakamura-san mo ie ni kaereba unagi no nedoko no yō na boroya-zumai da.
Nakamura may have a flashy lifestyle, but he goes home to a cramped dump at night.

被災地では、仮設住宅が鰻の寝床のように並んでいる。
Hisai-chi de wa, kasetsu-jūtaku ga unagi no nedoko no yō ni narande iru.
Rows of barracks have been thrown up in the disaster area to provide temporary shelter.

こんな鰻の寝床みたいな土地じゃ店舗には向かないな。
Konna unagi no nedoko mitai na tochi ja tenpo ni wa mukanai na.
A sliver of land like this (with almost no frontage) won't do for a business. / You could never make a business work on a strip of land like this, with almost no frontage.

🐟 Of land, buildings, or rooms. From the observation that eels, being eels, need a long but not a wide place to sleep.

↬ *tako-beya* たこ部屋, *usagigoya* うさぎ小屋

Unagi nobori 鰻登り "eel climbing"
skyrocket, soar, take off, go out of sight

新製品の人気はまさに鰻登りだ。
Shin-seihin no ninki wa masa ni unagi nobori da.
The popularity of the new product is simply soaring. / The new product is really taking off.

天候不順で、野菜の値段が鰻登りに上がっている。
Tenkō-fujun de, yasai no nedan ga unagi nobori ni agatte iru.
Vegetable prices are skyrocketing due to the bad weather.

🐟 Used primarily of such things as prices, which are expressed in numbers. According to one source the expression derives from the eel's manner of rising quickly in the water, while a second source claims it is from the eel's slippery climb up and out of your hands—and control—when you try to grasp it.

---

unsan-mushō 雲散霧消 "the clouds scatter, the fog disappears"

to go up in a puff of smoke, to disappear without trace, to be scattered on the winds

例外ばかり認めていたのでは、原則など雲散霧消してしまう。
Reigai bakari mitomete ita no de wa, gensoku nado unsan-mushō shite shimau.
If we allowed all kinds of exceptions to the rule, the general principle would disappear in a puff of smoke.

バブル経済の崩壊とともに、社屋の移転、新築の話は雲散霧消した。
Baburu-keizai no hōkai to tomo ni, shaoku no iten, shinchiku no hanashi wa unsan-mushō shita.
When the bubble economy burst, all the talk of companies moving to new premises and erecting new buildings went up in smoke.

uō-saō 右往左往 "going right and going left"

〜する to run about in utter confusion, to run pell-mell, to rush about like a headless chicken, to lose one's head, to get into a panic

こんなことでいちいち右往左往するなんて、みっともないよ。
Konna koto de ichiichi uō-saō suru nante, mittomo nai yo.
To let yourself get worked up over something like this really makes you look bad.

幹事の連絡の不行き届きで、みんなが右往左往させられてしまった。
Kanji no renraku no fu-yukitodoki de, minna ga uō-saō saserarete shimatta.
Because the (party's, meeting's) organizer was careless about notifying people, there was a lot of needless running around.

uogokoro areba mizugokoro ari 魚心あれば水心あり "if the fish feels that way, so will the water"

scratch my back and I'll scratch yours; logrolling

魚心あれば水心ありで、責任は誘った男だけじゃなく、誘われ
た女にもあるさ。
Uogokoro areba mizugokoro aride, sekinin wa sasotta otoko dake ja naku, sasowareta onna ni mo aru sa.
Responsibility lies not just with the man who tempted the woman, but also with the woman who allowed herself to be tempted. After all, it takes two to tango.

魚心あれば水心あり、その会社は富士商事の商談に乗った。
Uogokoro areba mizugokoro ari, sono kaisha wa Fuji-shōji no shōdan ni notta.
Seeing that there was something in it for both parties, the company took Fuji Trading up on its offer.

🐇 From a sense of mutuality between two entities, usually with both parties feeling positively about the other. And, yes, there's something fishy going on behind the scenes here, too.

usagi うさぎ (兎) rabbit, hare

Rabbitry has been in the myth, folklore, and language of Japan since at least the early 700s, when mentioned in the *Kojiki*. Considered a trickster, the rabbit also figures as the Japanese equivalent of the English "Man in the Moon," for some still hold that a rabbit can be seen hard at work pounding *mochi* on the face of a full moon. Only a few species exist in Japan today and, although they are equally prolific, Japanese rabbits have yet to achieve the same notoriety for copulating as they have in English.

Rabbits are counted *ippiki* 一匹 or, of all things, *ichiwa* 一羽, no doubt because of the size or resemblance of their ears to wings and some distant flight of fancy that found common ground with birds, which are normally counted in this way. Written 卯, the hare is fourth among the twelve signs of the Chinese zodiac.

Tonikaku とにかく（兎に角） "horns on a rabbit"
anyway, anyhow, in any case, at any rate, either way, even so, be that as it may

とにかく、彼に尋ねてみよう。
Tonikaku, kare ni tazunete miyō.
Anyway, I'll just ask him and see what's up.

とにかく、これ食べてごらんよ、美味しいから。
Tonikaku, kore tabete goran yo, oishii kara.
Don't give me that, just try it. It's really good.

とにかく、彼女は強情だ。
Tonikaku, kanojo wa gōjō da.
At any rate, she's one hardheaded woman.

※ The characters for rabbit and horn are said to be merely phonetic equivalents, though it is not a great leap to the notion that even in the unlikely event that rabbits were found to have horns, the speaker would still hold such-and-such to be the case, i.e., anyhow. But this is idle speculation.

Usagigoya うさぎ小屋 "a rabbit hut"
a rabbit hutch, warren

うさぎ小屋に住みたくて日本人は住んでいるんじゃないよ。
Usagigoya ni sumitakute Nihon-jin wa sunde iru n' ja nai yo.
Japanese don't live in small, cramped "rabbit hutches" because they want to, you know.

こんなうさぎ小屋に住むなんて、もうこりごりだ。
Konna usagigoya ni sumu nante, mō korigori da.
I'm sick and tired of living in a warren like this.

※ It was in 1979 that information from a confidential EC document containing the English expression was leaked to the press. The observation by an undiplomatic foreign diplomat that Japanese were living in rabbit hutches caused an uproar in Kasumigaseki, particularly within the Construction Ministry. Of course, the stoic Japanese citizenry was being told nothing they hadn't already known firsthand for generations, a fact which caused them to look upon Japanese officialdom's righteous indignation somewhat sardonically.

☞ *tako-beya* たこ部屋, *unagi no nedoko* 鰻の寝床

Usagitobi うさぎ跳び "a rabbit hop"
hop with one's hands clasped behind one's back

よし、1年生はうさぎ跳び100回だ。
Yoshi, ichinen-sei wa usagitobi hyakkai da.
All right all you freshmen, I want to see a hundred rabbit hops right now.

あいつうさぎ跳び200回やっても涼しい顔してる。
Aitsu usagitobi nihyakkai yatte mo suzushii kao shite 'ru.
He can do two hundred rabbit hops and still look as cool as a cucumber.

✌ From the physical resemblance of this activity to a rabbit in motion.

ushi うし (牛) cow

The fact that cattle have been plodding around Japan for the last two thousand years or so goes a long way toward explaining why these bovines figure so largely in the language. Their size, appetite, docility, and reputation for lethargy, as well as their observed ability to trample unsuspecting human fry underfoot all figure in idioms included herein.

These beasts of burden were long free from fear of being butchered because of Buddhist proscriptions, but in modern Japan, beginning in the Meiji period (1868–1912), domestic beef has been piled increasingly higher on the tables of the nation. In one Kansai area, the Matsuzaka breed is even fed beer to fatten it up, while marbling and softening its meat. Matsuzaka beef remains highly prized—and exorbitantly priced in today's competitive market.

The cow's moo is *mōmō* モウモウ, and cows, bulls, and calves are counted *ippiki* 一匹 or *ittō* 一頭. Written 丑, the cow is second among the twelve signs of the Chinese zodiac.

↪ *gyūho* 牛歩, *gyūjiru* 牛耳る

Ushi no shōben　牛の小便　"cow piss"
unending, long and drawn out

あの牛の小便みたいな街頭演説やめてくれないかなあ。
Ano ushi no shōben mitai na gaitō-enzetsu yamete kurenai ka nā.
I sure wish they'd do away with those campaign speeches that just seem to go on and on.

あの先生いったん説教を始めると牛の小便でうんざりだ。
Ano sensei ittan sekkyō o hajimeru to ushi no shōben de unzari da.
I'm sick of the way that once that prof starts in on us he drones on forever.

🐌 This picturesque idiom is used of interminable things, usually of speeches that just don't seem to end.

↪ *ushi no yodare* 牛のよだれ

Ushi no yodare　牛のよだれ　"cow drool"
long and slow; slower than molasses in January

うちの社長の訓辞はいつも牛のよだれのようだ。
Uchi no shachō no kunji wa itsumo ushi no yodare no yō da.
Our president's little pep talks are always such ho-hummers.

会議はなぜいつも牛のよだれのようなのだろうか。
Kaigi wa naze itsumo ushi no yodare no yō na no darō ka.
Why are meetings always so long and drawn out?

🐇 Most commonly of desultory discourse. Almost always followed by *no yō*.

↪ *ushi no shōben* 牛の小便

ushiro-yubi o sasareru 後ろ指をさされる "be pointed at behind one's back"

be the object of gossip

私は、後ろ指をさされるようなことは何もしていない。
Watashi wa, ushiro-yubi o sasareru yō na koto wa nani mo shite inai.
I haven't done anything to make people talk behind my back.

人から後ろ指をさされるようなことだけは、してはならない。
Hito kara ushiro-yubi o sasareru yō na koto dake wa, shite wa naranai.
Don't do anything that will cause you to be the object of gossip.

ushirogami o hikareru (omoi) 後ろ髪を引かれる（思い） "feel like the hair on the back of one's head is being pulled"

reluctantly, with a heavy heart

彼は後ろ髪を引かれる思いで故郷を後にした。
Kare wa ushirogami o hikareru omoi de kokyō o ato ni shita.
He left his hometown with a heavy heart.

彼女は後ろ髪を引かれる思いで年老いた母のいる家を出た。
Kanojo wa ushirogami o hikareru omoi de toshioita haha no iru ie o deta.

It was hard for her to leave her old mother alone. / She almost couldn't find it in her heart to leave her aged mother alone at home.

utsurigi (na) 移り気（な） "moving *ki*"

(noun) a caprice, whim; (adj.) capricious, changeable, fickle, whimsical, doesn't stick with anything for long

移り気な野中さんは今回5回目の転職をした。
Utsurigi na Nonaka-san wa konkai gokai-me no tenshoku o shita.
That Nonaka just can't seem to settle down. This makes the fifth time he's changed jobs.

うちの娘は移り気で、次から次へとお稽古ごとを始めるがどれも長続きしない。
Uchi no musume wa utsurigi de, tsugi kara tsugi e to okeiko-goto o hajimeru ga dore mo nagatsuzuki shinai.
My daughter's so changeable, always taking up some new hobby but never sticking with anything for long.

※ *tsugi kara tsugi e*: (changing) from one thing to another, one after another (a set phrase).

あんな移り気な男を信用するんじゃなかった。
Anna utsurigi na otoko o shin'yō suru n' ja nakatta.
I should have known better than to trust a fickle guy like him.

※ For comparison with *ki ga ōi*, see usage note under that entry.

☞ *ki ga ōi* 気が多い, *ki ga kawariyasui* 気が変わりやすい (example under *ki ga kawaru*)

uwaki 浮気 "floating *ki*"

an affair, a fling, hanky-panky, something on the side; cheating, two-timing, unfaithfulness, stepping out

父の浮気が母にばれて大騒ぎになった。
Chichi no uwaki ga haha ni barete ōsawagi ni natta.
The shit hit the fan when Mom found out about Dad having an affair.

浮気のつもりが本気になってしまって、とうとう妻とは離婚した。
Uwaki no tsumori ga honki ni natte shimatte, tōtō tsuma to wa rikon shita.
What started out as a casual affair turned out to be the real thing, and I ended up getting a divorce from my wife.

主人の浮気の相手と称する女が図々しく尋ねてきた。
Shujin no uwaki no aite to shō-suru onna ga zūzūshiku tazunete kita.
Some woman calling herself my husband's lover had the nerve to come to the house.

☞ *uwaki suru* 浮気する, *uwakippoi* 浮気っぽい

uwaki suru 浮気する "float one's *ki*"

carry on (with); (of a man) get a little (nookie, pussy) on the side, have an extramarital relationship (with), two-time, step out (on)

夫は浮気するような人じゃありません。
Otto wa uwaki suru yō na hito ja arimasen.
My husband's not the kind to cheat. / My husband would never fool around on me.

アンケートの結果、既婚者の半数以上が浮気したいと考えていることが分かった。
Ankēto no kekka, kikon-sha no hansū ijō ga uwaki shitai to kangaete iru koto ga wakatta.

The survey results showed that more than half of married men and women would like to have an affair.

⌘ Thanks in large measure to TV soaps, gossip shows, and weekly mags, *uwaki suru* appears to be on the way out. No, the nation's philanderers are not having second thoughts because of AIDS and staying at home in front of the boob tube with the kids to watch cartoons and eat popcorn; on the contrary, the activity itself has apparently become the *in* thing to do and now flourishes as perhaps never before. It's the word *uwaki suru* that people don't use any more. The media has found it necessary to rehabilitate a musty old noun in its stead, *furin* 不倫 (originally, unethical, immoral; by extension, an illicit sexual relationship), spiffed it up by appending *suru* to make it the *de rigueur* contemporary verb for that very special and now somehow almost respectable extracurricular activity. As with other artifices like *tabako suru* タバコする (do tobacco, hence "smoke") the jury is still out on whether the construction will remain in the language when its popularizers move on to something else.

☞ *uwaki* 浮気, *uwakippoi* 浮気っぽい

uwakippoi 浮気っぽい "like floating *ki*"

adulterous, cheating, two-timing; [usually of a man, not necessarily implying that he is an adulterer or cheater] have a roving eye

彼みたいな浮気っぽい人と一緒になると苦労するのは目に見えてる*よ。

Kare mitai na uwakippoi hito to issho ni naru to kurō suru no wa me ni miete 'ru yo.

Anybody can see that you're going to have nothing but trouble if you hook up with a two-timer like him.

* *me ni mieru*: lit., to be seen by the eye; to be certain, obvious.

⌘ *Uwakippoi,* like its less common synonym *uwaki na,* may also, though only rarely, be used to mean "not sticking to one thing for any length of time."

The consensus of the authors and our usage panelists (read "friends" here) is that *uwaki na* does not merit an entry, but we have chosen to include the following example of how it may be used.

浮気なマリ子は今の彼氏でもう8人目だよ。
Uwaki na Mariko wa ima no kareshi de mō hachinin-me da yo.
Mariko's so fickle that she's already on her eighth boyfriend.

☞ *ki ga ōi* 気が多い (#1), *uwaki* 浮気, *uwaki suru* 浮気する

uya-muya 有耶無耶 "to be, not to be"

vague, unclear, fuzzy; 〜になる to be left up in the air, unresolved, vague; 〜にする to leave (something) up in the air, unresolved, vague

戦後の混乱の中で、事件の真相は有耶無耶になってしまった。
Sengo no konran no naka de, jiken no shinsō wa uya-muya ni natte shimatta.
In the midst of all the postwar confusion it became impossible to tell what the truth of the incident was.

これは大事なことなんだから、有耶無耶にしないでくださいよ。
Kore wa daiji na koto nan da kara, uya-muya ni shinai de kudasai yo.
This is a very important matter so please do not try to gloss over it.

uzō-muzō 有象無象 "with form, without form"

the rabble; the riffraff; every Tom, Dick and Harry; everyone and his brother

有象無象の自称「宮沢賢治研究家」がいるけど、本当に深く勉強している人は少ない。
Uzō-muzō no jishō "Miyazawa Kenji kenkyū-ka" ga iru kedo, hontō ni fukaku benkyō shite iru hito wa sukunai.

There are legions of self-proclaimed scholars of Miyazawa Kenji, but very few are really doing serious research.

🐝 宮沢賢治 Miyazawa Kenji (1896-1933) was a famous Japanese poet and writer of children's stories.

有名人の周りには、有象無象の人たちが金魚の糞のようについてくるものだ。
Yūmei-jin no mawari ni wa, uzō-muzō no hitotachi ga kingyo no fun no yō ni tsuite kuru mono da.
Famous people attract all kinds of riffraff like flies.

🐝 See 金魚の糞 (*kingyo no fun*, goldfish droppings). In this vivid and common figure of speech, the droppings of the goldfish, which tend to trail after the fish until becoming detached, are likened to human hangers-on.

wakai tsubame 若い燕 "a young swallow"

a young male lover, a gigilo

あの中年女優は若い燕と同棲している。
Ano chūnen-joyū wa wakai tsubame to dōsei shite iru.
That middle-aged actress is shacking up with some young stud.

京子最近若い燕ができたらしいわよ。
Kyōko saikin wakai tsubame ga dekita rashii wa yo.
It looks like Kyoko's found herself a young bohunk.

🐝 Of a young man who has attached himself to an older woman and is usually kept by her as a lover. Said to have originated during the Meiji period (1868–1912) when a famous woman's rights activist received a letter written by a painter (to whom she was later married by common law), in which he referred to himself as a *wakai tsubame*.

warugi 悪気 "bad *ki*"

an evil intention; malice

小沢さんに悪気がないのは分かっているが、それでも腹が立つ。
Ozawa-san ni warugi ga nai no wa wakatte iru ga, sore de mo hara ga tatsu.
I realize Ozawa's intentions weren't bad, but it still makes me mad.

悪気はなかったんだが、ついうっかりして忘れてしまった。
Warugi wa nakatta n' da ga, tsui ukkari shite wasurete shimatta.
I didn't mean anything by it; it just completely slipped my mind.

悪気のない冗談のつもりが、あいつすっかり怒っちゃった。
Warugi no nai jōdan no tsumori ga, aitsu sukkari okotchatta.
I was just makin' a harmless joke, but he really exploded.

悪気のある男じゃないんだが、あの無神経さにはまいるよ。
Warugi no aru otoko ja nai n' da ga, ano mushinkei-sa ni wa mairu yo.
He doesn't try to be an asshole, it's just that he's so damn thoughtless.

(warui) mushi ga tsuku （悪い）虫がつく "a bad bug attaches (itself)"

have (get) a boyfriend (lover)

彼女は、箱入り娘だから虫がつかないように親がいつも目を光らせている。
Kanojo wa, hakoiri-musume da kara mushi ga tsukanai yō ni oya ga itsumo me o hikarasete iru.
She's led a sheltered life, her parents always making sure there're no guys sniffing around her (that she doesn't get mixed up with some guy).

悪い虫でもついたのか、最近彼女帰りが遅いらしいのよ。
Warui mushi de mo tsuita no ka, saikin kanojo kaeri ga osoi rashii no yo.

Maybe she's got a boyfriend. Seems like she's been getting home later and later.

🌱 Used almost exclusively about women, particularly unmarried or widowed ones. Less commonly used of married women who are having an affair. *Warui* appears with the idiom with great regularity.

↬ *mushi* 虫

wayō-setchū 和洋折衷 "Japanese and Western mixture"

a mix (mixture) of Japanese and Western styles

この本は英語と日本語が入り交じっているから、和洋折衷ですね。
Kono hon wa eigo to nihongo ga irimajitte iru kara, wayō-setchū desu ne.
This book could be called a mixture of the Japanese with the Western as it contains both English and Japanese.

家じゃ畳の部屋にベッドで寝て、ご飯と味噌汁の後でコーヒー飲んで、という和洋折衷で暮らしていますよ。
Uchi ja tatami no heya ni beddo de nete, gohan to misoshiru no ato de kōhī nonde, to iu wayō-setchū de kurashite imasu yo.
At home, life is a mixture of the Japanese and the Western: my bedroom floor's covered in tatami but I sleep in a bed; I eat rice and miso soup, then have a cup of coffee.

現代の日本では純日本式の生活をしている人は少数派で、大多数の人は衣食住のすべての面、特に食と住において和洋折衷になっています。
Gendai no Nihon de wa jun-nihonshiki no seikatsu o shite iru hito wa shōsū-ha de, dai-tasū no hito wa i-shoku-jū no subete no men, toku ni shoku to jū ni oite wayō-setchū ni natte imasu.
In present-day Japan people living in a purely Japanese way are in the minority. When it comes to food, clothing, and shelter (and especially

in food and shelter), most people have adopted a mixture of Japanese and Western styles.

🐍 Another four-character compound containing the characters for Japan (和) and the West (洋) is 和魂洋才 (*wakon-yōsai*), which literally means "a Japanese soul with Western learning." In the Meiji era (1868–1912) Japan imported Western learning wholesale but at the same time strove to maintain its own cultural identity. Although this four-character compound is rarely used in conversation today, you might well come across it when reading about Japanese history, so it is perhaps worth including in your passive vocabulary.

yabuhebi やぶ蛇 "a snake in the brush"

ask for it (trouble), stir up a hornets' nest; wake a sleeping dog, not know when to leave well enough alone, put one's foot in it

やぶ蛇になるからそのことは話さない方がいいよ。
Yabuhebi ni naru kara sono koto wa hanasanai hō ga ii yo.
You probably shouldn't mention it, or you'll just stir up a hornets' nest. / You'll just be asking for trouble if you bring that up.

お父さんに小遣いせびったら、やぶ蛇になっちゃって、成績のことで怒られちゃった。
Otōsan ni kozukai sebittara, yabuhebi ni natchatte, seiseki no koto de okorarechatta.
I was buggin' my old man for some spending money when the shit hit the fan, and he started in on me about my grades.

この件では仕入れ先にクレームをつけない方がいいよ。支払いのことを問題にされたらやぶ蛇になる。
Kono ken de wa shiire-saki ni kurēmu o tsukenai hō ga ii yo. Shiharai no koto o mondai ni saretara yabuhebi ni naru.
In this case, we'd better not register a complaint against the supplier. If

they bring up the matter of payment, we'll find ourselves with a different can of worms.

🐍 Shortened from *yabu o tsutsuite hebi o dasu* 薮をつついて蛇を出す, or literally, "poke around in the brush and drive out a snake," it means to say or do something uncalled for and thereby worsen one's position.

yajiuma やじ（野次）馬 "a heckling horse"

a rubberneck, gawker, curious bystander (onlooker)

その火事現場の周りは野次馬でいっぱいだった。
Sono kaji-genba no mawari wa yajiuma de ippai datta.
Curious bystanders were all around the scene of the fire.

野次馬のせいで救急車の到着が遅れた。
Yajiuma no sei de kyūkyūsha no tōchaku ga okureta.
The ambulance was delayed by rubberneckers.

🐍 Possibly from the original meaning of "a difficult horse to break" or, according to one theory, from a shortening of *oyajiuma,* or "an old male horse," *oyaji* meaning old man. Although the word *yaji* means heckling, as in *yaji o tobasu* ヤジを飛ばす, a *yajiuma* is not a heckler. Confusing but true.

yamai wa ki kara 病は気から "illness comes from *ki*"

the mind rules the body, no sickness is completely physical

「病は気から」というが、あの人も奥さんを亡くしてからすっかり落ち込んで病気がちになってしまった。

"Yamai wa ki kara" to iu ga, ano hito mo okusan o nakushite kara sukkari ochikonde byōki-gachi ni natte shimatta.

He's a living example of what they say about the mind ruling the body; he's been depressed and sickly ever since he lost his wife.

「病は気から」ですよ。そんな暗い顔してちゃ治るものも治りゃしない。元気出して。
"Yamai wa ki kara" desu yo. Sonna kurai kao shite 'cha naoru mono mo naorya shinai. Genki dashite.

Remember, "Mind over matter." Walking around with a long face like that's not going to help anything. Cheer up.

🐵 Can be used to cheer up an ill person, though care must be taken to use it only if the illness is not too serious, for the implication is that since the ill person's attitude itself is causing his distress, it can't be all that bad. History bears this out. Upon visiting a hospital for atomic bomb victims in Hiroshima, one former Japanese prime minister caused quite an uproar when he thoughtlessly told one patient that it was "all a mental thing." Sure.

↪ *ki de ki o yamu* 気で気を病む

yamazaru 山猿 "mountain monkey"

a rustic; a clodhopper, a boor

あんな山猿に会社を乗っ取られてたまるもんか。
Anna yamazaru ni kaisha o nottorarete tamaru mon ka.

If you think I'm going to stand by while some hick takes over the company, you've got another think coming.

若い頃は山猿と馬鹿にされていた彼も、今では売れ子の詩人になった。
Wakai koro wa yamazaru to baka ni sarete ita kare mo, ima de wa ureko no shijin ni natta.

Once treated like a country bumpkin, he's a best-selling poet now.

❧ The original meaning is a wild mountain monkey. Metaphorically it became a derisive term for an unschooled person from the country, untutored in the niceties of urban life.

yanagi no shita ni itsumo dojō wa inai 柳の下にいつもどじょうはいない。 "There is not always a loach under the willow."

there is a limit to luck (from the tale of a man who once caught a loach under a certain willow tree but was never able to repeat the feat)

去年のダービーでは大穴を当てたが、柳の下にいつもどじょうはいないということか。
Kyonen no dābī de wa ōana o ateta ga, yanagi no shita ni itsumo dojō wa inai to iu koto ka.
Last year I made a killing on a sleeper in the derby, but no such luck this year.

前の試験はたまたまヤマが当たっただけでしょう。柳の下にどじょうは二匹いないよ。
Mae no shiken wa tamatama yama ga atatta dake deshō. Yanagi no shita ni dojō wa nihiki inai yo.
I just lucked out on the last test. No way it'll ever happen again.

yaruki やる気 "*ki* to do"

ambition, desire, drive, enthusiasm, fight, get-up-and-go, motivation, will

やる気がある人だけに来てもらいたい。
Yaruki ga aru hito dake ni kite moraitai.
We want only motivated people.

しょっちゅう遅刻するのはやる気のない証拠だ。
Shotchū chikoku suru no wa yaruki no nai shōko da.
Coming late all the time is proof that you're not into your work.

やる気のない選手はスタメンからはずせ。
Yaruki no nai senshu wa sutamen kara hazuse.
Take everybody out of the starting lineup who's not ready to put out.

社長のワンマン経営のせいで若手の社員はすっかりやる気をなくしている。
Shachō no wanman-keiei no sei de wakate no shain wa sukkari yaruki o nakushite iru.
All the younger employees are losing their drive because the boss runs the company like a one-man show.

彼も早く立ち直って、やる気になってくれればいいんだが。
Kare mo hayaku tachinaotte, yaruki ni natte kurereba ii n' da ga.
Everything would be all right if he could pull himself out of his slump and get back into things.

みんな、もっとやる気を出してがんばろうよ。
Minna, motto yaruki o dashite ganbarō yo.
Come on, you guys. Let's get with the program (get cracking).

成功するもしないも君のやる気次第だ。
Seikō suru mo shinai mo kimi no yaruki shidai da.
Whether or not you succeed depends entirely on how bad you want it.

給料は歩合制ですからやる気次第でいくらでも稼げますよ。
Kyūryō wa buai-sei desu kara yaruki shidai de ikura de mo kasegemasu yo.
You'll be working on commission, so how much you earn is entirely up to you.

賢一君もついにやる気を起こして、今では見違えるように張り切っている。

Ken'ichi-kun mo tsui ni yaruki o okoshite, ima de wa michigaeru yō ni harikitte iru.
Even old Kenichi is into it now. You ought to see him; he's a changed man.

やる気が起きないってまさか鬱病の始まりじゃないだろうね。
Yaruki ga okinai tte masaka utsubyō no hajimari ja nai darō ne.
So you can't get interested in anything, huh? I hope you're not starting to get depressed.

この前までやる気満々だったのに、一体どうしたんだろう。
Kono mae made yaruki manman datta no ni, ittai dō shita n' darō.
You were all fired up until just the other day. What went wrong?

yōi-bantan 用意万端 "everything ready"

everything is ready and set

用意万端整いましたので、会場の方へどうぞ。
Yōi-bantan totonoimashita no de, kaijō no hō e dōzo.
All is set and ready to go, so if you'd just like to make your way to the assembly hall, please.

↳ *yōi-shūtō* 用意周到

yōi-shūtō 用意周到 "exhaustive preparation"

mindfulness, cautiousness, prudence, thoroughgoing preparation, to be prepared for all eventualities, to be thoroughly prepared

雨靴まで履いて来たとは、ずいぶん用意周到だねえ。
Amagutsu made haite kita to wa, zuibun yōi-shūtō da nē.
He was really well prepared; he had even come wearing his gumboots (galoshes).

用意周到に準備したつもりだったのに、地図を忘れて来ちゃったよ。
Yōi-shūtō ni junbi shita tsumori datta no ni, chizu o wasurete kichatta yo.
I thought I'd thought of everything, but then I ended up forgetting the map.

いつ外泊してもいいように、バッグに着替えと洗面用具入れて歩いてるんですか。用意周到な人と言うべきか、遊び人と言うべきか……。
Itsu gaihaku shite mo ii yō ni, baggu ni kigae to senmen-yōgu irete aruite 'ru n' desu ka. Yōi-shūtō na hito to iu beki ka, asobinin to iu beki ka . . .
What? She always goes round with a change of clothes and some toiletries in her bag "just in case"? I don't know whether to call her well prepared or simply loose.

☞ *yōi-bantan* 用意万端

yōki (na) 陽気（な） "bright *ki*"

bright, cheerful, happy, outgoing

君んちのお母さんて陽気な人なんだなあ。
Kimi n' 'chi no okāsan te yōki na hito nan da nā.
Boy, your mom sure is a cheerful person.

原田さん陽気だから一緒にいるとこっちまで楽しくなっちゃう。
Harada-san yōki da kara issho ni iru to kotchi made tanoshiku natchau.
Harada's such a happy-go-lucky guy that it sort of rubs off on you when you're around him.

ぱっと陽気に騒いで嫌なことは忘れようぜ。
Patto yōki ni sawaide iya na koto wa wasureyō ze.
Hey, man, let's party down and forget all the bad shit.

☞ *inki (na)* 陰気（な）

yōtō-kuniku 羊頭狗肉 "a sheep's head, but dog meat"

cry wine and sell vinegar, make extravagant (and false) claims for a product, false advertising

テレビのコマーシャルとは大違いじゃないの、羊頭狗肉の商法だわ。
Terebi no komāsharu to wa ōchigai ja nai no, yōtō-kuniku no shōhō da wa.
It's nothing like the TV commercial at all. That's blatantly false advertising.

面白そうなテーマで、講師の肩書も立派だったのに、全然つまらない羊頭狗肉の講演だった。
Omoshirosō na tēma de, kōshi no katagaki mo rippa datta no ni, zenzen tsumaranai yōtō-kuniku no kōen datta.
The subject looked interesting, and the lecturer had impressive credentials, but it turned out to be a really boring lecture. I felt like I'd been swindled.

yowaki (na) 弱気(な) "weak *ki*"

gutless, irresolute, spineless, timid, weak-kneed

断られるのが怖いなんて、そんな弱気なことでどうするんだ。
Kotowarareru no ga kowai nante, sonna yowaki na koto de dō suru n' da.
How are you going to get anywhere if you're always quaking in your boots because you think you'll be turned down?

彼の場合は慎重というより弱気ですよ。
Kare no bāi wa shinchō to iu yori yowaki desu yo.
In his case, he's not so much cautious as downright timid.

Also 気弱な *kiyowa na*.
↪ *ki ga chiisai* 気が小さい, *ki ga yowai* 気が弱い; *ki ga tsuyoi* 気が強い, *tsuyoki (na)* 強気(な)

yowamushi 弱虫 "a weak insect"

a baby, coward; sissy, pussy, weakling, weenie, wuss, wimp, candy ass; (of a boy) a momma's boy, a girl

弱虫、毛虫、はさんで捨てろ。
Yowamushi, kemushi, hasande sutero.
Cry baby! Cry baby!

そんな弱虫でどうする。
Sonna yowamushi de dō suru.
You're a big sissy, aren't ya!

☞ *mushi* 虫, *nakimushi* 泣き虫

yubi 指 finger

It should come as no surprise that all five fingers have Japanese names, starting with the thumb or *oya-yubi* ("parent finger"). Japanese women use their thumb to indicate a man by raising it in a "thumbs up" gesture, often accompanied by a comment like *Kore ga urusai,* which roughly means that their boyfriend or husband won't let them do what they want to do. The index finger is called the *hitosashi-yubi,* or the finger you use to point at people. Known only as the *naka-yubi* ("middle finger"), the longest finger on the hand comes out short in the name game. The ring finger is known as the *kusuri-yubi*, or "medicine finger," because, being the weakest of the fingers and therefore the least likely to inflict pain, it's the one that was traditionally used to mix and apply concoctions to all kinds to injuries. The last and least is the *ko-yubi,* or "little finger," which gets a lot of use by Japanese men, who make a fist and stick it up when they're talking about women or their amorous adventures.

By the way, closing the index finger and the thumb in a circle, as an

American might do to make the OK sign, means "money," though it can also be used for OK. If it's toes that you want to talk about, just affix *ashi no* to *yubi* and you have, quite logically, a "foot finger."

Ushiro-yubi o sasareru 後ろ指をさされる "be pointed at behind one's back"
be the object of gossip

私は、後ろ指をさされるようなことは何もしていない。
Watashi wa, ushiro-yubi o sasareru yō na koto wa nani mo shite inai.
I haven't done anything to make people talk behind my back.

人から後ろ指をさされるようなことだけは、してはならない。
Hito kara ushiro-yubi o sasareru yō na koto dake wa, shite wa naranai.
Don't do anything that will cause you to be the object of gossip.

Yubi ippon (mo) furesasenai 指一本（も）触れさせない "not let someone lay even one finger on something"
don't let someone lay a finger on

彼女には指一本触れさせない。
Kanojo ni wa yubi ippon furesasenai.
You lay even so much as one finger on her! / Lay a finger on her and you're in for it!

先祖代々のこの土地に、誰であろうと、指一本も触れさせない。
Senzo-daidai no kono tochi ni, dare de arō to, yubi ippon mo furesasenai.
This property has been in the family for generations, and I'm not about to let anyone lay a finger on it (get their hands on it).

Yubi o kuwaeru 指をくわえる "have one's finger in one's mouth"

---

(1) stand around (without doing anything) (2) look on longingly

(1) 彼が乱暴されているのを、指をくわえて見ていたというのか。
Kare ga ranbō sarete iru no o, yubi o kuwaete mite ita to iu no ka.
You mean you just stood there and watched while he was being assaulted? / Don't tell me you just stood around with your finger in your ear (picking your nose) while he was getting beaten up?

(2) 彼は幸せそうな家族の姿を、指をくわえて見ていた。
Kare wa shiawase-sō na kazoku no sugata o, yubi o kuwaete mite ita.
He watched the happy family enviously.

yudan-taiteki 油断大敵 "carelessness is the greatest enemy"

danger comes when you least expect it; there is many a slip twixt the cup and the lip; Be very careful! Be on your guard! Watch your step!

あいつは意外と口が軽いから、うっかりしたことは言えないね。油断大敵だ。
Aitsu wa igai to kuchi ga karui kara, ukkari shita koto wa ienai ne. Yudan-taiteki da.
You wouldn't think it but he's a real chatterbox, so you've got to be careful what you say. A word to the wise.

やさしいとたかをくくって試験に臨んだのが油断大敵さ、不合格だったよ。
Yasashii to taka o kukutte shiken ni nozonda no ga yudan-taiteki sa, fugōkaku datta yo.
I really slipped up big this time. I thought the exam was going to be a cinch, but guess who ended up failing.

yūdō-jinmon 誘導尋問 "leading interrogation"

a leading question

女房の誘導尋問にひっかかって、へそくりがばれてしまったよ。
Nyōbō no yūdō-jinmon ni hikkakatte, hesokuri ga barete shimatta yo.
I got caught off guard by a leading question, and my wife found out about the money I'd been squirreling away.

母は、私が今誰とつきあってるのか知りたくて、誘導尋問してくるんだけど、その手にはのらないわ。
Haha wa, watashi ga ima dare to tsukiatte 'ru no ka shiritakute, yūdō-jinmon shite kuru n' da kedo, sono te ni wa noranai wa.
My mother always wants to know who I'm going out with and keeps asking leading questions, but I'm not falling for that one.

yūjū-fudan 優柔不断 "indecisive and irresolute"

indecision; to be indecisive, to vacillate, to waver, to shilly-shally

今度の上司は優柔不断で、新しい企画案を出しても取り上げてもらえないんだよ。
Kondo no jōshi wa yūjū-fudan de, atarashii kikaku-an o dashite mo toriagete moraenai n' da yo.
Our new boss is incapable of making a decision. Try putting forward a new planning proposal—it'll never see the light of day.

いつまでも優柔不断なこと言ってたから、彼女は別の人と見合いしてさっさと結婚したんじゃないか。
Itsu made mo yūjū-fudan na koto itte 'ta kara, kanojo wa betsu no hito to miai shite sassa to kekkon shita n' ja nai ka.
You never stopped hemming and hawing, so she went off and got married to some guy she'd been introduced to by relatives.

yūkei-mukei 有形無形 "with shape, without shape"

visible and invisible, material and spiritual, concrete and abstract, tangible and intangible

友だちから有形無形の援助をしてもらって、とても助かりました。
Tomodachi kara yūkei-mukei no enjō o shite moratte, totemo tasukarimashita.
I received a great deal of support from my friends, both material and moral, which really helped a lot.

彼はよい家柄に生まれたことで、有形無形の恩恵を受けている。
Kare wa yoi iegara ni umareta koto de, yūkei-mukei no onkei o ukete iru.
Being born with a silver spoon in his mouth, he had a headstart in life in innumerable ways, both tangible and intangible.

長期にわたって有形無形の圧力をかけられて、ついに屈した。
Chōki ni watatte yūkei-mukei no atsuryoku o kakerarete, tsui ni kusshita.
After a long spell of having all manner of pressure brought to bear on me, I've finally thrown in the towel.

yukue-fumei 行方不明 "whereabouts unclear"

to be missing; whereabouts unknown

妻が家出して行方不明になってから、もう半年になります。
Tsuma ga iede shite yukue-fumei ni natte kara, mō hantoshi ni narimasu.
It's already been six months now since my wife left home and disappeared.

長いこと行方不明だった本が、机の裏から出てきたよ。
Nagai koto yukue-fumei datta hon ga, tsukue no ura kara dete kita yo.
That book that was missing for so long has turned up behind my desk.

※ When people move house without informing others of their new address, post that is delivered to their former address is returned to the sender stamped

移転先不明 (*itensaki-fumei*, new address unknown). The Japanese for "of no fixed abode," 住所不定 (*jūsho-futei*), is now commonly used in reference to the homeless.

yūmei-mujitsu 有名無実 "the name exists, but the reality doesn't"

nominal, titular, in name alone, famous (but unjustly so)

名医だという話だったけど、あの先生の評判は有名無実だよ。
Meii da to iu hanashi datta kedo, ano sensei no hyōban wa yūmei-mujitsu da yo.
He was supposed to be an excellent doctor, but his reputation turned out to be without any foundation in fact.

あんな有名無実なヒヤリングは、いくらやっても無駄だ。
Anna yūmei-mujitsu na hiyaringu wa, ikura yatte mo muda da.
There's no use holding any more meaningless "hearings" like that.

社長と言っても、僕の肩書は有名無実なんですよ。
Shachō to itte mo, boku no katagaki wa yūmei-mujitsu nan desu yo.
I am CEO in name only.

yūmō-kakan 勇猛果敢 "very brave and decisive"

dauntless courage and decisiveness

強者ぞろいの中でも、彼は抜きんでて勇猛果敢だった。
Tsuwamono zoroi no naka de mo, kare wa nukinde 'te yūmō-kakan datta.
Even in the midst of such mighty men, he stood out as being the bravest and the boldest of them all.

司令官みずから勇猛果敢に戦った。
Shirei-kan mizukara yūmō-kakan ni tatakatta.
With a total disregard for his own safety the commander courageously threw himself into the thick of battle.

zako 雑魚 "various fish"

small fish; small fry

今日は雑魚ばかり釣れた。
Kyō wa zako bakari tsureta.
I just caught a bunch of garbage (small) fish today.

雑魚は相手にせず、大物だけを狙え。
Zako wa aite ni sezu, ōmono dake o nerae.
Don't bother with the small fry, go for the bigwigs.

警察は大がかりな摘発作戦に出たが、検挙したのは雑魚ばかりだった。
Keisatsu wa ōgakari na tekihatsu-sakusen ni deta ga, kenkyo shita no wa zako bakari datta.
The police began a large-scale roundup of criminals, but ended up netting a bunch of small-time crooks.

☞ *zako-ne* 雑魚寝

zako-ne 雑魚寝 "sleep together like various fish"

sleep together in a huddle

旅行社の手違いで、小さな部屋に他の客と一緒に雑魚寝させられた。
Ryokō-sha no techigai de, chiisana heya ni hoka no kyaku to issho ni zako-ne saserareta.

Thanks to a slipup on the tour company's part, we had to sleep all huddled up with other guests in one room.

その不法入国者達は6畳のアパートに雑魚寝しているところを検挙された。
Sono fuhō-nyūkokusha-tachi wa roku-jō no apāto ni zako-ne shite iru tokoro o kenkyo sareta.
When the illegal immigrants were picked up, they were all sleeping packed into one six-mat room.

❈ From the hodgepodge of small fish landed in nets. Often used of men and women sleeping huddled together in one room.

☞ *zako* 雑魚

zeitaku-zanmai 贅沢三昧 "concentration on luxury"

burn the candle at both ends, give oneself over to a life of pleasure, sow one's wild oats, live for pleasure

若い頃、贅沢三昧の生活をした罰があたったんでしょうか。年取ってからは苦労続きです。
Wakai koro, zeitaku-zanmai no seikatsu o shita batsu ga atatta n' deshō ka. Toshitotte kara wa kurō-tsuzuki desu.
When I was young, I burned the candle at both ends, but it seems I'm paying for it now. As I get on in years, I'm having nothing but trouble.

ブランド物を買いあさって、贅沢三昧をしていたバブル全盛の頃が懐かしいな。
Burando-mono o kaiasatte, zeitaku-zanmai o shite ita baburu-zensei no koro ga natsukashii na.
I miss the days of the bubble economy, buying designer goods and indulging in every whim.

zendai-mimon 前代未聞 "never heard of before"

unheard of, unprecedented, unparalleled (in history), record-breaking, rare, unusual

宗教団体による、この前代未聞の犯罪には、日本中がショックを受けた。
Shūkyō-dantai ni yoru, kono zendai-mimon no hanzai ni wa, Nihon-jū ga shokku o uketa.
Japan was shocked by the unprecedented scale of the crime committed by the religious cult.

役人が役所の内情を暴露した本を書くなんて、前代未聞だね。
Yakunin ga yakusho no naijō o bakuro shita hon o kaku nante, zendai-mimon da ne.
It's unheard of for a civil servant to write a book exposing the inner workings of the Japanese bureaucracy.

zengo-fukaku 前後不覚 "before and after, no recollection"

to be dead to the world, out for the count, in a stupor, to pass out

ゆうべまた、調子にのって飲み過ぎて、前後不覚になったらしい。何も覚えていないんだ。
Yūbe mata, chōshi ni notte nomisugite, zengo-fukaku ni natta rashii. Nani mo oboete inai n' da.
I got carried away again last night, drank myself silly, and apparently passed out. I don't remember a thing.

夕べは疲れていたので、前後不覚に10時間以上も寝てしまった。
Yūbe wa tsukarete ita no de, zengo-fukaku ni jūji-kan ijō mo nete shimatta.
Last night I was so tired that I just conked out and slept for over ten hours.

zento-yōyō 前途洋々 "The road ahead is broad and wide."

one's future prospects are good; the outlook is good; you've got a bright (promising) future before you; the future's looking good (rosy); the future's coming up roses

一流大学卒業、一流企業へ就職、とまさに前途洋々だねえ。
Ichiryū-daigaku sotsugyō, ichiryū-kigyō e shūshoku, to masa ni zento-yōyō da nē.
What with you graduating from a top university and now getting a job with a major company, your future's certainly looking rosy.

出世間違いなし、前途洋々の青年だって仲人さんが言ったから結婚したのに……。
Shusse machigai nashi, zento-yōyō no seinen datte nakōdo-san ga itta kara kekkon shita no ni …
To think that I married him because the matchmaker said he was certain to get promoted, that he was a young man with a bright future . . .

❀ There is a four-character compound with the opposite meaning to this, which is 前途多難 (*zento-tanan*). Its literal meaning is "on the road ahead there are many difficulties." In more idiomatic English we might say someone "has got their work cut out for them" or "is in for a rough ride ahead." See the examples below.

かえったばかりのカメの赤ちゃんはやっと海へ入っていった。でもまだまだこれから前途多難だ。
Kaetta bakari no kame no akachan wa yatto umi e haitte itta. Demo mada mada kore kara zento-tanan da.
The newly hatched baby turtles managed to make their way to the sea. But many many obstacles still lie ahead.

企画会議はなんとか通ったが、まだまだ前途多難だよ。
Kikaku-kaigi wa nan to ka tōta ga, mada mada zento-tanan da yo.
We managed to get our plan accepted by the project committee, but we're still facing an uphill struggle.

zettai-zetsumei 絶体絶命 "desperate body, desperate life"

a desperate (critical) situation, a (tight) corner, a bad fix, a real bind, up the creek (without a paddle)

007は、何回も絶体絶命の危機に直面しながら、いつも助かることになっている。
Zero-zero-sebun wa, nankai mo zettai-zetsumei no kiki ni chokumen shinagara, itsumo tasukaru koto ni natte iru.
James Bond is forever getting into impossibly tight corners, but he always manages to get out of them again.

もうごまかしはきかない。絶体絶命だ。横領がばれてしまった。
Mō gomakashi wa kikanai. Zettai-zetsumei da. Ōryō ga barete shimatta.
None of your excuses are going to work this time. You're in deep trouble. They've found out you've been cooking the books.

zukan-sokunetsu 頭寒足熱 "a cold head and warm feet"

keeping the head cool and the feet warm

昔から頭寒足熱は健康に良いとされてるね。
Mukashi kara zukan-sokunetsu wa kenkō ni yoi to sarete 'ru ne.
It's always been said that keeping your feet warm and your head cool is good for the health.

部屋中こんなに暑くしてちゃ、頭がのぼせるよ。頭寒足熱を心がけなくちゃ。
Heya-jū konna ni atsuku shite 'cha, atama ga noboseru yo. Zukan-sokunetsu o kokorogakenakucha.
If you keep your room as hot as this, the blood will rush to your head. Keeping your feet warm but your head cool is the way to do it.

✤ This four-character compound contains a traditional piece of Japanese folk wisdom that is of particular cultural interest. By keeping the air temperature in a room quite low (by letting the outside fresh air in), we are less prone to catching colds (as germs thrive in a warm, stuffy environment), and we are better able to keep a cool head and think clearly. However, if we don't keep our feet warm, we feel crotchety and bad tempered. How do the Japanese maintain this healthy equilibrium between a cool head and warm feet? Simple. They invented the *kotatsu*, a low square table covered with a quilt, under which a small electric heater is placed (before the days of electricity, charcoal was used). You sit on the floor with your legs under the quilt, and your feet stay nice and warm.

INDEX

A
abandon oneself to despair 160
abandoned 433
ability being its own best advertisement 456, 541
abominable 78
absurd 78, 352
abusive language 38
academic 24
acquire 393, 560
act big 300
act like a stranger 545
action speaks louder than words 60
active 75
ad hoc 478
adapting 478
addict 298
adding insult to injury 425
admire 28
adulterous 618
advance by leaps and bounds 455
adverse reaction 369
adversity makes strange bedfellows 77
affair 617
affected 300
affinity 128

age 441
aggressive 594
agitated 243
agony 503
airhead 41, 579
all at once 132
(all) at sea 15
all by one's lonesome 442
all directions 503
all ears 479
All is set and ready to go 628
all of something that one can stand 91
all one's heart 152
all one's might 152
all or nothing 144
all over 421
all probability 166
all smiles 329
all talk 426, 430
all the rage 454
all there 242, 523
almost 557
also-ran 373
always a winner 367
amazing 379
ambiguous 545
ambition 626
amiable 216

amiable person 265
angry 30, 96, 546
annoy 261
anticipation 302
anticlimax 482
antsy 225
anxiety 306, 339
anxious 211, 225, 274
anyhow 579, 612
anyway 579, 612
apery 493
apple of one's eye 467
ardor 325
aristocratic 197
arm 597
around the clock 51
aroused 243
arrest 123
arrogance 40, 305
arrogant 350
articulate 85
artless and unaffected character 569
as long as one is alive and kicking 383
as one 134
asinine 492
ask for it 425, 578
ask for it (trouble), stir up a hornets' nest 623

ask for trouble 425, 578
ask one's heart 411
ask oneself 164
asked for it 161
asking for trouble 431
asking too much 423
ass 579
ass in a lion's skin 581
ass-licker 139
assume a (certain) attitude 276
astonished 99
astounded 99, 385
at a (total) loss 15
at a loss 332
at a loss for an answer 32
at a total loss 79
at any rate 579, 612
at each other's throats 199
at sea 79
attend 186
attention 310
attention was diverted 283
attentive 247, 286
audacious 52
audacity 40
authentic 526
avoid 141
avoid being seen 386
aware 246, 263, 342
awkward 313, 343

B

babe in the woods 121
baboon 106
baby 419, 631
back 494
back and forth 151
back down 326
back in one's element 402
back off 393

back out 326, 393, 562
back something 193
back to the wall 371
backbone 292, 309
bad blood 199
bad fix 641
bad humor 417
bad mood 105, 417
bad play 493
bad-mouth 360
badger 407, 534
baffled 332
baldy 544
barefaced 344
barely 110
bargain-basement prices 455
bashful 510
bastard 73, 198
bat 65, 347
bath 190
battle-ax 65
be into 419
be that as it may 579, 612
beam 385
beaming with joy 329
beanpole 173
beanstalk 173
bear in mind 263
beast 142
beat 108
beautiful scenery 62
bee 85
beetle 544
befuddled 332
begin 564, 565
behind the times 25
believe 240
belly 95
belly button 104
bent (out of shape) 417
bent out of shape 96

beside oneself 220
besieged 506
betray oneself 37
bewildered 79
beyond description 78
beyond one 237
beyond reproach 497
big (tall) talk 538
big baby 419
big head 24
big job 556
big laugh 104
big mouth 70
Big Three 487
big, round glasses (sun-glasses) 577
big-headed 24
biggest fish that gets away 448
bird 584
birdbrain 542
birds of a feather 407, 470
bit 319
bit much 380
bitch 65
bite one's lip 364
blab 359
black (pass) out 245
black eye 186
black out 287, 338
blackhearted 96
blah 228
blame oneself 244
blameless 497
bland 408
blessed (gifted, endowed) with both brains and beauty 485
blister 401
blood relations 47
bloodshed 46
bloom (hit one's peak) late

in life 539
blow hot and cold 219
blow one's own trumpet 160
blow up 546
blown away 316, 521
blown-away 99
blows hot and cold 296
blue 136, 209, 234
blue-blooded 197
bluntly 549
boar 138
boast 90
boasting 538
body 187
bold as brass 52
bonanza 130
bone 114
bonkers 213
book of secret teachings 582
boor 494, 625
boring 408
born talker 361
bossy 12
both good points and bad points 155
both merits and demerits 155
both pros and cons 155
bother 259, 261
bothered 255, 259, 262
bothersome 302
bow 489
bow to 33
boy who cried wolf 463
boyfriend 422
boyfriend (lover) 621
brace up 280, 282
brag 413
bragging 538
brains and beauty 485

brass balls 510
brave 52, 280
bravery 475
brazen 344, 510, 511
break one's concentration 207
break someone's concentration 282
bream 537
breast 408
brief reign 396
bright 25, 221, 629
bright (promising) future 640
bright-faced go-getter 527
bring oneself to do 233
bring someone around 261
bring up 49
broke 465
broken 420
broken off 517, 576
brooding 136
brow(s) 376
brown-noser 139
brush up 600
buck up 280, 284
buff 298
bug 415
bulldog 534
bulldoze 79
bullish 594
bummed 234
bummed out 224, 230, 239
bundle up 394
bunhead 542
buoyant 129, 213
buoyed up 289
burn the candle at both ends 638
bush warbler 601
bushed 13
business is booming 522

business is on the up and up 522
business is slow (bad) 183
bust ass 116, 394
bust one's buns 394
busy 378
busy (eager) beaver 347
busy bee 347
butt in 363
buttocks 513
button one's lip 177
bystander 624

C

call black white 606
call someone names 38
calligraphy 401
calling it quits 564
calm and collected 477, 540
calm down 32, 238, 281
calm oneself 279
calm oneself down 278
calmness 102
can handle it 327
can picture 382
can't concentrate on 561
can't get down to 561
can't get into it 215
can't get to first base 558
can't handle 558
can't keep a secret 358
can't keep one's mind on 253
can't keep one's mouth shut 358
can't seem to shake 322
can't stand up to 25
can't take one's eyes off 377
candy ass 419, 631

canned 354
caprice 312, 616
capricious 231, 312, 616
care 262, 306, 310
carefree 313, 327, 459
careful 272, 286, 341
carefully laid plans 507
carp 344
carry 496
carry on 617
carrying a torch 34
cart before the horse 118
casting one's lot with another 126
casting pearls before swine 42, 431
casual 427
cat 428
cat and mouse 153
cat's paw 139
catch one's attention 382
cats and dogs 199
caught up (with one's work) 555
cautious 526
cautiousness 628
centipede 72
ceremony 545
chain reaction 477
champ at the bit 236
chance of a lifetime 501
chance to show what one can do 599
change of heart 219, 507
change of mind 507
change of pace 293
change one's mind 219
change rapidly 433
changeable 616
chaos 516
charming 295
cheapskate 513

cheat on (fudge) the count 483
cheating 617, 618
check out 388
check out every lead 512
checkered 98
cheeky 344, 426
cheerful 75, 629
chemistry's wrong 418
chest 408
chewy 350
chic 221
chicken 207, 587
chicken feed 455
chicken out 326
chicken-livered 317
chickenhearted 207, 317
chickenheartedness 458
childhood friend 48
childish 476
chill 486, 487
chills 486
chip in 363
chivalry 475
choice 528
choked with sorrow, all choked up 410
chow hound 41
chugalug 133
chutzpa 510
cirrocumulus 157
clam up 177
classics 470
claw 591
clean up a place before one leaves 554, 584
clean up after someone 516
clean up someone's mess 516
cleaned out 465
clear 85
clear as day 546

clear as day(light) 124
clear as mud 545
clearly 124, 381, 560
clemency 167
clever 346
click 603
clink 43
clodhopper 494, 625
close call 308
close shave 308
close up like a clam 177
close-mouthed 359
clothes make the man 372
cloud 112, 157
co-prosperity 370
coaxing (wheedling, flattering) (tone of) voice 438
cock-a-hoop 129
cockiness 126
cocky 465, 511
coexistence 370
cold (frightening, exciting) enough to give one goose bumps 586
cold days 489
collect one's thoughts 284
collect oneself 284
collector 590
comb 512
come 22
come around 247
come back to one's senses 247
come to 247
come to bloodshed 46
come to one 246
come to one's senses 379
comfort 336
comfortable 327
coming up roses 640
common consent 134

common or garden-variety event, no big deal, ten a penny 446
commotion 85
communication 149
compare notes 109
compassionate 250
compatible 206
competition 168
competitive 173
complacent satisfaction 162
complain 364
complete rundown 122
conceit 126
conceited 300
concern 301, 339
concerned 255
concrete and abstract 635
confidence 165
conscience-stricken 244
consciousness 524
consider 386
considerate 220, 223, 247, 271, 341
consideration 339
consolation 336
constrained 303
contacts 185
contender 539
content 240
control 82
convince someone to do something 261
cool 221, 427, 477, 540
cool as a cucumber 104, 477, 540
cool down 32, 416
cool head 540, 641
cool off 32
cooler 43
cooling-off period 476
cooperating 450

cop out 326
copy 493
copycatting 493
cordoned off 18
cormorant 595
cornered rat 371
could(n't) care less 171, 253
counting one's chickens before they hatch 552, 583
courage 636
courteous 349
cow 613
coward 419, 631
cowardly 526
cracked 213, 298
crackpot 297
craftsmanship 525
crafty old fox 607
cramp someone's style 22
crane 593
crane chains 499, 593
crane fly 173
cranes 499
crazy 213, 297, 298
crazy about 379
crazy about 419
cream of the crop 528
creep 73, 198
creepy 314
crème de la crème 528
crib 493, 582
critical 360
critical moment 308
cross 105
cross-grained 321
crow 189
crow's-feet 190
crud 198
cry wine and sell vinegar 630

crybaby 419
cubbyhole 432
cuckoo 183
cue ball 544
cultivate a (business) relationship 187
cunning 492
cunning person 551
cur 142
cure all 432
curious bystanders 624
cursing 38
curtains 421
cut corners 564
cut in 363
cut one to the quick 412
cut something loose 564
cut the Gordian knot 156

D

daily (common, commonplace, ordinary) occurrence 446
damn the torpedos 138
dampen 281
danger comes when you least expect it 633
daredevil 52
dark 137
dash 75
dauntless 636
dawn on one 246
dead to the world 639
deaf 398
deal with a matter decisively 156
death 77
death's door 421
decide 97
decisiveness 636
decoy 33

deeply impressed 392
deer caught in the headlights 101
defiance 40
defiant 92
dejected 127, 278
delicate white fingers 512
delicious 13
delight written all over one's face 329
delightful 295, 346
dense 46
depressed 127, 209, 215, 224, 239, 278
depressing 137
deserted 585
deserve what you get 161
desire 626
desire (for) 147
desire (to eat) 365
desired effect 432
despair 160
despair gives courage to a coward 371
desperate (critical) situation 641
desperation 160
desperation of a cornered rat 371
despondent 278, 325
despotic husband 567
details 522
determined 216, 249, 350
developing your abilities 502
devil of a time 504
devotee 298
diamond on a dunghill is still a diamond 367, 537
diarrhea of the mouth 358
die a dog's death 142
die in vain 142

die peacefully 77
different as night and day 534
difficult 83, 114, 321, 556
diffident 215
dignity 307
dim-witted 28
dimwit 41
dingdong 151
diplomacy 68
diplomatic 68
dire distress 504
directly 549
dirt cheap 455
dirty look 389
dirty old man 106
disagreeable 320
disappear without trace 609
disappointed 230, 364
discomfort 303
discouraged 127, 325
discover 342
discuss 109
disease 44
disgusted 158
disgusting 83, 320, 411
dishearten 281
disheartened 278
disinclined 242
dislike 256, 418
disorderly crowd 600
disperse 366
disposition 299
disruption 516
dissemble 434
distract 282
distracted 207, 239, 253, 283
disturbed 520
disturbing 259
dither 339
divergent views 338

diversify 563
diversion 293
divert one's attention 273
divert someone's attention 282
diverted 222
DIY 447
dizzying 245
do a good job 268
do one's best 566
do something 566
do-it-yourself fanatic 447
docile 112
dog 138
dog tired 13
dog-eat-dog world 158
dog-paddle 143
dog-tired 108
doing good business 522
dominate 82
don't care 102, 171
don't care (much) for 256
don't feel 237
don't feel (like doing) 236
don't feel like 227
don't get the feeling 237
don't intend to 227
don't know what to do 32
don't let someone lay a finger on 632
don't like 256
don't like someone's looks 383
don't sweat the small stuff 233
don't think 237
don't toot your horn 541
done and dusted 131
done in 13, 108
dope 542
dote on 435

double (dual) personality 449
double-crossed 177
doubt 76
doubtful 93
dove 99
down 189, 215, 224, 234, 239
down in the dumps 127, 132
down to business 117
down-and-outer 373
downcast 278
downhearted 127
dream come true 180
dreary 137
drink 436
drive 328, 626
drop in the bucket 536
drop one's guard 252, 291
drop out 562
drowned rat 445
drowsiness 439
dubious 93
duck 179
dull 408
dull-witted 27
dumbell 41
dummy 542
dump 543
dunners 591
dupe 179
dwindling out 482

E

eager-beaver 404
eagerness 460
ear 397
ear to the ground 397
earnestness 116
earthworm 400
ease off 290
easy 235
easy lay 514
easy mark 179
easy to be around 232
easy to get along with 328
easy way 59
easygoing 304, 327, 459
eat 362, 436
eating 406
ebb and flow 151
echo 469
educational background 69
eerie 314
egghead 544
ego trip 126
either way 579, 612
elated 129
elbow 107
electrical cords 544
elite corps 528
elusive 509
embezzle 565
emotional rollercoaster 132
empathy 182
empty 111
empty threat 374
emulate 592
encouraged 289
encouragement 336
endless battle 404
endure 496
enduring 321
enemies 77
energetic 573, 585
energetic 75
energy 74, 328
enforcer 590
engrossed 406
enigmatic 545
enjoy popularity 454
enlightened 379
enthusiasm 325, 460, 626
enthusiast 298
enthusiastic 193, 210, 229, 271
equivocal 545
evasive 85
even Homer sometimes nods 491
even so 579, 612
eventful 98
eventually 574
ever so polite 136
every direction 503
every dog and his brother 430
every dog has his day 141
every miller draws water to his own mill 67
every move one makes 134
every possible means 563
every Tom, Dick and Harry 430, 619
every trick in the book 563
every which way 503
everyday occurrence (affair) 446
everyone and his brother 619
everything is ready 628
everything under the sun 563
evidently 124
evil 96
evil intention 621
exaggerating 508
excitable 203
excited 20, 46, 213, 409
excruciating pain 502
exemplary behavior 107
exhalted 197
exhausted 108
expand 563

expansive 233, 556
experience firsthand 86
explode 546
explosive 547
express 362
extemporaneously 478
extramarital relationship 617
extraneous 54
extravagant (and false) claims for a product 630
exultant 129
eye 377
eyebrow(s) 73, 376
eyes get big 385

F

face 184
face full of joy 329
face lit up with joy 329
facing the same fate 126
fail miserably after a good start 482
failure 373
faint 245, 287, 338
faint (barely audible, thin) voice 172
faint (shallow) breathing 421
fainthearted 207, 251, 317, 526
faintheartedness 458
fair 61
fair and square 498
faithfully 498
fake 300, 493
fall between two stools 11
fall on one's knees 489
fall unconscious 338
false advertising 630

familiar 335
family happily united 129
famous (but unjustly so) 636
fan 298, 419
fanatical 419
fantastic 330
far and wide 503
farsighted 507
fashionable 450
fast runner 21
fast start and a slow finish 482
fast to put the make on a woman 556
faultless 184
favor 466
favorite 467
fear 339, 500
fearless 52
feathering one's own nest 517
feed one's face 362
feel (like) 240
feel (something) in one's bones 417
feel a pang of conscience 244
feel at ease 232
feel bad 288, 320
feel better 210, 235
feel differently about 219
feel dizzy 378
feel faint 245
feel funny 215
feel good 319
feel great 295, 319
feel ill 295
feel ill at ease 248
feel like 201, 204
feel like a load (weight) has been lifted from

one's shoulders 217, 235
feel like doing 208, 226, 257
feel like one has already done something when one hasn't 258
feel low 325
feel rushed 339
feel that way, feel like 529
feel well 295
feeling 530
feeling lonely 442
feeling sick 88
feeling(s) 293, 305, 317
feign (put on an act of) ignorance or innocence 434
feisty 92, 173, 249
female announcer 603
fervor 325
fickle 231, 433, 616
fight 292, 626
fight desperately 15
figment of one's imagination 266
finally 574
find a diversion 273
find and keep 436
find out 342
find out about 399
fine hair 437
fine-tooth comb 512
finger 632
finger 591
fingernail 591
fingers 512
fire 356
fire and water 71
fire them up 521
fired 353, 354
firm 350, 594
fish 437, 637
fit as a fiddle 405

fit for a king 13
fixer-upper 337
fizzle out 517, 576
fizzling out 482
flat 230
flat out 51
flatter oneself 289
flattery 42
flawless 184, 569
fleabite 171
flexibility 478
flexible 29
flighty 514
fling 617
flip one's lid 30
flip out 30, 214, 222
flip-flop 219, 433
flirtatious 231
floccus 112
floored 99
flowery language 39
fluency 166
flunky 139
flushed 233
flustered 243
flux 433
foggiest idea 79
follow one's heart 411
fool 41, 542, 579
foolhardy 50, 138
foolishness 579
foot the bill 159
footloose and fancy-free 58
for a change 293
for peanuts 455
for real 116
forehead 109
forget (one's worries) 222
forget one's troubles 268
forget oneself 406
form up 70
forthright 84

fox 331
fox fire 334
foxed 332
frame of mind 266
frank 84
frankly 549
fraught (pregnant) with meaning 135
freak out 30
free 188, 555
freeload 533
freely 166, 170, 473
fresh 426
fret (over) 264, 274
friend from childhood 48
friendly 335
friendly chat 113
frightened out of one's wits 316
frog 174
from all over 503
from the start 29
frown 376
frozen in fear 101
frugal 592
fuddy-duddy 372
fudge 483
full deck 28
full of (good) ideas 223
full of hope 413
full particulars 122
full steam ahead 169
funny feeling 417
furrow one's brows 376
fuss 274
fussy 321
future prospects 640
fuzzy 619

G

gag 492

gaggle 600
gain 560
gallantry 475
game 249
gamut of human emotions 300
gangster 53
gawker 624
general release 143
generosity 311
generously 473
genius in the family 572
gentle 250
gentle on the outside 67
genuine article 526
geometrical (exponential) increase 444
get 560
get (jump, delve) into something 356
get (take) one's mind off 273
get a grip 281
get a little (nookie, pussy) on the side 617
get a lot of bang for your buck 59
get ahead of oneself 212
get all hopped up (about) 229
get along 87, 206
get along (get on) well 603
get bad vibes 418
get behind something 117, 193
get better 598
get careless 277
get down to it 117
get fired 355
get going 229
get hold of 559
get hold of oneself 281

get in someone's way 22
get in the mood to do 233
get in the mood 257
get into 229, 326
get into a panic 610
get into doing something 210, 271
get involved (in) 562, 564
get mad and you'll live to regret it 547
get married 394
get on one's nerves 256, 259
get one's two cents worth in 363
get others to do your work 553
get out 393, 562
get over an important hurdle 589
get rich quick 130
get rid of 356
get someone's attention 282
get someone's hopes up 275
get something off one's chest 410
get the attention of 382
get the ax 355
get the notion (that) 240
get the wrong idea 274
get to one 261
get together 113
get together to discuss something 370
get turned on 229
get up on the wrong side of the bed in the morning 417
get wind of 342, 399
get-up-and-go 626

gets around 185
getting ahead 345, 478
getting on in the world 478
giddy 378
gigilo 590, 620
gingerly 500
girl 419, 631
girlfriend 471
give (lend) a helping hand 110
give an ear to 399
give in to 33
give one's right arm for someone 110
give oneself away 37
give oneself over to a life of pleasure 638
give oneself to 395
give oneself to a man 88
give somebody a pep talk 521
give someone a dirty look 519
give someone a workout 413
give something one's all 115
give something up 562
give up 351
gives you the creeps 320
glasses 577
gloomy 136, 137
glowworm 120
glum face 603
go 22
go (be) crazy 206, 214, 222
go against the grain 256
go along uncritically with something 518
go for broke 144
go on and on about 90

go out like a light 245, 287
go out of sight 609
go to 186
go to a lot of trouble 368
go to bed with a man 395
go to one's head 126
go to town 599
go too far 359
go toward 23
go up in a puff of smoke 609
gobbledegook 516
goby 78
going to 201
goldfish 322
good (irreproachable) conduct 107
good at 598
good cheer 129
good disposition 216, 265
good person 265
good sense of smell 90
good-for-nothing 53
good-hearted 216
good-natured 216
goof off 277
goose bumps, goose pimples, gooseflesh 586
gossip 632
grand 197
great distress 16
great presence of mind 540
great talents are slow in maturing 539
greatness late in life 539
green 514
grimacing 422
grimalkin 65
grin and bear it 422
grind 98
grinning like a Cheshire cat 329

grope blindly in the dark 15
grounding in the classics 471
grumble 364
grumpy 417
guilty 244
gullible 596
gut-wretching 409
gutless 630
gutsy 249, 510
guzzle 133

H

habitual liar 463
had it 421
hair 178, 319
hale and hearty 405
half-assed 102
half-baked 51
half-done 51, 102, 517, 576
half-finished 51, 517, 576
halfhearted 51, 324
ham actor 52
handwriting 401
handyman 337
hang by a hair 308
hang on 282
hang on to (keep) one's job 354
hang tough 280, 350
hanger-on 322
hanky-panky 617
happily married 473
happy 346, 629
happy family (home) 129
happy-go-lucky 327
hard (tireless) worker 347
hard as one can 152
hard fight 15
hard of hearing 398

hard to get along with 321
hard work and effort 368
hard worker 38, 98, 404
hard-nosed 218, 594
hardhat 572
hardheaded 249
hare 611
harried 339
hassle 556
hasty 212, 225
hate someone's guts 383
hates to lose 173
have a fire lit under one 515
have a hard time 16
have a lot of irons in the fire 231
have a mind of one's own 249
have a minute 555
have a nose for 90
have a screw loose 213
have actually done 392
have both oars in the water 242
have enough 240
have guts 510
have had enough of 158
have had one's fill 240
have it in for someone 383
have misgivings 445
have no effect 35
have no use for 256
have one's feelings hurt 288
have one's hands full 559, 567
have one's head up in the clouds 20
have one's ruffled feathers smoothed 416
have one's share snatched

away at the last moment 571
have some doubts 356
have someone's best interests at heart 341
have something on one's mind 255, 259, 262
have something stolen that was almost in one's hand 571
have trouble concentrating on 253
hawk 540
hazy 14
head for 23
headache 26, 301
headstrong 249
health 74
hear of 398, 399
heard about all one wants to hear of something 399
heart 292, 328, 510
heart and mind 305
heart in one's mouth 409
heart is filled 409
heart sinks 224
heart's in the right place 292
heart-to-heart talk 97
heartbreaking 409
heartrending 409
heavy heart 127
heavyhearted 234
hell 11
help 110
herd of cats 600
here one minute, gone the next 509
heron 484
hesitate 445
high 495

high morals 107
high spirits 129, 213
high turnover 89
high-flying 573, 585
high-handed 350
highfalutin phrases 39
hint 75
hips 348
hit a sore spot 398
hit it off 128, 206
hit on 562
hit the jackpot 130
hit where it hurts 398
hitting the bull's-eye 120
hitting the mark 120
hoity-toity 350
hold back nothing 115
hold on 282
hold one's own 598
hold someone back 22
hold sway over 82
hole in the wall 432
home alone 442
honey-tongued 360
hood 53
hop 613
hopped up 46
horseface 607
hot 243
hot and bothered 46
hot stuff 126
hot to trot 46
hot under the collar 96
hot-tempered 224
hotheaded 224
hounded 339
how many times have I told you 360
how one looks at it (things) 266
huddle 109
human wave tactics 165

humble 349
humongous 245
hunch 417
hungry 95
husband 458, 567

I

idiot 542, 579
ignis fatuus 334
ill 189
ill at ease 192, 313, 343
illness 44
illness brought on by emotional fatigue 267
imagine 411
imbecile 542
immersed 406
imminent 388
impartial 61
impatience can be expensive 548
impatient 212, 225
impending 388
impertinent 426
imperturbable 540
impetuous 212
impolite 350
imposing 197
impractical 20
impress 414
impromptu 478
improve 598
improve oneself 501
impudent 344
in a day 155
in a fog 79
in a good mood 289
in a hurry 236
in a rush 236
in any case 579, 612
in debt (hock) 353

in love 532
in love with yourself 162
in name alone 636
in one ear and out the other 35
in one shot 132
in one's right mind 242
in the dark 392
in the end (final analysis) 574
in the mood 226
in the red 21
in the same boat 126
inches away from 145
inclination (to do) 324
inclined to 201, 226
incoherence 516
incomplete 51
inconsistency 516
incredulous 93
indecision 634
indecisive 634
independence 57
independent 61
indication 198
indifferent 102, 427
inexcusable 78
infantile 476
infatuated 357
influential 185, 573, 585
informal 232
informant 139
inhibited 207
inner strength 328
innermost thoughts 305
innocence 570
innocent 169
innocent-looking 424
ins and outs 122
insane 213, 222, 297
insanity 297, 368
insect 415

insect- (worm-, moth-, etc.) eaten 420
insensitive 102
insipid 408
insolence 40
insolent 426
insularism 505
insularity 505
insults 38
integrity 497
intellectual 24
intend to 201, 204
intensity 325
interest (in) 147, 324
interested in 203, 204, 388
interested in (awaken to) sex 148
interfere 22, 356, 362
intolerable 380
intrepid 52
intuitively shared thoughts 149
inviting trouble 431
iron-jawed 249
irreconcilable 61
irresolute 630
irritate 261
island-nation mentality 505
isolated 585
it takes all kinds 168
it won't last 396
it's all in one's head 266
it's the thought that counts 292

J

jab someone with one's elbow 107
Jack of all trades and master of none 337
Jack Sprat and his wife 458
jack-o'-lantern 334
jail 43
jam-packed train 374
Japanese and Western styles 622
Jekyll and Hyde 449
jerk 73, 198
jewel beetle 544
jig is up 63
joke 493
jump on the bandwagon 518
jump the gun 162
just a shade 319
just asking for it 180
just don't like 418
just know (something is wrong) 417
just like (no different/no better than) the others 407, 470
just right 221
just the person we need 568
just the ticket 568
juvenile 476

K

keen on 203
keep an eye on 380, 385
keep it up 396
keep on one's toes 376
keep one's eye on 388
keep one's eyes peeled 595
keep one's mouth shut 177
keep one's wits about one 376
keep the faith 287
keep to oneself 597
kick back 288
kids can turn out better than their parents 572
kill two birds with one stone 150
kind 250
kindred spirit 128
kiss 365
kite 571
knackered 108
knit one's brows 376
knock off 493
know 392
know a thing or two about 378
know better 387
know how to spot something good 378
know something backwards and forwards 380
know something inside and out 380
knowledgeable 378
knucklehead 41
koi 344
kowtow 489

L

lackadaisical 228
lackey 139
ladle 474
lady-killer 91
laid-back 216, 227, 304, 327, 328, 459
lamblike 191
land 559
largess 311
last ditch effort 154
last gasp retort 154
last legs 421
last thing one needs (wants) to see 383
last-ditch stalling 81
late (slow) developer 539

late bloomer 539
laugh 90
law of the jungle 158
lay 565
lay (put) one's life on the line 188
lay someone off 356
lead in one's pants 350
leading question 633
learn 393
leave 562
leave (something) up in the air 619
leave a fox to guard the henhouse 431
leave a place like one found it 554, 584
leave a strong impression 412
leave something half-dead 101
lech 106
left up in the air 619
legit 195
legitimate 195
lend a hand 563
lend an ear to 400
leniency 167
let down 230
let it all hang out 233
let one's conscience be one's guide 411
let one's guard down 252, 291
let one's mind wander 281
let someone go 356
let something get to one 262
let something pass 387
let something slip 359
let up 252, 277, 290, 291
lick one's chops 457

light-headed 245
lighthearted 210, 217, 235, 304
like 254, 466
like a fish out of water 402
like a ghost in the night 509
like a house on fire 128
like a lot 379
like a weight has been lifted from one's shoulders 210
like father, like son 175
like food better than sex 147
like mad 206
like mother, like daughter 175
like the ladies 91
like the ladies (men) 231
like the plague 141
like-minded 128, 206
lily-livered 207, 317
limit to luck 626
limp 351
line up 70
lining one's own pockets 517
lip(s) 363
listen to 399, 400
listless 228
little more than 178, 197
live (for something / to do something) 419
live and breathe (something) 419
live for pleasure 638
lively 75
liver 315
loach 55
load off one's mind 410, 414
logrolling 610

lone wolf (loner) 144, 463
long and drawn out 614
long and slow 614
long face 607
long fuse 227
long line 50
long-faced 136, 364
long-suffering 321
long-winded 358
look after 284
look as if one could not kill (hurt, harm) a fly (flea) 424
look askance 389, 519
look at 386, 387, 388
look daggers 389, 519
look favorably upon 466
look forward to 123
look on longingly 632
look over 387, 595
look toward 386
looker 601
looking good (rosy) 640
looking pleased with yourself (smug) 575
loony 297
loose 514
loose lips 358
lord it 465
lose (all the) fizz 230
lose concentration 281
lose consciousness 245, 287
lose face 186
lose heart 230, 325
lose it 207, 214, 222
lose one's head 610
lose one's marbles 213, 214
lose one's mind 222
lose one's nerve 326
lose one's zest for life 252

lose oneself in   406
lose touch   472
lose track   208
loser   373
losing one's job   353
lot of work   114
louse   511
lousy (poor) actor   52
love triangle   488
lovebirds   473
lover   422, 590, 620
loving couple   65
low   234, 495
low profile   349
low spirits   209
luck   56
lucky day   141
lugubrious   136
lukewarm   324
lump in one's throat   409
lunacy   299
lunatic   297

M

machismo   475
mackerel   483
mackerel cloud (sky)   157
mad   30, 213, 222
madcap   50, 138
made in heaven   473
made your bed   161
madhouse   85
madman   297
madness   297, 299, 368
make a killing   59, 130
make a lasting impression   392
make a move   566
make a pig of oneself   39
make a sour face; scowl   422, 447

make no bones   102
make one sick   256
make one want to gag   83
make oneself at home   280
make someone (want to) do something   261
make the first strike   500
make up one's mind   97, 125
making a fortune   130
making a fresh start   507
making a mountain out of a molehill   508
making a name   478
making a success   478
male chauvinism   54
malice   621
mandarin duck   472
maniac   297
manliness, masculinity   475
material and spiritual   635
matters of extremely minor importance   522
maverick   144, 463
maximize returns and minimize effort   59
meaningful   135
measure up   194
meddle   356
meek   207, 251
meet   389, 468
melancholy   136, 239
men and women of all ages   480
men wrapped around her little finger   601
mental anguish   306
mental fatigue   340
meticulous   557
mettle   328
midair somersault   577
milling crowd   600

million laughs   104
mimicry   493
mind   262
mind is taken off something   283
mind one's tongue   361
mind rules the body   624
mind's someplace else   254
mindfulness   628
minuscule   109
miscount   483
misfortunes seldom come alone   425
missing   635
mistake   18
mistrustful   274
mixed opinion   338
mock   90
mockery   493
model of composure   540
model wife and mother   480
mole   139, 403
mole cricket   464
mollified   416
momma's boy   419, 631
money politics   323
monkey   490
monkey business; monkey see, monkey do   493
monologue   164
mooch   533
mood   293, 530
moody   296
more interested in food than sex   147
more than one can ask (hope) for   180
more than one deserves   391
more ways than you could shake a stick   563
morose   136

moth drawn to flame 425, 578
motivation 626
motormouth 361
mouse 442
mousiness 458
mousy 112
mouth 357
mouth is watering 457
mouthwatering 13
move 414
moving 412
mullet 573
mumbo jumbo 493
munificence 311
music 474
musical note 474
must be imagining things 266
mutual love 532
mutual understanding 128
mystery man 604
mystery woman 604
mystified 332

N

nailed to the floor 350
naive person 121
naivety 570
namby-pamby 526
narcissistic 162
narrow margin 89
natural 328
nature 299
nausea 88
nauseating 83
navel 104
nearly shit one's pants 316
neck 353
neck and neck 194
need 457
needless to say 140
nerve 510
nerve-racking 211
nervous exhaustion 340
nervously 500
nest egg 582
neurosis 267
neutral 61
never do anything to hurt someone 23
next to nothing 172, 455, 536
nice 250
nick of time 308
night blindness 587
night owl 62
night person 62
night-blind person 587
nine cases out of ten 166
ninny 542
nitwit 579
no admittance to women 461
no chance of 339
no complaints 327
no fooling 116
no longer in contact 472
no match for 25, 83
no risk of 339
no sign of life 433
no such luck 626
no sweat 235
no taste for 228
no way around it 496
noble 197
nobody 373, 604
nobody acting 581
nobody to blame but yourself 161
nobody's fool 551
nobody's perfect 491
nod one's head 355
nominal 636
non-partisan 61
nonchalance 102
nonchalant 427
nonsensical 352
noodles 333
nose 89
not be chewy 351
not be interested (in) 228
not be oneself 220
not be ready to 227
not be very sticky 351
not bite 559
not buy 559
not fall for 559
not faze someone 176
not have a clue 79
not have enough help 557
not have one's feet on the ground 20
not know what one is doing 379
not know when to shut up 361
not like 228
not much more than 178, 197
not outgoing 597
not pressing 66
not very nice 196
not very sociable 597
not vital 66
nothing ventured, nothing gained 580
notice 263
notice (pay attention to) one 270
notion (to do) 324
nuts, nutty 206, 214, 222, 297, 298
nyctalopia 587

O

object of gossip 615, 632
obscure 545
obsessed 26
obviously 124, 140, 381
occur to 263
occur to one 342
octopus 541
of one accord 134
off limits to women 461
off one's rocker 206, 213, 297
offended 288
old (bad) habits die hard 536
old dog 64
old eagle is better than a young crow 367, 537
old fox (coon) 64, 551
old school 25, 372
old tricks 45
old-fashioned 372
on a par with 194
on bended knee 489
on edge 243, 268
on one's guard 269, 376
on one's mind 301
on one's toes 268
on target 120
on the ball 221
on the level 498
on the lookout for 269
on the same wave length 206, 603
on your guard 633
once a winner, always a winner 367, 537
once in a lifetime 150, 501
once-in-a-lifetime meeting 122
one extreme or the other 338
one heart and mind 151
one man's meat is another man's poison 168
one mind and body 151
one step short of 145
one that got away 448
one visitor after another 499
one voice 134
one's heart's desire 166
one-sided love 34
onlooker 624
only the strong survive 158
open and aboveboard 498
open for interpretation 545
open to the public 143
open up 291
openhandedly 473
openly and fairly 498
opinionated 218
opportunist 196, 588
ordinary parents have ordinary children 175
ornery 92
out 454
out for the count 639
out of control 558, 559
out of hand 29
out of luck 140
out of one's element 402
out of one's mind 206, 208
out of sorts 417
out of the ordinary 330
out of this world 569
out-of-bounds to women 461
outdo oneself 268
outgoing 629
outlook is good 640
outrageous 78
outspoken 84
over my dead body 383
overdrink 39

overeat 39
overloaded 434
overloaded electrical outlet 544
overnight 155
overpolite 136
overpowered 277
owl 62
own two feet 57

P

packed train 374
painful 409
painless death 77
pains 306, 310
painstaking 557
pandemonium 11
paper cranes 499, 593
paradise 77
paralyzed 93
paranoia 105
paranoid 76
parasite 53
parents may have children who are much better than they are 572
parrot 468, 469
partial 420
partial paralysis 93
parting shot 154, 374
pass away in peace 77
pass muster 589
pass oneself off 301
pass out 287, 639
pass the buck 575
passed on to 561
passel of good-for-nothings 600
pat oneself on the back 160
patchy 14

patient, patience   227, 276, 321
patsy   179, 181
pay attention to   262, 263, 272, 285
peanuts   455
peevishness   182, 415
pellucid   546
penniless   465
people of all ages and both sexes   480
perceive   342
perfect   569
perfect wife and mother   481
perfection   184
perfectly   560
persecution complex   105
persevere   276
persistent   321
persistent person   534
person from nowhere   604
personable   265
personal gain   517
pet   467
petering out   482
pheasant   307
phony   300
pick at   19
pick up on   246
picturesque   62
piddling sum   536
piece of cake   235
pig   41
pigeon   99, 179
pigheaded   27
pigpen, pigsty   43, 543
piker   513
pit   543
pitiful   264, 409
pittance   172
placated   416

place in one's heart   203
place to sleep   608
plain and simple   546
plain at the nose on your face   140
plain to see   124
plan to   201
planning   507
plant   33, 139
play the field   231
playing possum   552
pleasant   216, 295, 319
please everyone   94
pleased as Punch   129, 329
pleasing   319
plucky   249
plutocracy   323
pocket   436
pointy-headed   24
poke one's nose into   356
polite   68, 349
politeness   136
pompous   300
ponder   356
pony   582
popular   452, 454
popular, trendy   450
popularity   450
pose   301
postage stamp-size piece of ground   432
potbelly   95
potentially explosive   152
pour over   595
pout   364
powerful   573, 585
practice   600
preaching to deaf ears   605
preaching to the wind   605
premature   162
premonition   417
preoccupied   26

preparation   628
prepared for all eventualities   628
preparedness   302
preposterous   78
pretend   301
pretending to be asleep   552
pride   305
prince   49
princess   49
priorities all wrong   118
private   597
profound   135
promoting one's own interests   67
prosaic   408
proud   413, 465, 90
proud as a peacock   92, 575
prudence   628
psyche them up   521
psycho   297
psychosomatic illness   267
publicity seeking   35
publicity stunt   35
puerile   476
puff up one's chest   413
pull oneself together   284
pull the wool over someone's eyes   606
pull yourself together   287
pulling in the crowds   499
punk   53
pure as the driven snow   169
purple prose   39
purse   69
pushed out of shape   105
pushover   251
pussy   419, 510, 631
pussycat   191, 251, 429
put (leave) something behind one   496

put in a good word for 363
put in an appearance 186
put on 393
put on a good show 268
put on airs 300
put one's back to something 496
put one's foot down 249
put one's foot in it 623
put one's mind to 210
put one's shoulder to the wheel 351
put ones' heads together, huddle (up) 370
put oneself in someone's place 391
put out 514
put some fire in their belly 521
put the country's needs before one's own 390
put your heads together 109
put the make on 562
putting all one's energy into 152
putting in my two cents 362
puzzled 332
pyramid 444
pyramid scheme 443

Q

quality 525
queue 50
quick 25, 221
quick dip 190
quick on one's feet 27
quick on the uptake 31
quick return 578
quick rise to the top 345
quick temper 546
quick thinker 27
quick to fight 556
quick-tempered 224
quick-witted 31
quicksand 17
quiet 112
quiet man of action 60
quiet or well mannered 429
quite a hand at 598

R

rabbit 611
rabbit hutch 612
rabble 619
raccoon dog 550
radar trap 443
rail 173
raise someone's expectations 275
ram (push) through 79
rapid progress 455
rare 639
rash 212, 225, 514
rat 442, 55, 73, 198
ratchet-jaw 358
ratchet-mouth 358
rattlebones 173
reach 557
reactionary 372
read 561
read each other's mind 149
readiness 302
ready (for anything) 269
ready oneself 282
ready to 204
ready to take one's punishment 375
real bind 641
real McCoy 526
real talker 520
real thing 526
realize 246, 557

reap what you sow 161
rear 513
reassurance 336
reassuring 414
rebuff 107
receptive to new things 29
recharge one's batteries 250
reciprocal affection 532
reckless 50, 138
recklessness 40
record-breaking 639
red snapper 537
refinement 307
regain consciousness 247
regain one's composure 238, 278
regal 197
regard 339
regret 244
regrettable 264
regroup 284
regular 195
regurgitate 469
reject 497
rejection 528
rejection (of foreign tissue or organ) 369
related by blood 47
relax 32, 192, 250, 252, 277, 279, 280, 288, 290, 291
relaxation 293
relaxed 232, 328, 335, 459
reliance upon others 553
relief 235, 414
relieved 210, 217, 235
reluctant 242
reluctant to start anything 514
reluctantly 179, 615
remorseful 244
remote 585

repentant 244
research 470
reserved 597
resigned to one's fate 375
resolute 287, 350
resolve 97
resolved 216
responsibility 192
rest 250, 288
restless 225, 339
retire 393
retirement 194
reveal one's true character 37
revolting 411
ride in on someone's coattails 518
riffraff 619
right down the street 388
right for one 87
right off 29
right over there 388
right person in the right place 568
right-mindedness 523
rings a bell 392
rise and fall of human affairs 59
risk one's life 188
rough skin 485
round and round 153
round to the nearest whole number 519
round-eyed 385
rounded shoulders 438
roving eye 91, 618
rub one the wrong way 256
rubberneck 624
rubbing salt into the wound 425
ruffled 243
ruin one's health 189

rumors 481
run (stand) for (election/office) 529
run about in utter confusion 610
run off at the mouth 358
run over the budget 21
run pell-mell 610
running wild 558
rush about like a headless chicken 610
rush-hour train 375
rustic 494, 625

S

sad 239, 264
sad face 603
saddened 239
same wavelength 128
sane 242
sanity 523
sardine 157
satisfied 240, 416
saturnine 136
save one's ass 575
say 362, 363
say too much 359
scandalous 78
scarcity value 329
scared (half) to death 316
scared spitless (stiff) 316
scared to death 410
scatter out 366
scattered on the winds 609
scheming 96
scholastic credentials 69
schools 168
scoundrel 55
scowl 447
scratch my back and I'll scratch yours 610

screw 565
screw oneself up 269, 326
screwball 297
scrutinize 595
scumbag 53
scuzzball 41
sea bream 537
sealed off 18
second to none 569
secondary smoke 120
see 381
see eye to eye 128
see in one's mind 411
see no evil, hear no evil, and speak no evil 490
see through 561
seesaw 151
seize the initiative 500
select few 528
selection 528
self-admiration 162
self-advertisement 35
self-conceit 162
self-congratulation 162
self-destructive 425, 578
self-esteem 305
self-interest 517
self-reliance 57
self-reliant 163
self-respect 305
self-satisfaction 126
self-seeking 67
self-sufficiency 163
self-supporting 163
selfish 313
selfless service for the common good 390
seniority 440
seniority system 440
sense 342
senseless 149
sensitive 313

seriousness 116, 117
serpent 100
serves him (you) right 314
serves you right 161
set back on one's heels 277
set one's teeth on edge 83
settle down 32, 238, 278, 281, 394, 416
settled 131
sex appeal 145
sexually attractive 148
shadow 322
shady past 533
shake (hands) on it 566
shake it out 192
shake one's head 355
sham 493
shameless 344
shamus 139
shark 485
sharp 25, 221, 346
sharp eyes 334
sheep, sheepish 111, 112
shilly-shally 634
shin 533
shivers 486
shocking 78
short 495
short fuse 224, 546, 547
short temper 546
short temper is costly (shortens life) 548
short time 155
short-lived reign 396
short-tempered 224, 547
shortage of workers 557
shorthanded 434, 557
shoulder 191
shoulder to shoulder 194
show one's skill 599
show one's true colors 37
show up 186

shower affection 49
shower someone with abuse 38
shudder 486, 487
shy 510, 597
sick 295
sick (and tired) 91
sick to one's stomach 295, 411
sickening 296, 411
sickness 44, 624
side (up) with 193
sign 198
sign that someone is around 111
simplicity 570
sincerely 498
sincerity 116
sing a different tune 433
sing one's own praises 160
single people 58
sink in 392
sinking heart 127
sissy 419, 631
sit down 352
sit on one's hands 350
sit right across from 113
sitting on a powder keg 152
skate 564
skeleton in the closet 533
skilled 598
skin 86, 486
skin of one's teeth 308
skinhead 544
skinny person 173
skinnybones 173
skunk 73, 198
skyrocket 609
slammer 43
slave 116
slave (to the passions) 139
sleep all huddled up 638

sleep around 514
sleep with a man 88
sleepiness 439
slick talker 360
slight stoop 438
slip into unconsciousness 245, 287
slippery 509
sliver of land 608
slob 41
sloppy 85
slow 28, 514
slow business 227
slow down 252
slow on the uptake 46
slow to act 350
slow walk 81
slow-witted 27
slower than molasses in January 614
sly (crafty) fellow 551
sly old dog 607
sly old fox 551
small fish 637
small fry 637
(small) token of one's appreciation 318
smart 25, 31, 221, 346, 492
smart aleck 511
smarter 30
smidgen 319
smile with one's eyes 385
smiling from ear to ear 329
smooth operator 360
smugness 162
snake 100
snap 235
snapper 537
snitcher 31
snort 90
so many men, so many minds 168

soaked to the bone 445
soar 609
society 69
soft in the head 28
soft on women 91
soft-shelled turtle 534
solace 336
solicitude 339
soliloquy 164
solve a problem once and for all 156
someone to watch 508
someone who stands in one's way 384
somersault turn 577
something on the side 617
somewhat 75
song 455
sophomoric 476
sorry 244
sound (feel) someone out 270
sound (good) health 405
sour look 422
sow one's wild oats 638
spare no pains 115
spare tire 95
sparse 83
speak one's mind 84
speak the same language 128
speaking volumes 135
speed trap 443
spider 366
spineless 526, 630
spirit 292
spirited 218
spit bath 190
split personality 449
spoil quickly 21
spoiler 33
sponge off (one's parents) 533
spooked 314
spread oneself (a little) thin 231
spunky 249
spur-of-the-moment 312
sputter 517, 576
spy 139
squat 495
stabbed in the back 177
stale 230
stalking horse 33
stand around 632
stand on formality 545
stand one's ground 92, 249
start 564, 565
start to notice boys (girls) 148
start with a bang and end with a whimper 517, 576
startling 379
stay out of trouble 308
stay quiet 308
stay somewhere forever 115
staying power 328, 396
steadfast 287
steal a kiss 365
steamroll 79
steel oneself 269
steeplejack 572
step out (on) 617
stepping out 617
stew 264, 274
stick out 382
stick to something 276
stick-in-the-mud 372
sticks to anything 396
sticky 350
stiff neck 192
stingy 513
stomach 95

stooge 139
stool pigeon 139
stop doing something 567
stop paying attention 239, 281
stormy 98
straight ahead 138
straight ahead (and damn the torpedos) 50
straight as a die 497
strained 313
strand someone 23
strength of one's convictions 309
stressful 211
strike at the heart of the matter 156
strike it rich 130
strike oil 130
strong 280, 287
strong opponent 539
strong-minded 173, 218
strong-willed 173, 218, 249
struggle 368
strung-out 211
strutting about like a peacock 575
stubborn 27, 249
stuck up 305
study guide 582
stuff oneself 39
stupefied 245
stupendous 245
stupid 542
stupidity 579
stupor 639
success 478
succulent 13
sucker 179, 181
suit 87
suit one's taste 361
sulky, sullen 136

summon one's courage 282
sunglasses 577
support 193
support something 193
surprised 349
surrounded 18
surrounded on all sides 506
survival of the fittest 158
suspecting 274
suspicion 76
suspicious 93, 274
swaggering 538
swallow 589
swallow (something) whole, swallow a story hook, line, and sinker 596
swamped 434
swearing 38
sweat blood 504
sweet 250
swimmingly 169
swing from joy to sorrow 132
sycophant 139
sympathy 128

T

tacit understanding 149
taciturn 136
tactful 220
tad 319
tagalong 322
tail 591
take (good) care of 284
take a break 567
take a breather 250
take a drastic step or measure 156
take a fancy to 203, 254
take a load off 352
take away someone's wheels 23
take care 272, 286
take charge of 82
take comfort 414
take great pains 368
take it easy 32, 279
take note 286
take off 609
take offense 288
take one's eyes off 384
take one's hat off to 28
take one's mind off one's problems 268
take over 194
take pains 114, 272, 284
take sides 193
take someone at his word 118
take someone seriously 118
take something (someone) wrong 274
take something to heart 262, 315
take time 556
take to 203, 254
take too much for granted 423
taken aback 277, 521
taking a new lease on life 507
taking mitigating circumstances into consideration 167
talent 406
talented amateur 337
talk 363
talk (very well or fast) 520
talk a good show 426, 430
talk big 426, 430
talk black into white 484
talk to 363
talk up a storm 268
tall 495
tame ending 482
tangible and intangible 635
tapped (out) 465
tarnished 186
tasteless 408
teeth 82
telepathy 149
tell over and over 360
temper of yours will be the death of you 549
temperament 299
temperamental 203
ten to one 166
ten-foot pole 141
tenacious 249
tendency 75
tense 211, 268, 313, 343
tenterhooks 500
terrified 316
terse 85
tête-à-tête 113
that feeling 529
the good and the bad 80
there is many a slip twixt the cup and the lip 633
thick and thin 71
thief 31
thin 334
thin (sparse) mustache 56
think 240
think about 255, 341
think aloud 164
think better of 219
think hard 356
think like 201
think of 246, 341
thinking aloud 164
thoroughly prepared 628
thoughtful 220, 223, 247, 271
thoughtlessly 427

thousand cranes   593
three-legged race   450
throat   457
through with   21, 564
throw a punch   562
throw a wet blanket on   281
throw cold water on   281
throw his weight   582
throw oneself into something   351, 394
throw oneself on the mercy of   395
throw out one's chest   413
throw someone to the lions (wolves)   575
thrown together   126
thumb one's nose   520
thunderstruck   521
tied to someone's apron strings   515
tiger   580
tight corner   641
tight-lipped   359
tightfisted   592
tightwad   513
time is not yet ripe   162
time to show one's stuff   599
timid   215, 251, 510, 526, 630
timidity   458
timidly   500
timorous   112, 215
tiny   109
tiny plot of land   432
tired   20
tireless worker   404
tirelessly   170
titular   636
tizzy   339
to the bone   392
to the point   85

toady   139
toil   116
token of my appreciation   318
token of one's appreciation   292
tongue   520
too many chiefs and not enough Indians   24
too much   380
toot your horn   456
tooth   82
top-heavy   24
tops   569
total despair   160
totally absorbed   406
touch   75, 414
touch-and-go   308
touch-and-go situation   152
touched   208
touching   412
touchy   224, 321
tough   173, 249, 594
tough on the inside   67
transfixed   101
trap   17
trapped (like a rat)   63
treasure   582
trial and error   504
tried his hand   565
trifling details   522
trip someone up   19
triumphant   129
triumvirate   487
troubling   302
trust a wolf to watch over sheep   431
try everything   566
try (push) hard   114
try to be like someone   592
try to do two things and fail at both   11

tug at one's heartstrings   412
turn one's back on   497
turn to   386
turn to others for help   553
turning over a new leaf   507
turtle   534
twinkling of an eye   155
twist everything to suit oneself   484
two-bagger   41
two-timing   617, 618
tyrant in his own home   567

U

umbrella   348
unable to believe one's ears   400
unable to do   558
unable to figure out   237
unaffected   328
unanimously   134
unappreciated or unnoticed hard work   181
unassertive   251
unbalanced   208
unbending   350
unbiased   61
unblemished record   497
uncanny feeling or sensation   314
unclear   619
uncomfortable   248, 303, 313, 343
unconcerned   102
unconscious   149
undaunted   52
under a lot of pressure   268
under a strain   268
under one's thumb   515
under siege   506

INDEX 667

under stress 211
uneasy 248, 303
unending 614
unenthusiastic 324
unfaithfulness 617
unfinished 517, 576
unflappable 104
unfortunate 264
unheard of 639
unimportant details 522
uninhibited 233
uninterested 228
uninteresting 408
united by ties of common interest 77
universal 37
universities 168
unmentionable 78
unnecessary 54
unparalleled 639
unpardonable 78
unperturbedness 102
unpleasant 296, 320
unpopular 454
unpopulated 111
unprecedented 639
unprincipled 196
unprincipled person 588
unready 227
unrealistic 20
unrequited love 34
unresolved 619
unrestrained 166
unrestricted 166
unrivalled 569
unscrupulous 344
unspeakable 78
unusual 639
unutterable 78
unwavering 287
unwilling 242

unwind 250
unyielding 218
up for 204
up in the clouds 132
up the creek 641
up to here with 91, 158
up-and-coming 508, 527
upbeat 413
uppermost in one's thoughts 285
ups and downs 98
ups and downs of life 59
upset stomach 295
upstanding (moral) character 107
uptight 192, 211, 274, 343
use confusion 85, 516
use one's head 33, 271
use some means (way) 565

V

vacillate 634
vague 14, 619
vanity 126, 305
vapid 408
vegetable 525
vengeance 71
verge 145
very little 172
very small amount (of money) 536
vicissitudes of life 59
vigorous 573, 585
vigorously 170
visible and invisible 635
visit 22, 186
visitors 499
visualize 382
vitality 74, 328
vogue 450
voice of authority 594

volatile situation 152
volcanic 203, 224

W

waist 348
wait for an opportunity to do something 592
wait impatiently for 123
wake a sleeping dog, not know when to leave well enough alone 623
wake up 247, 379, 387
waking up 440
wale 401
walking papers 354
want 457
want to 204
want to do 208, 257
want to do everything 231
warm 250
warm days 489
warm feet 641
warren 612
wary 376
wash one's hands of 21
waste 42
watch one's P's and Q's 361
watch over someone's shoulder 385
watch your step 633
water off a duck's back 35, 176, 605
waver 634
way one feels 293, 317
way out there 297
weak 351
weak-kneed 251, 317, 351, 526, 630
weak-willed 251
weaken 252

weakling 419, 631
weal 401
wear 393
weasel-worded 545
weathercock 196, 588
weenie 207, 419, 631
weird 314
well behaved 191, 429
well suited 87
well suited for the job (role) 568
welt 401
wet behind the ears 514
whale of a difference 534
what is born of a cat will catch mice 175
what is learned in the cradle is carried to the grave 536
wheal 401
when all is said and done 574
when it rains, it pours 425
whereabouts unknown 635
whim, whimsical 312, 616
whiner 419
whisper 172
whistling in the wind 605
white fingers 512
whole bag of tricks 563
whole story 122
wholeheartedly 498
wide circle of acquaintances 185
wife 458, 471
wild 352, 419
wild (unfounded) rumors 481
wild boar 137
wild duck 179
will 626
will-o'-the-wisp 334

willful 249, 313
willpower 328
wily (crafty) old dog 551
wimp 419, 510, 631
wimpish 526
win 560
wind at one's back (in one's sails) 169
wind knocked out of you 127
windbag 361
wink at something 387
wiped out 465
wise-ass 511
wishy-washy 14
with a heavy heart 179, 615
with fear and trembling 500
without a friend in the world 506
without a second thought 473
without artifice 569
without beating about the bush 549
without charm or cuteness 196
without effect 103
without feeling a thing 103
without looking back 473
without mincing words 549
without preamble 549
without regret 473
without stopping 132
without thinking 427
witty 221
wobbly (rubbery) legs 48
wolf 462, 467
wolf in sheep's clothing 434
woman announcer over a PA system 602

woman's touch 471
women 146
wonder 356
wonder about 259
wonder to oneself 164
wonderful dexterity 166
wool-gather 281
word from on high 594
word is law 594
work day and night 51
work far away from 549
work hard 64
work like crazy 394
work oneself into a lather 202
work oneself up 326
work until one drops 394
workaholic 98, 404
worked up 46, 269, 326
worked up about nothing 202
workhorse 38, 98
working together 450
works like a dog 98
worn down 215
worn out 13, 108
worried 409
worried to death 220
worrisome 302
worry 255, 259, 274, 301, 306, 339, 341
worry (needlessly) about 264
worry oneself sick 202
worry over 26
worrying 259
wrapped up 406
wring one's hands 225
writhe in agony 502, 504
wrought up 243
wuss 419, 631

Y

yellow 317
yellow-bellied 317
yes-man 139
young and energetic (enthusiastic) 527
young at heart 249
yummy 13

Z

zeal 325
zero 579